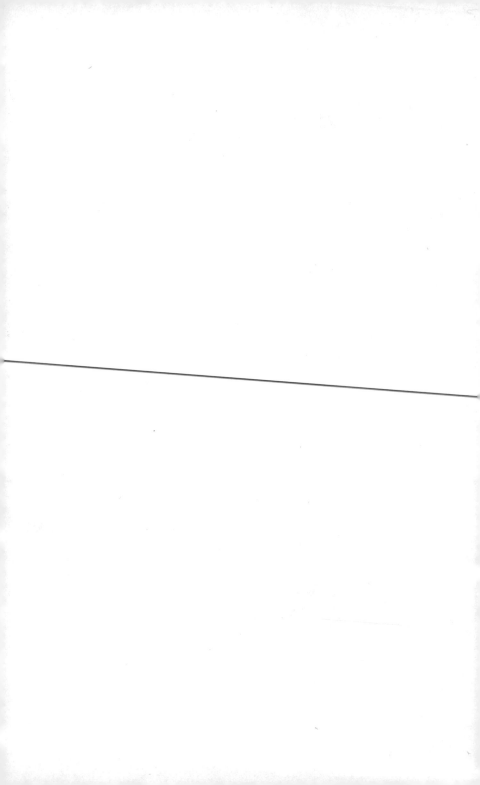

Homemade Cookies

Other cookbooks by Farm Journal

FARM JOURNAL'S COUNTRY COOKBOOK
FREEZING & CANNING COOKBOOK
FARM JOURNAL'S COMPLETE PIE COOKBOOK
LET'S START TO COOK
COOKING FOR COMPANY
HOMEMADE BREAD
AMERICA'S BEST VEGETABLE RECIPES
HOMEMADE CANDY
BUSY WOMAN'S COOKBOOK

BY THE FOOD EDITORS OF *FARM JOURNAL*

Homemade Cookies

Edited by

NELL B. NICHOLS

FARM JOURNAL FIELD FOOD EDITOR

Photography Supervised by

AL J. REAGAN

FARM JOURNAL ART STAFF

DOUBLEDAY & COMPANY, INC.

GARDEN CITY, NEW YORK

Contents

	page
Choice Homemade Cookies from Countryside America	9
How to Bake Good Cookies Every Time	14
How to Pack Cookies for Mailing	21
Bar Cookies	22
Drop Cookies	71
Rolled Cookies	122
Refrigerator Cookies	172
Molded Cookies	186
Pressed Cookies	217
Meringue Cookies	224
Cookie Confections	231
Pie-Bar Dessert Cookies	252
Ready-Made Cookies	263
Cookies to Make from a Mix	273
Cookies Children Will Love to Make	286

Cookies for Special Occasions   306

Index   309

COLOR ILLUSTRATIONS

Robert E. Coates

Heaps of Cookies   *facing page*   257

William Hazzard/Faraghan Studio

Cookie Assortment   *facing page*   64

Hoedt Studios

Christmas Cookie Church   *facing page*   193

Al Reagan

After-School Welcome   *facing page*   128

Mel Richman, Inc.

Cookie Barnyard   *facing page*   256

Celebration Cookies   *facing page*   129

Ready for Holiday Guests   *facing page*   192

Bruce Harlow

Eight-in-One Recipe   *facing page*   65

Homemade Cookies

Choice Homemade Cookies from Countryside America

Golden brown cookies, warm and fragrant from the oven—could anything taste better? And what arouses greater enthusiasm—watch the children head for the cookie jar when they return home from school. Notice how your husband lingers in the kitchen if the spicy aroma of cookies, spread on cooling racks, greets him. Doesn't he take seconds—and sometimes thirds?

Don't you yourself recall your mother's wonderful date bars or whatever was her specialty? Maybe your own son, as a serviceman, appreciated your boxes of cookies . . . "love from home." Eating homemade cookies is happiness that builds memories to treasure.

This cookbook contains superior recipes representing all types of cookies; among them are sure to be some you associate with your childhood. We include the best cookies published in FARM JOURNAL through the past twenty years—many of them from country kitchens. But we also feature original Test Kitchen recipes that never before appeared in print.

First in this book you will find recipes for the Big Six traditional cookies—bar, drop, rolled, refrigerator, molded and pressed cookies. The way you handle the dough determines the family to which a cookie belongs—whether you bake it in a pan and cut the cookies with a knife; whether you shape it into rolls and refrigerate them to bake later; roll the dough out thin and use a cutter to form shapes; drop it from a spoon right onto the baking sheet; shape it into balls with your hands; or squirt it from a cookie press.

Newest among the traditionals are the refrigerator cookies, known as icebox cookies before electric refrigerators became commonplace. These are special for women who want to bake thin, crisp cookies without bothering with rolling pin and cookie cutters. It's so much easier, they insist, just to slice dough and bake it.

When Europeans came to America from overseas to establish homes in a new world, the women brought along their treasured cookie recipes, sometimes written down, sometimes memorized. We include some of these old-time specialties, adapting them to the ingredients and appliances and tools we have and to flavors we like. Some of these first colonists made room in their crowded baggage for sandbakelser molds and hand-carved springerle boards or rolling pins. Those who could not bring either the board or rolling pin to use for making these picture cookies improvised by pressing butter molds or glass dishes with cut designs on the rolled cookie dough. You will find in this book up-to-date recipes for Sandbakelser and Springerle and other cookies that originated in many lands. Italy, for example, produced Florentines—rich, melt-in-the-mouth, chocolate-covered cookies flavored with candied orange peel and almonds.

Americans made their own cookie discoveries. Chocolate chip cookies are the classic example. Developed by a Massachusetts home economist who cut up chocolate and added it to her cookie dough when she found her raisin box empty, the cookies caught on at once and skyrocketed to popularity across the country. This book offers you a variety of recipes for this kind of cookie. Try our Cape Cod Chocolate Chip Cookies (molded), Soft Chocolate Chippers (drop) and Chocolate Chip Bars to see which kind you and your family like best.

Cry Baby Cookies, molasses-flavored drop cookies that contain such good things as coconut, nuts, raisins, rate tops with navy men. The first recipes for these cookies are believed to have evolved in kitchens of Maryland's Eastern Shore. Bake them when you want a big batch of cookies to please men. The recipe makes about 9½ dozen cookies, but you can freeze part of the dough to bake later if you like.

Jumbo Sugar Cookies are another all-American treat. The sugar-cinnamon top scents the kitchen delightfully while they bake. One of our home economists who tested this recipe baked a batch and took them to a P.T.A. food sale. They sold fast at 10¢ each! These big cookies are first cousins of Snickerdoodles, an early American, but you handle the dough differently and the ingredients vary somewhat. You'll find recipes for both in our book.

Meringue cookies, or kisses, have been special-occasion treats for generations, the favorite way to use leftover egg whites that accumulated in kitchens where lots of baking was done. You'll be surprised how many appetizing ways this cookbook gives for flavoring meringue cookies and making them distinctive.

Many of our native cookies, once enjoyed, disappeared along

with the special need for them. Boom Cookies are an example. They were giant size—about 5" in diameter—molasses/coffee-flavored cookies, which hungry lumberjacks joyfully ate at the Boom in Minnesota, a sorting station when logs were floated down the St. Croix River. Gone is the cook shack, the circumstance and the cookies, but our Soft Molasses Cookies in smaller sizes have the same taste provided by molasses, spices and instant coffee powder. It is one recipe of many in this cookbook for molasses cookies.

Christmas and cookies go together, although every season has its cookies. Certainly women bake more cookies for the holidays than at any other time. One reason is the visiting that goes on around the countryside during Yuletide. The traditional refreshments for open houses consist of Christmas cookies with coffee, wine or a fruit drink. In the Bethlehem, Pennsylvania, area, this visiting is called "putzing." It's when a family welcomes neighbors and friends who come to see their crèche under the Christmas tree. The "putz" is the crèche and the name comes from *putzen,* which to Germans means to decorate.

There are many reasons for Christmas cookies other than sharing the treats with visiting friends. They make ideal gifts from the home kitchen to neighbors, shut-ins, business associates and other friends. There also are gift boxes to mail, children home from school eager to feast on Mother's cookies. Cookies are an important part, too, of refreshments served at parties given by clubs and other organizations. And in many homes, Christmas cookies help decorate the gala tree.

Cookies such as White Christmas and brown Spiced Christmas Cookies and Pepper Nuts—the kind grandmothers of Swiss and German descent used to keep in their apron pockets to reward grandchildren for good behavior—still are baked at Christmastime (see Index for the recipes). We give suggestions for decorating these and many other cookies, though all are good plain also. It's the opinion of women who contributed their choice recipes, that the trims justify what they cost in time and effort.

You'll observe recipes in this book that call for frostings, white and tinted to top or coat the cookies and sometimes to put them together in pairs for sandwiches. This dress-up helps both their appearance and disappearance!

You'll find many recipes that call for fillings. In fact, all of the traditional cookie types lend themselves to fillings. One of the favorite types is the bar cookies in which the filling bakes between two layers of dough, sometimes in a jelly roll pan. Some women lament that cookies go so fast, even though they want them to appeal and please. Mothers sometimes have to hide cookies to save them for serving at some special occasion. One mother stores some of her cookies in empty rolled oat boxes because the children never think of looking there for cookies.

To make cookie baking pleasant and memorable, enlist the help of the family, especially with Christmas cookies. You may prefer to bake the cookies and let the children help decorate them—gingerbread boys and animals for Christmas, for instance. Or dream up your own ways to stimulate their interest. We give recipes for making farmyard cookie animals (see Cocoa Cookie Barn), a cookie family, as well as recipe, patterns and directions for making a Christmas gingerbread church. This makes a great Christmas centerpiece and the children will love to help.

In fact, we have included a special section for junior cooks with cookie recipes in their language and with extra how-to detail.

Important as traditional cookies are in our collection, we include many other newer types. Cookie confections have many loyal boosters. These are the easy-to-make cookies that children like to fix for their friends, and also to eat. But homemakers as well like to make cookies that are little work and taste really good. Some of them are no-bake cookies, and several of them require brief *cooking* in a saucepan!

Cookie confections are close kin to candies. You often make them with ready-to-eat cereals or with rolled oats, crackers or vanilla wafers substituting for flour. Many ingredient goodies contribute to their popularity—raisins, marshmallows, chocolate pieces, coconut, nuts.

One of our new cookie triumphs is what we call the pie-bar dessert cookie. It's a cross between a bar cookie and a piece of pie. These luscious cookies that taste like pie salve the calorie-counter's conscience.

Since many women today must stretch time, this book offers quick ways to speedily glamorize packaged store cookies you can keep in your cupboard. The recipes show you how to add homemade touches to cookies you buy.

Today's appliances have speeded up and simplified cookie making. The electric mixer can be used to mix all or part of the dough (see "How to Bake Good Cookies Every Time"). It especially excels for quickly and easily creaming the fat and sugar until light and fluffy, and for thoroughly blending in the eggs and flavoring. The freezer enables women to keep baked cookies or the dough for baking cookies on hand for months.

Most of the recipes in this cookbook are for use in homes located in areas with an altitude under 5,000 feet. But because families living in the mountain states also like homemade cookies, we include the Colorado Basic Cookie Mix for high altitude baking. The basic mix can be used for a wide variety of excellent cookies.

We also give you the recipes for two other popular basic mixes (for altitudes under 5,000 feet): Cookie Starter and Eight-in-One Sugar Cookies. And you'll find many excellent basic recipes with several variations.

For your convenience, we have selected and listed for you cookies appropriate for mailing; to serve at women's luncheon and tea parties; to sell at bazaars; to pack in lunchboxes; to offer at coffee parties; for children to bake; we also list cookies of foreign origin and Christmas specialties.

No one knows where cookies originated, but their name comes from the Dutch word *koekje,* which gets a mention in this old, anonymous American jingle:

> "The British call it biscuit
> And it's *koekje* to the Dutch
> But no matter what you call it
> All cookies please us much."

How to Bake Good Cookies Every Time

You will bake wonderful cookies with the recipes in this cookbook *if* you follow them carefully. To assure you the greatest satisfaction with your results, we pass on some of the points we watch in our Test Kitchens.

COOKIE INGREDIENTS

Flour — Use all-purpose flour in our recipes unless otherwise specified. If a recipe calls for sifted flour, spoon it lightly into measuring cup and level off with straight edge of knife or spatula. Some busy women skip the sifting (we don't recommend) and instead stir the flour in the canister or other container to incorporate air. If you then spoon it lightly into measuring cup and level it off, you sometimes get approximately the same amount as in sifting, but *often you get a little more*. Avoid tapping the cup filled with flour; this packs it.

Fats — The fats called for in this book are butter, regular margarine (in sticks), lard, shortening (it comes in 1- to 3-lb. cans) and salad oil (vegetable). Soft, tub-type margarines are whipped and so contain air and less fat than regular margarine. Use the fat the recipe calls for with one exception: You can substitute shortening for half of the butter listed. For instance, instead of using 1 c. butter, you can use ½ c. each of butter and of shortening.

Many women prefer to use butter in refrigerator cookies because it gets very hard when chilled; the dough slices neatly and evenly. Regular margarine also gives satisfactory results if you freeze the dough or chill it until very cold before slicing.

Pack solid fats firmly in measuring cup and level off. Bring them to room temperature before you start to combine and mix ingredients.

Sugar — Use granulated white sugar (cane or beet) unless otherwise specified. When a recipe calls for brown sugar, use light brown unless dark is designated. Superfine sugar is very fine granulated sugar.

Confectioners sugar (called powdered sugar in many areas) should be free of lumps before measuring. Some recipes call for sifted confectioners sugar.

Molasses — Use light molasses unless recipe calls for the dark. You can use either type, but the dark has deeper color and stronger flavor. The light comes from the first boiling of sugar cane, the dark from the second boiling.

Eggs — Recipes in this cookbook were tested with medium to large eggs. If you have small eggs, break two of them into a ¼-cup measure. A medium egg measures about ¼ cup. You can measure the correct amount for the recipe you are using. Since eggs are often the only liquid in cookies, the size used affects the results.

Milk and Cream — When your recipe calls for sweetened condensed milk, read the label on the can to make sure that's what you have. Evaporated milk and sweetened condensed milk both come in cans; they *cannot* be used interchangeably. Recipes calling for buttermilk were tested with commercial cultured type. You can substitute evaporated milk for fresh milk if you mix it with an equal amount of water. A few recipes list packaged instant dry milk powder as an ingredient.

In case you do not have sour milk, measure 1 tsp. vinegar or fresh lemon juice into a ¼-cup measure. Fill with milk and let stand several minutes; then stir and use. (For 1 c. sour milk, use 1 tblsp. vinegar or fresh lemon juice in a 1-cup measure.)

Cream in the recipes is either heavy or whipping (30 to 35% butterfat), coffee or light (18 to 20% butterfat), dairy half-and-half (10 to 12% butterfat) or dairy sour (commercial with 20% butterfat). Do not substitute one kind for another. Our recipes use commercial dairy sour cream.

Chocolate — Recipes in this book may call for one of four kinds of chocolate: unsweetened, semisweet, sweet cooking and no-melt unsweetened chocolate in envelopes. Use the designated type. You can substitute unsweetened chocolate squares for no-melt chocolate when recipe directs it may be done. Melt the squares in a heavy bowl set in a pan of hot, not boiling water, or put the chocolate in the top of a double boiler over hot water. You also can melt it in a small pan over very low heat, stirring constantly, but do watch closely, for chocolate scorches easily. Cool melted chocolate before adding it to other ingredients. Many recipes use chocolate pieces: semisweet, semisweet mint-flavored chocolate and milk chocolate—all have different flavors. Women quite commonly refer to these chocolate pieces as chocolate chips.

If you do not have unsweetened chocolate when ready to bake cookies, you can use 3 tblsp. unsweetened cocoa and 1 tblsp. butter for 1 square unsweetened chocolate. When a recipe calls for cocoa, use the unsweetened.

Peanut Butter — Unless a recipe designates crunchy peanut butter, we used smooth peanut butter in testing.

Rolled Oats — Use either the quick-cooking or regular kind as specified.

Raisins — Seedless raisins, from grapes without seeds, are designated in most recipes, although a few call for seeded raisins, from grapes with seeds that are removed, as the first choice.

Food Color — There are two kinds, liquid and paste. You can use the type you prefer. We found in our testing that the paste gives especially vivid colors, but use it sparingly. Liquid food colors are more widely available. Add them drop by drop until you get the shade you desire. It is easy to mix these colors. For instance, 3 drops of red and 2 of yellow food color make orange.

Decorating Sugars and Candies — Packaged coarse sugar in glistening white and many colors is widely available. Among the other favored cookie decorations are silver, gold and colored dragées, tiny candies of one or many colors and chocolate shot (jimmies).

Nuts — Store nuts in refrigerator or freezer if they are to be kept several days or weeks before use. To chop nuts, spread on wooden board. Hold top of sharp knife close to surface of board with one hand, then move knife handle up and down, and around in a semicircle with other hand so blade contacts uncut nuts. Nut choppers do a good job, too, and so does the electric blender. Chop nuts very fine if recipe calls for grated nuts, or put them through food chopper or chop in blender. When a recipe lists ½ c. nuts (or other measurement), we usually used pecans or walnuts.

UTENSILS AND TOOLS

The tools and utensils you use can simplify cookie baking and contribute to good results. It is especially important to use the pan sizes designated in recipes. Here are the utensils and tools that were especially helpful to home economists perfecting these cookie recipes in our Test Kitchens:

Graduated measuring cups
Measuring cups for liquid
Mixing bowls
Electric mixer (portable or stationary)
Wooden spoon
Small spatula for spreading frosting
Measuring spoons
Double boiler
Rolling pin
Stockinet cover for rolling pin
Pastry cloth
Cookie cutters
Baking sheets — two or more, at least 2" shorter and narrower than the oven. Shiny baking sheets are best for delicate browning. If you have only one baking sheet, use an inverted baking pan for a second one. Or cut heavy-duty aluminum foil to fit your baking sheet. Arrange cookie dough on it while one batch bakes. When the cookies are done, remove them and transfer the foil with the cookies for baking to the hot baking sheet. Put in the oven at once.
Baking pans of standard sizes — 8 and 9" square, 13 x 9 x 2" and 15½ x 10½ x 1" jelly roll pan
Broad spatula for removing cookies from baking sheets
Wire cooling racks
Timer
Cookie press

MIXING COOKIES THE RIGHT WAY

Every recipe in this cookbook gives precise directions for mixing the dough, but here are a few general pointers:
Bring ingredients to room temperature before you combine and mix them. This is especially important with solid fats.
Use the electric mixer at medium speed for creaming fats (beating them until light), for creaming together fats and sugar and to blend in eggs and flavorings. You can beat these foods until light and fluffy by hand with a wooden spoon, but we used the electric mixer extensively in testing the recipes. Either add the dry ingredients with the electric mixer at low speed, or mix them in with a wooden spoon.
If the cookie dough seems too soft, chill it an hour or longer. As it becomes firm enough to handle easily, work with a small amount at a

time, leaving the remainder in the refrigerator until you are ready for it. If the dough still seems too soft after chilling, bake a test cookie. If it spreads too much, work 1 to 2 tblsp. flour into the dough.

Here are some of the reasons why your cookie dough is sometimes a trifle too soft: skimpy flour measurement; flour stored in humid place; too generous fat measurement; melted or very soft fat instead of fat at room temperature; large eggs instead of medium size; mixing dough in a very warm kitchen.

When the dough seems too dry, bake a test cookie. If it is dry and crumbly, work 1 to 2 tblsp. soft butter or cream into dough with your hands.

Here are some of the reasons why cookie dough sometimes is a trifle too dry: flour stored in place with low humidity; too generous flour measurement; skimpy fat measurement; soft tub-type margarine instead of regular kind; skimpy liquid measurement; cold fat, such as butter taken directly from refrigerator; small eggs instead of medium size.

Flour has remarkable ability to absorb moisture from the air and to release moisture when stored in a dry place. There is a slight variation in the amount of moisture, due to atmospheric conditions, it can take up in a recipe.

COOKIE BAKING POINTERS

Be sure to heat oven to the correct temperature before putting cookies in to bake. When you bake one batch at a time, place baking sheet on rack in center of oven. If baking two batches at the same time, divide the oven into thirds with racks. Use cool baking sheets for all bakings; cookies spread too much on warm sheets.

Notice whether the recipe calls for a greased baking sheet. If it does, rub the surface lightly with unsalted fat, such as shortening. Some doughs are rich enough that cookies will not stick to ungreased baking sheets and pans. (Ungreased sheets or pans are easier to wash.)

Check cookies for doneness at end of the shortest baking time given in the recipe. When only one baking time is given, test 2 minutes before it ends. Try to avoid overbaking—it makes cookies dry. (Tests for doneness for the different cookie types are given with the recipes.) *Use a timer.*

Remove cookies from baking sheet with wide spatula at once, unless recipe specifies otherwise. When left on baking sheet even a few minutes, they continue to cook. Some recipes direct leaving cookies on baking sheet briefly before removing them. These cookies are fragile and easily broken when hot.

Spread cookies in a single layer on cooling racks. When cooling bar cookies in pan, set it on rack. You cut most bar cookies when cool or at least partly cool. Use a sharp knife.

When a frosting appears with a recipe, it makes enough to frost that amount of cookies unless noted otherwise. So when using the frosting for another cookie, use your judgment about whether it will be enough, too much, or whether you'll have to double the recipe.

HOW TO STORE COOKIES

Once your cookies are baked and thoroughly cooled, store them correctly and in a cool place if possible. This helps them to retain appetizing freshness. Here's the way to do it:

Crisp Cookies — Store in container with loose-fitting lid. If they soften despite your care, spread them on a baking sheet before serving and heat them 3 to 5 minutes in a slow oven (300°).

Soft Cookies — Store them in a container with a tight-fitting lid. If they seem to dry out, add a piece of apple, orange or bread, but replace fruit or bread frequently. You can freshen soft cookies. Before serving, put them in a casserole, cover and heat 8 to 10 minutes in a slow oven (300°).

Bar Cookies — It often is convenient to store them in the pan in which they baked. Lay a piece of plastic wrap over top of cookies; then cover pan with its lid or with foil.

HOW TO FREEZE COOKIES AND COOKIE DOUGH

You can freeze either baked cookies or cookie dough for 9 months to a year. Space in the freezer may determine whether you freeze them baked or unbaked in dough form. Frozen dough frequently takes up less space than baked cookies. Since frosted cookies freeze less satisfactorily than unfrosted, most women prefer to add the frosting shortly before serving them. This gives them a fresh taste. Here's the way to freeze cookies and cookie dough:

Baked Cookies — Layer thoroughly cooled cookies in a rigid container, such as a sturdy box, lined with plastic wrap or aluminum foil. Separate the layers and top with plastic wrap, which clings to them and keeps out the air, or with aluminum foil in which you can seal cookies. Seal foil lining and top covering. Close box, label and freeze. Let cookies thaw unwrapped in package 10 to 15 minutes before serving.

Cookie Dough — Put dough for *drop* cookies in frozen food containers and cover tightly. Or wrap in plastic wrap sealed with freezer tape, or in aluminum foil. Place the wrapped dough, when frozen, in a plastic bag. When ready to bake, thaw dough just enough so that you can drop it from a spoon.

Pack and freeze *molded* cookie dough like drop cookie dough. When ready to bake, thaw dough just enough so that you can shape it.

Arrange cutout dough for *rolled* cookies in layers in a sturdy box lined with plastic wrap or aluminum foil. Separate layers with plastic wrap or with foil you can seal as for drop cookies. Cover tightly, seal and label. Or spread cookie cutouts on a baking sheet and freeze; then package in the same way. The frozen cutouts are rigid and easier to pack. Put frozen cutouts on baking sheet and bake; no need to thaw.

Shape *refrigerator* cookie dough in rolls of the desired size, wrap tightly in plastic wrap and seal ends with tape, or wrap in aluminum foil. When ready to bake remove from freezer, let thaw just enough so that you can slice the rolls with a sharp knife. You can thaw them in refrigerator for 1 hour and slice.

Freeze dough for *bar* cookies in the pan in which you will bake it. Cover dough with plastic wrap, then with pan lid or foil.

How to Pack Cookies for Mailing

Once you've baked and cooled good cookies, you may get the desire to share some of them with members of your family who are away from home or with friends who live too far away for you to take your prizes to them. You can mail them successfully. No homemade gift travels more extensively than cookies. And no food tastes better to the recipient. If you want your cookies to reach their destination in tiptop condition, follow these rules, which we have tested:

Choose the right cookie for mailing (see Index for suggestions). Soft drop, bar and fruit cookies travel well, while thin, crisp cookies (refrigerator and rolled types) are likely to crumble.

Select a strong packing box; a pasteboard box is not strong enough. Line the box with plastic wrap or aluminum foil.

Have plenty of filler on hand to use between layers of wrapped cookies. You can use shredded or crushed tissue paper, waxed paper or aluminum foil. Popped corn sometimes is used, but occasionally it molds, especially in overseas shipments.

Wrap each cookie separately, or two cookies, back to back, in plastic wrap; fasten with tape.

Place a layer of filler on bottom of box for a cushion. Arrange wrapped cookies close together in neat rows to fill box with some of the filler between each layer. If sending more than one kind of cookie, put the heaviest ones in the bottom of the box.

Spread layer of filler on top. Then lay folded paper napkins or towels on top. Enclose your gift card. Close the box. It should be so full that you have to exert light pressure to close it. Tape box shut. (It's a good idea to write on top the name and address of the person to whom you are mailing the cookies.)

Wrap box with heavy wrapping paper and tie securely. Stick on the clearly addressed label.

Mark the box "FRAGILE—HANDLE WITH CARE," and "PERISHABLE." If you are sending the package overseas, send it by air parcel post if you can.

Bar Cookies

Brownies, rich, moist and fudge-like, top the list of bar cookies. But there are many wonderful-tasting competitors, for the bar cookie family is large. All the cookies you make by spreading dough in a pan and cutting it, after baking, into bars, squares, diamonds and other shapes are generally called "bar cookies."

When women across country send us their favorite cookie recipes, the brownie contributions come in great numbers. Some of them appear on the following pages. They may sound alike but each is different. Try them and find out which you, your family and friends like best—Candy-Top Brownies that make you think they're baked fudge, less sweet California Chocolate Brownies so luscious when topped with whipped cream peaks and frozen, Brownies for a Crowd baked in a jelly roll pan, handsome Two-Tone Brownies and other varieties.

Compare them with the other bars you make from recipes in this section—elegant Cheesecake Squares that melt in the mouth; gently spiced Chocolate/Orange Bars; English Tea Squares with strawberry jam filling. The homemaker who shares the recipe for the Tea Squares says: "They're simply divine, especially when faintly warm."

Bar cookies are so versatile because you can custom-cut them. The size depends mainly on whom you are cutting them for. So consider the sizes indicated in our recipes as suggestions.

Naturally, you want smaller, daintier cookies to serve at a women's party than to pack in a lunchbox or tote to the field to refresh men at work.

Some of our bar cookies can be served for dessert—Frosted Carrot Bars, for instance (cut them somewhat larger than usual). They taste so good that no one will dream the humble vegetable is an ingredient.

Bar cookies make good snacks for people of all ages. Plantation Peanut Cookies or Chocolate Chip Bars will generate special enthusiasm among teen-agers.

Bars are the easiest cookies to bake. You skip rolling, cutting, dropping or shaping the dough and there's only one batch to put in and take from the oven.

Do cut the bars when the cookie is slightly warm or completely cooled unless the recipe designates otherwise. If cut when hot, some bars crumble. Here are other pointers:

Avoid overmixing the dough — makes cookie tops hard. Overmixing the dough will result in a tough textured cookie.

Spread the dough evenly in the pan so all the bars will have the same thickness and texture (some areas in the pan may overbake if spread thinly).

Use the pan size the recipe indicates. If larger, the dough will be thin and unless you reduce the baking time, the cookie will be dry and tough; if smaller, the dough will be thick and may require a longer baking time.

Bake cookies only until they are done. Overbaked cookies are hard and dry; if underdone, doughy. Use the time given in the recipe as a guide for doneness, but also apply the standard tests. Cookies are done if when pressed lightly with a finger, they retain a slight imprint; a toothpick inserted in the center of cake-like bars comes out clean.

BROWNIES FOR A CROWD

Save time—bake cookies in one big pan; they're moist and keep well

½ c. regular margarine	¼ tsp. salt
1 c. sugar	½ c. chopped walnuts
4 eggs	6 tblsp. regular margarine
1 tsp. vanilla	6 tblsp. milk
1 (1 lb.) can chocolate syrup	1 c. sugar
(1½ c.)	½ c. semisweet chocolate pieces
1 c. plus 1 tblsp. sifted flour	1 tsp. vanilla
½ tsp. baking powder	

Beat ½ c. margarine with 1 c. sugar until light and fluffy. Beat in eggs, two at a time, and 1 tsp. vanilla. Mix well. Stir in chocolate syrup.

Sift together flour, baking powder and salt. Stir into chocolate mixture. Add nuts. Pour into well-greased 15½ x 10½ x 1" jelly roll pan and spread evenly.

Bake in moderate oven (350°) 22 to 25 minutes, or until slight imprint remains when touched lightly with finger. Remove pan to rack, and let cookies cool.

Meanwhile, combine 6 tblsp. margarine, milk and 1 c. sugar in saucepan; stir to mix. Bring to a boil and boil 30 seconds. Add chocolate pieces; stir until mixture thickens slightly and cools. Stir in 1 tsp. vanilla. Spread over cooled cookies, then cut in 2½ x 1" bars. Makes 5 dozen.

CANDY-TOP BROWNIES

These candy-like cookies win compliments; they're good travelers

2 c. sugar	½ c. chopped walnuts
2 eggs	1 egg, beaten
4 squares unsweetened chocolate	2 tblsp. light cream
½ c. butter or regular margarine	2 tblsp. butter or regular
½ c. flour	margarine
2 tsp. vanilla	

Combine 1 c. sugar and 2 eggs; beat.

Melt 2 squares chocolate with ½ c. butter; add to egg mixture. Blend in flour, 1 tsp. vanilla and nuts. Spread in greased 8" square pan.

Bake in moderate oven (350°) 25 to 35 minutes; cool on rack.

Combine remaining 1 c. sugar, beaten egg, cream, 2 squares chocolate, 2 tblsp. butter and 1 tsp. vanilla. Bring to a boil, stirring constantly. Remove from heat and stir until of spreading consistency. Spread over cooled brownies. Cut in 2" squares. Makes 16.

CALIFORNIA CHOCOLATE BROWNIES

These are less sweet than most brownies so you may want to frost them or sprinkle on confectioners sugar . . . they're good keepers

½ c. shortening	¾ c. sifted cake flour
1 c. light corn syrup	¼ tsp. baking powder
2 squares unsweetened chocolate, melted	¼ tsp. salt
	¾ c. chopped nuts
2 eggs, well beaten	Vanilla Cream Icing (see Index)
½ tsp. vanilla	

Cream shortening until fluffy. Gradually beat in corn syrup until thoroughly mixed and light and fluffy. Stir in melted chocolate. Add eggs and vanilla.

Sift together cake flour, baking powder and salt. Add ¼ c. at a time to creamed mixture. Fold in nuts. Pour into well-greased 8″ square pan.

Bake in moderate oven (350°) 30 to 35 minutes, or until slight imprint remains when touched lightly with finger. Set pan on rack to cool completely. Then frost with Vanilla Cream Icing, if desired. Cut in 2″ squares. Makes 16.

Variations

Brownies Made with Cocoa: Omit unsweetened chocolate. Sift 6 tblsp. cocoa with flour. Add 2 tblsp. additional shortening.

Snow Peaked Brownies: When brownies in pan are cool, cut in squares. Do not frost. Remove brownies, one at a time, to baking sheet covered with waxed paper. Beat ½ c. heavy cream until it peaks when beater is removed. Beat in 2 tblsp. sugar and ½ tsp. vanilla. Top each brownie with a teaspoonful of whipped cream, forming a peak. Freeze. When frozen, place in plastic bag and return to freezer. Will keep in good condition up to 3 months.

COTTAGE CHEESE BROWNIES

Two chocolate layers with luscious cheese filling between

3 squares unsweetened chocolate	½ tsp. lemon juice
½ c. butter	½ c. unsifted flour
1¼ c. sugar	½ tsp. baking powder
1½ tsp. vanilla	¼ tsp. salt
1 tblsp. cornstarch	½ c. chopped walnuts
¾ c. creamed cottage cheese	½ tsp. almond extract
3 eggs	

Melt chocolate and 6 tblsp. butter over hot water.

Cream remaining 2 tblsp. butter, ¼ c. sugar and ½ tsp. vanilla. Add cornstarch, cottage cheese, 1 egg and lemon juice; beat until smooth. Set aside.

Beat remaining 2 eggs until thick. With a spoon, gradually stir in remaining 1 c. sugar. Beat with spoon until thoroughly mixed. Stir in chocolate mixture.

Mix and sift together flour, baking powder and salt. Stir into chocolate mixture. Mix in nuts, remaining 1 tsp. vanilla and almond extract. Spoon half of batter into bottom of greased 9" square pan. Spread evenly.

Cover with cottage cheese mixture. Carefully spoon remaining batter over top. With a spoon, zigzag through batter. Bake in moderate oven (350°) 35 minutes. Cool in pan set on rack 10 minutes, or cool completely. Cut in 2¼" squares. Makes 16.

HALLOWEEN THREE-DECKER BROWNIES

These orange-and-black treats are brownies in gala, holiday dress

First Deck:

2 squares unsweetened chocolate
½ c. butter
1 c. sugar
2 eggs, beaten
½ tsp. vanilla
½ c. sifted flour
½ c. chopped pecans

Second Deck:

1 c. confectioners sugar
2 tblsp. soft butter
2 tsp. milk
½ tsp. vanilla
3 or 4 drops orange food color
(or use mixture of yellow and red to make orange)

Third Deck:

¼ square unsweetened chocolate   1½ tsp. butter

To make first deck, combine chocolate and butter; melt over hot water. Beat in sugar, eggs and vanilla. Stir in flour and nuts. Bake in greased 8" square pan in slow oven (325°) 30 to 35 minutes. Cool in pan on rack.

To make second layer, combine confectioners sugar, butter, milk and vanilla to make a smooth mixture. Tint orange with food color. Spread over brownies in pan. Chill 10 minutes.

To make third deck, combine chocolate and butter; melt over hot water. Drizzle from small spoon over top of brownies. Cool in pan on rack, and cut in 2" squares. Makes 16.

MOCHA BROWNIES

The chocolate/coffee team is tops—do try the frosted brownies

2 squares unsweetened chocolate
⅓ c. butter or regular
  margarine
2 eggs
1 c. sugar
1 tsp. vanilla

¾ c. sifted flour
½ tsp. baking powder
¼ tsp. salt
2 tblsp. instant coffee powder
½ to ¾ c. chopped walnuts
  (optional)

Melt chocolate and butter together over very low heat, stirring constantly. Set aside to cool.

Beat eggs until light; gradually add sugar and beat until light and fluffy. Add vanilla. Combine with chocolate mixture and mix well.

Sift together flour, baking powder, salt and coffee powder; stir into chocolate mixture and mix well. Fold in nuts. Pour into greased 8″ square pan.

Bake in moderate oven (350°) 30 minutes, or until a slight imprint remains when fingertips touch center top. Cool in pan set on rack, then cut in 2″ squares. Makes 16.

Variation

Frosted Mocha Brownies: Bake brownies as directed. After brownies in pan are cool, but before cutting them, spread with this frosting: Melt 1 square unsweetened chocolate with 1 tblsp. butter or margarine over hot water (or over very low heat, stirring constantly). Blend in 1½ tblsp. very hot and strong liquid coffee and about 1 c. sifted confectioners sugar, enough to make a frosting that spreads smoothly and easily.

ORANGE BROWNIES

The new twist in these brownies is the delicate fresh orange taste

2 squares unsweetened chocolate
½ c. butter
2 eggs
1 c. sugar
1 tsp. vanilla

½ tsp. grated orange peel
½ c. sifted flour
⅛ tsp. salt
1 c. chopped walnuts

Melt chocolate and butter. Beat eggs; beat in sugar gradually. Beat in butter and chocolate, vanilla and orange peel.

Stir in flour, salt and nuts. Pour into greased 8″ square pan.

Bake in moderate oven (350°) 20 to 25 minutes. Do not over-bake. Cut in 2″ squares. Cool on racks. Makes 16.

Variation

Double Chocolate Brownies: Stir in ½ c. semisweet chocolate pieces along with the nuts.

PINEAPPLE/CHOCOLATE BARS

Pineapple and chocolate unite tastily in these two-tone specials

¾ c. shortening

½ c. sugar

3 eggs

1 tsp. vanilla

½ tsp. ground cinnamon

½ tsp. salt

1 tsp. baking powder

1 c. sifted flour

¼ c. chopped nuts

2 squares semisweet chocolate, melted

1 (8½ oz.) can crushed pine-apple, well drained (⅔ c.)

Combine shortening, sugar, eggs and vanilla; beat until mixture is creamy.

Sift together cinnamon, salt, baking powder and flour. Add to shortening mixture. Stir in nuts.

Divide batter in half. To one half add melted chocolate; spread in greased 9″ square pan. To second half add pineapple; spread over chocolate mixture in pan.

Bake in moderate oven (350°) 35 minutes. Cool in pan on rack. When cool, cut in 3 x 1″ bars. Makes 27.

TWO-TONE BROWNIES

Color contrast of the dark and light layer provides a happy change

⅓ c. shortening

1 c. sugar

2 eggs

½ c. sifted flour

½ tsp. baking powder

½ tsp. salt

1 tsp. vanilla

1 c. chopped nuts

1½ squares unsweetened chocolate, melted

Cream shortening and sugar until light and fluffy; beat in eggs.

Sift dry ingredients together and add to creamed mixture. Mix thoroughly. Stir in vanilla and nuts.

Divide dough in half. To one half, add
greased 8″ square pan. Spread remaining half of

Bake in moderate oven (375°) about 20 minutes,
pick inserted in center comes out clean. Cool in pan set
minutes, or cool completely, then cut in 2″ squares. Makes 1

BUTTERSCOTCH BROWNIES

Quick-and-easy cookie squares have glossy, caramel-colored tops

1 (6 oz.) pkg. butterscotch pieces	1 c. sifted flour
¼ c. shortening	1 tsp. baking powder
1 c. brown sugar, firmly packed	½ tsp. salt
2 eggs	½ c. coarsely chopped walnuts
½ tsp. vanilla	

Melt butterscotch pieces and shortening in double boiler over hot
water. Remove from heat and stir in brown sugar; cool 5 minutes.

Stir eggs and vanilla into butterscotch mixture to blend thoroughly.

Sift together flour, baking powder and salt. Blend into batter. Stir
in nuts. Spread in greased 13 x 9 x 2″ pan and bake in moderate oven
(350°) about 25 minutes. Set pan on rack. While still warm, cut in
2″ (about) squares (cookies are especially good warm from the
oven). Makes about 2 dozen.

PEANUT BUTTER BROWNIES

Delightful treat for those in your family who like a chewy cookie

6 eggs	1 tblsp. vanilla
3 c. sugar	4 c. unsifted flour
1½ c. brown sugar, firmly packed	1½ tblsp. baking powder
1 c. peanut butter	1½ tsp. salt
½ c. shortening	½ c. chopped peanuts

Combine eggs, sugars, peanut butter, shortening and vanilla; blend
thoroughly.

Add dry ingredients; mix only until dough is smooth. Spread evenly
in two lightly greased 15½ x 10½ x 1″ jelly roll pans (or three
13 x 9 x 2″ pans). Sprinkle with peanuts.

Bake in moderate oven (350°) 25 minutes. Cut in 3 x 1″ bars and
cool in pans on racks. Makes about 8 dozen.

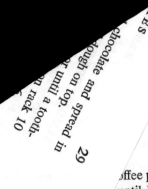

chocolate and spread in
dough on top.
on until a tooth-
on rack 10

29

IES

...d brittle—they're really that good

1 c. sugar
2 c. sifted flour
1 (6 oz.) pkg. semisweet
chocolate pieces
½ c. finely chopped almonds

...ffee powder, salt and almond extract. Gradu-
a... ...until light and fluffy.

Sti... ...ocolate pieces. Press batter into ungreased 15½ x 10½ x 1... ...pan. Sprinkle almonds over top.

Bake in mode... ...e oven (375°) 23 to 25 minutes, or until golden brown. Set pan on rack; cut in 2½ x 1½″ bars while warm. When cool, remove from pan. Makes 40.

N O T E : If you want to break the cookies in irregular pieces, cool baked cookie dough in pan on rack, then break it in pieces with your fingers. Cookies are crisp.

CHOCOLATE CHIP BARS

Keep your cookie jar filled with these for a good hostess reputation

1 c. butter or regular margarine
1 c. light brown sugar, firmly packed
1 tsp. vanilla
⅛ tsp. salt

2 c. sifted flour
1 (6 oz.) pkg. semisweet chocolate pieces
1 c. chopped pecans or walnuts

Beat butter with sugar until mixture is light and fluffy. Beat in vanilla.

Blend salt with flour and stir into beaten mixture, mixing well. Fold in chocolate pieces and nuts. Press into ungreased 15½ x 10½ x 1″ jelly roll pan.

Bake in moderate oven (350°) 20 minutes. While warm, cut in 2½ x 1½″ bars. Cool in pan on rack. Makes 3 dozen.

CHOCOLATE FUDGE COOKIES

There's a citrus tang in these rich bars fast-made with a cake mix

2 eggs
½ tsp. baking soda
½ c. melted butter
1 tblsp. grated orange peel
1 (about 19 oz.) pkg. devil's food cake mix

½ c. sifted flour
1 (6 oz.) pkg. semisweet chocolate pieces
⅔ c. chopped walnuts
Confectioners sugar

In a mixing bowl, beat eggs with baking soda. Beat in butter. Add orange peel, cake mix and flour. Stir until all ingredients are moistened (mixture will be stiff). Stir in chocolate pieces and nuts.

Turn batter into greased 15½ x 10½ x 1" jelly roll pan; spread dough evenly over bottom of pan using fork tines. Bake in moderate oven (350°) 12 to 13 minutes, or until toothpick inserted in center comes out clean. (Cookies will not appear to be done.) Place pan on rack to cool. While still warm, cut in 1½" squares; sift confectioners sugar generously over top. Makes about 5½ dozen.

CHOCOLATE MERINGUE BARS

This cookie has everything—eye and appetite appeal and fine flavor

¾ c. shortening
½ c. sugar
½ c. brown sugar, firmly packed
3 eggs, separated
1 tsp. vanilla
1 tsp. baking powder
¼ tsp. baking soda

¼ tsp. salt
2 c. sifted flour
1 (6 oz.) pkg. semisweet chocolate pieces
½ c. flaked coconut
½ c. chopped nuts
1 c. brown sugar, firmly packed

Beat together shortening, white sugar and ½ c. brown sugar until light and fluffy. Beat in egg yolks and vanilla to mix well.

Sift together baking powder, baking soda, salt and flour. Add to creamed mixture. Pat into greased 13 x 9 x 2" pan. Sprinkle top with chocolate pieces, coconut and nuts.

Beat egg whites until frothy; gradually add 1 c. brown sugar, beating constantly. Beat until stiff. Spread over cookie dough in pan.

Bake in moderate oven (375°) 25 to 30 minutes. Set pan on rack to cool, then cut in 3 x 1" bars. Makes about 3 dozen.

CHOCOLATE MOLASSES COOKIES

You mix these in a saucepan. Molasses gives the new flavor

½ c. butter or regular margarine
¼ c. molasses
¾ c. brown sugar, firmly packed
1 egg
1 c. sifted flour

½ tsp. salt
½ tsp. baking soda
1 (6 oz.) pkg. semisweet
    chocolate pieces

Heat butter and molasses. Add brown sugar; stir over low heat until sugar is melted. Cool.

Beat egg until light. Add to cooled molasses mixture.

Sift together flour, salt and baking soda. Add with chocolate pieces to molasses mixture. Mix well. Spread in greased 13 x 9 x 2" pan.

Bake in moderate oven (350°) 20 minutes. Set pan on rack to cool. When cool, cut in 3 x 1" bars. Makes 39.

CHOCOLATE/ORANGE BARS

Delicately spiced, orange-flavored bars with chocolate-nut topping

1 c. butter or regular margarine
1 c. light brown sugar, firmly
    packed
1 egg yolk
1 tblsp. grated orange peel
2½ c. sifted flour

⅛ tsp. salt
½ tsp. ground allspice
2 (6 oz.) pkgs. milk chocolate
    pieces
⅓ c. chopped walnuts

Beat butter, brown sugar and egg yolk until well blended. Beat in orange peel.

Sift together flour, salt and allspice. Stir into beaten mixture. Mix well. Spread batter in greased 13 x 9 x 2" pan.

Bake in moderate oven (375°) 15 to 20 minutes, until browned. Remove from oven and top at once with milk chocolate pieces, spreading with spatula as they melt. Sprinkle with nuts. Cool in pan set on rack, then cut in 3 x 1" bars. Makes 39.

CHOCOLATE/WALNUT COOKIES

Black walnuts lend flavor to these country-kitchen chocolate cookies

1 c. sugar	1 tsp. baking powder
2 eggs, well beaten	¼ tsp. salt
2 squares unsweetened chocolate	1 c. finely chopped black walnuts
½ c. butter or regular margarine	1 tsp. vanilla
1 c. sifted flour	Sifted confectioners sugar

Gradually add sugar to eggs. Melt chocolate with butter; stir into eggs.

Sift together flour, baking powder and salt. Add to first mixture with nuts and vanilla.

Bake in greased 15½ x 10½ x 1" jelly roll pan in moderate oven (350°) 12 to 15 minutes. Cool slightly in pan; dust with confectioners sugar. Cool completely in pan on rack; cut in diamonds, triangles or 1¾" bars. Makes about 7 dozen.

COCOA BARS

A cake-like bar with economical nut and cereal topping—good

2½ c. shortening	1 tblsp. vanilla
2½ c. sugar	2 tsp. salt
1 c. light corn syrup	2½ c. unsifted flour
8 eggs	1 c. chopped walnuts
1⅓ c. cocoa	1 c. oven-toasted rice cereal

Cream shortening and sugar until fluffy. Beat in corn syrup; beat in eggs, one at a time. Blend in cocoa. Add vanilla, salt and flour and blend.

Spread dough into two lightly greased 15½ x 10½ x 1" jelly roll pans (or three 13 x 9 x 2" pans). Combine nuts and cereal; sprinkle over dough.

Bake in moderate oven (350°) about 30 minutes. Cool in pans on racks, then cut in 3 x 1" bars. Makes about 8 dozen.

N O T E : Cereal topping may absorb moisture during storage. To restore crispness, open container of cookies 2 hours before serving.

FUDGE NUT BARS

Luscious fudge nut filling bakes between two layers of cookie mixture

1 c. butter or regular margarine
2 c. light brown sugar, firmly
  packed
2 eggs
2 tsp. vanilla
2½ c. sifted flour
1 tsp. baking soda
1 tsp. salt
3 c. quick-cooking rolled oats

1 (12 oz.) pkg. semisweet
  chocolate pieces
1 c. sweetened condensed milk,
  (not evaporated)
2 tblsp. butter or regular
  margarine
½ tsp. salt
1 c. chopped nuts
2 tsp. vanilla

Cream together 1 c. butter and sugar. Mix in eggs and 2 tsp. vanilla. Sift together flour, soda and 1 tsp. salt; stir in rolled oats. Add dry ingredients to creamed mixture. Set aside while you make filling.

In a saucepan over boiling water, mix together chocolate pieces, sweetened condensed milk, 2 tblsp. butter and ½ tsp. salt. Stir until chocolate pieces are melted and mixture is smooth. Remove from heat, and stir in nuts and 2 tsp. vanilla.

Spread about two-thirds of cookie dough in bottom of a greased 15½ x 10½ x 1″ jelly roll pan. Cover with fudge filling. Dot with remainder of cookie dough and swirl it over fudge filling.

Bake in moderate oven (350°) 25 to 30 minutes, or until lightly browned. Cut in small (2 x 1″) bars. Cool in pan on racks. Makes about 6 dozen.

HOSTESS BAR COOKIES

Tempting layered cookies with chocolate tops resemble candy bars

¾ c. butter
¾ c. sifted confectioners sugar
1 tsp. vanilla
1 tblsp. light or heavy cream
2 c. sifted flour
1 (6 oz.) pkg. butterscotch pieces
2 tblsp. light or heavy cream

¼ c. confectioners sugar
1 c. chopped pecans
½ c. semisweet chocolate pieces
2 tblsp. light or heavy cream
¼ c. confectioners sugar
1 tsp. vanilla

Combine butter, ¾ c. confectioners sugar, 1 tsp. vanilla, 1 tblsp. cream and flour in bowl; mix well to form dough. Pat into ungreased

13 x 9 x 2" pan. Bake in slow oven (325°) 25 minutes. Set pan on rack to cool.

Meanwhile, melt butterscotch pieces in small saucepan over low heat, stirring constantly until smooth. Remove from heat; add 2 tblsp. cream and ¼ c. confectioners sugar and beat until smooth. Fold in pecans. Spread over baked cookie in pan.

Melt chocolate pieces over low heat, stirring constantly. Remove from heat; stir in 2 tblsp. cream, ¼ c. confectioners sugar and 1 tsp. vanilla. Spread on top of filling on cookies. Cut in 3 x 1½" bars. Makes about 2 dozen.

INDIAN BARS

They're extra-moist chocolate brownies, and that means wonderful

1 c. butter or regular margarine	1½ c. sifted flour
2 squares unsweetened chocolate	1 tsp. baking powder
2 c. sugar	2 tsp. vanilla
4 eggs, slightly beaten	1 c. chopped pecans

Melt butter and chocolate over low heat. Add sugar and eggs; mix thoroughly.

Sift flour with baking powder; stir into creamed mixture. Mix in vanilla and nuts.

Bake in a greased 13 x 9 x 2" pan in moderate oven (350°) 35 to 40 minutes. Cool completely in pan set on rack. Cut in 3 x 1½" bars. Makes about 2 dozen.

N O T E : You can cut the recipe in half to make 12 cookie bars. Use an 8" square pan for baking the cookie mixture.

MARBLEIZED SQUARES

Light brown and dark chocolate variegate attractive, crinkled tops

½ c. butter or regular margarine	1 c. sifted flour
6 tblsp. sugar	½ tsp. salt
6 tblsp. brown sugar, firmly packed	½ tsp. baking soda
	½ c. broken walnuts
1 egg	1 (6 oz.) pkg. semisweet
½ tsp. vanilla	chocolate pieces

Beat butter until light; add white and brown sugars and beat until light and fluffy. Beat in egg and vanilla to mix thoroughly.

Sift together flour, salt and baking soda, and add to first mixture. Stir in nuts. Spread in greased 13 x 9 x 2″ pan. Sprinkle chocolate pieces evenly over top.

Place in moderate oven (350°) 1 minute. Remove from oven and run a knife through dough to marbleize it. Return to oven and bake 12 to 14 minutes. Set pan on rack. When cool, cut in 2″ (about) squares. Makes 2 dozen.

OATMEAL/CHOCOLATE BARS

Thick chewy bars that carry well to picnics and other gatherings

1½ c. brown sugar, firmly packed	1 tsp. salt
¾ c. sugar	1½ tsp. ground cinnamon
1 c. shortening	¾ c. milk
3 eggs	4 c. quick-cooking rolled oats
1 tsp. vanilla	1 (12 oz.) pkg. semisweet
2¼ c. sifted flour	chocolate pieces
1 tsp. baking soda	

Cream sugars with shortening until light and fluffy. Beat in eggs and vanilla.

Sift together flour, soda, salt and cinnamon. Add to creamed mixture along with milk. Stir in oats and chocolate pieces.

Spread batter in greased 15½ x 10½ x 1″ jelly roll pan. Bake in moderate oven (350°) about 30 minutes. While warm, cut in 2 x 1″ bars, but cool completely in pan on rack. Makes about 6 dozen.

SEA FOAM COOKIES

They get their name from meringue top; excellent flavor combination

½ c. shortening	1 tsp. baking soda
½ c. sugar	½ tsp. salt
½ c. brown sugar, firmly packed	3 tblsp. milk
2 eggs, separated	1 (6 oz.) pkg. semisweet
1 tsp. vanilla	chocolate pieces
2 c. sifted flour	1 c. brown sugar, firmly packed
2 tsp. baking powder	¾ c. chopped salted peanuts

Cream shortening with sugar and ½ c. brown sugar until light and fluffy. Beat in egg yolks and vanilla.

Sift together flour, baking powder, soda and salt; stir into creamed mixture alternately with milk. (The dough will be stiff.) Press dough into greased 13 x 9 x 2″ pan. Sprinkle evenly with chocolate pieces.

Beat egg whites until soft peaks form; gradually add remaining 1 c. brown sugar and beat, until very stiff and glossy. Spread over dough in pan. Scatter peanuts evenly over top.

Bake in slow oven (325°) 30 to 35 minutes. Cool in pan set on rack, then cut in 3 x 1″ bars. Makes 39.

SPICY CHOCOLATE BARS

Chocolate, always good, is even better in this richly spiced cookie

1½ c. shortening	2 tsp. salt
1½ c. sugar	4 tsp. ground cinnamon
1½ c. brown sugar, firmly packed	1 tsp. ground cloves
4 eggs	1 tsp. ground nutmeg
2 tsp. vanilla	2 c. semisweet chocolate pieces
4 c. unsifted flour	(12 oz. pkg.)
2 tsp. baking soda	

Cream shortening and sugars until fluffy. Beat in eggs, one at a time. Add vanilla.

Blend in dry ingredients; add chocolate pieces. Spread evenly in two ungreased 15½ x 10½ x 1″ jelly roll pans. Bake in moderate oven (375°) 20 minutes. Cut in 3 x 1″ bars; cool in pans on racks. Makes about 8 dozen.

NOTE: Instead of adding chocolate pieces to the batter, you can sprinkle them over top of dough before baking. Cookies may also be baked in three 13 x 9 x 2″ pans instead of the two jelly roll pans.

TOFFEE COOKIE SQUARES

Rich cookies that taste like toffee. Bake them for Christmas presents

½ c. butter or regular margarine	½ tsp. salt
½ c. shortening	2 c. sifted flour
1 c. brown sugar, firmly packed	1 (6 oz.) pkg. semisweet
1 egg yolk, unbeaten	chocolate pieces
1 tsp. vanilla	½ c. chopped nuts

Cream together butter, shortening, brown sugar and egg yolk. Stir in vanilla, salt and flour.

Pat mixture into lightly greased 15½ x 10½ x 1" jelly roll pan. Bake in slow oven (325°) 15 to 20 minutes.

Melt chocolate pieces; spread over warm baked mixture. Sprinkle with chopped nuts; cut in 2" squares while warm. Cool in pan on rack. Makes 3 dozen.

COCONUT/MOLASSES WUNDERBARS

A molasses/coconut candy, chocolate-coated, inspired this duplicate of the flavor combination in cookies—they're mighty good eating

½ c. butter or regular margarine	1 c. sifted flour
¾ c. brown sugar, firmly packed	¼ tsp. salt
¼ c. dark molasses	1 c. flaked coconut
2 eggs	4 (¾ oz.) milk chocolate candy
1 tsp. vanilla	bars

Cream butter and brown sugar until light and fluffy. Beat in molasses, eggs and vanilla to mix well.

Mix flour and salt thoroughly; gradually stir into creamed mixture. Stir in coconut.

Spread in greased 9" square pan. Bake in moderate oven (350°) about 25 minutes, or until lightly browned. Remove from oven and set pan on rack. Immediately place chocolate candy, broken in pieces, over the top. When chocolate melts, spread it evenly over top.

Cool completely in pan, then cut in 1½" squares. Makes 3 dozen.

FILLED OATMEAL BARS

It's the taste of chocolate-coated raisins that makes these so good

1 (15 oz.) can sweetened condensed milk (not evaporated)	1⅓ c. brown sugar, firmly packed
	1½ tsp. vanilla
	2 c. sifted flour
2 squares unsweetened chocolate	¾ tsp. salt
2 c. seedless raisins	½ tsp. baking soda
1 c. butter or regular margarine	2½ c. quick-cooking rolled oats

Combine sweetened condensed milk and chocolate; heat over boiling water until chocolate melts, stirring occasionally. Remove from heat; stir in raisins. Set aside to cool slightly.

Beat butter until light; beat in brown sugar and vanilla until fluffy.

Sift together flour, salt and baking soda; add rolled oats. Mix with creamed mixture until crumbly.

Press half of dough evenly into ungreased 13 x 9 x 2" pan. Cover with chocolate mixture. Sprinkle with remaining half of dough; press down slightly.

Bake in moderate oven (375°) about 25 minutes, or until golden brown. Set pan on rack to cool. Cut, while slightly warm, in 2 x 1" bars. Makes about 4 dozen.

SPICY APPLE BARS

Cut cookies larger and serve warm with vanilla ice cream on top for a compliment-winning dessert

½ c. shortening	1 tsp. ground cinnamon
1 c. sugar	½ tsp. ground nutmeg
2 eggs	¼ tsp. ground cloves
1 c. sifted flour	1 c. quick-cooking rolled oats
1 tsp. baking powder	1½ c. diced peeled apples
½ tsp. baking soda	½ c. coarsely chopped walnuts
½ tsp. salt	Sifted confectioners sugar
1 tblsp. cocoa	

Cream together shortening and sugar until light and fluffy; beat in eggs, one at a time.

Sift together flour, baking powder, baking soda, salt, cocoa and spices; add to creamed mixture. Stir in rolled oats, apples and nuts. Spread in greased 13 x 9 x 2" pan.

Bake in moderate oven (375°) about 25 minutes. Cool slightly in pan on rack; cut in 2 x 1½" bars. Sprinkle with confectioners sugar. Makes about 2½ dozen.

APPLESAUCE FUDGIES

The applesauce keeps the cookies moist longer than most brownies

2 squares unsweetened chocolate	1 c. sifted flour
½ c. butter	½ tsp. baking powder
½ c. sweetened applesauce	¼ tsp. baking soda
2 eggs, beaten	¼ tsp. salt
1 c. brown sugar, firmly packed	½ c. chopped walnuts
1 tsp. vanilla	

Melt chocolate and butter together.

Mix applesauce, eggs, sugar and vanilla. Sift dry ingredients into applesauce mixture. Stir until blended; add chocolate and stir well.

Pour into greased 9″ square pan. Sprinkle with walnuts. Bake in moderate oven (350°) 30 minutes. Cut in 2¼″ squares and cool in pan on racks. Makes 16.

APRICOT BARS

Color-bright bits of apricot and fruity topping make these luscious

1 c. dried apricots	1 tsp. baking powder
1 c. boiling water	¾ tsp. salt
½ c. butter or regular margarine	2 tsp. orange juice
2 c. brown sugar, firmly packed	2 tsp. lemon juice
2 eggs	1 tsp. grated orange peel
1 tsp. vanilla	2 tsp. soft butter
1 tsp. grated orange peel	1 c. sifted confectioners sugar
1¾ c. sifted flour	½ c. chopped walnuts

Put apricots in small bowl; pour on boiling water. Let stand 5 minutes. Then drain and cut in small bits with kitchen scissors.

Cream together ½ c. butter and brown sugar until light and fluffy; beat in eggs, vanilla and 1 tsp. orange peel.

Sift together flour, baking powder and salt; blend into creamed mixture. Stir in apricots.

Spread in greased 15½ x 10½ x 1″ jelly roll pan and bake in moderate oven (350°) about 20 minutes. Let cool in pan set on rack 10 minutes.

Meanwhile, blend orange and lemon juices, 1 tsp. orange peel, 2 tsp. butter and confectioners sugar, beating until smooth. Spread on cookies that have cooled 10 minutes in pan. Sprinkle with walnuts, pressing them in lightly so they will adhere to cookies. Complete cooling, then cut in 2¼ x 1¼″ bars. Makes about 56.

LUSCIOUS APRICOT BARS

Tang of apricots makes these special

⅔ c. dried apricots
½ c. butter
¼ c. sugar
1⅓ c. sifted flour
1 c. brown sugar, firmly packed
2 eggs, well beaten

½ tsp. baking powder
¼ tsp. salt
½ tsp. vanilla
½ c. chopped almonds
Confectioners sugar (optional)

Rinse apricots; cover with water and simmer 10 minutes. Drain, cool and chop.

Combine butter, white sugar and 1 c. flour; mix until crumbly. Pack into greased 9″ square pan. Bake in moderate oven (375°) 20 minutes.

Gradually beat brown sugar into eggs. Sift together remaining flour, baking powder and salt. Add to egg mixture; mix well. Add vanilla, ¼ c. almonds and apricots. Spread on baked layer. Sprinkle with remaining nuts.

Bake in moderate oven (350°) about 20 minutes. Cool in pan on rack. Cut in 1½″ squares. If you wish, sprinkle lightly with confectioners sugar. Makes 2½ dozen.

CRAN/APRICOT SCOTCHIES

Red filling has luscious tang, contrasts beautifully with snowy coating

1 c. apricot pulp (cooked dried apricots put through food mill), or drained and strained canned apricots
½ c. cooked or canned whole cranberry sauce
½ c. sugar
1 tblsp. flour
1 tblsp. lemon juice
2 tblsp. orange juice

2 tsp. butter
1½ c. brown sugar, firmly packed
¾ c. butter or regular margarine
2 eggs
1 c. flaked coconut
3¾ c. sifted flour
2 tsp. cream of tartar
1 tsp. baking soda
1 tsp. salt
Confectioners sugar (for coating)

Combine apricot pulp, cranberry sauce, sugar mixed with 1 tblsp. flour, lemon and orange juices and 2 tsp. butter in saucepan. Bring to a boil, stirring constantly. Reduce heat and simmer, stirring constantly, 5 minutes. Set filling aside to cool before using.

Cream together brown sugar and ¾ c. butter until light and fluffy. Beat in eggs. Add coconut; stir to mix.

Sift together flour, cream of tartar, baking soda and salt; stir into creamed mixture. Pat half of mixture into greased 13 x 9 x 2" pan.

Spoon cooled filling evenly over dough in pan. Sprinkle remaining half of dough over top (it will be crumbly, but will spread and cover during baking).

Bake in moderate oven (350°) 30 minutes. Cool in pan on rack. Cut in 3 x 1" bars and roll in confectioners sugar. Makes about 3 dozen.

NOTE: The filling is rather soft when cookies come from oven, but it firms when cooled completely. If you want to serve cookies before thorough cooling, use 1½ tblsp. flour instead of 1 tblsp. to thicken filling.

CHERRY/WALNUT BARS

Pink-frosted cookies with shortbread base, rich candy-like topping

2¼ c. sifted flour	½ tsp. vanilla
½ c. sugar	1 (2 oz.) jar maraschino cherries
1 c. butter	½ c. chopped walnuts
2 eggs	1 tblsp. softened butter
1 c. brown sugar, firmly packed	1 c. confectioners sugar
½ tsp. salt	½ c. flaked coconut (optional)
½ tsp. baking powder	

Mix flour, sugar and 1 c. butter until crumbly. Press into ungreased 13 x 9 x 2" pan. Bake in moderate oven (350°) 20 minutes, or until crust is lightly browned.

Blend together eggs, brown sugar, salt, baking powder and vanilla.

Drain and chop cherries, reserving liquid. Stir chopped cherries and walnuts into blended mixture. Spread on top of baked crust. Return to oven and bake 25 minutes. Remove from oven; cool in pan on rack.

Combine softened butter and confectioners sugar with enough reserved cherry liquid to spread. Spread on cookies; sprinkle with coconut, if you wish. When icing has set, cut in 2 x 1" bars. Makes 48.

MARSHMALLOW/CHERRY BARS

Tall, dainty-pink marshmallow topping with dots of red cherries

¾ c. butter or regular margarine
⅓ c. brown sugar, firmly packed
1½ c. sifted flour
2 envelopes unflavored gelatin
½ c. cold water
2 c. sugar

½ c. cherry juice and water
1 (8 oz.) jar maraschino cherries,
  drained and chopped
½ c. chopped almonds
3 drops red food color
½ tsp. almond extract

Combine butter, brown sugar and flour; mix well and press into ungreased 13 x 9 x 2" pan. Bake in slow oven (325°) 30 minutes. Set aside to cool.

Soften gelatin in ½ c. water.

Combine white sugar and juice drained from cherries (with enough water added to make ½ c.). Bring to a boil over medium heat and boil 2 minutes. Remove from heat and stir in softened gelatin. Beat with electric mixer at medium speed until very stiff, about 20 minutes (mixture climbs beaters as it thickens).

Fold in cherries and almonds. Add food color and almond extract. Spread on top of baked crust in pan. Let stand at room temperature until topping sets. Cut in 2 x 1" bars. Cover pan with lid or foil and leave in a cool place until time to serve. Makes about 48.

HERMITS—SEA-VOYAGE COOKIES

You don't have to tax your imagination to appreciate how marvelous New England Hermits tasted to men at sea. Canisters, lovingly filled and tucked into chests, went on clipper ships from Massachusetts to many faraway places. Eyes brightened when the cookies appeared, for they brought remembrances of home. Good travelers and keepers.

These hearty American cookies, spiced and fruited, never went out of style. Good today served with hot coffee. Our recipe comes from Cape Cod.

NEW ENGLAND HERMITS

Roll cookies in confectioners sugar for a homey, quick dress-up

½ c. butter	1 tsp. ground cinnamon
½ c. sugar	½ tsp. ground cloves
2 eggs	¼ tsp. ground nutmeg
½ c. molasses	⅛ tsp. ground allspice
2 c. sifted flour	3 tblsp. chopped citron
½ tsp. salt	½ c. chopped raisins
¾ tsp. baking soda	½ c. currants
¾ tsp. cream of tartar	¼ c. chopped walnuts

Cream butter with sugar until light and fluffy. Beat in eggs and molasses.

Sift together flour, salt, baking soda, cream of tartar and spices; stir into creamed mixture. Stir in citron, raisins, currants and nuts.

Spread batter evenly in greased 13 x 9 x 2" pan. Bake in moderate oven (350°) about 20 minutes, or until done. (Touch lightly with fingertip. If no imprint remains, cookies are done.)

Set pan on rack to cool, cutting in 3 x 1" bars while slightly warm. Cool completely before removing from pan. Makes 39.

TEATIME CURRANT COOKIES

Remember how Grandma's currant teacakes tasted? Moist, tender!

1 c. dried currants	1¾ c. sifted flour
1 c. water	¼ tsp. salt
½ c. salad oil	1 tsp. baking soda
1 egg	½ c. chopped pecans
1 c. sugar	1 c. sifted confectioners sugar

Place currants and water in 1-qt. saucepan; bring to a boil. Remove from heat, add salad oil and let cool.

Beat egg slightly; gradually add sugar, beating until thoroughly mixed. Beat in thoroughly cooled currant mixture.

Sift flour, salt and baking soda together and add to currant mixture. Stir in nuts.

Spread in greased 13 x 9 x 2" pan; bake in moderate oven (375°) 20 minutes (test for doneness with a wooden toothpick). Remove from oven and set pan on rack to cool 10 minutes. Cut in 2¼ x 1" bars (about) and roll in confectioners sugar. Cool completely on racks. Makes 4 dozen.

CHINESE CHEWS

Distinctive, marvelous in taste and good keepers if you hide them

1 c. sugar	1 c. chopped pitted dates
¾ c. sifted flour	1 c. chopped nuts
1 tsp. baking powder	2 eggs, beaten
¼ tsp. salt	Confectioners sugar

Sift sugar, flour, baking powder and salt into bowl. Stir in dates and nuts.

Add eggs; mix thoroughly. Spread in greased 15½ x 10½ x 1″ jelly roll pan. Bake in moderate oven (375°) about 20 minutes.

Cut in 2 x 1″ bars while warm; sprinkle lightly with confectioners sugar. Cool in pan set on rack. Makes about 6 dozen.

DATE-FILLED OAT COOKIES

Lemon peel and spices give tantalizing fragrance, distinctive taste

1 c. chopped dates	¾ tsp. ground cinnamon
½ c. sugar	½ c. light brown sugar, firmly
¼ c. orange juice	packed
½ c. water	1 tsp. grated lemon peel
1 c. sifted flour	½ c. butter or regular margarine
¼ tsp. salt	¼ c. milk
¼ tsp. baking soda	1½ c. quick-cooking rolled oats
¼ tsp. ground nutmeg	

Combine dates, sugar, orange juice and water in small saucepan. Cook, stirring, until thick; set aside to cool. You'll have about 1¾ c. filling.

Sift together flour, salt, baking soda, nutmeg and cinnamon. Add brown sugar and lemon peel, blending well. Blend in butter with pastry blender, as for pie crust. Add milk; stir in rolled oats.

Spread half of dough in greased 8″ square pan. Spread date filling evenly over top.

Roll remaining half of dough between sheets of waxed paper into an 8″ square to fit pan. Fit dough over filling.

Bake in moderate oven (350°) 25 to 30 minutes. Cool in pan set on rack. Cut in bars about 2½ x 1″. Makes 2 dozen.

DATE/NUT BARS

These cake-like cookies and coffee make great evening refreshments

1 c. sifted confectioners sugar	½ tsp. baking powder
1 tblsp. oil	¾ c. chopped nuts
2 eggs, beaten	1 c. chopped dates
¼ c. sifted cake flour	1 tsp. vanilla
¼ tsp. salt	Confectioners sugar (for tops)

Add 1 c. confectioners sugar and oil to eggs; blend well.

Add sifted dry ingredients. Stir in nuts, dates and vanilla.

Pour into greased 9″ square pan. Bake in slow oven (325°) 25 minutes. Cool slightly in pan on rack. Cut in 3 x 1″ bars; sprinkle with confectioners sugar. Makes 27.

DATE SANDWICH BARS

Easy to tote when you're asked to bring cookies. They'll win praise

¼ c. sugar	1 c. brown sugar, firmly packed
3 c. cut-up dates	1¾ c. sifted flour
1½ c. water	½ tsp. baking soda
¾ c. soft butter or regular margarine	1 tsp. salt
	1½ c. quick-cooking rolled oats

Mix sugar, dates and water, and cook over low heat until mixture thickens. Stir to prevent scorching. Set aside to cool.

Thoroughly mix butter and brown sugar. Beat until fluffy.

Stir flour, baking soda and salt together. Stir into the brown sugar-butter mixture. Add rolled oats and mix well. Divide in half and spread one part into greased 13 x 9 x 2″ pan. Flatten and press it down with hands so the mixture will cover the bottom of the pan.

Spread the cooled date mixture on top. Sprinkle evenly with the second half of the rolled oat mixture. Pat it down lightly with hands.

Bake in hot oven (400°) 25 to 30 minutes, or until a delicate brown. Remove from oven; while warm, cut in 2 x 1½″ bars. Remove bars at once from pan to racks to finish cooling. Makes about 30.

FRENCH BARS

Delicate as spice cake. Dress up cookies with Orange Butter Frosting

2¼ c. brown sugar, firmly packed
4 eggs, well beaten
1½ c. soured evaporated milk
  (see Note)
1½ tsp. baking soda
2¼ c. unsifted flour
1 tsp. ground cinnamon

½ tsp. salt
1½ c. chopped walnuts
1½ c. cut-up dates
1 c. toasted flaked coconut
Orange Butter Frosting (recipe
  follows)

Add sugar to eggs and beat until thick. Stir in soured evaporated milk.

Blend in dry ingredients. Stir in nuts, dates and coconut. Do not overmix batter.

Spread dough evenly in two lightly greased 15½ x 10½ x 1" jelly roll pans (or three 13 x 9 x 2" pans). Bake in moderate oven (350°) about 20 minutes. Cool in pans on racks. Frost if desired, and cut in 2½ x 1" bars. Makes 80.

N O T E : To sour evaporated milk, pour 1½ tblsp. vinegar into a 2-cup measure. Add evaporated milk until measurement is 1½ c. Stir well and set aside a few minutes before using.

Orange Butter Frosting: Combine 1 lb. confectioners sugar, sifted, with ¼ c. butter, ¼ c. orange juice, ½ tsp. salt and 1 tsp. grated orange peel. Beat until creamy. Spread on cooled bars. (Let frosting set before cutting cookies).

NUT AND FRUIT BARS

It's wonderful how fast these date cookies sell at Christmas bazaars

3 eggs
1 tsp. vanilla
1 c. sugar
1 c. sifted flour
½ tsp. salt
1 tsp. baking powder

1 c. chopped walnuts
1 (8 oz.) pkg. pitted dates
1 (6 oz.) jar maraschino
  cherries, drained
Confectioners sugar

Combine eggs and vanilla. Beat well. Add sugar and flour sifted with salt and baking powder; blend well. Stir in nuts and fruits.

Bake in greased 15½ x 10½ x 1" jelly roll pan in moderate oven

(350°) 30 minutes. Cool in pan on rack. Cut in 2″ squares. Sprinkle with confectioners sugar. Store in airtight box. Makes 3 dozen.

ORANGE/DATE BARS

These are "candy cookies"; roll moist bars in confectioners sugar

½ lb. pitted dates	1 tsp. baking soda
2 tblsp. flour	1¾ c. sifted flour
1 c. water	½ tsp. salt
¾ c. shortening	½ c. chopped nuts (optional)
1 c. brown sugar, firmly packed	1 (16 oz.) pkg. candy orange
1 tsp. vanilla	slices (gumdrops)
2 eggs	

Put dates, 2 tblsp. flour and water in small saucepan. Bring to a boil and cook until mixture is thick. Set aside to cool.

Cream shortening, brown sugar and vanilla until light and fluffy. Beat in eggs.

Sift together baking soda, 1¾ c. flour and salt; add to creamed mixture. Stir in nuts. Spread half of dough in bottom of greased 13 x 9 x 2″ pan.

Cut candy orange slices in lengthwise thirds; cover dough in pan with candy arranged in straight rows crosswise in pan. Spread cooled date mixture on top of orange slices. Carefully top with remaining half of dough.

Bake in moderate oven (350°) 40 minutes. Cool in pan on rack, then cut between orange slices to make bars about 2 x 1″. Makes about 4 dozen.

ORANGE/DATE DAINTIES

Orange/date flavors blend and lift these out of the commonplace

1 c. finely cut dates	1 c. sifted cake flour
1 c. orange juice	¼ tsp. baking soda
2 tsp. grated orange peel	½ tsp. baking powder
¼ c. regular margarine	⅛ tsp. salt
½ c. sugar	¼ c. orange juice
1 egg	¾ c. crushed corn flakes

Combine dates and 1 c. orange juice in heavy pan. Cook over low heat, stirring, until mixture is thick and smooth. Cool slightly; stir in orange peel and set aside.

Beat together margarine and sugar until light and fluffy. Beat in egg to blend well.

Sift together cake flour, baking soda, baking powder and salt. Add alternately with ¼ c. orange juice to beaten mixture, beating after each addition.

Spread batter in lightly greased 15½ x 10½ x 1″ jelly roll pan. Top batter with reserved orange-date mixture, spreading evenly. Sprinkle corn flakes over the top.

Bake in moderate oven (375°) about 25 minutes. Set pan on rack; while still hot, cut in 2″ squares. Makes about 40.

TREASURE BARS

Nuts, coconut, dates or chocolate are the hidden treasure in these

1 c. sifted flour	½ tsp. baking powder
½ c. brown sugar, firmly packed	¼ tsp. salt
½ c. butter	1 c. chopped walnuts
2 eggs	1 c. shredded coconut
1 c. brown sugar, firmly packed	½ c. chopped dates or semisweet
1 tsp. vanilla	chocolate pieces
1 tblsp. flour	

Combine 1 c. flour and ½ c. brown sugar; cut in butter. Press into greased 13 x 9 x 2″ pan. Bake in moderate oven (350°) 12 minutes. Cool on rack 5 minutes.

Meanwhile, beat eggs slightly. Add 1 c. brown sugar gradually, beating until light and fluffy. Blend in vanilla.

Sift together 1 tblsp. flour, baking powder and salt. Stir into egg mixture. Stir in nuts, coconut and dates. Spread over baked crust. Return to oven and bake 25 minutes. Cool in pan on rack, then cut in 2½ x 1½″ bars. Makes about 2½ dozen.

CALIFORNIA LEMON BARS

Hostess favorite—rich cookies, great with beverages and ice cream

1 c. sifted flour	2 tblsp. flour
½ c. butter or regular margarine	1½ c. confectioners sugar
¼ c. confectioners sugar	1 tsp. vanilla
2 eggs, beaten	2 tblsp. melted butter or
1 c. sugar	margarine
½ tsp. baking powder	1 tblsp. milk (about)
2 tblsp. lemon juice	

Blend 1 c. flour, ½ c. butter and ¼ c. confectioners sugar as for pastry. Press into ungreased 8" square pan. Bake in moderate oven (350°) 20 minutes.

Combine eggs, sugar, baking powder, lemon juice and 2 tblsp. flour. Pour onto baked bottom layer and bake in moderate oven (350°) 25 minutes. Cool slightly in pan.

Combine 1½ c. confectioners sugar, vanilla, 2 tblsp. butter and enough milk to make mixture of spreading consistency. Spread on top of baked cookies in pan. Cool in pan on rack, then cut in 2½ x 1¼" bars. Makes 1½ dozen.

LEMON MERINGUE BARS

These cookies taste like lemon meringue pie—and that's good!

½ c. butter or regular margarine	2 tsp. finely grated lemon peel
½ c. sifted confectioners sugar	½ c. sugar
2 eggs, separated	½ c. chopped walnuts
1 c. sifted flour	16 walnut halves
¼ tsp. salt	

Cream butter until light and fluffy. Gradually beat in confectioners sugar. Beat in egg yolks to blend.

Combine flour and salt; sift into egg yolk mixture. Stir in lemon peel. Spread evenly in greased 8" square pan.

Bake in moderate oven (350°) about 10 minutes, until lightly browned. Remove from oven. Set oven regulator to hot (400°).

Beat egg whites until they form stiff moist peaks; gradually beat in ½ c. sugar, blending well. Stir in chopped nuts. Spread meringue evenly over baked layer. Return to hot oven (400°) and bake about

5 to 7 minutes, until lightly browned. Remove from o...
tially cool in pan set on wire rack. Cut in 2″ squares and
square with a walnut half. Makes 16.

LEMON/COCONUT SQUARES

Delicate texture, fresh lemon flavor make these cookies special

Cookie Dough:
1½ c. sifted flour
½ c. brown sugar, firmly packed
½ c. butter or regular margarine

Filling:
2 eggs, beaten
1 c. brown sugar, firmly packed
1½ c. flaked or shredded coconut
1 c. chopped nuts
2 tblsp. flour
½ tsp. baking powder
¼ tsp. salt
½ tsp. vanilla

Frosting:
1 c. confectioners sugar
1 tblsp. melted butter or regular
  margarine
Juice of 1 lemon

Mix together ingredients for cookie dough; pat down well in buttered 13 x 9 x 2″ pan. Bake in very slow oven (275°) 10 minutes.

To make filling, combine eggs, sugar, coconut, nuts, flour, baking
powder, salt and vanilla. Spread on top of baked mixture. Bake in
moderate oven (350°) 20 minutes.

While still warm, spread with frosting made by combining confectioners sugar, melted butter and lemon juice. Cool slightly; cut in 2″
squares. Complete cooling in pan on racks. Makes about 24.

LEMON LOVE NOTES

Snowy confectioners sugar coating contributes to the cookies' charms

½ c. butter
1 c. sifted flour
¼ c. confectioners sugar
1 c. sugar
2 tblsp. flour
½ tsp. baking powder
2 eggs, beaten
2 tblsp. lemon juice
2 tsp. grated lemon peel

Mix butter, 1 c. flour and confectioners sugar. Press into an un-

ke in moderate oven (350°) 8 minutes or
on rack.

flour and baking powder. Add eggs, lemon
Pour evenly over baked, cooled mixture in

n (350°) 25 minutes. (Top puffs up in bak-
.) Cool in pan on rack and cut in 2″ squares.
ners sugar, if desired. Makes 16.

COFFEE COOKIE BARS

A hearty cookie, moist and tasty—a fine coffee accompaniment

1 c. brown sugar, firmly packed	½ tsp. baking soda
¼ c. shortening	½ tsp. salt
1 egg	½ c. hot, strong coffee
1 tsp. vanilla	½ c. raisins
1½ c. sifted flour	½ c. chopped nuts
½ tsp. ground cinnamon	Caramel Icing (recipe follows)
½ tsp. baking powder	

Cream sugar and shortening until light and fluffy. Beat in egg and
vanilla.

Sift together flour, cinnamon, baking powder, baking soda and
salt, and add alternately with hot coffee to creamed mixture. Stir in
raisins and nuts.

Spread dough in greased 13 x 9 x 2″ pan. Bake in moderate oven
(350°) 25 minutes. While hot, spread with Caramel Icing. Set pan
on rack to cool, then cut in 2 x 1″ bars. Makes about 4 dozen.

Caramel Icing: Combine 3 tblsp. brown sugar, firmly packed, 3 tblsp.
butter and 1 tblsp. dairy half-and-half, light cream or milk in 1-qt.
saucepan. Bring to a boil. Remove from heat and gradually add 1 c.
sifted confectioners sugar, beating constantly. If icing is not smooth,
place over low heat, stirring constantly, until lumps of sugar disappear. Makes enough to ice cookies baked in a 13 x 9 x 2″ pan.

FRUIT BARS

Excellent cookies to mail for gifts—they're good keepers

2 c. seedless raisins	1 c. sugar
1½ c. chopped mixed candied fruit	1 c. brown sugar, firmly packed
	2 eggs, beaten
1 c. chopped walnuts	4½ c. sifted flour
½ c. orange or pineapple juice	2 tsp. ground cinnamon
2 tsp. vanilla	2 tsp. baking powder
1 c. butter or regular margarine	1 tsp. baking soda

Rinse raisins in hot water, drain; dry on towel.

Combine raisins, candied fruit, nuts, juice and vanilla; let stand.

Cream together butter, sugars and eggs. Sift together dry ingredients and add in thirds to creamed mixture; mix until smooth. Add fruit mixture; blend well. Let stand 1½ hours in refrigerator, or overnight.

When ready to bake, spread dough in greased 15½ x 10½ x 1" jelly roll pan. Bake in hot oven (400°) 15 to 20 minutes, until lightly browned. Cool in pan set on rack. When cool, cut in bars about 3 x 1". Makes about 4 dozen.

RAISIN-FILLED BARS

Cooked raisin filling produces cookies that are good—like raisin pie

2 c. raisins	1½ c. quick-cooking or regular rolled oats
1⅓ c. water	
3 tblsp. cornstarch	1 c. melted butter or regular margarine
2 tblsp. cold water	
1 c. sugar	1½ c. sifted flour
1 tsp. vanilla	1 tsp. baking soda
1 c. brown sugar, firmly packed	½ tsp. salt
	1 c. chopped nuts

To make filling, cook raisins in 1⅓ c. water until tender. Dissolve cornstarch in 2 tblsp. cold water. Add sugar and cornstarch to raisins; stir until mixture thickens. Remove from heat, add vanilla and set aside to cool.

Add brown sugar and oats to melted butter; mix well.

Sift together flour, soda and salt; add to sugar-butter mixture. Stir in nuts. Pack half of mixture into bottom of greased 9" square pan. Spread raisin filling evenly on top. Then top with remaining crumb mixture.

Bake in moderate oven (350°) 30 minutes. Set pan on rack to cool 10 minutes, or cool completely, then cut in 3 x 1" bars. Makes about 27.

FAVORITE HONEY BARS

These chewy cookies are good. Play smart and double the recipe

½ c. shortening	½ tsp. baking powder
½ c. sugar	¼ tsp. salt
½ c. honey	1 c. quick-cooking rolled oats
1 egg, well beaten	1 c. flaked coconut
⅔ c. sifted flour	1 tsp. vanilla
½ tsp. baking soda	½ c. chopped nuts

Cream shortening, sugar and honey until light and fluffy. Add egg and blend.

Sift flour with soda, baking powder and salt; add to creamed mixture. Add oats, coconut, vanilla and nuts.

Spread in greased 15½ x 10½ x 1" jelly roll pan; bake in moderate oven (350°) 20 to 25 minutes. Cool in pan on rack. When cool, cut in 2½ x 1½" bars. Makes about 3 dozen.

NOTE: To trim, sprinkle confectioners sugar over tops of bars before serving.

HONEY/ALMOND TRIANGLES

A honey-almond topping bakes right on these rich, tasty cookies

½ c. butter	1¾ c. sifted flour
¼ c. sugar	½ c. sugar
2 tblsp. honey	2 tsp. baking powder
2 tblsp. milk	¼ tsp. salt
1 c. chopped, slivered or sliced almonds	½ c. butter
	1 egg
1 tsp. almond extract	

In saucepan combine ½ c. butter, ¼ c. sugar, honey, milk, almonds and almond extract. Bring to a full rolling boil, stirring constantly. Set aside to cool slightly.

Sift together flour, ½ c. sugar, baking powder and salt. With pastry blender, cut in ½ c. butter until particles are very fine.

Beat egg with a fork until blended; add to crumb mixture, tossing with a fork to mix. Gather dough and work with hands until mixture holds together. With lightly floured fingertips, press evenly over bottom of lightly greased 15½ x 10½ x 1″ jelly roll pan.

Pour honey-almond topping over dough and spread evenly. Bake in moderate oven (350°) 20 to 25 minutes, or until a deep golden color. Place pan on rack at least 10 minutes, or until cool. Cut in 2½″ squares, then cut each square diagonally to make triangles. Makes 4 dozen.

HONEYED LEMON SLICES

Honey and lemon blend their flavors in these superlative cookie bars

1 c. brown sugar, firmly packed	1 c. honey
2 c. sifted flour	2 tblsp. butter
½ c. butter or regular margarine	¼ c. lemon juice
1 c. cookie coconut	3 eggs, beaten

Blend together brown sugar, flour, ½ c. butter and coconut. Pat two-thirds of mixture into ungreased 9″ square pan.

In small saucepan, cook together honey, 2 tblsp. butter, lemon juice and eggs, stirring constantly, until mixture thickens. Cool and spread over mixture in pan. Sprinkle remainder of brown sugar mixture over top.

Bake in moderate oven (350°) 40 minutes. Cut in 1½″ squares and cool in pan on rack. Makes about 3 dozen.

LEBKUCHEN

Spicy German Christmas cookies with glazed tops—good keepers

¾ c. honey	1 tsp. ground cinnamon
¾ c. sugar	1 tsp. ground allspice
1 large egg	¼ tsp. ground cloves
1 tsp. grated lemon peel	⅓ c. chopped citron
1 tblsp. milk	½ c. chopped blanched almonds
2¾ c. sifted flour	1 c. sifted confectioners sugar
½ tsp. salt	4 tsp. water (about)

In large saucepan heat honey slightly, but do not boil. Remove from heat and stir in sugar. Beat in egg, then add lemon peel and milk.

Sift together flour, salt, cinnamon, allspice and cloves. Stir, a little at a time, into honey mixture. Stir in citron and almonds. Form dough into a ball; wrap in waxed paper and chill several hours or overnight.

Divide dough in half and let stand 15 to 20 minutes to warm slightly to make spreading in pans easier. Spread each half in a greased 13 x 9 x 2" pan (use a metal spoon moistened in water to spread dough).

Bake pans of dough separately in hot oven (400°) about 15 minutes, or until lightly browned. (Or test for doneness by touching lightly with fingertip. If no imprint remains, cookies are done.)

Place pans on cooling racks and brush cookie tops at once with confectioners sugar mixed with enough water to make a smooth icing. While still warm, cut in 3 x 1" bars or diamond shapes; remove from pans to cool on racks. When cool, store cookies in airtight containers. They will keep several weeks. Four or five days before serving, a cut apple or orange placed in canisters mellows and improves flavor of cookies. Makes about 6 dozen.

ENGLISH TEA SQUARES

Jam-filled bars are all-purpose cookies—serve with tea or coffee

¾ c. butter or regular margarine	¼ tsp. ground allspice
1 c. sugar	1 c. chopped almonds or walnuts
1 egg	½ c. strawberry jam
1 tsp. vanilla	3 tblsp. confectioners sugar
2 c. sifted flour	

Beat butter until light; add sugar and beat until light and fluffy. Beat in egg and vanilla to blend well. Stir in flour, allspice and almonds.

Spoon about half of mixture into lightly greased 9" square pan. Carefully spread strawberry jam over top. Top with remaining dough.

Bake in moderate oven (350°) 40 to 45 minutes, or until delicately browned. Remove to cooling rack and sift confectioners sugar over top. When cool, cut in 1½" squares. Makes 3 dozen.

JINGLE JAM BARS

You bake cake-like batter on berry jam and cut it in luscious ribbons

¼ c. butter	¾ c. sifted cake flour
1 c. red raspberry jam	1 tsp. baking powder
4 eggs	1 tsp. salt
¾ c. sugar	Confectioners sugar
1 tsp. vanilla	

Melt butter in 15½ x 10½ x 1" jelly roll pan. Mix jam with butter and spread evenly over bottom of pan.

Beat eggs until thick and lemon colored. Add sugar, 1 tblsp. at a time, beating after each addition. Add vanilla.

Sift together remaining dry ingredients and fold into egg mixture in 2 parts. Spread batter evenly over jam mixture in pan. Bake in hot oven (400°) 15 to 18 minutes. Remove from oven and let stand in pan for 5 minutes.

Then invert pan on sheet of wrapping paper or towel lightly dusted with confectioners sugar. Let stand 2 or 3 minutes. Then lift pan gradually, allowing cake to fall out slowly. Assist carefully with spatula, if necessary.

Cut cake crosswise in two equal pieces. Invert one piece over the other so that jam edges are together. Use paper to assist in turning one piece over the other. Cut in 2½ x 1½" bars. Cool on racks. Makes 20.

N O T E : You can use strawberry, apricot or other jam instead of raspberry.

MARMALADE BARS

If you're looking for a superb go-with for tea or coffee, here it is

1 c. orange marmalade	1½ c. sifted flour
½ c. chopped pecans	1 tsp. baking powder
½ c. flaked coconut	¼ tsp. baking soda
½ c. regular margarine	¼ tsp. salt
1 c. brown sugar, firmly packed	1 c. quick-cooking rolled oats
1 egg	Orange Confectioners Frosting
2 tblsp. orange juice	(recipe follows)

Combine marmalade, pecans and coconut. Set aside.

Beat margarine and brown sugar until light and fluffy. Beat in egg and orange juice to mix well.

Sift together flour, baking powder, soda and salt. Add to beaten mixture. Fold in rolled oats. Spread half of dough into well-greased 13 x 9 x 2" pan. Drop teaspoonfuls of marmalade mixture over dough and spread evenly to cover. Drop remaining half of dough over top. Carefully spread over filling.

Bake in moderate oven (350°) 35 to 38 minutes. While warm, frost with Orange Confectioners Frosting. Cool in pan set on rack, then cut in 3 x 1" bars. Makes 39.

Orange Confectioners Frosting: Combine 2 tblsp. soft margarine, 1½ c. sifted confectioners sugar and 2 to 3 tblsp. orange juice (or enough to make a frosting of spreading consistency). Beat until smooth.

SWEDISH ALMOND SHORTBREAD

A crisp bar, subtly flavored with toasted almonds; sugar-sprinkled

2 c. butter	½ tsp. salt
1 c. sugar	1 c. toasted slivered almonds
6 c. unsifted flour	Sugar (for top)
1 tblsp. vanilla	

Cream butter and sugar until fluffy. Work in flour, vanilla and salt. Roll out dough to fit two ungreased 15½ x 10½ x 1" jelly roll pans (or three 13 x 9 x 2" pans).

Sprinkle with almonds and sugar. Cut unbaked dough in 2½ x 1½" bars. Bake in moderate oven (350°) about 15 minutes. Immediately recut bars along same lines. Cool in pans on racks. Makes 80.

BRAZIL NUT BARS

Distinctive holiday cookies with a rich, nutty flavor—try them

2 c. sifted flour	1 c. light brown sugar, firmly packed
2 tsp. baking powder	
¾ tsp. salt	2 eggs, beaten
½ tsp. ground cinnamon	1 tsp. vanilla
½ c. shortening	1 c. thinly sliced or chopped Brazil nuts
⅓ c. butter or regular margarine	
	1 egg white

Sift together flour, baking powder, salt and cinnamon.

Cream together shortening, butter and brown sugar until light and fluffy. Add eggs and vanilla; beat until light. Add sifted dry ingredients and half of nuts. Spread in greased 15½ x 10½ x 1" jelly roll pan, or two 8" square pans.

Beat egg white slightly. Brush over dough; sprinkle with remaining nuts. Bake in moderate oven (350°) 20 to 30 minutes. Cut in 2 x 1" bars. Cool in pans on racks. Makes about 6 dozen.

BROWN SUGAR CHEWS

No-fat cookies have crisp crust, and chewy, sweet walnut centers

1 egg	¼ tsp. salt
1 c. brown sugar, firmly packed	¼ tsp. baking soda
1 tsp. vanilla	1 c. chopped walnuts
½ c. sifted flour	

Combine egg, brown sugar and vanilla. Mix thoroughly.

Sift together flour, salt and baking soda; stir into brown sugar mixture, then stir in nuts.

Spread in greased 8" square pan. Bake in moderate oven (350°) 15 to 18 minutes. Cool in pan on rack, then cut in 1½" bars. (Chews are soft when warm.) Makes 25.

BROWN SUGAR/NUT BARS

Cut these chewy cookies in small squares—they're rich, satisfying

1 lb. brown sugar	1 tsp. baking powder
1 c. butter	½ tsp. salt
2 eggs	1 c. coarsely chopped walnuts
2 c. sifted flour	

Cook sugar and butter in top of double boiler over hot water until sugar dissolves. Cool.

Add eggs, one at a time, beating thoroughly after each addition. Stir in remaining ingredients. Spread in ungreased 15½ x 10½ x 1" jelly roll pan. Bake in moderate oven (350°) 25 minutes. While hot, cut in 2" squares or desired size. Cool in pan on rack. Makes about 35.

BUTTERSCOTCH STRIPS

Cookies three ways—strips, man-size squares and a four-layer stack

½ c. butter
2 c. brown sugar, firmly packed
2 eggs
2 c. sifted flour
2 tsp. baking powder

½ c. chopped nuts
½ tsp. salt
2 tsp. vanilla
Confectioners sugar

Melt butter, add to sugar and cool. Blend in eggs. Stir in remaining ingredients.

Spread in lightly greased 13 x 9 x 2″ pan. Bake in slow oven (325°) about 30 minutes. While still warm, cut into 24 strips about 3 x 1½″. Roll in confectioners sugar. Cool on racks. Makes 2 dozen.

NOTE: These may be cut in 12 (3 x 3″) squares for man-size cookies.

Variation

Butterscotch Stack: Mix dough as directed and divide into four equal portions. Roll or pat out each portion into an 8″ circle between two pieces of waxed paper (draw an 8″ circle on counter top for guide).

Chill circles in refrigerator until top piece of paper can be peeled off easily; transfer circles on waxed paper to lightly greased baking sheets.

Bake in slow oven (325°) about 20 minutes. You may bake two at a time by using both oven shelves; be sure to exchange top and bottom baking sheets after 10 minutes in the oven for even browning.

Remove from baking sheet and cool on rack. When cool, peel off paper. Stack circles, spreading each with filling of whipped cream or scoops of softened ice cream. Freeze. To serve, let stand at room temperature about 15 minutes. Cut into wedges. Makes 10 to 12 servings.

CHEESECAKE BARS

They taste like cheesecake and that means rich and luscious

⅓ c. butter or regular margarine
⅓ c. brown sugar, firmly packed
1 c. sifted flour
½ c. chopped walnuts
¼ c. sugar

1 (8 oz.) pkg. cream cheese
1 egg, beaten
2 tblsp. milk
1 tblsp. lemon juice
½ tsp. vanilla

Cream butter and brown sugar until light; add flour and chopped walnuts. Cream with spoon until mixture forms crumbs. Set aside 1 c. mixture for topping. Press remaining crumb mixture into ungreased 8″ square pan.

Bake in moderate oven (350°) 12 to 15 minutes. Set pan on rack to cool.

Combine white sugar and cream cheese; beat until smooth. Add egg, milk, lemon juice and vanilla. Beat thoroughly to mix. Spread evenly in pan over baked crumbs. Sprinkle reserved 1 c. crumbs over top.

Bake in moderate oven (350°) 25 to 30 minutes. Set pan on rack to cool. Cut in 2 x 1″ bars and store in refrigerator. (Cookies are perishable and must be kept in refrigerator until eaten.) Makes 32.

FROSTED CARROT BARS

Carrots are the mystery ingredient in these wonderfully moist cookies

4 eggs
2 c. sugar
1½ c. salad oil
2 c. sifted flour
2 tsp. baking soda
2 tsp. ground cinnamon
1 tsp. salt

3 c. finely grated carrots (9 medium)
1½ c. flaked coconut
1½ c. chopped walnuts
Cream Cheese Frosting (recipe follows)

Beat eggs until light; gradually beat in sugar. Alternately add salad oil and flour sifted with soda, cinnamon and salt. Mix well.

Fold in carrots, coconut and walnuts. Spread evenly in two greased 13 x 9 x 2″ pans.

Bake in moderate oven (350°) 25 to 30 minutes. Set pans on racks and cool. Spread with Cream Cheese Frosting, then cut in 3 x 1″

bars. Remove from pans and place in covered container. Store in refrigerator or freezer. Makes 6½ dozen.

Cream Cheese Frosting: Blend 1 (3 oz.) pkg. cream cheese with 1 tblsp. dairy half-and-half or whole milk. Add 2½ c. sifted confectioners sugar, 3 tblsp. dairy half-and-half or whole milk (or enough to make a frosting of spreading consistency), 1 tsp. vanilla and ⅛ tsp. salt. Beat to mix.

PENUCHE DREAM BARS

And we give you a chocolate variation—try both and take your pick

Bottom Layer:

½ c. shortening	½ tsp. salt
½ c. brown sugar, firmly packed	2 tblsp. milk
1 c. sifted flour	

Top Layer:

2 eggs	½ tsp. baking powder
1 c. brown sugar, firmly packed	1 (3½ oz.) can flaked coconut (1⅓ c.)
1 tsp. vanilla	
½ tsp. salt	1 c. chopped pecans
2 tblsp. flour	

For bottom layer, cream shortening and brown sugar until light and fluffy. Mix together flour and salt; add to creamed mixture. Stir in milk. Pat evenly in greased 9″ square pan.

Bake in slow oven (325°) about 20 minutes, until light brown. Remove from oven.

To make top layer, combine eggs, brown sugar and vanilla; beat until mixture thickens.

Sift together salt, flour and baking powder; add to egg mixture. Mix well; stir in coconut and pecans. Spread evenly over baked bottom layer.

Bake in slow oven (325°) about 20 minutes, until golden brown. Set pan on rack and let cool, then cut in 2¼ x 1″ bars. Makes 3 dozen.

Variation

Chocolate Dream Bars: Make and bake bottom layer as for Penuche Dream Bars, but use ⅓ c. butter or regular margarine instead of ½ c.

shortening. Make top layer, substituting 1 (6 oz.) pkg. semisweet chocolate pieces for the coconut. Spread on baked layer and bake 15 to 20 minutes. Cool in pan on rack. Spread Easy Chocolate Icing on top and cut in 2¼ x 1″ bars.

Easy Chocolate Icing: Melt 1 tsp. butter with 1 square unsweetened chocolate over warm, not boiling, water. Remove from heat and stir in 1½ to 2 tblsp. hot water. Add enough sifted confectioners sugar (about 1 c.) to make icing that spreads easily. Beat until smooth. Makes enough to ice from 3 to 4 dozen cookies, depending on size, or a 9″ square pan of cookies.

PLANTATION PEANUT COOKIES

Cookies look and taste much like peanut brittle—a teen-age favorite

½ c. butter or shortening	1 c. sifted flour
½ c. brown sugar, firmly packed	¼ tsp. baking soda
1 egg, slightly beaten	½ tsp. ground cinnamon
1 tsp. vanilla	½ c. coarsely chopped salted
½ c. finely chopped salted peanuts	peanuts

Cream butter until light; beat in brown sugar until fluffy. Beat in 2 tblsp. beaten egg and vanilla to mix well. Add the ½ c. finely chopped peanuts.

Blend together flour, baking soda and cinnamon; add to creamed mixture. With floured fingers, pat dough on greased baking sheet to make a rectangle 14 x 10″. Brush top with remaining egg and sprinkle with coarsely chopped peanuts.

Bake in slow oven (325°) 20 to 22 minutes. Press lightly with finger. If a slight imprint remains, cookies are done. Use care not to overbake. While warm, cut in 3½ x 1½″ bars (or break in irregular pieces). Cool in pan on rack. Makes 2 dozen.

PECAN CHEWS

Easy-to-make cookies with a caramel, toasted-nut flavor

¾ c. butter
1½ c. brown sugar, firmly packed
1 egg
1 tsp. vanilla

½ tsp. salt
2 c. sifted flour
1 c. chopped toasted pecans
(see Index)

Cream butter and brown sugar until light and fluffy. Beat in egg, vanilla and salt. Blend in flour and nuts.

Spread dough in lightly greased 15½ x 10½ x 1″ jelly roll pan. Bake in moderate oven (375°) about 15 minutes, or until lightly browned. Cool in pan on rack, then cut in 3 x 1″ bars. Makes about 4 dozen.

NUT-CRESTED COOKIE SQUARES

Serve these candy-like cookies during the holidays with fruit punch

1 c. butter
1 c. brown sugar, firmly packed
1 tsp. vanilla
1 egg
2 c. sifted flour

⅛ tsp. salt
1 (6 oz.) pkg. semisweet
chocolate pieces
½ c. finely chopped nuts

Cream butter until fluffy; add brown sugar and beat until light. Add vanilla and egg; then add the flour and salt. Blend well.

Spread evenly about ¼″ thick on greased baking sheet. Bake in moderate oven (350°) 15 minutes.

Meanwhile melt chocolate pieces.

Remove baking sheet from oven and at once spread melted chocolate over top to frost evenly. Sprinkle with nuts. Cut in 2″ squares while still hot. Cool in pan on racks. Makes about 4 dozen.

Cookie Assortment. Everyone can choose his favorite. Inside jar, clockwise, starting top left: French Bars (page 47), Peanut Butter Brownies (page 29), Cocoa Bars (page 33) and Swedish Almond Shortbread (page 58).

Eight-in-One Recipe. Seven varieties of delicious crisp cookies from one recipe, Walnut/Cinnamon Squares (pages 67–68). One batch makes about six dozen — great to take to church suppers or bazaars.

SOUTHERN PRALINE BARS

Rich butterscotch flavor makes these chewy, frosted bars favorites

½ c. lard	1 tsp. salt
1½ c. brown sugar, firmly packed	2 tsp. vanilla
2 eggs	¾ c. chopped pecans
1½ c. sifted flour	Praline Frosting (recipe follows)
1 tsp. baking powder	

Melt lard in 2-qt. saucepan. Add remaining ingredients, except frosting, and mix well. Spread in greased 13 x 9 x 2″ pan.

Bake in moderate oven (350°) 25 to 30 minutes. Cool slightly in pan on rack, then spread with Praline Frosting. When cool, cut in 2 x 1½″ bars. Makes about 2½ dozen.

Praline Frosting: Melt together in saucepan 2 tblsp. butter, ¼ c. brown sugar, firmly packed, and 2 tblsp. light cream or milk. Stir in about 1 c. sifted confectioners sugar (enough to make a frosting of spreading consistency) and beat until smooth.

Variation

Coconut Praline Bars: Substitute ¾ c. flaked coconut for the pecans and bake as directed.

SWEDISH HEIRLOOM BARS

Dainty tea-party cookies accented with cinnamon—a women's special

1 c. sugar	2 c. sifted flour
1 c. shortening	½ tsp. salt
½ tsp. vanilla	1 tblsp. ground cinnamon
1 egg, separated	1 c. finely chopped nuts

Cream sugar, shortening and vanilla until mixture is light and fluffy. Beat in egg yolk.

Sift together flour, salt and cinnamon; stir into creamed mixture and mix well. Spread dough in greased 15½ x 10½ x 1″ jelly roll pan (dough will be spread thin).

Beat egg white until frothy and spread over top of dough. Sprinkle nuts evenly over egg white topping.

Bake in moderate oven (350°) about 20 minutes. Cool in pan on rack 10 minutes, then cut in 2 x 1½″ bars. Makes about 50.

SPEEDY COOKIES SUPREME

Quick and easy—youngsters like the pronounced brown sugar flavor

2 c. brown sugar, firmly packed　2 c. sifted flour
2 eggs　　　　　　　　　　　　　1 c. broken nuts
½ c. butter or shortening

Combine 1 c. brown sugar, 1 egg, beaten, butter and flour. Blend thoroughly. Press dough onto greased large baking sheet (about 17 x 14").

Beat the remaining egg and spread over top of dough on baking sheet; sprinkle with ½ c. brown sugar, then with nuts. Scatter remaining ½ c. brown sugar over top.

Bake in moderate oven (350°) about 15 minutes, until light brown. Cool on baking sheet set on rack 10 minutes, then cut in 2" squares, or desired shapes. Makes about 4½ dozen.

TOFFEE STICKS

These take more time to make than many bars, but they are worth it

¾ c. butter or regular margarine　1 (6 oz.) pkg. butterscotch pieces
½ c. brown sugar, firmly packed　¼ c. light corn syrup
1 egg yolk　　　　　　　　　　　1 tblsp. water
1 tsp. vanilla　　　　　　　　　　¼ tsp. salt
¼ tsp. salt　　　　　　　　　　　Toasted slivered almonds
1½ c. sifted flour　　　　　　　　　(for top)
2 tblsp. shortening

Blend together butter, brown sugar, egg yolk, vanilla and salt. Stir in flour. Spread mixture in greased 13 x 9 x 2" pan.

Bake in moderate oven (350°) 20 minutes, or until nicely browned. Cool slightly in pan on rack.

Combine shortening, butterscotch morsels, corn syrup, water and salt in saucepan. Heat and stir until smooth; spread over top of baked dough. Sprinkle on almonds. Allow topping to set, then cut in 2 x 1" sticks. Makes about 4 dozen.

WALNUT BARS

Chewy nut cookies have crackly tops—they disappear fast

¾ c. sifted flour	2 c. brown sugar, lightly packed
¼ tsp. salt	2 eggs
¼ tsp. baking soda	1 c. coarsely chopped walnuts

Sift together flour, salt and soda. Add sugar and eggs, mix well; then beat quickly until fluffy. Add nuts.

Bake in greased 9″ square pan in moderate oven (350°) 30 minutes. Cool in pan on rack, then cut in 2 x 1″ bars. Makes about 32.

WALNUT/CINNAMON SQUARES

This recipe and variations make eight different kinds of cookies

1 c. butter	2 c. sifted flour
1 c. sugar	1 tsp. ground cinnamon
1 egg, separated	1 c. finely chopped walnuts

In a mixing bowl, cream together butter and sugar. Beat in egg yolk to mix thoroughly.

Sift together flour and cinnamon; stir into creamed mixture and mix thoroughly. Spread dough evenly over bottom of lightly greased 15½ x 10½ x 1″ jelly roll pan.

Beat egg white slightly; brush over top of dough. With fingertips, smooth surface. Sprinkle nuts over dough and press in.

Bake in very slow oven (275°) 1 hour. While still hot, cut in 1½″ squares; cool in pans on racks. Makes about 5½ dozen.

Variations

Austrian Almond Squares: Make dough for Walnut/Cinnamon Squares, but substitute 1 tsp. ground nutmeg for the cinnamon and 1 c. chopped or sliced almonds for the walnuts. Bake as directed.

Orange/Pecan Flats: Make cookies as directed for Walnut/Cinnamon Squares, but add 1 tblsp. grated orange peel along with egg yolk. Omit cinnamon and use chopped pecans instead of walnuts.

Turkish Cardamoms: Make cookies as directed for Walnut/Cinnamon Squares, but substitute 1 tsp. ground cardamom for the cinnamon and 1 c. chopped filberts or hazelnuts for the walnuts.

Macadamia Nut Gingers: Make cookies as directed for Walnut/Cinnamon Squares, but substitute 1 tsp. ground ginger for the cinnamon and use finely chopped roasted salted macadamia nuts instead of walnuts.

Peanut Salts: Make cookies as directed for Walnut/Cinnamon Squares, except use 1 c. brown sugar, firmly packed, instead of white sugar. Omit cinnamon, and use salted roasted peanuts instead of walnuts.

Brown Sugar Spice Crisps: Make cookies as directed for Walnut/Cinnamon Squares, substituting 1 c. light brown sugar, firmly packed, for the white sugar. Use 1½ tsp. ground cinnamon instead of 1, and add ¾ tsp. ground nutmeg, ¾ tsp. ground ginger and ¼ tsp. ground cloves along with cinnamon. Omit walnuts, topping only with egg white.

Lemon or Lime Sugar Crisps: Make cookies as directed for Walnut/Cinnamon Squares, but add 2 tblsp. grated lemon or lime peel along with egg yolk. Omit cinnamon and walnuts.

GOLDEN COCONUT DIAMONDS

You brush icing on these Danish cookies luscious with coconut

1 c. butter
1 c. sugar
Few drops yellow food color
1 c. flaked coconut
2 c. sifted flour

1 c. sifted confectioners sugar (about)
2 tblsp. light rum, or about 1 tsp. rum flavoring plus 2 tsp. water

Cream together butter and sugar until light and fluffy. Beat in food color; stir in coconut. Gradually stir in flour to make a smooth dough.

With lightly floured fingertips, press dough evenly over bottom of greased 15½ x 10½ x 1″ jelly roll pan. Bake in slow oven (325°) 25 to 30 minutes, or until lightly browned.

Mix confectioners sugar and rum to make a thin icing. While cookies are hot, drizzle on icing and quickly brush it over cookies to form a glaze. While still warm, cut cookies in 8 lengthwise strips, then diagonally in 1″ wide strips to make diamonds. Cool in pan on rack. Makes about 80.

CRUMBLE COOKIES

This three-generation family recipe came from England with the home-maker's grandmother. Easy to make, great with tea or milk

1 c. dark brown sugar, firmly packed	1 c. butter
	2¼ c. sifted flour

Combine all ingredients in large bowl of electric mixer; beat at medium speed to mix thoroughly. Press over bottom of ungreased 13 x 9 x 2″ pan.

Bake in moderate oven (350°) 15 to 17 minutes, or until golden brown. Set pan on rack. Cut in 2″ squares while warm; let cool a few minutes before removing from pan. Makes about 28.

FROSTED MOLASSES CREAMS

Coffee flavors these molasses cookies and the frosting they wear

½ c. shortening	¾ tsp. salt
½ c. sugar	¼ tsp. baking soda
1 egg, beaten	1 tsp. ground cinnamon
½ c. molasses	½ tsp. ground cloves
⅓ c. strong, hot coffee	Creamy Coffee Icing (recipe follows)
1½ c. sifted flour	
1½ tsp. baking powder	

Cream together shortening and sugar; blend in egg, molasses and coffee.

Sift together dry ingredients; add to creamed mixture and blend well. Pour into greased and waxed-paper lined 13 x 9 x 2″ pan.

Bake in moderate oven (350°) 25 minutes. While warm, frost with Creamy Coffee Icing. Cool in pan on rack, then cut in 3 x 1″ bars. Makes about 39.

Creamy Coffee Icing: Cream ¼ c. butter or margarine with 2 c. confectioners sugar. Add about 2 tblsp. cold coffee, enough to make an icing of spreading consistency; mix until smooth.

OATMEAL SHORTBREADS

Try these nutty, not-too-sweet cookies as an accompaniment to cheese

1½ c. sifted flour   ⅔ c. quick-cooking rolled oats
⅔ c. brown sugar, firmly packed   1 c. butter

Combine all ingredients in large mixing bowl. With pastry blender or fingers, cut or rub ingredients together until well blended and crumbly. Press firmly and evenly into greased 15½ x 10½ x 1″ jelly roll pan. (Lightly flour fingertips if necessary to prevent sticking.)

Bake in slow oven (300°) 40 to 45 minutes, or until deep golden. While still hot, cut in 2 x 1½″ bars. Cool in pan on rack. Makes about 4 dozen.

Drop Cookies

Bite into plump, golden drop cookies and you'll often discover happy surprises in our recipes—dates, raisins, currants, cherries, nuts, chocolate pieces, citron, coconut and other treats. These are the substantial family cookies that usually travel successfully and keep well (if you hide them). They fill more cookie jars than any other kind and contribute much to the fame of country kitchens.

Next to bars, drop cookies are the easiest type to make. True, you do have several bakings, but if pressed for time, you can divide the dough and freeze part of it to bake when you have a little leisure or want to serve freshly baked cookies with coffee to business callers or neighbors who stop by.

Many cookies that once were rolled and cut now are represented in the drop cookie family. Try Grandma's Soft Sugar Cookies in this section and see if they don't remind you of the rolled cookies you used to eat at your grandmother's house. They're big and fat, with a glistening sprinkle of sugar and a raisin decoration in the center.

It's a real sacrifice not to give honorable mention to many of our drop cookie recipes. For instance, Hampshire Hermits, in which the flavors of citron and Lemon Glaze blend so harmoniously. And if you like fig cookies, you'll want to try California Fig Cookies. They're *really* good.

The dough for drop cookies is soft enough to drop from a spoon. Use a kitchen spoon rather than a measuring spoon, and take slightly rounded rather than level spoonfuls (unless recipe specifies otherwise). Push dough off the spoon with a rubber spatula or another spoon. Make the drops the same size and peak them up so they will bake evenly and look attractive. Bake them *just until done,* or until a slight imprint remains when you touch a cookie lightly with your finger. Remove from baking sheet unless the recipe directs otherwise. If left on a hot sheet, they continue to bake and may overbake.

You also will find several crisp cookies in this section that start as drops of dough. Sesame Wafers are an excellent example. So are see-through, party lace cookies, flat or rolled (after baking) the Swedish way.

The generous collection of oatmeal cookie recipes includes the favorites of the countryside, be they crisp, chewy or soft. Among them are Rookie Cookies, which, as some women know from experience, greatly please men.

ALMOND JEWELS

Cookies bright as a Mexican fiesta with that Chinese-almond taste

2 c. sifted flour	1 egg
½ tsp. baking powder	¾ tsp. vanilla
¼ tsp. salt	¾ c. chopped almonds
½ c. butter or regular margarine	Gumdrops
¾ c. sifted brown sugar, firmly packed	Almonds (for tops)

Sift together flour, baking powder and salt.

Cream butter; add sugar gradually; cream until light and fluffy. Beat in egg and vanilla; stir in chopped nuts. Add dry ingredients and mix.

Drop teaspoonfuls of dough 1½ to 2″ apart onto lightly greased baking sheet. Decorate tops with pieces of bright gumdrops (not licorice) and insert lengthwise slices of almonds in cookie centers.

Bake in moderate oven (350°) 12 to 15 minutes. Cool cookies on racks. Makes 3½ dozen.

ANISE DROPS

Cookies make their own creamy white topping while they bake

3 eggs	½ tsp. salt
1 c. plus 2 tblsp. sugar	1 tsp. anise extract or 3 tblsp.
1¾ c. sifted flour	anise seeds
½ tsp. baking powder	

Beat eggs with electric mixer at medium speed until fluffy. Gradually add sugar, beating constantly. Continue to beat for 20 minutes.

Reduce speed of mixer to low and add flour sifted with baking powder and salt. Beat in anise extract. Drop dough by teaspoonfuls about ½″ apart onto well-greased baking sheet, swirling dough to make a round cookie. Let stand at least 8 hours to dry, preferably overnight.

Bake in slow oven (325°) about 10 minutes, or until cookies are a creamy golden color, not brown, on bottom. Remove cookies to rack to cool. Makes about 50.

BLACK WALNUT COOKIES

Tastes like sour cream cookies Grandma served with applesauce

½ c. shortening	1 tsp. ground cinnamon
¾ c. sugar	½ tsp. salt
1 egg	¼ tsp. baking soda
½ tsp. vanilla	½ c. dairy sour cream
2 c. sifted flour	½ c. chopped black walnuts
1 tsp. baking powder	

Cream shortening and sugar until light and fluffy. Beat in egg and vanilla.

Sift together dry ingredients. Add to creamed mixture, alternately with sour cream. Stir in walnuts.

Drop by teaspoonfuls about 2″ apart onto greased baking sheet. Press flat with bottom of drinking glass, dipping glass into sugar before pressing each cookie.

Bake in moderate oven (375°) 9 to 12 minutes. Remove cookies and cool on racks. Makes 4½ dozen.

BEST-EVER BUTTERSCOTCH COOKIES

One of the best-tasting cookies ever baked in Countryside Kitchens

1 tblsp. vinegar	1 tsp. baking soda
1 c. evaporated milk (about)	½ tsp. baking powder
½ c. butter or regular margarine	½ tsp. salt
1½ c. brown sugar, firmly packed	⅔ c. chopped walnuts or pecans
2 eggs	Brown Butter Frosting (recipe
1 tsp. vanilla	follows)
2½ c. sifted flour	Walnut or pecan halves

Put vinegar in a 1-cup measure; add evaporated milk and set aside.

Beat butter until light; add brown sugar and beat until mixture is light and fluffy. Beat in eggs and vanilla to blend thoroughly.

Sift together flour, baking soda, baking powder and salt.

Stir evaporated milk and add alternately with dry ingredients to creamed mixture. Stir in chopped nuts. Drop rounded tablespoonfuls of dough about 2½" apart onto lightly greased baking sheet.

Bake in moderate oven (350°) 10 to 12 minutes, or until lightly browned and barely firm to touch. Remove cookies and cool on racks. When cool, spread with Brown Butter Frosting and press a walnut or pecan half in each cookie. Makes about 5 dozen.

Brown Butter Frosting: Melt ½ c. butter in small saucepan and cook over medium heat, stirring constantly, until butter stops bubbling and is nut-brown in color (do not scorch). Combine with 2 c. sifted confectioners sugar and 2 to 4 tblsp. boiling water; beat until smooth and of spreading consistency. Makes enough to frost about 5 dozen cookies.

BUTTERSCOTCH DROPS

These soft, chewy, delicious, easy, economical cookies always please

1 c. shortening	3½ c. sifted flour
2 c. brown sugar, firmly packed	1 tsp. baking soda
2 eggs	1 tsp. salt
½ c. buttermilk or water	

Mix shortening, brown sugar and eggs. Stir in buttermilk.

Sift together flour, soda and salt, and add to first mixture. Chill.

Drop by teaspoonfuls about 2" apart onto lightly greased baking sheet. Bake in hot oven (400°) 8 to 10 minutes until set (almost no imprint when touched with finger). Makes 6 dozen.

CASHEW DROPS

Pleasant surprise: biting into a whole-cashew center

½ c. butter or regular margarine	¾ tsp. baking soda
1 c. brown sugar, firmly packed	¼ tsp. salt
1 egg	⅓ c. dairy sour cream
½ tsp. vanilla	1¾ c. whole cashew nuts
2 c. sifted flour	Golden Butter Glaze (recipe
¾ tsp. baking powder	follows)

Cream butter and sugar until light and fluffy. Beat in egg and vanilla to mix thoroughly. Add sifted dry ingredients alternately with sour cream, blending well. Carefully fold in nuts.

Drop by well-rounded teaspoonfuls 2″ apart onto greased baking sheet.

Bake in hot oven (400°) 8 to 10 minutes. Remove cookies and cool on racks. Top with Golden Butter Glaze, if desired. Makes about 4 dozen.

Golden Butter Glaze: Melt ½ c. butter in saucepan over medium heat until it turns *light* golden brown (use care not to overbrown). Remove from heat and add 3 c. sifted confectioners sugar, 1 tsp. vanilla and enough hot water (3 to 4 tblsp.) to make a glaze that will spread smoothly. Beat well. Makes enough to frost or glaze 4 dozen cookies, depending on size.

CORN FLAKE COOKIES

Coconut takes the spotlight in these extra-good, crisp cookies

2 c. sifted flour	1 c. brown sugar, firmly packed
1 tsp. baking soda	2 eggs, well beaten
½ tsp. salt	1 tsp. vanilla
½ tsp. baking powder	2 c. flaked or shredded coconut
1¼ c. shortening	2 c. corn flakes
1 c. sugar	

Sift together flour, soda, salt and baking powder.

Cream shortening; gradually add sugars; beat until light. Add eggs and vanilla.

Combine dry ingredients and creamed mixture; add coconut and corn flakes.

Drop small teaspoonfuls 1½″ apart onto greased baking sheet.

Bake in moderate oven (350°) 8 to 10 minutes, or until delicately browned. Spread on racks to cool. Makes 8 dozen.

CREAM CHEESE DROP COOKIES

Lemon and cheese flavors blend tastily in these drop cookies

¾ c. butter	2 tsp. grated lemon peel
1 (3 oz.) pkg. cream cheese	2 c. sifted cake flour
1 c. sifted confectioners sugar	1 c. chopped pecans
1 tblsp. lemon juice	Sifted confectioners sugar (for
1 tsp. vanilla	rolling)

Cream butter and cream cheese until light and fluffy. Gradually add 1 c. confectioners sugar, beating thoroughly. Stir in lemon juice, vanilla and lemon peel. Add flour and mix well. Stir in nuts.

Drop by scant teaspoonfuls about 2" apart onto ungreased baking sheet. Bake in slow oven (300°) about 25 minutes, until set but not brown. While hot roll in sifted confectioners sugar. Cool on racks. Makes 4 dozen.

GUESS-AGAIN COOKIES

The slightly salty, crisp bits in these rich cookies are potato chips!

1 c. butter or regular margarine	2 c. sifted flour
½ c. sugar	½ c. crushed potato chips
1 tsp. vanilla	½ c. chopped pecans

Beat butter, sugar and vanilla until light and fluffy. Add flour, potato chips and nuts; mix well.

Drop by scant teaspoonfuls 2" apart onto ungreased baking sheet. Flatten by pressing with bottom of drinking glass, greased and dipped in sugar (grease and sugar glass as needed).

Bake in moderate oven (350°) 10 to 11 minutes. Remove to racks to cool. Makes about 5 dozen.

MAPLE WAFERS

You can bake these maple cookies even if you live far from sugar bush country. Try frosting on your favorite sugar cookies, too

3 tblsp. butter or regular margarine	1 tsp. cream of tartar
	½ tsp. baking soda
½ c. maple-blended syrup	¼ tsp. salt
1 egg, beaten	¾ c. chopped nuts
2 tblsp. milk	Maple Frosting (recipe follows)
1 c. sifted flour	

Melt butter. Remove from heat and stir in maple syrup. Add egg and milk and mix well.

Sift together flour, cream of tartar, baking soda and salt. Add to maple syrup mixture; blend well. Fold in nuts. Chill thoroughly (batter thickens).

Drop dough by teaspoonfuls 2" apart onto lightly greased baking sheet. Bake in hot oven (400°) 8 to 10 minutes. Remove cookies and cool on racks. When cool, spread with Maple Frosting. Makes about 2 dozen.

Maple Frosting: Heat ¼ c. butter until light golden brown. Stir in 1 c. sifted confectioners sugar, ⅛ tsp. salt, ¾ to 1 tsp. maple flavoring and 1 tblsp. hot water, or enough to make frosting that will spread smoothly on wafers.

POTATO CHIP COOKIES

Something different! These chewy cookies will be the talk of your next coffee party when you reveal what's in them

1 c. shortening	1 tsp. vanilla
1 c. sugar	2 c. sifted flour
1 c. brown sugar, firmly packed	1 c. crushed potato chips
2 eggs	

Beat shortening until light; gradually add white and brown sugars, beating constantly. When light and fluffy, add eggs, one at a time, beating after each addition. Add vanilla and beat to blend thoroughly.

Stir in flour, then fold in potato chips. Drop by rounded teaspoonfuls 2″ apart onto lightly greased baking sheet. Flatten with floured fork tines.

Bake in moderate oven (350°) 12 to 15 minutes, or until light golden brown. Spread on racks to cool. Makes about 5 dozen.

SALTED PEANUT COOKIES

Red-skinned and creamy white peanuts dot these brown cookies

1 c. shortening	1 tsp. baking powder
2 c. brown sugar, firmly packed	½ tsp. baking soda
2 eggs	2 c. quick-cooking rolled oats
1 tsp. vanilla	1 c. corn flakes
2 c. sifted flour	1 c. salted peanuts (skins on)

Cream shortening and brown sugar until light and fluffy. Beat in eggs to mix thoroughly. Beat in vanilla.

Sift together flour, baking powder and soda; stir into creamed mixture. Then fold in rolled oats, corn flakes and peanuts. Drop by rounded teaspoonfuls 2″ apart onto greased baking sheet.

Bake in moderate oven (350°) 10 to 12 minutes. Spread on racks to cool. Makes about 7 dozen.

SESAME WAFERS

Dainty, crisp and rich-flavored—taste-testers were enthusiastic

¾ c. melted butter or regular margarine	1 c. Toasted Sesame Seeds (recipe follows)
1½ c. light brown sugar, firmly packed	1¼ c. sifted flour
	¼ tsp. baking powder
1 tsp. vanilla	¼ tsp. salt
1 egg	

Cream butter and sugar until light and fluffy. Add vanilla and egg; beat to mix thoroughly. Stir in sesame seeds.

Sift together flour, baking powder and salt; stir into creamed mixture. Drop half teaspoonfuls of dough about 2″ apart onto lightly greased baking sheet.

Bake in moderate oven (375°) about 5 to 6 minutes, or until edges brown (bottoms of cookies brown and burn quickly). Remove from oven and transfer cookies at once to racks to cool. Makes about 7 dozen.

Toasted Sesame Seeds: Spread seeds in a shallow pan and heat in a moderate oven (350°) about 20 minutes, until they turn a pale brown; stir occasionally. Remove from oven and cool. (Watch while they are in the oven to prevent scorching.)

SOUR CREAM DROP COOKIES

New version of old-time sour cream cookies uses dairy sour cream

1 c. shortening	½ tsp. baking soda
2 c. sugar	3 tsp. baking powder
1 tsp. vanilla	1 tsp. salt
3 eggs	1½ c. chopped walnuts
1 c. dairy sour cream	2 tblsp. sugar
5 c. sifted flour	1 tsp. ground cinnamon

Beat shortening until light; add 2 c. sugar and beat until fluffy. Beat in vanilla and eggs to mix thoroughly. Beat in sour cream.

Sift together flour, baking soda, baking powder and salt. Add to creamed mixture. Fold in chopped nuts. Chill 1 hour, or until dough is easy to handle.

Drop dough by teaspoonfuls about 2″ apart onto lightly greased baking sheet.

Combine 2 tblsp. sugar with cinnamon. Lightly grease bottom of drinking glass (2¼″ in diameter) and dip in cinnamon/sugar mixture. Press cookies flat.

Bake in moderate oven (350°) about 12 minutes. Remove to racks to cool. Makes about 6 dozen.

CHOCOLATE BANANA COOKIES

Delicious way to salvage very ripe bananas—tasty, moist cookies

1 c. sugar	2½ c. sifted flour
⅔ c. shortening	2 tsp. baking powder
2 eggs	¼ tsp. salt
1 tsp. vanilla	¼ tsp. baking soda
1 c. mashed bananas (2½ medium)	Chocolate Frosting (recipe follows)
1 (6 oz.) pkg. semisweet chocolate pieces, melted	

Beat together sugar and shortening until mixture is light and fluffy. Beat in eggs and vanilla, mixing well. Add bananas and melted chocolate.

Sift together flour, baking powder, salt and baking soda. Add to beaten mixture. Drop by teaspoonfuls about 2″ apart onto lightly greased baking sheet.

Bake in moderate oven (350°) 10 minutes. Remove cookies and cool on racks; then frost with Chocolate Frosting, if desired. Makes about 5 dozen.

Chocolate Frosting: Combine 2 tblsp. soft butter, 2 squares unsweetened chocolate, melted, 3 tblsp. warm water and 2 c. sifted confectioners sugar. Beat until smooth.

CHOCOLATE CHEESE COOKIES

Crisp cookies with a delicate flavor of chocolate and cream cheese

½ c. butter	2 squares semisweet chocolate,
½ c. shortening	melted and cooled slightly
1 (3 oz.) pkg. cream cheese	2¼ c. sifted flour
1½ c. sugar	1½ tsp. baking powder
1 egg	½ tsp. salt
½ tsp. vanilla	2 tblsp. milk
	½ c. chopped nuts (optional)

Beat butter, shortening and cream cheese until light. Gradually add sugar, beating until mixture is light and fluffy. Beat in egg, vanilla and melted chocolate.

Sift together flour, baking powder and salt. Add alternately with milk to chocolate mixture. Stir in nuts.

Drop by teaspoonfuls 2″ apart onto lightly greased baking sheet. Bake in moderate oven (350°) about 15 minutes. Remove cookies and cool on racks. Makes about 4½ dozen.

N O T E : Use unsweetened instead of semisweet chocolate for a more pronounced chocolate flavor.

CHOCOLATE HERMITS

Make dainty, tea-size or man-size cookies according to your needs. Top with a chocolate confectioners sugar frosting (see Index)—a decorative curl for dainty cookies, a generous covering for others

1⅓ c. sifted flour	3 squares unsweetened
2 tsp. baking powder	chocolate, melted
½ tsp. salt	1 tsp. vanilla
1 tsp. ground cinnamon	⅓ c. milk
½ c. shortening	1 c. chopped raisins
1 c. sugar	1 c. chopped nuts
1 egg, well beaten	

Sift together flour, baking powder, salt and cinnamon.

Cream shortening; add sugar gradually; cream until fluffy.

Add egg to creamed mixture with chocolate; blend well. Add vanilla and milk. Stir in dry ingredients, raisins and nuts. Mix well; chill 30 minutes.

Drop by teaspoonfuls about 2" apart onto greased baking sheet. Bake in moderate oven (350°) 15 minutes. Remove cookies and cool on racks. Makes 2 dozen.

CHOCOLATE MARSHMALLOW CAKELETS

Cookies resemble little cakes, ideal for cold weather because chocolate topping sometimes gets sticky when it's hot and humid

½ c. shortening	½ c. chopped walnuts
1 c. brown sugar, firmly packed	18 regular marshmallows
1 egg	(about), cut in halves
1¾ c. sifted flour	1 (6 oz.) pkg. semisweet
½ tsp. baking soda	chocolate pieces
½ tsp. salt	2 tblsp. butter
½ c. cocoa	½ tsp. ground cinnamon
½ c. milk	

Beat shortening until light; add brown sugar and beat until fluffy. Beat in egg to blend.

Sift together flour, baking soda, salt and cocoa. Beat flour mixture alternately with milk into creamed mixture. Stir in walnuts.

Drop rounded teaspoonfuls of dough 2" apart onto lightly greased baking sheet. Bake in moderate oven (350°) 12 to 15 minutes. Remove from oven and top with marshmallow halves. Set pan on rack until cookies are cool enough to handle.

Melt chocolate pieces with butter; stir in cinnamon. Holding cookies in hand, use a small spatula and swirl their tops with chocolate mixture to cover marshmallows. Cool cookies on racks. Makes about 3 dozen.

CHOCO-MARSHMALLOW COOKIES

Fat marshmallows atop chocolate cookies go fancy with frosting

1¾ c. sifted cake flour	1 tsp. vanilla
½ tsp. salt	¼ c. milk
½ tsp. baking soda	18 regular marshmallows, cut in
½ c. cocoa	halves
½ c. shortening	Cocoa Frosting (recipe follows)
1 c. sugar	36 pecan halves (½ c.)
1 egg	

Sift together flour, salt, soda and cocoa.

Cream shortening and sugar; add egg, vanilla and milk, beating well. Add dry ingredients and mix. Drop by teaspoonfuls about 2" apart onto greased baking sheet.

Bake in moderate oven (350°) 8 minutes (don't overbake). Remove from oven and press a marshmallow half, cut side down, on top of each cookie. Bake 2 minutes longer. Remove cookies and cool on racks. Top with Cocoa Frosting, then with a pecan half. Makes 3 dozen.

Cocoa Frosting: Combine 2 c. sifted confectioners sugar, 5 tblsp. cocoa and ⅛ tsp. salt. Add 3 tblsp. soft butter or margarine and 4 to 5 tblsp. light cream. Blend until smooth.

CHOCOLATE POTATO COOKIES

A homey pioneer favorite made with buttermilk—moist, good keepers

½ c. shortening	1½ c. sifted flour
1 c. brown sugar, firmly packed	½ tsp. salt
1 egg	½ tsp. baking soda
1 tsp. vanilla	¾ c. buttermilk
2 squares unsweetened chocolate, melted	½ c. chopped walnuts or pecans
	½ recipe for Chocolate Frosting
½ c. unseasoned mashed potatoes (room temperature)	(see Index)

Cream together shortening and brown sugar until light and fluffy. Beat in egg and vanilla to mix well. Add chocolate and mashed potatoes and beat until smooth.

Sift together flour, salt and baking soda; add alternately with buttermilk to creamed mixture. Stir until smooth, then add nuts. Drop by rounded teaspoonfuls 2" apart onto greased baking sheet.

Bake in hot oven (400°) about 10 minutes, or until cookies, when touched with finger, spring back (do not overbake). Let remain on baking sheet a minute or two before removing to racks for cooling. While *still warm,* spread on Chocolate Frosting. Makes 4½ dozen.

CHOCOLATE SANDWICH TREASURES

Favorite of a Pennsylvania woman—keeps well, sells fast at bazaars

1 c. milk	4 c. sifted flour
5 tblsp. flour	2 tsp. baking soda
1 c. confectioners sugar	½ tsp. baking powder
1 c. shortening	½ tsp. salt
¼ tsp. salt	1 c. buttermilk
½ c. shortening	¾ c. boiling water
2 c. sugar	½ c. cocoa
2 eggs	2 drops red or green food color
1 tsp. vanilla	(optional)

To make filling, combine ½ c. milk with 5 tblsp. flour and mix to a smooth paste. Add remaining ½ c. milk. Cook over medium heat, stirring, until mixture thickens. Set aside to cool.

In large mixer bowl, beat at medium speed confectioners sugar, 1 c. shortening and ¼ tsp. salt until light and fluffy. Add cooked mixture and continue beating until fluffy. Set aside while you bake cookies. (You'll have 2½ cups.)

To make cookie dough, beat ½ c. shortening until light; gradually add white sugar and beat until mixture is light and fluffy. Beat in eggs and vanilla to mix well.

Sift together 4 c. flour, baking soda, baking powder and ½ tsp. salt. Alternately add with buttermilk to creamed mixture.

Pour boiling water over cocoa and stir to mix. Cool and add to dough, mixing well.

Drop by teaspoonfuls (not heaping) 1″ apart onto lightly greased baking sheet. Bake in moderate oven (350°) 8 minutes. Remove from pan and cool on racks.

When cookies are cool, put together in pairs with filling spread between. You'll use 2 c. to fill cookies. Tint remaining ½ c. filling a delicate pink or green with 2 drops red or green food color, or leave filling untinted. Drop a little on top of each cookie sandwich. A nut or flaked coconut may be placed on top for decoration. Makes 5 dozen filled cookies.

NOTE: When the Pennsylvania homemaker who contributed this recipe wants to give the cookies a special appeal for guests, she divides the filling in quarters and places each part in a small bowl. She leaves one part creamy white, tints the other three delicately with food color—pink, green and yellow-orange. Then she decorates the tops of the sandwiches with a bit of the filling, adding nuts or flaked coconut for a trim.

FLORENTINES DIRECT FROM ITALY

Many American tourists in Europe resolve, once they get home, to duplicate the Florentines they ate in Italy. These cookies are almost a confection—half candy, half cookie. They are rich, sweet and excellent with coffee for evening refreshments. It's the combination of flavors—candied orange peel, chocolate and cream—plus the crisp texture that makes the cookies so rewarding.

Their name comes from the city of Florence, according to most food historians, back in the 15th or 16th century.

Our taste tests revealed that many people on this side of the Atlantic Ocean prefer a little less candied orange peel than Europeans like. Our recipe calls for ¾ cup finely chopped peel, but there's no law against using 1 to 1½ cups of it.

FLORENTINES

Lacy cookies for special occasions, painted with melted chocolate

¾ c. heavy cream
¼ c. sugar
¼ c. sifted flour
½ c. very finely chopped slivered blanched almonds

¾ c. very finely chopped candied orange peel (4 oz. pkg.)
2 (4 oz.) bars sweet cooking chocolate

Stir cream and sugar together to blend well. Stir in flour, almonds and orange peel. Drop by scant teaspoonfuls about 1¼″ apart onto heavily greased and floured baking sheet. *Flatten cookies with spatula;* they will be about ½ to ¾″ apart after flattening.

Bake in moderate oven (350°) about 10 to 12 minutes, until cookies brown lightly around edges. (Centers of cookies will be bubbling when you remove them from oven.) Let stand 2 or 3 minutes or until they become firmer. Place on wire rack or waxed paper to cool.

Meanwhile, melt chocolate over hot, not boiling, water. When cookies are cool, turn upside down and brush with melted chocolate. Let dry several hours or overnight at room temperature to give chocolate time to set. (In hot, humid weather, use chocolate confection coating, melted, instead of sweet cooking chocolate.) Store in covered container in refrigerator or freezer. Makes about 4 dozen.

FROSTED DROP BROWNIES

Frost some cookies white, some with chocolate to provide interest

½ c. butter or regular margarine
¾ c. sugar
1 egg
2 squares unsweetened chocolate, melted
1¾ c. sifted flour
½ tsp. baking soda
½ tsp. salt
½ c. milk
1 tsp. vanilla
½ c. chopped nuts
Shiny White Icing or Chocolate Icing
36 walnut or pecan halves

Cream butter and sugar until fluffy. Add egg and beat well. Stir in melted chocolate.

Sift together flour, baking soda and salt. Add alternately with the milk to the chocolate mixture. Stir in vanilla and nuts.

Drop by teaspoonfuls 2″ apart onto ungreased baking sheet; bake in hot oven (400°) 8 to 10 minutes. Remove cookies and cool on racks. Drop 1 tsp. Shiny White or Chocolate Icing onto center of each cookie and swirl with a fork. Top with walnut or pecan halves. Makes 3 dozen cookies.

Shiny White Icing: Add enough cream or milk to 2 c. sifted confectioners sugar to make icing of spreading consistency. Add ½ tsp. vanilla. (Tint part of the icing a delicate pink with a few drops red food color. Flavor with peppermint extract, if you like.)

Chocolate Icing: Add 1 square unsweetened chocolate, melted, to 1 c. sifted confectioners sugar; beat in enough cream or milk to make icing of spreading consistency. Add ½ tsp. vanilla.

MALTED CHOCOLATE DROPS

Just the cookie chocolate lovers adore—try the frosted variation

⅔ c. butter or regular margarine	¼ tsp. salt
¾ c. sugar	¼ c. cocoa
2 eggs	1 c. chocolate-flavored instant
1 tsp. vanilla	malted milk powder
2 c. sifted flour	¼ c. water
2 tsp. baking powder	1 c. chopped walnuts

Beat butter and sugar together until light and fluffy. Beat in eggs and vanilla to mix well.

Sift together flour, baking powder, salt, cocoa and malted milk powder. Add alternately with water to creamed mixture. Fold in nuts. Chill several hours.

Drop teaspoonfuls of dough 2″ apart onto greased baking sheet. Bake in moderate oven (350°) about 12 minutes. Remove cookies and cool on racks. Makes about 4 dozen.

Variation

Frosted Malted Chocolate Drops: When cookies are cool frost with Chocolate Malt Frosting.

Chocolate Malt Frosting: Melt 1 square unsweetened chocolate and 1 tblsp. butter over very low heat (or over hot water), stirring constantly. Mix in 1 tblsp. warm water, 2 tblsp. chocolate-flavored instant malted milk powder, 2 tblsp. light cream or dairy half-and-half and 1 c. sifted confectioners sugar, or enough to make a frosting of spreading consistency.

PENNSYLVANIA DUTCH COOKIE-PIES

A teen-age enthusiasm. Filling is good with other cookies, too

1½ c. sugar	½ tsp. cream of tartar
¼ c. shortening	½ tsp. baking soda
½ c. cocoa	1 tsp. salt
1 egg	¾ c. buttermilk
1 tsp. vanilla	Fluffy Refrigerator Filling
2 c. sifted flour	(recipe follows)

Cream together sugar and shortening until light and fluffy. Beat in cocoa and egg. Add vanilla.

Sift together flour, cream of tartar, baking soda and salt; add alternately with buttermilk to creamed mixture. Mix well.

Drop by teaspoonfuls about 2″ apart onto greased baking sheet. Bake in moderate oven (375°) 10 to 12 minutes. Remove cookies to racks and cool.

Spread flat sides (bottoms) of cooled cookies with Fluffy Refrigerator Filling and put together in pairs. (If you like, you can sprinkle filling with flaked coconut before putting together.) Makes 26 cookie-pies.

Fluffy Refrigerator Filling: Place 2½ tblsp. flour in 1-qt. saucepan. Measure ½ c. milk. Add a little milk to flour and stir to make a smooth paste. Add remaining milk; cook and stir until mixture thickens. Cool.

In a small mixing bowl, cream together ½ c. butter or shortening, ½ c. sugar, ⅛ tsp. salt and 1 tsp. vanilla until light and fluffy. Slowly add thickened flour-milk mixture, beating constantly, until filling is light and fluffy. Makes about 1¾ cups.

N O T E : You will have ⅓ to ⅔ c. filling left over after using for Pennsylvania Dutch Cookie-Pies. The woman who shares this recipe says it's a planned leftover. She stores the filling in a covered jar in the refrigerator and uses it to spread on other cookies or cupcakes she bakes. The filling in the refrigerator remains soft and fluffy. She often doubles the recipe to make more filling to refrigerate.

PINEAPPLE/CHOCOLATE CHIP COOKIES

Big recipe for family—good keepers, have mild pineapple flavor

½ c. butter	4 c. sifted flour
½ c. shortening	½ tsp. baking soda
1 c. brown sugar, firmly packed	½ tsp. salt
1 c. white sugar	1 c. chopped walnuts
2 eggs	1 (6 oz.) pkg. semisweet
1 tsp. vanilla	chocolate pieces
1 c. crushed pineapple with juice	

Cream together butter, shortening and sugars until light and fluffy. Beat in eggs, one at a time, and vanilla. Stir in pineapple.

Sift together flour, baking soda and salt; divide in half. Add first half to creamed mixture. When well blended, add second half. Stir in nuts and chocolate pieces.

Drop batter by teaspoonfuls 2" apart onto greased baking sheet. Bake in hot oven (400°) 15 minutes. Remove cookies to racks and cool. Makes about 7 dozen.

SOFT CHOCOLATE CHIPPERS

Children like to come home to these chocolate-dotted goodies

½ c. shortening	½ tsp. baking soda
1 c. brown sugar, firmly packed	½ tsp. salt
1 egg	¼ c. buttermilk
1 tsp. vanilla	1 (6 oz.) pkg. semisweet
1¾ c. sifted flour	chocolate pieces

Beat shortening until light; add brown sugar and beat until light and fluffy. Beat in egg and vanilla to blend well.

Sift together flour, baking soda and salt. Add alternately with buttermilk to creamed mixture. Beat until smooth. Add chocolate pieces and mix well.

Drop about 2" apart onto greased baking sheet. Flatten with a spoon. Bake in moderate oven (375°) 8 to 10 minutes, until lightly browned. Remove to cooling racks. Makes about 3 dozen.

SOUR CREAM CHOCOLATE COOKIES

These quick-to-make cookies have the good taste sour cream imparts

½ c. butter	¼ tsp. salt
1 c. brown sugar, firmly packed	¼ tsp. baking soda
1 egg	½ c. dairy sour cream
2 squares unsweetened	1 c. chopped walnuts
chocolate, melted	1 tsp. vanilla
1½ c. sifted flour	Cocoa Frosting (recipe follows)
¼ tsp. baking powder	

Cream together butter and brown sugar. Add egg and blend well. Beat in chocolate.

Sift together flour, baking powder, salt and soda; add to creamed mixture alternately with sour cream. Stir in nuts and vanilla.

Drop by teaspoonfuls about 2" apart onto greased baking sheet. Bake in moderate oven (375°) 8 minutes. Remove cookies and cool on racks, then frost with Cocoa Frosting. Makes 5 dozen.

Cocoa Frosting: Heat 3 tblsp. milk. Add 1½ c. sifted confectioners sugar, 3 tblsp. butter and 3 tblsp. cocoa. Blend together until of spreading consistency.

TWO-TONE JUMBLES

Try these 2-in-1 cookies—plain and chocolate sour cream treats

¼ c. shortening	2¾ c. sifted flour
¼ c. butter	½ tsp. baking soda
1 c. brown sugar, firmly packed	1 tsp. salt
½ c. sugar	1 c. dairy sour cream
1 tsp. vanilla	1 square unsweetened chocolate,
2 eggs	melted
1 c. chopped walnuts or pecans	

Beat together shortening, butter, brown and white sugars and vanilla until light and fluffy. Beat in eggs to mix well. Stir in ½ c. walnuts.

Sift together flour, baking soda and salt. Add alternately to creamed mixture with sour cream. Divide dough in half. Add chocolate to one half.

Drop chocolate dough from teaspoon 2″ apart onto lightly greased baking sheet. Drop equal size spoonfuls of plain dough next to and touching chocolate mounds (they will bake together as one). Sprinkle with remaining ½ c. nuts, pressing them in lightly.

Bake in moderate oven (375°) about 12 minutes, until almost no imprint remains after touching center of cookie with finger and until lightly browned. Remove cookies to racks to cool. Makes about 3½ dozen.

TWO-WAY COOKIES

As easy to bake chocolate/orange and coconut cookies as one kind

4 c. sifted flour	3 eggs
1 tsp. salt	1 tsp. vanilla
1 tsp. baking soda	½ tsp. orange extract
1 c. regular margarine	1 (6 oz.) pkg. semisweet
1 c. sugar	chocolate pieces
1¼ c. light brown sugar, firmly packed	1 (3½ oz.) can flaked coconut

Sift together flour, salt and baking soda.

Cream margarine until fluffy; gradually add sugars. Add eggs, one at a time, beating thoroughly after each addition. Add vanilla; blend. Add sifted dry ingredients. Mix well. Divide batter in half.

Add orange extract and chocolate pieces to one half dough and coconut to other half. Drop by rounded teaspoonfuls about 2″ apart onto greased baking sheet.

Bake in a moderate oven (350°) 12 to 15 minutes. Remove cookies and cool on racks. Makes about 6 dozen.

CARAMEL APPLE COOKIES

You can frost the cookies before freezing or just before serving

½ c. shortening
1⅓ c. brown sugar, firmly
   packed
1 egg
2¼ c. sifted flour
1 tsp. baking soda
½ tsp. salt
1 tsp. ground cinnamon

1 tsp. ground cloves
½ tsp. ground nutmeg
1 c. grated peeled apples
1 c. light raisins
½ c. apple juice
1 c. chopped walnuts
Caramel Icing (recipe follows)

Cream shortening, sugar and egg until light and fluffy. Sift together dry ingredients and add to creamed mixture. When well blended, stir in remaining ingredients, except icing.

Drop by level tablespoonfuls 3″ apart onto greased baking sheet. Bake in moderate oven (350°) about 12 minutes, or until lightly browned.

Remove cookies and cool on racks. When cool, spread with Caramel Icing. Makes about 4 dozen.

Caramel Icing: Combine ¼ c. butter and ¼ c. brown sugar, firmly packed, in saucepan; cook until sugar dissolves, about 3 minutes. Add 1½ c. sifted confectioners sugar, ¼ tsp. salt and 2½ tblsp. dairy half-and-half or light cream; beat until smooth. (If frosting becomes too thick when spreading on cookies, thin it by adding a little more cream.)

GLAZED APPLE COOKIES

These big, spicy cookies travel and keep well, taste wonderful

½ c. shortening
1⅓ c. brown sugar, firmly
   packed
1 egg
2 c. sifted flour
1 tsp. baking soda
½ tsp. salt
1 tsp. ground cinnamon
½ tsp. ground cloves
¼ tsp. ground nutmeg

1 c. coarsely chopped nuts
1 c. finely chopped peeled apple
   (2 medium)
1 c. raisins
¼ c. milk
1½ c. sifted confectioners sugar
1 tblsp. butter
½ tsp. vanilla
2½ tblsp. light cream or dairy
   half-and-half (about)

Beat together shortening and brown sugar until light and fluffy. Beat in egg to blend thoroughly.

Sift together flour, baking soda, salt, cinnamon, cloves and nutmeg. Stir half the dry ingredients into creamed mixture. Stir in nuts, apple and raisins; then stir in remaining half of dry ingredients and milk. Mix well.

Drop from tablespoon 1½" apart onto lightly greased baking sheet. Bake in hot oven (400°) 10 to 12 minutes. Remove cookies to racks and while still warm, spread with glaze.

To make glaze, combine confectioners sugar, butter, vanilla and enough cream to make glaze of spreading consistency. Beat until smooth. Spread on warm cookies. Makes about 3 dozen.

BANANA DROP COOKIES

Cake-like banana cookies are coated with cinnamon-sugar and bran

1 c. whole bran cereal
6 tblsp. sugar
½ tsp. ground cinnamon
1 c. sugar
½ c. shortening
¼ c. butter

2 eggs
1½ tsp. vanilla
1 c. mashed bananas (3 medium)
2½ c. sifted flour
3 tsp. baking powder
1 tsp. salt

Place bran cereal on sheet of waxed paper; roll fine with rolling pin. Add 6 tblsp. sugar and cinnamon; mix well. Set aside.

Beat 1 c. sugar, shortening and butter until light and fluffy. Beat in eggs and vanilla to mix thoroughly. Stir in bananas.

Sift together flour, baking powder and salt. Stir into banana mixture. Drop by teaspoonfuls into bran mixture and tumble until they are well coated. Place 2″ apart on greased baking sheet.

Bake in hot oven (400°) about 10 minutes. Remove cookies and cool on racks. Makes 4½ dozen.

CITRUS/NUT DROPS

Cookies flavored with orange and lemon, wear red cherry hats

½ c. shortening
¼ c. sugar
1 egg yolk
½ tsp. vanilla
2 tblsp. evaporated milk
1 tsp. grated orange peel

1 tsp. grated lemon peel
1¼ c. sifted flour
1 egg white, slightly beaten
¾ c. finely chopped nuts
Candied cherry halves (for tops)

Cream together shortening and sugar until light and fluffy. Beat in egg yolk, vanilla, evaporated milk and orange and lemon peels. Mix in flour.

Dip tablespoonfuls of dough in egg white. Lift out with fork, and dip one side in nuts. Place nut side up 2″ apart on greased baking sheet; press a cherry half into each.

Bake in slow oven (325°) 20 minutes. Remove cookies and cool on racks. Makes about 2 dozen.

CHRISTMAS DROP COOKIES

Gay with holiday colors, but festive for parties at all seasons

1 lb. dates, chopped
½ c. chopped walnuts
½ c. chopped maraschino
cherries
1 c. sugar

1 tsp. vanilla
3 egg whites, stiffly beaten
1 c. sifted flour
Maraschino cherry pieces (for tops)

Combine dates, nuts and cherries. Mix in sugar and vanilla. Add egg whites to fruit mixture alternately with flour. (If mixture is dry, add a little cherry juice.)

Drop by teaspoonfuls about 2″ apart onto greased baking sheet. Top with pieces of cherries.

Bake in moderate oven (350°) about 20 minutes, until lightly browned. Remove cookies and cool on racks. Store in tightly covered container. (They keep indefinitely, and are better with aging.) Makes 4 dozen.

CRY BABY COOKIES

They're favorites of men. That's why we give you a giant-size recipe

1 c. plus 2 tblsp. shortening	1 tsp. salt
1 c. plus 2 tblsp. sugar	1½ tsp. baking soda
1 c. light molasses	2 c. shredded coconut
2 eggs, well beaten	2 c. chopped walnuts
4¾ c. sifted cake flour	1½ c. raisins
1 tblsp. baking powder	1 c. milk

Cream shortening; beat in sugar, molasses and eggs.

Sift together flour, baking powder, salt and soda; combine with coconut, walnuts and raisins. Add alternately with milk to creamed mixture.

Drop tablespoonfuls 2″ apart onto greased baking sheet. Bake in moderate oven (375°) 10 minutes. Remove cookies and cool on racks. Makes about 9½ dozen.

DATE/NUT DROPS

Chewy cookies rich flavored with nuts, dates and brown sugar—good

2 c. chopped dates	1 tsp. vanilla
½ c. sugar	4 c. sifted flour
½ c. water	1 tsp. baking soda
1 c. butter or regular margarine	1 tsp. salt
1 c. sugar	1 tsp. ground cinnamon
1 c. brown sugar, firmly packed	1½ c. chopped nuts
3 eggs	

Combine dates, ½ c. sugar and water in saucepan. Cook, stirring occasionally, until mixture is the consistency of very thick jam. Cool.

Cream butter; add sugars gradually, beating until light and fluffy. Beat in eggs and vanilla.

Sift together dry ingredients. Add to creamed mixture, blending thoroughly. Stir in nuts and date mixture.

Drop by rounded teaspoonfuls about 2″ apart onto greased baking sheet. Bake in a moderate oven (375°) 12 to 15 minutes. Remove cookies and cool on racks. Makes 12 dozen.

OREGON DATE SURPRISES

Walnut-stuffed dates are the unusual ingredient in these cookies

36 pitted dates (8 oz.)	1¼ c. sifted flour
½ c. large walnut pieces (36)	½ tsp. baking soda
¼ c. butter or regular margarine	1 tsp. baking powder
¾ c. brown sugar, firmly packed	¼ tsp. salt
1 egg	½ c. dairy sour cream
1 tsp. vanilla	Vanilla Cream Icing (see Index)

Stuff each date with a walnut piece. Set aside.

Beat together butter and brown sugar until light and fluffy. Beat in egg and vanilla to blend well.

Sift together flour, baking soda, baking powder and salt. Add to creamed mixture alternately with sour cream. Add stuffed dates and stir until they are well coated with batter.

Drop from teaspoon about 2″ apart onto lightly greased baking sheet, allowing 1 date to each cookie. Bake in moderate oven (375°) about 10 minutes. Remove cookies and cool on racks. If you like, frost with Vanilla Cream Icing. Makes 3 dozen.

N O T E : If you shell walnuts, first soak them overnight in salt water. Then the nut meats will come out whole.

RAGGED ROBINS

These dainty cookies are ideal for serving with ice cream, puddings

2 eggs	1 c. chopped dates
½ c. sugar	2 c. corn flakes
1 tsp. vanilla	¼ c. confectioners sugar
1 c. chopped walnuts	

Beat eggs until lemon-colored; gradually beat in sugar and vanilla to blend thoroughly. Stir in walnuts and dates. Fold in corn flakes.

Drop by teaspoonfuls 2″ apart onto lightly greased baking sheet. Bake in moderate oven (350°) 12 to 15 minutes. Cool 1 or 2 minutes on baking sheet, then remove to cooling rack. While still warm, roll in confectioners sugar. When cool, store cookies in loosely covered container. Makes about 3½ dozen.

CALIFORNIA FIG COOKIES

A recipe from the state that grows figs—and knows how to use them

1 c. chopped golden or black figs (½ lb.)	1 tsp. vanilla
⅓ c. water	2 c. sifted flour
1 c. butter or regular margarine	2 tsp. baking powder
½ c. sugar	½ tsp. salt
½ c. brown sugar, firmly packed	Walnut or pecan halves (optional)
1 egg	

Cook figs with water, stirring frequently, until thickened, about 5 minutes. Set aside to cool.

Beat butter with both sugars until light and fluffy; beat in egg and vanilla to blend well.

Sift together flour, baking powder and salt. Mix into creamed mixture. Then stir in cooled figs.

Drop by teaspoonfuls about 2" apart onto lightly greased baking sheet. Press a walnut half on top of each cookie. Bake in moderate oven (375°) 10 to 12 minutes, until lightly browned. Remove cookies and cool on racks. Makes 4 dozen.

FAMILY COOKIES

These soft cookies contain healthful vegetable and fruit ingredients

1 c. regular margarine	4½ c. sifted flour
2 c. sugar	½ tsp. salt
3 eggs	1 tsp. baking soda
1 c. cut-up carrots, ground	¼ tsp. ground allspice
1 large apple, ground	¼ tsp. ground cloves
1 large orange, ground	½ tsp. ground nutmeg
1 c. dates, ground	1 tsp. ground cinnamon
1 c. raisins, ground	1 c. chopped walnuts

Beat margarine until light; gradually add sugar and beat until light and fluffy. Beat in eggs until well blended. Fold in carrots and fruits.

Sift together flour, salt, baking soda and spices. Add to first mixture. Fold in nuts.

Drop by teaspoonfuls 2" apart onto lightly greased baking sheet and bake in moderate oven (350°) 10 to 12 minutes. Remove cookies and cool on racks. Store in airtight container. Makes about 7½ dozen.

HOLIDAY FRUITCAKE COOKIES

Glamor cookies with gay green and red topknots—a yuletide treat

4 c. sifted flour	1 c. chopped pecans
1 tsp. baking soda	1 c. candied cherries, cut in
1 tsp. salt	quarters
1 c. shortening	2 c. cut-up dates
2 c. brown sugar, firmly packed	1 c. candied fruits and peels
2 eggs, beaten	Red or green candied cherries
⅔ c. buttermilk	(for tops)

Sift together flour, soda and salt.

Cream shortening; add brown sugar and eggs; beat until light and fluffy. Add buttermilk and sifted dry ingredients, then fold in nuts, cherries, dates and candied fruits. Chill dough.

Drop dough by teaspoonfuls about 2" apart onto lightly greased baking sheet. Top each cookie with green or red cherry half.

Bake in moderate oven (375°) 8 to 10 minutes. Remove cookies and cool on racks. Makes 8 dozen.

FRUITED DROP COOKIES

There are many ways to introduce healthful fruit, wheat germ and rolled oats in meals, but when it comes to pleasant eating, none surpasses Fruited Drop Cookies. The recipe comes from a Tennessee woman who invented it; she says the cookies are husband-inspired. Because her husband is a great cookie fan, she decided to make them contribute to his nutrition. Result: Fruited Drop Cookies. Once you make them, you'll know why the hearty, good-for-you cookies are so popular in her family.

FRUITED DROP COOKIES

Serve these with glasses of milk or with hot coffee for a treat

½ c. finely cut dried apricots	1 tblsp. lemon juice
½ c. chopped dried prunes	1½ c. quick-cooking rolled oats
½ c. seedless raisins	2 tblsp. wheat germ
¾ c. water	2 c. sifted flour
½ c. regular margarine	1 tsp. baking soda
½ c. sugar	½ tsp. baking powder
½ c. brown sugar, firmly packed	½ tsp. salt
1 egg	½ c. chopped nuts

Combine apricots, prunes and raisins with water in saucepan. Heat and simmer about 5 minutes, stirring frequently. (Mixture is thick; watch carefully.) Set aside to cool.

Beat margarine until light; gradually add white and brown sugars, beating until light and fluffy. Beat in egg and lemon juice to blend well. Add fruit, rolled oats and wheat germ and mix well.

Sift together flour, baking soda, baking powder and salt. Fold into fruit mixture along with nuts. Chill.

Drop dough by teaspoonfuls 1" apart onto lightly greased baking sheet. Bake in moderate oven (375°) 12 to 15 minutes. Remove cookies and cool on racks. Store in tightly covered container. Makes about 4½ dozen.

FRUITY GUMDROP COOKIES

Apples, gumdrops and raisins—no wonder the cookies are so tasty

2 c. sifted flour	1 egg, beaten
½ tsp. salt	¾ c. thick applesauce
2 tsp. baking powder	1 c. gumdrops, cut in small pieces
½ tsp. ground cinnamon	(no black candies)
½ c. shortening	1 c. raisins
½ c. sugar	

Sift together flour, salt, baking powder and cinnamon.

Cream shortening and sugar; add egg and applesauce; mix well.

Add flour mixture; stir until well blended; stir in gumdrops (no black candies) and raisins.

Drop by teaspoonfuls about 2" apart onto lightly greased baking sheet. Bake in hot oven (400°) 10 to 15 minutes, until lightly browned. Transfer to cooling rack. Makes 4 dozen.

N O T E : You can use drained, crushed pineapple or canned peaches, drained and mashed, instead of applesauce. Rolled oats may be substituted for the gumdrops.

HAMPSHIRE HERMITS

Tangy Lemon Glaze is perfect on these citron-flavored cookies

⅔ c. butter or regular margarine	¼ tsp. ground ginger
1 c. light brown sugar, firmly packed	¼ tsp. cloves
	¼ tsp. baking soda
2 eggs	⅛ tsp. salt
2 tblsp. dairy sour cream or buttermilk	1 c. chopped nuts
	½ c. chopped raisins or currants
1¾ c. sifted flour	½ c. finely chopped citron
1¾ tsp. ground cinnamon	Lemon Glaze (recipe follows)

Beat butter until light. Gradually add brown sugar and beat after each addition until light and fluffy. Beat in eggs, one at a time, beating to mix thoroughly. Stir in sour cream.

Sift together flour, spices, baking soda and salt. Add to creamed mixture and beat until batter is smooth. Gradually add nuts, raisins and citron.

Drop batter from tablespoon 2″ apart onto greased baking sheet. Bake in moderate oven (350°) about 12 to 15 minutes, until cookies are golden brown. Remove cookies to racks and while warm, brush with Lemon Glaze. Makes about 3 dozen.

Lemon Glaze: Add 2 tblsp. lemon juice to 1 c. sifted confectioners sugar. Stir until smooth; brush over warm cookies (glaze is thin and tart).

LEMON DROP COOKIES

Crushed candy sweetens, adds lemony flavor to dotted cookies

½ c. boiling water (about)
¼ c. dried currants
2 c. sifted flour
3 tsp. baking powder
1 tsp. salt
1 c. finely crushed candy lemon drops

¼ c. shortening
½ c. chopped candied cherries
1 egg, beaten
½ tsp. vanilla
⅓ c. milk

Pour boiling water over currants to cover; let stand 5 minutes. Drain and spread currants on paper toweling.

Sift together flour, baking powder and salt. Crush about ¼ c. lemon drops at a time between two sheets of aluminum foil; measure and stir each fourth at once into flour mixture before they stick together. Mix flour mixture and crushed lemon candy well. Blend in shortening with pastry blender until crumbly. Add cherries and currants.

Combine egg, vanilla and milk, and stir into flour mixture with fork. Stir until dough clings together in a ball.

Drop by teaspoonfuls about 1" apart onto greased baking sheet. Bake in moderate oven (350°) about 15 minutes. Transfer cookies to rack to cool. Makes about 3½ dozen.

MULTI-FRUITED DROPS

Crisp cookies—grated citrus peel enhances other fruit flavors

1 c. butter or regular margarine
1 c. sugar
1 c. brown sugar, firmly packed
2 eggs
1 tsp. vanilla
2 c. sifted flour
½ tsp. salt
1 tsp. baking powder

½ tsp. baking soda
1½ c. quick-cooking rolled oats
1 tblsp. grated orange peel
1 tblsp. grated lemon peel
1 c. chopped dates
1 c. seedless raisins
1 c. chopped nuts
1 c. flaked coconut

Cream together butter and sugars until light and fluffy. Beat in eggs and vanilla to mix thoroughly.

Sift together flour, salt, baking powder and soda. Mix into creamed mixture. Add remaining ingredients and mix well.

Drop from teaspoon about 2″ apart onto greased baking sheet. Bake in moderate oven (375°) 12 minutes. Remove to racks to cool. Makes about 8 dozen cookies.

OLD-FASHIONED HERMITS

Seeded raisins make country-kitchen treats tasty—good travelers

1 c. shortening	1 tsp. salt
2 c. brown sugar, firmly packed	1 tsp. ground nutmeg
2 eggs	1 tsp. ground cinnamon
½ c. cold coffee	1½ c. chopped nuts
3½ c. sifted flour	2½ c. seeded raisins or currants
1 tsp. baking soda	

Thoroughly mix together shortening, sugar and eggs. Stir in cold coffee.

Sift together dry ingredients and stir into shortening mixture. Stir in nuts and raisins. Chill at least 1 hour.

Drop rounded teaspoonfuls of dough 2″ apart onto lightly greased baking sheet. Bake in moderate oven (375°) 8 to 10 minutes. Test for doneness by touching lightly with fingertip. If almost no imprint remains, cookies are done. Use care not to overbake. Remove to racks to cool. Makes about 7½ dozen.

ORANGE COOKIES

For parties spread Orange Icing over tops of cake-like treats

⅔ c. shortening	½ tsp. salt
1 c. sugar	½ tsp. baking soda
2 eggs, slightly beaten	½ c. orange juice
1 tblsp. grated orange peel	½ c. chopped nuts
2¼ c. sifted flour	

Cream together shortening and sugar.

Combine eggs, creamed mixture and orange peel.

Sift together flour, salt and baking soda.

Add to creamed mixture alternately with orange juice; mix until well blended. Add nuts.

Drop by tablespoonfuls about 2″ apart onto greased baking sheet. Bake in moderate oven (375°) 10 minutes, or until golden brown. Remove cookies and cool on rack. Makes 3 dozen.

Orange Icing: Blend together 2½ tblsp. butter or regular margarine and 1½ c. sifted confectioners sugar. Stir in 1½ tblsp. orange juice and 2 tsp. grated orange peel. Blend until smooth.

ORANGE/CARROT COOKIES

Cheerful as Kansas sunflowers and kind to the budget—attractive, too

1 c. shortening	2 c. sifted flour
¾ c. sugar	2 tsp. baking powder
1 c. mashed cooked carrots	½ tsp. salt
1 egg	Golden Glow Topping (recipe
1 tsp. vanilla	follows)

Cream shortening and sugar until fluffy. Add carrots, egg and vanilla; mix well.

Sift together flour, baking powder and salt; add to carrot mixture; mix well. Drop batter by teaspoonfuls about 2″ apart onto greased baking sheet.

Bake in moderate oven (350°) about 20 minutes. Place cookies on racks to cool. While warm, spread with Golden Glow Topping. Makes 5 dozen.

Golden Glow Topping: Combine juice of ½ orange; grated peel of 1 orange, 1 tblsp. butter or regular margarine and 1 c. sifted confectioners sugar. Blend until smooth.

ORANGE/COCONUT CRISPS

Friends will make a point to stop by for these crisp 3″ cookies

2 eggs	2½ c. sifted flour
⅔ c. salad oil	2 tsp. baking powder
1 c. sugar	½ tsp. salt
¼ c. thawed frozen orange juice concentrate	1 c. cookie coconut

Beat eggs with fork until well blended. Stir in oil. Blend in sugar until mixture thickens. Stir in orange juice concentrate.

Sift together flour, baking powder and salt; add with coconut to egg mixture. Stir until well blended.

Drop by teaspoonfuls about 2″ apart on ungreased baking sheet. Stamp each cookie flat with bottom of drinking glass dipped in sugar. (Lightly oil glass, then dip in sugar. Continue dipping in sugar for each cookie.)

Bake in hot oven (400°) 8 to 10 minutes. Remove immediately from baking sheet to cooling rack. Makes 3 dozen.

N O T E : Balls of cookie dough, rolled in sugar, may be packaged and frozen for future use. To bake: remove as many balls as desired from package, place on baking sheet and let stand about 30 minutes at room temperature. Bake as directed.

ORANGE-GLAZED PRUNE COOKIES

Brown cookies with yellow topknots hold prune and orange flavors

2 c. brown sugar, firmly packed	1 tsp. ground cinnamon
1 c. butter or shortening	½ tsp. salt
2 eggs, beaten	2 c. chopped cooked prunes
½ c. milk	1 c. chopped walnuts
3½ c. sifted flour	1 tsp. vanilla
1 tsp. baking powder	Orange Glaze (recipe follows)
1 tsp. baking soda	

Cream together sugar and butter; stir in eggs and milk.

Sift together flour, baking powder, soda, cinnamon and salt; stir into creamed mixture. Add prunes, nuts and vanilla.

Drop by teaspoonfuls onto greased baking sheet. Bake in moderate oven (350°) 15 to 20 minutes, until lightly browned. Remove cookies and cool on racks.

Spread tops of cooled cookies with a thin layer of Orange Glaze. Makes 8½ dozen.

Orange Glaze: Combine 3 c. confectioners sugar, grated peel of 1 orange and ¼ c. orange juice. Blend thoroughly until smooth.

PRUNE COOKIES

Spiced drop cookies topped with prune hats—try these soon

2 c. sugar	½ tsp. ground allspice
1 c. shortening	1 tsp. ground cinnamon
3 eggs	¼ tsp. ground nutmeg
1 c. finely cut cooked prunes	¼ tsp. ground cloves
3 c. sifted flour	¾ c. chopped walnuts
1 tsp. baking soda	Cooked prunes, pitted (for tops)
½ tsp. salt	

Combine sugar, shortening, eggs and prunes; beat until well blended.

Sift together dry ingredients; add in thirds to beaten mixture. Stir in walnuts.

Drop dough from teaspoon about 2″ apart onto ungreased baking sheet. Top each with a quarter of a cooked prune, skin side up.

Bake in moderate oven (375°) 12 to 14 minutes. Remove cookies and cool on racks. Makes about 5 dozen.

N O T E : If batter seems too stiff, add a small amount of prune juice.

GOLDEN PINEAPPLE COOKIES

You paint cookie tops with pineapple juice-confectioners sugar icing

½ c. shortening	2 c. sifted flour
1 c. brown sugar, firmly packed	1½ tsp. baking powder
1 egg	¼ tsp. baking soda
1 tsp. vanilla	⅛ tsp. salt
1 (8½ oz.) can crushed pineapple	1 c. sifted confectioners sugar

Cream shortening with brown sugar until light and fluffy. Add egg and vanilla and beat well to mix thoroughly.

Drain pineapple, reserving juice. Add pineapple to creamed mixture. Sift together flour, baking powder, baking soda and salt; stir into creamed mixture.

Drop by teaspoonfuls 1½ to 2″ apart onto greased baking sheet. Bake in slow oven (325°) about 15 minutes, until golden. Remove from baking sheet and cool on racks.

Stir 4 tsp. reserved pineapple juice into confectioners sugar. Beat until smooth. Brush on cookies. Makes about 4 dozen.

PUMPKIN COOKIES

Children eat these soft cookies without making crumbs

½ c. shortening	4 tsp. baking powder
1¼ c. brown sugar, firmly packed	½ tsp. salt
2 eggs	½ tsp. ground cinnamon
1 tsp. vanilla	½ tsp. ground nutmeg
1½ c. mashed cooked or canned	1 c. raisins
pumpkin	1 c. chopped nuts
2½ c. sifted flour	

Cream together shortening and brown sugar. Add eggs; beat thoroughly. Mix in vanilla and pumpkin.

Sift together dry ingredients. Blend into creamed mixture. Stir in raisins and nuts.

Drop dough by heaping teaspoonfuls about 2″ apart onto greased baking sheet. Bake in a moderate oven (375°) about 15 minutes, until lightly browned. Remove cookies and cool on racks. Makes 5 dozen.

PUMPKIN/PINEAPPLE COOKIES

Taste like your best pumpkin pie with faint pineapple undertone

½ c. butter or regular margarine	1 c. quick-cooking rolled oats
1 c. brown sugar, firmly packed	2 c. sifted flour
½ c. sugar	½ tsp. baking powder
1 egg	½ tsp. baking soda
1 c. canned pumpkin	½ tsp. salt
½ c. drained crushed pineapple	2 tsp. ground cinnamon
1 c. coarsely cut-up pecans	¼ c. milk

Cream butter and sugars until light and fluffy. Beat in egg, then beat in pumpkin and pineapple. Stir in nuts and oats.

Sift together dry ingredients and add alternately with milk to creamed mixture.

Drop by teaspoonfuls about 2″ apart onto greased baking sheet.

Bake in moderate oven (350°) 8 to 10 minutes. Place cookies on racks to cool. Makes 6 dozen.

GRANDMA'S RAISIN COOKIES

To keep cookies until mealtime, hide them from your family

1½ c. seedless raisins	2 tsp. baking powder
1½ c. water	1 tsp. baking soda
1½ c. shortening	½ tsp. salt
2 c. sugar	1 c. chopped walnuts
2 eggs	Caramel Frosting (recipe
1 tsp. vanilla	follows)
4 c. sifted flour (about)	

Cover raisins with water and cook gently about 20 minutes. Drain, saving 1 c. liquid. Cool.

Beat shortening and sugar until light and fluffy. Beat in eggs and vanilla to mix thoroughly.

Sift together flour, baking powder, baking soda and salt. Stir into creamed mixture alternately with reserved 1 c. raisin liquid. Stir in raisins and nuts.

Drop dough from tablespoon 2″ apart onto greased baking sheet. Spread out with bowl of spoon. Bake in moderate oven (375°) 10 to 12 minutes. Place cookies on racks and while still warm, spread tops with Caramel Frosting. Makes 5½ dozen.

Caramel Frosting: Combine in saucepan 1½ c. brown sugar, firmly packed, ¾ c. evaporated milk and ¼ c. regular margarine. Cook until sugar dissolves and margarine is melted. Remove from heat and cool slightly. Add 1 tsp. vanilla and enough sifted confectioners sugar (about 3 c.) to make a frosting of spreading consistency. If frosting gets too thick, add a few drops of milk.

RANCH HOUSE RAISIN COOKIES

You cook the raisins before you stir them into the cookie mixture

½ c. raisins
1 c. water
1 c. brown sugar, firmly packed
½ c. shortening
1 egg
½ tsp. vanilla

1¾ c. sifted flour
½ tsp. salt
½ tsp. baking powder
½ tsp. baking soda
½ c. chopped nuts

Bring raisins to a boil with water. Cool thoroughly.

Cream sugar and shortening until fluffy. Add egg and vanilla. Beat to mix.

Sift together flour, salt, baking powder and soda. Alternately add to creamed mixture with cooled raisins (there should be ½ c. liquid with raisins; if not, add water to make ½ c.). Stir in nuts.

Drop dough by teaspoonfuls at least 2″ apart onto greased baking sheets.

Bake in moderate oven (350°) 10 to 12 minutes. Remove cookies and cool on racks. Makes 4 dozen.

RAISIN/CARROT COOKIES

Good family-style cookies that keep well if given a chance

1 c. sifted flour
¼ c. nonfat dry milk powder
¼ tsp. baking soda
1 tsp. baking powder
¼ tsp. ground nutmeg
¼ tsp. ground cinnamon
½ tsp. salt
⅓ c. shortening
⅓ c. brown sugar, firmly packed

½ c. molasses
1 egg, beaten
1 c. shredded carrots (or sweet potato)
1 tsp. grated lemon peel
½ c. ground or finely chopped raisins
1¾ c. quick-cooking rolled oats

Sift together flour, dry milk powder, soda, baking powder, nutmeg, cinnamon and salt.

Cream together shortening, sugar and molasses; add egg, then dry ingredients; stir until well blended.

Add carrots, lemon peel, raisins and oats; mix well. (If dough is too stiff, add a few drops of milk.) Chill.

Drop by teaspoonfuls about 2″ apart onto lightly greased baking sheet. Bake in hot oven (400°) 10 to 12 minutes, until lightly browned. Remove cookies and cool on racks. Makes 5 dozen.

RAISIN/KETCHUP COOKIES

Ketchup gives cookies a rose-beige color and faint spicy taste—fresh Lemon Glaze contributes pleasing piquant flavor contrast

1 c. regular margarine	½ tsp. baking soda
½ c. sugar	⅛ tsp. salt
½ c. light brown sugar, firmly packed	¼ c. tomato ketchup
	¾ c. raisins
2 eggs	½ c. chopped nuts
1 tsp. vanilla	Lemon Glaze (recipe follows)
2¾ c. sifted flour	

Beat margarine until light. Gradually add white and brown sugars, beating constantly. Beat until light and fluffy. Beat in eggs and vanilla to blend well.

Sift together flour, baking soda and salt. Stir into creamed mixture alternately with ketchup. Fold in raisins and nuts. Drop heaping teaspoonfuls of dough 2″ apart onto lightly greased baking sheet.

Bake in moderate oven (375°) 10 to 12 minutes, or until edges are browned and almost no imprint remains when touched lightly with fingertip. Remove cookies to cooling racks. Brush on Lemon Glaze while cookies are hot. Makes about 4 dozen.

Lemon Glaze: Combine 1½ c. sifted confectioners sugar with 2 tblsp. strained lemon juice; stir until smooth. If mixture is not thin enough to make a transparent glaze on cookies, add more lemon juice, 2 or 3 drops at a time until of right consistency. Makes ½ cup.

PECAN LACE ROLL-UPS

For women's luncheons tie bright ribbons around the crisp roll-ups

2 eggs	¼ c. melted butter or regular margarine
⅔ c. brown sugar, firmly packed	
1 tsp. vanilla	¼ c. sifted flour
	⅔ c. finely chopped pecans

Beat eggs until they thicken. Add brown sugar, 1 tblsp. at a time, beating constantly. Beat in vanilla to blend well. Slowly add slightly cooled butter. Fold in flour and pecans.

Place a tablespoonful of batter on well-greased baking sheet, spreading it to make a circle 4″ in diameter. Repeat process, having no more than 4 cookie circles 2″ apart on baking sheet at a time.

Bake in moderate oven (375°) 5 to 6 minutes, or until browned. Remove from oven and let cool about 30 seconds, then slip wide spatula under cookie to loosen it. Place the handle of a wooden spoon on one end of cookie and quickly roll up loosely to make a fat cylinder. Place on rack to cool. Repeat with other baked cookies. Then bake and roll the remainder of the batter in the same way (no more than 4 cookies at a time). Makes 15.

SWEDISH LACE COOKIES

The thin, crisp, brown lace-like cookie saddles or roll-ups always get attention. They're much easier to make than you may think

½ c. butter or regular margarine	1 tsp. baking powder
1½ c. regular rolled oats	1 tblsp. flour
1 egg	Dash of salt
⅔ c. sugar	

Melt butter and pour over rolled oats.

Beat egg until light; then beat in sugar. Stir together baking powder, flour and salt to blend. Add to egg mixture, then add rolled oats.

Drop tablespoonfuls of batter 3″ apart onto greased and lightly floured baking sheet. Bake in moderate oven (375°) about 8 to 10 minutes, until golden brown.

Place on cooling rack; let stand about 1 minute (cookies should still be hot and pliable). Lift cookies off quickly with wide spatula and place over broomstick, wrapped with aluminum foil, propped across two coffee or shortening cans or pans. Gently press cookies to make them the shape of a saddle. Work fast. If cookies get too cold, they break in shaping. You can return the baking sheet to the oven for a minute if they cool too fast. Makes about 20 cookies.

Variation

Lace Roll-Ups: While cookies are warm, roll up around handle of a wooden spoon to make fat cylinders. These cookies are easier to store than the saddle shapes.

WALNUT LACE COOKIES

These see-through cookies are thin, fragile, crisp and delicious

⅓ c. sifted flour
½ tsp. baking powder
⅛ tsp. salt
¼ c. butter or regular margarine

1 c. brown sugar, firmly packed
1 egg, slightly beaten
1 c. chopped walnuts

Sift together flour, baking powder and salt.

Blend butter, brown sugar and sifted dry ingredients with pastry blender as for pie crust. Add egg and mix thoroughly. Stir in walnuts.

Drop thin batter by half teaspoonfuls about 2" apart onto heavily greased baking sheet. (Cookies spread during baking.) Bake in moderate oven (375°) 5 to 6 minutes. Remove from baking sheet at once and cool on racks. Makes about 5½ dozen.

GINGER NUGGETS

Team these cookies with glasses of milk for after-school snacks

3 c. sifted flour
1 c. nonfat dry milk powder
1½ tsp. salt
2 tsp. baking soda
1 tsp. ground cinnamon
½ tsp. ground ginger

¼ tsp. ground cloves
1 c. shortening
1½ c. molasses
¼ c. sugar
1 egg

Sift together flour, dry milk powder, salt, soda and spices.

Cream together shortening, molasses and sugar.

Add egg, mix well. Add dry ingredients, and mix well. Chill.

Drop from teaspoon about 2" apart onto greased baking sheet.

Bake in moderate oven (375°) 10 to 15 minutes, until done. Remove cookies and cool on racks. Makes about 8 dozen.

MOLASSES/WHOLE WHEAT COOKIES

Raisins and whole wheat flour make these molasses cookies special

½ c. nonfat dry milk powder	1 tsp. vanilla
½ tsp. baking soda	2 eggs, beaten
2 tsp. baking powder	1 c. plus 2 tblsp. whole wheat
½ tsp. salt	flour
⅓ c. shortening	½ c. raisins
¾ c. molasses	

Sift together dry milk powder, soda, baking powder and salt.

Cream together shortening, molasses, and vanilla; add eggs, blend well.

Add sifted ingredients and whole wheat flour; stir until thoroughly mixed. Add raisins (whole, chopped or ground).

Drop by teaspoonfuls about 2″ apart onto lightly greased baking sheet. Bake in moderate oven (350°) 10 to 12 minutes, until lightly browned. Remove cookies and cool on racks. Makes 4 dozen.

PEANUT/MOLASSES COOKIES

Cookies fruited with prunes are a pleasing texture and flavor surprise

1 c. sifted flour	½ c. molasses
½ tsp. salt	½ c. crunchy peanut butter
1 tsp. baking powder	½ tsp. vanilla
¼ tsp. baking soda	1 egg
¼ c. shortening	2 tblsp. milk
¼ c. brown sugar, firmly packed	1 c. chopped, uncooked prunes

Sift together flour, salt, baking powder and soda.

Cream together shortening, sugar, molasses, peanut butter and vanilla. Add egg and milk; mix well. Add dry ingredients; stir until well blended. Add chopped prunes.

Drop by teaspoonfuls onto lightly greased baking sheet. Bake in moderate oven (375°) 10 to 15 minutes, or until done.

Transfer cookies to cooling rack. Store in tightly covered container. Makes 5 dozen.

SOFT MOLASSES COOKIES

Family-style, generous cookies like Grandma used to make—updated

1 c. butter or regular margarine	1 tsp. instant coffee powder
1 c. sugar	2 tsp. ground cinnamon
1 large egg	1 tsp. ground ginger
1 c. light molasses	½ tsp. ground cloves
4¾ c. sifted flour	¾ c. milk
3 tsp. baking soda	Raisins or walnut halves
½ tsp. salt	

Beat butter until light; gradually add sugar and beat until fluffy. Beat in egg to blend thoroughly; then beat in molasses.

Sift together flour, baking soda, salt, coffee powder and spices. Add to first mixture alternately with milk. Beat about 30 seconds.

Drop dough by heaping teaspoonfuls about 2" apart onto lightly greased baking sheet, using care to keep cookies round. Press a raisin in center of each cookie.

Bake in moderate oven (375°) about 12 to 15 minutes, or until done. Place cookies on racks to cool. Makes about 5½ dozen.

SOFT MOLASSES DROPS

Ideal for mailing overseas and wonderful eating at home and abroad

¾ c. butter	2 tblsp. molasses
1½ c. brown sugar, firmly packed	1 tsp. baking soda
3 eggs	3 c. sifted flour
1 tsp. vanilla	1 c. raisins

Cream together butter and sugar until light and fluffy. Beat in eggs and vanilla to mix well.

Combine molasses and baking soda. Add to creamed mixture. Gradually stir in flour. Add raisins.

Drop by teaspoonfuls 2" apart onto greased baking sheet. Bake in moderate oven (350°) 8 minutes, or until brown. Cool cookies on racks. Makes about 6 dozen.

SLAPJACKS

The Pennsylvania Dutch created these molasses/coconut cookies

¾ c. butter or regular margarine
3 c. brown sugar, not firmly
   packed
1 c. light or dark molasses
1½ tsp. baking soda
3 c. sifted flour
¼ tsp. salt
½ c. cookie coconut
½ c. chopped walnuts

Cream butter and brown sugar until light and fluffy. Blend in molasses.

Sift together baking soda, flour and salt; add to creamed mixture, beating to mix thoroughly. Add coconut and nuts. Chill thoroughly for several hours, or overnight.

Drop dough by teaspoonfuls 2" apart onto greased baking sheet. Bake in moderate oven (350°) 12 to 14 minutes. Cool 2 or 3 minutes on baking sheet before removing to cooling rack. Makes about 7 dozen.

COCONUT/NUTMEG COOKIES

Serve these with lemon sherbet for a wonderful flavor combination

1 (1 lb. 3 oz.) pkg. yellow or
   white cake mix
1 c. flaked coconut
½ c. butter or regular margarine
1 tsp. ground nutmeg
1 egg
2 tblsp. cold water

Combine all ingredients and mix until well blended.

Drop teaspoonfuls of mixture onto lightly greased baking sheet. Bake in moderate oven (350°) 12 to 15 minutes, until lightly browned. Transfer cookies to cooling rack. Makes 3½ dozen.

HONEYED GINGERSNAPS

Sugar sparkles on top of brown cookies—crisp outside, chewy within

⅔ c. sugar
¼ c. butter or regular margarine
1 tsp. ground ginger
½ tsp. ground cinnamon
½ tsp. baking soda
½ tsp. salt

½ tsp. vanilla
1 egg
½ c. honey
1½ c. sifted flour
Sugar for topping (about ¼ c.)

Combine ⅔ c. sugar, butter, ginger, cinnamon, baking soda, salt and vanilla in large mixing bowl. Cream until light and fluffy. Add egg and beat until very fluffy. Blend in honey. Add flour, a little at a time, and blend well.

Drop by teaspoonfuls 2½" apart onto lightly greased baking sheet. Sprinkle with sugar.

Bake in moderate oven (350°) 10 to 15 minutes, until lightly browned. Remove at once from baking sheet to racks to cool thoroughly. Makes about 4 dozen.

SWEDISH SPICE SPECIALS

Cardamom and orange peel contribute delightful, distinctive flavor

2 c. sifted flour
½ c. sugar
½ tsp. baking soda
½ c. light corn syrup
½ c. regular margarine or butter

1 tsp. ground cardamom
¼ tsp. ground ginger
¼ tsp. ground cloves
2 tsp. finely grated orange peel
1 egg

Sift flour with sugar and soda.

Combine corn syrup, margarine, spices and orange peel in saucepan; heat just until mixture boils and margarine melts. Remove from heat and cool.

Beat egg in large bowl. Slowly pour the cooled syrup into the egg. Stir in flour-sugar mixture all at once; blend well.

Drop by teaspoonfuls 2" apart onto greased baking sheet. Bake in moderate oven (350°) 10 to 12 minutes, until lightly browned. Transfer cookies to racks to cool. Makes about 3 dozen.

CIRCLE RANCH OAT COOKIES

Nicely spiced, big soft cookies—store airtight to retain freshness

1 c. shortening	1 tsp. baking soda
1½ c. brown sugar, firmly packed	¾ tsp. salt
	1 tsp. ground cinnamon
2 eggs	½ tsp. ground nutmeg
½ c. buttermilk	3 c. quick-cooking rolled oats
1¾ c. sifted flour	½ c. chopped walnuts
1 tsp. baking powder	¾ c. dried currants or raisins

Beat shortening until light; add brown sugar and beat until fluffy. Beat in eggs to mix well. Stir in buttermilk.

Sift together flour, baking powder, baking soda, salt, cinnamon and nutmeg; stir into beaten mixture. Stir in rolled oats, nuts and currants.

Drop dough by tablespoonfuls 2″ apart onto lightly greased baking sheet. Bake in hot oven (400°) about 8 minutes. Cool slightly on baking sheet; then remove to racks to complete cooling. Makes about 5 dozen.

N O T E : You can use sweet milk instead of buttermilk, but decrease baking soda to ¼ tsp. and increase baking powder to 2 tsp.

FRESH-FROM-THE-OVEN COOKIES

The contributor of the recipe for Oatmeal/Coconut Crisps and its variations keeps the dough in a tight container in her refrigerator for several days—sometimes a few weeks. It's a great recipe; she finds it easier to bake a few cookies at a time. And, in addition, she can always serve cookies with that wonderful fresh-from-the-oven aroma and taste.

OATMEAL/COCONUT CRISPS

Taste-testers voted these the best oatmeal cookies they've sampled

2 c. butter or regular margarine	3 c. sifted flour
2 c. brown sugar, firmly packed	2 tsp. salt
2 c. sugar	2 tsp. baking soda
2 tsp. vanilla	6 c. quick-cooking rolled oats
4 eggs	1½ c. flaked coconut

Cream together butter and brown and white sugars until fluffy. Stir in vanilla; then add eggs, one at a time, beating after each addition.

Sift together flour, salt and baking soda. Add to creamed mixture. Stir in rolled oats and coconut. Drop by teaspoonfuls about 2″ apart onto well-greased baking sheet.

Bake in moderate oven (350°) 10 to 15 minutes. Cool cookies on racks. Makes 14 dozen.

NOTE: You can omit the 1½ c. coconut and divide dough into thirds. Add ⅓ c. flaked coconut to one part, ⅓ c. raisins to second part and ⅓ c. chopped walnuts to the third part.

Variations

Oatmeal/Raisin Cookies: Use 1½ c. raisins instead of the coconut.
Oatmeal/Nut Cookies: Use 1½ c. chopped walnuts instead of the coconut.
Oatmeal/Butter Crisps: Omit the flaked coconut.

OATMEAL CHIPPERS

Nuggets of chocolate lift these cookies above the commonplace

½ c. butter or regular margarine	1 tsp. salt
½ c. shortening	1 tsp. ground cinnamon
1 c. sugar	1 tsp. ground nutmeg
1 c. brown sugar, firmly packed	2 c. quick-cooking rolled oats
2 eggs	1 (6 oz.) pkg. semisweet
1 tsp. vanilla	chocolate pieces
2 c. sifted flour	1 c. chopped walnuts
1 tsp. baking soda	

Cream together butter and shortening. Add sugars gradually, beating until light and fluffy. Beat in eggs and vanilla.

Blend in sifted dry ingredients, mixing thoroughly. Stir in oats, chocolate pieces and nuts.

Drop by rounded teaspoonfuls about 2" apart onto greased baking sheet. Bake in moderate oven (375°) 9 to 12 minutes. Remove cookies and cool on racks. Makes 8 dozen.

OATMEAL DROP COOKIES

Coffee party treats—apricot or other fruit jam adds a color note

½ c. butter or regular margarine	2½ c. sifted flour
½ c. shortening	1 tsp. baking soda
1 c. brown sugar, firmly packed	1 tsp. salt
¾ c. sugar	1 tsp. ground cinnamon
2 eggs	2 c. quick-cooking rolled oats
½ c. water	½ c. apricot jam
1 tsp. vanilla	

Cream together butter and shortening. Gradually beat in sugars until mixture is light and fluffy. Add eggs, water and vanilla. Beat well.

Sift together flour, soda, salt and cinnamon. Blend into creamed mixture. Stir in oats.

Drop rounded teaspoonfuls about 3" apart onto ungreased baking sheet. Make an indentation in each with tip of spoon. Fill with apricot jam (about ½ tsp.). Top with 1 tsp. dough.

Bake in hot oven (400°) 10 to 12 minutes. Remove cookies and cool on rack. Makes 4 dozen.

JEWELED OATMEAL DROPS

Gumdrops add chewy texture, color and flavor to these crisp cookies

1 c. shortening	½ tsp. baking soda
1 c. brown sugar, firmly packed	1 tsp. baking powder
1 c. sugar	¾ tsp. salt
2 eggs	2 c. quick-cooking rolled oats
1 tsp. vanilla	1 c. cut-up assorted gumdrops
2 c. sifted flour	(no black candies)

Beat shortening until light. Add sugars and beat until fluffy. Beat in eggs and vanilla to mix thoroughly.

Sift together flour, baking soda, baking powder and salt; add to beaten mixture. Mix well.

Stir in rolled oats and gumdrops. Drop by teaspoonfuls about 2" apart onto lightly greased baking sheet.

Bake in moderate oven (375°) about 10 to 12 minutes. Remove from baking sheet to rack and let cool. Makes 5½ dozen.

N O T E : Cut gumdrops with scissors moistened in cold water.

Variation

Orange Jeweled Oatmeal Drops: Substitute 18 candy orange slices, cut in small pieces, for the assorted gumdrops.

ORANGE/OATMEAL SCOTCHIES

An orange-coconut blend flavors these crisp brown oatmeal cookies

¾ c. shortening	1½ c. quick-cooking rolled oats
1½ c. brown sugar, firmly packed	½ c. flaked coconut
2 eggs	2 c. sifted flour
1 tblsp. grated orange peel	2 tsp. baking powder
6 tblsp. orange juice	½ tsp. baking soda
	½ tsp. salt

Cream shortening and sugar until light and fluffy. Beat in eggs to mix thoroughly. Then beat in orange peel and juice. Stir in rolled oats and coconut.

Sift together remaining dry ingredients; stir into first mixture.

Drop by teaspoonfuls 2" apart onto lightly greased baking sheet.

Bake in hot oven (400°) 8 to 10 minutes. Remove cookies and cool on racks. Makes about 5½ dozen.

OVERNIGHT MACAROONS

Easy-to-make, delicious, inexpensive—cookies look like brown lace

4 c. quick-cooking rolled oats	2 eggs, beaten
2 c. brown sugar, firmly packed	1 tsp. salt
1 c. salad oil	1 tsp. almond extract

Combine rolled oats, brown sugar and salad oil in large mixing bowl; mix well. Cover and let stand overnight.

In the morning, blend eggs, salt and almond extract into oat mixture. Let stand 5 minutes.

Drop batter from teaspoon 2″ apart onto lightly greased baking sheet. Bake in slow oven (325°) 15 minutes. Remove cookies and cool on racks. Makes 4 dozen.

SCOTCH MOLASSES COOKIES

Thin, crisp oatmeal cookies have attractive lacy edges. Good!

¾ c. sifted flour	½ tsp. ground cloves
½ c. sugar	2½ c. quick-cooking rolled oats
2 tsp. baking powder	1 c. raisins
½ tsp. salt	⅔ c. melted shortening
2 tsp. baking soda	1 egg, beaten
1 tsp. ground cinnamon	¾ c. molasses
½ tsp. ground nutmeg	1 tblsp. milk

Sift together dry ingredients.

Combine oats and raisins; sift flour mixture over top.

Combine remaining ingredients in bowl. Pour over dry ingredients; mix well. Drop by teaspoonfuls 2 to 3″ apart onto greased baking sheet.

Bake in moderate oven (350°) 8 to 12 minutes. Spread on racks to cool. Makes 3 dozen.

PUMPKIN/OATMEAL DROPS

Not too sweet; mild, spicy and good keepers if you hide them

¾ c. butter or regular margarine	½ tsp. salt
1½ c. sugar	1 tsp. ground cinnamon
2 eggs	½ tsp. ground nutmeg
1 c. canned pumpkin	⅛ tsp. ground cloves
1 tsp. vanilla	1½ c. quick-cooking rolled oats
1½ c. sifted flour	½ c. shredded coconut
2 tsp. baking powder	½ c. chopped nuts
½ tsp. baking soda	

Cream together butter and sugar. Beat in eggs; add pumpkin and vanilla.

Sift together flour, baking powder, soda, salt and spices. Stir into creamed mixture. Add oats, coconut and nuts.

Drop by teaspoonfuls 2″ apart onto greased baking sheet. Bake in moderate oven (375°) about 12 minutes. Remove cookies and cool on racks. Makes 6 dozen.

ROOKIE COOKIES

For hearty cookies that are extra-chewy use regular rolled oats

2 eggs	½ tsp. salt
2 c. brown sugar, firmly packed	4 c. regular rolled oats
1 c. melted butter or regular margarine	1 c. chopped nuts
	1 c. shredded coconut
2 c. sifted flour	½ c. raisins
1 tsp. baking powder	½ c. water (about)
½ tsp. baking soda	

Beat eggs; blend in sugar and butter.

Sift together flour, baking powder, soda and salt. Stir into egg mixture. Stir in remaining ingredients, adding enough water to moisten well. Mix thoroughly.

Drop by teaspoonfuls about 2″ apart onto greased baking sheet. Bake in moderate oven (350°) about 15 minutes. Remove cookies and cool on racks. Makes 6 dozen.

NOTE: For less chewy cookies use 3½ c. quick-cooking rolled oats instead of the regular.

WHEAT/OAT CRISPS

It's a wonder that anything so "good for you" can taste so good

¾ c. shortening	1 tsp. salt
1 c. brown sugar, firmly packed	½ tsp. baking soda
½ c. white sugar	3 c. quick-cooking rolled oats
1 egg	2 tblsp. wheat germ
¼ c. water	½ c. flaked coconut
1 tsp. vanilla	½ c. chopped nuts
1 c. stone ground whole wheat flour	¼ c. semisweet chocolate pieces (optional)

Beat shortening with sugars until light and fluffy. Beat in egg, water and vanilla until creamy.

Stir together flour, salt and baking soda to mix. Stir into creamed mixture and blend well. Add rolled oats, wheat germ, coconut and nuts. Drop by teaspoonfuls 2″ apart onto lightly greased baking sheet. Top each cookie with a chocolate piece.

Bake in moderate oven (350°) 12 to 15 minutes. Transfer cookies to racks to cool. Makes 5 dozen.

GRANDMA'S SOFT SUGAR COOKIES

Grandma centered seeded raisins in her memorable man-size cookies

1 c. sugar	3½ c. sifted flour
1 c. brown sugar, firmly packed	2 tsp. baking powder
½ c. butter	1 tsp. cream of tartar
½ c. shortening	¾ tsp. salt
2 eggs	¾ tsp. baking soda
1 tsp. vanilla	1 c. buttermilk
½ tsp. lemon extract	⅓ c. sugar (for tops)
1 tsp. ground nutmeg	Seeded raisins (or seedless)

Beat together white and brown sugars, butter and shortening until light and fluffy. Beat in eggs, vanilla and lemon extract to mix well.

Sift together nutmeg, flour, baking powder, cream of tartar, salt and soda. Add alternately with buttermilk to creamed mixture.

Drop tablespoonfuls of dough 2½″ apart onto greased baking sheet. With the back of the spoon's bowl, spread round and round with the outer edge of the cookies a little thicker than the centers. Sprinkle generously with sugar and place a fat seeded raisin in the center of each cookie.

Bake in hot oven (400°) about 10 minutes. For softer cookies, bake in hot oven (425°) about 8 minutes, or until no indentation remains when you touch the center of the cookie with your fingertip. Remove cookies and cool on racks. Makes 4 dozen.

POWDERED SUGAR COOKIES

Rich, dainty cookies that can be either molded or dropped

½ c. shortening
½ c. butter
1½ c. confectioners sugar
1 egg
1 tsp. vanilla
¼ tsp. almond extract
2½ c. sifted flour

1 tsp. baking soda
1 tsp. cream of tartar
¼ tsp. salt
1 c. chopped pecans
¾ c. confectioners sugar (for coating)

Beat shortening and butter until light; gradually add 1½ c. confectioners sugar, beating constantly. Beat in egg, vanilla and almond extract to mix well.

Sift together flour, baking soda, cream of tartar and salt. Add to creamed mixture. Stir in nuts.

Drop by teaspoonfuls 1″ apart onto ungreased baking sheet. (Or shape in 1″ balls.) Bake in hot oven (400°) 8 to 10 minutes. Remove to cooling racks, and while still warm, roll in confectioners sugar. When cool, roll in confectioners sugar again for snowy white coating. Makes about 6 dozen.

Rolled Cookies

When lights and decorations go up along main streets across the country, rolling pins and cookie cutters of many shapes soon come to light in the kitchen. Then, more than at any other season, rolled cookies have top popularity. By the time Christmas arrives, cookie stars, hearts, crescents, jaunty gingerbread boys and animals dangle from the branches of twinkling Christmas trees.

We tell you how to glamorize cookies by sprinkling them before baking with coarse white or colored decorating sugar, tiny colored candies, chocolate shot (jimmies), chopped nuts, silver and gold dragées and other simple trims. You can also spread baked cookies with frosting or a glaze, or put them together in pairs with frosting or filling. (Be sure to try our Raisin-Filled Cookies with a choice of three other fillings.)

If you want a picture-pretty tray or plate of cookies to set—as for a buffet supper—bake our beautiful Wild Rose Cookies, dainty Cheese/Jam Cookie Tarts and Frosted Diamond Cookies (a Pennsylvania Dutch specialty containing caraway seeds).

Among our rolled cookies are also some imported recipes from faraway places, all adapted to American tastes—Finnish Stars, Orange Wreaths from Mexico and Chinese Almond Cookies.

Do bake our traditionals. We recommend the Frosted Ginger Creams, an unforgettable molasses cookie. And don't miss the big recipe for Gingerbread Christmas Cookies, ideal for cutting into different shapes for yuletide. We also include Hard-Cooked Egg Cookies, a delightful yellow rolled cookie.

Some women bake rolled cookies the year around, time being their only limitation. But beginners and women inexperienced in rolling dough are sometimes loath to try them. It's really simple to roll cookie dough if you use good recipes and follow the rules. Number one is to chill the dough if it seems soft. When it gets firm, take only the amount you can work with at a time from the refrigerator.

Roll it on a pastry cloth with a stockinet-covered rolling pin. Rub a little flour into the cloth and stockinet with your hands to discourage the dough from sticking. Repeat if necessary, but be stingy with flour —adding too much makes cookies tough.

Roll from the center of the mound of dough as you do for pie crust. When you cut dough with the cookie cutter, start at the edges and work to the center. Dip the cutter in flour and shake off the excess. Repeat as often as necessary to prevent dough from sticking. Cut with pressure and keep scraps to a minimum by cutting cookies close together. For the last baking, gather the scraps, shape into a mound, roll and cut. These cookies will be less tender than those rolled only once.

If you do not have cookie cutters in assorted shapes, why not start a collection, adding one or two a year? Many women say this is a rewarding hobby. If you (or another family member) have artistic leanings you also can draw and cut patterns from cardboard. Grease the patterns well before laying them on the rolled dough; cut around them with a pointed knife.

Lift cutouts to the baking sheet on a wide spatula to avoid stretching them out of shape. Bake cookies only until delicately browned unless recipe specifies otherwise.

ALMOND QUARTER-MOONS

Recipe for the dainty crescents is from an almond grower's wife

2¾ c. sifted flour	1½ c. sugar
1½ tsp. baking powder	½ tsp. almond extract
¼ tsp. salt	2 eggs, beaten
¾ c. butter or regular margarine	½ c. ground unblanched almonds

Sift together flour, baking powder and salt.

Cream butter and sugar until light and fluffy. Add almond extract and eggs; beat well. Add sifted dry ingredients and almonds and mix well. Chill.

Roll dough about ⅛" thick. Cut with crescent-shaped cutter. Place about 2" apart on ungreased baking sheet. Bake in moderate oven (350°) 8 to 10 minutes. Remove cookies and cool on racks. Makes about 10 dozen.

SPECIAL-OCCASION JELLY COOKIES

Jelly in country kitchens is more than a spread for hot biscuits, toast or jelly roll. It's also a favored ingredient in many dishes, including cookies like these Almond/Jelly Cookies.

Jelly touches these crisp, rich cookies with bright color and supplies that luscious fruity flavor. They're at their best served the same day you bake them, although you can freeze them successfully to bring out on short notice when you want to give your guests a true country-kitchen treat. The combination of almond/jelly flavors makes these cookie sandwiches exceptional.

When we first made them, we used currant jelly, as suggested by the North Dakota woman who contributed this recipe. You can substitute any kind you especially like or have in your cupboard. We found both apricot and peach jams also made delightful fillings.

ALMOND/JELLY COOKIES

Grated almonds speckle cookie sandwiches filled with tart-sweet jelly

1 c. butter	⅛ tsp. salt
1 c. plus 2 tblsp. sugar	1 c. grated unblanched almonds
¼ tsp. vanilla	(about ¾ c. before grating)
1½ c. sifted flour	½ c. currant jelly

Beat butter until light; add sugar and vanilla and beat until fluffy. Add flour and salt, blended together, and then the almonds.

Cover bowl tightly and chill overnight or several hours.

Roll dough very thin with waxed paper placed over dough to make rolling easier. Cut with 2½" round cutter.

Place cookies 1" apart on lightly greased baking sheet and bake in slow oven (300°) 8 to 10 minutes, until they start to brown around edges. Remove cookies to cooling rack. While still warm, spread half of cookies with currant jelly and top with other half of cookies. Complete cooling on racks. Makes 3 dozen.

N O T E : You can crush almonds fine with a rolling pin if a hand-turned grater is not available.

APPLESAUCE ROLL-UP COOKIES

Slice and bake one roll; freeze the other roll for baking later

1¾ c. applesauce (16½ oz. can)   1 c. shortening
¾ c. cut-up dates   3 eggs
½ c. sugar   4 c. sifted flour
1 tblsp. grated orange peel   ¼ tsp. salt
1 c. chopped nuts   ½ tsp. baking soda
2 c. brown sugar, firmly packed

To make filling, combine applesauce, dates and white sugar. Cook over low heat, stirring until thick, about 12 minutes. Remove from heat; stir in orange peel and nuts. Set aside to cool (you'll have 3 c. filling).

Beat brown sugar with shortening until light and fluffy. Beat in eggs to mix well.

Sift together flour, salt and baking soda. Add to creamed mixture, and mix thoroughly. Divide in half. Roll each half about ¼" thick on waxed paper to make a 15 x 12" rectangle.

Spread 1½ c. filling over each half of dough. Roll up like jelly roll (each roll will be about 16" long). Wrap tightly in waxed paper and refrigerate overnight, or at least several hours.

With a sharp knife, cut dough in ¼" slices; place 1½ to 2" apart on lightly greased baking sheet. Bake in moderate oven (350°) about 12 minutes, until lightly browned. Transfer cookies to racks to cool. Store cookies in container with loose-fitting lid. Makes about 10 dozen.

NOTE: If cookies lose crispness on standing, spread on baking sheet and heat in slow oven (300°) about 5 minutes. If you like, sift confectioners sugar mixed with cinnamon over slightly warm cookies. Use the proportion of 1 tsp. ground cinnamon to ½ c. confectioners sugar. Especially good with coffee.

BROWN-EYED SUSANS

These yellow and brown cookies bring beauty to any tea table

1 c. butter or regular margarine	3¼ c. sifted flour
1 c. sugar	1 tblsp. baking powder
1 egg	1 tsp. salt
½ tsp. almond extract	⅓ c. semisweet chocolate
¼ tsp. yellow food color	pieces (64)

Cream butter and sugar together until light and fluffy. Beat in egg, almond extract and food color.

Sift together flour, baking powder and salt. Gradually blend into creamed mixture.

Turn dough onto lightly floured surface; knead gently to form a ball. Wrap in plastic wrap or waxed paper and chill several hours, or until dough can be handled easily.

Divide dough in fourths. Roll one fourth at a time to make a 12 x 6" rectangle. Cut each rectangle into strips ¾" wide and 6" long. On long side of strip cut slits ½" apart and three-fourths of the way through to opposite side. Roll each strip like a jelly roll. (Dough has tendency to break when rolled; hold roll together with fingers and pinch slightly on bottom when placing on baking sheet. This spreads the blossoms.) Place about 1" apart on ungreased baking sheet. Turn cut ends down a little to form flower petals. Center a chocolate piece, flat side up, in each flower.

Bake in moderate oven (375°) 8 to 10 minutes, until browned. Remove from oven; cool slightly on baking sheet set on rack. Remove from baking sheet and cool completely on racks. Makes about 64.

Variation

Festival Squares: Divide dough for Brown-Eyed Susans in half. Make flower cookies with one half, Festival Squares with the other half: Roll dough into two 12 x 6" rectangles. Cut in 2" squares with knife; then cut two ½" slits in each side of squares. Bake and cool like Brown-Eyed Susans. Then drop Vanilla Cream Icing in irregular amounts from teaspoon onto centers of cookies. For the most charming cookies, divide icing into four parts. Leave one white and tint the others with food color in pastel shades of pink, green and yellow. Makes 3 dozen.

Vanilla Cream Icing: Stir together 2 c. sifted confectioners sugar, ¼ tsp. salt and 1 tsp. vanilla; add enough milk or water (about 2 tblsp.) to make an icing that spreads easily. Beat well. Spread on cookies with pastry brush, or drop from spoon, as directed in recipe.

BUTTER CRISPIES

Freeze some of these to bring out for company—they're good keepers

1 c. butter	⅛ tsp. salt
1 c. sugar	¾ tsp. ground nutmeg
1 egg	1 tsp. baking soda
3½ c. sifted flour	½ c. buttermilk

Cream butter until light and fluffy. Gradually beat in sugar and egg.

Combine flour, salt, nutmeg and baking soda. Sift into creamed mixture alternately with buttermilk. Chill at least an hour or until firm.

Roll out a small part of dough at a time, keeping remaining dough in refrigerator until ready to roll. Roll very thin. Cut with 2½″ round or fancy cookie cutters. Place ¼ to ½″ apart on ungreased baking sheet.

Bake in moderate oven (350°) 8 to 10 minutes, until lightly browned. Remove from baking sheet to wire racks to cool. Makes 5½ dozen.

CHEESE/JAM COOKIE TARTS

Brown rims of cookie dough frame fruit jams of festive colors

1 c. butter	½ c. jam (grape, apricot, peach
1 (8 oz.) pkg. cream cheese	or berry)
2 c. sifted flour	

Beat together butter and cream cheese until light and fluffy. Blend in flour. Chill overnight.

Roll dough about ⅛″ thick and cut with 2″ round cutter. Spread tops with jam; arrange ½″ apart on ungreased baking sheet. (Cookies shrink during baking.)

Bake in moderate oven (350°) 10 to 12 minutes. Remove cookies and cool on racks. Makes about 6 dozen.

N O T E : Store cookies in container with loose lid in a cool place, or package and freeze them. To use if frozen, thaw in wrapper at room temperature about 15 minutes. To restore crispness to stored cookies, spread them on baking sheets and heat in slow oven (300°) about 5 minutes.

CHINESE ALMOND COOKIES

An Iowa country woman, member of a gourmet club, serves these with tea for dessert after an oriental-type meal.

The inspiration to make Chinese Almond Cookies followed a trip to California and an afternoon spent browsing around San Francisco's Chinatown. Back home in her farm kitchen, she set out to duplicate the cookies she saw in an oriental bakery and tasted in a Chinese dinner. Luckily, she used lard for shortening; this gave her product that characteristic texture that all authentic Chinese almond cookies have. By baking them in a slow oven, she achieved the right color—no browning except a delicate shading around the edges. Her cookies, with almonds centered on top, capture the delightful flavor that makes this type of cookie the top oriental favorite of Americans.

CHINESE ALMOND COOKIES

Go Chinese with these creamy white cookies, a top oriental favorite

1 c. lard, butter or regular margarine	½ tsp. baking soda
	½ tsp. salt
1 c. sugar	24 whole almonds (about), split
1 egg	lengthwise in halves
¾ tsp. almond extract	(about ¼ c.)
2¾ c. sifted flour	

Beat together lard and sugar until light and fluffy. Beat in egg and almond extract to blend well.

Sift together flour, baking soda and salt; add to creamed mixture. Shape dough with hands to form a ball.

Roll dough a scant ¼″ thick and cut with 2″ round cutter. Place 2″ apart on ungreased baking sheet. Put an almond half in the center of each cookie.

Bake in slow oven (325°) 15 to 20 minutes, or until cookies brown very lightly around edges. Carefully remove cookies with broad

After-School Welcome. It's nice to come home to Oatmeal/Molasses Cookies and a cold glass of milk (page 150). Makes six dozen cookies. Freeze some to serve with coffee to drop-in guests.

Celebration Cookies. Decorative, but simple to make: Chocolate Crackles, top (page 192); Toffee Sticks, right (page 66); Fruitcake Squares (page 236). They look — and taste — fancy.

spatula to cooling rack. (They are fragile when hot.) When cool, store in covered container in a cool place, or freeze. Makes about 3½ dozen.

CLOTHESPIN COOKIES

These fascinating cookies will be the talk of your coffee party

3¼ c. sifted flour
1 tsp. salt
2 tblsp. sugar
2 c. shortening

1¼ c. warm water
2 egg yolks
Chocolate/Marshmallow Filling
    (recipe follows)

Blend together flour, salt, sugar and ½ c. shortening as for pie crust. Stir in warm water. Then add egg yolks and mix well. Cover bowl and chill 1 hour.

Remove dough from refrigerator and roll in rectangle ¼" thick. Spread with ½ c. shortening. Fold one half of dough (greased top) over on other half; refrigerate another hour. Repeat this process two more times, each time spreading ½ c. shortening on dough.

Roll a fourth of dough at a time, leaving remaining dough in refrigerator until ready to work with it. Cut in strips 1" wide, 4" long. Wind each strip loosely around a clean wooden clothespin. Lay in ungreased 15½ x 10½ x 1" jelly roll pan.

Bake in hot oven (425°) 10 to 12 minutes. Place clothespins with cookies on cooling racks. In 2 or 3 minutes, gently twist pins and slip off cookies. (They are crisp and break easily so work carefully.) When cool, fill with Chocolate/Marshmallow Filling.

To fill, cut a small hole in corner of small plastic bag. Partly fill with Chocolate/Marshmallow Filling, leaving remaining filling in refrigerator until needed. Squeeze out filling, first into one end of cookie and then in other end to fill completely. Store filled cookies in refrigerator until serving time. Makes 9 dozen.

NOTE: Cookies may be refrigerated a few days and then filled. Or freeze cookies and fill them when needed.

CHOCOLATE/MARSHMALLOW FILLING

This luscious filling and the crisp cookies are great teammates

¼ c. flour
1 c. milk
½ c. butter
½ c. sugar
½ c. confectioners sugar

½ c. marshmallow creme
1 tsp. vanilla
2 to 4 squares unsweetened
    chocolate, melted and cooled

Mix flour with a little milk to make a smooth paste; add remaining milk and cook, stirring constantly, until mixture thickens. Set aside to cool.

Cream together butter and sugars until light and fluffy, using electric mixer on high speed. Add thickened flour-milk mixture and beat well. Then beat in the marshmallow creme and vanilla. Stir in chocolate. Cover and chill before using. Makes 2 cups.

N O T E : You can use 2 to 4 squares unsweetened or semisweet chocolate in the filling. What you use and how much is a matter of personal preference.

COCOA/MOLASSES COOKIES

Long-time favorites in Dutch neighborhoods in Hudson River Valley

1 c. butter
½ c. sugar
1 c. light molasses
1 egg
1 tsp. vanilla

3 c. sifted flour
1 tsp. salt
½ c. cocoa
Vanilla Glaze (see Index)

Cream butter and sugar until light and fluffy. Beat in molasses, egg and vanilla to mix well.

Sift together flour, salt and cocoa; stir into creamed mixture. Chill dough.

Roll dough rather thick, about ¼″, and cut into 4 x 2½″ rectangles. (Use an empty luncheon meat can for a cutter, or a 4 x 2½″ rectangular cutter or a knife. Cookies cut with the empty can or cutter have rounded corners.) Place ½″ apart on lightly greased baking sheet.

Bake in moderate oven (350°) about 10 minutes. Remove cookies and cool on racks, then spread with Vanilla Glaze. Makes 3 dozen.

CORNMEAL COOKIES

The unusual ingredient in these crisp, raisin treats is cornmeal

1½ c. sifted flour	¾ c. sugar
½ tsp. baking powder	1 egg
½ tsp. salt	½ tsp. lemon extract
½ c. cornmeal	¼ c. milk
½ tsp. ground nutmeg	½ c. chopped raisins
½ c. shortening	5 tblsp. sugar (for topping)

Sift together flour, baking powder, salt, cornmeal and nutmeg.

Beat together shortening and ¾ c. sugar until light and fluffy. Beat in egg and lemon extract. Alternately add milk and sifted dry ingredients. Beat until smooth. Stir in raisins.

Roll dough out on lightly floured board to ¼″ thickness; cut with 2½″ round cutter. Place 1″ apart on greased baking sheet; sprinkle with sugar. Bake in moderate oven (375°) 12 to 15 minutes. Remove cookies and cool on racks. Makes 29 cookies.

DATE PINWHEELS

Two-tone pinwheels add charm to a tray or plate of one-color cookies

1⅓ c. chopped dates	1⅓ c. brown sugar, firmly packed
½ c. sugar	2 eggs
½ c. water	2⅔ c. sifted flour
½ c. chopped nuts	½ tsp. salt
⅔ c. shortening	½ tsp. baking soda

Combine dates, sugar, water and nuts in saucepan; cook until thick. Set aside to cool.

Cream shortening; beat in brown sugar. Beat in eggs to mix thoroughly.

Sift together dry ingredients; add to creamed mixture and blend well. Chill thoroughly.

Divide dough in half; roll each half in a rectangle ¼″ thick. Spread each with date filling and roll up like a jelly roll. Wrap in waxed paper and chill overnight.

Cut dough in ⅛″ slices and place 1½″ apart on greased baking sheet. Bake in moderate oven (375°) 8 minutes, or until lightly browned. Remove cookies and cool on racks. Makes about 5 dozen.

PINK AND WHITE FROSTED DIAMONDS

Pennsylvania Dutch women of Moravian faith invented these cookies and named them Moravian seed cookies. Your fondness for them
will depend on how much you enjoy the flavor of caraway.

Tradition requires that you cut the pastry-like dough in diamond
shapes, frost them in white and sprinkle on coarse pink sugar.

Diamonds are easy to cut with a knife, although you can use a
cookie cutter if you have one. Just roll the dough in a rectangle and
cut 2″ diagonal strips one way, and then the other. And you have no
scraps of dough to reroll and bake.

FROSTED DIAMOND COOKIES

Guaranteed to please caraway fans—also to dress up the cookie tray

½ c. butter	1 tsp. caraway seeds
½ c. sugar	White Mountain Frosting
2 eggs	(recipe follows)
1 tsp. vanilla	¼ c. coarse pink decorating
3 c. sifted flour	sugar (about)
⅛ tsp. salt	

Beat butter until light; gradually add sugar and beat until mixture
is fluffy. Beat in eggs and vanilla to blend thoroughly.

Sift together flour and salt; add to creamed mixture. Stir in caraway seeds.

Roll dough thin, not more than ⅛″, and cut in 2″ diamonds with
sharp knife or cookie cutter. Place ½″ apart on lightly greased baking
sheet.

Bake in slow oven (325°) 10 to 12 minutes. Remove cookies and
cool on racks. Then spread with White Mountain Frosting and sprinkle with pink sugar. Makes about 6½ dozen.

White Mountain Frosting: Combine 1 c. sugar, ⅛ tsp. cream of tartar and ¼ c. water in small saucepan. Place over heat and stir until
sugar dissolves. Continue cooking syrup to soft ball stage (236°).

Meanwhile, add ⅛ tsp. salt to 1 egg white and beat until stiff. Pour
hot syrup in a fine stream into egg white, beating constantly until
frosting is of spreading consistency.

DOUBLE CREAM COOKIES

Tea party tidbits—tiny, rich cookies put together with frosting

1 c. soft butter	2 c. sifted flour
⅓ c. heavy cream	Creamy Frosting (recipe follows)

Mix together butter, cream and flour; chill thoroughly. Roll ⅛″ thick and cut in 1½″ rounds. Place on waxed paper heavily sprinkled with sugar and turn to coat circles.

Place about 2″ apart on ungreased baking sheet; prick tops with fork in three or four places. Bake in moderate oven (375°) about 8 minutes, until puffy, but not browned. Place cookies on racks to cool. Put together in pairs with Creamy Frosting. Makes about 5 dozen double cookies.

Creamy Frosting: Blend together ¼ c. butter, ¾ c. sifted confectioners sugar, 1 egg yolk and 1 tsp. vanilla or ¼ tsp. almond extract. Beat until smooth.

FIG BARS

The moist fig filling in these butter cookies is not overly sweet

1 c. butter	1 tsp. baking powder
2 c. brown sugar, firmly packed	1½ c. ground figs
3 eggs	1 c. water
1 tsp. vanilla	¾ c. sugar
1 tblsp. lemon juice	3 tblsp. flour
4 c. sifted flour	¼ c. chopped walnuts
1 tsp. salt	2 tblsp. orange juice
1 tsp. baking soda	

To make dough, cream butter and brown sugar. Add eggs, vanilla and lemon juice; beat. Stir together 4 c. flour, salt, baking soda and baking powder; blend into creamed mixture. Chill.

Meanwhile, prepare fig filling. Boil figs in water 5 minutes. Blend sugar and 3 tblsp. flour; stir into figs. Cook over low heat, stirring frequently, until thick. Stir in nuts and orange juice. Cool.

Divide chilled dough in half. Roll each half in a rectangle 18 x 12 x ⅛″ on well-floured pastry cloth. Cut into four 3″ wide strips. Put cooled filling down center of strips. Using a spatula, fold dough over filling. Cut strips in half; transfer strips, seam side down, to ungreased baking sheet, about 2" apart. Bake in moderate oven (375°) about 15 minutes. Transfer bars to racks to cool. Cut in 2" bars. Makes about 5 dozen.

FIG/ORANGE-FILLED SQUARES

Fork tines make decorative edge on two sides of plump turnovers

2 c. finely chopped dried figs	1 egg
½ c. white sugar	2 tblsp. milk
1 c. orange juice	1 tsp. vanilla
Dash of salt	3 c. sifted flour
½ c. sugar	½ tsp. salt
½ c. brown sugar, firmly packed	½ tsp. baking soda
1 c. shortening	

To make filling, combine figs, ½ c. white sugar, orange juice and dash of salt in small saucepan. Cook, stirring occasionally, until thick. Set aside to cool. You will have 2 cups.

Cream together ½ c. white sugar, brown sugar and shortening until light and fluffy. Add egg, milk and vanilla; beat well.

Sift together flour, ½ tsp. salt and baking soda; stir into creamed mixture. Chill dough at least 1 hour.

Divide dough into quarters. Roll one quarter at a time on lightly floured board to make a 12 x 8" rectangle. Cut crosswise into 6 strips, each 2" wide. Spread fig filling over half of strips; then top with remaining strips. Press lengthwise edges with floured tines of fork to seal. Cut in 2" lengths. Repeat with remaining portions of dough.

Place 2" apart on ungreased baking sheet and bake in moderate oven (350°) about 10 minutes. Transfer cookies to rack to cool. Makes about 4 dozen.

FINNISH STAR COOKIES

These decorative cookies are rich like pastry—with date filling

1 c. sugar	1 c. butter
1 c. finely cut dates (½ lb.)	½ c. water
1 c. water	1 tblsp. light cream or milk
1½ c. sifted flour	2 tblsp. sugar (for tops)

To make filling, combine 1 c. sugar, dates and 1 c. water in saucepan. Bring to a boil over medium heat; reduce heat to low and continue cooking and stirring until filling thickens. Set aside to cool.

Blend flour with ½ c. butter with pastry blender as for pie crust. Slowly add ½ c. water; mix well and chill thoroughly.

Roll dough ⅛" thick. Spread about a third of remaining ½ c. butter over half of dough. Fold buttered half over other half of dough and roll to ⅛" thickness. Repeat spreading with butter and rolling two more times.

Cut dough in 2½" squares. Cut 1" slash in each corner of squares and place about 1 tsp. cooled date filling on center of each square. Fold one point of each slashed corner to center to make pinwheel, and pinch edges to seal. Brush with cream and sprinkle with sugar.

Arrange about 2" apart on ungreased baking sheet and bake in hot oven (400°) about 10 minutes. Transfer cookies to racks to cool. Makes about 5 dozen.

FORTUNE COOKIES, AMERICAN STYLE

Bake fortune cookies for the next social gathering at your house; they're fun for people of all ages. The homemade version tastes better than the Chinese, but differs in shape—flatter, with a small center peak.

The recipe for Mom's Fortune Cookies comes from an Illinois woman who has been baking them off and on for more than 10 years. Stored in a covered container and put in a cold place or the freezer, they keep for several months. It's convenient to keep them on hand to bring out on short notice.

The Illinois mother always writes messages to insert in a few cookies she saves especially for her children. That explains the name of the recipe. Her motherly notes run from "I love you" and "It's your turn to feed the cat" to "You're an exceptional child—exceptionally untidy and sweet."

Adult messages are predictions, such as "You'll meet a stranger this week who will bring you happiness" and "If your birthday is between May 1 and August 25, this is your year for exciting travel."

Here's the recipe for the cookies. You'll enjoy using your imagination when you write the fortunes to enclose in them.

MOM'S FORTUNE COOKIES

These cookies liven up parties; make them ahead to have on hand

1 c. sugar	⅓ c. milk
⅔ c. shortening	3 c. sifted flour
2 eggs	3 tsp. baking powder
1 tsp. vanilla	½ tsp. salt

Cream sugar and shortening until light and fluffy. Beat in eggs, vanilla and milk to mix thoroughly.

Sift together flour, baking powder and salt. Stir gradually into creamed mixture. Chill well.

Roll dough ⅛" thick and cut with 2" round cutter. Place about 1" apart on ungreased baking sheet.

Type or write your own messages on little slips of paper; fold small and place like tent in center of each cookie on baking sheet. Place another cut-out cookie on top and press edges together to seal.

Bake in hot oven (400°) 10 to 12 minutes. Remove cookies and cool on racks. Makes about 5½ dozen.

FRUIT BLOSSOM COOKIES

Charming as an old-fashioned flower garden in full bloom

⅔ c. shortening	1½ tsp. baking powder
¾ c. sugar	¼ tsp. salt
1 egg	2 tblsp. milk
½ tsp. vanilla	Citrus/Raisin (or other) Filling
2 c. sifted flour	(recipe follows)

Cream together shortening and sugar. Add egg; beat until light and fluffy. Add vanilla.

Sift together dry ingredients. Add to creamed mixture along with milk. Divide dough in half. Chill 1 hour.

Roll out half of dough; keep the rest chilled. Roll ¹⁄₁₆ to ⅛" thick. Cut with 2" scalloped cookie cutter. Place about ½ tsp. Citrus/Raisin Filling in centers of half the cookies. Place 1½" apart on greased baking sheet. Cut out centers of remaining half of cookies with 1" round cutter; place on filled bottoms and press edges with fork to seal. Repeat this process with remaining half of dough.

Bake in moderate oven (350°) 10 to 12 minutes. Transfer cookies to racks to cool. Makes about 2 dozen.

CITRUS/RAISIN FILLING

Do try the fruity variations—they add color and taste contrasts

¼ c. chopped seedless raisins	4 tsp. water
½ tsp. grated orange peel	2 tblsp. sugar
1 tblsp. orange juice	½ tsp. flour
½ tsp. lemon juice	⅛ tsp. salt

Combine all ingredients in heavy saucepan. Bring to a boil, stirring constantly. Cook over medium heat about 5 minutes, stirring occasionally. Cool. Makes about ¼ cup.

Variations

Fig Filling: Substitute chopped dried figs for the raisins.
Apricot Filling: Substitute finely chopped, soft, dried apricots for raisins and add 1½ tsp. orange juice, ¼ tsp. lemon juice, 3 tblsp. water and 1 tsp. flour.
Pineapple Filling: Combine in saucepan ¾ tsp. cornstarch and ¼ c. crushed pineapple, undrained. Cook until clear, stirring constantly. Cool.
Cherry Filling: Mash ¼ c. cherry pie filling. Add a few drops almond extract, if desired.

GINGER COOKIES FOR A CROWD

A big recipe to make when you wish to put cookies in the freezer

5½ c. sifted flour	1 c. shortening
1 tblsp. baking soda	1 c. sugar
2 tsp. baking powder	1 egg, beaten
1 tsp. salt	½ tsp. vanilla
¾ tsp. ground ginger	1 c. dark molasses
1 tsp. ground cinnamon	½ c. strong coffee

Sift together flour, soda, baking powder, salt, ginger and cinnamon.
Cream shortening; add sugar gradually; beat until light; add egg and vanilla.

Add molasses and coffee, then sifted dry ingredients; mix well; chill.

Roll out on lightly floured board ¼″ thick; cut with round 2″ cutter.

Place about 2″ apart on greased baking sheet. Bake in hot oven (400°) 8 to 10 minutes. Spread on racks to cool. Makes 12 dozen.

GINGERBREAD CHRISTMAS COOKIES

Few goodies you make in your kitchen say Merry Christmas more eloquently than gingerbread cookies. You may consider them old-fashioned, but they're as up to date as the carols you sing or the Santa Claus to whom children write such adorable letters. These spicy molasses cookies are especially inviting on Christmas trees, and lend themselves to decorating.

Aside from tradition and tastiness, gingerbread cookies have many qualities that recommend them. You can bake them ahead. They keep satisfactorily for weeks either in the freezer or a cool place. You can cut them in many fancy shapes, such as animals, stars, bells, Christmas trees or whatever forms you wish, including plain and scalloped rounds. And you can decorate them with raisins, currants, candies and white or tinted icing. The dark brown cookie makes an excellent background to show off the trimmings.

Our Gingerbread Christmas Cookies recipe makes cookies that do not break easily. For this reason alone they are a fine choice for Christmas trees. You can hang them on your big tree or a smaller one decorated entirely with cookies. The cookie tree can be a small evergreen. Or cut a flat triangular Christmas tree from a piece of softboard. Cover it with green felt and pin the cookies to the felt, using red and green ribbons you pull through holes made in the cookies before baking.

There are two ways to make the holes in the cookies: 1) Insert 1½″ length of drinking straw into each unbaked cookie in the place you want the hole. Remove the straws before cookies are cool. Pull green and red ribbons through the holes and tie in bows or loops. 2) For each cookie, loop a 5 to 6″ length of string on baking sheet. Press unbaked cookie on a string, leaving at least 1″ overlap to hold cookie securely.

If you have such a hospitality cookie tree, you will need a reserve supply of cookies to replace those your visitors enjoy taking off and eating. Our recipe for Gingerbread Christmas Cookies makes about 12 dozen 2½" round cookies. It's easy to cut the recipe in half if you want to bake a smaller batch.

GINGERBREAD CHRISTMAS COOKIES

Cookies are sturdy, crisp and hard—taste like gingerbread. The little pigs with pink icing curls for tails make a hit with a crowd

½ c. shortening	1 tsp. ground allspice
1 c. brown sugar, firmly packed	1½ c. dark molasses
2 tsp. baking soda	⅔ c. water
2 tsp. salt	6½ c. sifted flour (about)
1 tsp. ground cinnamon	Ornamental Icing (optional,
1 tsp. ground ginger	see Index)
1 tsp. ground cloves	

Cream shortening, sugar, baking soda, salt and spices together until light and fluffy. Beat in molasses. Stir in water.

Gradually stir in enough flour to make a stiff dough (about 6½ c.). Shape dough in ball with hands, wrap in plastic wrap or waxed paper and refrigerate several hours or overnight.

Roll out dough, a small amount at a time, ⅛ to ¼" thick. Cut with desired cutter; slip a broad spatula under cookie and transfer it to lightly greased baking sheet. Arrange cutouts a short distance apart on baking sheet (they spread very little).

Bake in moderate oven (350°) 10 to 12 minutes, or until cookies are lightly browned. Remove from baking sheet to racks and cool. Decorate with Ornamental Icing, if you wish. Makes about 12 dozen.

Gingerbread Boys: Cut rolled dough for Gingerbread Christmas Cookies with 6" gingerbread boy cutter. Place them about ½" apart on lightly greased baking sheet. Place heads of cutout boys on loops of string or insert drinking straws, as described. For each cookie, dip 3 raisins in slightly beaten egg white and press firmly, an equal distance apart, into cookie to represent shirt buttons (you'll need about 12 dozen raisins). For red buttons press in cinnamon candies (red hots) instead of raisins. Carefully move the legs and arms of the boys in different positions to provide animation and variety. Bake cookies, remove drinking straws, if used, and cool on racks. Decorate after cooling, or after freezing or storing. Use Ornamental Icing put through a decorating tube or small plastic bag with small hole cut in one corner. Use to draw faces on gingerbread boys, changing the features to give them a variety of expressions. The recipe for Gingerbread Christmas Cookies makes about 4 dozen 6″ Gingerbread Boys. **Gingerbread Pigs:** Cut the recipe for Gingerbread Christmas Cookies in half. Roll dough as directed, and cut with pig-shaped cookie cutter. Bake, cool and decorate with Ornamental Icing. You can outline each pig cookie with a thin white line of icing and make icing circles or dots for eyes. Tint a little icing pink with red food color and use it to make a curl on each pig cookie to represent its tail. Makes 64.

N O T E : Children delight in animal cookies. Among their favorites are rooster, hen, rabbit, reindeer and horse cookies.

OLD-FASHIONED GINGER CREAMS

Almost everyone cherishes memories of cookies especially enjoyed in childhood. Frosted Ginger Creams are more than a dream. A California homemaker-home economist developed her own recipe for Frosted Ginger Creams, the cookies she ate when a child on visits to an aunt.

She had never acquired the recipe—not written down. But when she had a home of her own, she baked ginger/molasses cookies until she duplicated the favorites of her childhood.

When we tested her recipe, every member of our taste panel gave the cookies an A-1 rating. Bake a batch soon. Your friends and family will rejoice in these old-fashioned treats.

FROSTED GINGER CREAMS

These white-iced ginger cookies are soft, flavorful—and keep well

1 c. shortening	½ tsp. baking powder
1 c. brown sugar, firmly packed	1 tsp. salt
2 eggs	2 tblsp. butter or regular
1 c. dark molasses	margarine
2 tblsp. vinegar	2 c. sifted confectioners sugar
5 c. sifted flour (about)	1 tsp. vanilla
1 tblsp. ground ginger	3 tblsp. milk or cream
1 tblsp. baking soda	

Cream together shortening and brown sugar until light; beat in eggs, one at a time, beating well to blend. Add molasses and vinegar.

Sift together 4 c. flour, ginger, soda, baking powder and salt; stir into batter. Add additional flour to make a soft dough easy to roll.

Roll dough on lightly floured surface; cut in 2 or 3" circles. Place about 1" apart on lightly greased baking sheet.

Bake in moderate oven (375°) 10 to 15 minutes. Remove cookies and cool on wire racks.

Meanwhile, blend butter and confectioners sugar together, add vanilla and milk and beat until smooth. Spread over tops of cooled cookies, leaving a ¼" rim of brown cookie around the white frosting. Store in airtight containers. Makes 5½ dozen.

GRAPEFRUIT SUGAR COOKIES

These dainty cookies make talk at tea parties—guests ask why they're so good. Candied peel is the secret

1 c. butter	½ tsp. salt
1¼ c. sugar	¾ c. finely chopped Candied
2 eggs	Grapefruit Peel (recipe
3 c. sifted flour	follows)
2½ tsp. baking powder	

Cream butter and sugar; add eggs and beat until fluffy.

Sift together dry ingredients; mix in grapefruit peel. Add to creamed mixture. Divide dough in half; place in covered container and chill in refrigerator several hours.

Roll dough about ¼" thick on floured board; cut with floured cutter.

Place 1 to 1½" apart on greased baking sheet and bake in moderate oven (375°) 8 to 10 minutes. Remove cookies and cool on racks. Makes about 5 dozen.

CANDIED GRAPEFRUIT PEEL

Keep this handy—it makes icings and cookies special

Select and wash thick-skinned grapefruit. Cut into quarters and remove pulp. Put peel in saucepan; cover with cold water. Weight down peel with a plate. Let stand several hours or overnight. Drain.

With scissors, cut peel into strips about ¼" wide.

Cover peel with cold water and slowly bring to a simmer (180°) in a saucepan. Remove from heat, cover pan and let stand about 1 hour; drain. Repeat process until peel no longer tastes bitter (about 3 times).

Cover again with water and boil until yellow peel is tender, about 15 minutes. Drain well in colander. Press out water. Pack peel firmly into measuring cup to measure.

Return peel to saucepan. For each cup of peel, add 1 cup of sugar. Place over medium heat; stir until sugar has dissolved (peel forms its own liquid).

Cook peel over medium heat, stirring frequently, until sugar syrup is concentrated; reduce heat to low (syrup should boil gently). Continue cooking until the grapefruit peel is semitransparent and most of the sugar syrup has boiled away.

Drain in colander. Separate pieces of peel on baking sheets and allow to stand until they feel fairly dry. Sprinkle with enough sugar to give a crystalline look.

Store in tightly covered cans, or in plastic bags in the freezer.

HARD-COOKED EGG COOKIES

Cinnamon and nuts splash the tops of the rich, tasty, yellow cookies

1 c. butter or regular margarine	3 c. sifted flour
1 c. sugar	1 egg, slightly beaten
1 egg	1 tsp. sugar
5 sieved hard-cooked egg yolks (about 1 c.)	2 tsp. ground cinnamon
	½ c. chopped nuts
1 tblsp. finely grated lemon peel	

Beat butter, 1 c. sugar and 1 egg to blend thoroughly. Add hard-cooked egg yolks and lemon peel. Stir in flour.

Roll dough about ¼″ thick on lightly floured surface; cut with 2″ round cutter. Place ½″ apart on ungreased baking sheet. Brush tops of cookies with slightly beaten egg.

Combine 1 tsp. sugar and cinnamon; sprinkle with nuts over cookies.

Bake in slow oven (325°) 20 to 25 minutes, or until delicately browned. Remove cookies and cool on racks. Store in container with loose-fitting lid to retain crispness. Makes about 52.

Variation

Molded Hard-Cooked Egg Cookies: Instead of rolling dough, shape in 1″ balls. Place 2″ apart on ungreased baking sheet. Flatten by pressing with lightly greased bottom of juice glass. Brush tops with slightly beaten egg, sprinkle with sugar-cinnamon mixture and nuts, and bake like cutout cookies. Makes about 68.

HONEY WAFERS

Honey, spices and bran make these crisp, dainty cookies delicious

½ c. butter	½ tsp. ground cinnamon
½ c. honey	¼ tsp. ground cloves
2 c. sifted flour	¼ tsp. ground allspice
1 tsp. baking soda	¼ c. crushed bran flakes

Cream together butter and honey.

Sift together flour, baking soda, cinnamon, cloves and allspice. Mix with bran flakes.

Combine dry ingredients with honey and butter. Chill 1 hour, or until firm enough to roll easily.

Roll ⅛″ thick on lightly floured board. Cut with floured cookie cutter. Place about 2″ apart on greased baking sheet; bake in moderate oven (350°) 8 to 10 minutes. Remove cookies and cool on racks. Makes 3 dozen.

EASTER LAMB COOKIES

Stand lambs in green cellophane grass on a tray for a centerpiece

1 c. regular margarine	½ tsp. baking powder
⅔ c. sugar	1 egg, separated
1 egg	1 c. cookie coconut
1 tsp. vanilla	¼ tsp. water
2½ c. sifted flour	2 drops red or blue food color

Beat together margarine and sugar until light and fluffy. Beat in 1 egg and vanilla to blend thoroughly.

Sift together flour and baking powder. Add to creamed mixture. Divide dough in half; wrap each half in waxed paper and chill.

On lightly floured surface, roll half of dough very thin, less than ⅛″ if possible. Cut with lamb cookie cutter or pattern.

Beat white from separated egg until foamy. Brush onto unbaked cookies. Sprinkle with half of cookie coconut. Place 1″ apart on greased baking sheet.

Bake in moderate oven (350°) 7 to 10 minutes. Place cookies on racks to cool.

Meanwhile, roll second half of dough; cut in same way, but decorate before baking with egg yolk paint: Beat yolk from separated egg with water; add food color. Paint on unbaked cookies; sprinkle with coconut and bake as for first half of cookies. Makes about 76 (38 from each half of dough).

LEMON/ALMOND RICHES

Almond daisies with red centers top these Christmas beauties

1 c. butter or regular margarine	1 tsp. water
1 c. sugar	2 tblsp. sugar (for tops)
1 egg, separated	2 c. whole blanched almonds
1 tblsp. finely grated lemon peel	(about ¾ lb.)
¼ tsp. salt	1 (4 oz.) pkg. candied cherries,
2 c. sifted flour	cut in halves
½ c. finely chopped blanched almonds	

Beat butter and 1 c. sugar together until light and fluffy. Beat in egg yolk and lemon peel.

Blend together salt and flour and stir into beaten mixture. Stir in chopped almonds. Shape dough in ball, flatten on lightly floured surface and roll ¼" thick. Cut with 2" round cutter.

Slightly beat egg white diluted with water; brush over tops of cookies. Sprinkle lightly with sugar. Press whole almonds around edge of cookies like daisy petals, 5 petals to a cookie. Place a cherry half, rounded side up, in center of each cookie.

Place cookies 1½" apart on lightly greased baking sheet. Bake in slow oven (325°) 15 to 17 minutes, or until cookies brown around edges. Remove cookies and cool on racks. Makes 3½ dozen.

Variation

Lemon-Flavored Riches: Omit almond daisy trim, placing a half candied cherry in center of each cookie before baking.

MINCEMEAT/CHEESE COOKIES

Perfect non-sweet addition to cookie tray—taste like mincemeat pie!

1 c. butter or regular margarine	1 (9 oz.) pkg. prepared
2 c. grated Cheddar cheese	mincemeat
(½ lb.)	½ c. water
2 c. sifted flour	

Cream butter until light; add cheese (at room temperature) and cream until well blended. Stir in flour; mix well and chill.

Meanwhile, cook mincemeat and water until slightly thickened. Set aside to cool.

Roll dough ⅛″ thick on lightly floured surface; cut in 2″ circles. Put half of circles about 1″ apart on lightly greased baking sheet. Place 1 tsp. cooled mincemeat mixture in center of each cookie on baking sheet. Top each with another circle of dough; press edges with fork to seal. Prick cookie tops in several places with tines of kitchen fork.

Bake in moderate oven (350°) 15 minutes, or until lightly browned. Remove cookies to racks to cool. Makes 3½ dozen.

MINCEMEAT-FILLED OATSIES

Substantial and luscious—men especially like this oatmeal cookie

1 c. sifted flour	¾ c. sugar
1 tsp. baking soda	5 c. quick-cooking rolled oats
¼ tsp. salt	1 c. prepared mincemeat
1 tsp. vinegar	1 tsp. lemon juice
½ c. milk	¼ c. water
½ c. butter or regular margarine	6 tblsp. sugar

Sift together flour, baking soda and salt.

Combine vinegar and milk; stir to mix and set aside.

Beat butter until light; gradually beat in ¾ c. sugar. Beat until fluffy.

Add half of flour mixture, the milk and then remaining flour mixture. Mix thoroughly and fold in rolled oats. Chill 4 hours or longer.

Meanwhile, combine mincemeat, lemon juice, water and 6 tblsp. sugar in saucepan. Bring to a boil, stirring constantly. Set aside to cool.

Roll dough, one-third at a time, leaving remaining dough in refrigerator until ready to work with it. Roll dough thin, about ⅛". Cut with 2½" round cutter.

Spread 1 tsp. cooled mincemeat mixture on half the cookies. Top with remaining cookies. Place 1" apart on ungreased baking sheet.

Bake in moderate oven (350°) 10 to 13 minutes. Remove cookies and cool on racks. Makes 3½ dozen.

Variation

Date-Filled Oatsies: Substitute 1 c. chopped dates for mincemeat in filling.

COUNTRY MOLASSES COOKIES

Make these cutouts as varied as the shape of your cookie cutters

1 c. sugar	1 tsp. baking soda
1 c. shortening	½ tsp. baking powder
1 c. light molasses	1 tsp. ground ginger
1 tblsp. vinegar	1 tsp. ground cinnamon
6 c. sifted flour	2 eggs, beaten
½ tsp. salt	

Combine sugar, shortening, molasses and vinegar in saucepan; bring to boil and cook 2 minutes. Cool.

Sift together flour, salt, soda, baking powder and spices.

Add eggs to cooled molasses mixture. Add dry ingredients and mix well. Chill.

Roll out dough on lightly floured board, about ⅛ to ¼" thick. Cut with cookie cutters of desired shapes; place 1" apart on greased baking sheet.

Bake in moderate oven (375°) 8 to 10 minutes, or until done. Transfer cookies to racks to cool. Makes about 12 dozen.

CRISP MOLASSES COOKIES

Fancy—spread cookies with white frosting, sprinkle with pink sugar

3 c. sifted flour
1 tsp. salt
1 tsp. baking soda
2 tsp. ground cinnamon
2 tsp. ground ginger
⅓ c. sugar

¾ c. shortening
1⅓ c. molasses
Nuts, colored decorating sugar or grated orange peel (for decorations)

Sift together dry ingredients; cut in shortening.

Heat molasses; add to flour mixture. Chill until stiff enough to roll (3 hours or overnight). Roll very thin, about $\frac{1}{16}''$, on lightly floured board. Cut with cookie cutter (leaves, butterflies, gingerbread men or other shapes). Decorate with nuts, colored sugar or orange peel.

Place about 2″ apart on lightly greased baking sheets. Bake in hot oven (400°) 7 to 8 minutes, or until lightly browned. Spread on racks to cool. Makes 6 dozen.

NOTE: To make drop cookies, do not chill dough. After mixing, drop from teaspoon about 2″ apart onto lightly greased baking sheet. Flatten with bottom of glass; bake as for rolled cookies.

MOLASSES WAGON WHEELS

Children adore these big cookies—with "spokes" of white icing

½ c. shortening
1 c. sugar
1 c. dark molasses
½ c. water
4 c. sifted flour
1 tsp. baking soda
1½ tsp. salt
1½ tsp. ground ginger
½ tsp. ground cloves

¼ tsp. ground nutmeg
¼ tsp. ground allspice
¼ c. sugar (for tops)
66 raisins (about ⅓ c.)
1 c. sifted confectioners sugar
¼ tsp. salt
½ tsp. vanilla
1 tblsp. light cream or dairy half-and-half

Cream shortening and 1 c. sugar until light and fluffy. Beat in molasses and water to mix thoroughly.

Sift together flour, soda, 1½ tsp. salt and spices; stir into creamed mixture. Chill several hours or overnight.

Roll dough ¼" thick. Press into 3" circles with large glass, or cut with 3" round cutter. Sprinkle tops with sugar. Place ¼ to ½" apart on greased baking sheet. Press 3 large raisins in center of each dough circle.

Bake in moderate oven (350°) about 12 minutes, until almost no imprint remains when touched lightly with finger. Remove from oven, but leave on baking sheet a few minutes before transferring to cooling racks.

Meanwhile, blend confectioners sugar, ¼ tsp. salt, vanilla and cream together until smooth. When cookies are cool, make spokes of wheel with icing put through small plastic bag, with small hole in one corner, and outline raisin center to simulate wheel's hub. Makes about 22.

NEW MOONS

Dainty crisp crescents shine with glaze—a special-occasion cookie

1 c. butter or regular margarine	1½ c. grated (not ground)
1¼ c. sugar	blanched almonds (½ lb.)
2 tsp. grated lemon peel	1 tsp. vanilla
¼ tsp. salt	2 c. sifted confectioners sugar
1⅓ c. sifted flour	2½ tblsp. boiling water
	1 tsp. vanilla

Cream butter and sugar until light and fluffy. Add lemon peel, salt, flour, almonds and 1 tsp. vanilla; mix thoroughly. Chill dough.

Roll dough ⅛" thick and cut with crescent cutter. Place about ½" apart on ungreased baking sheet. Bake in moderate oven (375°) 8 to 10 minutes.

Meanwhile, combine confectioners sugar, boiling water and 1 tsp. vanilla. Spread over tops of warm cookies. If glaze gets too thick to spread thinly on cookies, add a few drops of hot water. Place cookies on racks to complete cooling. Makes 10 dozen.

NORWEGIAN HEIRLOOM COOKIES

Cut in squares or diamonds—the granulated sugar coating sparkles

1 c. butter	2 c. sifted flour
½ c. sugar	1 c. finely chopped nuts
2 tsp. vanilla	¼ c. sugar (for coating)

Cream butter and ½ c. sugar until light and fluffy. Add vanilla and mix well. Stir in flour and nuts. Chill until firm enough to roll.

Roll dough ¼″ thick and cut with knife in 2″ squares or diamonds. Place ½″ apart on ungreased baking sheet.

Bake in moderate oven (375°) 8 to 10 minutes. While warm roll in sugar. Cool on racks. Makes 5 dozen.

N O T E : Put nuts through nut chopper twice or chop very fine with a knife.

NUT BUTTER COOKIES

Rich cookies—you may want to double recipe for special occasions

1 c. sifted flour	¼ c. apricot or red raspberry
⅓ c. sugar	jam (about)
⅔ c. finely chopped pecans	Viennese Chocolate Frosting
½ c. butter	(recipe follows)
	Pecan halves (about 18)

Sift together flour and sugar; add chopped pecans and mix well. Blend in butter with fork or pastry blender until dough holds together. (Dough will be crumbly.) Chill until easy to handle.

Roll dough on lightly floured surface to ⅛″ thickness. Cut in 2″ circles and place ½″ apart on ungreased baking sheet. Bake in moderate oven (375°) 7 to 10 minutes. Remove from oven and let stand 1 to 2 minutes before removing from baking sheet. Cool completely on racks.

Make sandwich cookies by spreading half the cookies with a thin layer of jam and topping with other half of cookies. Spread Viennese Chocolate Frosting on top of sandwiches and place a pecan half on top of each frosted sandwich. Makes about 1½ dozen.

Viennese Chocolate Frosting: Cream together 2 tblsp. butter and ⅓ c. confectioners sugar until light and creamy. Blend in 1 square unsweetened chocolate, melted and cooled.

CALL THEM DISHPAN OR OATMEAL/MOLASSES COOKIES

Big, chewy Oatmeal/Molasses Cookies, made from a recipe that appeared in Farm Journal, are enjoying great popularity in country kitchens. A farm woman in New York State likes to bake the 6 dozen cookies from our recipe in installments because it's easier to find time to get one baking sheet in the oven than several. (Also, her family thinks no cookie can surpass one just out of the oven.) She calls them Dishpan Cookies because the Illinois woman who contributed the recipe to Farm Journal said her grandmother mixed the dough in a dishpan.

Here's the way she makes the cookies in installments: "I shape the dough in rolls 3" in diameter, wrap them tightly in foil or plastic wrap and store them in the refrigerator or freezer—the freezer if I'm not going to bake them for a week or longer. When I want to bake cookies, I slice the dough ¼" thick and bake it as the recipe directs."

OATMEAL/MOLASSES COOKIES

A big recipe for big cookies—put some in freezer to have handy

8½ c. sifted flour	2 c. light molasses
1 tblsp. salt	4 eggs, beaten
2 tblsp. baking soda	¼ c. hot water
8 c. quick-cooking rolled oats	3 c. seedless raisins
2½ c. sugar	2 c. ground black walnuts or
1 tblsp. ground ginger	English walnuts
2 c. melted shortening	Sugar (for tops)

Reserve ½ c. flour. Sift together 8 c. flour, salt and baking soda.

In a very large bowl or dishpan, mix rolled oats, sugar and ginger. Stir in shortening, molasses, eggs, hot water, sifted dry ingredients, raisins and nuts. Work dough with hands until well mixed. Add the reserved ½ c. flour if needed to make dough workable.

Roll dough to ¼" thickness; cut with 3½" round cutter. Place 2 to 3" apart on lightly greased baking sheet. Brush with water and sprinkle with sugar.

Bake in moderate oven (375°) 8 to 10 minutes. Remove cookies to racks to cool. Makes 6 dozen.

OPEN-HOUSE COOKIES

When it's Christmas time in the Bethlehem, Pennsylvania, area, families visit from one neighbor's home to another to view one another's putz, or Nativity Scene. It's an old Pennsylvania Dutch custom, on these occasions, for the hostess to pass traditional cookies.

Many of them are in camel, donkey, star and other fascinating shapes. From women in this community come recipes for three of the favorites, Spiced Christmas Cookies (often called Brown Christmas Cookies), White Christmas Cookies and Pepper Nuts (Pfeffernuesse).

All three recipes make dozens of cookies. And all keep well so you can bake them ahead. Store them in airtight containers or package and freeze. The secret to success in making these treats is to chill the dough overnight before working with it. And do roll Spiced and White Christmas cookies very thin.

SPICED CHRISTMAS COOKIES

Crisp, brown and molasses-flavored cookies to decorate if you wish

1 c. butter	5 c. sifted flour
1½ c. brown sugar, firmly packed	1 tblsp. ground cinnamon
2 c. molasses	1½ tsp. ground ginger
2 tblsp. light cream or dairy half-and-half	½ tsp. ground cloves

Cream butter; gradually add sugar, beating until light and fluffy. Beat in molasses; blend in cream.

Sift together dry ingredients; stir into creamed mixture. Store in covered bowl in refrigerator overnight.

Roll dough thin, using floured pastry cloth on board and rolling pin. Cut in animal shapes.

Place 1 to 1½" apart on greased baking sheet. Bake in moderate oven (350°) 10 to 12 minutes. Remove cookies and cool on racks. Makes 19 dozen.

WHITE CHRISTMAS COOKIES

Sugar, spice and everything nice—cookies are crisp and straw-colored

1 c. butter	4 c. sifted flour
2 c. sugar	⅛ tsp. ground nutmeg
4 eggs, beaten	⅛ tsp. ground cinnamon

Cream butter; gradually add sugar and beat until light and fluffy. Beat in eggs.

Sift together dry ingredients; stir into creamed mixture (dough should be stiff). Store in covered bowl in refrigerator overnight.

Roll dough very thin, using floured pastry cloth on board and rolling pin. Cut in star shapes. Place 1 to 1½" apart on greased baking sheet.

Bake in moderate oven (350°) 10 to 12 minutes, or until crisp and straw-colored. Remove cookies and cool on racks. Makes 16 dozen.

PEPPER NUTS

Store these spicy, hard cookies in airtight containers. You can add a slice of apple to mellow them

3 eggs, beaten
3½ c. brown sugar, firmly packed
4 c. sifted flour
1 tsp. baking powder

2 tblsp. ground cinnamon
1 tblsp. ground cloves
Ornamental Icing (see Index)
Red cinnamon candy (optional)

Combine eggs and sugar; beat well.

Sift together dry ingredients; add gradually to egg-sugar mixture (dough will be very stiff).

Divide dough. Roll with hands on lightly floured board into rolls the thickness of your middle finger. Cut in ½" slices. Place 1 to 1½" apart on greased baking sheet.

Bake in slow oven (300°) 30 minutes. Remove cookies and cool on racks.

Shortly before serving you can top each pepper nut with a dab of Ornamental Icing and a red cinnamon candy (red hots), if you like. Makes 27 dozen.

ORANGE WREATHS

Recipe is from Mexico where cookies accompany hot chocolate

½ c. butter or regular margarine
¼ c. sugar
2 tsp. grated orange peel
3 egg yolks, well beaten

2 c. sifted flour
2 tsp. baking powder
1 egg white, beaten until foamy

Cream butter, sugar and orange peel together until light and fluffy. Beat in egg yolks and mix well.

Mix and sift together flour and baking powder; add a little at a time to the creamed mixture. Beat after each addition until dough is moderately stiff.

Roll dough on lightly floured surface to ½" thickness. Cut with 2½" doughnut cutter. Place about 2" apart on lightly greased baking sheet. Brush tops of cookies with egg white.

Bake in moderate oven (375°) about 20 minutes, or until golden brown. Remove from baking sheet and cool on racks. Makes about 1 dozen.

N O T E : Gather scraps of dough and centers of rings together in a ball; roll, cut and bake.

PARTY WHIRLS

Pretty pink, brown and cream-colored cookie pinwheels—delicious

1 c. butter	½ tsp. salt
1 c. sugar	½ tsp. ground cinnamon
2 eggs	3 drops red food color
½ tsp. vanilla	½ square semisweet chocolate,
3 c. sifted flour	melted

Beat together butter and sugar until light and fluffy. Beat in eggs and vanilla to blend well.

Sift together flour, salt and cinnamon; add to creamed mixture. Divide dough in thirds. Tint one-third pink with red food color (stir in food color with a spoon); color the second part brown with melted chocolate, and leave the last third untinted.

Roll each third of dough separately on lightly floured waxed paper into a 13 x 10" rectangle. Cover baking sheet with waxed paper; hold over untinted dough, invert and remove waxed paper from top of dough on baking sheet. Flip pink rectangle of dough over onto untinted dough and remove waxed paper from it. If edges are not quite even, straighten them by gently rolling with a rolling pin. Then turn chocolate dough onto pink dough and remove waxed paper from it. Straighten edges if necessary. Chill until firm.

Remove dough from refrigerator and roll up tightly as for jelly roll, using waxed paper under dough to help shape the log. Wrap tightly in waxed paper and chill. If you do not want to bake the cookies within three days, cut the long log in half, wrap each log in aluminum foil and store in freezer until ready to bake.

To bake, cut dough in ⅛ to ¼" slices with sharp knife. Place ½" apart on ungreased baking sheet and bake in hot oven (400°) about 8 minutes. Remove cookies to cooling racks. Makes about 7 dozen.

AMERICAN SAND TARTS

Crisp cookies, thin as paper, have true buttery flavor, nut trim

1 c. butter	1 egg white, slightly beaten
2¼ c. sugar	Almonds or peanuts
2 eggs	Ground cinnamon
4 c. sifted flour	

Cream butter and sugar until light and fluffy. Beat in eggs, mixing well. Stir in flour. Chill dough thoroughly.

Roll dough very thin and cut with 2½" round cutter. Brush centers of rounds with egg white and put ½ almond or peanut in center of each cookie. Brush again with egg white and sprinkle nuts with a trace of cinnamon.

Place cookies about ½" apart on ungreased baking sheet. Bake in hot oven (400°) about 5 minutes. Remove cookies to cooling racks. Makes about 12 dozen.

SCOTCH SHORTBREAD COOKIES

Buttery-rich, extra-good cookies—tint the dough if you like

1 c. butter
¾ c. confectioners sugar
2 c. sifted flour

Cream butter until light. Add sugar (sift if not smooth) and beat until light and fluffy. Add flour and mix to make a soft dough.

Pat or roll on floured surface to ⅓ to ½" thickness. Cut with 2½" cookie cutter or knife. (You can gently flute edges with fingers as for pie crust. Or decorate by pricking cookies with fork.)

Bake on ungreased baking sheet in slow oven (325°) about 20 minutes, until cookies are very delicately browned. Remove cookies and cool on racks. Makes 28 to 30.

STAR COOKIES

Sugar cookies cut in yuletide star shape. Icing will glamorize them

3 c. sifted flour	1¼ c. sugar
2 tsp. baking powder	1 tsp. vanilla
½ tsp. salt	1 egg
½ c. shortening	1 tblsp. milk
½ c. butter or regular margarine	

Sift together flour, baking powder and salt.

Cream shortening and butter with sugar until light and fluffy. Add vanilla, egg and milk; beat thoroughly. Add dry ingredients and mix well. Chill dough 1 hour for easy handling.

Divide dough in fourths; roll out each portion ⅛″ thick. Cut with 2½″ star-shaped cookie cutter. Place 1½ to 2″ apart on greased baking sheet.

Bake in moderate oven (375°) 8 to 10 minutes. Remove cookies and cool on racks. Makes 7 dozen.

SPRINGERLE—THE PICTURE COOKIE

Springerle is a time-tested, German Christmas cookie with many fans on this side of the Atlantic Ocean. It's one of the first cookies to bake for the yuletide since it needs to mellow from 5 to 8 weeks. Often it's baked and waiting for Christmas even before Thanksgiving.

Traditionally, you sprinkle anise seeds over the surface on which you let the cookie dough stand overnight. You can use oil of anise instead of the seeds if you prefer. Our recipe gives directions for both flavorings.

These are picture cookies. You stamp the designs on the rolled cookie dough either with a board or rolling pin in which designs of birds and flowers are carved. You will find both the boards and rolling pins in housewares departments, especially in late autumn; occasionally you can find interesting old ones in antique shops.

In our tests we discovered it is somewhat easier to use the design board instead of a roller. Certainly this is true for inexperienced springerle bakers. It is important to press the board down firmly on the rolled dough so it leaves a clear print of the design. Lift the board off the dough with steady hands to avoid blurred pictures. If you use the rolling pin, roll it with a little pressure across the sheet of dough *only once.*

Adding too much flour produces a hard cookie. If the dough sticks to board or pin, use care in flouring it. We found chilling the dough 1 hour before rolling helps. Be sure not to roll the dough too thin, for if you do, it's almost impossible to get good imprints.

Making these cookies is a two-day operation because after rolling the dough you let it stand overnight (at least 10 hours) at room temperature before baking. Store the baked cookies in a container with a tight lid and set them in a cool place.

One more pointer: The cookies should not be brown—just a hint of yellow around the edges.

SPRINGERLE

Give these cookies time to mellow—they're well worth waiting for

4 eggs	¼ tsp. salt
2 c. sugar	2 tblsp. melted butter
4 c. sifted cake flour	1 tblsp. anise seeds
1 tsp. baking powder	

Using electric mixer at low speed, beat eggs in large bowl. Gradually add sugar, then beat at medium speed about 10 minutes. (You can use a hand rotary beater, but if you do, increase beating time to 30 minutes.)

Sift together flour, baking powder and salt; blend into egg mixture alternately with butter, mixing well. Cover dough with waxed paper or foil and chill 1 hour.

Dust surface lightly with flour and pat out or roll half of the dough at a time to almost, but not quite, ½" thickness.

Lightly flour springerle board and press it firmly down on dough. Lift board up carefully so as not to mar lines of the design. If board sticks to dough, lightly flour it and the top of the dough. Then brush off flour after removing board. (If you use springerle rolling pin, roll the dough to a flat sheet ½" thick. Then roll over it with springerle rolling pin just once to press in designs.)

Lightly grease baking sheet and sprinkle evenly with anise seeds.

Lift dough carefully to baking sheet, cover loosely with waxed paper and let stand overnight.

When ready to bake, cut dough to cookie size along lines made by

springerle board (or rolling pin). Separate on baking sheet by ½"
space.

Bake in moderate oven (350°) 5 minutes, then reduce heat to
slow (300°) and continue baking about 10 minutes longer. Remove
cookies and cool on racks. Makes about 3½ dozen.

NOTE: You can use 6 drops anise oil instead of the anise seeds.
Add it to the beaten eggs. Superfine granulated sugar gives the best
results in this recipe, but you can use regular granulated sugar.

RAISIN-FILLED COOKIES

Dark fruit filling shows through window in tender, light brown cookies

½ c. shortening	2½ c. sifted flour
1 c. sugar	¼ tsp. baking soda
2 eggs	½ tsp. salt
1 tsp. vanilla	Raisin Filling (recipe follows)

Mix together shortening, sugar and eggs. Stir in vanilla and mix
thoroughly.

Sift together flour, soda and salt. Blend into sugar/egg mixture.
Chill thoroughly.

Roll dough thin, about ¹⁄₁₆", and cut with 2½" round cutter.
(Or use any desired shape cutter.) Place half of cookies 1" apart on
lightly greased baking sheet. Spread a generous teaspoonful of cooled
Raisin Filling on each. Cut centers out of other half of cookies, using
a small heart, star or other shaped cutter. Place over cookies on
baking sheet. Press edges together with floured fork tines or fingers.

Bake in hot oven (400°) 8 to 10 minutes, or until cookies are
lightly browned. Spread on racks to cool. Makes about 3½ dozen.

Raisin Filling: In a small saucepan, combine 2 c. ground or finely
cut raisins, ¾ c. sugar and ¾ c. water; cook slowly, stirring constantly, until mixture thickens. Remove from heat; stir in ½ c.
chopped walnuts (optional) and 1 tsp. finely grated lemon or orange
peel. Cool before using.

Variations

Prune-Filled Cookies: Cook 2⅔ c. prunes; drain and mash (you
should have 2 c.). Substitute for raisins in Raisin Filling.

Date-Filled Cookies: Substitute 2 c. finely cut-up or ground dates for raisins in Raisin Filling.

Raisin Turnovers: Cut cookie dough in 3″ instead of 2½″ rounds. Place 1 tsp. Raisin Filling on each cookie. Fold over and press edges to seal. Bake like Raisin-Filled Cookies. Makes about 6 dozen.

NOTE: You can use prune or date filling instead of Raisin Filling to make turnovers.

GRIDDLE COOKIES—BACK IN STYLE

Grandmother used to bake cookies on the griddle to avoid heating the oven in midsummer. Children stopping in her kitchen, hopeful of a handout, remembered how good the warm cookies were with glasses of cold lemonade or bowls of ice cream. No childhood eating experience could be more memorable. So it's good news that the cookies again are coming off griddles to please people of all ages.

Give freezers the thanks. Today's cooks roll and cut the dough and stack the circles with foil between like hamburger patties. As they are wrapped in packages and frozen, it's easy to bring the desired number out. Bake them in your electric skillet—at the table, if that's convenient.

RAISIN GRIDDLE COOKIES

Keep packages of dough in your freezer to bake on short notice

3½ c. sifted flour	1 tsp. ground nutmeg
1 c. sugar	1 c. shortening
1½ tsp. baking powder	1 egg
1 tsp. salt	½ c. milk
½ tsp. baking soda	1¼ c. raisins

Sift dry ingredients together into bowl. Cut in shortening until mixture is mealy.

Beat egg, add milk and blend. Add egg mixture and raisins to flour mixture. Stir until all the ingredients are moistened and dough holds together.

Roll on lightly floured board to ¼″ thickness. Cut with 2″ round cookie cutter.

Heat griddle until a few drops of water dance on it. (Do not overheat griddle.) Oil griddle lightly and place cookies on it. As the bottoms brown, the tops become puffy. Then turn and brown on other side. Serve warm. Makes about 4 dozen.

Variation

Lemon Griddle Cookies: Make dough for Raisin Griddle Cookies, but omit raisins and add 1 tsp. grated lemon peel. Bake as directed.

LEMON SUGAR COOKIES

A time-tested recipe that makes bar, rolled and drop cookies

½ c. butter or regular margarine	1½ tsp. baking powder
1 c. sugar	2 c. sifted flour
1 egg	¼ c. milk
½ tsp. vanilla	1 egg white, slightly beaten
2 tsp. grated lemon peel	(optional)
¼ tsp. salt	Sugar (optional)

Cream butter and sugar thoroughly. Add egg, vanilla and lemon peel. Beat until mixture is light and fluffy.

Sift dry ingredients. Stir into creamed mixture together with milk. Divide dough in half. Chill 1 hour.

Roll out half of dough on floured board, keeping the other half chilled until ready to use. Roll ¼" thick.

Cut into bars and place about 2" apart on greased baking sheet.

If desired, brush with slightly beaten egg white and sprinkle with sugar. Repeat with remaining dough.

Bake in moderate oven (350°) 12 to 15 minutes. Remove cookies and cool on racks. Makes 2 dozen.

Variations

Chocolate Chip Cookies: Add ½ c. semisweet chocolate pieces to dough.

Grease and flour two 9" square baking pans. Spread half the dough in each. Bake in moderate oven (350°) 25 minutes, or until light brown.

While still warm cut into 3" squares. Cool in pan on racks. Makes 1½ dozen.

Nut/Sugar Cookies: Mix ½ c. finely chopped nuts into dough. Roll dough and bake as directed.

Coconut Cookies: Add ½ c. shredded coconut. Make drop cookies and place 2″ apart on greased baking sheet.

Raisin Cookies: Add ½ c. seedless raisins. Make drop cookies and place 2″ apart on greased baking sheet.

Spiced Sugar Cookies: Add ¼ tsp. ground nutmeg and ½ tsp. ground cinnamon to dough, omitting lemon peel. Roll dough. Bake as directed.

SUGAR COOKIES

Sugar-topped, old-fashioned cookies—men say: "Make them bigger"

1 c. shortening	3 c. sifted flour
1 c. sugar	1 tsp. salt
1 c. dairy sour cream	1 tsp. baking powder
3 egg yolks, beaten	½ tsp. baking soda
1 tsp. vanilla	Sugar (for tops)

Cream shortening and sugar thoroughly; add sour cream, egg yolks and vanilla.

Sift together dry ingredients; add to creamed mixture, blending well; chill.

Shape into balls, working with small portions at a time, keeping remaining dough chilled.

Roll out ⅛″ thick on lightly floured surface. Cut with floured 2½″ cutter (sprinkle cutouts with sugar).

Place about 2″ apart on greased baking sheet. Bake in moderate oven (375°) about 15 minutes. Transfer cookies to racks to cool. Makes 6 dozen.

THUMBPRINT COOKIES

Rich and tender rather than sweet—beautiful on tray or plate

¾ c. butter or regular margarine	½ tsp. salt
1 (3 oz.) pkg. cream cheese	¼ tsp. baking powder
2 c. sifted flour	⅓ c. jam or jelly
2 tblsp. sugar	

Cream together butter and cream cheese until light and fluffy.

Sift together flour, sugar, salt and baking powder. Stir into creamed mixture, blending thoroughly.

Roll out on lightly floured surface into a square about ½" thick. Cut into 1½" squares.

Place about 1" apart on ungreased baking sheet. With your thumb make an indentation in center of each cookie. Fill with ½ tsp. jam or jelly.

Bake in a moderate oven (350°) 20 to 25 minutes. Remove cookies and cool on racks. Makes 2½ dozen.

N O T E : For fancy cookies, use jellies or jams of different kinds and colors.

WEDDING RING COOKIES

Gold and silver cookies—ideal for bridal showers, anniversaries

1 c. butter	1 tblsp. water
1¾ c. sifted flour	1 egg white, lightly beaten
1½ tsp. grated lemon peel (optional)	½ c. coarsely chopped blanched almonds
1 tblsp. light cream or dairy half-and-half	⅓ c. yellow sugar
	Silver dragées

Blend butter and flour with pastry blender until mixture is crumbly. Add lemon peel, cream and water; mix with hands to form a stiff dough. Shape in ball and refrigerate to chill thoroughly.

Divide dough in half; keep one half in refrigerator while working with other half. Roll dough on lightly floured surface to ¼" thickness. Cut out rings with doughnut cutter. Brush one side of rings with egg white; dip this side of cookies in almonds. Press almonds lightly so they will adhere. Sprinkle with yellow sugar. Repeat with remaining half of dough.

To make double rings, cut one ring and link it through another ring on lightly greased baking sheet. Decorate one of the rings with silver dragées.

Bake 6 double rings at a time in hot oven (425°) about 8 minutes, or until cookies brown around edges. Remove from oven and let cookies cool on baking sheet a few minutes. Transfer with metal spatula to cooling racks. Makes 18 to 19 double rings.

N O T E : You can bake some of the decorated rings singly for guests who like smaller servings than the double rings.

WILD ROSE COOKIES

These cookies are buttery rich, like shortbread, and party pretty

1 c. butter or regular margarine	2¼ c. sifted flour
½ c. very fine granulated sugar (super fine)	Pink decorating sugar
	Yellow decorating sugar, or tiny
¼ tsp. vanilla	yellow candies

Cream butter with sugar until light and fluffy; beat in vanilla.

Divide flour in thirds. Stir first third into creamed mixture and blend well. Repeat with second third and then with last third. Knead gently until smooth, about 5 minutes. Shape in ball, wrap in clear plastic wrap or waxed paper and chill several hours, or overnight.

Divide dough in fourths. Pat one portion at a time ¼" thick on lightly floured surface. Cut with 2½" round scalloped cutter. Place dough cutouts ½ to 1" apart on ungreased baking sheet. Sprinkle liberally with pink sugar, leaving ¾" circle in center uncovered.

Cut a circle of stiff paper about the same size of cookies and cut out a ¾" circle in center. Lay on cookie and carefully spoon yellow sugar into hole in paper; lift off paper. Or, if you can find small yellow candies, use them for cookie centers.

Bake in slow oven (325°) 12 to 15 minutes, until firm, but do not brown. Transfer cookies to racks and cool. Makes 5 dozen.

N O T E : You can bake the cookies after adding pink sugar, cool them and add dots of frosting, tinted yellow, to make the centers. Use ½ recipe for Ornamental Icing. For dainty teatime cookies, use a 1" round, scalloped cookie cutter.

ORNAMENTAL ICING

Write and draw on cookies with this icing to give them a festive look

1½ to 2 c. confectioners sugar
1 to 2 tblsp. slightly beaten egg white (about)

Combine confectioners sugar with enough egg white to make an icing you can put through decorating tube or small plastic bag with small hole cut in one corner, but which will have enough consistency to hold its shape on cookies. A second batch of icing can easily be made if needed.

CHRISTMAS COOKIE CENTERPIECES

You can bake rolled cookies and put them together to make charming yuletide centerpieces. It takes time to bake the cookies, to build with them and to add decorations, but when you see the way the children and guests of all ages admire your creation, you'll know the minutes were well spent.

The trick is to divide the work. Bake the cookies ahead and freeze them or store them in a cold place. It helps to have them on hand when you are ready to start assembling the scenes.

We give you recipes, patterns and directions for two cookie centerpieces. Take your pick of a country barnyard scene, made with chocolate-flavored cookies, or a Christmas church built with sugar cookies. Snow (frosting) trims both of them.

SUGAR-SYRUP CEMENT

This sweet syrup holds cookies in place when building with them

For Barn: Melt ½ c. sugar in a heavy shallow skillet (at least 12″ across); use lowest heat to melt sugar. For silo, melt another ½ c. sugar.

For Church: Melt 2 c. sugar.

Stir constantly while sugar melts, so that it won't burn. Keep syrup on medium heat while you use it. Be sure to use a wide skillet, so you can dip edges of long cookies into the syrup easily, as you put pieces together.

Work slowly when putting barn or church together. Make sure pieces are "glued" firmly before adding another.

General Directions: Enlarge patterns as indicated (each square equals 1 square inch) and cut from cardboard. Use them to cut cookie pieces.

Dust cardboard patterns with flour and cut around them with a sharp knife.

Bake cookie pieces one day; assemble and decorate cookie scene the next (or store baked cookies in freezer).

Check baked cookies against patterns; trim edges with a sharp knife while cookies are still warm.

GINGER COOKIE CHURCH

Put cookie pieces together with "cement"; arrange trees and fence,
build gumdrop bushes and blanket with icing—use photo as guide

1 c. shortening	1 c. dark corn syrup
1 c. brown sugar, firmly packed	2 eggs, beaten
1 tblsp. grated lemon peel	5½ to 6 c. sifted flour
1 tblsp. ground cinnamon	1 tsp. salt
1 tblsp. ground ginger	1¼ tsp. baking soda

Cream shortening; add brown sugar, lemon peel and spices; blend.
Bring syrup to a boil; pour into creamed mixture; stir until well blended.

Add eggs and blend.

Sift 3 c. flour with salt and baking soda; add to mixture. Stir in 2½ c. flour, a little at a time.

Turn out on lightly floured surface and knead about 10 minutes, using remaining ½ c. flour if necessary.

Chill 1 hour.

Separate dough into several sections. (It is slightly stiffer than ordinary dough. This prevents crumbling.) Roll out each section to ¼" thickness. Transfer to greased baking sheet; smooth out dough with rolling pin. Dust patterns for church pieces with flour; place over dough and cut out with sharp knife. Mark "logs" on doors and sides of church with a two-tined fork or a knife.

Bake in moderate oven (375°) 12 to 15 minutes for large pieces, 5 to 7 for smaller pieces. Remove cookies and cool on racks.

Snow Icing: Place 1 lb. confectioners sugar in mixing bowl. Beat 3 egg whites slightly with a fork; add to confectioners sugar and beat with electric mixer on low speed for 1 minute. Add 1 tblsp. white vinegar; beat 2 minutes more at high speed, or until stiff and glossy —as for stiff meringue. Use as directed to decorate cookie church.

To Assemble Church: Cover heavy cardboard 20 x 18" with cotton. Wet your thumb and push a path through the cotton, leading to the church door.

Diagrams show how church and steeple go together. First, fasten colored cellophane or tissue paper over windows of church with flour paste.

Cut fence pieces and weave together (see photo)

Fence Post (Cut 10)

F

Spire
(Cut 4)

Top of Tower
(Cut 1)
Base for Spire

Fence for Church (Cut 4)

B
Roof of Church (Cut 2)

Flat Sides
of Tower
(Cut 2)

Sides of
Tower
to fit over
Roof
(Cut 2)

C

Cut
Window

D

Door
of
Church
(Cut 2)

Sides of Church (Cut 2)

A

Back and Front of Church (Cut 2)

Cut out door in front;
cut window with small
cookie cutter. Leave
back of church solid.

E

Floor of Church (Optional Cut 1)

If you plan to use a Christmas
tree light or tiny flashlight
inside the church, you can't
use a cookie floor.

Each square = 1 square inch

F

B

C

A

D

Assemble church walls; glue walls to floor with Sugar-Syrup Cement.

To put roof on church, dip slanting edges of walls on one side of church into Sugar-Syrup Cement and quickly set roof in place, carefully lining up top edge with peak of walls and leaving about a 1" overhang on 3 other sides. Repeat on other side of church.

Add doors, open wide.

Assemble steeple, spire first, then tower; center on top of church roof.

Cookie Trees: To make trees stand up straight, dip the long, right-angle edge of tree brace (X-2 or Y-2) into Sugar-Syrup Cement and press it at right angle against tree cookie, so bottom of tree and bottom of base are flush.

Gumdrop Bushes: You'll need 1 large green gumdrop and 3 dozen (or more) small green gumdrops for each bush. Break toothpicks into different lengths; use them to attach small gumdrops to large gumdrop base, hiding it completely. Sprinkle with confectioners sugar.

To Decorate Church: Spread Snow Icing liberally on church, trees

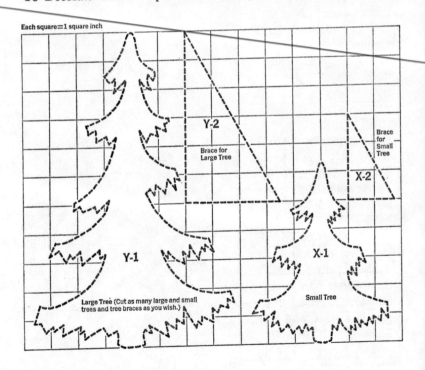

Each square = 1 square inch

Y-2 · Brace for Large Tree

Brace for Small Tree · X-2

Y-1 · Large Tree (Cut as many large and small trees and tree braces as you wish.)

X-1 · Small Tree

and fence after they've been put together (see photo). Icicles will form naturally if you apply icing from the top.

Sprinkle with confectioners sugar while icing is still moist, for a look of new-fallen snow. Shake sugar through a fine sieve.

COCOA COOKIE BARN

A good "building dough" especially flavored for chocolate lovers

1⅓ c. shortening	1 tsp. baking soda
2 c. sugar	1 tsp. salt
2 eggs	½ c. cocoa
4⅔ c. flour	½ c. milk
2 tsp. baking powder	

Cream shortening and sugar until light and fluffy; add eggs and beat well.

Sift together dry ingredients; add alternately with milk to creamed mixture, mixing well. Chill dough.

Roll out small amount of dough at a time ⅛″ thick on lightly floured pastry cloth. Cut desired shapes (see patterns).

Bake on greased baking sheets in slow oven (325°) 10 to 15 minutes. Remove cookies and cool on racks.

White Decorating Frosting: Combine 2 egg whites, 1½ c. sugar, ⅓ c. water, 2 tsp. light corn syrup and ⅛ tsp. salt in top of double boiler; beat 1 minute. Cook over boiling water, beating constantly, until mixture stands in stiff peaks. Remove from heat; transfer to mixing bowl; beat until smooth. Use at once.

Red Decorating Frosting: Beat together 4 c. confectioners sugar, ⅛ tsp. salt, 2½ tsp. red food color, 6 drops yellow food color and 4½ to 5 tblsp. milk until of stiff spreading consistency.

To Assemble Barn Scene: Cover heavy cardboard 30 x 20″ with foil. Set decorated barn and silo at one end. Frost board with another batch of White Decorating Frosting, leaving unfrosted area for pond; swirl frosting for drifts. Don't worry if the roof isn't quite straight—just cover the defects with frosting.

Make pretzel fence. Set decorated animals and trees in frosting snow (prop with toothpicks till frosting dries).

Silo: Cut 30 circles from dough with 2″ cookie cutter. Bake, cool and glue in a stack with Sugar-Syrup Cement.

Animals and Trees: Use any cookie cutters you have, or make your

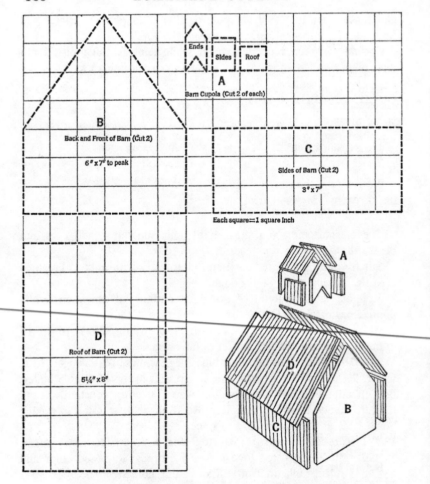

Ends

Sides   Roof

A

Barn Cupola (Cut 2 of each)

B

Back and Front of Barn (Cut 2)

6″ x 7″ to peak

C

Sides of Barn (Cut 2)

3″ x 7″

Each square=1 square inch

D

Roof of Barn (Cut 2)

5¼″ x 8″

A

D

B

C

own patterns by tracing from magazines or cards. Give animals character by drawing features (wings, ears, eyes) in dough with toothpick before baking.

To Decorate Barn: Use Red Decorating Frosting for sides of barn and silo. Apply with small-blade spatula to make ridges (see photo).

Use 1 batch of White Decorating Frosting for roof of barn, cupola, to make peak of silo and (with decorating tube) for features on animals, trees, barn windows and doors.

COOKIE FAMILY IN A CHRISTMAS HOUSE

Cookie dolls all dressed up for the holidays—a whole family of them in a cozy Christmas House—are an ideal gift for children. They will tote this present around until they finally can no longer resist eating them.

Children will sense the love you put into the homemade gift. Most of them will keep the pretty house and store their personal treasures in it.

We give you the recipe and patterns for making the Cookie Family and directions for the Christmas House.

COOKIE FAMILY

It's easiest to bake cookies one day and decorate them the next

⅔ c. shortening	3¼ c. sifted flour
1½ c. sugar	2½ tsp. baking powder
2 eggs	½ tsp. salt
1 tsp. vanilla	Decorating Frosting
1 tblsp. milk	

Mix shortening, sugar and eggs. Stir in vanilla and milk.

Sift together flour, baking powder and salt. Blend into creamed mixture. Chill.

Roll out dough ⅛" thick on floured board or pastry cloth. Dust cardboard patterns with flour. Lay patterns on dough and cut out designs with point of paring knife. Use spatula to move to lightly greased baking sheet. Do not stretch dough.

Before baking Cookie Girl, insert a short piece of paper drinking straw in dough through which to tie hair bow.

Bake in hot oven (400°) 5 to 7 minutes, until lightly browned. Transfer cookies to racks to cool. Cool before frosting. Makes 7 cookie families.

Decorating Frosting:

⅓ c. butter or regular margarine
3 c. sifted confectioners sugar
1½ tblsp. water (about)

Cream butter and sugar thoroughly. Add enough water to make frosting of spreading consistency.

PATTERNS FOR THE COOKIE FAMILY
(*Each square = ½ inch*)

Divide frosting into 7 small dishes and add food color as follows:

White: ⅓ c. for Father's and Boy's shirts, and for dress trimmings.

Brown: Add 2 tsp. cocoa to ¼ c. frosting. For eyes, hair for Father, Mother's and Boy's shoes.

Pink: Add red to ¼ c. frosting. For Mother's dress.

Red: Add red plus small amount of yellow to 2 tblsp. frosting. For Girl's dress, all mouths.

Green: Add green to 2 tblsp. frosting. For Boy's trousers.

Yellow: Add yellow to 1 tblsp. frosting. For Girl's hair.

Orange: Add yellow plus small amount of red to 2 tblsp. frosting. For Dog.

Let one color frosting dry well before using second on the same cookie.

Spread frosting with narrow spatula. Use paint brush for facial features.

When frosted cookies are completely dry, add white trim on dresses, using decorating tube.

Use narrow red ribbons to tie cookies onto sheet of white cardboard that fits into hosiery-type box.

CHRISTMAS HOUSE

Decorate a hosiery-type box about ¾" to 1" thick to look like a house for the cookie family. Sketch a design to fit box lid (suggestions follow). A red house looks especially festive. To make it, cover lid and bottom of box separately with red wrapping paper. On the lid, paste a roof cut from gray paper; draw shingles on roof. Add a scalloped cornice along roof edge, cut from white paper. Cut a window from yellow paper; cut a Christmas tree from green paper and decorate it with colored signal dots (from stationery store). Paste tree on window and window on house. Add white shutters and white window frame. Cut a white door and paste it in place. Cut dark green bushes and gold lanterns to paste on each side of door. Finally, decorate door with wreath cut from an old Christmas card.

To mount cookies, cut a piece of stiff cardboard to fit inside box. Arrange cookies and mark where holes for ribbon should be made: on both sides of man's neck, both sides of woman's waist, through hair-ribbon hole in girl's head and on opposite side, on both sides of boy's neck and on both sides of dog's neck. Make holes with ice pick or sharp knife. Tie cookies in place with ¼" red ribbon.

Refrigerator Cookies

Making refrigerator cookies is a two-act performance. Act one: mix, shape and freeze or refrigerate the dough; act two: slice and bake. The action may take place days, weeks or months apart. It's this division of work that elevates refrigerator cookies to first place among summer homemade cookies.

Even if it's hot and humid, you can slice off just enough cookies to meet your immediate needs and bake them quickly without heating the kitchen too much. Country women like to bake the cookies right after breakfast before the sun turns on full heat. Of course the cookies are favorites at all seasons, but summer is their heyday.

You need only a few rules for successful refrigerator cookies. One is to shape the dough in smooth, firm rolls with your hands. Make them the diameter you want your cookies; they spread little in baking. Wrap them tightly in waxed paper, twisting both ends to seal. If you freeze the dough, overwrap with foil. Or wrap them with foil or plastic wrap, taping edges. Most cookie doughs will keep well 3 to 5 days in the refrigerator, 6 months in the freezer.

Use a knife with a long, sharp blade to slice the dough from ⅛ to ¼" in thickness. The thinner the slices, the crisper the cookies will be. Be sure they are cut to the same thickness so they will bake in the same number of minutes. Bake them until they are lightly browned unless recipe directs otherwise. If you add nuts to the dough, chop them very fine or they will make it difficult to slice cookies neatly.

Refrigerator cookies need no decoration. But for special occasions you can sprinkle waxed paper with decorating sugar or with tiny multicolored candies, finely chopped nuts, chocolate shot (jimmies) or finely crushed stick candy. Turn the roll of cookie dough round and round on the waxed paper to coat it with the decoration. Then wrap and chill or freeze. When baked, the cookies have fancy rims.

You can also tint light-colored dough with food color or press a nut or drop a dab of jelly on cookie slices just before you bake them.

Or top ready-to-bake cookies with peaks of meringue, tinted if you like. Our Meringue-Topped Cookies are tasty beauties, especially when you flavor the meringue with peppermint, tint it pink and sprinkle with pink sugar—or coconut or chocolate shot.

Filled refrigerator cookies are so easy to fix. When the slices of dough are on the baking sheet, drop a bit of filling on each one and lay another cookie on top. Try our fruity Mincemeat/Lemon Filling. You can also put *baked* refrigerator cookies together with filling to make sandwiches—to prove that two cookies taste better than one!

For cookies that are on the salty rather than the sweet side, make Old Salts. They're a great snack or appetizer. Our Molasses Almond Cookies are unusual, too—the topping bakes right with the cookies. Our recipe suggests that you shape both the rolls of dough and topping in rolls 1″ in diameter. This produces small cookies which are ideal for tea and other parties. You may prefer to double the recipe and make 2″ rolls.

You'll find recipes for many kinds of refrigerator cookies that are wonderful with ice cream, sherbet, iced or hot tea and coffee, lemonade and other fruit drinks. They also are perfect partners for party punch.

ALMOND REFRIGERATOR COOKIES

A simplified, American version of Chinese cookies—crisp, lacy, rich

1 c. butter or regular margarine	½ tsp. almond extract
2 c. sifted flour	1 egg yolk
¾ tsp. salt	1 tblsp. water
¾ c. sugar	½ c. blanched almonds, cut in
½ tsp. vanilla	halves (see Index)

Cut butter into flour with pastry blender as for pie crust. Work in salt, sugar, vanilla and almond extract with hands. Shape in two long rolls 1 to 1½″ in diameter. Wrap tightly in plastic wrap or waxed paper and refrigerate 1 hour, or until firm.

Cut rolls in ¼″ slices and place 1″ apart on lightly greased baking sheet. Brush top of each cookie sparingly with egg yolk mixed with water. Press an almond half in center of each.

Bake in hot oven (400°) 8 to 10 minutes, or until lightly browned. Cool slightly on baking sheet before removing to cooling rack. (If you do not cool them a little on baking sheet, they will crumble.) Makes about 6½ dozen.

RICH ANISE COOKIES

Keep several rolls in the refrigerator—excellent with ice cream

1 c. butter or regular margarine	½ tsp. vanilla
1 (3 oz.) pkg. cream cheese	2½ c. sifted flour
1 c. sugar	½ tsp. salt
1 egg yolk	2 tsp. anise seeds, crushed

Cream butter, cream cheese and sugar together until light. Add egg yolk and vanilla and beat until light and fluffy.

Combine flour, salt and anise seeds. Blend into creamed mixture until smooth. Shape in two rolls about 2″ in diameter on lightly floured waxed paper. Wrap rolls tightly in waxed paper and chill at least 2 hours or overnight.

Cut dough in thin slices, about ⅛″ thick; place about 2″ apart on ungreased baking sheet. Bake in moderate oven (350°) 10 to 12 minutes, or until cookie edges are browned. Remove cookies and cool on racks. Makes about 6 dozen.

Variation

Rich Nutmeg Cookies: Omit anise seeds from Rich Anise Cookies and add 1 tsp. ground nutmeg with the flour.

BUTTERSCOTCH REFRIGERATOR COOKIES

Keep a few cans of dough in freezer to bake on short notice

3½ c. sifted flour	2 c. brown sugar, firmly packed
1 tsp. salt	2 eggs, well beaten
1 tsp. ground cinnamon	2 tblsp. warm water
1 tsp. baking soda	1 tsp. vanilla
½ c. shortening	1 c. chopped nuts
½ c. butter	

Sift together flour, salt, cinnamon and soda.

Cream shortening and butter; gradually add sugar; beat until light. Add eggs, water and vanilla; mix well.

Combine dry ingredients and creamed mixture; blend well. Add nuts.

Shape dough into roll 2" in diameter. Wrap tightly in waxed paper and chill thoroughly—overnight for best results. When ready to bake, cut in ⅛" slices.

Bake 1½" apart on ungreased baking sheet in hot oven (400°) 10 to 12 minutes. Spread on racks to cool. Makes 6 dozen.

BLACK WALNUT COOKIES

Descendant of Pennsylvania Dutch slapjacks—cookies taste great

6 c. sifted flour	2¼ c. brown sugar, firmly packed
1 tsp. salt	½ c. sugar
½ tsp. baking soda	2 eggs, beaten
1 tsp. cream of tartar	2 tsp. vanilla
1¾ c. butter or regular margarine	1½ c. black walnuts
	1½ c. flaked or shredded coconut

Sift together flour, salt, soda and cream of tartar.

Cream butter; add brown and white sugars gradually and beat until fluffy. Add eggs and vanilla; mix well.

Grind nuts and coconut together in food chopper using medium blade, or use blender. Add to creamed mixture. Add sifted dry ingredients and blend well. Chill.

Shape dough in four rolls about 2" in diameter. Wrap tightly in waxed paper and chill thoroughly.

Cut rolls in ⅛" slices; place about 1" apart on ungreased baking sheet. Bake in moderate oven (350°) 10 to 12 minutes. Remove cookies and cool on racks. Makes 8 to 9 dozen.

BLUSHING REFRIGERATOR COOKIES

The pink glow of cookies contrasts charmingly with their gay red tops

1 c. butter	5 drops red food color
½ c. sugar	2¾ c. sifted flour
½ c. brown sugar, firmly packed	½ tsp. baking soda
2 eggs	½ tsp. salt
1 tsp. vanilla	Red decorating sugar (for tops)

Combine butter, sugars, eggs and vanilla; beat until very light. Add food color.

Sift together flour, baking soda and salt. Stir into first mixture. Mix with hands until dough is smooth. Shape in two rolls, each 2" in diameter and about 9½" long. Wrap tightly in waxed paper, twisting ends. Chill in refrigerator overnight or a couple of days, or freeze.

When ready to bake, cut dough in thin slices, about ⅛" thick, with a sharp knife. Arrange ½" apart on ungreased baking sheet. Sprinkle tops with red sugar.

Bake in hot oven (400°) 6 to 8 minutes. Remove from baking sheet and cool on racks. Makes 8 dozen.

Variations

Chocolate Wafers: Make like Blushing Refrigerator Cookies, only omit food color and red decorating sugar, and add 2 squares unsweetened chocolate, melted and cooled, to butter. Sprinkle tops of wafers before baking with finely chopped nuts or green decorating sugar, or decorate them, when cool, with Ornamental Icing (see Index).

Filled Refrigerator Cookies: Make half of recipe for Blushing Refrigerator Cookies, but omit food color and red decorating sugar. Place half of the cookies on baking sheet; top each with ½ tsp. Mincemeat/Lemon Filling, then top with another cookie and bake as directed. Makes 2 dozen.

Mincemeat/Lemon Filling: Stir together ¼ c. prepared mincemeat, 2 tblsp. chopped walnuts and 2 tsp. grated lemon peel.

CHOCOLATE COOKIE SANDWICHES

Fill with pastel pink and green frosting for a festive party tray

½ c. shortening	1¾ c. sifted flour
½ c. sugar	1 tsp. salt
1 egg	½ tsp. baking powder
3 tblsp. milk	Peppermint Frosting (recipe
2 squares unsweetened chocolate, melted and cooled	follows)

Cream shortening and sugar until fluffy; beat in egg, milk and chocolate.

Sift together flour, salt and baking powder. Stir into creamed mixture. Shape dough in two smooth rolls about 2" in diameter, 6" long. Wrap each in waxed paper and chill several hours until firm, or overnight.

Slice rolls thin, about ⅛", with sharp knife. Place 1½" apart on lightly greased baking sheet. Bake in moderate oven (375°) 7 to 10 minutes (watch carefully). Remove cookies and cool on racks. Spread half the cookies with Peppermint Frosting. Top with remaining cookies. Makes 2½ dozen.

Peppermint Frosting: Combine 2 c. sifted confectioners sugar, 1½ tblsp. butter and 2½ tblsp. dairy half-and-half or light cream. Beat until smooth. Add 3 to 4 drops peppermint extract. Divide in half; to one part add 3 drops red food color, to the other, 2 drops green food color.

CHOCOLATE FILLED COOKIES

Partially melted chocolate candy wafers form the luscious filling

1 c. butter	2½ c. sifted flour
1 c. sugar	¼ tsp. cream of tartar
1 egg	40 thin round chocolate candy
1 tsp. vanilla	wafers

Cream butter and sugar until light and fluffy. Add egg and vanilla. Beat well.

Sift flour and cream of tartar; add to creamed mixture and beat until blended. Chill until dough is firm enough to handle. Then shape dough in two rolls, each about 10″ long. Wrap tightly in waxed paper or plastic wrap and chill overnight.

Cut one roll of dough in ⅛″ slices. Place 20 rounds 1 to 1½″ apart on ungreased baking sheet. Place a chocolate wafer on each. Top with 20 more rounds of dough. Press dough circles together, completely covering chocolate wafers. Repeat with other roll of dough.

Bake in moderate oven (375°) about 10 minutes, or until cookies are delicately browned. Transfer cookies to racks to cool. Makes 40.

N O T E : Work with half of dough at a time, keeping the remaining dough in refrigerator.

CHOCOLATE MINT WAFERS

Chocolate/mint flavors complement each other in these thin cookies

¼ c. heavy cream	⅛ tsp. peppermint extract
1 tblsp. vinegar	2 c. sifted flour
½ c. shortening	¾ c. cocoa
1 c. sugar	½ tsp. baking soda
1 egg	¼ tsp. salt

Combine heavy cream and vinegar in measuring cup; set aside. Cream together shortening and sugar; stir in egg and peppermint extract.

Sift together remaining dry ingredients; add alternately with heavy cream to creamed mixture. Mix thoroughly. Divide dough in half and shape into two rolls. Wrap tightly in waxed paper and chill several hours in refrigerator.

Cut dough in ⅛" slices with sharp knife; place 1½" apart on ungreased baking sheet. Bake in moderate oven (350°) 15 minutes. Remove cookies and cool on racks. Makes 3 dozen.

EASY DATE FILL-UPS

For crisper cookies refrigerate filling and add just before serving

½ c. butter	1 tsp. vanilla
½ c. lard	2½ c. sifted flour
½ c. dairy sour cream	2 c. quick-cooking rolled oats
¾ c. brown sugar, firmly packed	1¼ c. halved dates (8 oz.)
2 tsp. baking soda	½ c. sugar
1 tsp. salt	¼ c. water

Blend together butter, lard, dairy sour cream, brown sugar, baking soda, salt and vanilla. Add flour and oats and mix well.

Divide dough in half. Shape each part in a roll 2" in diameter. Wrap in foil or waxed paper and refrigerate overnight, or at least 8 hours. (For faster chilling place in freezer.)

To bake, cut dough in ⅛" slices; place about 1" apart on ungreased baking sheet. Bake in moderate oven (350°) 8 to 12 minutes, or until light golden brown. Remove cookies and cool on racks.

To make filling, combine dates, white sugar and water in saucepan. Cook over medium heat until thick and smooth, stirring constantly. Cool until lukewarm.

At serving time, spread half of cooled cookies on bottom sides with date filling; top with remaining cookies. Makes about 4 dozen.

Variation

Austrian Cookie Rounds: Omit the date filling. Melt together in custard cup, set in hot water, ½ c. semisweet chocolate pieces and 1 tblsp. shortening. Spread on half of cookies while still slightly warm to coat them with a glaze. Let harden. Before serving, spread a thin layer of currant or other red jelly on the unglazed cookies and top with a glazed cookie, glazed side up.

FINNISH SHORTBREAD COOKIES

Rich cookies, a treat from Finnish kitchens—we give you variations

2 c. butter	⅛ tsp. salt
1 c. sugar	Chopped almonds
4 c. sifted flour	Sugar (for tops)

Cream butter and 1 c. sugar thoroughly. Add flour and salt. Shape in long, slender rolls 1″ in diameter. Wrap rolls tightly in waxed paper and chill thoroughly.

Cut dough in ½″ slices; place ½ to 1″ apart on ungreased baking sheet. Press each circle down with your thumb. Sprinkle with almonds, then with sugar.

Bake in hot oven (400°) 7 to 10 minutes. (Cookies should not brown.) Remove cookies and cool on racks. Makes about 14 dozen.

N O T E : You can take the dough from the refrigerator and bake cookies whenever convenient. It's a good idea to chill the dough at least 24 hours.

Variations

Easter Shortbreads: Prepare dough for Finnish Shortbread Cookies; chill thoroughly (do not form in rolls). Divide chilled dough in thirds, and work with one part at a time. Roll dough ⅓″ thick on lightly floured surface. Cut first third of dough with Easter bunny cookie cutter; arrange ½″ apart on ungreased baking sheet. Do not sprinkle with almonds. Bake in hot oven (400°) 8 minutes. Remove cookies and cool on racks. Repeat with second third of dough, but cut with chicken cookie cutter. Then roll and cut last portion of dough with an Easter cross cookie cutter. (All cutters are from 2 to 2½" at longest or widest place.)

When all cookies are cool, frost tops with Tinted Frosting. Use pink dragées for bunny eyes, green dragées for chicken eyes and three silver dragées to decorate each cross (one dragée centered in each extension of the cross). Spread frosted cookies out in tight container with waxed paper between layers if they are to be held a few hours or a couple of days before serving. Set in a cold place. Cookies are especially handsome served on a purple or black lacquer or a silver tray. Makes 5 dozen.

Tinted Frosting: Beat together until smooth 2 c. sifted confectioners sugar, 1 tsp. vanilla and 3 to 4 tblsp. milk, enough to make a frosting of spreading consistency. Divide in thirds. To one part, add 1 drop of red food color to make a delicate pink frosting for the bunnies; to the second part, add 2 drops yellow food color to make frosting for chickens; and to the last third, add 1 drop green food color to make a pale green frosting for the crosses.

FRESH LEMON COCONUT COOKIES

Lemon peel provides a fresh citrus taste that's wonderful with coconut

¼ c. butter	¾ c. shredded coconut
¼ c. shortening	1¾ c. sifted flour
1 c. sugar	½ tsp. salt
1 egg	2 tsp. baking powder
2 tsp. grated lemon peel	

Cream together butter, shortening and sugar. Add egg and beat until light and fluffy. Add lemon peel and coconut; stir to blend.

Sift together dry ingredients; stir into creamed mixture. Divide dough in half and shape into rolls. Wrap tightly in waxed paper and store in refrigerator at least several hours.

Cut dough in thin slices with sharp knife; place 1½" apart on ungreased baking sheet. Bake in hot oven (400°) 10 minutes. Remove cookies and cool on racks. Makes about 4 dozen.

LEMON THINS

Just right to escort ice cream, sherbet, light puddings and fruits

1 c. butter or regular margarine	½ tsp. baking powder
½ c. sugar	⅛ tsp. salt
1 egg, beaten	1 tblsp. lemon juice
2 c. sifted flour	½ tsp. grated lemon peel

Cream together butter and sugar; add egg; mix well.

Sift together flour, baking powder and salt; combine with sugar mixture. Add lemon juice and peel.

Form into rolls 1½ to 2" in diameter; wrap tightly in waxed paper and chill.

Slice very thin. Bake 1½" apart on ungreased baking sheet in moderate oven (375°) 8 to 10 minutes. Remove cookies and cool on racks. Makes 5 to 6 dozen.

MERINGUE-TOPPED COOKIES

Beauties—pink, peppermint-flavored meringue with pink sugar trim

1 c. butter or regular margarine	½ tsp. cream of tartar
1½ c. sugar	¼ tsp. almond extract
3 eggs, separated	Colored decorating sugar,
2 tsp. grated orange peel	decorating candies or flaked
3 c. sifted flour	coconut (optional)
¼ tsp. salt	

Beat butter until light. Add ¾ c. sugar and beat until light and fluffy. Beat in egg yolks and orange peel to blend well.

Stir together flour and salt; add to creamed mixture. Shape in two rolls 1½" in diameter. Wrap tightly in waxed paper, twisting ends, and refrigerate overnight.

Cut dough in ¼" slices. Place about 1" apart on ungreased baking sheet.

Beat egg whites with cream of tartar until foamy. Gradually add remaining ¾ c. sugar and beat until stiff, but not dry. Fold in almond extract. Drop by teaspoonfuls onto cookie slices. Sprinkle top of meringue with colored sugar, decorating candies or flaked coconut.

Bake in moderate oven (350°) 10 to 12 minutes, or just until delicately browned. Remove cookies to cooling rack. Makes about 5 dozen.

NOTE: For fascinating holiday cookies, tint meringue with food color; omit almond extract and flavor with other extracts. Use peppermint extract for pink or green meringues, lemon extract for yellow meringues and orange extract for orange-colored meringues (mixture of red and yellow food color makes orange). Sprinkle tops of meringues with colored sugar to match color of meringue, or with decorating candies, silver or other colored dragées, flaked coconut or chocolate shot (jimmies). A tray of these handsome, buttery rich cookies provides decorative and delicious hospitality for a party or open house.

MINCEMEAT REFRIGERATOR COOKIES

Mincemeat is the seasoning in this big recipe—makes 9 dozen

¾ c. butter	3 c. sifted flour
1 c. sugar	½ tsp. baking soda
1 egg	½ tsp. salt
½ tsp. vanilla	1 tsp. ground cinnamon
1 tsp. finely grated lemon peel	½ c. chopped walnuts
¾ c. prepared mincemeat	

Cream together butter and sugar until light and fluffy. Beat in egg, vanilla and lemon peel. Stir in mincemeat.

Sift together flour, baking soda, salt and cinnamon; gradually add to creamed mixture, mixing well. Stir in nuts.

Divide dough in half. Place each part on a lightly floured sheet of waxed paper and form in a roll 1½" in diameter, about 12" long. (Sprinkling waxed paper with a little flour helps you to shape smooth rolls.) Wrap rolls in waxed paper and refrigerate several hours, overnight or 2 or 3 days.

With sharp knife, cut dough in ⅛" slices; place 1½" apart on ungreased baking sheet. Bake in moderate oven (375°) about 10 minutes. Remove cookies to cooling racks at once. Makes 9 dozen.

MOCHA NUT COOKIES

Chocolate and coffee combine in these distinctive cookies

½ c. shortening	½ c. chopped walnuts or pecans
1 c. sugar	1 c. sifted flour
1 egg	¼ tsp. salt
2 squares unsweetened chocolate, melted	1 tsp. baking powder
	2 tsp. instant coffee powder

Cream together shortening and sugar. Add egg and beat until light and fluffy. Stir in chocolate and nuts.

Sift together dry ingredients and add to creamed mixture; blend thoroughly. Divide dough in half and shape into rolls. Wrap tightly in waxed paper; chill in refrigerator at least several hours.

Cut dough in ⅛" slices; place 1½" apart on ungreased baking sheet. Bake in moderate oven (375°) 15 minutes. Remove cookies and cool on racks. Makes about 6 dozen.

MOLASSES/ALMOND COOKIES

Little coffee-flavored molasses cookies with a baked-on topping

½ c. shortening	¼ tsp. salt
3 tblsp. light molasses	¼ tsp. baking soda
1 tsp. instant coffee powder	½ c. butter
½ tsp. vanilla	½ c. confectioners sugar
1½ c. sifted flour	½ c. chopped almonds

Beat shortening until light. Gradually beat in molasses. Stir in coffee powder and vanilla.

Sift together flour, salt and baking soda. Add to molasses mixture. Form dough into a roll 1" in diameter, about 13" long. Wrap tightly in waxed paper, twisting ends, and chill in refrigerator 2 hours or overnight.

Combine butter, confectioners sugar and almonds. Shape in roll 1" in diameter; wrap tightly in waxed paper, twisting ends. Chill 2 hours or overnight.

To bake, cut each roll in ¼" slices; place dough slices about 1" apart on ungreased baking sheet and top with almond slices. Bake in moderate oven (350°) 10 to 12 minutes. Remove cookies and cool on racks. Makes about 4 dozen.

OATMEAL/MAPLE COOKIES

Whole wheat flour and maple flavoring give the cookies distinction

1 c. soft butter	1 c. quick-cooking rolled oats
1 c. brown sugar, firmly packed	¼ c. chocolate shot (jimmies)
1 tsp. maple flavoring	¼ c. finely chopped walnuts
1½ c. whole wheat flour	

Cream butter, brown sugar and flavoring together until fluffy. Stir in flour and oats; mix until blended.

Divide dough in half. Shape each half into a roll 1½" in diameter. Roll one roll in chocolate shot and the other in nuts. Wrap tightly in waxed paper; chill several hours or overnight.

Cut ¼" slices and place 1½" apart on ungreased baking sheet. Bake in moderate oven (350°) 12 to 15 minutes. Cool on baking sheet until firm before removing to cooling rack. Makes 6 dozen.

OLD SALTS

Perfect snack—hide or they'll disappear. Salted tops, sweet inside

1 c. shortening	¼ tsp. salt
1 c. sugar	½ tsp. baking powder
1 egg	½ tsp. baking soda
1 tsp. vanilla	3 c. quick-cooking rolled oats
1¼ c. sifted flour	Salt (for tops)

Cream shortening and sugar until light and fluffy. Beat in egg and vanilla to mix thoroughly.

Sift together flour, ¼ tsp. salt, baking powder and soda; add to creamed mixture. Stir in rolled oats.

Divide dough in quarters and place each part on sheet of lightly floured waxed paper. Shape in roll 1" in diameter and about 12" long. Wrap in waxed paper and chill several hours or overnight. (It's easier to shape soft dough on waxed paper lightly floured.)

Cut in ¼" slices (dough will be crumbly and cannot be cut thinner). Sprinkle tops lightly with salt. Place about 1" apart on greased baking sheet.

Bake in moderate oven (375°) 10 to 12 minutes. Let stand a couple of minutes before removing from baking sheet to rack for cooling. Makes about 12 dozen.

SIX-IN-ONE REFRIGERATOR COOKIES

You make 18 dozen cookies of six flavors from one batch of dough

2 c. butter	½ c. shredded coconut
1 c. sugar	½ c. finely chopped pecans
1 c. light brown sugar, firmly	½ tsp. ground nutmeg
packed	1 tsp. ground cinnamon
2 eggs, beaten	1 square unsweetened chocolate,
1 tsp. vanilla	melted
4 c. flour	¼ c. finely chopped candied
1 tsp. baking soda	cherries
½ tsp. salt	

Cream butter. Gradually add sugars; cream until light and fluffy. Add eggs and vanilla; mix well.

Sift together flour, soda and salt; gradually add to creamed mixture, beating well after each addition.

Divide dough in six parts. Add coconut to one part; pecans to second; nutmeg and cinnamon to third; melted chocolate to fourth; and candied cherries to fifth. Leave the last portion plain. Chill 30 minutes, or longer.

Shape dough into six rolls about 1¾" in diameter. Wrap tightly in plastic wrap or waxed paper and refrigerate overnight, or freeze.

When ready to use, slice with sharp knife in ⅛" slices. (If frozen, thaw just enough to slice.) Place on lightly greased baking sheet.

Bake in moderate oven (375°) 10 to 12 minutes, until lightly browned. Remove cookies and cool on racks. Makes 18 dozen.

Molded Cookies

Christmas Cane Cookies tied with red ribbons . . . two-color cookie snails, or Swirls . . . Chocolate Bonbon Cookies with shiny pink Peppermint Glaze . . . Mexican Fiesta Balls dotted with cherries and fragrant with coffee—these will give you an idea of charming cookies you can make with recipes in this section.

Our molded cookies come in many sizes and shapes. Among the tasty tidbits are Spanish Wedding Cakes made from lemon-flavored cookie dough wrapped around almonds. Frosted Yule Logs resemble short, fat pencils coated with nuts. And Honeyed Yo-Yos are big, plump cookies sweetened and flavored with honey and brown sugar. Put together in pairs with apricot or other jam between, they really look like yo-yos. Men especially think they're right, both in size and taste.

This cookbook contains several superior recipes for sugar cookies. But our Molded Sugar Cookies take second place to none of them. They won several blue ribbons at fairs for the woman who shares the recipe with you. If you like sugar cookies that are golden and crisp on the outside and soft within, this recipe is for you.

Molded cookies especially delight women who like to create beautiful food and who like to shape dough with their hands. The technique can give you the same sort of satisfaction an artist experiences from molding clay.

Though fascinating, these cookies are not difficult to make, nor unduly time consuming. But do plan to spend enough time to achieve artistic results.

Rules are few—it's imaginative work and defies many cut-and-dried regulations. The dough has to be right. If it's too soft, chill it until you can easily handle it.

Balls of dough are the beginning of many molded cookies. Some of them retain their spherical shape during the baking, while others, such as Snickerdoodles, flatten. Some cookies are flattened before you put them in the oven. Use the bottom of a glass tumbler, greased lightly every time you press it on the dough. Some recipes recommend that you dip the glass lightly in flour or in sugar. And you flatten some cookies with the floured tines of a fork, pressed crosswise and then lengthwise to make a design.

Gather cheer, if you're new at this baking art, by reminding yourself that the more cookies you mold, the faster you'll do it well. Mothers report that some children excel in shaping cookie dough. Give them an opportunity to participate.

ALMOND BUTTERBALLS

Right for teas, parties, receptions—a hostess favorite

1 c. butter or regular margarine	2 c. sifted flour
¼ c. confectioners sugar	1 c. chopped almonds
1 tsp. vanilla	Confectioners sugar (for coating)
⅛ tsp. almond extract	

Cream butter and ¼ c. confectioners sugar until light and fluffy; add flavorings.

Stir in flour and almonds; blend well.

Form dough into tiny balls; place about 1" apart on ungreased baking sheet. Bake in moderate oven (350°) about 20 minutes.

Roll cookies in confectioners sugar while warm. Cool on racks. Makes about 6 dozen.

BLACK WALNUT CRESCENTS

Serve these with applesauce for a great winter supper dessert

½ c. butter	2 tsp. vanilla
½ c. shortening	2 c. sifted flour
⅓ c. sugar	½ c. chopped black walnuts
2 tsp. water	Confectioners sugar (for dipping)

Cream butter and shortening until light; add sugar, cream until light and fluffy. Beat in water, vanilla, flour and nuts. Chill 4 hours, or overnight.

Shape dough in rolls about 15" long and ½" in diameter; then cut in 3" lengths. Shape in crescents.

Place about ½" apart on ungreased baking sheet, and bake in slow oven (325°) 12 to 15 minutes. Do not let cookies brown. Cool slightly on baking sheet, then remove from baking sheet and dip in confectioners sugar. Place on racks to cool. Makes about 44.

NOTE : Black walnuts have a pronounced flavor. If you wish to decrease it, put 2 tblsp. chopped black walnuts in a ½ c. measure and fill with chopped walnuts, English-type.

CHRISTMAS CANE COOKIES

There's a hint of peppermint in these entwined red and creamy white butter cookie strips, shaped like canes for the yuletide

1 c. butter or regular margarine	½ tsp. salt
1 c. sifted confectioners sugar	½ tsp. red food color
1 egg	¼ c. crushed red and white
1½ tsp. vanilla	peppermint candy
½ tsp. almond extract	¼ c. sugar
2½ c. sifted flour	

Beat butter and confectioners sugar until mixture is light and fluffy. Beat in egg, vanilla and almond extract to blend well.

Mix flour and salt and stir into creamed mixture. Divide in half. Blend food color into one half. Work with ¼ plain dough and ¼ tinted dough. Keep remainder of dough in refrigerator until you are ready to use it.

Take 1 tsp. plain dough and roll with hands into a strip 4″ long. Then roll 1 tsp. tinted dough into a strip the same length. Lay the two strips side by side and twist together, holding both ends of strips, to make a red and white striped rope. Place the rope on ungreased baking sheet and curve one end to make the cane's handle. Repeat, making one cane at a time so the dough will not dry out and be difficult to twist and shape. Place canes about 1″ apart on baking sheet (12 will fit on one baking sheet). Then repeat with remaining portions of dough.

Bake in moderate oven (375°) about 10 minutes. Remove from baking sheet at once. Combine candy and white sugar; sprinkle on hot cookies. Cool on racks. Makes about 4 dozen.

EASY CANE COOKIES

Cookies are dappled with red flakes of peppermint candy—tie the canes with Christmas ribbons for a festive look

1 c. butter or regular margarine	2½ c. sifted flour
1 c. confectioners sugar	½ tsp. salt
1 egg	½ c. crushed red and white
1 tsp. vanilla	peppermint candy
¼ tsp. peppermint extract	2 tblsp. sugar

Beat together butter and confectioners sugar until light and fluffy. Beat in egg, vanilla and peppermint extract to blend well.

Combine flour and salt and stir into creamed mixture. Wrap dough in waxed paper and chill at least 1 hour.

When ready to shape, mix crushed candy with white sugar. Roll 1 level measuring tablespoonful of dough on surface sprinkled with small amount of crushed candy mixture to make a 6″ rope. Place on greased baking sheet. Curve one end down to form handle of cane. Repeat until all the crushed candy mixture and dough have been used.

Bake in moderate oven (375°) about 12 minutes, until lightly browned. Remove at once from baking sheet and cool on racks. Makes about 3½ dozen.

N O T E : You can use stick candy of different colors and different extracts instead of the peppermint candy.

CHOCOLATE BONBON COOKIES

Tiny cookies with a shiny red peppermint glaze—for holiday parties

2 c. sifted flour	1 square unsweetened chocolate,
½ tsp. baking powder	melted
½ tsp. salt	1 tsp. vanilla
½ c. butter or regular margarine	Peppermint Glaze (recipe
½ c. sugar	follows)
1 egg	Silver dragées, nuts or canned
	frostings (for decorations)

Sift together flour, baking powder and salt.

Cream butter and sugar together until light and fluffy. Beat in egg, melted chocolate and vanilla. Stir in flour mixture, a third at a time, blending well. The dough will be stiff.

Roll rounded teaspoonfuls of dough, one at a time, into balls between hands. Place balls about 2″ apart on lightly greased baking sheet.

Bake in moderate oven (350°) about 12 minutes, until firm. Remove from baking sheet to wire racks. Repeat until all dough is baked. Cool thoroughly.

To glaze cookies, arrange at least 1″ apart on racks over waxed paper. Spoon Peppermint Glaze over to cover cookies completely (scrape glaze that drips onto waxed paper back into bowl). Spoon a second coating of glaze over the cookies; let cool. Trim with silver dragées, nuts or frostings from pressurized cans. Makes about 31.

N O T E : For Christmas holidays, use green frosting to make holly leaves, dots of red frosting for holly berries.

PEPPERMINT GLAZE

Perfect for chocolate cookies; tint glaze pink or green if you wish

3 c. sifted confectioners sugar	¼ tsp. red food color (optional)
2 to 3 tblsp. water	¼ tsp. peppermint extract

Combine all ingredients and beat until smooth. The glaze should be thin enough to pour from a spoon. If it gets too thick while working with it, add a few drops of water and beat until smooth. Makes about 1 cup.

Variation

Vanilla Glaze: Omit peppermint extract and red food color; add ½ tsp. vanilla and make glaze as directed.

CAPE COD CHOCOLATE CHIP COOKIES

A great 20th century cookie that rates among the all-time champions

1 c. butter or regular margarine	1 tsp. baking soda
¾ c. brown sugar, firmly packed	1 tsp. salt
¾ c. sugar	1 (6 oz.) pkg. semisweet
2 eggs	chocolate pieces
1 tsp. vanilla	½ c. chopped walnuts
2¼ c. sifted flour	

Cream butter until fluffy; gradually add sugars and beat until light and fluffy. Beat in eggs and vanilla, mixing well.

Sift together flour, baking powder and salt; add to creamed mixture and blend. Stir in chocolate pieces and nuts. Chill dough several hours or overnight.

Roll dough by teaspoonfuls between palms of hands and place 2″ apart on greased baking sheet. Flatten balls with fingertips to make flat rounds. Bake in moderate oven (350°) 10 to 12 minutes, or until light golden brown. Cool a few minutes on baking sheets before removing to racks to cool. Makes about 6½ dozen.

HOSTESS CINNAMON BALLS

Cookie balls wear cinnamon-walnut-sugar coating—they're special

½ c. butter or regular margarine	1 tsp. baking powder
1 c. sugar	¼ tsp. salt
1 egg, unbeaten	½ c. finely chopped nuts
1 tsp. vanilla	1 tblsp. ground cinnamon
1¼ c. sifted flour	1 tblsp. sugar

Cream butter and 1 c. sugar. Add egg and vanilla; beat well for 2 minutes with electric mixer at medium speed.

Sift together flour, baking powder and salt; add to creamed mixture; chill.

Mix nuts, cinnamon and 1 tblsp. sugar.

Mold dough into walnut-size balls; roll each in nut mixture.

Place balls 2½″ apart on greased baking sheet. Bake in moderate oven (350°) 12 to 15 minutes. Remove cookies and cool on racks. Makes about 20.

CHOCOLATE CRACKLES

Use confectioners sugar to put designs on these soft chocolate party cookie balls. The tops crackle in baking—a hostess favorite

2 eggs
1 c. sugar
1 tsp. vanilla
3 squares unsweetened chocolate, grated
2 c. finely grated (chopped very fine) pecans (7½ oz.)

¼ c. finely ground dry bread crumbs
2 tblsp. flour
¾ tsp. ground cinnamon
⅛ tsp. salt
¼ c. confectioners sugar (for coating)

Beat eggs with sugar and vanilla to blend well. With spoon, mix in chocolate, pecans, bread crumbs, flour, cinnamon and salt. Chill dough until easy to handle.

Shape part of dough at a time in 1″ balls, leaving remaining dough in refrigerator until ready to work with it. Roll balls in confectioners sugar and arrange 1″ apart on greased baking sheet.

Bake in slow oven (325°) 12 to 15 minutes (they will be soft and crackled on top). Remove cookies and cool on racks. Store in tightly covered container. Makes about 3½ dozen.

EASY CHOCOLATE CRACKLES

These cookies made with cake mix have a moist, fudge-like center

1 (1 lb. 2½ oz.) pkg. devil's food cake mix
2 eggs, slightly beaten

1 tblsp. water
½ c. shortening
Confectioners sugar (for coating)

Combine cake mix, eggs, water and shortening. Mix with a spoon until well blended.

Shape dough into balls the size of walnuts. Roll in confectioners sugar.

Place 1½″ apart on greased baking sheet. Bake in moderate oven (375°) 8 to 10 minutes. Remove cookies and cool on racks. Makes 4 dozen.

Ready for Holiday Guests. Top to bottom, left: Gingerbread Boys (page 139), Fudge Nut Bars (page 34), Lemon Love Notes (page 51). In blue container: cherry-centered Pecan Cookies (page 207), Mexican Seed Cookies (page 203).

Christmas Cookie Church. Bake cookies ahead, freeze or store. Patterns and directions for assembling plus recipes for cookies, Snow Icing and Sugar Syrup Cement (page 164). Let the family help.

CHOCOLATE MACAROONS

If you like chocolate and chewy cookies, these will please you

½ c. shortening	2 c. sugar
4 squares unsweetened chocolate	4 eggs
2 c. sifted flour	2 tsp. vanilla
2 tsp. baking powder	Confectioners sugar (for coating)
½ tsp. salt	

Melt together shortening and chocolate.

Sift together flour, baking powder and salt.

Add sugar to chocolate, stirring until smooth. Add eggs singly, beating well after each; add vanilla.

Add flour mixture; blend thoroughly.

Chill dough 2 to 3 hours.

Dip out rounded teaspoons of dough; form into small balls. Roll each in confectioners sugar. Place about 2" apart on lightly greased baking sheet.

Bake in moderate oven (375°) about 10 minutes. (Do not overbake. Cookies should be soft when taken from oven.) Remove cookies and cool on rack. Makes 5 to 6 dozen.

COCONUT CRISPIES

Crisp cookies with crinkled tops—perfect with ice cream

½ c. regular margarine	1 c. sifted flour
½ c. sugar	½ tsp. baking soda
½ c. brown sugar, firmly packed	½ tsp. salt
1 egg	½ c. crushed corn flakes
½ tsp. vanilla	½ c. flaked coconut

Beat together margarine and white and brown sugars until light and fluffy. Beat in egg and vanilla to blend well.

Sift together flour, baking soda and salt. Stir into creamed mixture. Fold in corn flakes and coconut. Chill until dough can easily be shaped in balls.

Shape dough by teaspoonfuls in little balls; place 2" apart on lightly greased baking sheet. Bake in moderate oven (350°) about 10 minutes, or until cookies are lightly browned. Remove at once from baking sheet to racks to cool. Store these thin crisp cookies in container with loose-fitting lid. Makes 50.

NOTE: You'll need 2 c. corn flakes to make about ½ c. crushed.

VIENNESE CRESCENTS

Use almonds in crescents for the Vienna version; or use pecans, shape in balls and you have Mexican Wedding Cakes

1 c. butter	2½ c. sifted flour
¾ c. sugar	1 c. ground almonds (or pecans)
1½ tsp. vanilla	Confectioners sugar (for coating)

Cream butter until light; gradually add sugar and beat until light and fluffy. Beat in vanilla.

Gradually blend in flour and nuts. Chill dough thoroughly so it will handle easily.

Form teaspoonfuls of dough into crescents; place ¾" apart on ungreased baking sheet. Bake in moderate oven (350°) 12 to 15 minutes, or until lightly browned. Cool slightly; remove from baking sheet and, while warm, roll in confectioners sugar. Cool on racks. Makes about 7½ dozen.

CRISSCROSS COOKIES

A winner because it has that wonderful lemon/brown sugar taste

4 c. sifted flour	2½ c. brown sugar, firmly packed
1½ tsp. baking soda	1½ tsp. vanilla
2 tsp. cream of tartar	1 tsp. lemon extract
1 tsp. salt	3 eggs, beaten
1⅓ c. shortening	

Sift together flour, soda, cream of tartar and salt.

Cream shortening; add brown sugar gradually. Add vanilla, lemon extract and eggs; beat until light and fluffy. Add sifted dry ingredients and mix until smooth. Chill several hours.

Roll level tablespoons of dough into balls the size of a small walnut. Place about 1" apart on greased baking sheet. Press lightly with tines of fork, making a crisscross pattern.

Bake in moderate oven (375°) 8 to 10 minutes. Remove cookies and cool on racks. Makes 8 dozen.

HEIRLOOM DANISH COOKIES

A rich version of sugar cookies; dress them up for the holidays

½ c. shortening
½ c. regular margarine
1 c. sugar
1 egg
1 tsp. vanilla

2 c. sifted flour
½ tsp. baking soda
½ tsp. cream of tartar
2 to 3 tblsp. sugar (for tops)

Cream together shortening, margarine, 1 c. sugar, egg and vanilla until light and fluffy.

Sift together flour, baking soda and cream of tartar. Gradually stir into creamed mixture to make a smooth dough. Chill thoroughly.

Roll dough in ¾" balls; place 1½" apart on ungreased baking sheet and flatten with fork. Sprinkle with sugar.

Bake in slow oven (325°) 12 to 15 minutes. Remove cookies to racks to cool. Makes about 6 dozen.

NOTE: You can tint cookie dough and sprinkle with colored sugar to match. A few red and green cookies are pretty in a Christmas gift package.

DOUBLE TREAT COOKIES

Cookies full of children's favorites—better make a triple batch

2 c. sifted flour
2 tsp. baking soda
½ tsp. salt
1 c. shortening
1 c. sugar
1 c. brown sugar, firmly packed

2 eggs
1 tsp. vanilla
1 c. peanut butter
1 c. chopped salted peanuts
1 (6 oz.) pkg. semisweet
chocolate pieces

Sift together flour, baking soda and salt.

Beat together shortening, white and brown sugars, eggs and vanilla until fluffy. Blend in peanut butter. Add sifted dry ingredients. Stir in peanuts and chocolate pieces.

Shape batter into small balls and place about 2" apart on ungreased baking sheet. Flatten with a drinking glass dipped in sugar. Bake in moderate oven (350°) 8 minutes, or until brown. Transfer cookies to racks to cool. Makes 7 dozen.

GREEK EASTER COOKIES

Excellent with coffee! These cookies are rich, but not very sweet

½ c. butter	7 c. sifted flour
1 c. sugar	3½ tsp. baking powder
½ c. salad oil	1 tsp. salt
½ c. melted shortening	1 egg yolk
⅔ c. milk	2 tblsp. milk
2 eggs	2½ tblsp. sesame seeds
1 tsp. vanilla	

Cream butter until light and fluffy; gradually beat in sugar, salad oil, melted shortening and milk. Beat in 2 eggs and vanilla.

Sift together flour, baking powder and salt, and gradually add to creamed mixture to make a soft dough.

Shape in 1½" balls and work each ball under fingers on lightly floured surface to make a rope 7 to 8" in length. Twist each strip of dough and shape in double twist, making 2 loops like a figure 8 with ends overlapping slightly. Place about ½" apart on ungreased baking sheet.

Combine egg yolk and milk; brush on cookies. Sprinkle with sesame seeds.

Bake in moderate oven (350°) about 20 minutes, or until golden. Cool slightly on baking sheet on rack; then remove from baking sheet and cool completely on racks. Makes about 5 dozen.

FOUR-FROM-ONE ANGEL COOKIES

This cookie cookbook contains many favorite recipes from Farm Journal readers, among them these Angel Cookies. An upstate New York woman says: "They are our best-liked cookies. It's a big recipe that makes about nine dozen so I make four different kinds.

"I divide the dough in quarters and bake the first portion plain. I roll the balls of dough from the second portion in flaked or cookie coconut. To the third, I add ½ c. semisweet chocolate pieces, to the fourth, ½ c. chopped salted peanuts."

You may think of other ways to introduce variety and interest to the cookie plate or tray.

ANGEL COOKIES

Keep a supply in your freezer ready to serve with coffee or tea

1 c. butter or regular margarine	4½ c. sifted flour
1 c. lard	2 tsp. baking soda
1 c. sugar	2 tsp. cream of tartar
1 c. brown sugar, firmly packed	2 tsp. salt
2 eggs	1 c. chopped nuts
2 tsp. vanilla	White sugar (for dipping)

Cream together butter, lard and white and brown sugars. Beat in eggs, one at a time, to mix thoroughly. Add vanilla.

Sift together flour, baking soda, cream of tartar and salt. Add to creamed mixture. Stir in nuts. Chill dough until it is easy to handle.

Shape dough in balls the size of walnuts; dip tops in sugar. Arrange about 2″ apart on lightly greased baking sheet. Sprinkle several drops of water on each cookie.

Bake in moderate oven (350°) 15 minutes. Remove cookies and cool on racks. Makes 9 dozen.

N O T E : You can divide the ingredients in half to bake 4½ dozen cookies.

GINGER BLOSSOM COOKIES

Nuts make cream-colored centers for brown cookies—attractive

¾ c. shortening	1 tsp. ground cinnamon
1 c. brown sugar, firmly packed	½ tsp. ground cloves
¼ c. light molasses	2 tsp. baking soda
1 egg, beaten	¼ tsp. salt
2¼ c. sifted flour	25 blanched almonds
1 tsp. ground ginger	

Cream shortening and sugar; add molasses and egg; blend well. Sift dry ingredients; add to creamed mixture; mix well.

Roll into balls about 1½″ in diameter; place 2½″ apart on greased baking sheet. Flatten slightly; press almond in center of each.

Bake in moderate oven (350°) 12 to 15 minutes. Remove cookies and cool on racks. Makes 25.

CRACKLE-TOP GINGER COOKIES

To make cookie tops glisten, sprinkle with sugar before baking

1 c. shortening	2 tsp. baking soda
2 c. brown sugar, firmly packed	2 tsp. ground ginger
1 egg, well beaten	1 tsp. vanilla
1 c. molasses	1 tsp. lemon extract
4 c. sifted flour	Sugar (for tops)
½ tsp. salt	

Cream shortening; gradually add brown sugar. Blend in egg and molasses; beat until light and fluffy.

Sift together dry ingredients; gradually blend into creamed mixture. (Dough should be soft but not sticky, or tops won't crackle.)

Add vanilla and lemon extract. Chill about 4 hours, or until dough can be handled with light dusting of flour on hands and board.

Shape dough into balls about 1½" in diameter. Place 3" apart on greased baking sheet. (Do not flatten.)

Bake in moderate oven (350°) 12 to 15 minutes, or until brown. Sprinkle with sugar, then remove from baking sheet with pancake turner. Spread on racks to cool. Makes about 30.

HONEY/NUT COOKIES

Good keepers if you hide them—rich and crisp but not too sweet

1 c. butter or regular margarine	1 tsp. ground cinnamon
¼ c. honey	1 c. chopped walnuts
2 c. sifted flour	Confectioners sugar (for tops)

Cream butter until light; add honey and beat to mix thoroughly. Sift flour and cinnamon together; beat into creamed mixture. Stir in nuts.

Shape in 1½" balls; place about 2" apart on lightly greased baking sheet. Flatten with bottom of drinking glass dipped in flour. Bake in slow oven (325°) 15 minutes, or until lightly browned. Cool on baking sheet a few minutes; place on racks and while still warm, dust with confectioners sugar. Makes about 5 dozen.

HONEYED YO-YOS

Put flat sides together with jam—big sandwiches resemble yo-yos

1 c. shortening	3½ c. sifted flour
1 c. brown sugar, firmly packed	2 tsp. baking soda
3 eggs	¼ tsp. salt
⅓ c. honey	¾ c. apricot jam
1 tsp. vanilla	

Cream together shortening and brown sugar until light and fluffy. Beat in eggs. Add honey and vanilla and beat to mix thoroughly.

Sift together flour, baking soda and salt. Add to creamed mixture. Chill overnight, or several hours until firm.

Shape dough in balls the size of large walnuts. Place 2" apart on ungreased baking sheet. Bake in moderate oven (350°) 10 to 12 minutes, until almost no imprint remains when you press cookie lightly with finger. Transfer cookies to racks and cool.

Put flat bottom sides of cookies together in pairs with apricot jam (or other fruit jam) between. Makes about 2½ dozen.

JELLY DIAGONALS

Use jelly, jam or preserves of another color for half the batch for contrast—try apricot and grape preserves for interesting effect

¾ c. butter	½ tsp. baking powder
⅔ c. sugar	½ tsp. ground nutmeg
1 egg	¼ tsp. salt
2 tsp. vanilla	¼ c. apricot jam or preserves,
2 c. sifted flour	or currant jelly

Cream butter until light; add sugar and beat until fluffy. Beat in egg and vanilla to mix thoroughly.

Sift together flour, baking powder, nutmeg and salt. Stir into creamed mixture; mix thoroughly.

Divide dough in quarters. Form each part into a roll about 12" long, ¾" in diameter. Place two rolls at a time 4" apart on ungreased baking sheet; have the rolls at least 2" from edges of baking sheet. Make a depression about ⅓" deep lengthwise down the center of each roll. You can do this with a knife handle. Fill the cavity with jam, preserves or jelly (you'll need about 1 tblsp. for each roll).

Bake in moderate oven (350°) 15 to 20 minutes, until lightly browned around edges. While warm, cut in diagonal slices, about 10 to a roll. Cool cookies on racks. Makes 40.

BRAZILIAN LACE-EDGED COOKIES

Lacy edges give these cookies a gay look—nice for entertaining

¼ c. soft butter or regular	1 c. sifted flour
margarine	1 tsp. ground cinnamon
1½ c. brown sugar, firmly packed	1 c. chopped Brazil nuts
2 tblsp. water	

Cream butter; add sugar gradually and cream until light and fluffy. Blend in water.

Sift flour and cinnamon; add nuts. Combine mixtures.

Shape dough in small balls, about 1″. Place 2″ apart on greased baking sheet.

Bake in slow oven (325°) about 15 minutes.

Remove from oven; let stand about 30 seconds before lifting from baking sheet with wide spatula. (If cookies get too crisp to come off smoothly, return to oven and heat about a minute to resoften.) Remove cookies and cool on racks. Makes about 5 dozen.

LEMON ANGEL COOKIES

Lemon-filled meringue tops these lovely hostess specials

⅔ c. shortening	1 tsp. salt
1 c. brown sugar, firmly packed	1 tsp. baking soda
2 eggs	3 egg whites
1 tsp. vanilla	¾ c. sugar
2 c. sifted flour	Lemon Filling (recipe follows)

Beat shortening with brown sugar until light and fluffy. Beat in the 2 eggs, one at a time, and vanilla to mix well.

Sift together flour, salt and baking soda and add to creamed mixture. Chill dough 1 hour.

Beat egg whites until foamy; add sugar gradually and beat until stiff peaks form. Set aside.

Shape chilled dough into balls, using 1 tsp. dough for each ball.

Place 2″ apart on ungreased baking sheet. Flatten to ⅛″ thickness with bottom of 2″ juice glass.

Top each cookie with 1 tsp. meringue. With the spoon, make a hollow in center of meringue on cookie. Bake in slow oven (325°) 10 to 12 minutes, or until cookies are cream-colored. Cool cookies on racks, then fill depressions in meringue on top of cookies with lukewarm Lemon Filling. Store cookies in refrigerator until time to serve them. Makes 4 dozen.

N O T E : You can fill these cookies with other fillings, jelly or jam or whipped cream just before serving.

LEMON FILLING

Filling on meringue-topped cookies will have a dull, yellow look

1 c. sugar	3 egg yolks
2 tblsp. cornstarch	¼ c. lemon juice
¼ tsp. salt	1 tsp. grated lemon peel
¼ c. water	1 tblsp. butter

Combine ½ c. sugar, cornstarch and salt in small saucepan, mixing well. Stir in water. Cook over low heat, stirring constantly, until mixture thickens (it will not be clear).

Beat together egg yolks and ½ c. sugar. Blend a little of the hot mixture into egg yolks, then add to mixture in saucepan. Cook over low heat, stirring constantly, about 2 minutes, or until mixture thickens; remove from heat.

Stir in lemon juice, lemon peel and butter. Cool until lukewarm.

LEMON SNOWBALLS

A great hostess favorite—pure white cookies accented with lemon

½ c. shortening or butter	¼ tsp. cream of tartar
⅔ c. sugar	3 tblsp. lemon juice
2 tsp. grated lemon peel	1 tblsp. water
1 egg	½ c. chopped nuts
1¾ c. sifted flour	Confectioners sugar (for coating)
½ tsp. baking soda	

Cream together shortening, sugar and lemon peel until light and fluffy. Add egg; beat until smooth.

Sift together flour, baking soda and cream of tartar. Add to creamed mixture alternately with lemon juice and water.

Stir in nuts. Chill dough.

With floured hands, form dough into small balls and place 1" apart on ungreased baking sheet. Bake in moderate oven (350°) 8 to 10 minutes. Remove from sheet and roll immediately in confectioners sugar. Cool on racks. Makes 3½ dozen.

Variation

Orange Snowballs: Omit lemon peel and lemon juice. Substitute grated orange peel and orange juice. Use pecans for nuts.

MEXICAN FIESTA BALLS

Chocolate, coffee and maraschino flavors blend in these gala cookies

1 c. butter	½ tsp. salt
½ c. sugar	1 c. finely chopped nuts
2 tsp. vanilla	½ c. chopped drained maraschino
2 c. sifted flour	cherries
¼ c. cocoa	1 c. confectioners sugar (for
1 tblsp. instant coffee powder	coating)

Beat butter until light; gradually add sugar. Beat until light and fluffy. Add vanilla and beat to blend well.

Sift together flour, cocoa, coffee powder and salt; gradually add to creamed mixture. Blend in nuts and cherries; chill until easy to handle.

Shape dough into balls 1" in diameter and place 1" apart on ungreased baking sheet. Bake in slow oven (325°) 20 minutes. Remove cookies to cooling racks and, while warm, roll in confectioners sugar. Makes 5 dozen.

MEXICAN SEED COOKIES

Anise and sesame seeds give these thin sugar cookies a new taste

1 tblsp. whole anise seeds	1 egg
2 tblsp. boiling water	2 c. sifted flour
⅔ c. sugar	1 egg, lightly beaten
¾ c. butter or regular margarine	⅓ c. toasted sesame seeds (see
⅛ tsp. baking soda	Index)

Combine anise seeds and boiling water and let stand.

Beat together sugar and butter until fluffy. Beat in soda and 1 egg. Drain anise seeds and add to mixture.

Stir in flour, a little at a time, and mix well. Wrap dough in waxed paper and chill overnight.

When ready to bake, roll dough into ½″ balls. Place about 3″ apart on ungreased baking sheets. Flatten to ¹⁄₁₆″ thickness with the bottom of a glass. Brush tops with lightly beaten egg. Sprinkle each with toasted sesame seeds.

Bake in hot oven (400°) 7 to 8 minutes, or until lightly browned. Remove cookies and cool on racks. Makes 6 dozen.

MEXICAN THUMBPRINTS

The custard filling bakes in these rich and luscious party cookies

1 egg yolk	½ c. sugar
1 tblsp. sugar	2 egg yolks
1 tblsp. flour	1 tsp. vanilla
¼ tsp. vanilla	2¼ c. sifted flour
Dash of salt	1 tsp. baking powder
½ c. heavy cream	⅛ tsp. salt
1 c. butter	

To make filling, blend 1 egg yolk with 1 tblsp. sugar, 1 tblsp. flour, ¼ tsp. vanilla and dash of salt in top of double boiler. Add the cream gradually and blend well. Cook over water, stirring constantly, until custard is thick and smooth. Cover surface of custard with waxed paper or plastic wrap. Chill thoroughly.

To make cookies, beat butter until light; gradually add ½ c. sugar and beat until fluffy. Beat in 2 egg yolks and 1 tsp. vanilla to blend well.

Sift together 2¼ c. flour, baking powder and ⅛ tsp. salt. Mix into egg yolk mixture to blend thoroughly. Chill dough until easy to handle, at least 1 hour.

Shape heaping teaspoonfuls of dough into balls; place 1″ apart on ungreased baking sheet. With thumb, press medium-size indentations in each dough ball. Put ¼ tsp. filling in each.

Bake in moderate oven (350°) 13 to 15 minutes, or until light brown. Remove cookies and cool on racks. Makes 4½ dozen.

MOLASSES BUTTERBALLS

Easy to make and really delicious—brown cookies in white dress

1 c. butter or regular margarine	2 c. finely chopped walnuts
¼ c. molasses	Confectioners sugar (for
2 c. sifted flour	coating)
½ tsp. salt	

Cream butter; add molasses.
Sift flour and salt; stir in nuts.

Add flour mixture to creamed mixture; blend well. Shape dough into small balls, about 1″ in diameter.

Place about 1″ apart on ungreased baking sheet. Bake in moderate oven (350°) 25 minutes, or until lightly browned. Roll in confectioners sugar while warm. Cool cookies on racks. Makes about 4 dozen.

SPICY MOLASSES BALLS

Brown sugar adds to the tastiness of these spicy, country specials

¾ c. shortening	2 tsp. baking soda
1 c. brown sugar, firmly packed	1 tsp. ground cinnamon
1 egg	1 tsp. ground ginger
¼ c. molasses	½ tsp. ground cloves
2½ c. sifted flour	Sugar (for dipping)
¼ tsp. salt	

Cream shortening and brown sugar; blend in egg and molasses.
Sift together remaining ingredients, except sugar; stir into creamed

mixture; mix well. Shape into ¾" balls; dip tops in sugar. Place 2" apart on greased baking sheet.

Bake in moderate oven (350°) 12 to 15 minutes. Remove cookies and cool on racks. Makes about 4 dozen.

PARTY PINKS

Crisp cookies with pink tops bring glamor to festive entertaining

¾ c. butter or regular margarine	1½ c. sifted flour
1½ c. sifted confectioners sugar	¼ tsp. salt
1 tsp. vanilla	1 egg white, slightly beaten
3 drops red food color (about)	1 c. finely chopped pecans
1 egg yolk	

Cream butter, sugar and vanilla until light and fluffy. Add food color to make a delicate pink. Take out ¼ c. mixture and refrigerate.

To remainder of creamed mixture add egg yolk, flour and salt; mix thoroughly. Shape in balls about 1" in diameter. Dip in egg white, then in nuts.

Place 1½" apart on ungreased baking sheet. Bake in moderate oven (350°) 10 minutes. Remove from oven and quickly make indentation in each cookie by pressing with back of ¼ tsp. measuring spoon (round bowl). Return to oven and bake about 7 minutes longer.

Transfer from baking sheet to racks. When cool, place ¼ tsp. reserved pink creamed mixture in the center of each cookie. Makes 3 dozen.

PEANUT/APPLE COOKIES

Apple gives these cookies their moistness, peanut butter, the flavor

½ c. shortening	½ c. grated peeled apple
½ c. smooth peanut butter	1½ c. sifted flour
½ c. sugar	½ tsp. baking soda
½ c. brown sugar, firmly packed	½ tsp. salt
1 egg	½ tsp. ground cinnamon
½ tsp. vanilla	

Cream together shortening, peanut butter and sugars until light and fluffy. Beat in egg, vanilla and apple to mix well.

Sift together remaining dry ingredients; stir into creamed mixture to blend well. Chill several hours.

Work with a fourth of dough at a time, leaving remaining dough in refrigerator until ready to use. Shape in 1" balls and place 1½" apart on greased baking sheet. Flatten balls with a fork moistened in cold water.

Bake in moderate oven (350°) 12 to 15 minutes. Remove cookies and cool on racks. Makes about 5 dozen.

PEANUT BLOSSOM COOKIES

Chocolate stars make pretty centers and make cookies look festive

1 c. shortening	2 tsp. baking soda
1 c. sugar	1 tsp. salt
1 c. brown sugar, firmly packed	2 tblsp. milk
2 eggs	½ c. sugar (for dipping)
1 c. peanut butter	Chocolate candy stars for
3½ c. sifted flour	centers (about 1 lb.)

Cream shortening, 1 c. white sugar and brown sugar together until light and fluffy. Beat in eggs and peanut butter.

Sift together flour, baking soda and salt and stir into creamed mixture. Add milk and mix.

Shape in 1 to 1½" balls with hands; dip in ½ c. sugar and arrange 2 to 3" apart on lightly greased baking sheet. Bake in moderate oven (350°) 7 minutes. Remove from oven and quickly press a small chocolate candy star in center of each cookie. (Candy will fall off cookie when cooled unless it is pressed in before cookie is completely baked.) Return to oven and bake 5 to 7 minutes longer.

Remove from baking sheet to racks and cool. Makes about 10 dozen.

PEANUT DROPS

These cookies have crisp, ragged tops with flashes of red cherries

¼ c. butter or regular margarine	¼ c. butter
½ c. peanut butter	⅓ c. sugar
½ c. brown sugar, firmly packed	1 egg
½ c. sugar	½ c. chopped salted peanuts
1 egg	3 c. corn flakes
1¼ c. sifted flour	¼ c. chopped drained
¼ tsp. baking soda	maraschino cherries
¼ tsp. salt	

To make cookie dough, beat ¼ c. butter and peanut butter together;

gradually add brown sugar and ½ c. white sugar and beat until light and fluffy. Beat in 1 egg to mix thoroughly.

Sift together flour, baking soda and salt. Add to first mixture; mix well.

Make topping by creaming together ¼ c. butter and ⅓ c. white sugar. Add remaining ingredients and beat well.

Shape cookie dough into 1" balls; place 2" apart on lightly greased baking sheet and flatten with a fork. Top each cookie with about 2 tblsp. topping.

Bake in moderate oven (375°) 12 to 15 minutes. Transfer cookies to racks to cool. Makes 34.

PECAN BONBONS AND LOGS

For variety bake part of dough in logs—bonbons are very pretty

2 c. sifted flour	2 tsp. vanilla
¼ c. sugar	2½ c. finely chopped pecans
½ tsp. salt	Confectioners sugar (for coating)
1 c. butter or regular margarine	

Sift flour, sugar and salt into mixing bowl. Blend in butter and vanilla with pastry blender. Add 2 c. nuts.

Shape half the dough into ½" balls. Roll in remaining nuts. Place about 1½" apart on greased baking sheet and bake in moderate oven (350°) 15 to 20 minutes. Cool cookies on racks.

Roll remaining dough into logs; bake. While warm, roll in confectioners sugar. Makes 4 dozen.

PECAN COOKIES

Jewel-like centers make these a pretty addition to the party tray

2 c. ground pecans	⅓ c. strawberry preserves
⅔ c. sugar	18 candied or maraschino
½ tsp. salt	cherries, cut in halves
2 egg whites	

Combine pecans and sugar. Add salt and egg whites and mix until mixture is completely moistened.

Form into small balls (mixture will be moist). Place about 2" apart on ungreased baking sheet. Press a small hole in center of each ball with your fingertip. Fill with strawberry preserves. Top with cherry halves, cut side down.

Bake in moderate oven (350°) about 15 minutes. Remove from baking sheet at once to prevent sticking. Cool on racks. Makes 3 dozen.

PECAN DROPS

The brown beauties with red-cherry trim are perfect for Christmas

1 c. butter or regular margarine	2 c. sifted flour
½ tsp. salt	1 c. finely chopped pecans
½ c. sifted confectioners sugar	Candied cherries, cut in sixths
1 tblsp. vanilla	

Blend together butter, salt, sugar and vanilla. Add flour and pecans; mix well; chill.

Shape into small balls; place about 2" apart on lightly greased baking sheet. Press small hole in center of each ball with fingertip; insert piece of cherry in each. Bake in moderate oven (350°) about 15 minutes. Remove cookies and cool on racks. Makes 5 dozen.

PECAN FINGER COOKIES

Pecan halves in cookie jackets—a tasty addition to the teatime tray

1 c. butter	¼ tsp. salt
½ c. sugar	1 c. pecan halves
2 tsp. vanilla	¼ c. confectioners sugar (for
2 c. sifted flour	coating)

Beat butter until light; add sugar and vanilla and beat until mixture is fluffy.

Blend together flour and salt; stir into creamed mixture and mix well. With the fingers, shape rounded teaspoonfuls of dough around each pecan half. If dough is soft, chill before using. Cut pecan halves in two if necessary.

Place about 1" apart on lightly greased baking sheet; bake in moderate oven (350°) 15 to 18 minutes, or until a light brown. While cookies are still warm, roll in confectioners sugar. Cool on racks. Makes about 4½ dozen.

Variation

Coconut/Pecan Finger Cookies: Before baking cookies, dip them in

1 egg white beaten lightly with 1 tblsp. water and roll in ¾ c. flaked coconut.

PECAN PUFFS

Pecan cookie balls are snowy white with confectioners sugar coating

½ c. butter
½ c. regular margarine
6 tblsp. confectioners sugar
6 tblsp. water
2 tsp. vanilla

2 c. sifted flour
1 c. finely chopped pecans
¾ c. confectioners sugar (for coating)

Place butter, margarine, 6 tblsp. confectioners sugar, water, vanilla, flour and nuts in bowl. Mix with electric mixer at medium speed. Chill dough briefly, about 1 hour.

Pinch off pieces of dough about the size of walnuts. Roll between hands to form balls. Place 1½" apart on ungreased baking sheet. Bake in moderate oven (350°) 18 to 20 minutes. While warm, roll in confectioners sugar. Cool on racks. For a heavier coating, roll again in confectioners sugar when cool. Makes 4 dozen.

PEPPARKAKOR

Black pepper gives "bite" to these Swedish gingersnaps

1 c. sugar
1 c. butter or lard
1 c. light molasses
1 tsp. baking soda
1 tsp. salt

1 tblsp. ground ginger
½ tsp. black pepper
3½ c. sifted flour
Sugar (for dipping)

Cream sugar and butter until light and fluffy. Beat in molasses.

Sift together baking soda, salt, ginger, pepper and flour; add to creamed mixture and beat to mix well. Chill dough until easy to handle.

Shape dough with hands into balls the size of large marbles. Dip in sugar before baking. Place 1½" apart on lightly greased baking sheet.

Bake in moderate oven (350°) 12 to 15 minutes, or until lightly browned. Cool on baking sheet 1 minute, then transfer to rack to cool completely. Makes about 7 dozen.

PRETZEL COOKIES

Pretzel shape adds charm to a tray of assorted cookies—rich-tasting

⅔ c. butter
½ c. sugar
½ tsp. vanilla
3 eggs

⅛ tsp. salt
3 c. sifted flour
½ c. sugar (for dipping)
½ c. finely chopped walnuts

Cream butter with ½ c. sugar until light and fluffy. Beat in vanilla and 2 eggs to mix thoroughly. Combine salt and flour; add to creamed mixture. Knead dough until smooth. Set aside for 1 hour or longer.

Take up small portions of dough (the size of large walnuts) and roll under hands on pastry cloth or board into 7″ lengths with the diameter of a pencil. Form in pretzel shapes. Brush with remaining egg, slightly beaten, then dip tops in remaining ½ c. sugar and nuts.

Place about 1″ apart on ungreased baking sheet; bake in slow oven (325°) about 25 minutes, or until cookies are a very light brown. Remove cookies and cool on racks. Makes about 40.

RIBBON COOKIES

Colorful cookies for your party—serve them with steaming hot coffee

1 c. butter or regular margarine
1½ c. sugar
1 egg
1 tsp. vanilla
2½ c. sifted flour
1½ tsp. baking powder
½ tsp. salt

¼ c. chopped candied red cherries
¼ c. chopped candied green cherries
⅓ c. semisweet chocolate pieces, melted over hot, not boiling, water
¼ c. chopped pecans

Cream butter and sugar until light and fluffy. Add egg and vanilla; beat.

Sift together flour, baking powder and salt; blend half into butter-sugar mixture; stir in remaining flour mixture until blended.

Divide dough in three parts. Add red cherries to one, green cherries to second and chocolate and pecans to the third part.

Line bottom and sides of 9 x 5 x 3″ loaf pan with foil. Pat red cherry dough into bottom of pan; pat chocolate dough over this; pat green cherry dough over top. Press each layer down firmly. Cover and refrigerate for several hours.

Turn out of pan. Cut in half lengthwise. Slice each bar in ⅛″ thick slices. Place 1½″ apart on ungreased baking sheet. Bake in hot oven (400°) 10 to 12 minutes. Remove cookies and cool on racks. Makes 8 dozen.

SANDBAKELSER

In Sweden these fragile sand tarts are served upside down on blue plates—or fill upright tarts with whipped cream at serving time

⅓ c. blanched almonds	1 egg white
½ c. butter	1 tsp. vanilla
½ c. sugar	1¼ c. sifted flour

Put almonds through fine blade of food chopper twice. Set aside. Mix together well butter, sugar, unbeaten egg white and vanilla. Stir in flour and almonds. Cover and chill 2 hours or longer.

With lightly floured fingers, press dough over bottom and sides of sandbakelser molds (they're like tiny fluted tart pans). Press dough as thin as possible, or about ⅛″ thick. Set on ungreased baking sheet.

Bake in moderate oven (350°) about 12 minutes, or until very delicately browned. Cool 3 minutes or until molds are cool enough to handle. Tap molds lightly on table to loosen cookies. Cool on racks. Makes 2½ to 3 dozen, depending on size of molds and thinness of cookies.

SAND BALLS

Honey enhances flavor; roll twice in sugar for snowy white coating

1 c. butter	¼ tsp. salt
½ c. confectioners sugar	1 tsp. vanilla
2 tblsp. honey	¾ c. chopped walnuts
2¼ c. sifted flour	Confectioners sugar (for coating)

Cream butter, confectioners sugar and honey together thoroughly. Add flour, salt, vanilla and nuts. Mix with hands, if necessary, to blend well.

Form into balls 1″ in diameter and chill thoroughly.

To bake, place cookie balls 2½″ apart on greased baking sheet. Bake in moderate oven (375°) 14 to 17 minutes. While still warm, roll in confectioners sugar. Cool cookies on racks. Then roll in confectioners sugar again. Makes 4 dozen.

SNICKERDOODLES

Generations of boys and girls have returned home from school happy to find the kitchen fragrant with cinnamon-sugar and the cookie jar filled with freshly baked Snickerdoodles. These cookies are just as popular today as they were long ago. The Pennsylvania Dutch proudly claim them as their invention, but the cookies were not strangers in New England homes, for most of the very old regional cookbooks with age-yellowed pages include the recipe, as do later editions. Good recipes always have journeyed from one section of the country to another because women like to share their favorites. Evidence of this is the thousands of recipes they sent to FARM JOURNAL for possible use in this cookbook.

Recipes undergo changes with the years. Originally, Snickerdoodles often were either rolled or drop cookies, sprinkled with sugar and cinnamon. Many women today prefer to shape the dough in small, even-sized balls and to roll them in a cinnamon-sugar mixture, the true Cape Cod way. The molded cookies come from the oven in almost perfect rounds. Our recipe is for this kind.

SNICKERDOODLES

The crisp cookies with crinkly sugar-cinnamon tops always please

½ c. butter or regular margarine	2 tsp. cream of tartar
½ c. lard	1 tsp. baking soda
1½ c. sugar	¼ tsp. salt
2 eggs	2 tblsp. sugar
1 tsp. vanilla	1 tsp. ground cinnamon
2⅔ c. sifted flour	

Beat butter and lard until light; add 1½ c. sugar and beat until fluffy. Beat in eggs and vanilla.

Sift together flour, cream of tartar, baking soda and salt; add to beaten mixture.

Combine 2 tblsp. sugar and cinnamon.

Shape dough in small balls, about 1″, and roll in sugar-cinnamon mixture. Place 2″ apart on ungreased baking sheet. Bake in hot oven (400°) 8 to 10 minutes. (Cookies flatten during baking.) Remove cookies and cool on racks. Makes about 6 dozen.

SWIRLS

These decorative, two-color cookies will provide party conversation

1 c. butter or regular margarine	½ tsp. vanilla
½ c. sifted confectioners sugar	¼ tsp. almond extract
2¼ c. sifted flour	3 drops red food color
¼ tsp. salt	12 drops yellow food color

Beat butter until light; add confectioners sugar and beat until fluffy.

Sift together flour and salt and blend well into creamed mixture. Divide dough in half. Leave one half plain and blend vanilla into it with electric mixer on low speed. To remaining half add almond extract and food colors to produce an orange-colored dough. Chill thoroughly.

Take 1 teaspoonful plain dough and shape into a pencil-like roll 6″ long. Repeat with tinted dough. (If dough gets warm while working with it and sticks to surface, lightly flour surface.) Lay the two rolls side by side on ungreased baking sheet and coil them. Repeat with remaining dough, leaving 1″ between coils.

Bake in hot oven (400°) about 8 minutes, or until cookies are set but not browned. Remove cookies and cool on racks. Makes 3 dozen.

CRACKLED SUGAR COOKIES

An old-fashioned cookie: subtle lemon flavor, pretty, crinkled top

1 c. shortening (part butter)	¼ c. sugar
1½ c. sugar	1 tsp. grated orange peel
6 egg yolks, or 3 eggs, beaten	½ tsp. grated lemon peel
1 tsp. vanilla	2 tblsp. finely chopped black
½ tsp. lemon extract	walnuts
½ tsp. orange extract	½ tsp. ground nutmeg
2½ c. flour	1 tblsp. brown sugar
1 tsp. baking soda	2 tblsp. sugar
1 tsp. cream of tartar	¼ c. chocolate shot (jimmies)

Cream shortening and 1½ c. sugar until fluffy. Add yolks and flavorings; beat.

Combine flour, baking soda and cream of tartar; add to creamed mixture. Shape in 1″ balls. Divide balls in thirds.

Combine ¼ c. sugar with orange and lemon peels; roll one-third of balls in mixture.

Roll second third of balls in mixture of nuts, nutmeg, brown sugar and 2 tblsp. sugar.

Roll remaining balls in chocolate decorations (jimmies).

Place cookie balls about 2″ apart on ungreased baking sheet. Bake in moderate oven (350°) 12 to 15 minutes. Remove cookies and cool on racks. Makes about 5 dozen.

JUMBO SUGAR COOKIES

Extra-crisp, big, thin cookies with crinkled tops sell fast at bazaars

2 c. sugar	1 tsp. baking soda
1 c. shortening	1 tsp. salt
2 eggs	1 tsp. ground cinnamon
2 c. sifted flour	(for tops)
2 tsp. cream of tartar	2 tblsp. sugar (for tops)

Beat together 2 c. sugar and shortening until light and fluffy. Beat in eggs to mix thoroughly.

Sift together flour, cream of tartar, baking soda and salt. Stir into creamed mixture. On lightly floured waxed paper, form dough into four rolls, each about 12″ long and 1 to 1¼″ in diameter. Cut in 1″ slices. Dip tops of cookies in mixture of cinnamon and 2 tblsp. sugar. Place 3″ apart, cinnamon-sugar sides up, on greased baking sheet.

Bake in moderate oven (375°) about 12 minutes. Let stand on baking sheet 1 minute before removing to cooling racks. Makes 4 dozen.

MOLDED SUGAR COOKIES

Have won blue ribbons in baking contests—crisp crust, soft interior

2½ c. sifted flour	1 c. butter
2 tsp. cream of tartar	1 tsp. vanilla
1 tsp. baking soda	1 c. sugar
½ tsp. salt	2 eggs, beaten

Sift together flour, cream of tartar, baking soda and salt.

Cream butter, vanilla and sugar until light and fluffy. Add eggs and beat well. Add sifted dry ingredients, a fourth at a time, stirring to mix thoroughly. Chill 1 hour.

Shape dough in 1″ balls and place 2½″ apart on greased baking sheet. Flatten by pressing with bottom of drinking glass coated with sugar. (Dip bottom of glass in sugar before flattening each cookie.)

Bake in moderate oven (375°) 8 minutes, or until golden. Remove cookies to racks to cool. Makes about 5½ dozen.

DOUBLE VANILLA BARS

These cookies, twice flavored with vanilla, win praise and disappear fast. Keep Vanilla Sugar on hand for a gourmet touch in baking

5 egg yolks	3¾ c. sifted flour
1 c. plus 2 tblsp. sugar	⅛ tsp. salt
2 tsp. vanilla	Vanilla Sugar (recipe follows)
1 c. butter	

Beat egg yolks until light. Gradually beat in sugar, beating after each addition. Then beat 3 minutes longer. Beat in vanilla.

With pastry blender, cut butter into flour mixed with salt until particles are fine. Add to egg mixture and blend. Then knead with hands until dough is smooth. Chill 1 hour.

Pinch off dough, about 1 tblsp. at a time; flour hands and roll into strips about 2″ long and ½″ thick. Place 1″ apart on ungreased baking sheet.

Bake in moderate oven (350°) 12 to 15 minutes, or until golden brown. Cool about 3 minutes before removing from baking sheet to racks. Carefully dip each cookie while warm into Vanilla Sugar to coat completely. Cool, then dip again in Vanilla Sugar. (If you wish, you can use sifted confectioners sugar instead of the Vanilla Sugar.) Makes about 5½ dozen.

Vanilla Sugar: Sift 1 (1 lb.) pkg. confectioners sugar into a container with a tight-fitting lid. Split a vanilla bean (available at many spice and flavoring counters) lengthwise; cut up and add to container of sugar. Cover and let stand 3 days or longer before using. Sugar will keep for months if tightly covered. You will need about half of it to coat these cookies.

SPANISH WEDDING CAKES

You wrap these cookies with lemon flavor around almonds

1 c. butter
¼ c. sifted confectioners sugar
1 tblsp. grated lemon peel
1 tblsp. water
2½ c. sifted flour

¼ tsp. salt
½ c. whole blanched almonds (about)
¾ c. confectioners sugar (for coating)

Cream butter until light and fluffy. Stir in ¼ c. confectioners sugar, lemon peel and water.

Mix flour with salt; beat into butter mixture. Knead with hands until dough is light.

Pinch off 1 heaping teaspoonful of dough at a time; press it flat and then press it around a whole almond to cover completely. Shape like a little loaf. Place about 1" apart on lightly greased baking sheet.

Bake in moderate oven (350°) about 15 minutes, or until cookies start to brown around bottom. Take care not to overbake. Remove from baking sheets and cool 2 or 3 minutes on racks, then roll in confectioners sugar. Cool completely and then roll again in confectioners sugar. Store in airtight container. Makes about 4 dozen.

FROSTED YULE LOGS

Shape of yule logs adds interest to Christmas cookie tray or box

1 c. butter or regular margarine
¾ c. sugar
1 egg
1 tsp. vanilla
3 c. sifted flour

½ tsp. ground nutmeg
¼ c. sugar
1 c. finely chopped pecans
1 egg white

Beat butter until light; add ¾ c. sugar and beat until light and fluffy. Beat in egg and vanilla to blend well.

Sift together flour and nutmeg; stir into creamed mixture. Shape dough into fat pencil-shaped rolls, each about 2" long, to represent yule logs.

Combine remaining ¼ c. sugar and pecans. Beat egg white slightly. Dip yule logs into egg white and then roll in nut mixture. Place 1" apart on lightly greased baking sheet.

Bake in moderate oven (375°) about 10 minutes, until browned. Remove cookies and cool on racks. Makes 6 dozen.

Pressed Cookies

Give a cookie press to a woman who likes to bake and turn her loose in her kitchen. Sweet things happen—like tender-crisp, buttery-rich cookies in many designs. Spritz, the highly revered Swedish pressed cookies, are the kind most frequently made, but different forms or shapes, flavors and decorations result in great variety. It seems incredible that so many delicacies can come from the same dough until you start using a press.

Among the designs in spritz that attract attention are the letter cookies. You'll find two recipes for them in this section, Lindsborg Letter Spritz, from a Swedish-American community in Kansas, and Lemon Cookie Letters.

You'll want to try our Royal Crowns, a splendid pressed cookie in which hard-cooked egg yolks are an ingredient.

As the term "pressed" suggests, you put the dough through a cookie press with one of a variety of plates inserted to produce cookies of the shape desired. Women who bake this kind of cookie consider it easy and quick.

The beauty of pressed cookies is partly in their design or shape. They all taste wonderful. Serve them undecorated or fancied up as you wish. You can top them, before baking, with bits of candied fruits, raisins, currants or chopped nuts. Or you can add decorations after baking, arranging them in designs and securing them to the cookie with drops of corn syrup or egg white. Use coarse colored sugar, multicolored tiny candies, dragées or tiny red cinnamon candies for the trims. And if you're in the mood, tint the dough with food color before you put it in the press.

The dough for pressed cookies needs to be right. Butter is the first choice of fats, but you can use regular margarine or shortening. Be sure to have the fat at room temperature before you start to mix the dough. Beat it with the electric mixer at medium speed until soft, or beat it with a spoon. Gradually add the sugar, beating all the time, and continue beating until the mixture is light and fluffy, but do not overbeat.

When the dough is ready, test it by pressing a small amount through the press. It should be pliable and soft, but not crumbly. Unless the dough is soft or the recipe directs that you chill it, work with it at room temperature. Dough that's too cold crumbles. When the dough seems too soft, add 1 to 2 tblsp. flour; if too stiff, add 1 egg yolk.

Put about one-fourth of the dough in the press at a time. Hold the press so it rests on the baking sheet unless you are using a star or bar plate. Press dough onto a cool baking sheet; if it is warm, the fat in the dough melts and the cookies will not adhere to the sheet when you lift off the press. Do not remove press until the dough forms a well-defined design. You may need to wait a few seconds to give it time to cling to the baking sheet. You will not need to exert pressure on the press or the handle if the dough is right.

Pressed cookies are rich. Bake them on an ungreased baking sheet until they are set. You bake some pressed cookies until lightly browned around the edges, while others are not browned at all.

ORANGE/CHEESE COOKIES

Rows of ridges on cookies make them look like little washboards

1 c. butter or regular margarine	1 tblsp. orange juice
1 (3 oz.) pkg. cream cheese	2½ c. sifted flour
1 c. sugar	1 tsp. baking powder
1 egg	Dash of salt
1 tblsp. grated orange peel	

Combine butter and cream cheese; beat until light. Gradually add sugar, beating until mixture is fluffy. Beat in egg, orange peel and juice to blend thoroughly.

Sift together flour, baking powder and salt. Add to creamed mixture, blending well.

Put plate with narrow slit in cookie press. Put a fourth of dough into press at a time and press rows of strips of dough about 1″ apart onto ungreased baking sheet. With knife, mark strips in 2″ lengths.

Bake in moderate oven (375°) 8 to 10 minutes, until very delicately browned. Immediately cut strips into pieces on knife marks. Remove cookies and cool on racks. Makes about 12½ dozen.

NOTE: Sprinkle some of the cookies before baking with chocolate shot (jimmies) for a tasty, interesting touch.

PEANUT BUTTER PRESSED COOKIES

Glamorize peanut butter cookies by shaping them with cookie press

¾ c. butter or regular margarine
3 tblsp. peanut butter
½ c. sugar
1 egg yolk
½ tsp. vanilla or almond extract
1¾ c. sifted flour
¼ tsp. salt

Beat together butter and peanut butter until light. Gradually beat in sugar, beating until light and fluffy. Beat in egg yolk and vanilla to blend thoroughly.

Sift together flour and salt. Add to creamed mixture; mix to a smooth dough.

Fit desired plate into cookie press. Put one-fourth of the dough in cookie press at a time. Force cookies 1″ apart onto ungreased baking sheet. Bake in moderate oven (375°) 8 to 10 minutes, or until delicately brown. Remove cookies and cool on racks. Makes about 3 dozen.

ROYAL CROWNS

A tasty, unusual, regal addition to the holiday cookie collection

4 hard-cooked egg yolks
½ tsp. salt
1 c. butter or regular margarine
⅔ c. sugar
½ tsp. almond extract
2½ c. sifted flour
Red or green candied cherries

Force egg yolks through a coarse sieve with back of spoon. Add salt and mix.

Cream together butter and sugar until light and fluffy. Add almond extract and egg yolks. Add flour and mix well.

Place dough in cookie press. Force dough through crown design 1 to 2″ apart onto lightly greased baking sheet. Decorate with bits of candied cherries.

Bake in moderate oven (375°) 7 to 10 minutes. Remove cookies and cool on racks. Makes 6 dozen.

SPRITZ

Change shape of these tender cookies with different press plates

1 c. butter
⅔ c. confectioners sugar
1 egg
1 egg yolk

1 tsp. almond extract, vanilla or
¼ c. grated almonds
2½ c. sifted flour

Combine butter, sugar, egg, egg yolk and almond extract. Work in flour.

Use a fourth of the dough at a time; force it through cookie press 1″ apart onto ungreased baking sheet in desired shapes. Bake in hot oven (400°) 7 to 10 minutes, or until set but not browned. Remove cookies and cool on racks. Makes 4 to 6 dozen, depending on size.

CHOCOLATE SPRITZ

The potent chocolate flavor of these crisp cookies delights many. They add charming contrast to a tray of light-colored spritz

1 c. butter or regular margarine
⅔ c. sugar
1½ squares unsweetened
   chocolate, melted
3 egg yolks

1 tsp. vanilla, or ¾ tsp. almond
extract
⅛ tsp. salt
2½ c. sifted flour

Cream butter with sugar until light and fluffy. Beat in chocolate, egg yolks and vanilla. Stir salt into flour to mix thoroughly. Work into creamed mixture, a little at a time.

Divide dough into fourths and put each part through cookie press ½ to 1″ apart on ungreased baking sheet. (Use whatever shaped disk in press you like.)

Bake in hot oven (400°) 7 to 10 minutes, until cookies are set, but do not brown. Remove at once to racks to cool. Makes about 7 dozen.

NOTE: See recipe in Index for Date/Nut Kisses if you want to use leftover egg whites in a delicious treat.

SPRITZ CHOCOLATE SANDWICHES

Pretty-as-a-picture, special-occasion spritz taste simply great—slender cookies with chocolate filling and chocolate-nut ends

1 c. butter or regular margarine	½ tsp. salt
1¼ c. sifted confectioners sugar	Buttery Chocolate Frosting
1 egg	(recipe follows)
1 tsp. vanilla	1 c. chopped walnuts
2½ c. sifted flour	

Beat butter until light; gradually add sugar, beating after each addition. Beat until light and fluffy. Beat in egg and vanilla to blend well.

Sift together flour and salt. Gradually add to creamed mixture, mixing well.

Put star plate in cookie press. Place a fourth of dough in press at a time. Press out to make 2½" strips about 1" apart on ungreased baking sheet.

Bake in hot oven (400°) 6 to 8 minutes, or until very delicately browned. Place cookies at once on cooling rack. When cool, put cookies together in pairs with Buttery Chocolate Frosting between. Dip ends of sandwiches in the frosting and then in chopped nuts. Makes 69 sandwiches.

Buttery Chocolate Frosting: Beat 3 tblsp. butter until light and fluffy. Add 1½ squares unsweetened chocolate, melted. Beat in ¾ tsp. vanilla, ⅛ tsp. salt, 3½ c. sifted confectioners sugar and enough dairy half-and-half or light cream (about 6 tblsp.) to make frosting of spreading consistency.

PINEAPPLE SPRITZ

Decorate them with silver or colored dragées for special occasions

1½ c. butter or regular margarine	4½ c. sifted flour
	1 tsp. baking powder
1 c. sugar	Dash of salt
1 egg	Silver and colored dragées
2 tblsp. thawed frozen pineapple juice concentrate	(optional)

Beat together butter and sugar until light and fluffy. Beat in egg and pineapple juice concentrate to blend thoroughly.

Sift together flour, baking powder and salt. Add to creamed mixture, blending well. (Dough will be stiff.)

Put rosette or other plate into cookie press. Put a fourth of dough in press at a time. Press out dough designs about 1″ apart onto ungreased baking sheet. Decorate with silver and colored dragées.

Bake in moderate oven (375°) 8 to 10 minutes, until firm but not brown. Remove at once from baking sheet to cooling racks. Makes 9 dozen.

SCANDINAVIAN SPRITZ

Crisp, buttery-tasting, fragile—serve with fruit punch or coffee

2¼ c. sifted flour	¾ c. sugar
½ tsp. baking powder	3 egg yolks, beaten
¼ tsp. salt	1 tsp. almond extract, or ¼ c.
1 c. butter or regular margarine	grated almonds

Sift together flour, baking powder and salt.

Cream butter; add sugar gradually and beat until light. Add egg yolks and almond extract. Add dry ingredients; work with hands if dough seems crumbly.

Using a fourth of dough at a time, force it through cookie press 1 to 2″ apart onto ungreased baking sheet in desired shapes. Bake in hot oven (400°) 7 to 10 minutes, until set but not brown. Remove cookies and cool on racks. Makes about 6 dozen.

LEMON COOKIE LETTERS

Cookie initials will honor a guest, a school team or any occasion

1 c. butter or regular margarine	1 egg
½ c. sugar	2½ c. sifted flour
½ c. brown sugar, firmly packed	¼ tsp. baking soda
1 tsp. grated lemon peel	⅛ tsp. salt
1 tblsp. lemon juice	

Beat butter until light; beat in sugars until light and fluffy. Beat in lemon peel and juice and egg to blend thoroughly.

Sift together flour, baking soda and salt. Add to creamed mixture, blending well.

Fill press with a fourth of dough at a time. Press letters about 1″ apart on ungreased baking sheet. Bake in moderate oven (375°)

10 to 12 minutes, until light brown on edges. Remove from baking sheet to cooling racks. Makes about 8½ dozen.

LINDSBORG LETTER SPRITZ

A Kansas version of Swedish spritz—they always start conversation

1 c. butter or regular margarine	2 c. sifted flour
¾ c. sugar	1 tsp. baking powder
1 egg yolk	⅛ tsp. salt
¾ tsp. almond extract or vanilla	

Cream butter with sugar until light and fluffy. Beat in egg yolk and almond extract. Beat until very fluffy.

Sift together flour, baking powder and salt; gradually add to creamed mixture, beating with mixer on low speed. Beat just enough to blend. Shape dough in ball, wrap in waxed paper and chill several hours or overnight.

Let dough warm slightly before using (very cold dough does not easily leave press). Using cookie press with star-shaped disk, press out dough in long, straight strips on cold, ungreased baking sheet.

Cut each strip in 4" pieces and shape in letters such as S, R, A, B, Y, U and O (or shape as desired). You will need to add pieces of dough to form some letters. Place ½ to 1" apart on ungreased baking sheet.

Bake in moderate oven (350°) 8 to 10 minutes, or until edges of cookies are a golden brown. Remove cookies to wire racks and cool. Makes about 6 dozen.

N O T E : To store, pack in containers in layers with waxed paper between. Freeze or keep in a cool place.

Meringue Cookies

The old-fashioned name for these small, airy clouds of flavorful sweetness we call meringue cookies is "kisses." By whatever name, they're delicious. Serve them with red-ripe strawberries or juicy sliced peaches and cream or ice cream. Or garnish ice cream sundaes with our little puffs, Miniature Meringues. And if wondering what dessert to take to the picnic, consider non-gooey meringues as the companion to fruit to eat from the hand—grapes, sweet cherries or pears.

Meringues are versatile—you can use your ingenuity to add charm and flavor to them. For a Valentine luncheon or party, bake our Jeweled Meringues, dotted with tiny red cinnamon candies, in heart shape. Add chopped dates and nuts to meringue cookies and you have our Date/Nut Kisses, which enhance any assortment of holiday or special-occasion cookies.

Tint meringue in pastel shades with food colors before baking for color-schemed effects at showers and receptions. Sprinkle coarse red sugar over meringue rosettes and you'll have our Holiday Party Kisses. They look like lovely red and white roses on the cookie tray at open houses and inspire word bouquets to the hostess.

Meringues are easy to make. Beat the egg whites with the electric mixer at medium speed until foamy. Continue to beat while you gradually add the sugar. Then beat until mixture is stiff and glossy. Drop it from a teaspoon to form peaks or put it through a pastry tube with the rosette or one of the other tips. Space the meringues about 1″ apart on greased baking sheets or on brown paper spread on baking sheets. Bake until set; then remove from baking sheet and cool on racks in a place free of drafts. Notice the time for baking listed in the recipe you are using. Some meringue cookies come from the oven white, while others take on a delicate beige around the edges.

Thrifty women to this day think meringue cookies are the best way to use leftover egg whites.

COCONUT KISSES

If you like macaroons you'll enjoy these chewy, moist cookies

¼ tsp. salt
½ c. egg whites (4 medium)
1¾ c. sugar

½ tsp. vanilla or almond extract
2½ c. shredded coconut

Add salt to egg whites and beat until foamy. Gradually beat in sugar. Continue beating until mixture stands in stiff peaks and is glossy. Fold in vanilla and coconut.

Drop by heaping teaspoonfuls 2″ apart onto greased baking sheet. Bake in slow oven (325°) 20 minutes, or until delicately browned and set. Remove from baking sheet and cool on racks. Makes about 3 dozen.

Variations

Walnut Kisses: Substitute finely chopped walnuts for the coconut in recipe for Coconut Kisses.

Chocolate/Coconut Kisses: Follow directions for making Coconut Kisses, but stir in 1 square unsweetened chocolate, melted and cooled until lukewarm, before folding in coconut.

CORN FLAKE KISSES

An inexpensive sweet to serve with apples or grapes for dessert

¼ tsp. salt
2 egg whites
1 c. sugar

1 tsp. grated orange peel or
vanilla
3 c. corn flakes

Add salt to egg whites and beat until foamy. Gradually beat in sugar. Continue beating until mixture stands in peaks and is glossy. Fold in orange peel and corn flakes.

Drop by teaspoonfuls 2″ apart onto greased baking sheet. Bake in moderate oven (350°) 15 to 18 minutes, or until set and delicately browned. Remove from baking sheet and cool on racks. Makes about 3 dozen.

DATE/NUT KISSES

You can depend on these easy-to-make party treats to please

3 egg whites	1 tsp. vanilla
1 c. sugar	¾ c. chopped walnuts
¼ tsp. salt	¾ c. chopped dates

Put egg whites, sugar, salt and vanilla in top of double boiler; stir to blend. Place over boiling water and beat with rotary beater until mixture stands in peaks. (To prevent meringues from being lumpy, scrape bottom and sides of pan occasionally with rubber scraper.) Stir in nuts and dates at once.

Drop heaping teaspoonfuls of mixture about 2″ apart onto lightly greased baking sheets (let one sheet wait while you bake the other).

Bake in slow oven (300°) 12 to 15 minutes, or until very lightly browned. Remove from baking sheet immediately and cool on racks. Makes about 40.

N O T E : Date/Nut Kisses offer an ideal way to use the 3 leftover egg whites when you make Chocolate Spritz (see Index).

HOLIDAY PARTY KISSES

Red and green rosettes—the small meringues are perfect for Christmas

3 egg whites	¾ c. sugar
⅛ tsp. salt	Red and green decorating sugar
⅛ tsp. cream of tartar	

Beat egg whites with electric mixer at medium speed until froth starts to appear. Add salt and cream of tartar. Continue beating for 5 minutes, or until soft peaks form. Gradually add half the white sugar, beating constantly; then beat 5 minutes. Add remaining half of white sugar in the same way. After beating for 5 minutes, continue beating until the sugar is completely dissolved.

Remove beater and place the meringue mixture in a pastry tube with rosette end. Press it out to make rosettes 1″ apart on brown paper spread over a baking sheet. (Or drop mixture from teaspoon.) Sprinkle half the meringues with red sugar, the other half with green sugar.

Bake in very slow oven (250°) 1 hour, or until meringues are firm, but not browned. (When done, meringues should lift off paper easily.) Remove from paper and cool on racks. Makes 26.

N O T E : When making meringues or kisses, or anything that uses only egg whites, slip the leftover yolks into a wire sieve immersed in a pan of simmering water. Simmer for 5 minutes. Remove and dry, then press the yolks through the sieve. Use to garnish salads, cooked buttered vegetables, creamed vegetables, soups and other dishes. One wonderful way to salvage egg yolks is to make Hard-Cooked Egg Cookies or Royal Crowns (see Index).

DEBBIE'S PEPPERMINT KISSES

A 12-year-old Hoosier girl bakes these for her mother's parties

4 egg whites	1½ c. brown sugar, firmly
¼ tsp. salt	packed
¼ tsp. cream of tartar	1 (12 oz.) pkg. semisweet
1 tsp. peppermint extract	chocolate pieces

Beat egg whites, salt, cream of tartar and peppermint extract together until soft peaks form.

Add brown sugar gradually, beating all the time. Beat until stiff peaks form.

Set aside 48 chocolate pieces and fold remainder into egg white mixture.

Drop teaspoonfuls 1″ apart onto plain paper spread on baking sheet. Top each with a chocolate piece.

Bake in slow oven (300°) 20 to 25 minutes, or until set and slightly brown. Remove from paper while slightly warm, this way: Remove paper from baking sheet, spread a wet towel on the hot baking sheet and place the paper of kisses on top. Let stand only 1 minute. The steam will loosen the kisses and they will slip off easily on a spatula. Makes about 4 dozen.

N O T E : Instead of plain paper, you can line the baking sheet with waxed paper.

PINK KISSES

These lovely pink meringues are chewy like coconut macaroons

1 (3 oz.) pkg. strawberry flavor gelatin	⅔ c. egg whites (about 5 to 7)
1 c. sugar	¾ tsp. almond extract
¼ tsp. salt	1 (3½ oz.) can flaked coconut

Combine gelatin, sugar and salt.

Beat egg whites at high speed on electric mixer, gradually adding gelatin-sugar mixture. Add almond extract and continue beating until glossy and stiff peaks form. Stir in coconut.

Place brown paper on baking sheet. Drop mixture by heaping teaspoonfuls about 1″ apart onto paper. Bake in very slow oven (275°) 35 to 40 minutes. Remove from paper and cool on racks. Makes 62.

Variation

Pink Raspberry Kisses: Substitute raspberry flavor gelatin for the strawberry, and bake as directed.

JEWELED MERINGUES FOR ENTERTAINING

These cookies have an easy-do aspect: You put the meringues in the oven in the evening, turn off the heat and forget them until morning when they'll be baked. Place them in a container, cover loosely with waxed paper and set in a cool place.

If you wish, you can freeze them. Wrap each meringue in plastic wrap and place in a plastic bag, or wrap with heavy-duty aluminum foil. They'll stay in good condition up to a month. To use, take meringues from bag or remove foil and let stand at room temperature in their individual wraps for 4 to 6 hours. Then unwrap and serve.

The cinnamon candies do not melt during baking. In addition to contributing flashes of bright color to the snowy-white meringues, and a texture contrast, they provide a taste of cinnamon. They're especially appropriate for the yuletide season and for Valentine parties, when touches of red in food are so inviting. Many hostesses like to serve the meringues with ice cream.

JEWELED MERINGUES

Especially pretty for a Valentine special—if shaped like hearts

2 egg whites	½ tsp. vanilla
⅛ tsp. salt	½ c. red cinnamon candies (red
½ tsp. cream of tartar	hots)
¾ c. sugar	

Beat egg whites until foamy. Add salt and cream of tartar. Beat until stiff peaks form. Add sugar, 1 tblsp. at a time, beating after each addition. Stir in vanilla. Fold in candies.

Drop mixture by teaspoonfuls 1 to 1½" apart onto lightly greased baking sheet. Place in moderate oven (350°); turn off heat. Leave in oven overnight. (Do not open oven door before at least 2 hours have passed.) Meringues do not brown. Remove from baking sheet and cool on racks. Makes 25.

MERINGUES À LA BELLE

Crackers give these crunchy, crisp kisses a faint salty taste

3 egg whites	1 tsp. vanilla
¾ c. sugar	⅔ c. crushed saltine crackers
½ tsp. baking powder	½ c. chopped nuts

Beat egg whites until frothy. Gradually add sugar, beating until meringue stands in soft peaks; scrape bottom and sides of bowl occasionally with rubber spatula. Blend in baking powder and vanilla. Fold in crackers and nuts.

Drop mixture by rounded teaspoonfuls 1" apart onto two lightly greased baking sheets. Bake one sheet at a time in slow oven (300°) about 20 minutes. Remove from baking sheets at once and cool on racks. Makes about 3 dozen.

MINIATURE MERINGUES

Serve these atop or alongside fruit, chocolate or other sundaes

1 large egg white	⅓ c. very fine granulated sugar
Few grains salt	(superfine)
	¼ tsp. vanilla

With electric mixer at medium speed, beat egg white and salt until mixture stands in soft, tilted peaks. Beat in sugar, 1 tblsp. at a time; continue beating until sugar is dissolved. (Rub a little of mixture between thumb and forefinger to determine if grains of sugar are dissolved.) Stir in vanilla.

Drop by rounded teaspoonfuls 1″ apart onto well-greased baking sheet. Bake in very slow oven (250°) 45 minutes, until firm and crisp, but not browned. Remove with metal spatula to wire racks to cool. Store in container with loose-fitting lid, or freeze in tightly covered container. Use to garnish ice cream or as an accompaniment to it. Makes 20 to 24.

BIT O' NUT SWEETS

Meringue cookies that taste like candy. So little work and so good

2 egg whites	½ c. chopped dates
2 c. brown sugar, firmly packed	½ c. chopped candied lemon
2 c. sliced Brazil nuts	peel, or other candied fruit

Beat egg whites until stiff. Beat in brown sugar gradually. Work in nuts, dates and lemon peel. Drop by teaspoonfuls 1″ apart onto greased baking sheet.

Bake in very slow oven (250°) 30 minutes. Remove from baking sheet immediately and cool on racks. Makes about 5 dozen.

Variation

Double Date Sweets: Omit candied lemon peel, and increase amount of chopped dates to 1 c.

Cookie Confections

To make cookie confections is to cook young. They're short on work, long on good eating.

No need to get out your electric mixer to make cookie confections. Nor will you have to heat the oven for some of them. Holiday Fruit Bars, for instance. Full of good things, such as dates, candied cherries, nuts and vanilla wafers, the bars are "No-Bake." Chocolate/ Peanut Crunchers also skip the oven.

Another characteristic of many cookie confections is the absence of flour from the ingredient list. Substituting for it often are foods made with flour or from grains, such as graham crackers, whole or in crumbs, vanilla wafers, rolled oats and other cereal representatives from supermarket shelves.

All cookie confections are a cross between cookies and candy; those that contain no food made with flour or cereals are more candy-like. Date/Coconut Balls and Carnival Candy Cookies are two tasty examples. It's this union of cookie and candy qualities that makes them "confections."

Look at the recipe for Basic Graham Cracker Mix and the intriguing cookies in which it appears. You press the mix into a pan, spread or pour on something luscious, bake, cool and cut it into bars. For example, an easy chocolate filling makes Fudgies distinctive; the refreshing lemon tang in Lemon-Filled Bars explains why hostesses like to serve them with fruit salads.

You'll find great variety in our cookie confections. In some— Swedish Almond Creams, for instance—you lay graham crackers over the bottom of the pan, top with filling and bake. You take a couple more steps with Graham Cracker Bars: Top the filling with a layer of graham crackers and spread on frosting. These are make-ahead specials; you refrigerate them overnight before cutting in bars and serving. You get them ready the day before your party.

The adaptability of cookie confections deserves as much credit for their astonishing success as the ease with which you fix them.

They're the answer to so many occasions. For snacking they have few equals and Potpourri Cookies are outstanding in this category. To make them you melt together chocolate pieces, marshmallows and butter and pour the mixture over crisp, oven-toasted rice cereal, salted peanuts and broken pretzel sticks. Your friends will enjoy nibbling on them while watching television with you.

Today's youngsters like quick results and turn to confection-making —easier to make than candy, and the results are foolproof. Join the ranks of up-to-date cooks and build up your repertoire of cookie confections from the recipes that follow.

BASIC GRAHAM CRACKER MIX

This is the starting point for any of the four recipes that follow

2¼ c. graham cracker crumbs
½ c. melted butter
½ c. sugar

Combine all ingredients, and use as directed.

COCONUT CARAMEL BARS

With the basic mix on hand, you can have cookies in 20 minutes

Basic Graham Cracker Mix   ⅓ c. light or heavy cream
28 caramels (½ lb.)   1 c. flaked coconut

Press two-thirds Basic Graham Cracker Mix over bottom of 13 x 9 x 2″ pan.

Melt caramels with cream over hot water. Stir in coconut. Spoon here and there over crumbs in pan. Spread carefully to cover crumbs. Sprinkle with remaining third of graham cracker mix; press down firmly.

Bake in moderate oven (375°) 15 minutes. Cool partially in pan set on rack; then cut in 3 x 1″ bars, or any desired size. Makes 39.

Variation

Nut Caramel Bars: Substitute 1 c. chopped nuts for coconut in Coconut Caramel Bars.

FUDGIES

The easy-to-make fudge filling makes these chocolate-delicious

Basic Graham Cracker Mix
1 (15 oz.) can sweetened
  condensed milk (not
  evaporated)

1 (6 oz.) pkg. semisweet
  chocolate pieces
½ c. chopped nuts

Press two-thirds Graham Cracker Mix over bottom of 13 x 9 x 2" pan.

Heat sweetened condensed milk in saucepan. Blend in chocolate pieces and stir until mixture thickens. Stir in nuts. Pour evenly over mix in pan. Sprinkle with remaining third of mix. Press down firmly.

Bake in moderate oven (375°) 15 minutes. Cool slightly in pan set on rack; then cut in 2" squares, or desired size. Makes 2 dozen.

LEMON-FILLED BARS

Serve these tangy lemon bars with dessert fruit cups and salads

Basic Graham Cracker Mix
2 eggs, slightly beaten
½ c. water
1 c. sugar

3 tblsp. lemon juice
2 tsp. grated lemon peel
2 tblsp. butter

Press all but 1 c. Graham Cracker Mix over bottom of 13 x 9 x 2" pan.

Combine remaining ingredients, except mix, in saucepan. Cook over low heat, stirring constantly, until very thick and clear. Pour over basic mix in pan. Sprinkle on remaining mix; press down.

Bake in moderate oven (375°) 20 minutes. Partially cool in pan set on rack; then cut in 3 x 1" bars, or desired size. Makes 39.

MATRIMONIAL GRAHAM BARS

You'll like the happy marriage of date and graham cracker flavors

Basic Graham Cracker Mix
1½ c. halved pitted dates

⅔ c. water
¼ c. sugar

Press two-thirds of Basic Graham Cracker Mix over bottom of 13 x 9 x 2" pan.

Cook dates, water and sugar together until thick and smooth, stirring frequently. Spoon here and there over crumbs in pan; spread carefully to cover. Sprinkle remaining third of basic mix over date filling; press down firmly.

Bake in moderate oven (375°) 15 minutes. Partially cool in pan set on rack; then cut in 3 x 1″ bars, or desired size. Makes 39.

CANDY BAR COOKIES

Here's the top favorite new recipe from an experienced cookie baker

½ c. butter or regular margarine	1 c. flaked coconut
1 c. fine graham cracker crumbs	1 c. broken nuts
1 (6 oz.) pkg. semisweet chocolate pieces	1 (15 oz.) can sweetened condensed milk (not evaporated)
1 (6 oz.) pkg. butterscotch pieces	

Melt butter in 13 x 9 x 2″ pan. Sprinkle graham cracker crumbs evenly over bottom of pan. Then sprinkle on chocolate pieces. Next sprinkle on butterscotch pieces, then the coconut. Sprinkle on nuts. Dribble sweetened condensed milk over top.

Bake in moderate oven (375°) about 25 minutes. Set pan on rack and cut in 3 x 1″ bars when partly cooled, but while still warm. Remove from pan when cool. Makes 39 bars.

CHOCOLATE/COCONUT BARS

Many popular cookies contain graham crackers—here's a good one

2 c. crushed graham crackers	1 (15 oz.) can sweetened condensed milk (not evaporated)
¼ c. sugar	
½ c. melted butter or regular margarine	2 c. flaked coconut
	1 (6 oz.) pkg. semisweet chocolate pieces

Combine graham crackers, sugar and butter. Mix well and pat into ungreased 13 x 9 x 2″ pan. Bake in moderate oven (350°) 15 minutes.

Combine sweetened milk and coconut. Spread on baked layer. Return to oven and bake 15 minutes longer.

Melt chocolate pieces and spread over baked layers. Cool in pan set on rack, then cut in 2½ x 1¼″ bars. Makes about 3 dozen.

DATE MALLOW CHEWS

Three sure-fire goodies in these bars: dates, nuts and marshmallows

½ c. butter
1 (10½ oz.) pkg. miniature
  marshmallows
1¼ c. cut-up dates
2 c. graham cracker crumbs

½ c. chopped nuts
1 square semisweet chocolate
2 tblsp. milk
1 tblsp. butter
1 c. confectioners sugar

Melt ½ c. butter in 3-qt. saucepan. Add marshmallows and cook over low heat until melted, stirring constantly. Stir in dates, graham cracker crumbs and nuts. Press into buttered 9″ square pan.

Combine chocolate, milk and 1 tblsp. butter in small saucepan over low heat; stir constantly until chocolate and butter are melted. Stir in confectioners sugar. Spread over mixture in pan. Let stand in pan until set, then cut in 1½″ squares. Makes 3 dozen.

DATE/MARSHMALLOW BALLS

Skip-the-oven cookies, sweet and rich—a real confection treat

1½ c. chopped dates
1¼ c. chopped nuts
2 c. miniature marshmallows

3½ c. graham cracker crumbs
1 (6½ oz.) pkg. fluffy white
  frosting mix

Combine dates, 1 c. nuts, marshmallows and 2½ c. graham cracker crumbs. Mix thoroughly.

Prepare frosting mix as directed on package. Add to the date mixture and mix until completely moistened.

Combine remaining ¼ c. nuts and 1 c. graham cracker crumbs in small bowl.

Form date mixture into 1½″ balls. Roll in graham cracker crumbs and nuts. Store in covered container at least 12 hours to mellow. Makes 3 dozen.

FRUITCAKE SQUARES

This holiday bar cookie was rated "yummy" by taste-testers

6 tblsp. butter or regular margarine
1½ c. graham cracker crumbs
1 c. shredded coconut
2 c. cut-up mixed candied fruit
1 c. dates

Flour
1 c. coarsely chopped walnuts or pecans
1 (15 oz.) can sweetened condensed milk (not evaporated)

Melt butter in 15½ x 10½ x 1" jelly roll pan. Sprinkle on crumbs; tap sides of pan to distribute crumbs evenly. Sprinkle on coconut. Distribute candied fruit as evenly as possible over coconut.

Cut dates into a small amount of flour so they won't stick together. Distribute dates over candied fruit. Sprinkle on nuts. Press mixture lightly with hands to level it in pan. Pour sweetened condensed milk evenly over top.

Bake in moderate oven (350°) 25 to 30 minutes. Cool completely in pan on rack before cutting in 1½" squares. Remove from pan. Makes 70.

GRAHAM CRACKER BARS

Simple start with graham crackers ends up with elegant cookies

30 graham crackers
1 c. brown sugar, firmly packed
½ c. butter or regular margarine
½ c. milk
1 c. flaked coconut

1 c. graham cracker crumbs
2 c. confectioners sugar
5 tblsp. melted butter
3 tblsp. dairy half-and-half
½ tsp. vanilla

Line bottom of greased 13 x 9 x 2" pan with 15 graham crackers.

In saucepan, combine brown sugar, ½ c. butter, milk, coconut and graham cracker crumbs. Bring to a boil and cook, stirring constantly, until thick, about 10 minutes. (Mixture burns easily.) Spread evenly on top of whole graham crackers in pan. Top with remaining 15 graham crackers to cover.

Beat together confectioners sugar, melted butter, dairy half-and-half and vanilla until mixture is smooth. Spread on top of graham crackers in pan.

Cover with waxed paper and let stand in refrigerator overnight before cutting in 3 x 1" bars. Makes 39.

JIFFY CANDY COOKIES

Children like to make these cookies that taste like candy bars

18 graham crackers, broken into small pieces
1 (15 oz.) can sweetened condensed milk (not evaporated)
1 (6 oz.) pkg. semisweet chocolate pieces
½ c. chopped pecans
½ c. flaked coconut

Combine all ingredients. Pour into greased 8" square pan. Bake in moderate oven (350°) 35 minutes.

While warm, cut in 1½" squares and place on cooling rack. Makes about 25.

N O T E : These cookies will firm when cool.

MAGIC COOKIE BARS

Cut bars to fit appetites—these cookies are almost like candy

½ c. regular margarine, melted
1½ c. graham cracker crumbs
1 c. chopped nuts
1 (6 oz.) pkg. semisweet chocolate pieces
1 (6 oz.) pkg. butterscotch pieces
1½ c. flaked coconut
1 (15 oz.) can sweetened condensed milk (not evaporated)

Cover bottom of 13 x 9 x 2" pan with melted margarine. Sprinkle evenly with graham cracker crumbs.

Sprinkle nuts, then chocolate pieces, butterscotch morsels and coconut over crumbs. Pour sweetened condensed milk over coconut.

Bake in moderate oven (350°) 25 to 30 minutes, until lightly browned. Cool in pan set on rack 15 minutes, then cut in 3 x 1½" bars. Lift from pan with spatula and complete cooling on rack. Makes 2 dozen.

PRALINE COOKIES

"Child pleasers" . . . these candy-like cookies are made in minutes

24 graham crackers
1 c. light brown sugar, firmly packed
½ c. butter or regular margarine
1 c. chopped pecans

Line the bottom of a greased 15½ x 10½ x 1" jelly roll pan with graham crackers.

Place brown sugar and butter in small saucepan; bring to a rolling boil over medium heat and cook 1½ minutes. Remove from heat. When mixture has stopped bubbling, stir in nuts. Spoon it on and spread over graham crackers.

Bake in moderate oven (350°) 10 minutes. Cool in pan on rack, then cut in 2 x 1″ bars. Makes about 48.

SEVEN-LAYER BARS

Just layer ingredients in pan—easy and delicious

¼ c. butter or regular margarine
1 c. graham cracker crumbs
1 c. shredded coconut
1 (6 oz.) pkg. semisweet chocolate pieces

1 (6 oz.) pkg. butterscotch pieces
1 (15 oz.) can sweetened condensed milk (not evaporated)
1 c. chopped nuts

Melt butter in 13 x 9 x 2″ pan. Sprinkle crumbs evenly over butter; tap sides of pan to distribute crumbs evenly. Sprinkle on coconut, chocolate and butterscotch pieces.

Pour sweetened condensed milk (not evaporated) evenly over top. Sprinkle on nuts and press lightly into pan.

Bake in moderate oven (350°) 30 minutes. Cool in pan on rack, then cut in 2 x 1″ bars. Makes about 40.

SWEDISH ALMOND CREAMS

Creamy almond candy on crisp graham crackers—wonderful taste

15 graham crackers
¼ c. light or heavy cream
¾ c. sugar
¼ c. light corn syrup

½ c. butter
¾ c. sliced almonds
¼ tsp. almond extract

Arrange graham crackers to cover bottom of heavily buttered 13 x 9 x 2″ pan.

Combine cream, sugar, corn syrup and butter in small saucepan; boil 3 minutes. Stir in almond slices and extract. Pour over crackers in pan.

Bake in moderate oven (375°) 10 minutes, or until lightly browned. Partially cool on rack, then cut in 3 x 1″ bars. Makes 39.

THREE-LAYER CHOCOLATE SQUARES

The cookies to make when your oven is busy—they taste wonderful

½ c. butter or regular margarine	1 tsp. cornstarch
¼ c. cocoa	2 tsp. sugar
½ c. sifted confectioners sugar	3 tblsp. light cream or
1 egg, slightly beaten	evaporated milk
2 tsp. vanilla	1 tsp. vanilla
3 c. graham cracker crumbs	2 c. sifted confectioners sugar
½ c. chopped pecans	1 (9¾ oz.) sweet chocolate
¼ c. butter or regular margarine	candy bar

Melt ½ c. butter. Add the following ingredients, one at a time, stirring after each addition: cocoa, ½ c. confectioners sugar, egg, 2 tsp. vanilla, cracker crumbs and pecans. Stir until mixture is well blended, then press it into lightly greased 13 x 9 x 2" pan.

Melt ¼ c. butter. Combine cornstarch and 2 tsp. sugar; add to butter and blend thoroughly. Add cream; cook, stirring constantly, until thick and smooth. Cool; add 1 tsp. vanilla and 2 c. confectioners sugar. Blend well and spread over first layer. (Drop by teaspoonfuls and spread carefully—this is a stiff mixture.)

Melt chocolate bar over hot water; spread it over the cream filling. Cool in pan on rack, and cut in 1" squares before chocolate sets completely. Makes about 9 dozen.

HALLOWEEN TREATS

Let your youngsters make these cookies for trick or treat visitors

2 c. sugar	1 tsp. vanilla
⅔ c. milk	1¼ c. crumbled soda crackers
6 tblsp. peanut butter	(40 squares)

Heat together sugar and milk in 2-qt. saucepan; boil 3 minutes. Remove from heat; add peanut butter. Then add vanilla and crackers. Mix well. Cool, then form into 1" balls. Makes 34.

COCONUT/CORN FLAKE CRISPIES

Chocolate topknots help to make party cookies out of the cereal base

3 egg whites	2 c. crushed corn flakes
¼ tsp. salt	1⅓ c. flaked coconut
1 c. sugar	½ c. chopped pecans
1 tsp. vanilla	

Beat egg whites until frothy; add salt and gradually beat in sugar. Continue beating until very stiff and glossy. Stir in vanilla, corn flakes, coconut and pecans.

Drop heaping teaspoonfuls of dough 2″ apart onto ungreased brown wrapping paper covering baking sheet.

Bake in slow oven (325°) 15 to 18 minutes, until set and delicately browned. Remove from oven and lift off paper holding cookies; lay wet towel on hot baking sheet. Place paper of cookies on towel; let stand 1 minute (steam will loosen cookies). Lift cookies with spatula to cooling rack. Makes 40.

Variations

Chocolate/Coconut Crispies: Make like Coconut/Corn Flake Crispies, but stir 2 squares unsweetened chocolate, melted and slightly cooled, into batter. Bake as directed.

Chocolate-Topped Crispies: Melt together over hot water 1 (6 oz.) pkg. milk chocolate pieces, 2 tblsp. shortening and 2 tblsp. shaved paraffin. Hold the baked cookies, one at a time, in the hand and dip tops in mixture.

PEANUT CHEWS

Peanut butter fans will like these crunchy cookies—fine for snacks

9 c. corn flakes	¼ c. butter or regular margarine
1½ c. sugar	¾ c. water
¼ tsp. salt	2 tsp. vanilla
¾ c. light corn syrup	½ c. crunchy peanut butter

Place corn flakes in a bowl.

Combine sugar, salt, corn syrup, butter and water in saucepan. Bring to a boil and reduce heat. Continue to cook to the hard ball stage (250°), using care not to overcook.

Remove from heat and stir in vanilla and peanut butter. Pour mixture over corn flakes.

Toss with a fork to cover corn flakes with syrup completely. Work quickly.

Drop in clusters onto waxed paper. Makes about 40.

PEANUT BUTTER DROPS

A quick confection; nutritious too—children like these

1 c. sugar	4 c. ready-to-eat high protein
1 c. light corn syrup	cereal
½ c. peanut butter	1 c. thin pretzel sticks, broken in 1″ lengths

Mix sugar and syrup in large saucepan. Bring to a boil over medium heat; cook about 30 seconds. Remove from heat and add peanut butter. Stir until smooth. Stir in cereal and pretzel sticks.

Drop by tablespoonfuls onto waxed paper. Makes about 4½ dozen.

DATE/COCONUT BALLS

Snowy coconut decorates these baked-in-a-skillet date cookies

2 tblsp. butter	½ c. chopped nuts
1 c. sugar	2 c. oven-toasted rice cereal
2 eggs, beaten	1 c. flaked coconut
1 c. chopped dates	

Put butter in heavy skillet with sugar, eggs and dates. Cook over medium-low heat, stirring constantly, until mixture leaves sides of skillet. (Mixture burns easily.)

Remove from heat; add nuts and cereal. Shape in 1″ balls with hands; roll in coconut. Store in tightly covered container (cookies are good keepers). Makes 38.

COCONUT CRISPS

Cookie bars, luscious with dates, nuts and snowy coconut topknots

6 c. oven-toasted rice cereal	¼ tsp. salt
1 c. chopped walnuts	1 c. chopped dates
¾ c. butter or regular margarine	1 tblsp. vanilla
1¼ c. sugar	2 tblsp. lemon juice
2 tblsp. milk	1 (3½ oz.) can flaked coconut

Combine cereal and walnuts in greased 13 x 9 x 2″ pan.

Combine butter, sugar, milk, salt and dates in saucepan. Cook to the soft ball stage (240°); stir occasionally. Remove from heat and add vanilla and lemon juice.

Pour hot syrup over cereal/nut mixture; stir lightly to coat cereal. Spread mixture evenly in pan. Sprinkle coconut over top and press mixture firmly into pan. Let set 4 hours or longer.

When firm, cut in 3 x 1¼″ bars. Makes 2½ dozen.

POTPOURRI COOKIES

Perfect snack to munch on while watching television or visiting

1 (6 oz.) pkg. semisweet chocolate pieces	2 c. salted Spanish peanuts
½ c. butter or regular margarine	2 c. raisins
1 (10 oz.) pkg. marshmallows	2 c. broken pretzel sticks (about ½″ lengths)
4 c. oven-toasted rice cereal	

Melt chocolate pieces, butter and marshmallows in top of double boiler over simmering water. Stir to blend.

Combine rice cereal, peanuts, raisins and broken pretzel sticks in a greased large bowl. Pour melted chocolate mixture over and stir to coat all pieces. With two teaspoons form into clusters; drop onto greased baking sheets. Cool until set. Makes 5 dozen.

PUFFED-UP RICE FINGERS

Candied fruits add color and flavor to these crunchy cereal bars

5 c. puffed rice
¼ c. diced mixed candied fruit
½ c. coarsely chopped nuts
½ c. sugar
¾ c. dark corn syrup

⅓ c. water
½ tsp. salt
1 tblsp. butter or regular margarine

Spread puffed rice in shallow pan and heat in moderate oven (350°) about 10 minutes. Then turn into a greased large bowl. Stir in fruit and nuts.

In medium-size saucepan stir together sugar, corn syrup, water and salt. Cook over medium heat to soft ball stage (236° on candy thermometer). Stir in butter.

Stir hot syrup mixture into puffed rice until evenly coated. Using greased hands, pack mixture firmly into greased 13 x 9 x 2" pan. Cut in 3 x 1" bars. Makes 39.

CHOCOLATE OATSIES

Shortcut to hospitality—make these fast-fix, candy-good cookies

2 c. sugar
½ c. milk
¼ c. butter or regular margarine
⅓ c. cocoa

3 c. quick-cooking rolled oats
½ c. flaked or shredded coconut
½ c. peanut butter
1 tsp. vanilla

Combine sugar, milk, butter and cocoa in saucepan. Boil 1 minute. Remove from heat.

Mix in rest of ingredients.

Drop by teaspoonfuls onto waxed paper. Makes 30.

FARMHOUSE CHOCOLATE CRUNCH

These chewy cookies containing black walnuts are cousins of candy

⅔ c. butter or regular margarine
½ c. light corn syrup
1 tsp. salt
3 tsp. vanilla
1 c. brown sugar, firmly packed

4 c. quick-cooking rolled oats
2 (6 oz.) pkgs. semisweet chocolate pieces
½ c. chopped black walnuts

Melt butter in a large saucepan. Add syrup, salt, vanilla, brown

sugar and rolled oats; mix well. Press into a well-greased 15½ x
10½ x 1" jelly roll pan.

Bake in hot oven (425°) 12 minutes. During the last 2 minutes
of baking, sprinkle on chocolate pieces. When they melt, remove pan
from oven and spread chocolate evenly to cover top. Sprinkle with
chopped nuts. Cut in 1½" squares while still warm. Cool in pan on
rack. Recut when cool. Makes about 70.

PEANUT CANDY-BAR COOKIES

Chewy, toffee-like bars topped with tasty peanut-chocolate

2 c. quick-cooking rolled oats	1 tsp. vanilla
1 c. graham cracker crumbs	½ c. salted peanuts
¾ c. brown sugar, firmly packed	1 (6 oz.) pkg. semisweet
½ c. melted butter	chocolate pieces
½ c. dark corn syrup	½ c. peanut butter
¼ tsp. baking soda	

Combine all ingredients, except chocolate pieces and peanut butter. Spread or press into greased 13 x 9 x 2" pan. Bake in moderate
oven (375°) 15 to 20 minutes, or until light golden brown.

Meanwhile, melt together chocolate pieces and peanut butter over
hot water. Spread over baked cookie while warm. Cool slightly in pan
set on rack, then cut in 3 x 1" bars. Makes 39.

CEREAL SLICES

These crunchy confection cookies really rate high with youngsters

½ c. butter	4 c. assorted bite-size shredded
1 (10½ oz.) pkg. miniature	cereal biscuits (wheat, rice
marshmallows	and corn)
2 c. salted peanuts	

Melt butter in 3-qt. saucepan. Add marshmallows and cook over
low heat, stirring constantly, until melted. Stir in nuts and cereals
(oat puffs are good included in this combination).

Divide mixture in half on sheets of foil or waxed paper. Shape
each half in a 15" long roll, using fork and side of foil or waxed paper
to aid in the shaping. Wrap rolls tightly and refrigerate until firm. To
serve, cut in ½" slices. Makes 5 dozen.

CHOCOLATE/PEANUT CRUNCHERS

Chocolate-marshmallow mix covers salted peanuts and crisp cereals

¼ c. butter
1 (6 oz.) pkg. semisweet
    chocolate pieces
1 (10½ oz.) pkg. miniature
    marshmallows

1½ c. salted peanuts
2 c. assorted bite-size shredded
    cereal biscuits (wheat, corn
    and rice)

Melt butter in 3-qt. saucepan over low heat. Add chocolate pieces and marshmallows; cook and stir constantly until melted, smooth and syrupy. Stir in peanuts and cereal (oat puffs are good included in assortment).

Spread in buttered 9″ square pan, using 2 forks to spread evenly. When firm, cut in 1½″ squares. Makes 3 dozen.

SPICY CRUNCH

If you want a snack guests rave about, here's the recipe to use

3 c. puffed oat cereal
2 c. shredded rice, bite-size
    biscuits
2 c. shredded corn, bite-size
    biscuits
2 c. shredded wheat, bite-size
    biscuits
1 c. raisins

1 c. pecan halves
½ c. butter or regular margarine
1⅓ c. brown sugar, firmly
    packed
¼ c. light corn syrup
2 tsp. ground cinnamon
½ tsp. salt

Butter a large bowl and toss cereals, raisins and pecans in it to mix.

Combine butter, brown sugar, corn syrup, cinnamon and salt in a heavy skillet. Stir constantly over medium heat until boiling. Boil 3 minutes.

Pour the hot syrup over cereal mixture in the bowl; stir to coat thoroughly.

Spread on two buttered baking sheets. Cool. When firm, break into pieces. Makes about 2½ quarts.

APRICOT/COCONUT BALLS

The refreshing tart-sweet flavor of apricots pleases everyone

1 c. apricot preserves	2 c. flaked coconut
2 tblsp. butter	¼ c. currants (optional)
2½ c. vanilla wafer crumbs	½ tsp. rum flavoring (optional)

Combine apricot preserves and butter in saucepan. Bring to a boil. Stir in vanilla wafer crumbs, ½ c. coconut, currants and rum flavoring.

Place remaining 1½ c. coconut in shallow dish. Drop teaspoonfuls of apricot mixture into coconut and roll to coat thoroughly. Shape into balls. Place on waxed paper. Makes 3½ dozen.

HOLIDAY FRUIT BARS

Ideal no-bake fruit cookies for Christmas celebrations and gifts

½ c. butter	1 c. candied cherries, cut in
1 (10½ oz.) pkg. miniature	halves
marshmallows	1 c. dates, cut in halves
¾ c. chopped nuts	1½ c. vanilla wafer crumbs

Melt butter in 3-qt. saucepan. Add marshmallows; cook over low heat, stirring constantly, until melted. Add remaining ingredients; mix thoroughly.

Spread mixture in buttered 9" square pan, using fork to spread evenly. When ready to serve, cut in 1½" squares. Makes 3 dozen.

Variation

Cereal Christmas Fruit Bars: Substitute 1½ c. oven-toasted rice cereal for vanilla wafer crumbs.

ALMOND BARS

These skip-the-oven cookies are so easy to make and so good to eat

¾ c. blanched almonds	1½ tblsp. honey
¼ c. candied cherries	¼ tsp. almond extract
¼ c. toasted flaked or shredded	1 (4 oz.) pkg. sweet cooking
coconut	chocolate
1 tblsp. butter or regular	
margarine	

Grind almonds and cherries together. Add coconut.

Cream butter, honey and almond extract together; add ground mixture; mix well. Shape into large rectangle on waxed paper.

Melt chocolate; spread over top; chill until firm. Cut in 2½ x 2" bars. Makes 18 to 20.

ALMOND BONBONS

This new almond Christmas special adds distinction to the cookie tray

3 c. finely chopped blanched almonds (1 lb.)	1 tblsp. lemon-flavored iced tea mix
3 egg whites, stiffly beaten	Chocolate pieces or nuts (for centers)
1 tblsp. heavy cream	
1 tsp. almond extract	Sugar or tiny multicolored decorating candies
2 c. sifted confectioners sugar	
1 tsp. water	

Combine almonds, stiffly beaten egg whites, heavy cream, almond extract, confectioners sugar, water and tea mix. Stir until ingredients are well blended.

Butter hands lightly (mixture is somewhat sticky) and form in 1" balls around chocolate pieces or nuts (one in each ball). Roll half of balls in sugar, the other half in colored candies. Makes about 5 dozen.

CARNIVAL CANDY COOKIES

Colored marshmallows give a festive look to these chocolate drops

1 (6 oz.) pkg. semisweet chocolate pieces	2 tblsp. shortening
¼ c. peanut butter	1 c. salted peanuts
2 tblsp. light corn syrup	1 c. colored miniature marshmallows

Melt together in saucepan over low heat chocolate pieces, peanut butter, corn syrup and shortening. Stir until smooth. Cool slightly, then stir in peanuts and marshmallows; avoid overstirring.

Drop by teaspoonfuls onto waxed paper. Let set until firm. Makes about 2 dozen.

Variation

Peanut/Cereal Candy Cookies: Use ½ c. salted peanuts and ½ c. oat puffs (cereal circles) in Carnival Candy Cookies instead of 1 c. salted peanuts.

CASSEROLE COOKIES

A Missouri school teacher contributed this recipe. She says she makes the confection cookies every yuletide season. The teachers take turns providing candy daily for their lounge the week before the holiday vacation. Casserole Cookies disappear quickly, which is adequate proof of their popularity.

You bake the cookie mixture in a casserole. A crust forms on top, but it disappears when you stir the hot cookies with a spoon. When mixture cools, you shape the cookies in 1″ balls and roll them in granulated sugar. The white sugar granules glisten on the dark cookie balls.

CASSEROLE COOKIES

A cookie-candy hybrid, baked in a casserole—inviting and rewarding

2 eggs	1 c. flaked coconut
1 c. sugar	1 tsp. vanilla
1 c. chopped walnuts	¼ tsp. almond extract
1 c. chopped dates	¼ c. sugar (for coating)

Beat eggs well; gradually add 1 c. sugar, beating until mixture is light and fluffy. Stir in nuts, dates, coconut, vanilla and almond extract. Turn into ungreased 2-qt. casserole.

Bake in moderate oven (350°) 30 minutes. Remove from oven and while still hot, stir well with wooden spoon. Let cool, then form into 1″ balls. Roll in ¼ c. sugar. Makes about 34.

COCONUT/DATE MARBLES

These attractive cookie marbles taste like date bars—party fare

1 egg	1 c. finely cut dates (8 oz.)
½ c. sugar	1 (7 oz.) pkg. cookie coconut
1 tsp. vanilla	½ c. finely chopped pecans
⅛ tsp. salt	4 drops red food color

Beat egg until foamy; gradually beat in sugar, vanilla and salt. Beat until fluffy. Stir in dates, ¾ c. coconut and pecans. Spread in greased 9" square pan.

Bake in slow oven (300°) about 30 minutes, or until golden. (Test by pressing lightly with fingertip. If cookie springs back, it is done.)

Set pan on rack to cool. Cut in 1½ x 1" bars. Roll each bar in hands to make a 1" ball. Tint half of the remaining coconut pink with red food color. Roll half the cookie balls in pink coconut, the other half in white. Makes about 4 dozen.

CHOCOLATE/PEANUT CLUSTERS

They'll remind you of candy, but you bake them like cookies—good

⅓ c. sifted flour	2 squares unsweetened
⅔ c. sugar	chocolate, melted
½ tsp. salt	2 tsp. light corn syrup
⅓ c. shortening	1 tsp. vanilla
1 egg	2½ c. unsalted peanuts

Sift flour, sugar and salt into bowl. Add shortening, egg, chocolate, corn syrup and vanilla; mix well. Add nuts.

Drop teaspoonfuls of dough 1" apart, onto greased baking sheet. Bake in moderate oven (350°) 8 minutes.

Cool cookies before removing to wire rack—they're very tender when hot! Makes 3 dozen.

Variations

Chocolate/Raisin Clusters: Use only 1½ c. peanuts and add 1 c. raisins.

Chocolate/Date Clusters: Use 1½ c. chopped walnuts instead of peanuts and 1 c. chopped dates.

DATE/NUT MACAROONS

They're moist, chewy, tasty and so easy to make. Try them soon

⅔ c. sweetened condensed milk (not evaporated)	1 c. chopped nuts
	1 c. chopped, pitted dates
1 c. flaked or shredded coconut	1 tsp. vanilla

Mix together all ingredients. Shape into balls and place about 1" apart on greased baking sheet.

Bake in moderate oven (350°) 10 to 12 minutes, until golden brown. Remove cookies and cool on racks. Makes about 2 dozen.

ROCKY ROAD FUDGE BARS

They're dual purpose—serve these treats as cookies or candy

½ c. light corn syrup	¼ c. peanut butter
½ c. sugar	½ c. chopped nuts
1 (6 oz.) pkg. semisweet chocolate pieces	2 c. miniature marshmallows

Combine corn syrup and sugar in saucepan; bring to a boil and boil 2 minutes. Stir in chocolate pieces and peanut butter; cool slightly. Add nuts and marshmallows, stirring just enough to distribute.

Spread evenly in buttered 9″ square pan. To serve, cut in 1½″ squares. Makes 3 dozen.

Variations

Rocky Road Fudge Slices: If desired, shape Rocky Road Fudge Bars mixture into two 10″ rolls. (Mixture is somewhat soft and is a little difficult to handle, but slices are very attractive.) Wrap rolls tightly in aluminum foil or waxed paper and refrigerate until firm. To serve, cut in ¼ to ½″ slices.

Cereal Rocky Road Fudge Slices: Make like Rocky Road Fudge Slices, but substitute 2 c. oat puffs (cereal circles) for the marshmallows.

SOUTHERN CANDY-COOKIES

Luscious butterscotch mix coats raisins, nuts and marshmallows

½ c. light corn syrup	2 c. light raisins (seeded)
½ c. brown sugar, firmly packed	½ c. chopped pecans
½ c. peanut butter	2 c. miniature marshmallows
1 (6 oz.) pkg. butterscotch pieces	

Bring to a boil corn syrup and brown sugar; boil 2 minutes. Remove from heat; blend in peanut butter and butterscotch pieces. Stir in raisins, pecans and marshmallows, using care not to overmix.

Drop by rounded teaspoonfuls onto waxed paper. To hasten setting, place in refrigerator. Makes about 3½ dozen.

COCONUT MARZIPANS

Fruit flavor gelatin contributes color and zip to these cookies

1 (3 oz.) pkg. fruit flavor
gelatin
2⅓ c. flaked or cookie
coconut (7 to 8 oz. pkg.)
½ c. sweetened condensed milk
(not evaporated)

¼ c. heavy or light cream
¼ c. sugar
¼ c. butter
1 c. confectioners sugar

Set aside 1 tblsp. gelatin to use in glaze. Combine coconut, sweetened condensed milk and remaining gelatin (strawberry, cherry, lemon, lime or orange). Mix thoroughly.

Form mixture into cookies in shape of berries or fruit to correspond to flavor of gelatin; let stand a few minutes.

Meanwhile, make glaze: Combine cream, sugar, butter and reserved gelatin in small saucepan. Boil 2 minutes; stir in confectioners sugar. Drop shaped cookies, one at a time, into glaze to coat. Lift out of glaze with fork, allowing excess to drip off. Place on waxed paper. (If necessary, thin glaze with a little milk while coating cookies.) Makes about 2½ dozen.

Pie-Bar Dessert Cookies

Our pie-bar dessert cookies, inspired by popular pies, prove there is something new under the sun—something mighty good to eat. The idea for this cross between cookies and pies came about through concern about calories.

Many Americans in this diet-conscious age try to skip dessert yet long for at least a few bites of delicious sweetness to top off the meal or to enjoy with coffee at evening social affairs. Our food editors in their travels around the country asked: "What is your favorite dessert? What would you choose if you were not counting calories?" Men promptly replied: Pies. And a surprising number of women gave the same answer.

With this in mind when we were working on this cookie book, some creative Test Kitchen work evolved our recipes for small cookies that taste like pies. We call them pie-bar dessert cookies. Taste-testers rated them as tasty as the pies from which they descend. We knew from that moment we had the right rich, satisfying miniature desserts.

The cookies, with the exception of Pumpkin Pie Squares, are finger food. It's easier to eat the spicy, pumpkin cookies with a fork. But there's nothing wrong about serving any of these pie-bar cookies on a small plate with a fork and coffee alongside.

Neither is there any reason why you can't cut these cookies a little larger, although if much bigger, you defeat the major reason for them —cookies small enough to please weight-watchers and permit them to have dessert without feeling guilty.

Which pie-bars taste best? Is it Sour Cream/Raisin, Golden Lemon, Brownie or Chess? Or are Pecan and French Apple Pie-Bars even better? Try all 15 of these exciting cookies and the variations before you decide.

CRAN/APPLE PIE-BARS

Sugar glistens on lattice top over cranberry-orange filling

2 c. sifted flour
½ tsp. salt
⅔ c. shortening
2 tblsp. butter or regular
    margarine
5 to 6 tblsp. water

1 (10 oz.) pkg. frozen cranberry-
    orange relish, thawed
1 c. finely chopped apple
⅓ c. sugar
Sugar (for top)

To make crust, combine flour and salt; cut in shortening and butter until particles are the size of small peas. Add water gradually, while stirring with a fork, until mixture is moist enough to hold together. Reserve ⅓ of dough to use for topping.

Roll remaining ⅔ of dough on floured surface to make a 14 x 9" rectangle. Place on ungreased baking sheet.

To make filling, combine cranberry-orange relish, apple and ⅓ c. sugar. Spread over pastry, leaving a ½" margin on all sides.

Roll out remaining ⅓ of dough. Cut in strips about ½" wide, half of them 14" long, the other half 9" long. Crisscross over filling to make a lattice top; fold lower crust up over. Sprinkle with sugar.

Bake in hot oven (400°) 30 to 35 minutes, or until pastry is golden brown. Cool in pan on rack. Cut in 2 x 1½" bars. Makes about 3½ dozen.

N O T E : Cookies lose some of their crispness after standing 24 hours. To serve them the second or third day after baking, heat them in a very slow oven (250°) about 10 minutes to restore crispness.

FRENCH APPLE PIE-BARS

Cookies never were better! That's the verdict of men taste-testers

2 c. sifted flour
1 tsp. salt
¾ c. shortening
4 to 5 tblsp. water
4 c. thinly sliced peeled
    apples

½ c. sugar
½ c. brown sugar, firmly packed
¼ c. flour
¼ tsp. ground cinnamon

To make crust, combine 2 c. flour with salt; cut in shortening until particles are size of small peas. Set aside 1 c. mixture. To the remainder, add water gradually, while stirring with a fork, just until dough is moist enough to hold together. Form into a square. Roll on floured board to a 14 x 10" rectangle. Fit into ungreased 13 x 9 x 2" pan.

Combine apples with white sugar. Place in pastry-lined pan.

Combine reserved crumb mixture with brown sugar, ¼ c. flour and cinnamon; sprinkle over apples.

Bake in hot oven (400°) 35 to 40 minutes, or until apples are tender and top is golden brown. Cool in pan on rack. Cut in 2" (about) squares. Makes 2 dozen.

BROWNIE PIE-BARS

A rich cream cheese crust holds the cake-like chocolate-nut filling

⅓ c. shortening	2 eggs
1 (3 oz.) pkg. cream cheese	⅓ c. flour
1¼ c. sifted flour	½ c. chopped nuts
½ tsp. salt	½ tsp. baking powder
4 to 5 tblsp. water	½ tsp. salt
½ c. butter or regular margarine	½ tsp. vanilla
2 squares unsweetened chocolate	¼ c. sifted confectioners sugar (for coating)
1 c. sugar	

To make crust, soften shortening with cream cheese (at room temperature). Add 1¼ c. flour and ½ tsp. salt. Mix just until particles are the size of small peas. Add water gradually, while stirring with a fork, until dough is moist enough to hold together.

Form dough into a square. Roll out on lightly floured surface to 14 x 10" rectangle. Fit into ungreased 13 x 9 x 2" pan.

To make filling, melt butter with chocolate in saucepan over very low heat. Stir in remaining ingredients, except confectioners sugar; beat to mix well. Pour into pastry-lined pan.

Bake in moderate oven (350°) 40 to 45 minutes. Cool in pan on rack; sprinkle with confectioners sugar. Cut in 2" (about) squares. Makes 2 dozen.

Variation

Frosted Brownie Pie-Bars: Omit sprinkling with confectioners sugar, and spread with this frosting: Melt together 1 (1 oz.) envelope no-melt unsweetened chocolate, or 1 square unsweetened chocolate, 2 tblsp. butter and 1 tblsp. milk. Stir in 1 c. confectioners sugar. Beat until smooth, adding a few drops of milk if necessary to make frosting of spreading consistency. Spread over cooled Brownie Pie-Bars.

DANISH CARAMEL PIE-BARS

We also give a speedy Americanized version of "caramelettes"

1½ c. sifted flour	1 egg
⅓ c. sugar	1 c. sugar
¼ tsp. salt	¾ c. light cream
½ c. butter	¾ c. sliced almonds

Combine flour, ⅓ c. sugar, salt and butter until mixture is crumbly. Blend in egg. Press mixture with fingers into bottom and ½" up sides of ungreased 9" square pan.

Melt 1 c. sugar in heavy skillet over medium-low heat, stirring constantly, until it turns a light caramel color. Add cream very slowly, stirring constantly. When mixture is smooth, remove from heat and stir in almonds. Pour into crust-lined pan.

Bake in moderate oven (350°) 30 to 35 minutes, or until edges are golden brown. Cool in pan on rack. Cut in 1½" squares. Makes 3 dozen.

Variations

American Caramel Pie-Bars: Make like Danish Caramel Pie-Bars, substituting this speedy filling for the one in which you melt the sugar: Combine ⅔ c. caramel sundae sauce, ¼ c. light cream, 1 tblsp. melted butter and ¾ c. sliced almonds. Pour into crust-lined pan and bake as directed.

Danish Caramel Tarts: Press crust for Danish Caramel Pie-Bars into 18 ungreased 2½" muffin-pan cups to cover bottom and ½" up sides. (Or use small tart pans.) Place rounded tablespoonfuls caramel filling in each muffin-pan cup. Bake in moderate oven (350°) about 25 minutes. Cool; loosen carefully and remove from pans. Makes 1½ dozen.

CHEESE PIE-BAR COOKIES

Between crisp undercrust and crumb top there's a velvety, lemon-flavored filling reminiscent of the best cheese cakes and pies

1¾ c. sifted flour	½ c. dairy sour cream
⅓ c. sugar	2 eggs
¼ tsp. salt	1 tsp. grated lemon peel
⅔ c. butter	⅓ c. sugar
1 (3 oz.) pkg. cream cheese	

Combine flour, ⅓ c. sugar and salt; using electric mixer on low speed, cut in butter until particles are fine like cornmeal. Set aside ⅓ of mixture for topping. Press remaining ⅔ of mixture into bottom of ungreased 9″ square pan. Bake in moderate oven (350°) 15 minutes.

To make filling, soften cream cheese by beating with sour cream. Blend in eggs, lemon peel and ⅓ c. sugar. Pour over crust in pan. Sprinkle with reserved crust mixture.

Bake in moderate oven (350°) 30 to 35 minutes, or until filling is set. Cool in pan on rack. Cut in 1½″ squares and store in refrigerator until serving time. Makes 3 dozen.

CHESS PIE BARS

For dessert cut larger squares; top with whipped cream or ice cream

1½ c. sifted flour	½ c. melted butter
¼ c. brown sugar, firmly packed	2 tblsp. milk
½ c. butter or regular margarine	1 tblsp. flour
1 c. brown sugar, firmly packed	2 eggs
½ c. sugar	½ c. chopped nuts

Combine 1½ c. flour and ¼ c. brown sugar; cut in butter, using mixer on low speed, until particles are fine. Press mixture into bottom of ungreased 13 x 9 x 2″ pan. Bake in moderate oven (375°) 10 minutes.

Meanwhile, combine remaining ingredients in mixing bowl; beat well. Pour over crust in pan; bake in moderate oven (375°) 20 to 25 minutes, or until golden brown. Cool in pan on rack; then cut in 2″ squares. Makes about 2 dozen.

Cookie Barnyard. Made of chocolate dough, decorated with red and white frosting, enclosed by pretzel fence. Patterns and directions for making barn (page 167); use any animal cookie cutters you have.

Heaps of Cookies. These are made from big recipes! Clockwise from left: Brazil Nut Bars (page 58), Crisscross (page 194), Country Molasses (page 146), Star (page 155) and Holiday Fruitcake (page 96).

FRENCH CHOCOLATE PIE-SQUARES

Chocolate creams is a good name for these specials

1⅔ c. graham cracker crumbs
¼ c. sugar
⅓ c. melted butter
½ c. butter
1 c. confectioners sugar

2 (1 oz.) envelopes no-melt
unsweetened chocolate or 2
squares unsweetened chocolate,
melted
2 eggs
1 tsp. vanilla

Combine graham cracker crumbs, sugar and melted butter. Set aside ⅓ of mixture for topping. Press remaining mixture into bottom of ungreased 9″ square pan.

Bake in moderate oven (375°) 8 minutes. (Omit baking, if you wish.)

To make filling, cream ½ c. butter with confectioners sugar until very light and fluffy. Blend in chocolate. Add eggs and vanilla; beat well. Spread over crust in pan. Sprinkle with reserved crust mixture. Refrigerate.

To serve, cut in 1½″ squares. Makes 3 dozen.

N O T E : Keep cookies in refrigerator. The filling softens at room temperature.

GLAZED JAM PIE-BARS

A cake-like filling bakes in a crust; spread jam and frosting on top

1⅓ c. sifted flour
½ tsp. salt
¼ c. shortening
¼ c. butter
3 to 4 tblsp. water
½ c. fruit or berry jam, or
preserves
½ c. butter

⅔ c. sugar
2 eggs
½ tsp. baking powder
½ tsp. salt
1 tsp. vanilla
1 c. sifted flour
Rum Frosting (recipe follows)

Mix 1⅓ c. flour and ½ tsp. salt. Using electric mixer at low speed, cut in shortening and ¼ c. butter until particles are fine. Add water gradually, while stirring with fork, until dough is moist enough to hold together.

Roll out dough on floured surface to a 14 x 10" rectangle. Fit into ungreased 13 x 9 x 2" pan. Spread jam over bottom.

To make filling, cream ½ c. butter and sugar until light and fluffy. Add eggs, baking powder, ½ tsp. salt and vanilla. Beat well. Blend in 1 c. flour. Spread carefully over jam-topped dough in pan.

Bake in moderate oven (375°) 30 to 35 minutes, or until golden brown. While warm spread with Rum Frosting. Cool in pan on rack, then cut in 2" (about) squares. (These cookies are good keepers.) Makes 2 dozen.

Rum Frosting: Blend together until smooth 2 tblsp. soft butter or regular margarine, 1 c. confectioners sugar, 1 tblsp. milk and ½ tsp. rum flavoring.

LEMON FLUFF PIE-BARS

Filling separates to form a creamy layer on bottom, spongy fluff on top, like lemon sponge pie. Cookies are light and refreshing

⅓ c. butter	¼ c. flour
¼ c. confectioners sugar	2 eggs, separated
1 c. sifted flour	1 tblsp. grated lemon peel
¼ c. butter or regular margarine	¼ c. lemon juice
1 c. sugar	1 c. milk

To make crust, soften ⅓ c. butter with confectioners sugar; blend in 1 c. flour. Press mixture into bottom of ungreased 9" square pan. Bake in moderate oven (350°) 12 minutes.

To make filling, cream together ¼ c. butter, sugar and ¼ c. flour. Beat in egg yolks, lemon peel and juice. Blend in milk.

Beat egg whites until they stand in peaks (stiff, but not dry). Fold into filling mixture and pour into baked crust.

Bake in moderate oven (350°) 35 to 40 minutes, or until deep golden brown. Cool in pan on rack and cut in 2 x 1" bars. Makes 3 dozen.

GOLDEN LEMON PIE-BARS

Crisp crust holds tart-sweet filling—a treat for lemon pie fans

1⅓ c. sifted flour	1 c. sugar
½ tsp. salt	2 tblsp. flour
½ c. shortening	2 eggs
2 to 3 tblsp. water	1 tblsp. grated lemon peel
⅓ c. butter	¼ c. lemon juice

To make crust, mix 1⅓ c. flour with salt; cut in shortening to form particles the size of small peas. Set aside ⅓ c. mixture for topping. To the remainder add water gradually, while stirring with a fork, until dough is moist enough to hold together.

Roll dough out on floured surface to make a 10″ square. Fit into ungreased 9″ square pan.

To make filling, cream butter with sugar. Blend in 2 tblsp. flour, eggs, lemon peel and juice. Pour into pastry-lined pan. Sprinkle top with reserved ⅓ c. crust mixture.

Bake in hot oven (400°) 30 to 35 minutes, or until golden. Cool in pan on rack. Cut in 1½″ squares. Makes 3 dozen.

MINCEMEAT PIE-BARS

For a holiday dessert cut in 3- or 4-inch bars, top with ice cream

2½ c. sifted flour	5 to 6 tblsp. water
1 tsp. salt	2 c. prepared mincemeat
1 c. shortening	2 tblsp. sugar (for tops)

Combine flour and salt; cut in shortening until particles are the size of small peas. Gradually add water, while stirring with a fork, until dough is moist enough to hold together.

Divide dough in half. Roll one part on floured surface to make a 14 x 9″ rectangle. Place on ungreased baking sheet. Spread mincemeat to within ½″ of edges.

Roll remaining half of dough to 14 x 9″ rectangle. Place on top of mincemeat; seal edges with a fork. Prick top generously with fork. Sprinkle with sugar.

Bake in hot oven (400°) 25 to 30 minutes, or until golden brown. Serve warm or cold, cut in 2″ (about) squares. Makes 28.

PECAN PIE-BARS

To serve these luscious cookies for dessert, top with whipped cream

½ c. butter	2 tblsp. flour
1¼ c. sifted flour	3 eggs
¼ c. sugar	1 tsp. vanilla
½ c. brown sugar, firmly packed	¼ tsp. salt
1 c. light or dark corn syrup	½ to 1 c. chopped pecans

To make crust, cut butter with 1¼ c. flour and sugar until particles are fine like cornmeal. Press into bottom of ungreased 9″ square pan. Bake in moderate oven (350°) 15 minutes.

Combine remaining ingredients in mixing bowl, beating until well blended. Pour over partially baked crust in pan.

Bake in moderate oven (350°) 30 to 35 minutes, or until golden brown and knife inserted in center comes out clean. Cool in pan on rack. Cut in 1½″ squares. Makes 3 dozen.

Variation

Chocolate Pecan Pie-Bars: Make like Pecan Pie-Bars, but in filling use light corn syrup and add 2 (1 oz.) envelopes no-melt unsweetened chocolate, or 2 squares unsweetened chocolate, melted. Bake 35 minutes after pouring filling into crust.

PUMPKIN PIE SQUARES

Serve these pumpkin squares with coffee for a perfect dessert after a big meal or for evening refreshments that will be talked about

1 c. sifted flour	¾ c. sugar
½ c. quick-cooking rolled oats	½ tsp. salt
½ c. brown sugar, firmly packed	1 tsp. ground cinnamon
½ c. butter or regular margarine	½ tsp. ground ginger
1 (1 lb.) can pumpkin (2 c.)	¼ tsp. ground cloves
1 (13½ oz.) can evaporated	½ c. chopped pecans
milk	½ c. brown sugar, firmly packed
2 eggs	2 tblsp. butter

Combine flour, rolled oats, ½ c. brown sugar and ½ c. butter in mixing bowl. Mix until crumbly, using electric mixer on low speed. Press into ungreased 13 x 9 x 2" pan. Bake in moderate oven (350°) 15 minutes.

Combine pumpkin, evaporated milk, eggs, white sugar, salt and spices in mixing bowl; beat well. Pour into baked crust. Bake in moderate oven (350°) 20 minutes.

Combine pecans, ½ c. brown sugar and 2 tblsp. butter; sprinkle over pumpkin filling. Return to oven and bake 15 to 20 minutes, or until filling is set. Cool in pan on rack and cut in 2" (about) squares. Makes 2 dozen.

DANISH RAISIN PIE-BAR COOKIES

Cookies have luscious soft filling—serve with a fork, if you like

1 c. butter or regular margarine	2 c. sifted flour
1½ c. sugar	½ tsp. salt
3 eggs	1 (1 lb. 6 oz.) can raisin pie
1 tsp. vanilla	filling (2 c.)

Beat butter with sugar until light and fluffy. Beat in eggs and vanilla to mix well.

Sift together flour and salt; add a little at a time to creamed mixture, beating after each addition. Divide dough in half. Spread one half in greased 15½ x 10½ x 1" jelly roll pan. Carefully spread raisin pie filling evenly over dough.

Drop remaining half of dough over filling with spoon or cake decorator to form a lattice (lattice spreads in the baking). Bake in moderate oven (350°) 28 to 30 minutes, or until golden. Set pan on rack to cool, then cut in 2½ x 1" bars. Cookies are best served the same day they are baked, or frozen. Makes 5 dozen.

RAISIN CREAM PIE-BARS

Tasty cookies are rich like raisin cream pie, so cut into small bars

½ c. butter	2 c. ground raisins
1¼ c. sifted flour	½ c. sugar
½ c. quick-cooking rolled oats	1 c. light cream
½ c. brown sugar, firmly packed	¼ tsp. salt
¼ tsp. salt	1 tblsp. lemon juice

To make crust, combine butter, flour, rolled oats, brown sugar and ¼ tsp. salt; mix until crumbly. Press 2 c. mixture into bottom of ungreased 9″ square pan. Set aside remainder of crumb mixture for topping.

To make filling, combine raisins, sugar, cream and ¼ tsp. salt. Cook, stirring, until thick. Remove from heat and stir in lemon juice. Spread over crust in pan. Top with reserved crumb mixture.

Bake in moderate oven (375°) 35 to 40 minutes, or until golden brown. Cool in pan on rack. Cut in 1½″ squares. Makes 3 dozen.

SOUR CREAM/RAISIN PIE-BARS

Praises skyrocket for these cookies inspired by sour cream raisin pie

1½ c. sifted flour	¾ c. sugar
½ tsp. salt	1 tblsp. flour
⅓ c. shortening	1 tsp. ground cinnamon
¼ c. butter or regular margarine	¼ tsp. ground nutmeg
2 to 3 tblsp. water	⅛ tsp. ground cloves
1 c. dairy sour cream	½ c. seedless raisins
2 eggs	¼ c. brown sugar, firmly packed

Mix 1½ c. flour with salt; cut in shortening and butter until particles are the size of small peas. Set aside ⅔ c. mixture for topping.

To remaining mixture, gradually add water, while stirring with a fork, until dough is just moist enough to hold together. Roll out on floured surface to make a 10″ square; fit into ungreased 9″ square pan.

Combine dairy sour cream, eggs, sugar, 1 tblsp. flour, spices and raisins; beat well to blend. Pour into pastry-lined pan.

Blend brown sugar into reserved crumb mixture; sprinkle over filling. Bake in moderate oven (375°) 30 to 35 minutes, or until light golden brown. Cool in pan on rack. Cut in 1½″ squares. Makes 3 dozen.

NOTE: The filling has a custard base. Store cookies in refrigerator if not used soon after baking and cooling.

Ready-Made Cookies

When you're too busy to bake cookies and the supply in the freezer has vanished, depend on packaged cookies from the supermarket to serve when company comes. Just transform the basic cookies with your own special touches and they will have both a homemade taste and also appearance.

Take Marshmallow Gingersnaps. All you do to glamorize the crisp, spicy cookies is to lay marshmallow halves on them and broil about 5 minutes. Then you spread on a speedy orange confectioners sugar frosting. They're yummy and easy to fix.

Flat oatmeal cookies respond kindly to dress-ups. For our Date Betweens, put the cookies together in pairs with a quickly cooked date filling for pleasing sandwiches.

Another type of store cookie you can personalize speedily is shortbread. For Fudge Shortbread Squares you arrange the square shortbread cookies in a pan, spoon on a fast-fix chocolate frosting and chill in the refrigerator until set. Then you cut them into 2″ bars.

You can accomplish so much with vanilla wafers plus imagination in so few minutes. Try Chocolate-Coated Wafers for an adventure in rapid cooking. After a few tries at "dress-ups," you'll be ready to branch out on your own in personalizing the cookies you buy.

Keep a few packages in the cupboard to fix up in a jiffy when you need something delicious to serve with tea, coffee, a fruit drink or ice cream. If friends telephone to say they're coming over, you can have a plate of pretty cookies ready for thoughtful hospitality by the time they arrive. They'll be impressed.

MARSHMALLOW GINGERSNAPS

Gingersnaps taste great topped with marshmallows, orange icing

15 regular marshmallows, halved   1 tsp. grated orange peel
30 gingersnaps   1 tblsp. butter
1 c. confectioners sugar   1 to 2 tblsp. orange juice

Place a marshmallow half, cut side down, on each gingersnap. Arrange on ungreased baking sheet and put in very slow oven (200°) 5 minutes. Remove from oven and press marshmallows down slightly.

Combine confectioners sugar, orange peel and butter, and add orange juice until of spreading consistency. Beat until smooth. Spread over marshmallow-topped gingersnaps. Makes 2½ dozen.

ORANGE/COCONUT TOPPERS

Orange/coconut top complements the spicy flavor of gingersnaps

2 tblsp. butter   2 tsp. grated orange peel
½ c. sugar   1 tblsp. orange juice
½ c. flaked coconut   4 dozen gingersnaps

Melt butter in small saucepan; stir in sugar, coconut, orange peel and juice. Spread a scant teaspoonful on each gingersnap, almost to edges.

Arrange on ungreased baking sheet and bake in very hot oven (450°) 5 minutes, or until topping is bubbly. Remove cookies and cool on racks. Makes 4 dozen.

DATE BETWEENS

Orange/date filling between oatmeal cookies makes a real treat

½ c. cut-up dates   2 tblsp. sugar
⅓ c. orange juice or water   40 small flat oatmeal cookies
1 tsp. grated orange peel
   (optional)

Combine dates, orange juice, orange peel and sugar in small saucepan. Cook over medium heat, stirring constantly, until thick.

Put cookies together in pairs with about 1 tsp. date filling between. Makes 20.

Variation

Date-Filled Specials: Substitute small flat butter cookies or vanilla wafers for the oatmeal cookies.

OATMEAL TOSCAS

Bake these cookies with Swedish almond topping only 5 minutes

¼ c. sugar	½ c. sliced almonds
1 tsp. flour	⅛ tsp. almond extract
2 tblsp. light cream or milk	2 dozen flat oatmeal cookies
2 tblsp. butter	

In a small saucepan combine sugar and flour; stir to mix. Add cream and butter. Bring to a full boil, stirring constantly. Remove from heat and stir in almond slices and almond extract. Place a teaspoonful on center of each oatmeal cookie. Place cookies on ungreased baking sheet.

Bake in very hot oven (450°) 5 minutes, or until topping is bubbly. Cool cookies on racks. Makes 2 dozen.

FUDGE SHORTBREAD SQUARES

Quick and easy fudge on shortbread cookies makes them festive

16 shortbread square cookies	1 (6 oz.) pkg. semisweet
½ c. sweetened condensed milk	chocolate pieces
(not evaporated)	½ c. chopped nuts
	½ tsp. vanilla

Arrange cookies in bottom of lightly greased 8″ square pan.

Cook condensed milk and chocolate pieces over low heat, stirring occasionally, until thick, smooth and shiny. Stir in nuts and vanilla. Spoon over cookies in pan; carefully spread to cover. (You can sprinkle 2 shortbread cookies, crumbled, over top if you wish.) Refrigerate until set.

Cut in 2″ squares to serve. Makes 16.

PEANUT/DATE SHORTIES

Date/peanut filling on shortbread cookies, topped with chocolate

½ c. peanut butter
2 tblsp. butter
1 c. cut-up dates
1 c. confectioners sugar
36 shortbread cookies

½ c. semisweet chocolate pieces
2 tblsp. butter
2 tblsp. milk
½ c. confectioners sugar

Combine peanut butter, 2 tblsp. butter, dates and 1 c. confectioners sugar; add a few drops of milk if necessary to mix. Place 1 teaspoonful of mixture on each cookie.

Melt chocolate pieces and 2 tblsp. butter in milk by heating over hot water. Stir in ½ c. confectioners sugar and beat until smooth and shiny. (Add more milk if necessary.)

Dip tops of cookies in chocolate frosting. Spread on racks until chocolate hardens. Makes 3 dozen.

AUSTRIAN TORTELETTES

Jelly spread between cookies and frosting is a tasty surprise

¼ c. red jelly or jam (about)
36 shortbread square cookies
 (10 oz. pkg.)
¼ c. sliced filberts

½ c. sugar
2 tblsp. milk
2 tblsp. butter
½ c. semisweet chocolate pieces

Spread about ½ tsp. jelly over top of each cookie. Sprinkle with filberts.

Combine sugar, milk and butter in small saucepan. Bring to a boil; boil 1 minute. Remove from heat and stir in chocolate pieces. Continue to stir until smooth and of spreading consistency. If mixture is not smooth and shiny, thin with a few drops of milk. Spread on tops of cookies. Additional sliced filberts may be scattered over tops of cookies before chocolate hardens. Makes 3 dozen.

Variation

Peanut Prizes: Omit jelly and filberts. Top each cookie with 1 tsp. peanut butter, then spread on chocolate mixture.

CARAMEL SUNDAE COOKIES

These quick-fix cookies will become favorites at your house

14 caramels (¼ lb.)
2 tblsp. light cream or dairy
half-and-half
2 tblsp. butter
½ c. confectioners sugar
¼ c. chopped nuts

⅛ tsp. peppermint extract
(optional)
4 dozen vanilla wafers
½ c. milk chocolate pieces
1 tblsp. shortening

Melt together over hot water caramels, cream and butter. Stir in confectioners sugar, nuts and peppermint extract. Place a scant teaspoonful on top each vanilla wafer.

Melt chocolate pieces and shortening over hot water. Stir to mix and spoon a small amount on top of caramel-topped wafers. Makes 4 dozen.

N O T E : Double the recipe for caramel mixture and chocolate topping for 1 (10 to 12 oz.) pkg. vanilla wafers.

Variations

Chocolate/Caramel Sundae Cookies: Substitute small chocolate cookies for the vanilla wafers.
Shortbread/Caramel Sundae Cookies: Substitute shortbread cookies for the vanilla wafers.
Butter Cookie/Caramel Sundae: Substitute small butter cookies for the vanilla wafers.

CHERRY/CHOCOLATE CREAMS

Maraschino cherries nestle in creamy fondant under the glaze

1 egg white
2 tblsp. maraschino cherry
juice
4 c. confectioners sugar
4½ dozen vanilla wafers

27 maraschino cherries, halved
and well drained
1 (6 oz.) pkg. milk chocolate
pieces
¼ c. maraschino cherry juice
2 tblsp. shortening

Beat together egg white, 2 tblsp. maraschino cherry juice and confectioners sugar. (Add a few drops of milk if too thick.) Place a teaspoonful of this fondant on top each vanilla wafer; press a cherry half, cut side down, on top.

To make glaze, melt together milk chocolate pieces, ¼ c. maraschino cherry juice and shortening in small saucepan. Stir until smooth. Place ½ tsp. glaze on top each cherry half on cookie, allowing it to run down on fondant topping. Makes 4½ dozen.

CHOCOLATE-COATED WAFERS

Fix vanilla wafers this way when you're having discerning guests

1 (6 oz.) pkg. mint or semisweet chocolate pieces	4 dozen vanilla wafers
2 tblsp. shortening	Cookie coconut or chopped nuts (optional)
2 tblsp. shaved paraffin	

Melt together chocolate pieces, shortening and paraffin over hot water. Stir to blend.

Dip vanilla wafers, one at a time, in chocolate mixture to coat. Lift out with 2 forks, allowing excess chocolate to drip off. Let harden on racks. If desired, decorate tops of wafers before topping hardens with cookie coconut, or with chopped nuts. Makes 4 dozen.

Variation

Butterscotch Favorites: Substitute butterscotch pieces for the chocolate pieces.

CHOCOLATE RUM BALLS

Cookies prettied up like this look and taste like chocolate candy

2 tblsp. butter	4 dozen vanilla wafers
1 c. confectioners sugar	½ c. milk chocolate pieces
1 to 2 tblsp. milk	1 tblsp. shortening
½ to 1 tsp. rum extract	1 tblsp. shaved paraffin

Melt butter in small saucepan over medium heat to a delicate brown. Blend in confectioners sugar. Gradually add milk until of spreading consistency. Stir in rum extract.

Spread mixture generously on bottom sides of half of vanilla wafers. Top with remaining half of cookies, bottom side down.

Melt milk chocolate pieces with shortening and paraffin over hot water; stir to blend. Drop cookie sandwiches into chocolate. Coat on both sides and lift out with 2 forks, letting excess chocolate drop off. Cool on racks. Makes 2 dozen.

MINT STUFFIES

Plain vanilla wafers, dressed up, become pretty party fare

3 tblsp. butter	1 to 2 tblsp. milk
2 c. confectioners sugar	4 dozen vanilla wafers
2 tblsp. crème de menthe, or	½ c. semisweet mint chocolate
½ tsp. peppermint extract and	pieces
a few drops green food color	1 tblsp. shortening

Combine butter, confectioners sugar, crème de menthe and enough milk to make frosting of spreading consistency. Put 1 scant teaspoonful of mixture on each vanilla wafer.

Melt mint chocolate pieces and shortening over hot water. Spoon over frosted vanilla wafers. Let cookies cool before serving. Makes 4 dozen.

PARTY-GOERS

Picture-pretty cookies. Gelatin both tints and flavors coconut

1 (3 oz.) pkg. strawberry flavor	2 tblsp. butter
gelatin	3 tblsp. milk
⅔ c. sweetened condensed milk	3 tblsp. sugar
(not evaporated)	1 c. confectioners sugar
2⅓ c. flaked coconut (7 oz.)	3 dozen vanilla wafers

Reserve 1 tblsp. gelatin for frosting; combine remaining gelatin and sweetened condensed milk. Stir in coconut. Refrigerate 1 to 2 hours.

To make frosting, combine reserved 1 tblsp. gelatin, butter, milk and white sugar; boil 2 minutes. Stir in confectioners sugar.

Shape chilled coconut mixture into ¾" balls; press one ball firmly down on each vanilla wafer. Spread frosting over topping and cookie. It may be necessary to thin frosting with a few drops of water while spreading on cookies. Makes 3 dozen.

NOTE: You can substitute gelatin of other flavors and colors, such as raspberry, cherry, lime, orange and lemon, for the strawberry flavor gelatin.

BOYS' SPECIAL

You can make one snack cookie sandwich using the ingredients given here—or you can make them by the dozen on short notice

1 tsp. peanut butter	4 or 5 miniature marshmallows
2 flat unfilled cookies (large butter cookies, chocolate chip, etc.)	6 to 8 semisweet chocolate pieces

Spread a thin layer of peanut butter on bottom side of a flat cookie. Top with marshmallows and chocolate pieces.

Broil until marshmallows are puffy and chocolate pieces appear melted. Top with another cookie, bottom side down. Makes 1 cookie sandwich.

CHILDREN'S SPECIAL

Their favorites combined—marshmallows, chocolate, peanut butter

½ c. peanut butter	1 square semisweet chocolate
24 chocolate chip or chocolate cookies	1 tblsp. butter
	1 tblsp. milk
12 marshmallows, halved	1 c. confectioners sugar

Spread 1 tsp. peanut butter in center of each cookie top. Place a marshmallow half, cut side down, on peanut butter centers.

In small saucepan, melt chocolate and butter with milk over low heat, stirring constantly. Stir in confectioners sugar. Beat until smooth, adding a few drops of milk if necessary for spreading consistency. Spread over marshmallow-topped cookies. Makes 2 dozen.

CHOCOLATE/COCONUT RIBBONS

Ribbons of chocolate decorate coconut bar cookies—really delicious

1 (6 oz.) pkg. semisweet chocolate pieces	½ c. peanut butter
	32 coconut bar cookies

Melt together over low heat, stirring constantly, chocolate pieces and peanut butter. Let stand until cool, but not set.

Arrange 4 coconut bars, in a single row with ends touching, on sheet of foil or waxed paper. Spread generously with the chocolate/peanut mixture.

Top with second layer of cookies, using half cookies at each end. Again spread with chocolate/peanut mixture. Repeat with third layer of cookies. Top with frosting, then a fourth layer of cookies.

Repeat procedure, using remaining 16 cookies. Wrap in foil or waxed paper and refrigerate several hours.

To serve, cut in ½" slices with a sharp knife. Cookies slice easier the day they are made because chocolate hardens more if left longer. If not used, place sliced cookies on plate and slip into a plastic bag. Makes 32.

FROSTED FIG BARS

Glamorize tiny fig-filled cookies this easy way for your tea party

30 fig-filled bar cookies	1½ tblsp. orange juice
(1 lb.)	1 tsp. grated orange peel
2½ tblsp. butter	½ c. cookie coconut
1½ c. sifted confectioners sugar	

Cut cookie bars lengthwise in halves.

Combine butter, confectioners sugar, orange juice and orange peel. Beat until smooth.

Place coconut in shallow dish.

Hold a half cookie in one hand; spread top with frosting, using a small spatula. Dip cookie top in coconut. Place on waxed paper. Makes 5 dozen.

Variation

Snowy Topped Fig Bars: Follow recipe for Frosted Fig Bars, but omit orange juice and peel and in their place use 1½ tblsp. light cream or milk and ½ tsp. vanilla. (Add enough cream or milk to make frosting of spreading consistency.)

LAZY DAISY SUGAR COOKIES

Good family dessert: these cookies with broiled tops, and ice cream

2 tblsp. melted butter
½ c. brown sugar, firmly packed
1 tblsp. light cream or milk

½ c. cookie coconut or finely
chopped nuts
12 large sugar cookies

Combine butter, sugar, cream and coconut. Spread a scant tablespoonful on each cookie.

Place cookies on ungreased baking sheet and broil until topping is bubbly. Remove cookies to rack to cool. Makes 1 dozen.

Cookies to Make from a Mix

A country cookie custom worthy of a wider adoption than it enjoys today is the use of a homemade cookie mix. Once you make it and have it on hand, it's no trick to bake a hurry-up batch of cookies. We give you recipes for a mix adapted to kitchens located in high country and two mixes for use in locations under 5,000 feet elevation.

BAKING COOKIES IN HIGH ALTITUDES

One of the easiest, quickest and most successful ways to bake good cookies if you live in a high altitude area is to use a reliable home-made mix. You can buy mixes in packages in mountainous regions that are adapted to high elevations, but it is an economy to make your own. Home economists at the Colorado State University Agricultural Experiment Station have developed a basic mix that is responsible for many of the best cookies that come from home ovens in high country. The recipe for it and for a variety of superior cookies made from it were evolved in the altitude laboratory where the various conditions due to different altitudes are simulated.*

Home economists at the Agricultural Experiment Station and women throughout the Western mountain region have told Farm Journal food editors about the pointers to heed in making the mix. They say it is important to follow the directions with precision be-cause at high altitudes recipes are more sensitive to slight changes than in lower places. Here are some of their suggestions: Measure accurately. Use the ingredients specified; substitutions will disappoint you. Be sure to use hydrogenated shortening, which is available in practically all food markets. It's a good idea to have all the ingredients at room temperature before you start combining them. (You will

* From *Cookie Recipes from a Basic Mix for High Altitudes* by Dr. Ferne Bowman and Dr. Edna Page, Colorado State University.

notice that baking powder is the variable ingredient in the following recipe. The amount for your altitude is given in a table that follows the recipe.)

COLORADO BASIC COOKIE MIX

9 c. sifted flour	1 tblsp. salt
3 c. instant nonfat dry milk powder	4 c. hydrogenated shortening
Baking powder (see table below)	4 c. sugar

Combine flour, dry milk powder, baking powder and salt. Sift together twice.

Soften shortening in 6-qt. (or larger) bowl with electric mixer at medium speed, or with large wooden spoon. Gradually add sugar, beating constantly, until mixture is light and fluffy.

Gradually add dry ingredients, blending them into mixture with electric mixer at low speed, or cut them in with pastry blender as for pie crust. Mixture will resemble coarse cornmeal.

Store in large covered container at room temperature. Mix will keep for several weeks. To use, stir with fork before measuring, then lightly spoon mix into measuring cup and level with straight edge of knife or spatula—do not pack it. Makes about 19 cups.

Amount of Baking Powder to Use

At 5,000 feet—3 tblsp.

At 7,500 feet—2 tblsp. plus ¾ tsp.

At 10,000 feet—1 tblsp. plus 1½ tsp.

If the altitude at which you live is not exactly 5,000, 7,500 or 10,-000 feet, use the one nearest to your altitude. For example, if your elevation is 6,000 feet, use the baking powder indicated for 5,000 feet.

FAVORITE COOKIES FROM THE BASIC MIX

Here are recipes for some of the best liked cookies made with the Colorado Basic Cookie Mix. Women in high country say they prefer to make comparatively small- or medium-size batches because the cookies are so quick to mix and bake. They like to serve them fresh and fragrant from the oven.

BROWNIES 1

6 squares semisweet chocolate
2 c. Colorado Basic Cookie Mix
2 eggs

¼ c. water
2 tsp. vanilla
½ c. chopped walnuts

Melt chocolate over hot water.

Combine all ingredients and blend thoroughly. Spread in greased and floured 9″ square pan and bake in moderate oven (350°) 25 to 30 minutes. Set pan on rack; when slightly cool, cut in 2 x 1½″ bars. Makes about 2 dozen.

BROWNIES 2

2 squares unsweetened chocolate
2 c. Colorado Basic Cookie Mix
2 eggs
½ c. brown sugar, firmly packed

¼ c. water
2 tsp. vanilla
½ c. chopped walnuts

Melt chocolate over hot water.

Blend all ingredients thoroughly. Spread in greased and floured 9″ square pan and bake in moderate oven (350°) 25 to 30 minutes. Set pan on rack; when slightly cool, cut in 2 x 1½″ bars. Makes about 2 dozen.

CHEWY DATE/NUT BARS

3 c. Colorado Basic Cookie Mix
2 tblsp. water
2 eggs
¼ c. brown sugar, firmly packed

1 tsp. vanilla
1 c. chopped dates
1 c. coarsely chopped walnuts

Blend all ingredients thoroughly. Spread in greased 13 x 9 x 2″ pan.

Bake in moderate oven (350°) 35 to 40 minutes. Cool in pan on rack, then cut in 2 x 1″ bars. Makes about 4 dozen.

CRISPY BARS

2 c. Colorado Basic Cookie Mix
¼ c. brown sugar, firmly packed
2 eggs
¼ tsp. salt
¾ c. brown sugar, firmly packed

1 tsp. vanilla
1 c. shredded or flaked coconut
1 c. oven-toasted rice cereal
1 c. broken walnuts

Combine cookie mix and ¼ c. brown sugar. Press into greased 9″ square pan.

Beat eggs until frothy; add salt. Gradually add ¾ c. brown sugar, beating until thick. Add vanilla, coconut, cereal and nuts. Mix thoroughly. Spread over layer in pan.

Bake in slow oven (325°) 25 to 30 minutes. Cool in pan on rack, then cut in 2 x 1½″ bars. Makes about 2 dozen.

DATE LAYER BARS

3 c. Colorado Basic Cookie Mix
1¾ c. quick-cooking rolled oats
1 lb. chopped dates
1 tblsp. lemon juice

1½ c. water
¼ c. brown sugar, firmly packed
2 tblsp. water

Combine cookie mix and rolled oats. Press 2½ c. of mixture into greased 13 x 9 x 2″ pan.

Combine dates, lemon juice and 1½ c. water; cook over low heat until mixture is the consistency of thin jam. Spread over crumb layer in pan.

Blend brown sugar and 2 tblsp. water into remaining crumb mixture. Sprinkle over date mixture in pan and press down lightly.

Bake in moderate oven (350°) 30 to 35 minutes. Cool in pan on rack, then cut in 2 x 1″ bars. Makes about 4 dozen.

PECAN BARS

2¼ c. Colorado Basic Cookie Mix
2 tblsp. water
3 eggs

1 c. brown sugar, firmly packed
½ tsp. vanilla
1 c. chopped pecans

Blend 2 c. cookie mix, water and 1 egg thoroughly. Spread in greased 13 x 9 x 2″ pan. Bake in moderate oven (375°) 8 to 10 minutes.

To make topping, beat 2 eggs until foamy. Add brown sugar, ¼ c. cookie mix and vanilla. Blend thoroughly. Stir in nuts. Spread over baked layer.

Return to moderate oven (350°) and bake 20 to 25 minutes. Cool in pan on rack, then cut in 2 x 1″ bars. Makes about 4 dozen.

CHERRY DROPS

3 c. Colorado Basic Cookie Mix
2 eggs

½ c. coarsely chopped drained
    maraschino cherries
½ c. chopped pecans

Blend cookie mix and eggs. Add cherries and nuts. Drop by teaspoonfuls about 2″ apart onto ungreased baking sheet.

Bake in moderate oven (375°) 10 to 12 minutes. Remove cookies and cool on rack. Makes 3½ to 4 dozen.

CHOCOLATE DROPS

2 c. Colorado Basic Cookie Mix
3 tblsp. cocoa
1 egg

2 tblsp. water
1 tsp. vanilla
½ c. chopped walnuts

Blend all ingredients thoroughly. Drop by teaspoonfuls about 2″ apart onto ungreased baking sheet.

Bake in moderate oven (375°) 10 to 14 minutes. Remove cookies and cool on racks. Makes 3 dozen.

CHOCOLATE CHIP COOKIES

4 c. Colorado Basic Cookie Mix
1 egg
2 tblsp. water
1½ tsp. vanilla

¼ c. brown sugar, firmly packed
1 (6 oz.) pkg. semisweet
    chocolate pieces
1 c. chopped walnuts

Blend all ingredients thoroughly. Drop by teaspoonfuls about 2″ apart onto ungreased baking sheet.

Bake in moderate oven (375°) 10 to 13 minutes. Remove cookies and cool on racks. Makes 5 dozen.

CRISP CHOCOLATE DROPS

4 squares semisweet chocolate
2 c. Colorado Basic Cookie Mix
2 tblsp. water

1 tsp. vanilla
½ c. chopped nuts

Melt chocolate over hot water.

Blend all ingredients thoroughly. Drop by teaspoonfuls about 2″ apart onto ungreased baking sheet.

Bake in moderate oven (375°) 10 to 12 minutes. Remove cookies and cool on racks. Makes 3 to 3½ dozen.

COCONUT COOKIES SUPREME

2 c. Colorado Basic Cookie Mix
1 egg
2 tblsp. water

1 tsp. vanilla
½ c. shredded coconut
½ c. chopped walnuts

Blend all ingredients thoroughly. Drop by teaspoonfuls about 2″ apart onto lightly greased baking sheet.

Bake in moderate oven (375°) 12 to 15 minutes. Remove cookies and cool on racks. Makes 3 dozen.

LEMON DROPS

2 c. Colorado Basic Cookie Mix
1 egg

1 tblsp. lemon juice
1½ tsp. grated lemon peel

Blend all ingredients thoroughly. Drop by teaspoonfuls about 2″ apart onto ungreased baking sheet.

Bake in moderate oven (375°) 10 to 12 minutes. Remove cookies and cool on racks. Makes 2½ dozen.

MINCEMEAT COOKIES

2 c. Colorado Basic Cookie Mix
½ c. prepared mincemeat
1 egg

½ tsp. vanilla
1 tblsp. water
½ c. chopped walnuts

Blend all ingredients thoroughly. Drop by teaspoonfuls about 2″ apart onto ungreased baking sheet.

Bake in moderate oven (375°) 10 to 12 minutes. Remove cookies and cool on racks. Makes 3 to 4 dozen.

OATMEAL COOKIES

1 c. raisins
2 c. Colorado Basic Cookie Mix
1 c. quick-cooking rolled oats
2 tblsp. brown sugar
½ tsp. ground cinnamon

½ tsp. ground allspice
1 egg
1½ tsp. vanilla
½ c. chopped walnuts

Cover raisins with water and simmer 5 minutes. Drain, reserving ½ c. raisin water.

Blend raisins and reserved ½ c. raisin water with remaining ingredients thoroughly. Drop by teaspoonfuls about 2" apart onto ungreased baking sheet.

Bake in moderate oven (375°) 13 to 15 minutes. Remove cookies and cool on racks. Makes 3½ to 4 dozen.

CINNAMON COOKIES

2½ c. Colorado Basic Cookie
  Mix
½ c. sugar
1 egg

1 tsp. vanilla
1½ tsp. ground cinnamon
¼ c. finely chopped nuts

Combine cookie mix, sugar, egg and vanilla; blend thoroughly. Combine cinnamon and nuts.

Form dough into small balls, about 1" in diameter; roll in cinnamon-nut mixture. Place 2" apart on ungreased baking sheet.

Bake in moderate oven (375°) 12 to 15 minutes. Remove cookies and cool on racks. Makes 3½ dozen.

MOLASSES COOKIES

4 c. Colorado Basic Cookie Mix
¼ tsp. ground cloves
½ tsp. ground cinnamon

½ tsp. ground ginger
1 egg
¼ c. molasses

Blend all ingredients thoroughly. Refrigerate dough 1 hour.

Form dough into small balls, about 1" in diameter; place 1 to 2" apart on lightly greased baking sheet. Flatten cookies with bottom of glass covered with damp cloth.

Bake in moderate oven (375°) 8 to 10 minutes. Remove cookies and cool on racks. Makes 5 to 6 dozen.

PEANUT BUTTER COOKIES

4 c. Colorado Basic Cookie Mix   1 egg
½ c. brown sugar, firmly packed   1½ tsp. vanilla
1 c. peanut butter   1 tblsp. water

Blend all ingredients thoroughly. Form dough into small balls, about 1" in diameter, and place 1 to 2" apart on ungreased baking sheet. Flatten cookies with tines of fork.

Bake in moderate oven (375°) 10 to 12 minutes. Remove cookies and cool on racks. Makes 7 dozen.

THUMBPRINTS

1 (3 oz.) pkg. cream cheese   9 drained maraschino cherries,
2 c. Colorado Basic Cookie Mix   cut in fourths
¾ tsp. vanilla   Jelly or tinted frosting
1 egg white, slightly beaten   (optional)
¾ c. finely chopped nuts

Soften cream cheese. Add cookie mix and vanilla and blend thoroughly. Form dough into small balls, about 1" in diameter. Dip into egg white, then roll in nuts. Place 1 to 2" apart on greased baking sheet and press top of each cookie with thumb.

Bake in moderate oven (350°) 5 minutes, or until puffy. Remove from oven and quickly press top of each cookie with thumb to make indentation.

Return to oven and bake about 10 minutes longer. Place cookies on racks to cool. Place a maraschino cherry quarter or a bit of jelly or tinted frosting in center of each cookie. Makes 2½ to 3 dozen.

SUGAR COOKIES

3 c. Colorado Basic Cookie Mix   ½ tsp. almond extract, or
1 egg   ¾ tsp. vanilla
     Sugar

Blend all ingredients thoroughly. Roll dough ⅛ to ¼" thick and cut with a round cookie cutter the size you like, or have. (Chill the dough 2 to 3 hours or overnight before rolling if it is difficult to handle.) Place 1 to 2" apart on ungreased baking sheet.

Bake in moderate oven (375°) 8 to 10 minutes. Place cookies on racks to cool. Sprinkle with sugar, or decorate as desired. Makes 3 dozen.

COOKIE STARTER

This mix is versatile. We give you seven good cookies to make with it

2¼ c. sifted flour
¾ tsp. salt
1 c. butter or regular margarine

Sift flour and salt into bowl.

Cut in butter until mixture resembles coarse bread crumbs.

Store in clean jar with tight-fitting lid. Keep in refrigerator or freezer. Makes 3 to 4 cups.

Tips on using mix

Let the crumbs reach room temperature before adding other ingredients. Loosen with a fork if mix is too compact. Your electric mixer can help you make cookie dough from the mix.

To short-cut cookie making, shape dough into roll; wrap and chill thoroughly. Slice and bake cookies as desired. When dough is cold, allow more time for baking. To get a thicker cookie, shape teaspoonfuls of dough with fingers and roll in palms of hands into balls; stamp with flat-bottomed glass and bake.

When you bake and then freeze, wrap cookies in foil or plastic wrap, or store them in freezer containers.

OLD ENGLISH GINGER CONES

If cookies break in rolling, return them to oven for 1 minute

1 c. Cookie Starter
¼ tsp. baking soda
1½ tsp. ground ginger
¼ tsp. ground nutmeg
¼ tsp. ground cinnamon

¼ c. dark brown sugar, firmly packed
1 tblsp. dark molasses
1 tblsp. buttermilk
Sifted confectioners sugar

Combine all ingredients, except confectioners sugar, and mix well. Form dough into ball; chill 2 hours.

Shape in 1″ balls. Roll in confectioners sugar, then pat very thin with glass dipped in confectioners sugar. Place 3″ apart on greased baking sheet.

Bake in moderate oven (350°) 4 minutes.

Remove cookies while still hot. Twist over wooden spoon handle and sprinkle with sugar. Cool on racks. Makes 1½ dozen.

BLIND DATES

You shape and bake dough around dates—add charm to cookie tray

1 (3 oz.) pkg. cream cheese (room temperature)	2 tblsp. confectioners sugar
	24 pitted dates
1 c. Cookie Starter	Sifted confectioners sugar
½ tsp. vanilla	

Combine first 4 ingredients. Form into four balls.

Chill dough 2 hours.

Work with one ball at a time, and roll ⅛″ thick on board dusted with confectioners sugar.

Cut in rounds with 2½″ cutter.

Place date in center of each round. (Date may be stuffed with nut, or use ½ date and 1 nut.) Fold edges over and pinch ends to points.

Place 1″ apart on lightly greased baking sheet, seam side down. Bake in moderate oven (350°) 10 to 12 minutes.

Sprinkle with confectioners sugar. Remove cookies and cool on racks. Makes 2 dozen.

ICE CREAM WAFERS

Wonderful ice cream accompaniment! Wafers are thin and crisp

1 c. Cookie Starter	⅓ c. sugar
½ tsp. vanilla	½ tsp. baking powder
1 egg yolk	Sifted confectioners sugar

Mix all ingredients, except confectioners sugar.

Chill dough thoroughly.

Sprinkle board and rolling pin with confectioners sugar. Roll small amount of dough ⅛″ thick.

Cut with small cookie cutter and place 1″ apart on greased baking sheet. Bake in moderate oven (350°) about 6 minutes, until cookies are lightly browned.

Dust with confectioners sugar. Remove cookies and cool on racks. Makes 3 dozen.

Variations

Oriental Almond Cookies: Make up Ice Cream Wafers recipe, substituting ½ tsp. almond extract for the vanilla.

Chill dough until firm enough to handle, about 1 hour.

Shape into balls about 1″ in diameter. Flatten with glass dipped in confectioners sugar.

Place cookies 3″ apart on lightly greased baking sheet.

Beat egg white with fork. Brush a little on each cookie.

Decorate each cookie with slivered, blanched almonds to make flower.

Bake in moderate oven (350°) about 12 minutes. Remove cookies and cool on racks. Makes 2 dozen.

Orange and Lemon Wafers: Make up Ice Cream Wafers recipe omitting vanilla and adding grated peel of 1 orange and grated peel of ½ lemon.

Roll out and cut cookies into different shapes. Place 1″ apart on lightly greased baking sheet. (Or roll into balls, using 1 teaspoon dough for each cookie. Dip fork into confectioners sugar and make waffle design by crisscrossing with fork. Don't mash cookies too flat.)

Bake in moderate oven (350°) 10 minutes. Decorate with strips of orange peel. Remove cookies and cool on racks. Makes 1½ dozen.

Sesame Cookies: Make Ice Cream Wafers recipe, substituting ¼ tsp. baking soda and ½ tsp. cream of tartar for baking powder. Add ½ c. toasted coconut and ¼ c. sesame seeds (if unavailable add another ¼ c. toasted coconut).

Mix ingredients well.

Shape dough into roll. Chill 15 minutes.

Slice ⅛″ thick and place 1″ apart on greased baking sheet. Bake in moderate oven (350°) 15 minutes, or until lightly browned. Remove cookies and cool on racks. Makes 2½ dozen.

N O T E : In Charleston, South Carolina, they're called Benne Cookies—benne is the colloquial name for sesame seeds.

Victorian Spice Cookies: Make up Ice Cream Wafers recipe using brown sugar instead of white, and ¼ tsp. baking soda instead of baking powder. Add ½ c. chopped walnuts, 1 tsp. cocoa, ⅛ tsp. ground nutmeg, ½ tsp. ground cinnamon and ¼ tsp. ground allspice.

Mix together all ingredients. Form into balls using 1 tsp. dough for each.

Put 1″ apart on greased baking sheet. Make hole in centers of cookies with fingertip. Place ¼ tsp. firm jelly in each hole.

Bake in moderate oven (350°) about 10 minutes, or until cookies are firm. Remove cookies and cool on racks. Makes 2½ dozen.

EIGHT-IN-ONE SUGAR COOKIES

Many women praised this mix when it appeared in Farm Journal

2 c. butter or regular margarine	6½ c. sifted flour
2 c. sugar	1 tblsp. cream of tartar
1 c. brown sugar, firmly packed	2 tsp. baking soda
4 eggs	¼ c. milk

Cream together butter and sugars until smooth and fluffy. Stir in unbeaten eggs, one at a time.

Sift together dry ingredients; add to creamed mixture alternately with milk. Mix thoroughly.

Divide dough in eight 1-cup lots. Wrap each tightly in foil or plastic wrap; freeze. Then place in plastic bag. To use, thaw dough just enough that you can shape or drop it. Place about 2″ apart on greased baking sheet and bake in moderate oven (375°) 10 to 15 minutes. Spread cookies on racks to cool. Mix makes 8 cups dough; each cup makes 2 to 3 dozen cookies, depending on the kind you bake.

N O T E : This dough, tightly wrapped, will keep several days in refrigerator. Freeze as recipe directs for longer storage.

Chocolate Chip Balls: Knead into 1 c. cookie dough, 1 tblsp. cocoa and ⅓ c. semisweet chocolate pieces. Shape into about 24 round balls; flatten slightly with spatula. Bake as directed.

Coconut/Almond Cookies: Knead into 1 c. cookie dough, 1 c. flaked coconut and ¼ tsp. almond extract. Shape into about 24 balls; place on greased baking sheet and press flat with spatula. Top each with a piece of candied cherry. Bake as directed.

Pecan Balls: Knead into 1 c. cookie dough, ½ c. finely chopped pecans and ¼ tsp. vanilla. Shape into 24 round balls. Bake as directed.

Ginger Cookie Balls: Stir into 1 c. cookie dough, 1 tblsp. dark molasses and ¼ to ½ tsp. ground ginger. Shape into about 24 balls (dip fingers occasionally in water so dough doesn't stick to hands). Bake as directed.

Gumdrop Cookie Balls: Mix into 1 c. cookie dough, ½ c. finely cut gumdrops (cut with scissors). Shape into 24 balls; crisscross with a fork. Bake as directed.

Fruit 'n Spice Drop Cookies: Stir into 1 c. cookie dough, ½ c. cooked and drained and chopped dried fruit, 2 tblsp. brown sugar, ¼ tsp. ground cinnamon and ⅛ tsp. ground cloves. Drop by teaspoonfuls 2″ apart onto greased baking sheet. Bake as directed. Makes 30.

Orange Wafers: Stir into 1 c. cookie dough, ¼ tsp. grated orange peel and ¼ c. sugar mixed with 4 tsp. orange juice. Drop by teaspoonfuls 2″ apart on greased baking sheet. Bake as directed. Makes 24 thin cookies.

Banana/Lemon Drops: Stir into 1 c. cookie dough, ¼ c. mashed ripe banana, ½ tsp. grated lemon peel and ¼ tsp. lemon juice. Drop 1 teaspoonful at a time into finely rolled corn flakes. Coat by turning gently with spoon. (Dough is very soft.) Place 2″ apart on greased baking sheet and bake as directed. Watch carefully so cookies do not scorch. Makes 2 dozen.

Cookies Children Will Love to Make

If your daughter has never baked cookies, you'll find easy-to-follow, step-by-step recipes in this section especially for beginning cooks. It's really *her* cookbook within *your* cookbook. They'll answer the questions she would otherwise have to ask you—will give her a feeling of independence and achievement. Let her use these recipes and she'll not have to bother Mother. What's more, she'll make good cookies.

After your youngster (boys like to bake cookies, too) has made these recipes successfully, she is ready to branch out and try other recipes on the preceding pages. We suggest, in a list preceding the Index, some of the easier ones that will appeal to young people.

The recipes in this section were developed in Farm Journal Countryside Test Kitchens especially for beginners in baking. We have taken them from our book for beginning cooks, Let's Start to Cook. These cookie recipes go into much more detail than the others and are easy to read and follow.

BAR COOKIES

These are the cookies that are easiest to bake. You spread the dough in a greased pan and bake it the way you bake cakes. Then you cut the cookie into squares or bars.

Here are some recipes for bar cookies almost everybody loves. So get out your measuring cup, mixing bowl and get going.

Do's for bar cookies

1. Do use the pan size the recipe recommends. If your pan is too large, the dough spreads thinner in the pan and it overbakes; the cookies will be tough and dry. If the pan is too small, the dough spreads too thick in it and the cookies may not bake through.

2. Do mix the dough the way the recipe directs. Overmixing gives bar cookies hard, crusty tops.

3. Do spread the dough evenly in the pan with a spatula or spoon so that all of it will bake in the same number of minutes.

4. Do watch the clock. When the time for baking is almost up, make the fingerprint test: When the cookies are lightly browned and a few minutes before the baking time is up, lightly press the top of the cookie with a fingertip. If your finger makes a slight dent or imprint that remains, the cookie is done. Overbaking makes cookies dry and crumbly.

5. Do cool the cookies in the pan at least 10 minutes before cutting. Cutting the bars while they are hot makes the cookies crumble.

FUDGE BROWNIES

For a surprise, frost these brownies with chocolate and white frostings and arrange like a checkerboard

2 (1-ounce) squares unsweetened chocolate	½ teaspoon salt
	1 cup sugar
⅓ cup soft shortening	2 eggs
¾ cup sifted flour	1 teaspoon vanilla
½ teaspoon baking powder	½ cup chopped or broken nuts

Start heating the oven to 350°. Lightly grease an 8 x 8 x 2-inch pan with unsalted shortening or salad oil.

Put the chocolate and shortening in the top of the double boiler and melt them over hot, not boiling, water. Or melt them in a small saucepan over low heat, watching all the time so chocolate won't burn. Cool until lukewarm.

Sift the flour onto a square of waxed paper or into a bowl and then measure. Sift the measured flour with the baking powder and salt. Set aside.

Beat the sugar and eggs together in a large bowl with a spoon, or with an electric mixer on medium speed, until light. If you use an electric mixer, stop the mixer two or three times and scrape sides of bowl with a rubber spatula.

Beat the cooled chocolate-shortening mixture and vanilla into the egg-sugar mixture. Stir in the flour mixture or beat it in with the electric mixer on low speed. Stir in the nuts and mix well. (If you like, you can divide the nuts in half. Stir ¼ cup into the cookie dough and sprinkle the other ¼ cup on top of dough in pan just before baking.)

Spread evenly in the greased pan with the back of a spoon or a spatula. Bake on the rack in the center of the oven 20 to 25 minutes. The crust on top will have a dull look when the cookie is done.

Remove the pan from the oven and set it on a wire rack to cool about 10 minutes, or until completely cooled, before cutting. Cut into 16 (2-inch) bars.

For a change

Before cutting the baked Brownies into squares or bars, sprinkle the top lightly with powdered sugar.

BROWNIES À LA MODE

Here's a dessert that you won't go wrong on if your friends or family are chocolate fans. (That means most Americans!) Bake the Fudge Brownies dough in a greased 9-inch round layer cake pan. Set the pan on a wire rack to cool. To serve, cut the cookie in pie-shaped pieces and top each triangle with vanilla ice cream. Pass a pitcher of chocolate sauce to pour over it. You can buy the sauce in a jar or can, or make it.

MAGIC PARTY SQUARES

The magic of these cookies is the way you frost them with milk chocolate candy bars. And their wonderful taste!

½ cup regular margarine or butter (¼ pound)	2 tablespoons water
	1 teaspoon vanilla
1 cup brown sugar, firmly packed	3 (1-ounce) milk chocolate candy bars
¾ cup sifted flour	
¾ cup quick-cooking rolled oats	¼ cup chopped nuts
1 egg	

Start heating the oven to 375°.

Put the margarine, brown sugar, flour and rolled oats in a medium bowl and mix well with a pastry blender. Be sure the margarine is evenly distributed. Add the egg, water and vanilla and beat with a spoon to mix thoroughly.

Spread evenly in an ungreased 9 x 9 x 2-inch pan with the back of a spoon or a spatula. Bake on the rack in the center of the oven about 22 to 25 minutes. The crust on top will have a dull look when the cookie is done.

Remove the pan from the oven and top at once with the chocolate candy bars. Let stand about 2 minutes or until the heat softens the candy. Spread the melted chocolate over the top of the cookie to make a frosting. Sprinkle the frosting with chopped nuts. Cool in pan on rack and cut into about 20 bars, or any number you like. (*Double Magic:* You can double this recipe and bake the cookie in a 13 x 9 x 2-inch pan. You'll need to bake it longer, about 35 to 40 minutes in all.)

CANDY BAR COOKIES

The 4-H Club girl who shares this recipe with us says the cookies taste like candy bars. Her friends agree

1 cup brown sugar, firmly packed	1 teaspoon salt
½ cup soft butter	4 cups quick-cooking rolled oats
½ cup light corn syrup	½ cup peanut butter
3 teaspoons vanilla	1 cup semisweet chocolate pieces

Start heating the oven to 350°. Grease a 13 x 9 x 2-inch pan with unsalted shortening or salad oil.

With a spoon or electric mixer on medium speed, mix the brown sugar and butter in a large bowl until light and fluffy. Add the corn syrup, vanilla, salt and rolled oats and beat on low speed to mix ingredients well.

Spread the mixture evenly in the greased pan with the back of a spoon or spatula. Bake on the rack in the center of the oven 15 minutes.

While the mixture bakes, mix the peanut butter and chocolate in a small bowl.

Remove the pan from the oven and at once spread the peanut butter-chocolate mixture evenly over the top to cover until the heat melts the chocolate. Cool in pan on rack, then cut into 27 bars and remove from the pan with a spatula.

RICH BUTTERSCOTCH BARS

*If you have a 1-pound box of brown sugar in the cupboard, use it.
Then you don't have to measure or roll out lumps*

1 pound brown sugar (2¼ to
   2⅓ cups, firmly packed)
1 cup soft butter
2 eggs
2 cups unsifted flour

1 teaspoon baking powder
½ teaspoon salt
1 cup coarsely chopped or
   broken walnuts

Cook the sugar and butter in the top of the double boiler over hot, not boiling, water until the sugar dissolves. Or cook them in a medium saucepan over low heat. Cool until lukewarm.

Start heating the oven to 350°.

Add the eggs, one at a time, to the butter-sugar mixture and beat thoroughly after adding each egg.

Stir together the flour, baking powder and salt to mix well. Add to the butter-sugar mixture and stir in the nuts.

Spread evenly in an ungreased 15½ x 10½ x 1-inch pan (jelly roll pan). Bake on the rack in the center of the oven 25 minutes or until the cookie is a delicate brown; a slight dent is left when you touch the top lightly with a fingertip.

Remove the pan from the oven and set it on a wire rack. Cut while hot into 40 bars, or as many as you like.

DATE LOGS

Chop and measure at the same time—cut the dates fine with scissors and let them drop into the measuring cup

¾ cup sifted flour
1 cup sugar
1 teaspoon baking powder
¼ teaspoon salt

1 cup pitted finely cut-up dates
1 cup chopped walnuts
3 eggs, well beaten
Confectioners sugar

Start heating the oven to 325°. Grease a 9 x 9 x 2-inch pan with unsalted shortening or salad oil.

Sift the flour onto a square of waxed paper or into a bowl and then measure. Sift the measured flour with the sugar, baking powder and salt into a medium bowl. Stir the finely cut dates, walnuts and the well-beaten eggs into the flour mixture.

Spread evenly in the
spatula. Bake on the r
or until the cookie is
touch the top lightly

Remove the pan f
completely cool. The
ber you like, and ro

You don't have
cookies got their r
a baking sheet. T
have to push the
spatula. If you h
make little peaks, the cookies will be esp

To give drop cookies a fancy look in a jiffy, press bits or nu
candied cherries on the center of each cookie before baking. Or
spread the baked and cooled cookies with cake frosting, either a
quick-to-fix confectioners sugar frosting or a packaged frosting mix.

CHOCOLATE/NUT DROPS

*Use a little showmanship and dress up these cookies—lightly press a
nut on each one before baking*

½ cup soft butter or regular
  margarine
6 tablespoons brown sugar
6 tablespoons honey
1 egg
1¼ cups sifted flour
½ teaspoon baking soda

½ teaspoon salt
Few drops hot water
½ teaspoon vanilla
1 (6-ounce) package semisweet
  chocolate pieces
½ cup chopped walnuts

Start heating the oven to 375°. Grease a baking sheet with unsalted shortening or salad oil.

Beat the butter, brown sugar and honey together until light and
fluffy. Add the unbeaten egg and beat well to mix.

Sift the flour onto a square of waxed paper or into a bowl and
then measure. Sift the measured flour with the baking soda and salt.

Stir into the creamed mixture.
Stir in the vanilla, chocolate p
Drop 2 inches apart from
Bake on the rack in the c
the cookies are a delic
the top lightly with
Remove the pa
slightly. Then r
spatula and s
36 cookies

292

HOMEMADE

MOL

dd the hot water and beat to mix.
eces and nuts.

a teaspoon onto a greased baking sheet.
nter of the oven 10 to 12 minutes or until
e brown; a slight dent shows when you touch
fingertip.

from the oven and set it on a wire rack to cool
move the cookies from the baking sheet with a wide
read them on a wire rack to finish cooling. Makes about

ASSES LOLLYPOP COOKIES

*onderful party favors and Christmas gifts for the young fry. You
can get skewers at dime stores and meat counters*

½ cup soft butter or regular margarine	1 teaspoon ground ginger
½ cup sugar	½ teaspoon ground cinnamon
1 egg	½ teaspoon ground cloves
½ cup light molasses	½ teaspoon ground nutmeg
2½ cups sifted flour	2 tablespoons water
¼ teaspoon salt	Wooden skewers, about 24, 4½ inches long
1 teaspoon baking soda	

Start heating the oven to 375°.

Beat the butter and sugar with an electric mixer on medium speed
or with a spoon until light and fluffy. Add the egg and molasses and
beat to mix well.

Sift the flour onto a square of waxed paper or into a bowl and
then measure. Sift the measured flour with the salt, baking soda and
spices. Add half of it to the molasses mixture and beat with the
electric mixer on low speed to mix. Add the water and stir until
smooth. Then mix in the second half of the flour mixture. Stir until
smooth.

Drop rounded tablespoonfuls of the dough 4 inches apart onto an
ungreased baking sheet. Insert the pointed end of a wooden skewer
(popsicle stick) into each cookie with a twisting motion.

Bake on the rack in the center of the oven 10 to 12 minutes or
until the cookies are a delicate brown; a slight dent shows when you
touch the cookie lightly with a fingertip.

Remove the pan from the oven and let it stand 1 minute. Then, with a wide spatula, carefully remove the lollypops to a wire rack to cool.

When the cookies are cool, decorate them as you like. One good way is to spread them with confectioners sugar mixed with a little milk until smooth and just thick enough to spread on the cookies. Use candies, raisins, tiny candy red hots, small gumdrops and chocolate pieces to make faces and flaked or shredded coconut for hair. Wonderful for a children's party or gifts to your friends. Makes about 24 large cookies.

ORANGE/COCONUT CRISPS

Use the orange juice as it comes from the can—just thaw

2 eggs	2½ cups sifted flour
⅔ cup salad oil	2 teaspoons baking powder
1 cup sugar	½ teaspoon salt
¼ cup frozen orange juice concentrate, thawed	1 cup packaged cookie coconut

Start heating the oven to 400°.

Beat the eggs with a fork or a wire whisk in a medium bowl. Stir in the salad oil and sugar and beat until the mixture thickens. Stir in the orange juice (do not dilute).

Sift the flour onto a square of waxed paper or into a bowl and then measure. Sift the measured flour with the baking powder and salt. Add with the coconut to the egg mixture. Stir to mix well.

Drop teaspoons of dough about 2 inches apart onto an ungreased baking sheet. Press each cookie flat with the bottom of a drinking glass, oiled lightly with salad oil and dipped in sugar. Dip the glass in the sugar before flattening each cookie. Bake on the rack in the center of the oven 8 to 10 minutes or until the cookies are a delicate brown; a slight dent shows when you touch the top lightly with a fingertip.

Remove the pan from the oven and take the cookies from the baking sheet with a wide spatula. Spread them on a wire rack to cool. Makes about 36.

TWICE-AS-GOOD COOKIES

Melted chocolate makes these chip cookies different

1 (6-ounce) package semisweet
    chocolate pieces
1 cup sifted flour
½ teaspoon baking soda
½ teaspoon salt
½ cup soft butter or regular
    margarine

½ cup sugar
1 egg
¼ cup warm water
½ cup chopped or broken
    walnuts

Melt ½ cup of the chocolate pieces in the top of the double boiler over hot, not boiling, water or in a small saucepan over low heat. Cool until lukewarm.

Sift the flour onto a square of waxed paper or into a bowl and then measure. Sift the measured flour with the baking soda and salt. Set aside.

Beat the butter, sugar and egg in the large bowl of the electric mixer, on medium speed, until the mixture is light and fluffy, or beat with a spoon.

Beat in the melted chocolate and warm water. Then beat in flour mixture on low speed just enough to mix, or mix in with a spoon.

Stir in the walnuts and the rest of the chocolate pieces with a spoon. Chill in the refrigerator at least 30 minutes.

Start heating the oven to 375°. Lightly grease a baking sheet with unsalted shortening or salad oil.

Drop rounded teaspoons of the dough onto the greased baking sheet about 3 inches apart. Bake on the rack in the center of the oven 10 to 12 minutes or until a slight dent shows when you touch the top lightly with a fingertip.

Remove the pan from the oven and take the cookies from the baking sheet with a wide spatula. Spread them on a wire rack to cool. Makes 36.

MOLDED COOKIES

If you have ever enjoyed modeling with clay, you'll love to make molded cookies. You shape the stiff dough with your hands, often into balls. To keep the dough from sticking to your hands, chill it thoroughly in the refrigerator. Then rub your hands lightly with flour or a little confectioners sugar before making the balls. You may have to flour or sugar your hands several times while shaping a batch of cookies.

Often recipes direct that you flatten the balls of dough after they are on the baking sheet. Sometimes you use a fork, sometimes the bottom of a glass, dipped in sugar. Then there are thumbprint cookies—you press a hollow in each cookie with your thumb, which you fill with goodies before or after baking. Some of the cookie balls flatten while they bake; some keep their shape. You'll find all kinds among our recipes.

SNACK TIME PEANUT COOKIES

For a snack that satisfies, serve these cookies with glasses of cold milk, cups of hot cocoa or fruit juice

½ cup soft butter or regular margarine	1 egg
½ cup peanut butter	1¼ cups unsifted flour
½ cup sugar	½ teaspoon baking powder
½ cup brown sugar, firmly packed	¾ teaspoon baking soda
	¼ teaspoon salt

In a medium bowl, beat the butter, peanut butter, white and brown sugars and the egg together until the mixture is light and fluffy.

Stir the flour, baking powder, baking soda and salt together in another medium bowl and then stir it into the peanut butter mixture. Chill the dough 1 hour, or until you can handle it easily.

Start heating the oven to 375°. Lightly grease a baking sheet with unsalted shortening or salad oil.

Shape the chilled dough into balls the size of large walnuts. Arrange them on the greased baking sheet about 3 inches apart. Dip a fork into flour and press it first one way and then the other to flatten each cookie and make a crisscross design.

Bake on the rack in the center of the oven until set, but not hard, or about 10 to 12 minutes. Remove from oven and spread cookies on rack to cool. Makes 36.

THUMBPRINT COOKIES

You make a hollow in the cookie balls with your thumb before baking to fill with treats when the cookies are cool

½ cup sifted confectioners sugar
1 cup soft butter or regular
   margarine
½ teaspoon salt

1 tablespoon vanilla
2 cups sifted flour
1 cup finely chopped or broken
   pecans

Sift the confectioners sugar and measure. Beat it, the butter, salt and vanilla together until fluffy.

Sift the flour onto a square of waxed paper or into a bowl and then measure. Stir the sifted flour and pecans into the confectioners sugar mixture. Mix well. Chill in the refrigerator at least an hour so dough will shape easily.

When you are ready to bake the cookies, start heating the oven to 350°.

Shape the chilled dough into small balls. Place them 3 inches apart on an ungreased baking sheet. Press a small hole in the center of each ball with your thumb tip.

Bake on the rack in the center of the oven about 15 minutes, or until lightly browned and set. Remove from oven and spread cookies on rack to cool. Makes 60 small cookies.

REFRIGERATOR COOKIES

Among cookies that were invented in American kitchens are the refrigerator cookies. They contain so much shortening that you have to chill them several hours before baking, which is how they got their name. The shortening makes refrigerator cookies especially crisp.

You shape the cookie dough into long rolls, wrap them in waxed paper, plastic wrap or aluminum foil and chill them in the refrigerator several hours or overnight. Then the shortening hardens and they're easy to slice and bake. If carefully wrapped so they won't dry out, you can keep the rolls of dough in the refrigerator 3 to 5 days. Then you can slice off and bake the cookies when you wish. Serve them warm from the oven—they're so good when freshly baked.

Or you can freeze the wrapped rolls of dough in the freezer and bake them any time within 6 months. When you're ready for some cookies, take the wrapped frozen dough from the freezer and leave it in the refrigerator for an hour, or on the kitchen counter 30 minutes. The rolls of dough will be just right for slicing. You will find many excellent refrigerator cookie dough rolls in the supermarket. All you have to do is slice and bake them.

Refrigerator cookies are thin and crisp. Remember that the thinner you slice them, the crisper they will be.

REFRIGERATOR SCOTCHIES

Shape the roll of refrigerator dough as big around as you want your cookies—2½ inches is a good size

1 cup soft butter or regular margarine	2 eggs
½ cup white sugar	1½ teaspoons vanilla
½ cup brown sugar, firmly packed	2¾ cups sifted flour
	½ teaspoon baking soda
	1 teaspoon salt

Beat the butter, white and brown sugars, eggs and vanilla until fluffy and well mixed.

Sift the flour onto a square of waxed paper or into a bowl and then measure. Sift the measured flour with the baking soda and salt. Add about half of it to the shortening-sugar mixture and stir to mix well. Gradually add the rest of the flour mixture, working it into the dough with the hands. Mix thoroughly.

Press and shape the dough into a long smooth roll about 2½ inches in diameter. Wrap it tightly in waxed paper or aluminum foil and chill several hours or overnight.

When you are ready to bake some of the cookies, start heating the oven to 400°.

Remove the dough from the refrigerator, unwrap it and cut off thin (⅛-inch) slices—eight slices from an inch of dough! Use a knife with a thin, sharp blade for slicing so the cookie edges will be neat. Rewrap the unused dough and put it back in the refrigerator. The dough will keep 3 to 5 days.

Place the slices a little distance apart on an ungreased baking sheet and bake on the rack in the center of the oven 6 to 8 minutes, or until cookies are lightly browned.

Remove the pan from the oven, lift the cookies from the baking sheet with a wide spatula and spread them on a wire rack to cool. This recipe will make about 75.

CHOCOLATE REFRIGERATOR COOKIES

Slices of chocolate and nuts—pretty, too, if you add fancy edges

1½ (1-ounce) squares unsweetened chocolate

½ cup soft butter or regular margarine

1 cup light brown sugar, firmly packed

1 egg

½ teaspoon vanilla

2 cups sifted flour

½ teaspoon baking powder

¼ teaspoon baking soda

¼ teaspoon salt

3 tablespoons milk

½ cup finely chopped nuts

Put the chocolate in the top of the double boiler and melt over hot, not boiling, water or melt it in a small saucepan over low heat. Cool until lukewarm.

Beat the butter and brown sugar with the electric mixer on medium speed or with a spoon until light and fluffy. Add the egg, chocolate and vanilla. Beat to mix thoroughly.

Sift the flour onto a sheet of waxed paper and then measure. Sift the flour with the baking powder, baking soda and salt into a medium bowl. Add some of it to the chocolate mixture, then add a little of the milk. Beat on mixer's low speed or with a spoon after each addition. Keep on adding the flour mixture and milk, first one and then the other, until all of these ingredients are used.

Stir in the nuts. They must be chopped very fine so the chilled dough can be sliced easily.

Shape the dough in two smooth rolls with your hands—make them about 2½ inches in diameter. Wrap them tightly in aluminum foil or waxed paper, twisting the ends of the paper so they will stay in place. Chill several hours or overnight.

When ready to bake the cookies, start heating the oven to 400°. Unwrap the rolls of dough and cut each into thin slices with a sharp knife. Place the slices a little distance apart on an ungreased baking sheet.

Bake on the rack in the center of the oven 6 to 10 minutes.

Remove the pan from the oven, lift the cookies from the baking sheet with a wide spatula and spread them on a wire rack to cool. Makes 46 to 48 cookies.

For a change

Fancy Edge Cookies: When you take the roll of dough from the refrigerator, sprinkle a sheet of waxed paper with little candies of many colors (nonpareils), chocolate shot (jimmies) or finely chopped nuts. Unwrap the roll of cookie dough and turn it around in these tiny candies to coat well. Then, slice and bake the cookies.

ROLLED COOKIES

Get out the rolling pin and cookie cutters before you start to make these cookies. They are a little more difficult to make than other cookies because you have to roll the dough, but this isn't hard if you chill the dough first and use the pastry cloth and stockinet-covered rolling pin. (Rub a little flour into the pastry cloth with your hand. It will disappear into the meshes in the cloth. Brush off any loose flour on the pastry cloth. Then roll the stockinet-covered rolling pin around on the pastry cloth.)

You can dress up rolled cookies in many ways. Just cutting them with various cookie cutters of many shapes gives them a different look. And you can sprinkle the unbaked cookie cutouts with sugar —white or colored—tiny candies or chopped nuts. Also you can spread the cooled, baked cookies with confectioners sugar icing—white or tinted with food color.

Bake these cookies only until they're light brown. Baking them longer will give you a tough, dry cookie.

EXTRA-GOOD SUGAR COOKIES

Sprinkle cookies with sugar before baking—they'll glisten

⅔ cup soft shortening	2 cups sifted flour
¾ cup sugar	1½ teaspoons baking powder
1 egg	¼ teaspoon salt
¾ teaspoon vanilla	4 teaspoons milk
¼ teaspoon almond extract	

Beat the shortening and sugar together until light and fluffy. Add the egg and beat to mix well. Add the vanilla and almond extracts. (You can use 1 teaspoon vanilla and omit the almond extract.) Mix thoroughly.

Sift the flour onto a square of waxed paper and then measure. Sift the measured flour with the baking powder and salt. Stir it into the sugar-shortening mixture along with the milk. Divide the dough in half and chill in the refrigerator 1 hour or until the dough is easy to handle.

Start heating the oven to 375°. Grease a baking sheet with unsalted shortening or salad oil.

Roll the dough, half of it at a time, from the center to the edge until it is ⅛ to ¼ inch thick. (The thinner you roll the dough, the crisper the cookies will be.) Cut with a 3- or 4-inch round cookie cutter.

Use a wide spatula to place the cookies ½ inch apart on the greased baking sheet.

Bake on the rack in the center of the oven 8 to 9 minutes, or until the cookies are light brown.

Remove the pan from the oven at once and use a wide spatula to place the cookies on a wire cooling rack. Makes about 24 cookies.

For a change

Polka Dot Cookies: Dot the tops of cooled Extra-Good Sugar Cookies with dabs of chocolate frosting.

Painted Cookies: Stir ¼ teaspoon cold water into 1 egg yolk. Divide the egg yolk among 3 or 4 small custard cups and tint each part a different bright color with food color of red, green, yellow and pink. Stir to mix the food color and egg yolk. When cookies are ready to bake, paint a design on the top of each with the tinted egg yolk. Use a small, clean, pointed brush for each color. If the egg yolk thickens while standing, add a few drops of cold water and stir.

Cookies on Sticks: Arrange popsicle sticks or wooden skewers with pointed ends on a greased baking sheet and place a round of cookie dough on the pointed end of each skewer. Allow at least ½ inch between each cookie. Bake like Extra-Good Sugar Cookies. Remove the pan from the oven and at once place a chocolate-coated candy mint on the center of each cookie. The candy will melt enough to stick to the cookie when it is cool. Use a wide spatula to place the cookies on wire racks to cool.

Funny Face Cookies: While Cookies on Sticks are hot, you can decorate them with chocolate pieces instead of mints to make the features of a funny face. Let Funny Face Cookies cool before handling them so that the decorations will stay on. Or frost the tops of the cooled cookies and decorate them with little candies and nuts.

CHOCOLATE PINKS

Flatter everyone by writing his name on the dark chocolate cookies

2 (1-ounce) squares un-
  sweetened chocolate
¾ cup soft shortening
1 cup sugar
1 egg
¼ cup light corn syrup

2 cups sifted flour
¼ teaspoon salt
1 teaspoon baking soda
1 teaspoon ground cinnamon
Pink Icing

Melt the chocolate in the top of the double boiler over hot, not boiling, water or in a saucepan over low heat. Cool until lukewarm.

Beat together the shortening, sugar and egg until light and fluffy. Stir in the chocolate and corn syrup.

Sift the flour onto a square of waxed paper or into a bowl and then measure. Sift the measured flour with the salt, baking soda and cinnamon into the chocolate mixture. Beat to mix well.

Divide the dough into three parts and chill it in the refrigerator at least 1 hour.

When you are ready to bake the cookies, start heating the oven to 350°.

Place ⅓ of the dough on a lightly floured pastry cloth. Keep the rest of the dough in the refrigerator until you are ready to roll it.

Roll the dough from the center to the edge ⅛ inch thick and cut it with a lightly floured cookie cutter. To avoid stretching the cookie cutouts, use a wide spatula to place them ½ inch apart on an ungreased baking sheet.

Bake on the rack in the center of the oven 10 to 12 minutes.

Remove the pan from the oven and take the cookies from the baking sheet with a wide spatula. Spread them on a wire rack to cool.

Roll, cut and bake the remaining two parts of the dough and the scraps, gathered together, in the same way.

When the cookies are cool, spread their tops with a creamy confectioners sugar icing, tinted pink. Makes about 30 to 36.

PINK ICING

1 cup sifted confectioners sugar
¼ teaspoon salt
½ teaspoon vanilla

1 to 1½ tablespoons light
  cream or water
Red food color

Sift the confectioners sugar onto a square of waxed paper or into a bowl and then measure. Put the measured powdered sugar, salt and vanilla in a small bowl. Add the cream or water and mix well with a spoon or with the electric mixer on low speed to make an icing that you can spread.

Tint the frosting pink with a few drops of red food color.

Spread it on the cookies with a spatula. Or make Pink Icing a little thicker, this way—use only about ¾ tablespoon of cold water or 1 tablespoon cream. Write names on the cookies with a toothpick dipped in the icing. Nice for a party.

GRANDMA'S MOLASSES COOKIES

They taste like molasses cookies Grandma used to make but they're topped with a sweet, shiny Sugar Glaze

4 cups sifted flour	½ cup soft shortening
1 teaspoon baking soda	¾ cup sugar
½ teaspoon baking powder	¾ cup light molasses
1 teaspoon salt	½ cup buttermilk
2 teaspoons ground ginger	Sugar Glaze (recipe follows)

Sift the flour onto a square of waxed paper and then measure. Sift the measured flour with the baking soda, baking powder, salt and ginger into a medium bowl. Set aside.

Beat the shortening in a large bowl with the electric mixer on medium speed or with a spoon until light and fluffy. Gradually add the sugar and beat until very fluffy.

Stir in a little of the flour mixture, then a little molasses and buttermilk. Keep adding the flour and the molasses and milk until you have used all of them. Start and end the mixing by adding some of the flour. Mix well.

Divide the dough into four parts. Cover and chill it at least 4 hours or overnight.

When you are ready to bake the cookies, start heating the oven to 400°. Lightly grease a baking sheet with unsalted shortening or salad oil.

Roll out ¼ of the dough at a time from the center to the edge to ¼-inch thickness if you want fat, soft cookies, or to ⅛-inch thickness if you want thinner, more crisp cookies. Use a floured cutter to make the cutouts. To avoid stretching the cutouts, use a wide spatula to place them about ½ inch apart on the baking sheet.

Bake on the rack in the center of th

Remove the pan from the oven an ing sheet with a wide spatula. Spre When partly cooled, spread with cookies.

SUGAR GLAZE

Put 2 cups sifted confectioners in a medium bowl. Stir until sm Molasses Cookies while they are

For a change

Gingerbread Boys: Cut the dough for Grandma's Molasses Cookies, rolled ¼ inch thick, with a floured gingerbread-boy cutter. Lift the cutouts with a wide spatula or pancake turner onto a lightly greased baking sheet. Press raisins into the dough for the eyes, nose, a mouth with a smile and shoe and cuff buttons. Use bits snipped from red or green gumdrops with scissors for coat buttons. Bake like Grandma's Molasses Cookies. You can move the legs and arms of the gingerbread boys on the baking sheet, before baking, to make them look as if they're dancing or running.

GIANT RAISIN COOKIES

Man-sized cookies big enough to satisfy the hungriest cookie eaters. There's a hint of orange flavor

½ cup raisins	4 cups sifted flour
1½ cups soft shortening	2 teaspoons salt
1½ cups sugar	1½ teaspoons baking powder
2 large eggs	⅓ cup milk
2 teaspoons vanilla	Sugar (for tops)
1 teaspoon grated orange peel	Raisins (for tops)

Cut the raisins coarsely with scissors.

Beat the shortening and sugar together in a large bowl with the electric mixer on medium speed or with a spoon until fluffy. Add the eggs, vanilla and orange peel. Beat well.

Sift the flour onto a square of waxed paper and then measure. Sift the measured flour with the salt and baking powder. Stir a little of

ortening-sugar mixture, then stir in a little milk.
until all the flour and milk are used.

t-up raisins.

dough into three parts and chill 1 hour or longer in the

heating the oven to 375°. Grease a baking sheet with un-
shortening or salad oil.

Roll one part of the dough at a time from the center to the edge on
lightly floured surface until a little less than ¼ inch thick.

Cut cookies by cutting around an empty 1-pound coffee can or its
lid with a small knife. Place them 1 inch apart on greased baking
sheets.

Sprinkle the circles of dough with sugar. Cut the raisins in strips
with scissors. Press the raisins into the cookies to make initials or
names.

Bake on the rack in the center of the oven 10 to 12 minutes, or
until a light brown.

Remove the pan from the oven and lift the cookies from the baking
sheet with a wide spatula. Place them on a wire rack to cool. Store
them in a jar with a loose lid. Makes 35.

COOKIE CONFECTIONS

Here are the easiest of all cookies to make. You don't bake them.
So get out a saucepan, stirring spoon and your measuring tools and
stir up a batch of cookies in a jiffy. We predict you'll have beginner's
luck with them—that means *good* luck.

BUTTERSCOTCH CRUNCHIES

*You can make these crunchy cookies with any ready-to-eat cereal
flakes. So look in your cupboard and take your pick*

2 (6-ounce) packages butterscotch pieces
½ cup peanut butter
6 cups corn flakes

In a large saucepan cook and stir butterscotch pieces and peanut
butter over medium heat until the mixture melts. Remove from the
heat and stir in the corn flakes with a spoon. Mix well.

Drop teaspoonfuls of the mixture onto a sheet of waxed paper. Let set. Makes 36.

NO-BAKE CHOCOLATE COOKIES

Stir these cookies up in a jiffy when something to nibble is in order. Let your guests help you make them

2 cups sugar	1 teaspoon salt
½ cup milk	3 cups quick-cooking rolled oats
1 stick butter or regular margarine (¼ pound)	1 teaspoon vanilla
	½ cup broken walnuts
3 tablespoons cocoa	1 cup flaked coconut

Put the sugar, milk, butter, cocoa and salt in a large saucepan and bring to a boil. Remove from the heat and stir in the rolled oats, vanilla, nuts and coconut.

Drop from a teaspoon onto waxed paper to make 48.

SAUCEPAN PEANUT COOKIES

Top favorites of schoolboys, fathers and new cooks. No wonder—use whatever cereal flakes you have

1 cup light corn syrup	1½ cups peanut butter
1 cup sugar	4 cups cereal flakes

Mix the corn syrup and sugar in a medium saucepan. Bring the mixture to a full boil. Remove from the heat and stir in the peanut butter and cereal flakes. Mix well.

Drop heaping teaspoonfuls onto a buttered baking sheet. Makes 48.

Cookies for Special Occasions

Once you've baked a variety of cookies from recipes in this cookbook, you'll want to choose the kinds you like but for different occasions. We list suggestions for you to consider to help you select a recipe to meet a special need.

Many cookies are exceptionally versatile and suitable for different occasions. For instance, some of those that originated in faraway places frequently are traditionals on the Christmas cookie tray but are also good travelers in lunchboxes. Children, of course, like just about all cookies, although those in our junior cookie section (see Cookies Children Will Love to Make in Index) and some of the cookie confections are probably most popular with them.

We based our selections primarily on the reactions of our tastetesters—men, women and children—and what women who contributed their favorite recipes to this cookbook told us about them. Many superior recipes in this book do not appear on our lists—these are merely suggested "starters."

(See Index for Recipes)

DAINTY HOSTESS COOKIES

Cheesecake Squares
Cheese Pie-Bar Cookies
Chess Pie-Bars
Chocolate Bonbon Cookies
Chocolate Cookie Sandwiches
French Chocolate Pie Squares
Grapefruit Sugar Cookies
Holiday Party Kisses
Jam/Cheese Cookie Tarts
Jeweled Meringues
Lemon/Coconut Squares

Meringue-Topped Cookies
Mocha Balls
Molasses/Almond Cookies
Nut Butter Cookies
Pumpkin Pie Squares
Ribbon Cookies
Royal Crowns
Spritz Chocolate Sandwiches
Swirls
Walnut Lace Cookies
Wild Rose Cookies

COMPANY AND COFFEE PARTY SPECIALS

Almond Butterballs
Butter Crispies
Chocolate Meringue Bars
Chocolate/Orange Bars
Date-Filled Oat Cookies
English Tea Squares
French Bars
Frosted Carrot Bars

Frosted Ginger Creams
Hampshire Hermits
Hard-Cooked Egg Cookies
Mom's Fortune Cookies
New Moons
Sesame Wafers
Southern Praline Bars

CHRISTMAS COOKIE FAVORITES

Brazil Nut Bars
Christmas Drop Cookies
Citrus/Nut Drops
Easy Cane Cookies
French Bars
Frosted Yule Logs
Fruitcake Squares

Gingerbread Christmas Cookies
Mincemeat/Cheese Cookies
Pretzel Cookies
Rich Anise Cookies
Spiced Christmas Cookies
Star Cookies
White Christmas Cookies

COOKIES FROM FARAWAY PLACES

Chinese Almond Cookies
Danish Raisin Cookies
Finnish Shortbread Cookies
Finnish Star Cookies
Florentines
Golden Coconut Diamonds
Greek Easter Cookies
Lebkuchen
Mexican Fiesta Balls

Orange Wreaths
Pepparkakor
Pepper Nuts
Sandbakelser
Spanish Wedding Cakes
Springerle
Swedish Almond Shortbread
Viennese Crescents

COOKIES FOR LUNCHBOXES

Chocolate Chip Bars
Chocolate Potato Cookies
Cornmeal Cookies
Fruity Gumdrop Cookies
Honeyed Yo-Yos

Indian Bars
Jeweled Oatmeal Drops
Orange/Carrot Cookies
Raisin-Filled Cookies
Rookie Cookies

GOOD SELLERS AT BAZAARS

Candy-Top Brownies
Chocolate Sandwich Treasures
Cocoa Bars
Cry Baby Cookies
Date-Filled Oat Cookies
Jumbo Sugar Cookies
Marshmallow/Cherry Bars
Nut and Fruit Bars
Oatmeal/Molasses Cookies
Snickerdoodles
Spicy Apple Bars
Two-Tone Jumbles

COOKIES THAT MAIL WELL

Applesauce Fudgies
Brownies for a Crowd
California Fig Cookies
Circle Ranch Oat Cookies
Fruit Bars
Glazed Apple Cookies
Grandma's Raisin Cookies
Hampshire Hermits
Multi-Fruited Drops
Oatmeal Chocolate Bars
Oregon Date Surprises
Pumpkin Cookies
Raisin/Ketchup Cookies
Two-Tone Jumbles

CHILDREN'S FAVORITES—TO EAT

Chocolate/Coconut Bars
Chocolate Marshmallow
    Cakelets
Chocolate/Peanut Crunchers
Date 'Mallow Chews
Double Treat Cookies
Grandma's Soft Sugar Cookies
Peanut Candy-Bar Cookies
Potpourri Cookies
Soft Chocolate Chippers

CHILDREN'S FAVORITES—TO MAKE

Butterscotch Crunchies
Candy Bar Cookies
Chocolate/Nut Drops
Chocolate Oatsies
Chocolate/Peanut Clusters
Chocolate/Peanut Crunchers
Chocolate Pinks
Chocolate Refrigerator Cookies
Date Logs
Date/Nut Macaroons
Extra-Good Sugar Cookies
Fudge Brownies
Giant Raisin Cookies
Grandma's Molasses Cookies
Jiffy Candy Cookies
Magic Party Squares
Molasses Lollypop Cookies
No-Bake Chocolate Cookies
Orange/Coconut Crisps
Peanut Butter Drops
Potato Chip Cookies
Refrigerator Scotchies
Rich Butterscotch Bars
Rocky Road Fudge Bars
Saucepan Peanut Cookies
Snack Time Peanut Cookies
Thumbprint Cookies
Twice-as-Good Cookies

Index

Almond
  Bars, 246
  Bonbons, 247
  Brittle Bars, 30
  Butterballs, 187
  Cookies, Chinese, 128
    Oriental, 283
  Creams, Swedish, 238
  Crescents, Viennese, 194
  /Honey Triangles, 54
  /Jelly Cookies, 124
  Jewels, 72
  /Lemon Riches, 144
  /Molasses Cookies, 183
  New Moons, 148
  Quarter Moons, 123
  Refrigerator Cookies, 173
  Shortbread, Swedish, 58
  Squares, Austrian, 67
Angel Cookies, 197
Anise: Cookies, Rich, 174
  Drops, 72
Apple
  Bars, Spicy, 39
  Cookies, Caramel, 90
  Cookies, Glazed, 91
  /Cran Pie Bars, 253
  /Peanut Cookies, 205
  Pie Bars, French, 253
Applesauce Fudgies, 39
Applesauce Roll-Up Cookies, 125
Apricot
  Bars, 40–41
  Coconut Balls, 246
  Filling, 137
  Scotchies, -Cranberry, 41
Austrian Cookie Rounds, 179
Austrian Tortelettes, 266

Banana
  Chocolate Cookies, 79
  Drop Cookies, 91
  /Lemon Drops, 285

Bar Cookies, see also Brownies
  Almond Brittle, 30
  Almond Shortbread, Swedish, 58
  Almond Squares, Austrian, 67
  Apple, Spicy, 39
  Applesauce Fudgies, 39
  Apricot, 40; Luscious, 41
  Brazil Nut, 58
  Brown Sugar Chews, 59
  Brown Sugar/Nut, 59
  Brown Sugar Spice Crisps, 68
  Butterscotch, Rich, 290
  Butterscotch Strips, 60
  Candy, 289
  Carrot, Frosted, 61
  Cheesecake, 61
  Cherry/Walnut, 42
  Chinese Chews, 45
  Chocolate
    Chip, 30
    Fudge, 31
    Meringue, 31
    Molasses, 32
    Spicy, 37
    Walnut, 33
  Cocoa, 33
  Coconut
    Diamonds, Golden, 68
    /Molasses Wunderbars, 38
  Coffee Cookie, 52
  Cran-Apricot Scotchies, 41
  Crumble Cookies, 69
  Currant Cookies, Teatime, 44
  Date-Filled Oat Cookies, 45
  Date Logs, 290
  Date/Nut, 46
  Date Sandwich, 46
  English Tea Squares, 56
  French, 47
  Fruit, 53
  Fudge Nut, 34
  Hermits, New England, 44
  Honey/Almond Triangles, 54

Bar Cookies (cont'd)
  Honey, Favorite, 54
  Hostess Cookies, 34
  Indian, 35
  Jingle Jam, 57
  Lebkuchen, 55
  Lemon, California, 50
  Lemon/Coconut Squares, 51
  Lemon or Lime Sugar Crisps, 68
  Lemon Love Notes, 51
  Lemon Meringue, 50
  Lemon Slices, Honeyed, 55
  Macadamia Nut Gingers, 68
  Magic Party Squares, 288
  Marbleized Squares, 35
  Marmalade, 57
  Marshmallow/Cherry, 43
  Molasses Creams, Frosted, 69
  Nut-Crested Squares, 64
  Nut and Fruit, 47
  Oatmeal/Chocolate, 36
  Oatmeal, Filled, 38
  Oatmeal Shortbreads, 70
  Orange/Date, 48
    Dainties, 48
  Orange/Pecan Flats, 67
  Peanut, Plantation, 63
  Peanut Salts, 68
  Pecan Chews, 64
  Penuche Dream, 62
  Pineapple/Chocolate, 28
  Praline, Southern, 65
  Raisin-Filled, 53
  Sea Foam Cookies, 36
  Speedy Cookies Supreme, 66
  Swedish Heirloom, 65
  Toffee Cookie Squares, 37
  Toffee Sticks, 66
  Treasure, 49
  Turkish Cardamoms, 67
  Walnut, 67
    /Cinnamon Squares, 67
Barn, Cocoa Cookie, 167–68
Black Walnut: Cookies, 73, 175
  /Chocolate Cookies, 33
  Crescents, 187
Blushing Refrigerator Cookies, 175
Boy's Special, 270
Brazilian Lace-Edged Cookies, 200
Brazil Nut Bars, 58
Brown-Eyed Susans, 126
Brown Sugar: Chews, 59
  /Nut Bars, 59

Spice Crisps, 68
Brownies
  à la Mode, 288
  Butterscotch, 29
  Candy-Top, 24
  Chocolate, California, 24
    Double, 28
  Cottage Cheese, 25
  Drop, Frosted, 85
  for a Crowd, 23
  from a Mix, 275
  Fudge, 287
  Halloween Three-Decker, 26
  made with Cocoa, 25
  Mocha, 27
  Orange, 27
  Peanut Butter, 29
  Pie-Bars, 254
  Snow-Peaked, 25
  Two-Tone, 28
Butter Cookie(s): /Caramel Sundae,
  267
  Crispies, 127
  Nut, 149
Butterscotch
  Bars, Rich, 290
  Brownies, 29
  Cookies, Best-Ever, 73
  Crunchies, 304
  Drops, 74
  Favorites, 268
  Refrigerator Cookies, 174
  Stack, 60
  Strips, 60

Candy Bar Cookies, 234
Candy Cookies, Carnival, 247
  Jiffy, 237
Cane Cookies, 188–89
Caramel
  Apple Cookies, 90
  Coconut Bars, 232
  Frosting, 105
  Icing, 52, 90
  Pie-Bars, American, 255
  Pie-Bars, Danish, 255
  Sundae Cookies, 267
  Tarts, Danish, 255
Carrot: Bars, Frosted, 61
  /Orange Cookies, 101
  /Raisin Cookies, 106
Cashew Drops, 74
Casserole Cookies, 248

Cereal Cookies, *see also* Confections, Individual Kinds
  Christmas Fruit Bars, 246
  Rocky Road Fudge Slices, 250
  Slices, 244
Cheese, *see also* Cream Cheese
  Chocolate Cookies, 80
  /Jam Cookie Tarts, 127
  /Mincemeat Cookies, 145
  /Orange Cookies, 218
  Pie-Bar Cookies, 256
Cheesecake Bars, 61
Cherry
  /Chocolate Creams, 267
  Drops, 277
  Filling, 137
  /Marshmallow Bars, 43
  /Walnut Bars, 42
Chess Pie Bars, 256
Children's Recipes, *see* Cookies Children Love to Make
Chinese Chews, 45
Chocolate
  Banana Cookies, 79
  Bars, -Pineapple, 28
    Spicy, 37
  Bonbon Cookies, 189
  Brownies, *see* Brownies
  /Caramel Sundae Cookies, 267
  Cheese Cookies, 80
  /Cherry Creams, 267
  Chip Balls, 284
  Chip Bars, 30
  Chip Cookies, 159
    Cape Cod, 191
    from a Mix, 277
    /Pineapple, 87
  Chippies, Soft, 88
  -Coated Wafers, 268
  Cocoa Bars, 33
  /Coconut Bars, 234
  /Coconut Crispies, 240
  /Coconut Kisses, 225
  /Coconut Ribbons, 270
  Cookie Sandwiches, 176
  Cookies, No-Bake, 305
  Crackles, 192
  Crunch, Farmhouse, 243
  /Date Clusters, 249
  Dream Bars, 62
  Drops, 277; Crisp, 278
  Filled Cookies, 177
  Florentines, 84

Frosting, *see* Frostings, Icings
Fudge Brownies, 287
Fudge Cookies, 31
Fudge Nut Bars, 34
Fudgies, 233
Hermits, 80
how to melt, 15
Macaroons, 193
Malted Drops, 86
Marshmallow Cakelets, 81
Marshmallow Cookies, 81
Marshmallow Filling, 130
Meringue Bars, 31
Mint Wafers, 178
Molasses Cookies, 32
/Nut Drops, 291
/Oatmeal Bars, 36
Oatsies, 243
/Peanut Clusters, 249
/Peanut Crunchers, 245
Pecan Pie-Bars, 260
Pie-Squares, French, 257
Pinks, 301
Potato Cookies, 82
/Raisin Clusters, 249
Refrigerator Cookies, 298
Rum Balls, 268
Sandwich Treasures, 83
Sour Cream Cookies, 88
Spritz, 220
  Sandwiches, 221
Squares, Three-Layer, 239
-Topped Crispies, 240
Twice-as-Good Cookies, 294
Wafers, 176
/Walnut Cookies, 33
Christmas
  Cane Cookies, 188
  Cookie Centerpieces, 163–68
  Cookies, Drop, 92
    Spiced, 151
    White, 151
  House, for Cookie Family, 171
Church, Ginger Cookie, 164–67
Cinnamon Balls, Hostess, 191
  Cookies, 279
  /Walnut Squares, 67
Citrus/Nut Drops, 92
Citrus/Raisin Filling, 137
Clothespin Cookies, 129
Cocoa
  Bars, 33
  Cookie Barn, 167–68

Cocoa (cont'd)
  Frosting, 82, 88
  /Molasses Cookies, 130
  substitute for chocolate, 16
Coconut
  /Almond Cookies, 284
  /Apricot Balls, 246
  Caramel Bars, 232
  /Chocolate Bars, 234
  /Chocolate Ribbons, 270
  Cookies, 160
    Supreme, 278
  /Corn Flake Crispies, 240
  Crispies, 193
  Crisps, 242
  /Date Balls, 241
  /Date Marbles, 248
  Diamonds, Golden, 68
  Kisses, 225
  Lemon Cookies, Fresh, 180
  /Lemon Squares, 51
  Marzipans, 251
  /Molasses Wunderbars, 38
  /Nutmeg Cookies, 112
  /Oatmeal Crisps, 115
  /Orange Crisps, 101, 293
  Orange Toppers, 264
  /Pecan Finger Cookies, 208
Coffee: Cookie Bars, 52
  Icing, Creamy, 69
Confections
  Almond Bars, 246
  Almond Bonbons, 247
  Almond Creams, Swedish, 238
  Apricot/Coconut Balls, 246
  Butterscotch Crunchies, 304
  Candy Bar Cookies, 234
  Candy Cookies, Carnival, 247
  Candy Cookies, Jiffy, 237
  Casserole Cookies, 248
  Cereal Slices, 244
  Chocolate
    /Coconut Bars, 234
    Cookies, No-Bake, 305
    Crunch, Farmhouse, 243
    Oatsies, 243
    /Peanut Clusters, 249
    /Peanut Crunchers, 245
    Squares, Three-Layer, 239
  Coconut
    Caramel Bars, 232
    /Corn Flake Crispies, 240
    Crisps, 242

  /Date Marbles, 248
    Marzipans, 251
  Date/Coconut Balls, 241
  Date Mallow Chews, 235
  Date Marshmallow Balls, 235
  Date/Nut Macaroons, 249
  Fruit Bars, Holiday, 246
  Fruitcake Squares, 236
  Fudge Bars, Rocky Road, 250
  Fudgies, 233
  Graham Bars, Matrimonial, 233
  Graham Cracker Bars, 236
  Halloween Treats, 239
  Lemon-Filled Bars, 233
  Magic Cookie Bars, 237
  Peanut Butter Drops, 241
  Peanut Candy Bar Cookies, 244
  Peanut Chews, 240
  Peanut Cookies, Saucepan, 305
  Potpourri Cookies, 242
  Praline Cookies, 237
  Puffed-Up Rice Fingers, 243
  Seven-Layer Bars, 238
  Southern Candy Cookies, 250
  Spicy Crunch, 245
Cookie
  Barn, Cocoa, 167-68
  Church, Ginger, 164-67
  Family, 169-70
  Mix, Colorado Basic, 274
    Eight-in-One Sugar, 284
    Starter, 281
Cookies Children Love to Make
  Brownies, Fudge, 287
  Brownies à la Mode, 288
  Butterscotch Bars, Rich, 290
  Butterscotch Crunchies, 304
  Candy Bar, 289
  Chocolate, No-Bake, 305
  Chocolate/Nut Drops, 291
  Chocolate Oatsies, 243
  Chocolate Peanut Clusters, 249
  Chocolate Peanut Crunchers, 245
  Chocolate Pinks, 301
  Chocolate Refrigerator, 298
  Cookies on Sticks, 300
  Date Logs, 290
  Date Nut Macaroons, 249
  Fancy Edge, 299
  Funny Face, 300
  Gingerbread Boys, 303
  Jiffy Candy Cookies, 237
  Magic Party Squares, 288

Cookies Children Love (*cont'd*)
Molasses, Grandma's, 302
Molasses Lollypop, 292
Orange/Coconut Crisps, 293
Painted, 300
Peanut Butter Drops, 241
Peanut, Saucepan, 305
Peanut, Snack Time, 295
Polka Dot, 300
Potato Chip, 77
Raisin, Giant, 303
Refrigerator Scotchies, 297
Rocky Road Fudge Bars, 250
Sugar, Extra Good, 299
Thumbprint, 296
Twice-as-Good, 294
Corn Flake/Coconut Crispies, 240
Corn Flake Cookies, 75
Corn Flake Kisses, 225
Cornmeal Cookies, 131
Cottage Cheese Brownies, 25
Cran/Apple Pie-Bars, 253
Cranberry/Apricot Scotchies, 41
Cream, *see also* Sour Cream
Cookies, Double, 133
Cream Cheese Drop Cookies, 75
Frosting, 62
Creamy Frosting, 133
Crescents
Black Walnut, 187
Viennese, 194
Crisscross Cookies, 194
Crumble Cookies, 69
Cry Baby Cookies, 93
Currant Cookies, Teatime, 44

Date(s)
Bars, Layer, 276
Betweens, 264
Blind, 282
/Coconut Balls, 241
/Coconut Marbles, 248
-Filled Cookies, 158
-Filled Oat Cookies, 45
-Filled Oatsies, 146
-Filled Specials, 265
Fill-Ups, Easy, 178
Logs, 290
Mallow Chews, 235
Marshmallow Balls, 235
/Nut Bars, 46
Chewy, 275
/Nut Drops, 93

/Nut Kisses, 226
/Nut Macaroons, 249
/Orange Bars, 48
/Orange Dainties, 48
/Peanut Shorties, 266
Pinwheels, 131
Sandwich Bars, 46
Surprises, Oregon, 94
Sweets, Double, 230
Double Treat Cookies, 195
Drop Cookies
Almond Jewels, 72
Anise, 72
Apple, Glazed, 91
Banana, 91
Black Walnut, 73
Brownies, Frosted, 85
Butterscotch, 74
Best-Ever, 73
Caramel Apple, 90
Cashew, 74
Chocolate
Banana, 79
Cheese, 80
Chippies, Soft, 88
Hermits, 80
Malted, 86
Marshmallow, 81
Cakelets, 81
/Nut, 291
Sandwich Treasures, 83
Christmas, 92
Citrus/Nut, 92
Coconut/Nutmeg, 112
Corn Flake, 75
Cream Cheese, 75
Cry Baby, 93
Date/Nut, 93
Date Surprises, Oregon, 94
Family, 95
Fig, California, 95
Florentines, 84
Fruitcake, Holiday, 96
Fruited, 97
Multi-, 99
Fruity Gumdrop, 97
Ginger Nuggets, 109
Gingersnaps, Honeyed, 113
Guess-Again, 76
Hermits, Hampshire, 98
Old-Fashioned, 100
Lemon, 99
Macaroons, Overnight, 118

Drop Cookies (cont'd)
Maple Wafers, 76
Molasses Lollypop, 292
Molasses, Scotch, 118
Molasses, Soft, 111
Molasses/Whole Wheat, 110
Oat, Circle Ranch, 114
Oatmeal, 116
Chippers, 116
/Coconut Crisps, 115
Jeweled, 117
Orange, 100
/Carrot, 101
/Coconut Crisps, 101, 293
-Glazed Prune, 102
/Oatmeal Scotchies, 117
Peanut/Molasses, 110
Peanut, Salted, 77
Pecan Lace Roll-Ups, 107
Pies, Pennsylvania Dutch, 86
Pineapple/Chocolate Chip, 87
Pineapple, Golden, 103
Potato Chip, 77
Prune, 103
Pumpkin, 104
/Oatmeal, 119
/Pineapple, 104
Ragged Robins, 94
Raisin/Carrot, 106
Raisin, Grandma's, 105
Raisin/Ketchup, 107
Raisin, Ranch House, 106
Rookie, 119
Sesame Wafers, 78
Slapjacks, 112
Sour Cream, 78
Chocolate, 88
Sugar, Grandma's Soft, 120
Powdered, 121
Swedish Lace Roll-Ups, 108
Swedish Spice Specials, 113
Twice-as-Good, 294
Two-Tone Jumbles, 89
Two-Way, 89
Walnut Lace, 109
Wheat/Oat Crisps, 120

Easter Cookies, Greek, 196
Lamb, 143
Shortbreads, 179
Egg Cookies, Hard-Cooked, 142
Eggs, how to measure, 15
Eight-in-One Sugar Cookies, 284

English Tea Squares, 56

Family Cookies, 95
Cookie Family, 169–70
Fancy Edge Cookies, 299
Fig Bars, 133
Cookies, California, 95
Filling, 137
Frosted, 271
/Orange Filled Squares, 134
Filling(s)
Chocolate/Marshmallow, 130
Citrus/Raisin, 137
Fluffy Refrigerator, 87
Lemon, 201
Mincemeat/Lemon, 176
Raisin, 157
Finnish: Shortbread Cookies, 179
Star Cookies, 134
Florentines, 84
Flour, how to measure, 14
Fortune Cookies, 135–36
Freezing Cookies, Cookie Dough, 19–20
French Bars, 47
Frosted Diamond Cookies, 132
Frostings, see also Glazes, Icings
Brown Butter, 74
Butter Glaze, Golden, 75
Caramel, 105
Chocolate, 79
Buttery, 221
Malt, 86
Viennese, 149
Cocoa, 82, 88
Cream Cheese, 62
Creamy, 133
Maple, 77
Orange Butter, 47
Orange Confectioners, 58
Peppermint, 177
Praline, 65
Red Decorating, 167
Rum, 258
Tinted, 180
White Decorating, 167
White Mountain, 132
Fruit Bars, 53
Holiday, 246
and Nut, 47
Fruit Blossom Cookies, 136
Fruitcake Cookies, Holiday, 96
Squares, 236

Fruited Drop Cookies, 97
  Multi-, 99
Fruit 'n Spice Drop Cookies, 285
Fruity Gumdrop Cookies, 97
Fudge Bars, Nut, 34
  Rocky Road, 250
  Shortbread Squares, 265
Fudgies, 233
Funny Face Cookies, 300

Ginger
  Cones, Old English, 281
  Cookie Balls, 284
  Cookie Church, 164–67
  Cookies, Blossom, 197
  Cookies, Crackle-Top, 198
  Cookies for a Crowd, 137
  Creams, Frosted, 140
  Nuggets, 109
Gingerbread: Boys, 139, 303
  Christmas Cookies, 138–39
  Pigs, 140
Gingersnaps, Honeyed, 113
  Marshmallow, 264
  Swedish (Pepparkakor), 209
Glaze(s)
  Golden Butter, 75
  Golden Glow Topping, 101
  Lemon, 98, 107
  Orange, 102
  Peppermint, 190
  Sugar, 303
Graham Bars, Matrimonial, 233
Graham Cracker Bars, 236
Graham Cracker Mix, Basic, 232
Grapefruit Peel, Candied, 141
Grapefruit Sugar Cookies, 141
Greek Easter Cookies, 196
Guess-Again Cookies, 76
Gumdrop Cookie Balls, 284

Halloween Treats, 239
Heirloom Danish Cookies, 195
Hermits
  Chocolate, 80
  Hampshire, 98
  New England, 44
  Old-Fashioned, 100
Honey
  /Almond Triangles, 54
  Bars, Favorite, 54
  /Nut Cookies, 198
  Wafers, 143

Honeyed Gingersnaps, 113
Honeyed Lemon Slices, 55
Honeyed Yo-Yos, 199

Ice Cream Wafers, 282
Icings, see also Frostings, Glazes
  Caramel, 52, 90
  Chocolate, 85
  Easy, 63
  Coffee, Creamy, 69
  Orange, 101
  Ornamental, 162
  Pink, 301
  Shiny White, 85
  Snow, 164
  Vanilla Cream, 127
Indian Bars, 35

Jam Bars, Jingle, 57
  /Cheese Cookie Tarts, 127
  Pie-Bars, Glazed, 257
Jelly: /Almond Cookies, 124
  Diagonals, 199
Jeweled Meringues, 228–29

Ketchup/Raisin Cookies, 107
Kisses, 225–28

Lace Cookies, 108–9
Lebkuchen, 55
Lemon
  /Almond Riches, 144
  Angel Cookies, 200
  Bars, California, 50
  Coconut Cookies, Fresh, 180
  /Coconut Squares, 51
  Cookie Letters, 222
  Drop Cookies, 99, 278
  -Filled Bars, 233
  Filling, 201
  Glaze, 98, 107
  Griddle Cookies, 159
  Meringue Bars, 50
  Pie-Bars, Fluff, 258
    Golden, 259
  Slices, Honeyed, 55
  Snowballs, 201
  Sugar Cookies, 159
  Sugar Crisps, 68
  Thins, 181
Lime Sugar Crisps, 68

Macadamia Nut Gingers, 68

Macaroons
  Chocolate, 193
  Date/Nut, 249
  Overnight, 118
Magic Cookie Bars, 237
Mailing Cookies, 21
Maple Frosting, 77
Maple/Oatmeal Cookies, 184
Maple Wafers, 76
Marbleized Squares, 35
Marmalade Bars, 57
Marshmallow
  /Cherry Bars, 43
  Choco-Cookies, 81
  Chocolate Cakelets, 81
  /Chocolate Filling, 130
  /Date Balls, 235
  Date Chews, 235
  Gingersnaps, 264
Marzipans, Coconut, 251
Meringue Cookies
  à la Belle, 229
  Bit o' Nut Sweets, 230
  Chocolate Bars, 31
  Coconut Kisses, 225
  Corn Flake Kisses, 225
  Date/Nut Kisses, 226
  Holiday Party Kisses, 226
  Jeweled, 228–29
  Lemon Bars, 50
  Miniature, 229
  Peppermint Kisses, Debbie's, 227
  Pink Kisses, 228
  Sea Foam Cookies, 36
  -Topped Cookies, 181
Mexican Fiesta Balls, 202
Mexican Seed Cookies, 203
Mexican Thumbprints, 203
Mincemeat
  /Cheese Cookies, 145
  Cookies, 278
  -Filled Oatsies, 145
  Filling, /Lemon, 176
  Pie-Bars, 259
  Refrigerator Cookies, 182
Mint Stuffies, 269
Mint Wafers, Chocolate, 178
Mix(es), Cookie
  Colorado Basic, 274
  Eight-in-One Sugar, 284
  Starter, 281
Mocha Nut Cookies, 183

Molasses, 15
  Balls, Spicy, 204
  Butterballs, 204
  /Coconut Wunderbars, 38
  Cookies, 279
    /Almond, 183
    Chocolate, 32
    /Cocoa, 130
    Country, 146
    Crisp, 147
    Grandma's, 302
    Lollypop, 292
    /Oatmeal, 150
    /Peanut, 110
    Scotch, 118
    Soft, 111
    /Whole Wheat, 110
  Creams, Frosted, 69
  Drops, Soft, 111
  Wagon Wheels, 147
Molded Cookies
  Almond Butterballs, 187
  Angel, 197
  Black Walnut Crescents, 187
  Brazilian Lace-Edged, 200
  Cane, Christmas, 188; Easy, 189
  Chocolate Bonbon, 189
    Chip, Cape Cod, 191
    Crackles, 192
    Macaroons, 193
  Cinnamon Balls, Hostess, 191
  Coconut Crispies, 193
  Crisscross, 194
  Double Treat, 195
  Easter, Greek, 196
  Heirloom Danish, 195
  Honeyed Yo-Yos, 199
  Honey/Nut, 198
  Jelly Diagonals, 199
  Lemon Angel, 200
  Lemon Snowballs, 201
  Mexican Fiesta Balls, 202
  Mexican Seed, 203
  Mexican Thumbprints, 203
  Molasses Balls, Spicy, 204
  Molasses Butterballs, 204
  Party Pinks, 205
  Peanut/Apple, 205
  Peanut Blossom, 206
  Peanut Drops, 206
  Peanut, Snack Time, 295
  Pecan, 207
    Bonbons and Logs, 207

Molded Cookies (cont'd)
Drops, 208
Finger, 208
Puffs, 209
Pepparkakor, 210
Pretzel, 210
Ribbon, 210
Sandbakelser, 211
Sand Balls, 211
Snickerdoodles, 212
Spanish Wedding Cakes, 216
Sugar, 214
Crackled, 213
Jumbo, 214
Swirls, 213
Thumbprint, 296
Vanilla Bars, Double, 215
Viennese Crescents, 194
Yule Logs, Frosted, 216
Mom's Fortune Cookies, 136

New Moons, 148
Norwegian Heirloom Cookies, 148
Nut(s), see also Individual Kinds
Butter Cookies, 149
Caramel Bars, 232
-Crested Cookie Squares, 64
and Fruit Bars, 47
/Sugar Cookies, 159
Nutmeg Cookies, Rich, 174

Oat Cookies, Circle Ranch, 114
Date-Filled, 45
/Wheat Crisps, 120
Oatmeal
Bars, Filled, 38
/Butter Crisps, 115
Chippers, 116
/Chocolate Bars, 36
Chocolate Oatsies, 243
/Coconut Crisps, 115
Cookies, 279
Drop Cookies, 116
Drops, Jeweled, 117
Macaroons, Overnight, 118
/Maple Cookies, 184
/Molasses Cookies, 150
/Nut Cookies, 115
/Orange Scotchies, 117
/Pumpkin Drops, 119
/Raisin Cookies, 115
Rookie Cookies, 119
Shortbreads, 70

Toscas, 265
Oatsies, Mincemeat-Filled, 145
Old Salts, 184
Orange
Butter Frosting, 47
/Carrot Cookies, 101
/Cheese Cookies, 218
/Coconut Crisps, 101, 293
/Coconut Toppers, 264
Confectioners Frosting, 58
Cookies, 100
/Date Bars, 48
/Date Dainties, 48
/Fig-Filled Squares, 134
Glaze, 102
-Glazed Prune Cookies, 102
Icing, 101
and Lemon Wafers, 283
/Oatmeal Scotchies, 117
/Pecan Flats, 67
Snowballs, 202
Wafers, 285
Wreaths, 152
Ornamental Icing, 162

Painted Cookies, 300
Party-Goers, 269
Party Pinks, 205
Patterns
for Cocoa Cookie Barn, 168
for Cookie Family, 170
for Ginger Cookie Church, 165–66
Peanut
Blossom Cookies, 206
Butter Brownies, 29
Butter Cookies, 280
Pressed, 219
Butter Drops, 241
Chews, 240
/Chocolate Clusters, 249
/Chocolate Crunchers, 245
Cookies: /Apple, 205
Candy Bar, 244
/Cereal Candy, 247
/Molasses, 110
Plantation, 63
Salted, 77
Saucepan, 305
Snack Time, 295
/Date Shorties, 266
Drops, 206
Prizes, 266
Salts, 68

Pecan
  Balls, 284
  Bars, 276
  Bonbons and Logs, 207
  Chews, 64
  Cookies, 207
  Drops, 208
  Finger Cookies, 208
  Lace Roll-Ups, 107
  Pie-Bars, 260
  Puffs, 209
Pennsylvania Dutch Cookie-Pies, 86
Penuche Dream Bars, 62
Pepparkakor, 210
Peppermint Frosting, 177
  Glaze, 190
  Kisses, Debbie's, 227
Pepper Nuts, 152
Pie-Bars
  Apple, French, 253
  Brownie, 254
  Caramel, Danish, 255
  Cheese, 256
  Chess, 256
  Chocolate Squares, French, 257
  Cran/Apple, 253
  Jam, Glazed, 257
  Lemon, Golden, 259
    Fluff, 258
  Mincemeat, 259
  Pecan, 260
  Pumpkin Squares, 260
  Raisin Cream, 261
  Raisin, Danish, 261
  Sour Cream/Raisin, 262
Pineapple
  Bars, -Chocolate, 28
  Cookies, /Chocolate Chip, 87
    Golden, 103
    Pumpkin, 104
  Filling, 137
  Spritz, 221
Pink Icing, 301
Pinwheels, Date, 131
  Party Whirls, 153
Polka Dot Cookies, 300
Potato Chip Cookies, 77
Potato Chocolate Cookies, 82
Potpourri Cookies, 242
Powdered Sugar Cookies, 121
Praline
  Bars, Southern, 65
  Cookies, 237

Frosting, 65
Pressed Cookies
  Lemon Letters, 222
  Orange/Cheese, 218
  Peanut Butter, 219
  Royal Crowns, 219
  Spritz, 220
    Chocolate, 220
    Chocolate Sandwiches, 221
    Lindsborg Letter, 223
    Pineapple, 221
    Scandinavian, 222
Pretzel Cookies, 210
Prune Cookies, 103
  -Filled, 157
  Orange-Glazed, 102
Puffed-Up Rice Fingers, 243
Pumpkin Cookies, 104
  /Oatmeal Drops, 119
  Pie Squares, 260
  /Pineapple, 104

Ragged Robins, 94
Raisin Cookies, 160
  /Carrot, 106
  Giant, 303
  Grandma's, 105
  Griddle, 158
  /Ketchup, 107
  Ranch House, 106
Raisin: -Filled Bars, 53
  -Filled Cookies, 157
  Filling, 157
    /Citrus, 137
  Pie-Bars, Cream, 261
    Danish, 261
    Sour Cream, 262
  Turnovers, 158
Raspberry Kisses, Pink, 228
Ready-Made Cookies
  Austrian Tortelettes, 266
  Boys' Special, 270
  Caramel Sundae, 267
  Cherry/Chocolate Creams, 267
  Children's Special, 270
  Chocolate-Coated Wafers, 268
  Chocolate/Coconut Ribbons, 270
  Chocolate Rum Balls, 268
  Date Betweens, 264
  Fig Bars, Frosted, 271
  Fudge Shortbread Squares, 265
  Marshmallow Gingersnaps, 264
  Mint Stuffies, 269

Ready-Made Cookies (cont'd)
    Oatmeal Toscas, 265
    Orange/Coconut Toppers, 264
    Party-Goers, 269
    Peanut/Date Shorties, 266
    Sugar, Lazy Daisy, 272
Refrigerator Cookies
    Almond, 173
    Anise, Rich, 174
    Black Walnut, 175
    Blushing, 175
    Butterscotch, 174
    Chocolate, 298
        Filled, 177
        Mint Wafers, 178
        Sandwiches, 176
    Date Fill-Ups, Easy, 178
    Filled, 176
    Lemon Coconut, Fresh, 180
    Lemon Thins, 181
    Meringue-Topped, 181
    Mincemeat, 182
    Mocha Nut, 183
    Molasses/Almond, 183
    Oatmeal/Maple, 184
    Old Salts, 184
    Scotchies, 297
    Shortbreads, Easter, 179
        Finnish, 179
    Six-in-One, 185
Ribbon Cookies, 219
Rocky Road Fudge Bars, 250
Rolled Cookies
    Almond, Chinese, 128
    Almond/Jelly, 124
    Almond Quarter-Moons, 123
    Applesauce Roll-Ups, 125
    Brown-Eyed Susans, 126
    Butter Crispies, 127
    Cheese/Jam Cookie Tarts, 127
    Chocolate Pinks, 301
    Christmas, Spiced, 151
    Clothespin, 129
    Cocoa Barn, 167–68
    Cocoa/Molasses, 130
    Cookie Family, 169
    Cornmeal, 131
    Cream, Double, 133
    Date Pinwheels, 131
    Easter Lamb, 143
    Egg, Hard-Cooked, 142
    Festival Squares, 126
    Fig Bars, 133

Fig/Orange-Filled, 134
Finnish Star, 134
Frosted Diamonds, 132
Fruit Blossom, 136
Ginger Blossom, 197
Gingerbread Boys, 139, 303
    Christmas, 139
    Pigs, 140
Ginger Church, 164–67
Ginger, Crackle-Top, 198
Ginger Creams, Frosted, 140
Ginger, for a Crowd, 137
Grapefruit Sugar, 141
Honey Wafers, 143
Lemon/Almond Riches, 144
Lemon Sugar, 159
Mincemeat-Cheese, 145
Mincemeat-Filled Oatsies, 145
Molasses, Country, 146
    Crisp, 147
    Grandma's, 302
    Wagon Wheels, 147
Mom's Fortune Cookies, 136
New Moons, 148
Norwegian Heirloom, 148
Nut Butter, 149
Oatmeal/Molasses, 150
Orange Wreaths, 152
Party Whirls, 153
Pepper Nuts, 152
Raisin-Filled, 157
    Giant, 303
    Griddle, 158
Sand Tarts, American, 154
Shortbread, Scotch, 154
Springerle, 156
Star, 155
Sugar, 160
    Extra-Good, 299
Thumbprint, 160
Wedding Ring, 161
White, 151
Wild Rose, 162
Rookie Cookies, 119
Royal Crowns, 219
Rum Frosting, 258

Sandbakelser, 211
Sand Balls, 211
Sand Tarts, American, 154
Sea Foam Cookies, 36
Sesame Cookies, 283
    Seeds, Toasted, 78

Sesame Cookies (cont'd)
  Wafers, 78
Seven-Layer Bars, 238
Shortbread
  Almond, Swedish, 58
  Austrian Tortelettes, 266
  /Caramel Sundae Cookies, 267
  Finnish, 179
  Oatmeal, 70
  Scotch, 154
  Squares, Fudge, 265
Six-in-One Refrigerator Cookies, 185
Slapjacks, 112
Snickerdoodles, 212
Sour Cream
  Chocolate Cookies, 88
  Drop Cookies, 78
  /Raisin Pie-Bars, 262
Southern Candy Cookies, 250
Spanish Wedding Cakes, 216
Speedy Cookies Supreme, 66
Spice Cookies, Victorian, 283
Spicy Crunch, 245
Springerle, 155–56
Spritz, 220–23
  Chocolate, 220
    Sandwiches, 221
  Lindsborg Letter, 223
  Pineapple, 221
  Scandinavian, 222
Star Cookies, 155
Storing Cookies, 19
Sugar Cookies, 160, 280
  Crackled, 213
  Eight-in-One, 284
  Extra-Good, 299
  Grandma's Soft, 120
  Grapefruit, 141
  Jumbo, 214
  Lazy Daisy, 272
  Molded, 214
  Powdered, 121

Spiced, 160
Sugar Glaze, 303
Sugar-Syrup Cement, 163
Sugar, Vanilla, 215
Swedish: Heirloom Bars, 65
  Lace Cookies, 108
  Spice Specials, 113
  Swirls, 213

Thumbprint Cookies
  for Children, 296
  Mexican, 203
  from a Mix, 280
  rolled, 160
Toasted Sesame Seeds, 78
Toffee Cookie Squares, 37
Toffee Sticks, 66
Topping, Golden Glow, 101
Treasure Bars, 49
Turkish Cardamoms, 67
Twice-as-Good Cookies, 294
Two-Tone Jumbles, 89
Two-Way Cookies, 89

Vanilla Bars, Double, 215
  Cream Icing, 127
  Sugar, 215
Viennese Crescents, 194

Walnut
  Bars, 67
  /Cinnamon Squares, 67
  Kisses, 225
  Lace Cookies, 109
Wedding Ring Cookies, 161
Wheat/Oat Crisps, 120
White Mountain Frosting, 132
Whole Wheat/Molasses Cookies, 110
Wild Rose Cookies, 162

Yo-Yos, Honeyed, 199
Yule Logs, Frosted, 216

JOHN MASTERS

To the
Coral Strand

London
MICHAEL JOSEPH

First published by
MICHAEL JOSEPH LTD
26 Bloomsbury Street
London, W.C.1
NOVEMBER 1962
SECOND IMPRESSION DECEMBER 1962
THIRD IMPRESSION AUGUST 1963

Set and printed in Great Britain by Tonbridge Printers Ltd,
Peach Hall Works, Tonbridge, Kent, in Times ten on
eleven point, on paper made by Henry Bruce at Currie,
Midlothian, and bound by James Burn at Esher, Surrey

For Alan and Nancy

Chapter 1

Margaret Wood walked slowly down the centre of the path, between the deep ruts of cart wheels. The sun streamed through the trees on her left hand, but the earth seemed dark.

Was it evening, then? She passed her hand in front of her eyes, and for a time afterwards could see nothing. She began to fall, and grasped a tree for support. Later, light returned, and she limped forward. Her shoes were red, and the red mud stained her bare legs.

The jungle fell back on the right and tall shapes began to glow among the trees. The sun spread an aura of orange light over the twisted façades and towers of four temples. All four stood on a stone platform raised a few feet above the level of the earth. The summits of the towers rose a little above the tops of the tallest trees. She leaned dizzily against the stone platform.

Was it evening, then? Twenty-four hours since he had died. Ten since the red earth rattled down on his coffin. Nine since she started walking.

The part of the platform where she rested, near the track, was almost undamaged. The nearest temple stood there, too, seemingly complete. Behind, tree roots and bushes grew through cracks in the stone. One of the other temples was little more than a ruin, another leaned crazily against the bole of a peepul tree which had grown up from the earth below. The light shone, under a flat lintel, into the interior of the temple which leaned against the peepul tree. It illumined a stone pillar, polished and glowing, the side facing her carved with the curved lines that turned it from a pillar to a phallus. The other three towers repeated the shape. Every tower rose by soaring steps, and every step was composed of a torrent of human beings in stone, but alive. Every human being coupled sexually with another, or others. Close to her head, where she had laid it

9

on the stone, a girl bent over, her long hair sweeping her bangled ankles, and a man powerful in his desire held her hips from behind. The stone girl smiled straight at the living woman.

Margaret closed her eyes and wept soundlessly. God had taken Henry from her and she was alone. Why? Where was His infinite mercy? Alone against this overpowering, thrusting animalism, which Henry had so despised . . . and feared. Alone, by herself, without his simple goodness, that had been able to shame her out of all passion.

She straightened her knees, and began to walk again.

'Been having a look at the local pornographic exhibition?' The man's voice was a little high-pitched, pleasant, slightly nasal. She jerked her head up and the words snapped out before she had time to think. 'Yes . . . No, of course not.'

The man stood in the road five feet from her, a walking-stick in his hand and his head bare. Through the blur of her recent tears his face sprang into violent focus, evenly lighted, grey against the orange glow among the trees. She stepped back a pace, and another, raising her arms. 'Keep away,' she gasped. 'Don't touch me!'

A shadow of astonishment crossed the man's blue eyes, then his expression altered. 'You're ill. You're out on your feet.' He took a pace towards her.

She backed away. The trees swayed and the earth heaved. 'Don't . . .' she began, and stopped. She stared more closely at him, one arm still raised. Was it possible that she had been mistaken? He stood there for inspection, his thin lips parted and his forehead wrinkled in an anxious frown. He was quite tall, clean shaven, his hair thick and dark, his eyes pale cold blue. His face was long and narrow, tapering to a strong pointed chin, his mouth wide. His khaki shirt flapped outside khaki drill trousers, and his desert boots were covered with the same red mud that covered her shoes. He held the walking-stick in his left hand, and his rolled sleeves showed thin muscular arms thickly covered with black hair, a silver wrist-watch strap round his left wrist.

She had not been mistaken. This was the man.

'Now, please,' he said. 'Let me help you before you fall down.' He smiled. 'I assure you I never assault women unless, in one way or another, they invite me to. You must be Mrs Wood.'

'My husband,' she began, and stopped. The red earth glowed at

10

her feet, and the sky was turning red. 'My husband . . . is dead.'

She saw him stepping quickly forward, his arm outstretched, and then the red light filled her eyes.

She was lying on her back, water on her face and in her eyes and hair. She sat up, feeling an arm supporting her, and looked dimly around. It was almost dark. A stream purled and splashed past her feet and she saw a dim white shape to the right. 'That's the old Forest Rest House,' she muttered, 'and this is the stream, the Shakkar.'

'Yes,' he said, 'I carried you here. You weigh quite a lot.'

'I'm not fat,' she said indignantly, sitting up straight.

'That's better. No, you're not fat, but you're not a sylph . . . Can you walk now, if you lean on me? If not, I'll get my car. I could be back in half an hour.'

'I can walk,' she said. He helped her up. Her knees trembled so that she almost fell. 'I think so. I've been walking a long time.'

He said, 'I apologise for my flippancy. I just parked my car in Lapri and walked straight past your mission. No one told me.'

She began walking, his stick in her hand. He walked at her side, comfortably matching his pace to hers; and as he walked, he talked – He was with McFadden Pulley, had been for a year. It's good, interesting work, he said, and worthwhile. He had never realised how much pioneering the British business firms did, and with no help from Government. At the moment, indeed, it was worse than that – there were prospects of active hostility from the socialistic-minded Congress. But McFadden Pulley would show them! At this very moment M.P. were on the track of new ore sources which, properly exploited, would create a whole new industry for India.

'What ores?' she asked involuntarily.

'Mainly manganese,' he said. 'Do you know anything about metals?'

She did not answer. His manifest enthusiasm had momentarily aroused her from her lethargy. But Henry was dead, and how could she care what *this* man did or thought? Anyway, he was only talking to keep her awake.

He rambled on. He was staying at his firm's Sabora quarries, just down the main road. She had visited them, of course? 'No . . . I mean, yes, once.' He loved this central Indian countryside.

11

He had been in these parts before. How long had she been in India?

'I landed in Bombay on August 15, 1947,' she said, and turned her head to stare at him, trying to see his face. There was no reaction.

'Independence Day,' he said. 'You've been here a year, then. I've been here seventeen years. There's a legend that a remote ancestor came here first in 1620, or thereabouts. Quite a long time.'

He turned to other subjects – the trees, the flowers, the wild animals. He asked her how much Hindustani she had learned and cross-examined her with Hindustani words and phrases.

Two miles, she thought. Two miles down the gently winding road, empty as a churchyard at this hour of the evening. Last time she met this man he'd been a lieutenant colonel in worn jungle-green uniform, with two rows of medal ribbons, and he'd been drunk. It was in Bombay, not far from Sir Andrew Graham's flat – Sir Andrew was the managing director of McFadden Pulley. Perhaps he'd just come away from the flat, too, or was on his way there to be interviewed for a job in civilian life. He'd obviously got the job – but surely not *that* day, in that state?

Her thoughts blurred and wandered. She wished she could lie down and sleep.

'Shall I carry you?' he asked. 'I could, you know. You're not really a bit heavy.'

'No,' she snapped.

His supporting arm pushed and joggled her, and she stumbled on. She didn't even know his name. He knew hers, because someone at the Sabora quarries must have mentioned the missionary couple buried in the jungles up the road, just over the border in Chambal State. Mentioned it, but not bothered to mention that Henry was dead. Perhaps they didn't know. Or care. Quiet, shy, Henry had never been anyone's hero. And now he'd gone, silently, with no one but herself as mourner.

A yellow light shone ahead, and the man said, 'Nearly there.' He raised his voice and called, '*Koi hai? Iddar ao, jaldi.*'

'There's no one,' she mumbled. 'No servants. We are missionaries.'

'But there is someone,' he said.

She recognised one of the nurses, a convert, walking towards

12

them, lamp upheld. She heard the man's rapid talk as the two of them helped her up the steps. Now he had lifted her, and was carrying her to the bedroom. Last night she had knelt all night in the chapel, praying over Henry's body . . . and before that she'd lain alone here while he crept towards death in the front room, where he had insisted they put him. Now she was really alone. She wanted to cry out, Don't leave me. The nurse was a dirty, unwilling girl, her face sulky even in this extremity. Margaret had learned enough Hindustani to understand that the man was saying, 'She's just tired. Stay with her. Give her something to drink, warm milk or tea, if she wakes up.'

She opened her eyes with a last effort, 'Thank you. What's your name?'

'Rodney Savage.'

When she awoke it was full morning and she was alone. She got up, and only then felt the blisters on her feet. She raised them and looked incuriously at the water-filled lumps spreading across the balls of her feet and between and under every toe. She prepared breakfast, ate hungrily and drank deeply, and went into the glare of the sun.

Her aching feet led her slowly down the dishevelled drive, a few yards along the road, and then left, towards the tiny chapel. Beside the chapel stood seven crosses. Six, the graves of men and women who had died in the mission hospital, were marked with simple stone crosses. Henry's had a wooden cross. Later, she must go to Sabora and ask the masons at the McFadden Pulley quarry to make her a tall, beautiful one for him. No, not bigger, just the same as the others: he would have wanted that.

She stood for a moment at the cross, looking down. What am I to do now? Go over to the ward and see the patients, as though nothing had happened? Write letters to the Society in England, asking for instructions? Begin packing my clothes?

Henry gave her no answer, on his grave the red earth lay silent, a little darker than the rest, but drying, fast sliding back into the breast of India.

She turned to the chapel. Its door hung open on a broken hinge and she slipped in. It seemed very dark inside, but hot. There were two benches on one side, two on the other, at the end a bare teak table, and on the table a wooden cross. The floor was of beaten

13

earth and the whole room was twelve feet square. She sat on one of the benches, staring at the cross, then slipped to her knees.

'Jesus Christ, our Lord,' she began, aloud, and stopped.

Her whisper hung in the enclosed darkness. A bat circled the room, brushing the silence with noiseless wings, and settled with a creeping sound back on its perch.

Henry was dead. His work, his life had been this mission. He had carried it forward through a thousand trials, a thousand disappointments. Now the work was hers. She clasped her hands together so tightly that the nails bit into the palms. She was so tired. Already they had written to her from England, accepting that she must close the mission when Henry's slow, inevitable march to death reached its end. It would be easy to give up, and leave this burning, desolate land to its heathenism, to the pagan sexuality, which could live even in dead stone and seemed to wink and laugh everywhere, just under the decorous surface of life.

'Give me strength to stay. I will not go,' she prayed. The mission, her husband's lifework, must live on in her, where he himself would live, inviolate.

She sat back on the bench, feeling the sweat run down between her thighs and under her breasts.

As clearly as though he were speaking to her now she heard the man's voice, Rodney Savage's voice: 'You've chosen a fine time to arrive, haven't you? Can't you read the traffic signs? One-way only, for us. That way.' And the vivid image of the man saying them, one upflung arm pointing out to sea, face grinning sardonically under the street lamp.

Now it was dawn that morning a year ago, August 15, 1947, India's Independence Day. She stood on the deck and watched the grey hot light spread under the monsoon clouds, and watched the approaching city grow out of the water. Henry lay in his bunk, weak and in pain with the first intimations of his illness. She remembered thinking, guiltily, as the Gateway of India slid past, that it was a strange moment to be arriving, bearing the dour messages of Lancashire nonconformist Christianity, in a country joyfully celebrating its reunion with its Hindu past. Henry had been here before, of course, many years. Henry felt nothing, no premonition, no despair. But Henry had faith.

By the evening of that day Henry felt a little better, but not well enough to go and see Sir Andrew. She quieted his fears on her account, left him in the cheap hotel, and went herself. McFadden Pulley's cement works at Sabora were close to the Lapri Mission and the firm had always been generous in its help.

It had drizzled slightly on her way, but when she came out after seeing Sir Andrew the rain had stopped. The streets were in pandemonium. Rockets fizzed across the sky, thunder flashes exploded everywhere, and bonfires flared in the roadways. Without warning a surging crowd, yelling and singing at the tops of their voices, had surrounded her, and she had felt a momentary panic. She found herself pressed against a lamp-post, close to a tall British officer. He was wearing a peaked military cap of pale khaki felt with a black cloth patch behind the big silver badge. The light shining directly on his shoulders showed his rank badges, the black crown and star of a lieutenant-colonel of a Rifle regiment – she had learned all that during the war. A heavy lanyard of twisted black and dark-green cord looped round his neck under the lapels of his tunic, and then divided at the top shirt button, one strand disappearing into each breast pocket. He wore two rows of medal ribbons, starting with the O.B.E. and then the Military Cross with two silver rosettes. Three M.C.s, she remembered thinking – he was a hero. Rodney Savage.

He noticed her, examined her, and after a while said, 'Frightened?'

'A little,' she said, smiling because her panic had gone. 'They seem so . . . wild.'

'Just off the boat?'

She nodded. 'This morning, very early. My husband is a medical missionary. He's been out before, but this is my first time.' She had to shout to make herself heard above the din. 'Have you been here long?'

That was when he said it, 'Can't you read the traffic signals? One-way only, for us. That way,' and the arm pointing seaward. That was also when she realised he was drunk. Nearly paralytic, her long nurse's training added. She found herself examining him with clinical interest. The lamp-post was supporting him, but his eyes were out of focus and his voice slow, the words kept separate by hard effort, each word slightly blurred.

She became frightened again, for her question seemed to

15

galvanise him into action. He took a step forward and stood, swaying slightly in the middle of the crowd. He raised his hand, and bellowed in a tremendous voice, 'Indians! Listen to me.' The people nearest to him turned in astonishment. The noise took a while to die down, but soon he stood in the centre of a dense circle of excited, dark faces.

'Indians,' he repeated, 'you are now independent . . .' The faces broke into smiles, and a dozen voices rose in eager shouts in a language she could not understand. A tall thin man in a dhoti shouted in English, 'And about time, too, don't you agree?'

The drunken colonel bawled, 'You are taking over this country as a gift from me . . .' He turned to the man in the dhoti and added, 'It is *not* about time, my friend, because you will make an unholy mess of it.'

She tried to move behind the lamp-post and out of sight. If he annoyed them, they would both be torn in pieces. These people were out of control.

The dhoti wearer translated for the crowd, who murmured loudly. The dhoti wearer said, 'But it is our country! You would not be denying that?'

'Certainly, I do! It is not your country. It is mine. I made it, from a hundred countries, I and my great-great-grandfather, and my great-grandfather, and so on. But don't forget my father, my father, whom you murdered yesterday because he loved you.' He raised his voice still more. 'I am sorry I do not speak Gujrati, but my friend here will translate for you . . . You are ignorant, superstitious, lazy buggers. You don't believe in India, because you're too, too small to understand India. Only understand your own dungheap . . .' She looked over her shoulder for a way of escape, but there was none. She was hemmed in. The colonel went on, 'Whassa name that little man, no clothes, spectacles, spinning wheel?'

'The Mahatma!' the English-speaker gasped. 'Oh, do not dare . . .'

'He understood,' the colonel shouted, 'so you shot him. Like my father . . . Well, aren't you going to kill me, too?'

The English-speaker hung his head as he mumbled a translation. The crowd fell silent. Margaret watched in numb astonishment.

The colonel threw his arms wide and began to talk in a language

16

she did not then understand, but now knew was Hindi. Simultaneously he embraced the English-speaker and shouted, 'It'll be all right!' In a moment he almost vanished under the yelling, weeping, laughing crowd. She saw him shaking hands, hugging everyone close to him, and kissing women on the cheek.

Slowly the crowd moved on down the street, singing louder than ever. Colonel Savage stood in the middle of the road, alone among trodden garlands and wilting flowers, the smoke of a bonfire drifting past. He raised both arms, palms extended and fingers spread wide and began to chant at the deep, light-flecked clouds over the city: 'Let us now praise famous men and our fathers that begat us. Let us call down God's blessing upon Robert Clive, First and Last Baron Clive of Plassey and of the County of something or other. And Warren Hastings, impeached by the mighty British nation for preserving their profits, extending their dominions, and loving India. And Stringer Lawrence and Eyre Coote, those much-underestimated soldiers. And Nicholson, Lawrence, Lawrence, Lawrence, Hodson, and Edwardes, the Old Firm, the muscular Christian moving men. And Mountstuart Elphinstone, Gent. and innumerable people called Battye and Coldstream, who usually died, without public comment, in places called Rumble-bellypore or Rotimakkanganj. And William Hickey, and Mr Justice Elijah Impey, and the great Elihu Yale, sometime chief despot of Madras. And Bobs Bahadur too, let us not forget him, O Lord, in spite of his well-known weakness in matters of administration.'

He stopped suddenly and staggered towards her. 'You were frightened,' he said accusingly. 'You'll never make a memsahib. You will be terribly polite, and afraid, and, and – hating them. I . . . I'm rude, and I'm not afraid, and . . . I love them. But it's time to go. That's the whole sad sad story. Time to go. *But I'm not going*. Never. See?'

He stood and examined her thoroughly. 'You're a good-looking woman, wonderful body. Would you care to take your clothes off? Take 'em off, and we'll make love in the street, here. Only proper thing to do, today.'

He put out his hand. She gathered her stunned wits and began to run. After a few seconds, realising no one was following, she looked over her shoulder. The colonel lay alone on his face at the

17

edge of the road, under the street lamp. For a time she hesitated, watching and waiting, then she turned again and hurried to the hotel . . .

It was stifling in the chapel now. She got up slowly, and found her knees stiff. She walked out into the leaden glare of day. Time to go – but, like him, she would not go. She crossed the road and entered the low hut that was the mission hospital's only ward.

Chapter 2

Major-general Ran Singh Dadhwal, known throughout the Indian Army as 'Max', spread his big hands on the table and looked up. '*Achcha*, so what do you propose to do now, Ranjit?'

The man opposite him, across the table, Mr Ranjit Singh, Indian Civil Service, was the Deputy Commissioner of the district. He was about thirty-six years of age, and wore a smart suntan suit with a white shirt and British cricket club tie – the Free Foresters, the general noted. The Deputy Commissioner was a Sikh, and today his long hair was bound up in a puggaree of dazzling pink. A polished steel bangle showed on his right wrist under the sleeve of his coat.

'I think we will have to be quite firm,' Ranjit Singh said. 'If we don't nip it in the bud now we will have worse trouble later.'

The general nodded. That's what he had expected to hear. Sikhs usually liked to be tough on everyone's foibles except their own. Also, there was the I.C.S. tradition. Eight hundred Englishmen hadn't ruled four hundred million Indians by forming committees. They'd gone out and done something, in person, at once. All Indians joining the I.C.S. had learned the lesson.

The general said, 'I can send a battalion down to manoeuvre in the area while you go in and haul out the ringleaders . . . but I presume you'll speak to the Governor before that. I mean, about what action is to be taken if they won't come. I don't want my chaps to drift into a battle. I want to know what the policy is before we go in. Otherwise, you'll have to do it with the police alone.'

The light changed and the two Indians glanced up. An Englishman stood in the open double doors, smiling. The general leaped to his feet. 'Rodney! What are you doing here?' He pumped the newcomer's arm. 'My God, it's funny seeing you in mufti again.

19

Just like before the war! Have you made your lakh yet, or is it a crore by now?'

The Englishman grinned and slapped the general's back. 'I am in this area because McFadden Pulley have sent me to study their cement operations. I'm in this dak bungalow because there was gossip that the Courageous General Sahib and the August Collector Sahib – they still use the old titles here, don't they? – were meeting to discuss yesterday's incident at Bhilghat.' He turned to the Sikh. 'You're the D.C.? I'm Rodney Savage.'

'Ranjit Singh,' the D.C. said, smiling.

'How's the policeman who . . . ?'

'Died this morning, in Bhowani hospital,' the D.C. said.

'Poor bastards,' Rodney said. 'They must be desperate.'

The general smiled at the remark. Rodney's instinctive reaction was for the Gonds, who had committed the outrage, rather than for the forces of law and order. Yet he had enforced the law often enough, as ruthlessly as he had fought the Japanese.

Rodney turned to him. 'I'm interrupting a conference – and that's what I meant to do. Look – if there isn't anything secret or high policy about this, can I help? I know Bhilghat pretty well. I was there before the war, and again once or twice in '46. And I've got a sort of family connection with the Gonds there. You don't *have* to listen to me . . . any more . . .' he grinned, 'but it's just possible that I might say something helpful.'

The general looked at the D.C. This was a civilian party, so far, and he'd have to abide by Ranjit Singh's decision. The I.C.S. didn't take kindly to advice from soldiers at the best of times, and now, with independence so recent, and Rodney an Englishman . . .

To his surprise the D.C. said, after only a small hesitation, 'Please do. Why don't you sit down?'

They all sat. Rodney said, 'In case it leaks out to your superiors that I was at this conference, I was just expressing McFadden Pulley's anxiety over the possible effects on our quarrying operations.'

'The story's simple enough,' the D.C. said. 'About a month ago the provincial government, in accordance with the policy of the Government of India, abolished the post of special assistant commissioner for Bhilghat –'

'The best young man's job in the I.C.S.,' Rodney murmured.

'Yes, but against national policy,' the D.C. said, smiling a little thinly. 'The Gonds have always been treated as a separate people, as savages. Their isolation from the rest of India, and other Indians, has been preserved and even reinforced. We cannot accept that. All Indians are – Indians. Bhilghat lies geographically in my district, Bijoli, and it has now been included in it. The Special Assistant Commissioner, who used to be responsible to the Governor direct, is now merely my own assistant. They gave me a new man . . .'

The general glanced at Rodney, expecting a groan or a sign of dismay; those were his own reactions at the time when the decision had been made. But Rodney showed nothing. The D.C. must also have expected disapproval, for he added quickly, 'We had to. The man there, though he was an Indian, had identified himself too closely with the Gonds . . . Yesterday the new man went down to discuss the building and staffing of a school for the Gonds. They opened fire on him, wounded him – he's still in hospital – and one of his police escort, the man who died.'

Rodney said, 'And you're planning to go back with more police, or some of Max's men in the background?'

'I am going to get hold of the headman and the elders, and I'm going to discuss schools,' the D.C. said. 'I don't propose to make much fuss about the affair yesterday, if they co-operate now. If they don't – then . . .' He shrugged.

Max watched his friend drumming his fingers on the table. He hoped he would come out with some idea that would save the Gonds from further trouble. They were a race of aborigines, living widely scattered over these Vindhya hills of Central India and completely out of touch with the modern world. They were not a relic of medieval times, nor yet of India's Golden Age, but of pre-history. They were pathetic and yet likeable. He wished that their individualism could somehow be preserved . . . but the new policy was right. A new India, a single India, conscious of its oneness, had to be created somehow, and fast.

Rodney said, 'Will you let me go down there alone, to talk to the headman?' The D.C. started to speak but Rodney raised his hand. 'Not as an official emissary. Suppose I had heard nothing of yesterday's affair and just happened to be driving down that way.

21

I don't think I'll be in any danger. I wouldn't go if I thought that. My hero days are over.' He smiled again, the wide grin that looked out of place under the cold blue eyes. That grin had always made Max smile, too, and he smiled now.

The D.C. said gently, 'I appreciate your offer, Savage – but I'm afraid I can't permit that. After all, I'm trying to make the Gonds realise that there's a new government of India – and that they're a part of it.'

Rodney said, 'Then why don't you and Max come with me?'

'We will increase the danger of a clash,' Max said.

The D.C. grimaced. 'We will, damn it, though it's an annoying thing to have to admit. And if they shoot me or the general, I'm afraid they will be in real trouble. I had thought of going down alone, of course, and decided it was not fair to them. After all, if they are willing to shoot at Parsad, how much more at me?'

'And to bore holes in a Thrice-Born of the I.C.S. is a heinous crime, indeed,' Rodney said with a straight face. The D.C. looked at him suspiciously, and then laughed.

Rodney said, 'Look, I have no position. But I do know these people. I think I can guarantee there won't be any trouble. If we fail, we'll fail without bloodshed. I believe it's worth trying.'

The D.C. made up his mind quickly. 'All right. When can you start?'

'Quarter of an hour,' Rodney said. 'I suggest we go in my company's jeep – we three, and Ratanbir. He's my orderly – I mean my chauffeur. Lately Havildar Ratanbir Burathoki, I.D.S.M., of the 1/13th Gurkha Rifles.'

The general sat up. 'Ratanbir? Is that the fellow who killed two Japanese officers with his *kukri* the night we—?'

The D.C. interrupted, smiling. 'We had better get ready . . .'

'Sorry,' the general said, 'Rodney and I haven't met for a long time. We'll have a good *gup* when we come back, eh? You must come and stay with us in Bhowani. Well, we can discuss that on the trip. Oh, and Janaki's coming out . . .'

But Rodney had gone, with a wave of the hand, and the D.C. was on his feet. 'An old army friend of yours? He's the man who got K. P. Roy, isn't he?'

The general said, 'Yes. He's more than a friend. He saved my career once.'

22

'Yours?' the D.C. said incredulously. 'I've never heard that you were the sort of chap to get into trouble.'

The general hesitated; but it was important to let the D.C. know what sort of man Rodney Savage was. He said, 'It was in Peshawar, not long after he'd joined – I had seven or eight years' service by then. We were an Indianised battalion, of course, and the fellow next junior to me got into moneylender trouble. He asked me to lend him two thousand chips out of the Treasure Chest or there'd be a stink, a court-martial . . . The stink would have been about a dishonest Indian. I felt it my duty to our reputation – there weren't so many of us in the service then – to help him. He put the lot on the horses, lost it, and disappeared. Then it was me who was in danger of a court-martial, and cashiering . . . one Indian instead of another. I told Janaki. She must have told Rodney, though I specially ordered her not to say anything – I had to face the music myself. Next day he came to the bungalow and gave me two thousand rupees.'

'Did he say where he got it?'

'No . . . I've always believed he stole it, but he never said a word, or I couldn't have taken it. It was bad enough anyway – but thinking of Janaki, what would happen to us, made me desperate.'

'A good friend, but a pretty ruthless character,' the D.C. murmured.

The general said, 'Yes, I suppose you'd have to say that . . . We kept on running into each other after that, on the Frontier. Then we commanded battalions in the same brigade in Burma. He was a hell of a good soldier.'

'Old India family?'

The general nodded. 'Yes. Very old.'

The D.C. said, 'Poor devils. They can't let go, even if they want to. Still, they had a long innings, and a good one, from their point of view . . . I'll be ready in a minute.'

The general picked up his red-banded hat and put it carefully on his head. He must tell his orderly and driver they were to stay here. Janaki was due later this afternoon to see how her Sabora Cottage Industry Co-operative was coming along. And, my God, he'd nearly forgotten – Sumitra was coming too. Not to look at Cottage Industries – out of boredom, more likely, and to preach birth control to giggling, nervous village women. Have to tell the

23

chowkidar to get her room ready ... Funny, Rodney turning up out of the blue. You couldn't agree with Rodney all the time about India. No Indian could. But you knew he loved India. You could fight happily with him. He sighed and went to his room to fill his tobacco pouch.

He and the D.C. were waiting on the veranda when a jeep drove up fast from the direction of the little town down the road. Rodney sat in the front seat beside a short Gurkha wearing khaki trousers, a white shirt, and a small round black cap. As the jeep stopped, Rodney swung easily into the back seat. 'Will you sit in front, Ranjit? Then they'll hit you first. Max and I will cower in the back. Thirty-two miles to Bhilghat – about an hour and a half on this road.'

They drove off. Max found his feet awkwardly placed on top of a large sack, that clinked as the jeep bounced along the rutted, muddy road, little more than a cart track. He cocked his head inquisitively, and the D.C. turned round in his seat.

Rodney Savage said, 'Rum. It helps.'

The jeep bumped on, often in four-wheeled drive and low gear in the deep reddish mud. The general fumbled for his pipe and began to fill it with his favourite mixture, a Benson and Hedges Special, which he ordered direct from London. Won't be getting this much longer, he thought, after the Prime Minister's warning that India must cut down imports.

The road wound up a low rise in short, steep zigzags, the outer edge marked by mud-splashed white stones. Momentarily from the top a long view spread out to the south, the foreground and middle distance all green under the jungle, the background dim blue, the whole filmed with a thin haze that reduced all dimensions to one, like a coat of paint on the surface. For a second the land seemed almost featureless, but, quickly, as the jeep's nose dipped down the far slope, he saw scattered cliffs, which marked the edge of gorges, and lines of rock on far escarpments, and the flash of water in a lake. Heavy white cloud formations sailing over from the southwest covered half the sky. Then they were grinding down in low gear, and he was looking under the ranked trees, where the wet leaves lay thick on the short grass, and there was a flock of goats and a young girl standing guard over them in the shade of a sal tree.

24

Something about his companion's attitude attracted his attention and he turned his head. Rodney Savage sat hunched forward, staring past Ratanbir's head at the landscape – no, not at it, but through and beyond it. His lips were slightly open and his whole being seemed to be projected forward – out of the bumping vehicle into the patterned sunlight and shadow of the jungle. He began to speak. 'Remember the mahua berries in July?' Max opened his mouth, then closed it. His friend was not speaking to him, nor to any of them.

'. . . They lie sticky and white under the trees everywhere in the jungle. The rain seems to fall directly through the trees then, because the monsoon has made the leaves heavy with all the water they can bear. The raindrops glisten on the berries. If you're near a village you see men and women and children gathering them, like ants . . . bent down, the baskets beside them, gathering up the berries and dropping them into the baskets. And someone has always started to boil them in the village, so if you're coming up-wind you can smell the sweet, fermenting smell from two miles away . . .'

He stopped, and when he spoke again it was in a different voice: 'What did that missionary in Lapri die of, Ranjit?'

'Dr Wood? Cancer. Did you know him?'

'No. I'd heard of them, of course. They are on M.P.'s books as worthy objects of our charity – and to leaven our profits with a little godliness.'

'It looks good on the balance sheets,' the D.C. said dryly. 'And, of course, the Raj had to stick together.'

Rodney laughed. 'What was he like – Wood?'

'A good man,' the D.C. said slowly. 'He'd been in India a long time but somehow never came to terms with it. He always looked a little surprised and horrified – at the heat, the dirt, the things his patients and the villagers did or didn't do. He was alone there for years, and then near the end of the war he went back to England and married the most competent nurse in the hospital where he'd been trained himself, years before. She's a good deal younger than he is – was. Northern Irish. Her name was Donoghue. A good-looking woman – good figure, auburn hair, and one of those skins that go with it, creamy and almost transparent but healthy.'

25

'I know,' Rodney said. 'I met her yesterday by accident. She'd been wandering round the jungles all day, in a daze. It must have been a blow.'

The D.C. said, 'I suppose she loved him. She certainly acted like it, and there must have been *something*, to bring her out here. But, you know, it wasn't what I'd call love. Perhaps it was religious fervour, or faith, or—'

'I met her once,' Max interposed. 'She's like an Indian woman, that's all. She married this man, and accepted him and his life and tried to make it her all. How well she succeeded' – he shrugged – 'no one can know. Perhaps she needed more time, and now he's gone.'

'The poor devil was ill the whole time since he came back last year,' the D.C. said.

'She must be absolutely lost,' Max said. 'And, hey, Rodney, that reminds me – congratulations on your engagement. When's the wedding?'

'October, in Delhi . . . We're getting near, Collector. *Asti janu, choro*. I think I'll stand up, if you don't mind.' The jeep slowed and Max thought, He's as sharp as ever. Calling Ranjit 'Collector' suddenly, like that, established the official relationships, and made an acknowledgement that the Sikh was in charge.

It would be easier if Rodney and the D.C. changed places, so that Rodney could hold on to the windshield, Max thought. But that would put the two Indians in the back seat. 'Here, hang on to my shoulder,' he said. He settled his red cap more firmly on his head, grasped his pipe between his teeth, and began to search the side of the road. They'd just passed milestone 28. If the Gonds meant business . . . The jeep swept round a sharp bend and lurched to a halt, throwing the passengers forward.

A sharp clattering sound from the hood made Max look up, and he saw an arrow turning in the air, to land beyond in the mud. Several large boughs blocked the road.

'No farther,' a voice called from the jungle in accented Hindi. 'Go back, or we will shoot, with guns.'

'Sit still, everyone,' the D.C. said sharply.

Rodney turned his face towards the jungle, from where the invisible voice had called. He spoke conversationally, in Hindi. 'Ohé, brother! Is Badal the *shikari* still alive?'

26

After a long pause the voice answered grudgingly, 'No, he is dead. Now, go back, or we will shoot.'

'Gulu, then? His younger brother.'

'Gulu's the chief now,' the D.C. muttered.

Rodney said, 'Tell Gulu, the chief, that Savage Sahib is here and wishes to talk to him about hunting. Savage Sahib, great-great-grandson of the Deliverer.'

There was a long pause, and then the voice said, 'I recognise you, sahib. Wait.'

Rodney sat down and said, 'We'll have a long wait. Gulu will be in the village.'

'Who was the Deliverer?' the D.C. asked curiously.

'William Savage.'

'The man who destroyed Thuggee?'

Rodney nodded. 'He spent a lot of time with the Gonds after that. It was nothing to do with the Thugs, as far as I can make out, that they call him the Deliverer. It was the British Government he saved them from, who were going to do something dreadful to them.'

'Build a school, perhaps,' the D.C. said dryly.

They all laughed, and then settled down to wait. Max examined the jungle curiously. There were probably half a dozen small dark men in there, with bows and arrows and a couple of ancient muskets trained on them from no more than fifteen feet – and he could see nothing. At least one man, probably two, had just run off through the heavy undergrowth towards the village – and he had heard nothing. He sighed and began relighting his pipe. If he could train his sepoys to move like that . . .

Heavier clouds piled up in the sky, and he felt hungry. Why had no one remembered to bring food? Probably because Rodney intended to ask the Gonds for it, to establish that they were guests. Who was it who'd written, 'If you want to make a friend, allow him to do you a favour'? Now Rodney would have to eat fried rat and raw ants. Thank God he himself was a Hindu and could properly refuse.

A man stood suddenly in the road five feet from the jeep's hood. He wore a loincloth, and nothing else, and carried a small long-handled axe in his hand. He was short, square, and very black, with short grizzled hair over a wide, angular, wrinkled face.

Rodney stood up. 'Gulu – greetings!' He stepped down from the jeep and walked forward. The two embraced formally, first clasping each other round the shoulders and then standing back and bowing, palms joined.

'May your belly always be full, sahib. You look well.'

They exchanged polite small talk for a few minutes. Then the old Gond said, 'Come to the village, and we will eat and drink. The mahua arrack from this year is good, though fiery, and I have a little left, a barrel, from last year.'

'Thank you,' Rodney said. 'I am with these friends – Ranjit Singh-sahib, Deputy Commissioner . . .'

Gulu the chief folded his thin, strong arms across his chest. 'I do not know him. He may not pass.'

The D.C., his face set, began to climb out of the jeep. Rodney said in a low voice, 'Very easy, Collector!' He turned back to the Gond. 'I think you do know him, Uncle. Whether or no – he is my friend and so is the other, the General-sahib, Dadhwal. And the driver, Havildar Ratanbir, a Gurkha. Him you know, he came with me before, when we were in the army.'

'Him I know,' the chief said. He went forward and embraced the Gurkha.

Rodney said, 'We are unarmed, all of us.'

The old Gond had returned to the middle of the road, arms folded, the axe blade over his right shoulder, his head high, silent, unsmiling.

Rodney said slowly, 'Was it not said, once, that the Deliverer and his seed, from then to the end of time, were Gonds? Free to eat and drink and hunt in all Gond lands? To demand the life of any Gond man, with or without reason? Put their own life into any Gond woman not already pregnant? Were these words only the promise of a Hindu *banniah*, to be forgotten when there is no profit to be made from them?'

God, the general thought, he's being hard on them. The promise must already have lasted a century and a quarter; and the deed Rodney was now helping the D.C. to accomplish would mean the end of the promise and the end of the kind of society that could give and keep it.

The old chief stood a minute longer, then bowed his head. 'It was said. I am sorry. They may come, as your friends. For no other reason.'

'We come as the representatives of the Government of India,' the D.C. said stiffly.

The old chief bowed ironically, and Max thought, we do not, we come under the protection of an Englishman, in our own country. Well, that's the way it was. Next year, the year after, it would be different. There was nothing to be done about it now, except be patient and understanding.

'Get in the jeep, Gulu,' Rodney said. The old man threw a few words over his shoulder into the silent jungle and climbed in. Two men appeared and dragged away the tree boughs. Ratanbir drove slowly on, Gulu now perched on the back seat between Max and Rodney.

It's all over, Max thought, all over bar the shouting. The Gonds were not fools and the only real problem was to reach them without creating another bloody incident.

As he had predicted, the tension relaxed all day, slowly but steadily. An hour after reaching the compact village – all the huts were very small, and two or three families lived in caves – they ate, and not mice or worms but a fine fish, with curried vegetables and chapatties. Outside the hut a short, heavy rain fell, darkening earth and sky. Inside, they sat on beaten earth and were served in silence by Gulu's grand-daughters. Gulu had vanished and did not reappear until mid-afternoon. By then the rain had stopped, the hot sun had dried the grass, and the appearance of able-bodied men in considerable numbers proved that the pickets and scouts had been recalled.

Then Gulu came, and Rodney talked with him for a long time outside, while he himself and Ranjit pretended to sleep in the hut. It would be undignified for the D.C. to hang around, aimless, while the Englishman talked, and this was a good way out. Rodney and Gulu were not far off, and Max, listening to their voices, caught enough to know that Rodney was not discussing the school, nor yesterday's attack on the Assistant Commissioner's party, but *shikar*. There were a good many tigers over to the west, across the border in Chambal State, the old Gond said. A man who went out from here, or from Lapri, could have good shooting. There was good fishing, also – he named four kinds of fish. Then they reminisced about Rodney's last visit, and two or three times Gulu cackled with laughter. Max heard the clink of bottles, and later the gurgle of liquid. He hoped Rodney knew what he was doing. The ice had to be broken, but if the Gonds were still in a state of fear and inner tension they might get fighting drunk. Rodney would be all right, but he and Ranjit could easily finish up with poisoned arrows in their guts.

'Now try the arrack, sahib,' he heard the chief say distinctly. 'That is this year's.' There was a faint female giggle. The grand-daughters were pretty girls, for Gonds, and young; they must be great-grand-daughters. The Gonds often consummated marriage at twelve or younger.

The sounds of talk and laughter increased outside and the D.C. sat up. 'About time we joined the party, I think,' he said. They brushed off their clothes and walked out. Twenty villagers were gathered by then, all men except for the two girls crouched in the background. A momentary silence greeted them, broken by Rodney calling, 'Sit down, Collector. I happen to have brought a little rum with me. Gulu has been telling me about the *shikar* . . .'

Then they all talked about *shikar*, which to these people meant food and life; and from there to the state of the few crops the Gonds grew, a little millet on the cleared hillside, a little rice in the bottoms. The D.C. never mentioned the object of his visit and Max thought, he's good, he has the I.C.S. stamp of confidence and firmness, plus an Indian's sense of community, of not being a stranger, however marvellous. As the dusk fell the girls brought little scraps of toasted, curried meat. Max ate without inquiring what they were. They would not be beef anyway, because the Gonds owned no cattle, only a few goats. Two young men lit a bonfire and at the edge of the circle women began to appear, squatting on their hunkers, loinclothed like the men, bare breasted, the younger ones with at least one baby, sometimes two, at breast, and another in the lap.

The murmuring increased, more food came, more people came. Full darkness crept up from the reed-rimmed shore of the lake. Arrack passed round, in bamboo mugs, teak bowls, and earthen-ware jars. An hour after dark a young man shuffled out in front of the fire and began to dance. Others joined him. Singing began, guttural and almost tuneless melodies that wandered about near the bottom of the scale. Small drums began to rattle and throb. On Max's right, Gulu squatted between Rodney and the D.C.

30

The two wide-mouthed girls crouched close behind Rodney. Max felt sure, from their protective, intimate attitude that Rodney had slept with them when he was last here. He wondered whether he would do so again tonight. Perhaps he would have to, to avoid upsetting the Gonds, if they had been offered to him as a special gift or because of his relationship with the Deliverer. Himself, he'd rather not. Gond women were really not attractive, and although Janaki would understand if he had to – he just didn't want to. He'd hardly ever wanted another woman than her. To be honest, hardly any other woman had ever wanted him – unlike Rodney. It must be a problem at times, that animal vitality which could at any moment make any woman, even the most respectable, suddenly think of bed. Ah, well, it wasn't likely to be a problem of his. He puffed contentedly at his pipe, noting that about two more rums would be enough for him.

The D.C. was saying, 'No – he died this morning. It was in his fate.' He spoke equably, as though the murder of a policeman on duty was a mere accident, which might have happened to anyone. Good, Max thought; really, it was an accident. A sudden outburst like that, from the Gonds, was an act of nature. There would be many more such, among many Indian tribes and peoples, before they could all be treated as rational human beings, answerable to a court of law for every action. And now the subject had been broached, and the old Gond was relaxed and full of rum and arrack.

The D.C. began to tell Gulu about the school he himself had been to, as a little boy in a Punjab village. Rodney got up, caught the two girls by the wrists and dragged them out, giggling and shrieking, into the centre of the circle by the fire. 'Now I shall dance,' he cried.

He began to gyrate and twist, his feet shuffling time with the beat of the nearest drum – there were a dozen different beats, half a dozen groups of dancers. Holding the girls tight, he danced with ludicrously suggestive movements, and most of the audience collapsed on to the grass, laughing with painful gasps. The girls dragged free and rushed into the shadow of a hut, where they hid their faces behind their hands and watched, cackling with laughter as loud as anyone.

After five minutes Rodney beckoned, and Ratanbir the Gurkha

31

stepped out into the firelight. Rodney seized a drum from a man collapsed with laughter and began to beat a subtle complex rhythm. Ratanbir, his face downcast and earnest, began to dance. Rodney sang, a haunting, repetitive melody.

Max poured himself another rum. The D.C. and the chief, their heads close together, were talking about schoolteachers. Where could they find a teacher who understood the Gond language? How could the village pay for such people? The Gurkha danced in slow grace, his powerful, squat body bending and turning as sinuously as a girl's. The audience was silent, except for the murmurs of Gulu and the D.C. The fire crackled and hissed as a few drops of rain fell. The underside of the trees reflected a diffuse yellowish light down on the thatched roofs of the huts, the dark heads, the babies sleeping in their mothers' arms.

Gulu the chief rose suddenly to his feet and clapped his hands with a short explosive sound. Ratanbir stopped dancing. Rodney let the rhythm of his drum die down in two more phrases, soft and softer. Gulu spoke a few short sentences in his own language, which Max could not understand. The D.C. leaned over to him and whispered, 'He's agreed. We won't build the school. We'll give them some money, and they'll build it themselves. We're getting a Gond-speaking teacher up from Jubbulpore. He never gave us a chance to tell him that before.'

The old man flung his arms wide in a motion that said, without the need for words, let joy be unconfined. The drums struck up, the singing redoubled, dancers gyrated wildly on the grass.

Rodney approached and Max got up, his hand out. 'Congratulations, Rodney.'

His friend looked tired now and his smile was a little grim. 'Thanks . . . I don't like it, you know.'

'What, education for the Gonds?'

Rodney looked back at the fire and the dancing figures. 'I don't know. Perhaps not even that. Certainly not bringing out these people's basic warmth and then – stabbing them in the back. Next time you come here it won't be like this. There'll be a political rally instead. Guest speaker – Mr Purshottamdass Tirthankardass, M.L.A.' He went abruptly over to the headman and said, 'Uncle, I am tired. With your permission, I shall go to sleep.'

'Thus early?' the old man said in surprise. 'You did not sleep at

32

all last time you came to Bhilghat.' The D.C. was looking up at Rodney, his expression compassionate. Rodney said, 'The Collector Sahib wishes to sit up all night, though. All Sikhs are mighty drinkers of rum, and the Collector Sahib is a champion among Sikhs.'

'That's a dirty trick,' the D.C. said in English. 'Well, I suppose even the worst hangover in history would be worth it.'

Gulu said, 'Very well, sahib.' He gestured with his chin. 'Your women are there.'

'Not tonight, Uncle. I could not do justice to them.'

He strode away towards the hut appointed for them. Max made his own apologies and followed. It was dark inside and there was no bed, only three flattened piles of dry grass. As Max entered he heard the rustling of grass and muttered, 'Which one are you taking, Rodney?'

'This one, in the corner.' A match flared and then the glow of a cigarette end. Now also the light from the fire outside, slipping in through a hundred tiny cracks in the walls, enabled Max to see. Rodney was sitting cross-legged in the middle of his pile of grass, the cigarette hanging from his lower lip and his face twisted up in the smoke. He bent forward to untie his shoe laces. Max sat down and followed suit.

Rodney loosened his belt and said, 'That's it. Not a very complicated toilette.' He sat there, just as he had in the jeep, staring towards the open doorway and the shadowed jungle, lit by the fire from the other side. He began to speak. 'Poor girls ... *She* smelled very different, and she was beautiful where these are ugly – to my eyes – but there was something of the same in her. A different relationship with a man. She was as passionate as these half-savage girls are, and they are like rutting animals, and like them, she'd never found that there was a war between men and women. There was none of the hostility you sometimes feel with our women. The moon was in the same phase as it is tonight, and it shone on her hair, her hair flowing like a dark river so that all I could see was hair and all I could feel was flesh, and all I could smell was ... India.'

'Who was it?' Max asked gently. 'I don't mean her name, but ...'

'My first Indian woman,' Rodney said. 'I wonder whether I've had my last. I'm engaged, remember? That's why I didn't go to the girls. Frances wouldn't understand. You know her?'

'No. She's John Clayton's sister, isn't she – the fellow who was your M.T.O. in Burma?'

'Yes. He was in McFadden Pulley's before he volunteered. He got me my job with them when I chucked the Service. His wife went home to put the kids in school, so Frances came out to housekeep for him, early in '47 ... Almost one year of total chastity for R. Savage. You ought to win some bets on that.' He laughed aloud, the strange mood vanished. 'Good night.'

The grass rustled and Max lay back, pillowed his head on his arms, and soon fell asleep.

Shortly before noon the next day the jeep ground over the brow of the last hill on the return journey, and Max saw the quarries and the pall of reddish dust that marked Sabora in the valley below. Now Rodney was driving, and Max sitting beside him. Rodney turned his head and said, '*Eh, atharsi!* Collector Sahib *lai utha.*'

Max watched, smiling, as the Gurkha gently moved his shoulder. The D.C. sat up, yawning and rubbing his bloodshot eyes. He looked very pale and dishevelled. As he adjusted the pink puggaree more firmly on his head, he muttered, 'God, I feel awful.'

'And two beautiful ladies to greet you when we arrive,' Rodney said cheerfully.

'Oh, no!' the D.C. cried. 'Who?'

'My wife and the Rani of Kishanpur – Sumitra,' Max said.

'Sumitra?' the D.C. said. 'I'd better hurry back to Bijoli, full speed. My wife will give me hell if she hears I've been meeting *her* in deserted dak bungalows at the back of beyond.'

'You must stay for a drink and lunch,' Max said; and then Rodney stopped the jeep in front of the dak bungalow. Max's orderly ran out, followed a moment later by two women. Max walked up the steps. 'Hullo, darling. The excitement's over.' He caught her hand momentarily and as he did he noticed that she was staring over his shoulder, her body tense. 'Rodney,' she said, 'Rodney Savage!'

Rodney came up then, a half-smile on his face. 'In person.' He held out his hand. 'How are you, Janaki?'

34

She dropped her eyes. 'This is the Rani of Kishanpur. Colonel Rodney Savage.'

The Rani said, 'Rodney – the famous Rodney.'

Rodney stood and stared at her, the half-smile still on his face. 'Sumitra.'

Max watched, fascinated, as they stood there, looking, gauging, Janaki between them. Sumitra had the classical rounded Indian beauty, wheat-gold skin, her black hair piled in a loose Western wave on top of her head. She wore a pale-blue sari, and high-heeled sandals. Janaki was much smaller, her figure in the patterned red sari seeming almost childlike beside the Rani's full-bosomed curves. Her cheekbones were higher and the eyes wider set in the small heart-shaped face; and she was darker than the other, and her heavy head of hair was swept down from a straight centre parting.

The Rani broke the silence. 'I have known about you for twelve years – since I married Dip. And now we meet.'

'I can say the same,' Rodney said.

Then the D.C. came up, and the men excused themselves and went to a spare bathroom to wash off the mud and dirt of the road and the Gond village.

'I didn't know you knew Kishanpur,' Max said, slapping cold water over his face.

Rodney said, 'That goes back a long time, too – to my great-grandfather. He and the Kishanpurs fought in the Mutiny together ... on opposite sides. Remember Sumitra Rawan, the Rani of Kishanpur?'

'My God!' Max said softly. 'That one. You really are mixed up with India, aren't you?'

The woman on the veranda was also a Rani of Kishanpur, and she was also called Sumitra; but when you mentioned those names, without qualification, it was taken for granted that you meant the famous heroine of 1857. She had led cavalry charges against the British in the Great Mutiny of that year, and had finally vanished, no one knew where or how. Some said it was to refuge in Nepal or Tibet; some said, into a Hindu *ashram;* some said, to lie unknown among the dead of the last great battle of the Mutiny.

Rodney said, 'She and my great-grandfather tried to kill each other – and fell in love. Things like that used to happen. They still

35

do . . . The two families have had a sort of foster-brother relationship ever since. They sent Dip Rao, the present Rajah, to stay with us in England for a time when he was a kid – he and I shared a nanny. The same with our parents and grandparents. But I have not met Sumitra, for reasons doubtless well known to you.'

The D.C. came in, curling his beard with his fingers. 'Well known to the entire population of India, I'm afraid. She's intelligent and, somehow, not selfish, though. And she's not a nymphomaniac. Whatever it is, it's not that . . . though I don't doubt she's – er, interested – and interesting.'

Max dried his hands, shaking his head. It was a sad business. Dip Rao Rawan, the Rajah of Kishanpur, was about Rodney's age – thirty-five or thirty-six. He'd married this girl from an old Mahratta family a good many years ago, about '36 – and hardly seen her since.

The French Riviera knew the beautiful Rani of Kishanpur. Kitzbühel and La Baule and Monte Carlo knew her; Claridge's and the Meurice and the Waldorf knew her – but, only very seldom, and for short visits, the ancient State of Kishanpur. Her love affairs, faithfully reported in shiny socialite papers and by word of mouth, were famous throughout the last years before the war, and during the war – which she had seemed to have spent shuttling between the Bahamas, New York, and Chile. It wasn't the affairs themselves that caused the furor so much as the bizarre objects of them: a Russian count who was certainly an impostor; a middle-aged American con man who'd later gone to jail; a Cuban painter who had almost, but not quite, become famous; a young Croat revolutionary who later suffocated himself in an asylum, using his own shirt . . . The list was long, and full of violent lights. Yet you couldn't help liking her when you met her; and though the big, dark eyes settled speculatively on all men, they had never seemed to Max to be predatory, still less, calculating. Rather they were inquiring, and direct – who are you, what are you, what makes you go? She was at home now, with Dip. He saw a good deal of them, for Kishanpur was only forty-seven miles east of his own headquarters in Bhowani.

'Shall we join the ladies?' he said formally.

'You're going to be my guests,' the D.C. said, 'though I think I

36

shall be sick if I even smell alcohol. I've got a couple of bottles of Black Label. My bearer should have put them out already.'

The three men walked together down the central passage and out on to the veranda. Rodney said, 'I'll be with you in a minute,' and went on down the steps to his jeep, parked in the shade of a tree across the drive. Max, turning aside to join the women at the small table set up with drinks, saw his friend lean in over the jeep side and put his hand on his chauffeur's shoulder. Ratanbir smiled ruefully and patted his own head. So even he, a Gurkha, had a hangover. It must have been a long night.

The Rani's husky, very French-sounding voice broke in on Max's thoughts: 'The colonel knows how to handle the natives, I see.'

Max answered shortly, 'When he has to, Rodney can handle anyone – one way or another.'

'So Dip tells me,' she said. 'Except, perhaps, himself.'

The jeep drove away and Rodney joined them. The D.C. rose to his feet, a glass of lemonade in his hand. 'Ladies and gentlemen – as Indians, I ask you to join me in a toast to an Englishman, who yesterday saved our government a great deal of embarrassment, and also probably saved a score of lives – Rodney Savage.'

Max quickly poured himself a lemonade and raised his glass. 'You were bloody marvellous, Rodney.'

The women murmured politely and sipped their fruit juice. Max began to relate the whole story, from the beginning. Every now and then Rodney threw in derisive comments and humorous pastiches of things seen, and soon they were all laughing. Max noticed the Rani's steady, weighing look fixed on Rodney. Janaki also was watching him, less obviously, and also seemed to be weighing, and judging, as though she had never met him before – although actually she knew him well. They had met soon after his marriage, when Rodney had first joined the 13th Gurkhas in Peshawar as a very young second lieutenant and he himself was a senior lieutenant of the Dogra Regiment – fifteen years ago, good heavens.

When he finished his tale, Rodney said, 'Taken by itself, without meaning, it was a good time – that trip to Bhilghat ... That's what people like me love about India. To us that *is* India. We haven't had much contact with people like you, for reasons you know as well as I do – our political dominance, our destruction of your class, your sulking in your tents. But we knew the poor, the peasants, those who live in the woods and the mountains . . . in the past, if you like.'

'Kept there, sometimes,' the D.C. interposed softly, brushing up his moustache.

'Yes . . . but damn it, Ranjit, the Gonds *are* different, so are the Bhils, and the Nagas, and the Mishmis, and . . .'

'And the Lahoulis?' the D.C. asked, naming a hill people who lived on the high northern border, touching Tibet. Those Rodney had named were more decidedly 'tribal,' mostly animist in religion and Stone Age in culture.

'The Lahoulis are a borderline case,' Rodney said. His face was eager and alive, his eyes sparkling.

The D.C. said, 'I'm afraid there can't be borderline cases now. There can't even be enclaves of quaint old customs, needing special handling till Doomsday. We haven't got the time. In England you couldn't accept the idea that the people of Lancashire were a special tribe which had to be specially handled, their speech preserved, schools kept away from them so that they'd always remain isolated. At least you never have. Nor can we accept the idea of "reservations", like the Americans.'

'Suppose they don't *want* to go to school?' Rodney said. 'Suppose they don't *want* to join the modern world?'

'They have no choice,' the D.C. said. 'History is marching in a certain direction, and they are going with it – whether they go willingly or get trampled on.'

Max sipped his lemonade and thought sadly, the D.C. was quite right; the Prime Minister was quite right; nevertheless, it was a pity. How many generations, how many short years, would pass before such a way of life as they had entered last night would vanish forever from the jungles, along with the handmade pottery, the wood crafted by their own hands, the weapons shaped by love and ancient skill? In all that village there probably were not ten rupees' worth of articles that had not been wholly made there.

'Go willingly or get trampled on,' Rodney repeated slowly. He stared into his orange juice. 'You'll have plenty doing both . . . and sometimes the people concerned won't even know which they want to do, or are doing. For God's sake, though, Ranjit, go as

38

slowly as you can, as carefully as you can. A tribal, patriarchal society may be a pain in the neck to you and Nehru, but it means a lot to the people who live inside it. It's all that holds them together – and not only the group, but the man himself, inside himself.'

He finished his juice quickly and poured out a whisky and soda. Sumitra of Kishanpur said, 'You seem to have found a solution, without going or getting trampled on.'

Rodney nodded, 'I travel all over India. I have responsibility. In a way, I'm getting many of the advantages of the Raj without the disadvantages – all India to roam in ... reasonable independence ... general control from the Viceroy – I beg his pardon, I mean the Managing Director ... policy from a board room in London. It doesn't seem very different, sometimes. And yet – it's strange, being an outsider. Just watching India, instead of being a part of it. On that basis I can't get trampled on. But sometimes I can hardly bear it. I was not born to be a bystander, not in India. I'd rather have the involvement, like last night – and the trampling.'

The D.C. said slowly, 'I'm afraid that's what it would be.'

The jeep drove up from the direction of the town. Ratanbir came to the veranda steps, saluted, and handed Rodney two letters.

'*Aru chhaina?*

'*Teti ho, hujoor.*'

Rodney said, 'Excuse me,' and opened one of the letters. Max turned to his wife with small talk, and Sumitra to the Deputy Commissioner. It took Rodney a long time to read the letters, and before he had finished them the D.C. told his servant to serve lunch.

Rodney stood up, folding the letters carefully and putting them in his pocket. 'I'll have to be off now,' he said, smiling. 'Thank you so much for the drinks. And thank you, Collector, for allowing me to come with you yesterday.'

Max rose. 'But, Rodney, aren't you staying for lunch? I thought ...'

'I'm afraid I'll have to go. Business before pleasure, you know, McFadden Pulley need me.'

'But surely ...'

He felt a sharp pain in his foot and grimaced involuntarily.

39

Looking down he saw that Sumitra, Rani of Kishanpur, had jabbed her stiletto heel into his instep. 'See you later, then,' she was saying, smiling sweetly, 'I'm going back tomorrow, but Max and Janaki will be here for a week, and you know you have a standing invitation to Kishanpur.'

'Thanks. Yes. Good-bye.' The Englishman ran quickly down the steps and jumped into the jeep. Ratanbir engaged gear and the little vehicle drove away.

Max said, 'I'm sure he said he'd have lunch here.'

Janaki said, 'Darling, you are very dense sometimes.'

'I was never supposed to be very bright,' Max said. 'What's the matter?'

'Couldn't you see? The letters.'

Chapter 3

After dinner General Dadhwal, dressed now in lightweight trousers of black cotton and a long, high-buttoning jodhpur coat of white silk, left the dak bungalow and walked slowly towards the town. Janaki told him he must go and see Rodney; he himself wasn't sure. Janaki said Rodney had had to make a tremendous effort to hide his shock while reading the letters. Janaki said she'd never seen a man hit by a bullet in a vital part of his body, but that's what it made her think of, watching Rodney from the corner of her eye. 'He didn't gasp or wince. I don't think a muscle of his face moved. He turned pale, then fought to get the colour back. His hands began to clench and he fought to make them relax. You must go . . .' All this in the darkened bedroom after lunch, while he prepared to take a nap.

But what right does a man have to intrude on another man, Max thought unhappily? Women don't understand. They can't hide their misery from another woman, so they don't try to. Every woman is part of the club, Womanhood. Someone's husband runs away, she likes her friends to come and comfort her. We don't. We're all as lonely as the single stag under the shade by the stream.

. . . After ten o'clock, and a hint of the first fresh breeze of the cold weather to come; not here yet, for it was only September, but promising to come, in the clear atmosphere and the fading rains . . .

The quarries, still ablaze with lights, were at the near end of the town, and McFadden Pulley's guest house nearer still, only a quarter of a mile from the dak bungalow. Light poured out from a front window, and there was a huge black car-shape silhouetted in front of it. He came close and saw that it was an old Bentley tourer. He shook his head and whistled in admiration. Those things went about six miles to the gallon. Rodney must be doing very well for himself. He squared his shoulders and walked up on to the veranda, and in through the double doors. A door on the left stood ajar and light streamed out over the coir matting on the hall floor. He knocked and called quietly, 'Rodney? It's Max.'

'Max? There's a man who's always welcome. Come on in.'

Rodney was sprawled in one of the long cane chairs that were the feature of every dak bungalow, club, and guest house in India, its arms extended into leg rests, his long legs raised on to them. Two bottles of whisky stood on the table beside him, one of them three-quarters empty. There were two zinc buckets on the floor, filled with ice and bottles of soda water. Half a dozen empty soda bottles stood in a military rank against the wall.

'Sit down. Pour yourself a drink.' His eyes were bloodshot and his voice a little slurred. 'I don't want to get drunk to forget,' Rodney said ' – only to remember. And perhaps to shake up the machinery inside my head. The old equipment doesn't seem to be able to deal with things quite as efficiently as it used to.'

Max poured a drink and sat down. 'What's happened? If I can ... Well, damn it, I'm here.'

'Because Janaki sent you, I'll bet. You can hide nothing from a good woman. You can hide anything from a good man – the better, the easier, if you follow me. And you are very very good, Max ... What shall I do? Rather, what *will* I do? Not what *should* I do. Certainly not! What *will* I do? Me, the ruthless chap looking after poor me. What will Me do? Wait till next week's thrilling instalment ... Will Me go willingly or will Me be trampled on? Will Me find a new way to Happiness? ... It was like having a lover, a married woman. You got her by force perhaps in the beginning – not rape-force, just power, and you didn't have to use it. Women like power because they need it. Yet they dislike you for having it, and dislike themselves for liking it ... So part of her always hated you for that, and another part was flattered. You were strong and the husband wasn't. Then in time you fell in love, and there were enough times of physical ecstasy, power and sensuality fused, so that she fell in love too, a little. You thought it would go on for ever. But it wouldn't, and her husband claimed her, softly, inevitably. You hadn't noticed it, but *the tide was going out*. She floated out and away. She had to.

42

High and dry, now your power's gone, the sheer hypnotic power of the erect and rampant stallion gone . . . You know the feeling, when a woman says sadly, "You'd better go now?" No, perhaps you don't, Max . . .'

'What's happened?' Max asked again, speaking very gently. Rodney was talking about the mysterious woman again, and yet Max was sure it wasn't really a woman. At least, not any one woman. He wondered suddenly whether his friend had become impotent. One of the letters might be from his doctor confirming that there was no cure.

Rodney put his hand in his pocket and brought out the two letters. Max did not think, from the clean folds, that he had looked at them since the first time at the dak bungalow. It was a rare man who could do that. 'This one is from McFadden Pulley. From Sir Andrew Graham, in person. He deeply regrets not having been able to tell us before, but the negotiations were of such delicacy that, etcetera, etcetera. In other words, the other chaps insisted on secrecy . . . McFadden Pulley, private sterling company, is being sold to a public company, Indian owned. The people who are floating the new company have declared as policy that all non-Indian executives will be replaced within five years, three quarters of them within one year. With generous compensation, of course – subject to Indian income tax of, say, 97 per cent.'

He drank unhurriedly, almost lovingly, from his tall glass.

Max said, 'But you've done well, Rodney. They may keep you for the five years.'

'I am the most recently acquired non-Indian, bar two youngsters in Bombay. Anyway, it's only a question of time . . . and I'm damned well not going to go on, business-as-usual, knowing that these chaps are playing Russian roulette with my head. No, I'd have to get out sooner or later, and it will be sooner – because of my addiction to duty. The new owners are a canny bunch. They're giving a nice directorship to an important Congressman. Guess who. L. P. Roy.'

'Oh, my God,' Max breathed. Rodney Savage was one of the few army officers whose name was known to political India. Two years earlier he had hunted down and shot the Communist fire-brand K. P. Roy, while the latter was causing riots and sabotage in Bhowani. The fact that K. P. Roy had also attempted to assassinate Mahatma Gandhi, and had caused the deaths of many innocent Indians, had been played down in Nationalist circles; Roy was anti-British, and that was enough. This man L. P. Roy, now to be a director of McFadden Pulley, had made an attempt to have Rodney court-martialled shortly after the incident. He was K.P.'s younger brother.

'A more dangerous character than K.P.,' Rodney said cheerfully. 'I rather liked K.P. He was a Communist, but he had a sense of humour. I haven't met L.P., but of course I've heard and read a good deal about him. His brother was a tiger – this one's a man, a twisted, tortured fanatic. As a matter of fact, it wasn't I who actually shot K.P. Another chap did . . . But it doesn't matter. I'm afraid, Max, it wouldn't matter if they promised to keep me on for thirty years. I've seen Indian businesses at work. This is where I discover I'm English. This is the parting of the ways.'

'You'd have stayed on in the army if they'd let you, wouldn't you?' Max said.

Rodney looked up, grinning with the slightly wolfish grin that Max remembered best about him; it had been most common when he was under strain, in battle. 'The Indian Army,' he said, 'is not an Indian business – yet. It rests exactly in the mode and tradition we made it. It will remain that way just as long as people like you are in charge. You don't think or act like an Indian, even though you do put on protective camouflage sometimes, like that jodhpur coat . . . That will change. Your political bosses don't like it now and they'll force the change. In a few years they'll find chaps who think their way, not yours, and they'll push them to the top. The pressure will come from inside, from underneath, too. Remember Iqbal?'

'Commanding the 9/21st Punjabis?'

'Yes. Just after the war nearly all his officers were Indian. His adjutant borrowed a battalion truck for non-military purposes – took his wife and kids to the flicks in it – not five hours after signing a strict order of Iqbal's against such practices. Iqbal sacked him. Well, the adjutant's wife was a friend of Iqbal's wife. Know what happened? Iqbal's wife refused to sleep with him unless he reinstated the chap as adjutant . . . Things like that will happen. There's an *Indian* way of dealing with them, I'm sure, and that's how they will be dealt with. But there's no British way of

44

dealing with them. Iqbal was helpless. Know what he did? Applied for more British junior officers. Of course, there weren't any to be had ... No, the bell has sounded. I realise now that I've been waiting for it, listening for it, ever since Independence. I got absolutely soused *that* night ... Perhaps that's what made yesterday, with the Gonds, so particularly wonderful. The roulette game's ended, the revolver's gone off, and I'm dead. *But I won't lie down*. I'm not going to go quietly. I'm going to fight, Max.'

Max poured himself another drink. He felt much more unhappy than Rodney seemed to. 'There must be lots of good jobs for you,' he said. 'You have so many friends here ...'

Rodney went on as though he had not spoken: 'I'm not going to go quietly, and I'm not going to stay quietly. Not like Great-aunt Mary ... great-aunt by marriage. She's still here. Running a hill station hotel on the road to Lansdowne. Her friends used to go up and down in tongas and ekkas, and break journey there over-night. She made a good living, and the place was always full of handsome, sunburned sahibs and pretty ladies and rosy children. Then they built a motor road, and the traffic went by without stopping, though most of her friends would at least have a cup of tea. Then her generation got old, or retired, or were killed. Then no one came, except a few Indians, who were terribly polite to her. For ten years no one at all. She's still there, nearly ninety, enormous wooden building, no servants but a crazy cook about the same age, with the same ideas and the same dreams, though he's a U.P. Muslim. She dresses every night for dinner in the gown she wore at Curzon's Viceregal Ball in '04, and eats a can of bully beef once a week, and the dust lies like a dense silent carpet over everything, and all the glass broken, and langurs swinging from the pines behind the house into the upstairs rooms. Is that what you'd like me to do?'

Max made a helpless gesture with his hands.

'What about smuggling? That's more like it, for me. What about armed dacoity? It's all here still, under the surface, the India my great-grandfather lived with, and the ones before him ... It wouldn't be hard to re-create the Pindaris, motorised. With a little bit of skill and luck a thousand properly led men could take over a province, or a district at least – all in the most proper

45

manner, votes and all . . . and I'd be in the background, just like the old days.'

'You can't turn the clock back, Rodney,' Max said.

'Who says?'

'No one can. Besides, you'd have to go back too far. For the past century and a half you've been building things up here, not tearing them down. You've done the work pretty well, too. *We* might tear ourselves apart – but you couldn't. Anyway, you're joking . . .'

'Believe me, I'm not.'

'Rodney, be patient. Just wait a bit. Remember your friends. India badly needs people like you, and there are enough of us, and we're strong enough not to have to take dictation from anyone, not even Nehru. If you want to stay, we'll find something good, and worthy of you.'

Rodney was looking at him, and seemed to be weighing his words. At last he said, 'Tomorrow I shall probably agree with you. I shall probably do just what you recommend. At this moment I want to fight. I know you've had the feeling. Twice in your life, eh? Once, when that fellow yelled at you to stop playing bloody Wog music in the mess.'

Max nodded. Rodney was referring to the incident which had given him his nickname, and made him popular with the inscrutable English. When he joined his Dogra battalion in 1927 the senior subaltern was a man who disliked educated Indians, though he loved the sepoys well enough. Max, the new second lieutenant, liked to play Indian music on the mess phonograph. The senior subaltern ordered him not to, in the language quoted by Rodney. Max respectfully refused to obey. The feud went on for three years until, in 1930, the senior subaltern seized his pile of records and smashed them on the stone floor. Max knocked him out. Hence the name 'Max', for 'Max Schmeling'; and hence one year's loss of leave privileges. A well-deserved punishment, Max thought. Right or wrong, the fellow was his senior officer, and there were other, proper channels of complaint.

Rodney continued: 'The second time was just after Independence, when Nehru and the boys wanted to promote some of the I.N.A. fellows, and you and Des and N. P. Satish and Chandra went and said that if they were made heroes, after what

46

they'd done to Indian prisoners in Singapore, you were going out.'

Max nodded again. The Japanese had formed the Indian National Army from Indian soldiers who fell prisoner into their hands in Malaya and Singapore. Himself, he had never felt strongly for or against the I.N.A., as an institution. There were many ways of being an Indian patriot in those days before Independence. But he and other Indian regulars could not forgive the I.N.A.'s treatment of such men as Hari Badhwar and Dhargalkar, who had refused to join it. Them the I.N.A. had hung up by the thumbs, tortured, starved for months in solitary confinement. When the Congress leaders wanted to idolise the I.N.A. Max knew again – he had to fight.

Rodney said, 'Well . . . I feel now that I have to fight. And even though tomorrow I may decide not to, the need to fight will be very close under the surface, just suppressed. Remember that, Max, remember.'

Max said, 'What about the other letter?'

'Ah, that. You ought to read that. It would make you cry. Cry for the gulf between people who are supposed to know each other pretty well. But I won't give it to you, because it is a caddish thing to do, to reveal the soul of a lady . . . This is from Frances Clayton, my ex-fiancée.'

'Ex!'

'It was written before the McFadden Pulley letter, so she knew nothing about that. She informs me she cannot face the prospect of living in India the rest of her life. I must go home to England, where brother John can guarantee me a good job with an M.P. subsidiary run by the people who own – used to own – M.P. She begs me to come to Delhi to discuss it. She's a nice girl, Max. Very nice. If you can call a woman of twenty-nine a girl. I suppose so. Unfortunately, I don't love her.'

'Don't say it!' Max cried. 'Go to Delhi and talk to her. It'll be all right.'

'I doubt it,' Rodney said, grinning. 'It took me time to get over Victoria Jones, the Anglo-Indian girl I met in Bhowani in '46, during the K. P. Roy affair. That was probably an attempt to avoid expulsion from India, the psychologists would say. There was an earlier love, which I shall never get over. Now I've spent a

47

year of chastity for the sake of Frances, who is a very decent young woman – but nice, don't forget that. Today, looking at Sumitra got me by the balls, and I'm sure I could love her if things worked out that way. But they won't . . . Meanwhile the manager of the cement works has informed me that the local harlots are superannuated, diseased, or both. He himself always sends to a little village called Pattan – it's hidden in the jungles behind Lapri – where there are a pair of beauties. I have already taken his advice. Ratanbir went with the company jeep to fetch the girls some time ago. He ought to be back any moment.'

'Ratanbir!' Max exclaimed. 'You wouldn't have . . .'

'No,' Rodney said, smiling the wolfish smile. 'I wouldn't have. I have never involved any soldier or servant or friend in anything of the kind, as far as in me lay. That is the sahib's way. I am no longer a sahib . . . I won't ask you to stay, because I know you – and I know Janaki. Thanks for coming. Good night, old boy.'

Max stopped in the doorway. 'For God's sake, Rodney, remember what I said. You're not alone.'

Rodney stood in the middle of the room, unswaying, smiling, saying nothing. Max strode heavily out and down the veranda steps. In the drive the headlights of the jeep flared on to him, half blinding him. When it had passed, slowing rapidly, he noticed two women, their saris drawn across their faces, sitting huddled together in the back seat behind the dark, stolid silhouette of Ratanbir.

Arrived back at the dak bungalow, Max felt very tired. I'm forty-four, he thought, but sometimes I feel like ninety. Perhaps it had something to do with the long fight for Independence, twenty years of being shot at from two sides, the anti-Indian British sneering at him for a Wog, the anti-British Indians sneering at him for a lackey. Rodney's reminding him of it had brought out the feeling of fatigue, of sheer exhaustion, that used to assail him. There had been days when he felt he had lost all his friends, all love, everything. Only an inner conviction that he was doing right, could indeed do no other, had supported him, and a sense that the tide must turn, and bring all to him – freedom, and respect, and love.

To his embarrassment he found Sumitra the Rani sitting in the main room with his wife. He had not had time to adjust his face,

48

and came in showing the heavy thoughts that had weighed on his mind, as after a bloody failure in Burma, and for the same reason – the inevitability, and the waste.

'What's happened? What's the matter with him?' Janaki was on her feet, her hand urgent on his sleeve.

He said, 'Quite a lot, I'm afraid.'

He sat down and told them, as briefly as he could, about Rodney's state. When he ended he looked up and saw tears glistening in his wife's lower lashes and a shining wet line down her left cheek. Sumitra's heavy, perfectly curved brows were bent down in a frown over her huge eyes. It was she who spoke first. 'A casualty of history. Just as the D.C. said.'

Janaki muttered, 'But it's dreadful. He wouldn't be a casualty if he didn't care.'

Sumitra said, 'Unfortunately, that is always true, everywhere, *nahin?*'

Her eyes shone and the frown had gone, and her face had taken back its ancient-seeming statuary beauty. She stood up, the rich sari rustling heavily over her thighs. She arranged the end of it lightly over her head, drawing it over the curve of her breast in a slow sweeping motion of great provocativeness.

'I will go to him,' she said. 'Casualties need nurses.'

After a moment of stunned inaction Max sprang to his feet. 'Sumitra, I don't think . . . he's drinking, you know. He must have put away a bottle by now. It's bound to hit him soon.'

'Perhaps I can stop him drinking,' Sumitra said, smiling slightly.

'Really,' Max mumbled, 'really, I wouldn't, I don't think you . . .'

She gazed at him steadily. 'You mean he has more than a couple of bottles to keep him company?'

'Yes', Max mumbled. He felt acutely uncomfortable. This woman was pure Indian by blood, by manner pure foreign – French perhaps, French grande-dame, courtesan, actress, God knows what.

'You're blushing like a schoolgirl, Max. I shall go to him. No, I'd rather walk.' She spoke with finality, and, trailing her hand in a small graceful gesture, left the room.

Max blew out his cheeks in a long sigh. 'I need another drink,' he said. 'She's incredible. Rodney's got two girls from some village there – tarts. Heaven knows what they'll be doing by the time Sumitra arrives ... She's *immoral!* And yet, I don't think she's going down there for her own sake, for her own gratification, do you? ... I suppose it's a wonderful thing to do, when you think of it, even though he has two tarts with him ... especially if he has two tarts with him.' He found the whisky in the corner cupboard and poured out a stiff peg. 'She doesn't give a damn. Poor Dip ... poor Rodney. I wish I knew what he was talking about, half the time. Some woman who's his ideal. They were lovers and then she left him ... grew away. He said it was inevitable. Because she was Indian? I'm not sure he said that, but I somehow feel that's what he meant.'

He was talking to himself, revolving his glass in his hand, staring at the tabletop, trying to see in its polished teak surface the solution of Rodney's riddles and allusions, trying to bring into the framework of his common sense these mysteries of sensitivity which so many others, especially Indians, knew about while he didn't. Well, I'm a Jat, he thought. We're supposed to be as dense as buffaloes ...

He looked up and saw his wife's head bent over the table, her hands to her face. The violence of her silent sobbing had loosened the fastenings of her hair, and already it was falling down. He stumbled to his feet, whispering, '*Kya hua, piari?*' and stretched out his hand to her. It brushed hard against her shaking head and completed the undoing of the smooth-swept hair. Her head bent farther down and her black hair swept out across the table, a shining river of light and shadow.

Max gasped, and staggered. 'Janaki!' he cried.

The hidden head nodded and the hair moved on the table, heaving and writhing and then lying again still, a dark river, frozen in motion. The hair fell back and her face came up, tear streaked, working, ugly in grief.

'Yes. Yes, it was I. All true. The love, why it came ... and what kind. What happened afterwards ... true ... all so many years ago ... I was not hurt, till now, now, when it's all been over so long. He's only hurt because he cared. And I can't do anything for him, I just can't ... I'm your wife. I always have been.' Again her head sank, and again the heavy sobbing filled the room.

The General looked at her a long time. Hers was the flowing

hair that haunted Rodney Savage's dreams. He himself was the husband who had possessed, but not possessed. The same man who had saved his career had taken his honour. A surge of anger rose slowly in him and his thick fingers clenched.

Why hadn't they run away together? Why was she still here? Why had she stayed with him all these years, fourteen years since the Peshawar days? Fourteen years of love, comradeship, affliction, partings, joinings, children. The woman of Rodney's dream was Janaki, but it was also India.

The astrologer had chosen the date for his marriage, but he'd had to change it – exigency of the service. So perhaps these sorrows were inevitable, no human being to blame. It seemed to him, as the anger sank and vanished, to be replaced by a deep thankfulness, that perhaps he could never suffer, now, as Rodney and Janaki had, and would.

He walked round the table, gathered his wife gently in his arms, so that her face rested against his shoulder, and carried her to their room, murmuring to her in their own language as he went.

Chapter 4

Frances Clayton turned the page and glanced up. The three over-stuffed armchairs were arranged in a group at the edge of the lawn, just in the shade of the trees. From behind the trees, beyond the low brick wall, came the hum of motor traffic and the steady clip-clop of a tonga pony's hoofs.

A sudden jangle of the tonga bell made her start. On the invisible road someone poured out a torrent of blurred, angry Hindustani. Someone else answered, other voices joined in ... Another near miss, another argument, Indians yelling and screaming at each other. Why couldn't they settle their differences sensibly, without hysterics and bad temper? And dust everywhere even though the rains were hardly over. Frowning, she looked at the men in the other two chairs.

'I think you're mistaking Roy's character. He's not cheap. It's not *you* he's against, but all British. And you're over-estimating his influence. The men who have floated the new company are out to make money . . .'

That was her brother John speaking. A ray of sunlight streaming through the branches had landed, like a magician, on his head, making the thin blond hairs vanish and turning the head into a pink football. His long face was pale, and he seemed worried, as usual. Well, now he'd got something to worry about.

He continued: 'You don't seem to realise that you've made more money for M.P. in one year than I have in twenty – well, say thirteen, not counting the years I was in the army. That bakelite deal which you suggested has been snowballing ever since.'

'I heard it was going well. But all I did was read that this American chemical wizard was in Bombay, and go and see him.'

'Yes, but no one else did. I wouldn't have.'

No, Frances thought, you wouldn't. You wouldn't want to push in on a stranger, even though his ideas might possibly produce business. You would remember that you were in the Shipping Department and this was the Coal Department's pigeon – if it was anyone's. You wouldn't risk wasting time you might have spent with a fishing rod. Sensibly, you would have worked out that the chances were a thousand to one against, and you would have been right. Rodney was just lucky.

'The truth is,' John continued, 'I am far more likely than you are to be in the first 75 per cent sacked.'

Rodney said, 'You can count me out of the musical chairs. I wrote to Graham yesterday, resigning my . . . commission in the Imperial Army of Scottish Merchants Trading to the East Indies.'

'You did!' Frances exclaimed. She laid down her book and gave up the pretence of reading. She smiled warmly at him. Since arriving in Delhi the day before yesterday he had said nothing about her letter. She had been afraid to broach the subject. Rodney was not a man you gave ultimatums to lightly. That was one of the things she liked about him. When they were married, there would be no doubt who wore the trousers. She despised henpecked husbands.

'I did,' Rodney said. He poured himself a stiff whisky with very little soda. Frances frowned. That was his third already. It was Sunday morning, yes, but hardly half past eleven yet. He was drinking much more than he used to. That was India again. It had a terrible effect on people.

Rodney said, 'Roy or no Roy, I'm not going to work for a Marwari-owned firm. I'm not saying they'll be more corrupt than us, or less efficient. I'm just saying they'll be different, in method and outlook and thought. I'm too old to change my whole personality.'

There was silence. Now should she ask, Frances wondered, now should she ask the obvious question – what *are* you going to do? Better let John ask it, she decided. A few minutes later he did. Frances waited, her hands tensed in her lap.

Rodney answered with another question. He said, 'Do you know what kind of jobs M.P. are going to offer us in England?'

'Not exactly,' John said, 'but it's not hard to guess. Something in the City. They're connected with investment banks and shipping.

I imagine we'd have to spend a year or two as glorified office boys, until we find our own level. You needn't worry.'

Rodney sat with head thrown back, staring up at the leaves. London, she thought. If he has to go to the City to work, I suppose we'd start in a semi-detached house in one of those ghastly suburbs you get to from London Bridge or Holborn Viaduct. It wouldn't take Rodney long to reach the top, though, and then they could move out to Surrey. Or perhaps Buckinghamshire. A big house that looked old but wasn't, with decent plumbing . . . a garden with a high wall round it; a tennis court; quiet, leafy roads, errand boys on bicycles, whistling, but not yelling at each other; voices that were never raised, and meat that tasted like meat; peace, and decency, and a soft light, air that did not feel as though they were rubbing sandpaper into your skin; the windows open winter and summer, no snakes or dust storms or howling monsoon rains flooding the drive and turning the lawn into a lake and carrying dead rats down the open drainage ditches . . . Her eyes slipped into focus and she found she was staring at the *mali*. He was squatting over the zinnia bed, the hose in his hand.

'Not now!' she called. '*Nahin, nahin! Pichche* . . . When the sun's off them.'

The *mali* salaamed and dragged the hose somewhere else. How often have I told him? she thought. They don't *listen*. Rodney was looking at her, frowning as though in thought. I ought to have learned better Hindustani in my time here, she thought. But I didn't want to.

Rodney said, 'Come out for a drive, Frances. We'll be back for lunch.'

She stood up at once. 'Wait a minute while I change my shoes.'

She went to her room and looked at herself in the mirror. A little more lipstick, smarter shoes, and . . . that dress looked dowdy. She changed quickly into a blue linen suit.

Rodney was waiting in the driver's seat of the huge old Bentley. That was a terrible waste of money, she thought. She hoped he wouldn't try to take it home. Besides costing a fortune in petrol it was rather flashy – not like an American car but . . . just too much. It would create a bad impression in England, especially in the kind of place they'd have to live in at first.

Rodney turned into the road and trod on the accelerator. The warm air rushed past and she put her hand to her head as her hair began to shake loose. Faster yet, the engine making a continuous burbling roar, bicyclists all over the road as usual, talking, hands on each other's shoulder, never looking where they were going, never thinking of giving a signal . . .

'Rodney!' she cried. 'Please go slower. It's not safe here in Delhi.'

Rodney whipped the Bentley round a traffic circle in a long, squealing skid, hurling gravel far out on to the grass lawns beyond. He slowed down. 'You are quite right,' he said gravely.

She tried to pat her hair back into place. 'Where are we going?'

'The Red Fort,' he said.

She felt a small twinge of unease. The Red Fort was very imposing, no one could deny that. It was not picturesque, like an English castle – it was just huge, with a gigantic wall all the way round. He would want to walk about inside it, among the formal gardens and mosques. If only he'd told her, she would have put on a pair of wedgies instead of these heels.

The car slipped noisily through the teeming traffic and soon drew up in the parking area outside the main entrance to the Fort. After helping her out Rodney stood awhile, gazing up at the Congress flag tugging gently at its staff. Then he walked on fast. She hurried to catch up with him, and laid her hand on his arm to slow him down. Sikh sentries stood stiff as ramrods, bayonets fixed on their rifles, beside the entrance. She thought Rodney would speak to the sergeant and other men standing nearby – he usually did, when he met Indian soldiers – but he passed without even looking.

Inside the arched gate they walked down the middle of a high-roofed bazaar. On either side shopkeepers called, and thrust out examples of their wares. Files of school-children scurried by, shepherded by young teachers in cheap, pretty saris. There was an overpowering smell of jasmine perfume.

Rodney said, 'You don't want to stay in India.'

She tightened her hand on his arm. What a place he'd chosen to speak about something so terribly important. She had rehearsed, many times, what she would say when this moment came. Now she found she had to search for the words, and go very carefully. She said, 'I – honestly, Rod, I don't. I haven't been here long enough. Lots of people say you always spend your first five years hating India. I don't know enough, the way you do. It can't be *home* for either of us, of course ... but it's been, well, a special place for you ... Not for me.' She hesitated and then got it out in a rush: 'It can't be such a special place for you any more now, can it? Darling, I do know what you feel, but there isn't anything else we can do, now, is there?' He did not answer, and she said again, 'Is there?'

'As a matter of fact, there is,' he said. 'The question is not Can, but Will. I'm still not certain what I'm going to do. I've never felt like this before in my life. I *will* do something, I mean I will make a decision – but I don't have any idea what it will be or what will cause it.'

He looked down at her, his face suddenly inquiring and almost anxious. 'Do you love me?' he asked.

She ought to cry out, 'Of course I do, I love you, I love you!' She could not say the words. She said, 'I don't think I honestly know what love is, Rod. I've never lost my appetite, or not been able to sleep, or felt simply swept away ... the things that are supposed to happen to people.'

They were passing under another huge arch of pink stone, walking down wide steps on to a gravelled walk between green lawns. 'I respect you,' she muttered, 'I like you, more than any man I've ever met. I know that I will come to love you ... and surely that's the only real love, the kind that comes slowly, after years, by living together and having affection and respect and – and mutual interests?'

'No,' he said.

She cried, 'But that's why we became engaged! I never pretended. I could have!'

'No, you never pretended,' he said wearily. 'It is entirely my fault.'

I should have lied, she thought in anguish. It's no use trying to be honest with men, not even Rodney. She *would* love him, it *would* come, deep, true, real love ... but how was she to pretend to have a 'fever', to shiver and shake and yearn, when she felt nothing of the kind – now? And the small nervous voice inside her

56

whispered, I don't want to shiver and shake and yearn and be miserable . . .

She must be sensible . . . He didn't like cities much. He was an open-air man. He liked mountains and sea. Perhaps it was the idea of the City, and suburbia, that was weighing on him. 'You don't have to take a McFadden Pulley job in London,' she said, speaking rapidly. 'We could go to Cornwall. Or Devon. Or Somerset. Don't ex-army officers often become chief constables of counties? . . . We could have a boat in Fowey, and a cottage on Bodmin Moor. You've talked a lot about Cornwall . . . the gorse on the cliff paths, the wonderful beaches . . . Tintagel . . .'

Rodney had stopped. He was looking at a white mosque close in front of them. He said aloud, 'If there be a heaven on earth, it is here, it is here, it is here.'

She tugged at his sleeve. 'Rodney . . .'

He said, still gazing at the mosque, 'This is the Pearl Mosque, the *Moti Masjid*. Which Mogul emperor had those lines inscribed? Was it here or at Shalimar? "If there be a heaven on earth . . ." '

She cried, 'But oh, Rod, it isn't, not any more, not for you!'

Rodney began to walk round the mosque, his head up and turned, examining it. Before she could catch him or warn him he had walked into a party of Indians coming in the other direction, knocking one man down.

Rodney glanced at the man as he struggled to get up. It looked like a cold, supercilious stare, but Frances knew that really there was no emotion in it of any kind. Rodney's feelings were somewhere else. He had not yet realised that it was he standing there, he who had knocked the man down.

The man was on his feet, dusting off his dhoti and adjusting the Gandhi cap on his mane of grey hair. He was a dark-visaged man with a heavy, square face, thin lips, and deep-set eyes. He snapped, in good but accented English, 'Do you expect Indians to hurry out of your way, still? There is Independence here now, you know.'

Rodney said, 'I didn't see you.' In another second, she was sure, he would have apologised, but the Indian didn't give him time: 'Because you are drunk! I can smell the whisky on your breath from here.'

The others of the group, two men and a pretty, languid woman, stood a little back and behind the speaker, as she stood behind Rodney.

Rodney said, 'Oh, for Christ's sake, shut up, and go away.'

One of the other men stepped forward pompously. 'Do you realise who you are insulting? This gentleman is L. P. Roy, M.L.A.'

Rodney stared at L. P. Roy, and bowed slowly. Straightening up, he said, 'And I am Rodney Savage, O.B.E., M.C.'

Frances watched, anxious yet aware of a warm glow of certainty. This must convince him.

The two men examined each other, the Indian tensed and angry, the Englishman loose, staring down, grinning with teeth bared.

Roy suddenly relaxed. He said, 'An employee of McFadden Pulley, I think. I saw your name on the list in the prospectus. Well, I am on the board to see that people like you do not continue to fatten on India.'

Rodney took her arm under his and walked away, towards the outer wall. Here, on a wide walk, marble water channels, but empty, ran under gateways of marble carved with such delicacy that they seemed to be made of lace. Rodney said, 'The women of the emperors sat here. The water flowed in the channels then, green and cool. The emperor sat on the *gaddi* on that marble bench, facing the crowd, some of them in the open and some under the pillars in the shade . . . Now, you must see how impossible it is.'

'Yes,' she said.

'I can't go. I will fight.'

She felt weak, and sat down on a bench. A passing Indian couple examined her curiously. Below her the wall dropped sheer for fifty feet. The ground down there was bare and brown and dusty, covered with thorn scrub. Ragged strips of canvas spread from thorn to thorn made a little shade for a gipsy family engaged in cooking their meal. Black-and-brown goats wandered among the thorn, standing on their hind legs to pluck leaves from the higher branches. Beyond, the haze of heat enveloped the view in a grey pall that united earth and sky.

He said, 'I have asked you to marry me. But we will stay in India.'

He stood beside her, but still not looking at her. He looked out over the land, to which he seemed to be speaking.

She was desperate for a place as a married woman. She could say yes, and hope he would change his mind.

The land out there, and the sky, and the grey haze densely enveloping them both, was hot and uncomfortable, full of dust. Sun and glare, anger and lust, and starved women lying dead in the gutter. She could not do it. There was no happiness here for her.

'Just because an Indian insulted you,' she said heavily. 'You're mad, Rodney.' She gathered strength. 'What are you going to fight? The Indian Government? L. P. Roy? You can't win. They'll break you, and the longer you hang on the worse it will be . . . John bends, but you won't. You'll break.'

'Perhaps,' he said; 'there's always that chance.' He spoke as though going into a battle, acknowledging the possibility of death.

'Have you fallen in love with someone else?' she asked suddenly.

He said, 'I have loved two other women. Hopeless cases from the beginning. I have met another. A generous, curious woman. I could manage to forget her if I left India.'

'Then . . .'

'Would you arrange to forget your right eye? Leave it behind on a hilltop and walk away?'

'If it hurt enough.'

He shrugged. 'That's the eye I see beauty with, and everything that's valuable and wonderful. The other one's for earning my living, protecting myself, all the necessary, material things.'

She burst out, 'How can you ask me to marry you if you are in love with someone else?'

He said, 'You are not promising me your love, are you? Respect and affection, remember? I can give you that . . . And, I told you, I do not love her – yet. Thank God. It looks like another hopeless case. But it's possible that I shall. It won't be the first time love has grown out of sex.'

She felt cold. 'Did you . . . have her?'

He said, 'Yes. After I got your letter. She is stimulating, and independent, and her views on sexuality are original. Well, I suppose they're not really, they're just old-fashioned – Hindu old-fashioned – but not immoral. She has no morals, of that kind.'

'Did you say . . . Is she an *Indian?*'

He turned then and looked at her. His expression was very sad.

59

He said, 'You were on the point of saying "native", weren't you? And meaning it . . . My poor Frances, you should never have met me. Yes, she's Indian.'

Frances groaned. Indian women. Natives. Of course, she had met scores of them socially, beautifully dressed, sophisticated, charming . . . and never been able to erase from her mind the idea that they were only disguised and painted sisters of the dark dirty beggar women with the matted hair, and the brown and wrinkled sweeper witches who cleaned the filth from the streets.

Rodney said, 'If we marry I shall stay physically faithful to you. But it must be in India. I can live without physical union with this woman – and others – but I cannot live without the atmosphere wherein they exist – this air, this dust, these smells, these skies . . . We'd better go back. It's nearly lunchtime.'

'Lunch!' she cried, but she got up. An American with a funny white cap was staring at her. She walked at Rodney's side, drying her tears with the back of her hand.

So it was sex. She had known from the beginning that Rodney was supposed to be a great lady's man. When he began to pay her attention she expected an early attempt at seduction. She had been glad, and delightfully surprised, that he had made no such attempt either before or during their engagement. She would not have agreed, anyway. She was a virgin and meant to remain one until they were married; but he had not even tried. Even his kisses had always been gentle and proper. She had seen nothing of the Casanova in him . . . but it must have been there all the time, held in check by God knows what will power, if he was desperate enough to turn to Indians. Had she driven him to such a thing? He must be frantic. If they did get married, she'd have to live with and assuage this beastly, animal side of him . . . yet she could not, would not give up the idea of marriage. Marriage was her only goal in life. No one but Rodney had asked her. She was twenty-nine.

She drew a deep breath and said, 'Rod . . . we don't know each other . . .'

'Eh? I'm sorry, I didn't hear.'

She felt the hot flush covering her face and neck. She couldn't talk about it, she just couldn't. But she could do it.

60

She sat preoccupied, trying to conceal her trembling, during the drive back to the house at the far end of New Delhi. Before lunch she quickly downed two pink gins. John looked at her with eyebrows raised, for normally she never drank during the daytime; but Rodney did not notice. During the traditional curry and rice meal – why must we have it *every* Sunday? she thought – she drank two gin and tonics. Afterwards, still queasy at the stomach but exhilarated and determined in mind, she caught her brother's arm and muttered, 'Take a drive, John. A long one. Rod and I have to talk.'

'Oh. Oh, all right.' Now it was John who blushed and she thought crossly: the wretch! Does he think I do this all the time, that I can't wait till bedtime now that Rod's back, even after what presumably happened last night? But of course, with Rod's reputation, that's probably what he did think.

She waited, breathless, sitting in the drawing-room with a magazine, until Rodney got up and said, 'I'm going to take a nap.'

She waited again, until she heard the door of his bedroom close behind him down the passage, then went quickly, on tiptoe, to her own room, and took off her clothes. Naked, she glanced at herself in the mirror, and hurriedly averted her eyes. Her figure was all right, she supposed, but her femaleness looked terribly obvious. Coarse. She found a nightgown and slipped it on, brushed her hair and went to the door.

After a long moment of waiting, while the blood pounded in her head and her stomach felt painfully empty, so that she thought she would faint, she opened the door, ran across the passage in her bare feet, opened Rodney's door opposite, and went in.

He was lying on his back on the bed, staring at the ceiling, naked except for a sheet flung loosely across his belly and loins. Slowly the scarlet colour spread from her neck to her face, to her breasts, to her body, down her legs and up her back, to blend again at her neck. She tried to keep her head high, looking at him, but it sank of its own weight until she was staring at the small Persian rug on the floor.

He sat up. 'You don't have to do this, Frances.'

'I – I want to,' she whispered.

She didn't want to. Perhaps Rod could teach her to want to, someday. Now she was only empty and afraid.

'You're a liar,' he said. 'But the real trouble is I don't want to, either.'

'Rod!' She ran the few steps to the bed and flung herself on to it, crouching beside him, turning to hold him, pressing her breasts against him. She put her mouth to his and kissed him, opening her lips as she had never done before. She moved against him, and after a moment, feeling neither shame nor fear, only desperation, she pulled the sheet away, spread her legs and straddled him.

He lay back. 'Frances, it's too late. In the beginning, if I'd tried to create this kind of thing between us, perhaps it would be different now. Perhaps I'd possess your soul and be eager to follow your body anywhere in the world . . . But I didn't. It's my fault. But it's over.'

She would not surrender.

Nothing happened, no stir of emotion in herself or in him. She began to cry.

Rodney moved her over gently and eased the pillow under her head. 'You are a good-looking woman,' he said. 'It will come out all right, with someone else . . . But, Frances, don't have a purpose for love-making. And no duty. Just love, or desire, or both.'

She lay, her eyes closed and her face pressed into the pillow so that he should not see them. She controlled herself after a long hard struggle, and sat up. She said, 'You said you had an idea, about something to do in India. What was it?'

Through the haze of the recent tears she saw him looking at her with respect. 'You're a hell of a girl, Frances. But don't think of me any more. I mean it. This is the end . . . Yes, I have an idea. I think I can make a living, and lead the kind of life I want to, and be my own master, in India. I'm going to be a white hunter. I'm going to start a *shikar* camp for rich foreigners.'

He jumped out of bed, found his cheroots, lit one, and jumped back in. She found herself noticing dispassionately that he was a lean, well-muscled man, densely covered with black hair from the navel down to the loins, the chest broad, flat, and hairless. He smiled at her and waved the cheroot. 'Every year before the war they used to extract hundreds of thousands of dollars from Americans in Kenya and Uganda and Tanganyika, and what do they have there except game? We have the game, and we have *India*, too. India! Temples, maharajahs, nautch girls, the Taj Mahal, Nehru, tall bearded Gurkhas waving their keen-edged *chilamchis*, subtle sinuous Sikhs clamouring for more muezzins...'

She found herself smiling. She felt tired but calm. Rodney was not going to make love to her and it was quite proper and sensible to be sitting up in his bed in a transparent nightie, listening to him talking about his plans. That was how she had first met him, only then they'd been sitting on the sofa in the drawing-room. So, after two years, she was back where she'd started, minus a few clothes. She felt like a little station on a big railway line. Rodney's train might have stopped forever here, but it hadn't. He was on his way again.

He said, 'I've got the place, too. An abandoned Forest Rest House beyond Lapri. I had a good look at it last week. The firm leased it twenty years ago for some reason and have practically never used it. It's nearly falling down but it could be fixed and I know they'll transfer the lease to me. I'll have to raise a bit of money. It will cost four or five thousand rupees just to fix the Rest House. Then I've got to buy equipment, tents, camp beds, mosquito nets, rifles to hire out to the clients . . .'

'Station wagons?' she said.

He waved his cigar energetically. 'Not a hope. The road's jeepable from the main road as far as Pattan village, but after that there are just tracks climbing on to the escarpment. Besides, it isn't going to be that sort of safari. I don't want people riding around in station wagons thinking they've seen India. They've got to get out in the jungles, on their feet.'

She said, 'If you're really going to attract the rich ones, you'll have to provide some sort of comfort, Rod.'

'Well, yes, something ... But they must realise they're in a jungle, and in India ... Then I have to live. There will be servants' salaries, *shikaris*, baksheesh and what not to keep the villagers of Pattan in our pocket – and, the biggest expense, advertising, publicity. The scheme will sink like a stone unless people hear about it in America, and England ... I'm going to raise the money from my friends, if I can.

'I'm sure John will lend you some,' she said.

'I'm going to ask him,' he said. 'I think it will work, and pay a good return on the investment.'

She said, 'I'll lend you some, too.'

'My dear,' he began.

'I know ... but you can let me lend you some money, can't you?'

He got up, pulled on his trousers, and kissed her. 'Yes,' he said, 'out of affection, and respect. Now you'd better go.'

Chapter 5

Margaret Wood looked vexedly at the dense swirling crowd that filled Lapri from end to end. She would have to get through that somehow, unless she turned off into the fields, and that would mean scrambling through thorn fences and over irrigation ditches and beds of stinging nettles. It was too hot. The whirring sound of a small car engine made her turn her head. The car stopped beside her and she saw that it was the Deputy Commissioner of Bijoli, Mr Ranjit Singh.

He climbed out and said, 'I was just coming to pay you a call. I hope it's convenient.'

'Oh, yes,' she said. 'Please.' What's the time? she thought. About half past four. Tea with small cakes would be enough. If she could find anyone to prepare it. Today was the biggest day of the Hindu festival of Holi, one of the most important of the year. Whether officially Christian or not, everyone disappeared from the mission. She had to keep one of the nurses on duty by a combination of main force, threats, and bribery.

'May I give you a lift?' the Sikh said, and she cried, 'Oh, yes, please.' She waved her hand at the throng ahead. Ranjit Singh smiled. 'You should be in your oldest clothes today. I am.' She saw that his khaki shirt was splashed with violet and red spots and streaks. She suppressed a grimace of disgust. During Holi the Indians threw coloured dye over each other, over everything, and sometimes water that had been dyed pink and red and violet. Educated Hindus energetically denied it, but she had heard that the red liquid represented women's menstrual blood, and it was thrown about at this time because Holi was the feast of spring, of fertility, and lust. An extra source of disgust was that Holi always coincided closely with Easter. The actual truth of the legend didn't matter. Hindu India, in the essence, as she saw it in this buried, forgotten corner, was quite capable of such a bestiality. You only had to look at the Pattan temples to realise that the Hindus really worshipped sex and everything to do with it. Last year, during Holi, she and Henry had seen men dancing in the road at night with huge wooden phalli strapped to their waists.

They crawled forward in low gear, the little Austin worming its way through the singing, shouting, dancing crowd. Small bands blared on either side, bombs of dye burst on the closed windows, and the heat inside was stifling. A young man, laughing and happy, leaned over the bonnet and sent a long squirt of red water on to the windshield. Ranjit Singh switched on his windshield wipers and the young man laughed even harder.

She gasped, 'Look!'

There was Rodney Savage, among the crowd. A mob of men and girls surrounded him, and they were all pelting each other with powder. As she watched, a paper bag burst on his forehead, and pink liquid flowed down his face. His shirt and trousers were a motley mess of red and violet, hardly any of the original colour visible. Near him she saw his chauffeur, the Gurkha Ratanbir, in the same state.

'He's gone absolutely native,' she said, and flushed; 'I'm sorry, I didn't mean . . .'

The Sikh smiled. 'I know what you mean, Mrs Wood.'

Savage saw them in the car at that moment. He straightened, then bowed deeply.

'He's drunk,' she muttered, 'he must be.'

Ranjit Singh said, 'He may well be – but he doesn't have to be. As you said, he has identified himself with these people and does not need to be drunk to share their pleasures . . . and their pains, I suppose.'

They reached the end of the town at last, and pulled up in front of the mission bungalow.

She hurried up the steps. 'If you'll excuse me a moment . . .'

'Please . . . just a glass of water. I cannot stay long.'

They sat down on the rickety chairs on the veranda. The blare of bands came strong on the hot afternoon wind. Ranjit Singh sipped his water. His face was slightly pockmarked and he had shrewd, prominent eyes and thick, sensual lips. She had found him a pleasant visitor on the two or three occasions when he passed

66

through Lapri on his way to visit the Pattan valley behind. But his visits had been purely social, for Lapri itself was not in India but in the princely State of Chambal. She wondered what was the purpose of this present call and why he was spending so long sipping his glass of water.

The Sikh put down the glass. 'Do you see much of your neighbour in Pattan?'

'Colonel Savage. No!'

She realised she had spoken with considerable vehemence. The Sikh fixed his prominent eyes on her. 'That seems a pity. Another Englishman, so close. He must be lonely . . . until his first batch of clients arrive.'

'He has hardly spoken ten words to me since he came last October – five months ago,' she said. 'It does not upset me, I assure you. I am not lonely, and even if I were, he would be the last person I would want to see.' She paused to gather breath and then the rest of her anger poured out, unchecked. It felt good, rushing out like a released flood. 'We used to get many villagers from Pattan and the valley coming down to the Mission. Now, since he came and started to repair the Rest House – none. He encourages them *not* to come. He wants to be a little tin god there. He encourages them in their old horrible superstitions. He even made a sacrifice.'

'Not human, I'm sure,' the D.C. said. 'I think I would have heard of that, even as far away as Bijoli.'

'No – goats and a buffalo, I heard. In October.'

The D.C. nodded. 'At the time of Dussehra. The Gurkha regiments always do it, though it's not a usual custom among other Hindus.'

She said, 'I saw him with some men from Pattan one evening, a week ago. They were carrying a sambhur doe.'

The D.C. said, 'Of course it has been a very poor winter crop and the villagers are hungry. But it seems an odd way to ensure good hunting for his clients . . . Has he annoyed or molested you in any way?'

'No,' she said at once, 'not personally. Not since . . . well, he did once, a long time ago, not here, but I have forgotten it and I don't think he even remembers. I'm not being spiteful, Mr Ranjit Singh. Only, he's giving all Europeans a bad name, and he's a bad

67

influence. I'm sure he's setting up a little kingdom of his own. He's the only employer in Pattan, and can spread the money, which isn't even his, just as he likes. He has them eating out of his hand ... My nurses desert as fast as I can begin to train them. He ... he has women. I don't know how any decent women can even visit him, but they do. Mrs Dadhwal went, with the General, in December. The Rani of Kishanpur is there now, alone.'

'They are all old friends,' the D.C. said, 'except the Rani ... He has a catholic taste.'

'Catholic!' she cried. 'He's just – just a lecher.'

The D.C. paused a long time before speaking again. Then he said, 'You may be right, I do not know him well. I have only met him a couple of times, and the first time he did me and the Government of India a good turn. But I think you misjudge him if you believe that is all he is. Some men who pursue many women are seeking for an ideal – and some already have an ideal, but it's unattainable. It's important not to underestimate him ... How are your relations with Mr Faiz Mohammed and the Chambal authorities in general?'

Mr Faiz Mohammed was the administrator of the Lapri district, and so Mr Ranjit Singh's opposite number, over the border in Chambal. He represented the government of the State. She frowned in puzzlement as she began to answer. What had Mr Faiz Mohammed got to do with Rodney Savage? She said, 'Not as good as they used to be. There's been no actual trouble ... just pinpricks. It's hard to get to see Mr Faiz Mohammed when I want to. Just after my husband died the Chambal government gave an order requiring foreign missions to get authority before bringing any more missionaries into the State. We applied at once, that is, our headquarters in Manchester did. They're still doubtful whether they can find anyone to come out, but even if they do – Chambal hasn't given the permission. We had been seriously thinking of moving the mission to Pattan. Henry had talked to me about taking over the old Rest House. Then we'd have been in India, instead of at the mercies of the Chambal p   . They seem to be getting more fanatically Muslim every day ...   it we don't have a proper missioner, and Colonel Savage has the Rest House.'

The D.C. said, 'And I'm afraid you would not find the attitude of our government much more helpful. Who was it who said the missions too often acted like an ecclesiastical branch of the I.C.S.? Ah, I remember, it was Rodney Savage.'

'It's not true!' she cried angrily.

'I know it does not apply to you,' he said hastily. 'Mrs Wood, I must explain something to you in plain words, which you may have thought out for yourself . . . As you know, when the British left this country they left it divided up into two sovereign nations – India and Pakistan – and several hundred princely states, varying in size from a few acres to thousands of square miles. Nearly all those states have since acceded to one nation or the other.'

'You invaded Hyderabad only six months ago,' she said.

The D.C. smiled. 'Our politicians use a less blunt language, but, yes, we did invade Hyderabad, the largest and richest state of all – because we are determined that these anachronistic despotisms have no place in the modern world, and we are sure that they cannot survive alone, whatever their rulers might say. *We are determined*.' He repeated the phrase with emphasis, staring at her. Then he continued: 'Half a dozen states have still not joined either us or Pakistan. They are all situated in this part of India, they are all contiguous or practically so, and the largest of them, the ringleader of the resistance, if one might call it that, is Chambal – this state. The others, such as Kishanpur and Konpara, are small and by themselves do not matter. But Chambal borders India, here, and also borders Pakistan, three hundred miles west of here, in the Sind Desert. Its ruler, the Nawab, is a Muslim. Ninety per cent of its people are Hindu.'

'You are going to take over Chambal?' she said.

He smiled carefully. 'It's not quite as easy as that. We wish to avoid violence. We suspect there is an understanding between Chambal and the smaller uncommitted states, and possibly between all of them and Pakistan, that they will act together to resist any overt action on our part. We must move carefully. But if there should be military action – this is the main gateway into Chambal from India.'

'Of course,' she muttered. 'That's why General Dadhwal was visiting in December. Mr Faiz Mohammed had three policemen waiting on the frontier to escort him whenever he stepped back into Chambal.'

The D.C. said, 'General Dadhwal was merely, ah, enjoying a shooting holiday with Colonel Savage ... What I wish to tell you is this. After Chambal is incorporated into India, as we are determined that it shall be sooner or later, the position of the Lapri Mission will be greatly helped if it has not been identified with the Nawab's futile struggle against us. Rather, the reverse. We would appreciate any information that can be given to us about unusual activity, visits of Chambal generals, high officials, and so on. We have other means of getting information, of course, but few of them are as well placed and as ... innocent, as you. There is a lot of tension between us now, and anything – a border incident, another speech by Mr Roy, further defiance by the Nawab – is liable to make matters worse at any moment. What are Colonel Savage's relations with Mr Faiz Mohammed? Have you noticed or heard of him meeting Chambal officials here or elsewhere?'

The abrupt questions again surprised her. She shook her head. 'I don't know ... I haven't heard ... Pattan is in India ... he has no reason for dealing with Mr Faiz Mohammed.'

'Precisely,' the D.C. said. 'That's why it would be very interesting ... and, to me, sad, if he were. I'm sorry for him.'

'Sorry?' she exclaimed, and checked herself. That was not a charitable outlook. Henry would have reproved her for that. She said, 'Is he suspected?'

The D.C. stood up. 'He has enemies,' he said enigmatically. 'Now I must run the gauntlet of the crowd again. No use washing my car, or myself, until next week. Thank you so much – and don't hesitate to call on me for any assistance I can give you. My *tehsildar* at Sabora will always forward a message. He is a very reliable man.'

She watched the little Austin drive down the road, and slow to a crawl as it reached the outskirts of the crowd. Soon it was engulfed.

Colonel Savage a sort of a spy, a secret agent of Chambal ... It would fit what she had heard about him in the old days; but somehow it didn't fit the new Savage, dancing and singing in that crowd there, the Savage of Pattan. This man seemed to be withdrawing from power, rather than meddling with it. She had not sensed any intrigue. What annoyed her was a feeling that he exerted a secret pull, like that of a hidden magnet, back towards the jungle, and a barbaric, sensual past. It was a strong pull, and it seemed to affect everyone who could be reached by the power of his personality, or his money. It affected her.

His first batch of clients was coming any day now, she had heard. She wondered how it would go. It would certainly be nothing like the African safaris one read about . . .

She glanced at the little chapel down the road. Henry's grave was indistinguishable from those of his converts now. Sometimes there were only two people at Sunday morning prayer service. Henry had ordained her a lay preacher during his long illness, and she did her best to feel the inspiration . . . but how could she guide souls when her own floated lost and desolate, here in the jungle, unable to go, without purpose to stay?

Now they wanted her to be a spy. It sounded exciting. She would write secret messages, pay secret calls on the *tehsildar* at Sabora, creep stealthily through the jungle to Pattan and, unseen, watch Rodney Savage's intrigues. Angrily she kicked a small stone off the veranda. What would Henry have said? No one would have suggested it to him. He was incapable of doing any work but God's. The affairs of man had meant nothing to him.

The sun was setting behind the Chambal hills to the west. Soon it would be dark. Time to check the oil in the lamps, and the wicks, and see whether the buffalo milk had curdled in the pantry, and read another chapter of the Bible, and pray, and wonder, and wait.

Chapter 6

March, 1949. The intrepid white hunter strode tirelessly across the rolling hills, the topi shading his keen handsome face from the tropical sun. His clothes were well worn but, oh, so obviously the work of a West End tailor, and his fingernails were clean, for Colonel Savage, O.B.E., M.C., late of His Majesty's Indian Army, was first, last, and all the time a gentleman, and could no more be found with dirty fingernails than the Holy Roller down in Lapri could be dragged out from under a bus and, horror of horrors, have it revealed that the corpse was wearing off-white drawers. At the Colonel's heels trotted his faithful native servants, doglike devotion written all over their inscrutable Oriental faces . . .

I was wearing a pair of khaki shorts and Bandelkhand slippers, as a matter of fact. Chadi, Mitoo, and Ganesha wore slippers and loincloths, mere ball bags. I'd have worn the same if I'd thought we might run into the Holy Roller, but that didn't seem likely, and I prefer shorts. That woman hated me and I resented it. Hated, feared, and despised me. The unreason of it haunted me, so that I'd see her face in my imagination, wearing a number of expressions I'd never seen it wearing in real life – compassion, amusement, speculation. Very odd, in spite of her auburn hair and fine race-horse thighs.

It kept drizzling a warm rain, and I tried to think of Sumitra, to keep my mind off being tired. The sweat and rain ran salt into my mouth. My legs and chest and face were thorn-scratched and bleeding in a dozen places. My stomach felt empty as a drum, the skin drawn back from the front against my backbone by a sheer sucking emptiness, and my mouth like a pot of stale glue. Not a sight of game all day, and now we were almost home again – only about four miles to go.

Yesterday we'd done thirty-five miles, from Pattan to the Gond

72

village of Bhilghat. I'd sat up most of the night with Gulu the chief, arranging to get their help in producing game for my clients. The Gonds live so close to nature that they can do almost anything with wild animals. Now we were on our way back, another thirty-five miles. And Sumitra probably arrived yesterday, expecting to find me there . . .

All this because of the weather. Six days of rain now, to ruin scent, drive the animals to shelter, reduce visibility – just before my first clients came. Weather bad, crops bad. I knew the crops had been bad, but I didn't know quite how bad until a month or so ago when I found a child, a little girl of eight, lying in the path between the Rest House and Pattan village, almost in front of the old temples. She was starving to death, and had fainted. I carried her into the Rest House and fed her up, and swore I'd eat the same as the poorest people in Pattan until I really knew what it was like to starve. I found the poorest family in the village, and for a week ate exactly what they ate, no more, no less. Then I took my rifle and started poaching game for the village to eat. It might have been more helpful to give them some money, or go and beg grain from the Holy Roller – she had a few rupees for such charity, I believe – or go and tell Ranjit the D.C. . . . but life isn't all sense, thank God. These were my people and we were going to come through it together, by our own efforts.

Chadi, Mitoo, and Ganesha were the faithful natives, trotting at my heels. Actually they were padding along in slow time, almost as dead beat as I – not quite, because they were all three typical hillmen from the Vindhyas, wiry, no surplus flesh, the skin tight on the bones but wrinkled at the joints, legs like match sticks with lengths of dark muscle cord wrapped over the bone and knotted here and there.

Chadi saw the stag first and touched my bare elbow. We all stopped. The stag was a monster, one of the best heads I've ever seen. He was feeding near the edge of the escarpment. Behind him the land dropped sharply away to the Shakkar valley, the Rest House, and the cart track from Pattan to Lapri. By then we were less than a mile from Pattan. The rain slanted gently from the northwest, not quite from the stag towards us, but diagonally. We sank down, the four of us, and stared at the stag. The three experts sniffed the air, looked at the trees, felt the earth. I couldn't help thinking, what a trophy! I could leave one of the men to mark his movements, and give H. Huntington Blauvelt or Lord Hillburn a near-record head – their first day. And we would still eat the carcass. My mouth began to water and my jaw to ache. No, this was food. Patten needed food, and I couldn't afford to risk losing it.

I wanted to shoot at once, but the beast was a good six hundred yards off, moving in and out among scrub teak and scattered bijasals. A flame-of-the-forest tree spread a kind of dull, wet-sheened scarlet light over him for a moment and my heart cried, don't fire, he lives here too, he walks these hills, and feels the earth underfoot, and the sun on his back, and smells the jungle at night, and caresses the does clustering round him. Then my jaw hurt more and saliva squirted out suddenly into the corner of my mouth and it hurt so much that I bit my tongue to avoid groaning aloud.

Chadi and Ganesha, the oldest and the youngest of the three, slipped away to the left. I understood well enough. They intended to drop over the edge of the escarpment and work along the slope below the stag until they were upwind of him. They'd have to get pretty close, in this weather. Then he'd raise his head and start moving, more or less towards me. We must not let him turn across the wind and down towards the Rest House, which he might easily do with the scent so indecisive and occasionally distorted by rain flurries.

When the others had been gone ten minutes Mitoo slipped away from my side. He would follow in their path, but closer to the top of the escarpment. When the stag began to move, he would come up to the crest line and show himself. No, that would be too crude. He would move subtly, make a noise that might mean anything, not enough to frighten the stag, enough to puzzle him. I had to remember that their hunting methods were based on the bow and arrow, and even the spear. They had no firearms, except one old blunderbuss in the village, which the government allowed them for the watchman. Nor could they afford cartridges.

I knelt beside a pterocarpus, my body hidden behind the bole, and watched the stag. My rifle was cocked now and I kept nervously examining the sights. Suppose I had hit a rock with the foresight sometime, and not noticed it? Suppose I'd bent the back-sight against a tree trunk?

The stag flung up his head and stared west, towards the edge of the escarpment. He took a couple of steps in that direction – away from me. My heart sank and my throat contracted in pain. None of the men were carrying any weapon but the long-handled hatchet.

The stag began to move along the edge of the escarpment. Now was the bad time. He was moving away from Chadi and Ganesha, but would not reach Mitoo for another couple of minutes. He only had to take a couple of steps to the right and he'd disappear over the edge. I had the sights on him, but there was no strength in my arms, and the rifle barrel wavered and swung so that sometimes I could see all of him above the foresight, sometimes the barrel blocked him out altogether, and bushes and trees kept obscuring him.

He went on, fast but not trotting, his head high, suspicion in the curve of his back and the set of his tail and the carriage of his great head. Another minute and I began to feel easier. He would be almost directly above Mitoo now.

He jerked his head sideways, stopped dead for a fraction of a second, then turned and trotted straight towards me. After a hundred yards his trot eased to a walk and he stopped, turned again. Another bad time – if he continued now in his original direction he'd disappear into a patch of thicker jungle, still nearly 500 yards away.

Mitoo appeared, rather to the left of where he must have been when he made his little sound. He stood now between the stag and the stand of dense jungle. The stag swung heavily round and broke into a full gallop. He passed me at thirty yards, and I hit him exactly behind the point of the left elbow. He dived head first on to his nose and never moved again, his head ploughing through the fallen leaves like a bulldozer, the horns remaining spread and upright.

They came, running, dancing, waving their axes in the air. I threw down my rifle and grabbed two by the waist, and we danced round the corpse, yelling. I broke it up by grabbing Ganesha's arm and shaking him. 'Run down to the village,' I shouted, 'and bring men to carry the stag. We cannot manage it by ourselves.'

Ganesha ran off, a huge grin splitting his dark narrow face. The two older men stopped their prancing, and we went slowly down over the edge of the escarpment towards Pattan.

We came in on a game trail that passes half a mile behind the temples, and about there met Ganesha and a dozen men carrying long bamboo poles, all trotting up the path and chanting a vigorous song: Question from Ganesha in front, 'Who saw the stag?' Response from the crowd behind, 'Who saw the stag, wah!' Then, in chorus:

> *'Chadi saw the stag, Chadi saw the stag, wah!*
> *The Gora Raja waited, the Gora Raja waited, wah!*
> *The Gora Raja fired, wah!*
> *We shall eat, we shall eat, wah!'*

Gora Raja means Pale Face King. That was me, and it was the best title, the sweetest in my ears, of any that I'd ever held. No one awarded it to me. I earned it.

We entered the village at about half past five in heavy rain. All the small boys ran out, shrieking and dancing and singing round me. I gave one of them my rifle to carry, and he put it on his shoulder and marched beside me like a bodyguard. I soon had a naked little girl in each hand and another riding on my shoulders, her thin legs clasped round my neck and her fists beating a tattoo on the top of my head. Their mothers and elder sisters were out, too, some smiling from the doorways, a couple of girls running out and throwing hurriedly made garlands round my neck. Mitoo's wife hugged me, and I held her naked waist with one arm and cried to Mitoo, 'Hey, this one wants to fornicate in the street in broad daylight. No wonder you look so tired.'

Mitoo yelled, 'She is a bottomless pit! She would like to be one of the stone women at the temples!'

The Pattan temples were covered with statues of communal love-making. For some time the near-famine had been scraping layers of repression and layers of modern organisation off the villagers. The temples and the kind of communal life they portrayed was now, again, very near the actuality. There wasn't a mixture of poverty and wealth. Everyone was the same – poor. One man's poverty or starvation affected everyone, because everyone shared in it. One man's good fortune affected everyone the same way, just as they were all dancing and laughing now. It was not at all hard to see in the present excitement, caused by the prospect of eating meat, that desire also would affect everyone. It only required a small step – forward or backward – for it, too, to be equally shared.

When we reached the headman's house the whole population of the village, about four hundred, was with us, except the men who had gone back up the hill. Lok Chand, the headman, came out of his little house, his wife behind him. They were both short, and usually cheerful, though they were no richer than anyone else. They both used to be fat, but had lost many pounds during the lean spell.

I called out to Lok Chand that we had killed a stag and he said, 'Do you think there is anyone here who doesn't know that? How shall I divide it?'

'The usual way,' I said. 'I do not want anything for myself.'

His wife pushed through the crowd, holding a brass jar of warm milk, and gave it to me. I drank some and passed it to Chadi, who drank and passed it to Mitoo. Everyone in Pattan was the same caste, a Sivaite sect of Sudras, except the village Brahmin. I had long ago been elected an honorary Sudra too, inasmuch as that mattered here. As the Brahmin and I had discussed several times, the Hinduism of Pattan seemed in many ways to be pre-Brahmin, Tantric and Rudric. Max had noticed it and commented on it during his visit in December.

I noticed that a couple of the older villagers who had been squatting outside the headman's house – combined hovel and byre would be a better word – were now arguing fiercely with each other, waving their arms, shaking their palms in the air, and gabbling away at high speed, though they kept their voices low. I called over the heads of the crowd, 'What is this, brothers? Should we quarrel when there is food?'

The two stopped, rather shamefaced, and the headman said, 'It is the old land dispute, sahib.'

'Are you two still quarrelling over five square yards of rock and one thornbush?' I cried. Everyone laughed. Lok Chand said, 'There is no bringing them to reason. I shall have to ask the Deputy Commissioner Sahib to settle it when he comes next.'

'The Deputy Commissioner?' I said. 'What do we in Pattan need

77

of him? Can we not settle our affairs by ourselves? Come here, brothers.' The two men came forward. 'It's that piece of land at the southeast corner of your maize field, eh?' I said to one.

'At the southwest corner of *my* maize field,' the other said.

'My father ...'

'My uncle ...'

'Who were one and the same person,' I bellowed. 'Shut up! ... Listen, will you accept my judgment? It will be either mine or the Sikh's. Make up your minds.'

The two old fools looked at each other. They spoke simultaneously. 'We will abide by your judgment, Gora Raja.'

'All right. Give me a coin, Lok Chand.' Lok Chand ran back into his house. Coinage wasn't used much in that village, where payments were made by exchange or barter or in kind. He came out with a two-anna piece. 'You,' I pointed to one of the old men, 'you will call either heads or tails when I flip this coin in the air. If you call it correct, the land will belong to you, but you will lease it to the other, without rental payment, for a period of ten years from this moment. If you call wrong, the opposite ... Call.'

He called wrong. 'It is settled,' I said.

'It is settled,' they said gravely. Their old wives appeared from nowhere, beaming at each other – they'd been glaring and glowering like little old witches for the past three months and more. I covered my eyes with the palm of my hand and cried, 'Those eyes! Take me away before I faint from desire.' More shrieking and cackling. I could have kissed them all.

I beckoned Lok Chand. 'Come with me a little way ...' We walked on between the houses, the crowd still with us. It was something like those old pre-war newsreels of Hitler entering Vienna or the Prince of Wales in the Welsh coal valleys: take your pick. I'd had the little naked girl wrapped round my neck all the time, and wondered whether any previous Solon gave his judgments wearing such a becoming scarf. I lowered her, smacked her behind, and told her to go home. She ran off, laughing.

'Listen, friend,' I said to Lok Chand. 'That stag is a big one, but it will not go far among four hundred. Tomorrow, leave behind in the village all the men I shall need as beaters and *shikaris*. Take a party of the rest to Bhilghat, and fish in the lakes.'

78

Lok Chand cried, 'The Gonds will kill us, sahib!'

I said, 'No, they won't. I have their chief's promise. Once a week, until your new crops ripen, you may take two hundred pounds of fish from their lakes and rivers.'

Lok Chand said, 'Sahib, in this weather not even our best fishermen will catch anything.'

I whispered in his ear. 'Dynamite. I have it and the detonators at the Rest House. Grimoo and Maldi and Taharu have all worked at the Sabora quarries, and know something of the business.'

Lok Chand dropped back, his palms joined. He had a deep sense of responsibility for his village, and usually no means to discharge that responsibility, being as helpless as the rest of them in the face of natural calamity and hardship. He was a good man.

By then we were almost at the temples. I went up the steps on to the great platform, followed by about half the original crowd – the rest had drifted back into the village. I took off my battered little garlands, kicked off my slippers, and went into the temple with the great red phallus, and hung the garlands carefully round the head of it. Most of the others came forward after me, with flowers they'd picked along the track, and green twigs, whatever they had in their hands, and laid their offerings at the base of the phallus.

Then we all looked at each other awhile, smiling in contentment, and I waved my hand and went on towards the Rest House. They, my people, turned back towards Pattan.

Sumitra was standing on the veranda when I came round the last bend in the track. She was wearing slim-cut fawn slacks of drill and a pale-blue silk blouse, with a wide belt and a big silver buckle. I went slowly up the steps to her, dirty and wet and smelling of woodsmoke and sweat. She held out a tall cold glass of lemonade. 'Congratulations. I hear it was a beauty.'

I nodded, busy drinking the lemonade.

'Too good for your clients,' she said. She laughed. 'Really, Rodney, you are impossible. Don't you have any sense of self-preservation?'

I didn't answer that, but I said, 'I'm sorry I wasn't here. Things got urgent and I had to go.'

She said, 'Don't worry. It was nice being alone for a change.'

It was getting dark under the rain clouds and Ratanbir had appeared to take the rifle from my hand. '*Ghusl tayyar chha*,' he said, saluting. I needed a bath more than anything just then, so I went in, with a word of apology to Sumitra.

Half an hour later, clean-scrubbed and dressed in a thin black dinner jacket and white trousers, I rejoined her. The butler brought us whisky and soda, and hot meat titbits to nibble on.

I said, 'I thought Dip was coming with you again.'

She said, 'He was. Then something turned up – a sudden visit by the Grand Wazir of Chambal. Dip had to stay.'

'Chambal?' I said. 'Oh, more bribes and threats, I suppose.'

She said, 'I suppose so . . . I had hell getting across the border yesterday, you know. The Chambal police practically turned my car, and all my luggage, inside out. It's that speech the Nawab made.'

'I know,' I said. Three days ago the Nawab of Chambal had made a fierce radio speech, all about how the great, ancient independent, and sovereign kingdom of Chambal would take no nonsense from anyone. And that was in response to a speech by L. P. Roy in Delhi, who'd said that India's patience was not inexhaustible, that India could not stand by for ever with folded hands while the Chambal despots threw democracy-loving citizens into jail and forced Hindus to eat beef at bayonet point.

'A pox on both your houses,' I said rather irritably. It didn't require much *nous* to realise that here at Pattan, peaceably going about my business, I was nevertheless in the firing line. Max had obviously done some snooping while on his shooting trip, and doubtless even now some Chambal general, bent over a map in Chambalpur, was announcing 'We'll stop them here' – with a large forefinger covering the words 'Lapri' and 'Pattan'.

'Aren't you going to take sides?' Sumitra asked. 'Or perhaps you already have?' Outwardly she looked very un-Indian, like a sun-tanned French brunette just in from riding round the grounds of her château. But her eyes, and the particular pose she adopted, relaxed in the long chair, and the set of her head, were pure Indian. Then there was something peculiarly Sumitra, special to her, which I recognised at once even though I'd seen her only three times: her eyes were alert, examining, and set, in the way a trigger is set, ready to go *tock* and set off a propellent charge of enormous power.

I wanted that charge to go off, aimed at me, though I knew it would be dangerous. I was lonely, and, busy as I kept myself, I could not prevent Janaki and Victoria Jones coming to me in my dreams – only to look at me with the helpless, puzzled look of people who see each other out of trains in a station, and then the trains begin to move in opposite directions, leaving me more lonely, more in need.

I said, 'No, I am not going to take sides.' I added in Hindi, 'I am a poor man of Pattan. Let the mighty ones fight over my head while I cultivate the soil.'

I reached out my hand, took hers, and said, 'I hope you've come to sleep with me.'

She let her hand lie in mine, and her eyes kept on mine, but the trigger notion was not in them so strongly now, or perhaps not at all, just a mirror-like self-inquiry.

'I don't know,' she said, 'I don't think so.'

I had a right to ask her, bluntly and without a gavotte of preparation. That first night she came to the Rest House and stayed the night – she and the two girls from Pattan. If I hadn't already seen Khajuraho and the Pattan temples I would have been hard put to it to know how to comport myself in such a situation. As it was, everything fitted into place, not only physically but spiritually. By morning my body was drained clean of any animal emotion whatever – love, hate, jealousy, anxiety, what have you. This was the original design: after the orgy those medieval Hindus went thus, empty, to the temple, to understand God. And so I had gone, empty, to Delhi.

She said, 'I have never slept with a cultivator of the soil.'

'*Quelle snob!*' I said; but it had always been clear that a man's mental state, his condition of tension and effort, what one might call being strung like a bow against his fate, meant more to her than the physical side. Her way and walk of life had not brought her into contact with a cultivator in rebellion against the soil, that was all. I was no longer in rebellion, and was digging my way into Pattan and rural Indian life so fast that in a year or two there'd be nothing left of me visible above ground.

She turned away her brilliant eyes and spoke to the night. 'I can see you want to fall in love. I don't wish to act as a substitute for Janaki, much as I admire her. And it wouldn't do you much good either, would it?'

Dip Rao, her husband, was a friend of mine and always had been, though we had not seen much of each other since boyhood. In the Western world, and in the old days, twinges of guilt would have assailed me about sleeping with a close friend's wife, but Sumitra's original kindness had altered that, at least in respect of her, and life in Pattan had confirmed the change. Here, in the pattern that seemed to be modelling itself on the ancient temple statuary, you slept *only* with friends' wives. After all, it is a situation which calls for a lot of understanding, sympathy, and affection.

'You have those two girls, I suppose, for your needs?' she said.

'Kunthi and Devi? I have been teaching them what I know of hygiene, sanitation, and elementary first aid. I think the village needs something like that. But I have not had them professionally since Sabora, in spite of the Holy Roller's tales to the contrary.'

She sank her hand on mine and squeezed it, 'Oh, Rodney, you are a fool! Why do you try to hurt yourself?'

She was as sharp as a razor. However energetically I sank into the life of Pattan I could not conceal from myself that something vital was missing; and that something was a woman of intelligence and power to share my secret life and thoughts. It was a desperate lack, and because of it I could not bring myself to waste my substance, the substance of my loneliness and need, on the frivolity of sheer fornication.

'This is impossible,' she said suddenly. She pulled her hand away and got up. 'I never thought it would be as hard as this. I'm going.'

She ran into the bungalow. It was nearly seven. She had 120 miles to go to Kishanpur. Well, she could always stop the night with Max and Janaki in Bhowani. She came out carrying a small suitcase.

I got up. 'Good-bye,' she said. 'Will you promise me something, Rodney? Send for those two girls. If you're going to give up the rest of the world, do it thoroughly. Otherwise – you'll get torn in pieces . . . Oh, I passed our elephants on the road. They'll be here tomorrow morning.'

She held out her hand and I raised it to my lips. A moment later she had slid behind the wheel of the Rolls shooting brake, and the lights came on, shining down the long avenue of the forest road to Lapri, and shining on the place by the stream, near the Irish bridge, where I had doused the Holy Roller with water, and then the red tail light shone dim and dimmer and she was gone.

After a long silent time, sitting slumped in the chair, I stirred myself and called for a double whisky. The rain clouds seemed to be lifting and perhaps my clients would not get soaked every day, though conditions would still be most unpromising. Tomorrow they'd arrive, Lord and Lady Poop, Mr J. Theophilus Hackenschmidt, Mr and Mrs whatever their bloody names were. My purpose in being here, my original object in becoming involved so closely with Pattan, was to prepare for them, and yet ever since the first preparations began, the clients had been taking shape in my mind as intruders.

The stretch of grass beside the Rest House, that had once been empty, was covered with big tents. Tomorrow I must move out into one of them myself. It wouldn't do for the clients to live in tents while the White Hunter, the paid servant, slept under a roof. We would use the Rest House for dining, bar, and common-room purposes. The servants' quarters and other smaller tents alongside them were full of servants. We had a Goanese butler and a Goanese cook, Carlos and Francis, respectively, and half a dozen bearers, plus sweepers and *bhistis* from Pattan. None of the men from outside was happy, and I'd had to pay vast sums to get them. The kind of servant who is at home in the jungle is apt to look primitive to the eyes of people straight from England or America – like my mother's old sweeper in Manali, who'd stride through the drawing-room while she was having a tea party, a full chamber pot in his hand, crying genially, 'Going to empty piss-paat, memsahib!' Conversely, such men as these, who knew how to handle all the complicated requirements of tourists, hated and feared the jungle. So they, even though Indians, were intruders too.

Tomorrow the rape would become final, the actual violation of Pattan. The peace would be broken, the enclosed entity shattered. I felt as though I were holding down a little girl, perhaps the naked nine-year-old who had ridden wrapped round my neck through the village just now, and guiding some ignorant foreign sod into her secret place. I felt terribly lonely, and for a moment fought against a frantic desire to send for Kunthi and Devi. Then my deeper longing won, and I called instead for dinner to be served at once.

The next morning dawned well, and the elephants arrived. These were half a dozen State elephants belonging to Dip Rao. He had to use them for ceremonial processions during Holi and again in October, for Dussehra. The rest of the time he was lending them to me, free of charge – in fact he was paying for their upkeep. I had promised to pay him back when we got going properly.

Later the first clients arrived. The hired cars made the journey from Bhowani Junction, where I went to meet the mail train, with only one puncture and no mechanical breakdowns. The clients rolled happily along with many Ohs! and Ahs! at the sight of the Romantic Orient. They thought the Rest House picturesque, the tents thrilling, and the servants amusing. At dinner the roast lamb was dreadful, but liberal lubrication with champagne did its work and by the end of the evening we all knew each other pretty well.

There were five of them – Lord and Lady Hillburn, Mr and Mrs Wilson, and H. Huntington Blauvelt. Hillburn was a shortish, fat fellow with a paunch and a face like a butcher's. The peeress – Cynthia, she told us to call her – was several inches taller, a natural blonde, long face, long legs, small breasts, hard blue eyes. She was obviously the boss, and the better athlete of that pair.

The Americans were the other way round. George Wilson was a rugged six-foot specimen, about forty-five, black hair cut short, an oil man from Wyoming. He assured me three times that his company had no connection whatever with teapots, and never did have. Baffled but polite, I agreed, and then he relaxed. His hunting equipment was workmanlike, and I enjoyed his manner. His weakness was an excessive fondness for his wife, Mother, as he called her. Dot Wilson was just what you'd have expected, a little plump friendly woman, totally unused to the wilds.

H. Huntington Blauvelt was the really important member of the group as far as we were concerned. Who hasn't read *The Doughboy and the Duchess*? Well, I hadn't until a month before, but apparently everyone else in the world had, certainly everyone in the

84

U.S.A., and even I had heard of it. He wrote it in 1919, and followed it with three or four flops – (John Clayton got all this from the Indian Government and they from the consulate in New York) and then he more or less disappeared from view, though making millions writing scripts in Hollywood, until the 1930's, when he emerged as a writer on shooting. Some of these later books I had read – *King of the Icefloes, Safari, An American Hunter*. Then he'd been a war correspondent, and just a couple of years ago had written something called *Return to the Duchess* . . . He'd had numerous wives, and looked like Apollo – thirty years on. He was bald but wore a toupee, not a very good one. His skin was a peculiar grey shade, odd in a man who spent so much time out of doors. He had blurred grey-blue eyes and a fine sensitive mouth.

Then there was John Clayton, come down to assist me in dealing with this first and all-important batch of clients. Frances sent her best wishes, he said. After that we did not mention her again.

We went to bed about eleven o'clock. The clients were excited, and I was keyed up. The next day we were kicking off with a tiger hunt on elephants.

Came the dawn. I checked that the clients had been awakened with *chota hazri*, and went back to the kitchen to see that breakfast was coming along. All well. I found the chief mahout in charge of the elephants. Work in progress there.

By 7.0 a.m. we had finished breakfast, but Blauvelt hadn't appeared. I went to his tent. He was lying in the camp bed, his face greyer than ever. His mouth twisted slightly when I entered, and he motioned wearily to the bedside table, where there was a glass of water and four bottles of pills. 'I'm sorry, Colonel . . . a touch of the old fever.'

'What a shame,' I said. The place stank of whisky, and I knew, if I looked, I'd see an empty bottle under the bed.

'It always does this to me,' he said. 'Been suffering with it since '24, when I went to Uganda.'

'Damned shame,' I said. Blauvelt's eyes flicked on to mine, passed by. He knew that I knew. One observed the amenities.

'I'll probably be all right tomorrow, maybe even this afternoon. The temperature usually goes down in the afternoon,' he said.

I nodded and slipped out. I'd have to rearrange the groupings on the elephants.

The elephants appeared, swinging round the corner of the Rest House in single file. They knelt and we climbed up into the howdahs on a little stepladder. I put myself on the lead elephant, with Lady Hillburn; Hillburn and Dot Wilson on the second; George Wilson and John Clayton on the third. Two spare elephants followed. Everyone had a good heavy rifle except Dot Wilson, who said, quite rightly, that she couldn't lift it. Naturally, John and I were not going to shoot except in emergency.

We rolled off down the drive, on to the cart track, left towards Pattan. The mahouts sagged comfortably on the elephants' necks. Everyone except John and me was wearing a huge quilted sola topi. Cynthia Hillburn wore a daringly cut bush shirt and khaki slacks.

We rolled majestically past the old temples, and Cynthia looked at the carvings with a clinical sort of interest. On through Pattan, where what was left of the population (half the men were out as beaters) lined the muddy path to watch us pass. Kunthi and Devi stood in a doorway in Kunthi's parents' house, looking very sexy. Lok Chand came out, made salaam, and told me the beaters had left two hours earlier. Chadi would meet me at the rendezvous and confirm that all was in order.

We heaved on, a convoy of little ships in line in the great ocean of the jungle. We passed a small lake set among red rocks, and there was a man burning brushwood on the far side. Two pictures came together before my eyes, unconnected in time or space but superimposed now by a combination of stimuli – I saw Rifleman Jitbahadur Gurung, dead the previous evening from a tribesman's rifle bullet through the chest, lying on a rough platform of logs. Nearby the battalion Brahmin intoned a prayer. My company *subadar* squatted beside me, and the flames were beginning to rise from the pyre. That picture was from 1937. Behind and in that picture there was the water of a lake, not this one, another, but it was water, and a pale grey-green light along the horizon, and I waited with shotgun ready. Above the crackle of the logs, where Jitbahadur burned in the first picture, I heard the whirring wings of the wild duck flighting, and felt my orderly stiffen behind me, and we crouched deeper into the reeds. That was a cold-weather dawn in the Punjab – 1936 perhaps?

The elephant rolled on.

But where else had I smelled the incense burning, and rich oils on a flame? I saw a man and a woman in gorgeous clothes kneeling over a brazier, and the flames leaping up red on to his face. The girl kept her head down and her sari drawn far forward, and I saw nothing of her skin. Hand in hand, round and round the fire they went in the ceremony of marriage. Now, as before, a second picture superimposed – this time a long file of men and women struggling up a stony path, a strong cold river beside them. Where was that? Why so many old men with sticks, and old women carried on beds on the shoulders of coolies?

'Badrinath,' I cried, 'the pilgrim road to Badrinath!'

'I beg your pardon?'

The peeress was staring at me. Hard as a bar of steel, I thought. I must make sure she got at least two good trophies, or she would see that the word went round – Savage is a fake.

I said, 'Sorry. My mind was wandering.'

'So it appeared,' she said, 'you were looking straight through me.'

'What a waste,' I said lightly, and then she smiled. I made sure we weren't touching in the howdah. No Francis Macomber stuff for me.

When we reached the rendezvous Chadi and Gulu, the Gond chief, and a dozen villagers were waiting there. We had covered four miles and were in scattered jungle near the head of the Shakkar River. Here the valley, which had been climbing gradually between the steep walls of the escarpments, spread and widened. The river was only a stream, and we looked south over a sea of waving tall brown grass, with a few trees dotted among it. It must have been an old lake bed, for it was quite flat, and nearly two miles long by a mile wide. Tigers frequently lay up in there, and it was just the country for a hunt from elephants, the only such area anywhere near Pattan.

The elephants knelt and we all got down. 'We'll have about half an hour here,' I told the clients, 'in case anyone wants to stretch his legs. Only don't go forward of this line, please.' They stood in a group, lighting cigarettes and talking.

Chadi said, 'There are two in the grass, sahib, a male and a female. The other pair may be in there still, but Gulu thinks they left during the night.'

I thanked Gulu. This hunt would have been impossible without the Gonds' help . . . and that stemmed from old William Savage. I was living on the reputation of my great-great-grandfather.

We ran through the plans again. The elephants were to get into position first. That meant moving forward about a quarter of a mile, to a point where the grass sea was just wide enough to take four elephants at a proper distance from each other, about a hundred yards. The villagers would extend the line, so that the tigers would not try to escape past the ends. When we were in position Mitoo would start down the grass from the far end, in the centre of thirty beaters.

More bloody tigers, I thought, that's what I need. At least one for Hillburn, assuming that Lady Hillburn and George Wilson got these two. I would have needed another except for Blauvelt's ague. He *had* to get a tiger sometime, and a good one, even if I put it in a cage and brought it to his tent so that he could stun it with a bottle. When viceroys and globe trotting grand dukes used to hunt tiger the maharajahs would have men trapping the beasts for a month beforehand, and cart them to the area, and release them only as the beat started. But those spacious days were gone, and I just didn't have the resources.

The elephants knelt again, we mounted, and moved forward, the villagers on the flanks. At the far end of the grass I heard the heavy boom of the village blunderbuss. We reached our position and waited. The hot, spring wind blew down the sea of grass, making long, curved waves, changing the colour and the brightness. The grass stood about six feet tall, with heavy tasselled tops. The elephants grunted and moved about. None of them were trained for this sort of thing.

A tremendous roaring boom made me jump, and our elephant backed and fidgeted. There was no sign of Hillburn in his howdah. Mrs Wilson, her fingers in her ears, was yammering with terror. That elephant was dancing about and curving up her trunk. Hillburn hauled himself up into view from the bottom of the howdah. His dear lady beside me snapped, 'Charles has shot at a bird.'

I had noticed a jungle hen rocketing skyward just after the shot. Damned fool. That would alert the tigers long before they were near us.

'Sorry,' Hillburn called to the company in general, 'I slipped, trying to keep my balance, and it went off . . . I say, can't you keep this animal still?'

My heart sank. We waited another ten minutes – fifteen, thirty. The beaters were coming very slowly. Now and then I saw an arm waving above the grass, and heard the clatter of pots and pans coming closer.

Cynthia Hillburn raised the heavy rifle and swung right. 'Mine,' she called, her eye to the sight and her cheek cuddled professionally into the butt.

I saw a tigress, a good one, creeping along on her belly almost directly towards the elephant on our right, Hillburn and Dot Wilson's. It was not Cynthia's tiger by a mile, but let *them* fight that out. She fired, and the tigress sank her head to the ground and never moved.

'Good shot!' I said, and had no time for more, as I saw her swing the rifle up to her shoulder again. This time it was a big male tiger, following at a hard gallop in his mate's tracks. George Wilson must have seen that if he didn't fire at once he was going to lose this one, too, because Hillburn had not even got his rifle into his shoulder, and the peeress was clearly a lady who shot first and discussed the niceties later – if at all. He fired. The tiger bounded into the air and began clawing at the head of Hillburn's elephant. The mahout scrambled back into the howdah, the elephant screamed and turned, ready to bolt. I took a big chance and, aiming at the tiger's hind quarters, fired, and blew it off the elephant on to the ground, where Wilson dispatched it with a final shot through the heart.

I reloaded – we were all using double-barrelled rifles, as I think they are safer with dangerous game. Cynthia reloaded. 'That's going to be all,' I said, 'I don't think there are any . . .'

But, by God, the rifle was whipping up into her shoulder again, and on came a third beast, this one a real monster of an old tiger with a magnificent ruff, heading along the same trail, straight for Hillburn.

I pushed Cynthia's rifle barrel up and yelled 'Yours,' to Hillburn. He was leaning far out over the front of the howdah. The mahout crouched underneath, lying almost flat. Blood ran from long claw stripes down the elephant's neck and forehead, and some of it had got on the mahout, who looked as though he had been mauled. From the corner of my eye I saw Cynthia's mouth set in a hard straight line. Hillburn fired both barrels at once. He dropped the tiger stone dead, but you can't fire both barrels of a big-game rifle without ill effects. Hillburn went straight over backwards, and out of the howdah altogether. As he fell, heavily, his lady snapped, 'Bloody fool,' put on her safety catch, and found a cigarette.

We had a picnic lunch by the lake we had passed on the way up. Everyone, except perhaps me, was in tremendous good humour, and very excited, even Cynthia in her cold-fish way. After pointing out that she knew the etiquette of shooting quite well, thank you, she indicated that I was quite a presentable male, for a colonel, Indian Army, and that she would tell me, in due course, when I was to be given the privilege of pleasuring her. George Wilson measured his trophy in every direction. Hillburn drank more champagne than he could carry, and showed us his bruises. He was turning purple-black already, all over his right shoulder. Then we went home to the Rest House, and sat up late – Blauvelt too. He talked a great deal and was very amusing, mostly at his own expense.

For the next day I had arranged a small-game beat. When we were almost ready to go – no sign of H. Huntington Blauvelt. I went to his tent and said sympathetically, 'The old trouble again?'

I don't know why I felt sympathetic. If the bastard didn't go out shooting, what could he write that would help us? But he looked grey and worn and vulnerable, and I liked him.

'No,' he said. 'A touch of dysentery, old man. Got it in Greenland, of all places, back in '38 ... some piece of seal meat the Eskimoes gave me. Never shaken it off.' His fine mouth was twisted in disgust. The place stank of alcohol – not whisky this time, something else, coarser and sweeter. I knew it wasn't whisky, because I'd counted the bottles in the bar at bed time, and at dawn, just to find out how much he did take. He'd had about a bottle during the afternoon and evening, but had not taken any to bed with him; and he didn't have any of his own. The bearer I'd allotted to him told me that. I sighed wearily. He must be getting arrack from the village. Well, I'd find out ... not that I could do anything about it.

'Hope you'll be better by afternoon,' I said, and left him.

We set off, myself again with Cynthia. I felt tired. After the others went to bed I'd sat up till nearly three in the morning, talking to Chadi, Mitoo, Ganesha, and Gulu about the leopard shoot planned for the next day after this. I did not expect this small-game beat to produce much. The leopard shoot had to succeed.

The beat was to be over a stretch of rolling upland jungle about half-way between Pattan, in the valley, and an even more isolated village called Dhain, on the hills to the west. The beaters – forty men from Pattan and ten from Dhain – were already in position outside Dhain. When we were ready, at nine o'clock, they'd drive towards us through the teak and sal jungle.

I spread the shooters out, giving each one a Pattan man as general factotum and helper, though none of them could speak English. I put Wilson and Cynthia Hillburn in the middle, where I expected the best game to come down a slight fold in the ground; Hillburn and John Clayton on the extreme right, where some animals might try to break past the line; and Dottie Wilson on the extreme left, with myself.

We waited. We waited a long time. You can't hurry game if you want to guide them, and the beaters had a long way to come, and they had to come slowly to make sure that no animals hid in the scrub until they had passed. Their line was long, fairly extended and the shape of an untidy crescent, the points towards us.

Hillburn got the first animal – a small lean boar. Dot Wilson had got over her initial nervousness, having found she could lift the lighter rifle, and I had left her and was standing by a tree more or less behind the centre of the line, where I could see everyone. Hillburn struggled to his feet – he had been lying down – waddled forward to inspect his trophy, kicked it, and waddled back.

Wilson fired next, about five minutes later, and got the stag out of a small herd of five chital that came straight at him at full gallop. The chital is a small and beautiful deer which I personally don't like shooting – it has white-spotted brown hide and a big white tail and a fine delicate head. Wilson dropped his cold with a single shot at about sixty yards. Dot Wilson fired at another chital, a doe, and, thank God, missed. Cynthia expertly polished off a small sambhur. Another long wait, then a bunch of weasels, rabbits, and jackals dashed out. Dot Wilson got a jackal in the hind leg, though

I was calling to her not to waste her shots. I killed it as it crawled away.

By then I was kneeling behind Cynthia Hillburn. A big boar charged out, head down, and passed close by us, going like an express train. The peeress never raised her rifle. 'I have not come here to shoot pig,' she drawled.

Then we had a long pause, with nothing moving. The rattle of the pots and the clangour of the tin cans on the ends of sticks came closer and closer. There was no tiger grass here and we could see a long way through the glades of the jungle. It was very hot. I could see the beaters clearly now, their thin legs working, right, left, right, pause, raise the stick, rattle-rattle, on again. When they had closed to about two hundred yards from us, I stood up, cupped my hands, and called, 'No more shooting, please.'

I saw Wilson jerk the bolt and eject the cartridge from his rifle. At my feet Cynthia Hillburn began to do the same, when a gigantic sambhur stag broke cover dead ahead of us, and no more than sixty yards away. He was as good as the one I'd got to feed the village. Where he could have been hiding that great bulk and that superb spread of horns, in that open jungle, I don't know -- but there he was, running at a gallop from right to left across our front, between us and the beaters.

Cynthia Hillburn slammed shut the bolt of her Mannlicher and in the same motion lifted it to her shoulder. As I jumped forward, she fired. I slammed the muzzle down into the ground with my foot, the sambhur leaped high in a long convulsive buck, and collapsed. It looked as if she'd got him clean through the neck, severing the spinal cord. A grunting, screaming cough from the farther trees made my hair stand on end. It broke down into a confused gobbling moan. I saw a beater writhing on the ground.

I stood over the Hillburn woman, a painful knot in my belly. If my rifle had been in my hand I would have shot her, but I'd put it down when I called to everyone to stop firing. I whispered, 'You selfish, self-indulgent bitch! You want a bayonet ramming up your cunt. Now get back to the Rest House, pack, and get out, at once.'

She looked pale, but composed. It was, after all, only a peasant, and a black one at that.

I ran to the wounded man. It was Piroo, the girl Kunthi's father.

The expanding bullet had gone straight through the sambhur's neck, without mushrooming much, and hit Piroo in the left shoulder, making a bloody mess of the collar bone. He was in agony and I opened my first-aid haversack and gave him a shot of morphia. Then with George Wilson's proficient help I bandaged the wound with a shell dressing and my shirt. Meanwhile one of the young men had run off as fast as he could go to the Rest House, to bring Ratanbir and the jeep to Pattan. Then a couple of strong men lifted Piroo and began to carry him down to the village. As I followed, I saw the peeress examining her trophy. Before she could stop me I snatched the Mannlicher from her hand and with a few savage swipes broke the antlers in several pieces. I don't suppose I did the rifle much good, either.

She said coldly, 'That was quite unnecessary . . . I will, of course, pay compensation to that man.'

'Our insurance covers that,' I said, 'and no compensation can pay for an act of pure, selfish murder, done to get a trophy. I told you to pack your bags and get out.'

'It was pretty bad luck,' John Clayton said awkwardly, 'I mean, the bullet going right on through. Of course Lady Hillburn shouldn't . . .' He always thought of money, our John. Why not? He was a businessman. He wasn't stingy, but to him this was a business venture, and his money, his savings, were involved.

'Look,' I said to the peeress, 'I'm going to Lapri with Piroo now. When I get back, I don't know how long that will be, you had better be gone.' Then I ran down the slope.

When we reached the Lapri Mission nearly an hour later Piroo was dopey with the morphia, and not in so much pain. I was driving the jeep, Ratanbir following in the Bentley. I left Kunthi and Chadi holding Piroo, and hurried into the shack that was the hospital. The Holy Roller was there, bending over a bed in the corner. She turned, and half raised one arm defensively.

'For Christ's sake!' I snapped. I recovered myself. 'I beg your pardon, Mrs Wood. I have a badly wounded man outside. Bullet through the left shoulder.'

She said, 'I am a nurse, you know, not a doctor . . . Bring him in, that door.'

We carried Piroo into the little operating room. It was small, clean, and primitive. She undid the bandages, and then began to

93

move with decision and certainty, cleaning the wound while the rest of us held him down. She talked to herself in a low voice: 'The clavicle is fractured ... compound ... shoulder blade irregular in the lower part. I can feel it – pierced by the bullet ... lacerated exit wound ... lucky he was not wearing any clothes to be driven into the hole. He must have a tetanus injection.'

She took a needle, filled it, gave him the injection, and wrote on his forehead with some purple dye: *TT* 2 *cc* 1230 19/3.

'He must go to the general hospital in Bhowani as soon as possible,' she said. 'He must get there before shock sets in.'

'I'm ready now,' I said. 'Is he?'

She nodded. I told Chadi that I was off. Chadi looked troubled, and Piroo reached out his right arm slowly and took my hand. He whispered, 'The sahib *log* ... the hunting ...'

'What do they matter when ...?' I began. But of course Chadi and Piroo were worrying about the success of my hunting camp. For the people of Pattan it might make the difference between near-starvation and a half-way decent life. Or was it my success they were worrying about? I couldn't follow the inner causes any further. Piroo was severely wounded and I, being responsible for him, ought to take him to Bhowani and see him into hospital.

Piroo said, 'You must not come, sahib.' He tried to sit up, his face working. 'The camp! The sahib *log!*'

I turned to Margaret Wood. 'He ought to have a nurse with him on the drive. Can you go?'

'No,' she said abruptly.

I glared at her; then told Chadi and Kunthi to carry Piroo out to the Bentley. I told Ratanbir to drive them to Bhowani hospital, fast but not too fast. Five minutes later they were gone. Margaret Wood and I stood alone in the road outside the hospital, opposite the tiny chapel and its graveyard.

'Why couldn't you go with him?' I said. 'He might need attention on the journey – trained attention,' I added, to forestall any criticism from her. *I* ought to have gone, but I knew Piroo would fret himself into a terrible state if I did. He thought my clients would starve to death, or die of terror in the wild Indian jungles, if I left them alone for even a few hours. Perhaps the Holy Roller had recognised all that, too, because she did not try to counter-attack

94

me. She said, 'I did not go because I cannot. I have two patients in there who need me.'

'Don't you have any other nurses trained, after all these years?' I said.

She turned on me like a panther, her dark-gold hair shaking heavy over her shoulders. 'I did have trained nurses,' she cried. 'I have trained eleven since I came here nearly two years ago. They have all gone! You have lured them away with your filthy money and your filthy life, the way you've lured back all the men.'

'Only four girls came to you from Pattan,' I said automatically. My temper rose. My nerves were throbbing and curling like a broken bridge cable. I snapped, 'And *then* came back because they don't want your damned religion rammed down their throats. They've got one of their own.'

'Organised lechery!' she cried. 'Worship of sticks and stones! But you are the real cause. Why can't you go away and leave me in peace?'

'Go away?' I said. 'I'm only starting. I'm going to be in Pattan for a long, long time. I shall be here long after you've appreciated the impudence of what you're doing, packed up and gone home, where you belong.'

I spoke with the assurance of temper. Actually I was not at all sure how the camp would go, especially after throwing out the peers in such a high-handed manner and getting no publicity from Blauvelt.

For a moment she seemed to lose all control of herself. 'I'll see that you go!' she cried. 'You wait! You're not as safe as you think you are! *I* know what you're doing!'

I felt in my pocket, fished out a handful of rupees, and threw them at her. 'For the treatment,' I said. 'Don't bother to send a receipt.'

Then I got into the jeep and drove away. In the rear-view mirror I saw her staring at the rupee notes in the road. Before I turned the corner she stooped and picked them up. I felt a sharp pang of pleasure at seeing her degrade herself; then realised that she had no choice. She needed the money for the mission, and the hospital. It was only myself I had degraded by that gesture. That did not improve my temper.

Halfway to the Rest House John Clayton passed me in his car

and I saw the Hillburns in it. He waved to me, rather nervously. The Hillburns sat up straight, ignoring me.

The Wilsons were sitting out on the lawn, in the shade of the big neem tree in the corner, overlooking the stream. H. Huntington Blauvelt's spot of dysentery seemed to have gone, for he was there, too, drinking pink gin. I ordered one for myself, drank it down, and ordered another. Wilson said, 'I want you to know, Colonel, that I would have done the same thing in your place.'

'And so would I,' Blauvelt said.

I thanked them. Dot Wilson looked a little glum. Partly the sight of blood, I thought, and partly the departure of the peerage. It was she who, a little later, said, 'It's so pretty here, isn't it?' She waved her hand at the tents, the Rest House, the Irish bridge, the heavy trees. 'So pretty. And quite different from what I expected, really.'

'What did you expect?' I asked. There was an edge to my voice, and in my mind I suddenly saw John Clayton's worried face. I added in an oily tone, 'If there's anything we can do, please let me know.'

Dot spread her plump hands. 'Well, India, you know ... the splendour and the spiritualism.' She burbled on. Yoga. Mysterious. *The Razor's Edge.* Nice maharajah, met in Lander, Wyoming, hunting antelope. *Lives of a Bengal Lancer.* H. Huntington Blauvelt was looking at me with real sympathy in his eye. He poured two gins, and thrust one into my hand. George Wilson said nothing. He liked the *shikar,* but he too had expected something different.

What they were saying, really, was that they were being cheated of India because they were being shown it by an Englishman. They wanted to be seated here, or in some more Oriental equivalent, but with a maharajah in my role, deep-thinking Hindus wandering in and out, a yogi (English-speaking) at the gate, ready to expound abstruse spiritual themes. I felt tired and a little ill. No place for me even here, if this were true.

We did nothing much that afternoon. In the evening John Clayton came back. I was glad he did not speak again about the Hillburns. I suppose he had realised that, though some of his savings were at stake, my whole life was.

The following morning Wilson and I fished – poor sport, unhappily – while Dot inspected the hand-loomed cloth I'd got some of the village women to start making, in bold patterns, for outside sale. At lunchtime we heard that Piroo was out of danger, though he'd be in hospital a month or so and might never be able to raise his left arm more than a few inches. In the evening we set out to sit up for panther. Again, Gulu and his Gonds had been at work for days on my behalf, the *machans* were ready, Blauvelt had no dysentery or ague, and I felt optimistic.

Optimistic, but unsettled. During the afternoon I had a sudden terrible yearning for Sumitra, as definite as a fever, which left me trembly and full of an appalling loneliness. That was succeeded by another, this one mixed with intense curiosity – what sort of woman, what sort of human being was she, really? – and with a violent, stallion-like desire.

Long before dusk we clambered up into the howdahs and rolled off along the cart track, past the temples, through Pattan with its usual crowd of onlookers, and then directly into the jungle, going slightly west of south. After a mile we came to the first *machan*, on the bank of a small stream, and Blauvelt scrambled down, carrying his rifle very professionally in the crook of his right arm. 'I ought to be back in half an hour or less,' I called down to him. A villager was there, tying up a lusty goat.

'Fine,' he answered. We left him gazing interestedly up at the *machan* in which he and I intended to sit. A few hundred yards farther on John Clayton and Dot Wilson got up into their *machan* and, farther on still, George Wilson and Ganesha, who had excellent night vision. Each *machan* had a goat tied up underneath it. I started back.

At the first *machan* Blauvelt was sitting on the ground, his head back against a tree trunk. He put a hand to his forehead when he saw me coming, and struggled to his feet. I climbed down. He looked grey and weary, the mouth twisted into the familiar scorn.

'A touch of the old neuralgia,' he said, 'got it at Saint-Mihiel in the trenches, in '18 . . .'

For a moment I thought I was going to lose my temper. But I couldn't, not with him. Instead, what I wanted to do came to me with great clarity and force. I wanted to get drunk with H. Huntington Blauvelt. The Wilsons were installed, there was no reason on earth why I should sit here, alone, and have my goat distract the leopards, if any, away from the Wilsons'. I untied the goat and it galloped off towards Pattan.

'I'll come back with you,' I said.

Blauvelt's eyes lit up and his face brightened. He licked his lips. Then he remembered the neuralgia. After all, he had his pride. This kind of drinking, to sodden oblivion, was better done alone. 'If my head gets any better,' he said, 'otherwise I'm afraid . . .'

'A couple of aspirins will fix that,' I said cheerfully. I felt good, bounding with vitality. We climbed back into the howdah and set out for the Rest House. On our way through Pattan I told Lok Chand to make sure that no one from the village left the houses after dark, so as not to disturb the leopards; and spoke to Gulu, who said he thought there were at least four leopards in the area, and all hungry. I felt better yet.

We rolled on. As we passed the temples Blauvelt said, 'You know, I've never had a look at those.'

'Now's the time,' I cried. 'We can see well enough. Besides, we have a lantern.'

Our elephant knelt and I lit the hurricane lantern I'd taken along. I also had a powerful flashlight. I told the head mahout to take all the elephants back to the Rest House, and warn the cook that two of us would be in for dinner, and we wanted a good one.

Blauvelt and I walked through the short grass to the platform and climbed up. Blauvelt shone the flashlight around – it was not fully dark yet, but without the light there were only vague shapes, no clear outlines. The wavering powerful beam picked up a red group towering above us on the wall of the nearest temple. 'My God!' Blauvelt muttered. It was a woman standing with right hip curved out in a pose of utter pride and joy in being a woman. Two men stood beside her, one cupping her right breast, the other pleasuring her loins. All three smiled proudly up at the night sky. Blauvelt stood transfixed, a dim insubstantial shadow-being linked by the bar of light to the real life up there in the stone. Jackals cackled in the jungle behind and Blauvelt moved the light on.

We walked slowly around, stumbling now and then, for Blauvelt held the light upwards and I too was looking up. There were many garlands and offerings on and around the base of the great phallus. When Blauvelt switched off the flashlight the more diffuse light of the hurricane lantern put us in the middle of a huge cave of darkness, peopled by these vital images of love – all kinds of love, for there were women holding babies, and couples holding hands, totally loving but not linked sexually at that moment, and an old man playing in the dust with his grandson, and children in a long frieze riding the buffaloes back to the village, as you could see them any day now if you went out to look.

After half an hour we left. 'I need a drink,' Blauvelt said.

'You shall have one,' I said. 'And so shall I. Many drinks.'

He didn't speak on the short walk to the Rest House. He didn't speak until we were sitting in the common-room, where the bar was, large brandy-and-sodas in our hands. He finished his in two gulps, and put it down with a sigh.

He looked at me. 'Colonel, you have been thinking you didn't get much value out of me, especially as I am a non-paying guest, eh?'

It was true, and I didn't attempt to deny it. 'It doesn't matter,' I said. 'After what I did to Lady Hillburn, and realising that tourists want something more exotically Indian, I don't think it's going to work anyway.'

He said, 'More exotic? Well, yes, you might fix up a bare-ass holy man or two, and a snake charmer, and maybe arrange a visit to a maharajah. You'd better do that, next time, because I shall write that you had it all *this* time. And I shall write about the near-record heads I got, thrilling days on the trail of the king of beasts, the hard comradeship of the jungle, the quiet luxury of the hunting lodge. And all of that will hinge on the central character – the tough, hard-bitten white hunter. Women swoon for him, but he doesn't give a damn. He'd as soon slap a beautiful countess's face as undress her.'

I poured myself another brandy.

'There are two kinds of truth, Colonel,' he said pontifically, 'and you know only one. I am going to write the best, most exciting piece, about you and about this place, that I've ever written. Then that will be truth for everyone who reads it, which is going to be approximately fifteen million people in the United States alone. Afterwards, when they start coming here in droves, you'll find that events will conform to what I've written, and you will conform to the character I've painted. You'll have to.'

I knew, without a moment's thought, that he was speaking the truth. That was just how it would be. The jungle recluse, dedicated to his village and his animals, the 'character' whom one had to meet . . .

'You'll have to,' he repeated bitterly. 'Once a certain image of you has been created, you have to conform to it. I know. *The Doughboy and the Duchess* was a freak. I didn't really feel at all like that. I was copying someone else, and it worked. Afterwards I tried to write the way I really wanted to . . . tender, sensitive, introspective things, about what makes men and women tick, without drama or excitement, no violence, all the action inward. They flopped. There was this enormous pressure on me to be the man who'd created that tough, sexy, the-hell-with-it bastard Bill Carden. Everyone thought it was autobiographical. Jesus, it wasn't even wish fulfilment . . . And what do you want to be?'

I couldn't answer him at once. I had wanted to be a good soldier, a good businessman, a good lover, many more or less unconnected things. Now I didn't know. Perhaps more than anything else I wanted to escape the present, and sink into Pattan. But, then, I felt lonely.

Slowly, with unusual hesitation, I tried to tell Blauvelt something of this. He listened, drinking from time to time, his sad eyes fixed intently on mine. He said at once, when I finished, 'Why haven't you got a village girl?'

I mumbled something unintelligible.

He said, 'As long as you hold aloof, it means you are not satisfied, you have not yourself accepted what you say you want. There's someone else, isn't there, and you're thinking she will come here to you . . . to complete your happiness? Well, she won't, and if she does, it won't be to sink into Pattan with you, but to drag you out . . . It happened to me, you know. I married my first wife in the full flush of fame after *Doughboy*. It seemed like the final touch of happiness – but remember, I wanted to sink into an introspective life, and she not only wanted to bring me back to the "real" outside world – she *was* that world. It failed after two years . . . I'm afraid, Rodney, you've got to marry someone who is interested in *you*, involved with *you*, not with what you *do*, or might do, or can do.'

100

I thought of Janaki. Yes, she had been involved in me; but now she was the other side of the wall, and would be for as long as Max lived, and, very probably, beyond that. Sumitra . . . Blauvelt's uncanny empathy had felt, through God knows how many protective layers, that her interest in all men was in their capacities and capabilities, not in them. And that this interest would not extend to a man's capacity for self-withdrawal. And, remember, he hadn't even met her.

Blauvelt said, 'You're here. You're going to stay here. Take a girl from Pattan, and settle down. This camp is going to be a success. I personally guarantee it. I'm going on to Chambalpur from here, as a guest of the Nawab – I don't know why they're inviting me, but I'm sure I'll find out soon enough what it is they want publicised . . . and I'll write the piece about you as soon as I get there. By mid-summer you'll be snowed under with applications.'

I knew why they were inviting him to Chambalpur – to put Chambal's case for independence before the world, especially the American public, in a roundabout sort of way. Well, that was the world I was trying to get away from, the world which involvement with Sumitra – or any other woman from 'civilisation' – would drag me back into.

Blauvelt stood up suddenly. 'Come on, let's send for a couple of girls. Break it up! Make up your mind. The temples, and Pattan . . . or this lady of yours, and the God-damned, stinking rat race outside. I know what *I* want. I want the temples . . . right now.'

I hesitated a little longer. It was easy for him. He didn't really mean that he wanted the lost, all-loving world of the temples – he meant he wanted it tonight, as a respite from the rat race. For me, the choice was permanent.

I made up my mind, by what process or accident I do not know. 'All right,' I said. I called for Ratanbir and told him to take the jeep and fetch Devi and Kunthi. He saluted woodenly and went out. One of the things I was giving up was being a sahib, with a sahib's standards, and it came surprisingly hard. A sahib does not involve his servant with his amours, or he will upset the man's sense of values and of his own position.

Half an hour later the girls slipped in, making deep *namasti*.

Kunthi had her war paint on – a diaphanous sari, made of material I'd given her, with no underclothes or bodice, her nipples painted red, reddish-blue lines drawn with face paint under the swell of her breasts to make them stand out more, and the sari itself slightly damped so that it clung to every curve and fold of her body. Devi never used those artifices. She was thin and intense, tonight looking almost demonic, her eyes huge and heavily rimmed with kohl in her small, pointed face.

I poured them drinks. Like most of the people of Pattan, they either didn't drink at all or they drank to extinction, but I hoped to keep them from passing out tonight.

I pulled Devi down on my knee. Kunthi went to Blauvelt. We fondled them and they smiled. We all drank. Blauvelt got excited. I told the girls to take their saris off, it wasn't going to make much difference. They did so, and danced a languid indecent dance, gliding round the table, bending over us and in front of us, singing softly in their high wavering voices.

We ate, off and on. Carlos the butler dropped the soup when he first came into the room, later became so uplifted that Blauvelt invited him to join us at the table. He looked nervously at me, but, as I said, this was good-bye to sahibdom, and I held him by the shoulders and forced him to sit down. Also Ratanbir. More girls appeared, and some men from Pattan.

At about two in the morning I had a great idea, the sort that often strikes at that hour. We went in a body, singing lewd songs, to the temples, and lit several bonfires on the platform. Ratanbir in the jeep brought along two or three cases of rum. No one wore any clothes, or, if so, they were peripheral and decorative rather than prurient in purpose. Devi's mother, Piroo's wife, for instance, wore a bodice but nothing else. Most men kept on their ragged puggarees. Many women wore the red *garghara*, the short swinging skirt of the peasant women, feeling that it was more proper – as the temple carvings often showed – to lift them or have them lifted while they danced and coupled, rather than go stark-naked. Blauvelt, forgetting which particular past he was re-entering, pranced about like a long, thin Pan, blowing tunelessly on someone's wooden pipe. He also took off his toupee and threw it away. Whatever I did I kept thinking of Sumitra.

It was said afterwards that the whole village of Pattan joined in the orgy on the old temple platform. This is not true. The population of Pattan was 403 at my last count before this, and there were some too old, some ill, some shocked, many tired, some disinterested. At dawn we had about forty present and active. The number had fluctuated all night, starting low, building, decreasing, increasing again. Nor was it an orgy, but a re-creation of the time and mood of the temples themselves, most religiously exact.

I saw the dawn coming. A greenish light spread fast over the eastern trees. The soaring temple towers, lit by the jumping red light of the fires on one side, all darkening into silhouette as the day drew on, made a most impressive and moving vision.

With Kunthi, Devi, and another woman, as a last triumphal act, I was trying to get into one of the most complicated of the interlocking positions shown in the carvings. It started with my standing on my head against a temple wall. Opposite me, between Kunthi's spread legs, I could see the model we were imitating, carved in red on another temple. Then, to the side, something alien and out of tune caught my eye. Out of tune because it was fearful, and shocked. It was the white, strained face of the Holy Roller, Margaret Wood.

She stood, frozen. I overbalanced, landed right way up, and walked over to her, the three women clinging to me wherever they could get a hold. Devi was by now on the edge of extinction.

'What can I do for you, madam?' I asked. I was not far from oblivion myself.

Her lips moved, whispering. 'A jackal . . . in the operating room . . . It has rabies.'

The light was strong but without any forewarning of the sun, yet. Devi slid slowly down my right side and collapsed gently, smiling, on the stone, her face to the sky.

The night was over.

'And you have no rifle, or anything?' I asked.

'No,' she whispered. 'No one in Lapri would help. They wouldn't even open the doors to me. It was dark. There was no one at the Rest House.' She was sweating, her face cold and wet and white.

I jumped down from the platform and climbed into the jeep. 'Get in,' I said. Like a sleepwalker she climbed in, looking straight ahead. On the platform the music and the shouting were dying, and men and women staggering home, others lying down where they were, out to the world.

I drove off. The light struck with a jolly warmth against my eyes and my head felt full of a joyous nothing. The road curved continuously when I wasn't looking, the cunning devil, so I had to swing the jeep nose fast and keep my wits about me or it would have slipped away from me. Once it got away and I had to dash in among the trees to catch it again. Margaret Wood bit off a cry but said nothing. The jeep seemed to want to fly and once or twice we actually took off, but there wasn't enough power, or the aerodynamics weren't quite right, and we returned to earth a few yards farther on.

The buildings of the mission were doing a cheerful fandango when I saw them, the bungalow on the left, chapel beyond, hospital on the right. 'Stop!' Her voice was sharp and full of panic.

'Whatsa matter? Jackal can't have escaped,' I said reasonably.

'Quick, behind the bungalow, *please*,' she cried.

'O.K., O.K.,' I said, and turned off.

Behind the bungalow she said, 'Stop!' and I stopped. 'Quick,' she grabbed me by the arm and dragged me up the back veranda steps, opened a door and jerked me inside.

'Jackal in here?' I asked in surprise. I knew she'd said the beast was in the hospital. But she had vanished. She came back with a pair of trousers and a shirt. 'Put these on,' she said. She'd got plenty of colour by now, and she wasn't cold or sweating any more.

Whims of women, I thought, and shrugged. I put on the clothes. They didn't fit very well and I couldn't get the trousers on because the leg hole had St Vitus's Dance, and when I had finally done it, by sitting down and holding the damned hole so that it couldn't escape, I got the other leg in the same hole. She was watching, and finally gave a sort of exasperated sigh and knelt down, dragged the trousers off me, and then with a couple of expert heaves and a wiggle, pulled them on properly.

'You'd better let me take the rifle,' she said.

'There's no need to be insulting,' I said, and walked out to the jeep and got the rifle. Then I followed her across the road to the hospital. One of the patients, wrapped in a blanket, was standing at a back window, peering in. It was a woman and I was glad I had made myself presentable. I peered in through the same window, the woman respectfully making room for me. I was looking into the little room where she had bandaged Piroo's shoulder. The jackal lay on the floor, slavering and panting deeply, obviously rabid. 'He went in, moaning, about four o'clock,' Margaret said. 'I heard the patients screaming ... I ran over and shut the doors ...'

I knocked out one pane of glass with the rifle butt, and, leaning in, shot the jackal through the head.

'All right?' I said.

She nodded wordlessly. 'One good turn deserves another,' I said, and walked back to the jeep.

'I'll drive you back,' she said. I frowned, and she added, 'You're as drunk as you were the first time we met.'

I said, with dignity, 'Madam, we have never met,' got into the jeep and drove back to the Rest House. Carlos, wan but fully clothed, was setting the table for breakfast. Two leopards, one very respectable and one magnificent, lay on the lawn with a grinning Chadi, Ganesha, and others squatted beside them and Wilson taking photographs. The hunting camp was going to be a great success. I seemed to have found my niche at last.

Three days later Blauvelt left for Chambalpur, the Wilsons for Agra, and John Clayton for Delhi. They were all very happy. Kunthi and Devi had installed themselves in one of the servants' quarters and were obviously my property. Dot Wilson had been deliciously titillated, George man-to-man approving. By chance a wandering *bhairagi* came by the day after the saturnalia, and I offered him a tree, a leaf roof, and the devotion of Pattan if he would be our yogi. He agreed, and took up residence. I had a letter from a friend in Delhi telling me that everyone was talking about how I had smacked Lady Hillburn's face and bodily thrown her out of the Rest House. My new suit of personality seemed to be settling into an excellent fit.

In the afternoon of the 23rd I was sitting on the veranda, reading my Sanskrit grammar, when I heard the whir of a small car, and Ranjit Singh, the D.C., drove up. I went down to greet him.

'What about some tea?' I said. 'The cook's off, so Ratanbir will make it, and it will have pepper in it.'

Ranjit grimaced, but did not smile. He looked worried, almost shamefaced, as much as a Sikh can look behind that imposing curled, black beard.

We chatted about nothing in particular until Ratanbir served the tea and left us. I noticed his shirt was dirty, but what the hell, so was mine.

After sipping his tea, with the pepper, and grimacing again, Ranjit abruptly set down his cup and looked at me. 'I've got bad news, Savage. You've got to leave Pattan.'

One's instinct is to repeat inanely some word or phrase that has shocked you. I try to resist it, and this time, after a pause, said reasonably, 'Don't be silly. I've only just come. I have a long lease.'

He flushed. 'It's been cancelled.'

I thought suddenly of Margaret Wood. She had sworn she would get rid of me, and now I had given her just the evidence she wanted. The Government of India, like the rest, exercises a fierce selectivity about its own past. You get a pat on the back for bringing the glory of Indian art to the world's attention. You get an expulsion order for re-creating the guiltless sensuality which made that art possible. 'The bitch!' I said aloud. 'Look, Ranjit, it's in the air here, in the people's minds, in their history and folklore.'

The D.C. stared at me with his best inscrutable I.C.S. face. I became desperate, and yet, at the edge of my mind, had a sharp realisation that Ranjit and I were playing, in reverse, a scene that had been enacted how many million times in the past century and a half – the alien consul trying to decide between two quarrelling natives – which is truth, which is invention to work off a grudge?

'She's furious because her converts and nurses leave,' I said, 'but it's nothing to do with me.'

Ranjit stroked his beard.

'She saw what she saw,' I pleaded. 'I'm not trying to deny it. I'm not trying to deny that you have to take a serious view of it. The Pandit would have a fit if it got out into world publicity. I know that. I'm only saying that it's not vice, here, but something else – tradition, love, something . . . Why are you taking sides with

106

a damned mission, trying to convert your own people away from your own religion, against me, who's trying to bring tourists into India and gain a lot of foreign exchange for you?'

Ranjit drank tea while I paused to gather breath. He said, 'You had better tell me just what did happen.'

The wily bugger. Well, I told him. I poured out the whole story of the hunting camp from beginning to end, including some sharp comments on the government's neglect of the near-famine situation in Pattan, which had driven me to poach game to feed them; and our illegal methods of killing fish for the same purpose; and my alliance with the Gonds; the tensions of the camp; Lady Hillburn; my state of mind; Blauvelt; the choice of sinking right into Pattan, or staying alone and lonely, yearning for something I couldn't have – I told him all.

I ended: 'So you see, it's not just a simple case of Satan debauching innocent villagers.

Without a word he handed me a long envelope. It was not sealed. The letter inside was addressed to me, and signed by the Governor of the province, Sir Chandragupta Chenur, another I.C.S. man. He informed me that under the provisions of section something or other of the Defence of India Act my lease of certain lands and buildings lying in the Pattan Reserved Forest (this meant the Rest House) was hereby terminated, as were my shooting leases over Blocks 3, 6, 7, 9, and 11. I was required to vacate the area by midnight on March 23 – three days hence.

I slammed the paper on the table. 'Christ, Ranjit, I've just been explaining!'

'Look again,' he said.

I looked again. The message said nothing new to me. But this time I noticed the date of the Governor's signature. It was March 19, the day of the leopard hunt – that is, before the affair at the temples.

Ranjit said, 'I am not required to give you any reason for the action, under the Act. *You* know that. And I have been specifically ordered – not by the Governor, by high political figures – not to say anything at all. But—' he fingered his tie, the same Free Foresters tie he had been wearing when I first met him – 'between gentlemen there are certain decencies . . . You are too close to the frontier with Chambal. The Nawab's recent speech decided the government to remove all possible sources of danger. You have had contacts with the Chambal authorities . . .'

'About the shooting!' I shouted. 'I've got to be able to cross the line when the game does. Look, the frontier's just over there.' I pointed across the Shakkar stream at the rise of rock on the far side of the valley, a mile away.

'I'm sure they would wish they had waited a few days,' Ranjit said, 'if they were ever to hear of this other business. That would have given them a much better case. But I suppose they never would have heard of it – nor I for that matter. You see, Savage, the real truth of the matter is that you have enemies, and the present tension allows them to act against you.'

'I have friends, too,' I said furiously. 'One word and I could have you torn in pieces, Ranjit. I could put the clock back here and in Bhilghat a long way, back to the time they killed your policeman down there! I could destroy your career, and the Governor's. I've only got to raise my finger and you'll have a thousand men in rebellion in these hills.'

He said sadly, 'You're right, I'm afraid. Which is why this order, instigated by malice though it is, is perhaps right, for India.'

I stood up. I wanted to pick up the table and smash the D.C.'s car to pulp with it. I didn't want to hit Ranjit. He was an impersonal servant, a disembodied force, pushing and shoving at me. 'I had it all settled,' I said, stammering with rage, 'I got out of your damned way. I left you to run the bloody country as best you could, and even then you had to send for me when you came across something you didn't understand. Now you're after me again, dragging me out of my hole in the ground. I didn't give a damn about Chambal. Force it in, let it join Pakistan, let it be independent, I didn't care. It wasn't my business any more. And now you, you . . .'

Ranjit stood up, too: 'I'm really sorry, Savage, and I'm deeply ashamed that it was I who had to deliver that order. But I had to, and I have . . . If there's anything I can do, now or afterwards, to help you, please tell me. I mean it.'

I did not answer. After a while, he was standing there with his hand out and I ignoring it; he turned away and got into his Austin and drove off.

I slumped back in my chair. For a time I just hated – nothing in

108

particular, everything. But I do not have the sort of temperament that can for long scrabble and batter at an irrevocably closed door. Now where? Back farther into the jungles? There were more remote places than this, deeper jungles, bigger and less penetrable hills, peoples still farther removed from the complex meanness of the century. There were Todas in high secret valleys of the Nilgiris; tribes in the back of Orissa whom only a dozen outsiders had ever heard of; Nagas, Abors, and Mishmis of the Assamese frontier – they were hard men, too, and they would fight harder to preserve their own ways. There would be other trails to walk, other girls like Kunthi and Devi, other fires in the night, other arrack, other dancing. And even as I thought of those places and those people I saw Ranjit, wearing the impeccable Western dress and the Free Foresters tie, advancing steadily, holding a pamphlet on planned economy in one hand and a pair of trousers in the other; and behind him, the Indian Army, and behind them, the dedicated faces of Jawaharlal Nehru, and L. P. Roy, and the ranked Gandhi caps, and the whey-cheeked teetotallers, the city planners, the vote getters, the speechmakers, the engineers with slide rules, the lawyers pleading *habeas corpus*, the university students carrying dingy banners – every one of them sprung from *my* mind, *my* work, *my* wounds. There was no denying that the creation of these people, this India, was the object, acknowledged or not, of my ancestors – but the wheel had turned full circle, the clock again reached twelve. They were forcing me back to the coral strand where old Jason Savage must have landed, if he ever existed – but where were the magnificent kings who had then walked the sands of Coromandel under golden umbrellas? Where were the Rajput knights who had put on their wedding silks – the same finery I had seen in one of those near-visions, beside the lake – and ridden out to die in hopeless battle against such as my ancestors? Where were their wives, who lit the pyres and leaped in, children in their arms? Where were the Madrassi sepoys who gave Clive the rice at Arcot and took only the water themselves, and yet had no knowledge of inferiority? Where now did I hear a man say, 'I have eaten your salt'? Where was the Rani of Kishanpur, splendid in steel armour, hating England and loving my great-grandfather? And the men in the stands of sugar cane along the bank of the Ravi, who gave you *gur* and milk to drink, and sat talking with you in dignity and pride and poverty at the corner of the house, in the shade? Where were the gentle lovers of Khajuraho and Pattan, and proud women who walked unveiled? Where was the splendour of India's soul, that met Jason Savage on that shore three centuries ago?

What had I done?

God damn them all. God damn them all.

Chapter 7

'Margaret Donoghue, you lazy thing, you, will you get out of bed now?'

Her mother's Londonderry brogue was strong, the voice laughing under the pretended sharpness. But Margaret couldn't get up. Her legs and arms lay like lead prolongations of a central core which had only just the strength to realise, and to hear, none to stir or lift. That's what it used to be like. Then strength would come very, very slowly as her mother clumped up the stairs and sat on the edge of the bed, and bent down to kiss her. Then the strength used to flow in, starting at the tips of her toes and the ends of her fingers.

Mother wasn't here. Rats scrabbled at the ceiling cloth. Or bats, or flying foxes, or horrible long centipedes, or scorpions, or shrews, or some of the small animals that had flitted across her path in the earliest dawn as she walked to the Rest House the night the jackal came. How long ago was that? A week. The rats would gnaw through the cloth and fall on her, helpless in the bed. She stared at the ceiling. It was a dim blur. Hard to know whether it was day or night outside. The ceiling swam into focus – no movement, no bulging and heaving, like sea waves, across from one end to the other, as the rats ran across, no squeak or gibber. The creaking continued.

She moaned, and turned her head. Wind, hot-weather wind. The window across the room was open and in the twilight she saw trees thrashing behind the empty servants' quarters. A spasm gripped her belly, she held on to herself with all her strength, leaned out of bed, fell to the floor, and crawled across the patched blue *durrie* on hands and knees to the bathroom. She grabbed the edge of the wooden toilet box, tried to pull herself up but could not, and relieved the agony where she knelt. Afterwards she hung

111

dizzy and blind for a time to the commode seat, then crawled back into the bedroom, clutched the sheet, tried to pull herself up, failed, and fell back to the floor. Floor and ceiling, heat and smell, receded on slow painful waves.

She was cold, shivering in a sleet-laden wind that slashed through her clothes and the flesh under them and the bones supporting the flesh and the marrow in the bones. She hung against a tree and screamed and screamed, alone in the forest with the swinging corpse of herself, hanged from the bough of a tree. The corpse's face – her own – was a flat white with no expression. Rain dripped from its face and chin and lay in shining oily drops in its hair. Now she recalled with perfect clarity that there had been no rain, and the corpse was not real.

It was worse than that. It was a straw-filled effigy of herself, wearing short skirt and blouse, the cardboard face painted white and wisps of reddish horse hair representing her own, the effigy dangling on a rope from the nearest tree to the chapel, on the side of the graveyard.

It was worse than that. The instant she saw the horrible thing she knew that she did not want to continue the work of the mission. She did not have the faith it needed. She had known that for a long time, but this show of hate had broken through the façade. When had she seen the effigy? In the dusk, when her bones already ached, but she was hoping the fever would pass, and had taken quinine and gone out for a breath of fresh air. How many days ago? Two, three, four?

Without faith, or purpose, why did she stay? Because she had promised Henry that she would. Not in so many words, but in her acceptance of marriage, in her comfortings during his last illness, which had said as plain as words, I will stay until another comes to replace me, however long that may be. But Henry had now become a vague figure whose face and eyes she could not recall, whose voice had vanished; and from England no other was coming, ever. They wrote, and hoped, but she knew.

She had felt totally empty, like a lake that has been steadily drained over a long period, until at last the water is gone; and after that the sun has worked on the damp earth and dried it, and there is finally neither water nor memory of water. There had been a crisis like this, in England, after the war, just before Henry came.

Twenty-eight years of age passed; the war passed; two of the inevitable nurses' affairs with handsome young doctors behind her; gone also three successive suitors in whom she had seen nothing, hard as she tried, except that they were men . . . and then the crisis of emptiness. Henry arrived in the middle of it, obviously in search of a trained nurse to be his wife – not the other way round. Yet as soon as he had approached her she accepted him – and at once the lake began to refill, and she knew again a sense of purpose, of fullness, of fulfilment.

She realised that she still lay on the floor. Rested now, with a great effort she pulled herself on to the bed, and lay there panting feebly. It was night, perhaps, but not late. The fourth night. She ought to be over it soon, one way or another. The darkness slowly, firmly closed in upon her. In an infinity of weariness she surrendered to it, in silence.

It was cool again, not cold. The coolness moved in waves, as all feeling had for a long time, down from her head, through her neck, across her breasts and belly, between her legs, under her buttocks. He head ached with a hollow pain. The hollowness kept her sane, for it enclosed the pain and made it come to her as from an immense distance, through a vacuum.

Why had the lake emptied itself again? *Because I did not love.* When had she noticed the desiccation, the dryness? At the moment of Henry's death, that was the truthful answer. It had taken half a year of loneliness after that before she could admit it to herself, and that brought her to – now. And what had made the next change, which she would never have admitted for another six months, except in the death-like honesty of this illness? What was it that brought once more a sense of life into her existence, as palpable as running water to refill the emptied, dried lake? The water was cold at first, bitter cold. She shivered at memories of anger – but anger meant life; of hate and striving – but with growing energy. Then, in the night, the night before the fever, or perhaps it was already upon her, the pulsing warm flood, her heart lifting and beating, faster and faster, her voice singing in the silence . . .

A man's head hung in a halo of light very close to her. Rodney Savage, his head a foot from hers, his eyes down, his lips slightly parted, a look of total absorption on his face. He was dressed, but very tired. The halo was a lantern on the table behind him. The blurred pink to the left, at the lower limit of her field of vision, was her own body, naked. He was sponging her down with a cold, wet sponge. The texture of substances became very clear, though distant. She was lying on one of the big, rough jail-made towels, near the outside edge of the bed. The wooden edge of the bed bit into her buttocks. Under the towel she felt the criss-cross pattern of the *newar* mattress.

She whispered, 'Do I look as you expected?'

He went on sponging, but turned his head slightly. 'Yes . . . better, as a matter of fact. Don't worry. It's only tit for tat, isn't it?'

She closed her eyes. It was intolerable that he should meet her, ask her to take her clothes off, and not even remember her, however drunk he had been. That had always annoyed her. And now, when he did see her naked, he still did not remember that first time, but only the other day, the time when frightened and lonely she had come upon that fantastic scene at the temples. Fantastic, and frighteningly wonderful.

Yes, it was a towel that she lay on. So he must have cleaned her of vomit and faeces, and taken away the sheets and clothes. She could not move her head, but the room smelled of soap and water.

'How long . . . ?' she whispered.

'Three, four hours,' he said. 'It's one o'clock in the morning. Roll over now, on your front.' His hands helped her, and she lay face down, feeling the cool sponge, hearing the tinkle of water as he wrung it out over an empty bucket, dipped it again in a full one, half-wrung it, put it to her back. 'You have a temperature of 104½,' he said. 'What have you got? Here—' she felt his hand slip into hers as it lay beside her – 'press my finger when I say the right word. Typhus? Malaria? Dysentery? Typhoid?' She squeezed his finger in her hand.

'Para,' she muttered into the pillow.

'Paratyphoid? Should I move you at once to Bhowani? I have the Bentley. Yes? No?' She squeezed again.

'No? You're too weak. I'm going to try to keep you warm and clean. There ought to be some glucose in the hospital, and I'll find that and give it to you. And I can get some milk and boil it. Nothing else until you can tell me. Is that right?'

114

The last word echoed and repeated in her head ... right-right-right-right, becoming fainter and fainter as her reserve of strength faded, rhythmically falling away in the repeated echo. She closed her hand tight on his finger and holding on to that drifted out on a heaving dark tide of sleep.

The light hurt her eyes, and someone whistling sounded like a shriek in her ears. She moved and the whistling stopped. It was daylight. She was wearing a man's pyjama coat and nothing else, and there were two blankets on the bed. She was sweating heavily.

'Something to drink,' he said.

She felt the spoon in her mouth, contracted her throat muscles and forced herself to swallow, again, again. When she could take no more she turned her head and muttered, 'Warm chicken broth ... Pills, labelled sulfaguanidine. Twenty at a time.'

She slept. She drank warm chicken broth, and knew from the taste that some sulfaguanidine must be ground up in it. Night time. She slept again.

She awoke to a hot morning light. He took her temperature, and said, 'A hundred exactly. Feel able to talk?'

She said, 'I didn't tell the D.C. anything. I never saw you do anything suspicious, or meet anybody except Mr Faiz Mohammed once or twice, and I didn't think it worth telling them that. Nor about ... the temples.'

He said, 'I know you didn't.'

She had to tell him now, while it was clear in her mind and he was here. At any moment he might vanish again, as he had come. 'Ranjit Singh stopped here on his way back the other day. He told me he had just given you the order cancelling your lease. I hadn't done anything, said anything, but I was pleased.' She looked at him, but he had his back turned to her. He must turn round and see her face; but he did not. She had to talk to his back as he went on mixing something in a bowl, a *degchi* of warm milk beside him on the table. 'Then that evening all the rest of the people here left. Two old women and a child left the hospital, though they were sick. Men came and carried them away. The sweeper left. The servant here.'

'It was nothing to do with me,' he said, still not turning.

'Oh, I know, I know – now! There was an effigy ...'

115

'You saw that? I hoped you had not. I cut it down and burned it.'

Then he did turn and come towards her, a mug in his hand. Dark pouches lay under his eyes, and a black stubble round his chin and jowl. He looked murderous, the pale-blue eyes shining feverishly.

'You're sick, too,' she muttered.

'Not sick – just tired.'

In the ocean of sleep there had been islands, painful islands. She had sat on pots, bones aching, clinging convulsively to something or someone. She had vomited, emptied her bowels, felt hot urine on her legs, drunk soup. Towels had been changed, and sheets, and blankets. Through the window now she could see blankets and towels and sheets and pyjama coats and shirts and dishcloths hanging on a clothes line. He must have washed them.

He said, when she had greedily finished the broth, suddenly aware of violent hunger pains, 'Now, should I take you somewhere where you can be properly looked after?'

'Are you going to Delhi?'

He shook his head impatiently. 'I don't know. That's not the question. Where should *you* go?'

She turned away. 'I'm staying here,' she said flatly. 'You can leave me now. By evening I shall be able to look after myself.'

'All right,' he said. 'But I shall bring Kunthi and Devi before I go. They're two girls from Pattan, and I've already given them some first-aid and hygiene training. Their normal profession is whore, but they'll look after you as long as you want them to.'

She mumbled, 'Thank you,' into the pillow.

'Now can I leave you safely for an hour or so?'

An hour! When before dark he was going away for ever. 'Yes,' she said.

'I'm off now, then. Go back to sleep.'

'I'm hungry,' she said resentfully. Did he have no awareness of any of her emotions or feelings?

'I'm sure you are. But no food now. Go back to sleep'

Sleep, she muttered, sleep, sleep, sleep. But against her will, she did. When she opened her eyes she saw a thin, dark Indian girl, her hair drawn tightly back from the high forehead, squatting on the floor near the head of the bed, her eyes fixed on her in an intense, unwinking stare. She recognised the girl at once as one who had been in his arms on the temple platform.

'What is your name?' she whispered.

'Devi,' the girl answered. 'He says you are to eat when you wake.' She stood up.

'Where is he?' she asked.

'Asleep,' she said over her shoulder as she went out towards the kitchen. 'I will awaken him.'

'No!' she cried.

'It is his order,' the voice said from the kitchen.

He did not come in until she had finished eating, and Kunthi had taken away the bowl, and also firmly made her change out of his pyjama coat into one of her own nightdresses. She sat up, pulling the sheet higher to her neck.

'Mind if I smoke a cheroot?' he said. 'I'll sit near the window.'

'Oh, please do,' she said. 'I'd like a cigarette, too.'

He found one of hers, put it in her mouth, and lit it. He puffed away at his cheroot. She saw that he had shaved and now looked a little less demonically villainous, though just as tired.

'I must go soon,' he said. 'I think you'll be all right. Kunthi and Devi will see that no harm comes to you. I've told them to tell Faiz Mohammed at once if you have a relapse . . . Don't take that effigy too hard, or your people leaving. There are all sorts of rumours flying around. The Chambal Army is going to move everyone out and dig defences against India . . . The Indian Army is coming through with guns and tanks, blasting everything before them with bombers. That's what's caused the flight, more than your excessive Christianity. . . . It did seem excessive to me.'

She said, 'I didn't feel very Christian when I lost my temper with you . . . when I tried to hate you.'

He said, 'You seemed more human to me then. Before, when I saw you, from what I heard . . . there seemed to be nothing but Christian resignation, turning the other cheek, love thine enemy. A saint in a church, palms joined, looking upward, beatific smile on the lips. Fixed beatific smiles make a woman look stupid.'

Her heart beat with a pleasant warmth. So he had thought about her! Why, oh, why, couldn't he have come earlier, when he was alone in Pattan, and discussed all this?

She said, 'I was lonely . . . afraid . . . afraid of India . . . bored

117

. . . frustrated. I am not a missionary, I have no real faith, I was terrified my husband would find out . . . But I did not want to show it. I wanted to stick it out, to do my job to the end, without failing. Sometimes . . . sometimes I used to think, lying awake in bed at night, that it was all a preparation. Once I told him at least that much, and he smiled and said "Yes, it was, a preparation for heaven." I didn't think so, but I could not say anything.'

He had listened with a sort of curious half-attention, his eyes sometimes fixed on hers, sometimes wandering round the room, his fingers fiddling with the sheet. Now ask me what I really felt, what I thought about you, she willed him; talk, talk about us; bring it all out of me; the right word, the right look, a touch, will do it . . .

He got up listlessly. 'It's the times. Something's pushing us out of India – rejecting us.'

'Yes!' she cried. 'We're in the same boat.'

'We're both being pushed out – you for trying to change old patterns, me for trying to get back to them . . . I must be on my way.'

'Where to?' she asked quickly. 'What are you going to do?'

He said, 'I don't know. I only know that they're not going to push me out . . . I dropped in that evening to return the clothes you lent me. Your husband's, I suppose? Also to tell you that you'd won, here.'

'No, no!' she cried.

'I also meant to tell you I didn't think you'd find your victory very real. Then I saw the effigy, and I knew I wouldn't have to say anything. Except good-bye . . . We didn't really affect each other at all. We just thought so, but really it was events, and times, which caught us both up and threw us against each other. There's no need for us to part as enemies.'

She looked at him and said, 'I am not your enemy. The opposite.'

'I'm sorry,' he said simply, and there was no way of knowing whether he understood but did not care, and was sorry; or did not understand, and was sorry; and no clear understanding, in her exhausted calm, of which of the two would be worse.

'Kunthi!' he called.

Another girl came in, the curvaceous one who had fallen down dead drunk on the platform. Margaret could see her now, more clearly than her smiling, clothed presence – her firm full breasts pointing to the sky, the legs parted, a beatific smile on her face, and every finished curve speaking of a woman's fulfilment.

Rodney spoke to her and she walked, hips swinging, into the other room, and came out with a bedding roll on her head. Rodney followed, returning with a suitcase.

'Your pyjama coats!' she cried. 'I saw two on the line . . . It must be lunchtime. You must have something to eat.'

But he shook his head, and Kunthi came in with the pyjamas and in a trice they were packed away in the suitcase.

'Good-bye,' he said.

'Good-bye,' she said. 'And – and thank you.' The door closed behind him and she whispered, 'With all my heart . . . Oh, God, oh, God,' and sank her head into the pillow.

Chapter 8

'Rodney!'

I'd heard that call twenty, thirty times the past few days, since arriving in Delhi. I couldn't walk in the street, have a drink at a bar, swim at the club pool, without a voice calling me. This time I was walking down the long corridor on the ground floor of the Imperial, and it was Max. He was wearing uniform and looked fit, burly, and businesslike. I had decided, long since, that he had learned about my love for Janaki, and had – sensibly and typically – realised that it had hurt me a great deal more than it could hurt him.

'What are you doing here?' he asked.

'Robbing a bank,' I said.

Max laughed. The usual conversation followed: Where was I staying? Good heavens, that flea pit! (I was staying at a small hotel in Old Delhi.) I must go and live with his cousin Hari. That, too, was as usual. Everyone invited me to stay, but I always refused. My old room was ready for me in John Clayton's bungalow, but I did not want to go there. Not that it would have been 'awkward'. The business with Frances was over and she knew it. She had already got a passage home about a month hence.

For politeness' sake I should have asked Max what he was doing in Delhi, knowing that his division was in Bhowani, but I didn't want to continue the conversation. Besides, I knew. Obviously he had been called up to discuss the increasing tension between India and Chambal. If India decided to deal with Chambal by force, Max was going to be the bullyboy.

'I've got to go,' he said finally, with a rather unconvincing look at his watch. He summoned up his courage. 'And, Rodney, old boy, you know, if there's anything I can do ... I have lots of friends – Daulat, Rikhye, P. R. Sethi—'

'Don't worry, Max,' I said, 'I'll come round with my hat in my hand before I have to sell the Bentley.' That was a lie, but what else could you say to a man like Max?

We parted and I went on out into the street and walked aimlessly towards Connaught Circus. It was hot then, at the very end of March, and I was not wearing a hat. Out in the bustle of the crowd, the clop of tonga pony hoofs and the rustle and murmur of people in my ears, dust rising by the hawkers' stalls, students lolling in the shade on the grass under the trees, bicycles ebbing to and fro like schools of fish ... I slipped back into the chain of thought which Max had interrupted – the morass of thought would be a better notion.

From the beginning, when the D.C. came to throw me out of Pattan, there had been interruptions, like finding Margaret Wood ill and alone at the mission, and, since then, these chance meetings. I could not decide whether the interruptions prevented me from achieving an orderly thought sequence, which would solve my problems, or mercifully yanked me out of a futile nose-chasing-tail hypnosis.

In the foreground, when I trod water in my swamp, all I could see was debt. John Clayton had put a lot of money into the hunting camp, and so had Frances. It had gone – not through my fault, but all the same it had gone, and I felt I owed it back. I had also lost all but a small amount of my own savings, and now had less than 300 rupees in the world, plus my pension. I wasn't going to starve, but neither was I going to be able to repay my debts.

So – I must get a job. Here I could feel my teeth gritting together, and a voiceless repetition of the words *In India*. Daulat, Rikhye, and P. R. Sethi, whom Max mentioned, were industrialists, owners of banks, airlines, cotton mills, God knows what else. P. R. Sethi was, in addition, a hell of a good man. Any of them, plus half a dozen others I could think of, would give me a good job, and were powerful enough, and independent enough to tell L. P. Roy to go to hell if he tried to prevent it.

Also, I wanted to meet Sumitra again.

Here all forward progress stopped, and the heavy mud of the morass began to rise about my hips and waist, clasping and dragging. Try as I might, I could think of no job that I would accept. No job that I would be offered, that is. There were plenty

121

that I would *not* be offered. For instance, I had already heard whispers of trouble between the new government and the Assam hill tribes, especially the Nagas. I saw the Nagas' point of view, and I saw the government's. I knew the Nagas – fought with them in the war – was an honorary Naga myself. If the government made me Special Commissioner for the Hill Tribes, and promised fifty years to me and my successors to bring the tribes into their new India – I'd go like a shot. But it was part of the problem that such a job *had* to be done by an Indian. It would make no difference if I crossed over into Pakistan, except that I could claim Pakistan citizenship by birth, having been born in Lahore. Even so, they would definitely not send me to Gilgit, Chitral, Waziristan, or any of the places where I wanted to be and where I could have done a good job. In brief, I didn't want what I could get and couldn't get what I wanted – and needed.

So, back to the money . . . By now I must have been round this circle 750 times. I wondered occasionally what Margaret Wood thought of me, when she recovered sufficiently to be aware that I was there. What I had to do in that forlorn bungalow I did in a trance. She was filthy, and I had to undress and wash her, many times. I don't suppose any man has ever had such a good-looking body under his hand and been so little aware of it. I remember briefly wishing it were Sumitra, that's all. I remember leaving with my suitcase, and I know she was saying something, but I have no idea what. I only hoped I hadn't been rude to her, unintentionally. She seemed a good, brave woman now that our troubles had got us below the squabbling level, and I didn't want to leave any bitterness.

So, back to the money . . . I saw that I was passing the Connaught Circus office of the Bombay-China Bank. I had told Max I was here to rob a bank. Well, why not? I had been thinking like a sahib. All the jobs I wanted, the jobs that no one would give me, were sahib's jobs. Such jobs had been created out of nothing by the British Raj. The Indians and Pakistanis were taking them over, using their own sahibs for the purpose – and we had created *them*, too.

There was no place for the English sahib, then. All right. Go back behind the day of the sahib, and what did you get? Merchant adventurers, soldiers of fortune, wandering mechanics . . . men who provided India with what it needed, or thought it needed, without any missionary or evangelical purpose. Translate that into today's conditions ... There was a shortage of lipstick, whisky, perfume, the luxuries which Indians crave as much as anyone else. Cars, big American cars, high-priced shotguns and rifles, cartridges. Wireless sets, ornate radiograms. There were laws against the importation of all these things, or heavy import duties. There were currency restrictions – but if you knew the right people you could easily get round all that, what with Portuguese territory touching India in Goa, bits of Pakistan to east and west, cordial dislike between all three nations, and not enough troops or police to guard the long borders. That was the sort of thing my ancestors would have been in, up to their necks. I could just see them, in wigs and heavy with sweat, working it all out in a back room off Chowringhee with a couple of tough, smoothly obsequious Bengali moneylenders to provide the initial working capital.

I found myself passing the Bombay-China Bank again. I needed working capital, first to pay off my debts, secondly to start this or any other venture of my own. I did not know any moneylenders and did not want to have them exercise any control over me. Inside the bank the British manager sat in the far corner, at a big desk of his own. Two Indian clerks worked at the counter and three at tables behind. Outside the door the bank guard sat on a stool, a shotgun in hand and a *kukri* hung in a red sash over one shoulder. He was a Gurkha. Obviously a pensioner, probably a *naik*, I thought from his appearance and manner. Not one of ours though, at least not during my service.

I walked on. It was a large step, to think of robbing a bank, though I did gamble with 'borrowed' money once, to help Max – Janaki, I should say. But, as I strode on, heedless of the sun burning down on my head and the crowds around me, I felt a distinct lightening. The morass seemed to be less gluey. This was not a sahib's thing to do. I would at least get rid of that damned albatross, which had been hanging round my family's neck for about a hundred and fifty years now.

Ratanbir, I thought. Ratanbir can make part of the reconnaissance. I can make the rest. I might rob the Bombay-China Bank, or I might not, but if I did I was going to do it properly, when it had a lot of money on hand, and get away without a trace, and have some means of converting the money, much of which would be traceable.

I hailed a tonga, and jolting along in the back, my mind working fast and constructively, drove to Old Delhi and my hotel, which was near the main railway station. I found Ratanbir polishing my shoes, though they were as bright as day already. I told him to go to New Delhi and make friends with the guards at the Bombay-China Bank. I gave him twenty rupees, and he saluted and went out. I looked at the closed door behind him, and thought, Max would not approve of this: rob a bank, all right, a chap might have to do that, but involve a soldier! Fine, Max, but you're still a sahib. You can afford to be; I can't.

I went down to the little bar and ordered a whisky and soda, then another.

'Colonel Savage?'

I just managed to repress a groan. I raised my head and turned. It was a slender middle-aged Indian, slightly bent, with thin, greying hair and a long crooked nose. He was wearing well-cut European clothes. He said, 'Forgive the impertinence,' and passed me a card. It read, *Mr Hussein Ali*, and underneath, *Chambali Industries Ltd.* I handed the card back.

He said in a low voice, 'I wonder if we could talk in your room, Colonel?'

The barman was out somewhere and I thought, what the hell. We went up to my room on the second floor.

Mr Hussein walked to the little balcony and peered out right and left. He tapped the wall. I watched, smiling. I love cloak-and-dagger stuff. He saw me, and smiled himself, rather charmingly. 'Silly,' he said, 'but one is a fool to omit small precautions.' He spoke with almost no accent. I had heard of him of course. He was an Ismaili, one of the Aga Khan's sect of Muslims. The family had gone to Zanzibar about fifty years earlier and made a fortune. Just before the war they returned to their homeland, which happened to be the State of Chambal, and now they owned practically every industry in the State – less the compulsory 15 per cent share that belonged to the Nawab.

I indicated a chair, and myself sat on the edge of the bed. He said. 'I have come to offer you a position, Colonel.'

124

I said, 'I'm afraid . . .'

He raised one hand. 'Not an ordinary position, or there would be no need for these precautions. I showed you my business card just now. I am also a member of His Highness's Wizarat.'

A Wizarat is the cabinet of a Muslim maharajah. (Muslim princes, by the way, are never called maharajah – always Nawab, Mir, Amir, or the like.) It was no surprise to learn that the richest man in Chambal, and its chief industrialist, had an official position with the Nawab's government.

He said, 'In business I can offer you a great deal of money, Colonel, because I am sure that with your talents you will earn it. But I am also sure you have been offered that by many others. I am not here to offer you money – but a task, for India.'

'For India?' I said, raising an eyebrow.

Hussein Ali said, 'Yes – for the India that still lives, and strives to find expression under the mean-spirited Congress rule. For the India of splendour, of great men, of heroes, if I do not embarrass your English reserve . . . I understand that the Indian Government expelled you from the Pattan Reserved Forest and ruined your most interesting enterprise, on suspicion that you were acting as a secret agent for us?'

I nodded. It was not quite accurate, but it was near enough.

He said, 'We wish to prove the Indians right, though there will be no secrecy about it. I am authorised to offer you a post as an agent of the Wizarat. Officially we would employ you as a brigadier, and you would have advisory duties with our armed forces – very real and important duties, I should add. Your military salary will be two thousand rupees a month. In your other capacity you will receive ten thousand rupees a month, with a suitable house, servants, et cetera.'

'What makes you think I am worth that much?' I asked. I have a high opinion of myself, but this was flying pretty high.

'First, our own observation,' he said. 'Second, your attitude and background as—'

'A sahib,' I said.

'Precisely. I can see that you now reject the word. Naturally, I have resented the idea, too . . . but you cannot in a moment undo what your predecessors have done. Whether you like it or not, you command respect, for you have conquered and ruled us. You have

a reputation for impartiality, incorruptibility – and decision ...
Third, we have the opinion of Mr Huntington Blauvelt.'

'My God!' I said. Blauvelt, the Wandering Minstrel, was affecting my life more than any one of a dozen people who were earnestly trying to.

Hussein nodded. 'Yes, Mr Blauvelt, who is at this moment visiting the State as a guest of His Highness. Mr Blauvelt has certain – problems, but he is a singularly acute observer, even when apparently in no condition to observe anything.'

'All right,' I said. 'Now tell me, what are you trying to do, in the State? And what is my job to be?'

He started at once to tell me, and I made an approving note. He had had the sense to realise that he must make up his mind about my reliability before approaching me at all. It would be no good hemming and hawing and fencing once he reached me.

'His Highness is determined to maintain Chambal's independence from both India and Pakistan,' he said.

All right, I thought. With luck, he might just manage it. Hyderabad, a slightly larger state, had tried, and Nehru had sent in the Indian Army. Two days – no Hyderabad. But Chambal had the enormous advantage of touching Pakistan as well as India, and so could not be treated quite so cavalierly, besides giving the Nawab the chance to play the two big nations off against each other.

'We are determined,' Hussein continued, 'to maintain the old values of India. Most of our people are Rajputs and Jats, as you know. They reject the sickly Hinduism of Bengal. They reject Congress demagoguery. They are warriors. Three centuries ago they took the oath of allegiance to His Highness's ancestor, and they are determined to uphold it. His Highness, for his part, while remaining a devout Muslim himself, rejects the intolerant spirit of Pakistan. There has never been any penalisation of Hindus in Chambal, and there never will be.'

'There'd better not be,' I said. Rajputs and Jats were not people who took kindly to oppression.

'We reject democracy, bureaucracy, socialism, and communism,' Hussein said. 'Chambal has always been ruled by a sovereign, respectfully advised by the Wizarat. Under that rule there has been peace and plenty, and as much freedom as a

126

reasonable man might ask. If a man wants to have a say in our government, let him rise by his own efforts until he sits in the seats of power – as Faiz Mohammed rose, from a butcher's son, to be Subadar of Lapri – and as a score of others so rose, whom I can name. If a man has not that ability, let him keep his mouth shut, till his soil, and obey the orders of those who have proved themselves his betters... We will advance materially, but through the enterprise of our own leaders, not on the plans of clerks sitting in Delhi – or Karachi.'

And you, doubtless, will make your tenth or twentieth million, pounds sterling, I thought. That did not bother me. I knew a good deal about Chambali Industries Ltd. Yes, they made money – but it all went back into new enterprises, certainly as well chosen as any government could do, and backed by a single man's drive and determination.

'That is what we are going to achieve,' Hussein said. 'We have a hard struggle ahead of us. You will have heard of our preparations to put our case to the United Nations, if need be. Other political and financial arrangements I will not bother you with now, though you will have to learn about them in due course. One political matter, though, will fall in your province – that is, the winning of the uncommitted states of Bandelkhand to our side. Their rulers all have the same point of view as His Highness. They too wish to preserve a way of life more suited to India than this cheap democracy. If they allow India to absorb them, not only will they themselves become landless paupers but their kingdoms will vanish, losing the identity of a thousand years – sometimes much more, as with Konpara – to become so much more raw material for Nehru's socialist experiments. . . . We believe you can exert great influence on the ruler of Kishanpur at least, perhaps also the Rajah of Konpara, through your family connections and your own personality. We want you to persuade them to join Chambal.'

'Why should they?' I asked.

Hussein stretched out his hands, turning them palms upward in a very Indian gesture, which I was pleased and reassured to see. He was, otherwise, so cosmopolitan, so much the international financier, that he could have been a Rothschild or a Morgan or a Baring, discussing some steel merger in Belgium. He said, 'In Chambal we already have twelve rajahs happy to admit the

127

Nawab's suzerainty, and all those twelve and their ancestors have ruled their lands without interference for a long time, subject only to the orders of His Highness on matters of common concern . . . I think it should not be hard to persuade Dip Rao Rawan that it is better to become the thirteenth rajah, than to disappear totally.'

I agreed, while thinking privately that those small states like Kishanpur and Konpara were probably expendable, in the Chambal view. If they could be persuaded to join Chambal, or to try to do so, the Indian Government would certainly not permit them; but it would have to turn its efforts to bringing them back into the fold and would find it hard to deal with Chambal at the same time. Of course, if the mergers *could* be managed, so much the better . . . If I had to deal with Kishanpur, I would meet Sumitra.

Hussein stood up. 'I have nothing more to say, Colonel. I shall leave you to think it over, and would ask for a reply within forty-eight hours. I am at Chambal House, in New Delhi.'

He looked straight at me, and the small, piercing dark eyes almost glittered. 'I think you are a man who has an ideal for this country, as I have. I am offering you a post as important for the future as any you have ever had in the past. Work of value to the spirit. Something you can fight for. And afterwards, when we have achieved our independence, there will be a secure place for you, and even higher rewards – in business or government, as you wish. We shall need you.'

He went out. I had controlled my feelings during his stay, but now I let them go. The first thing I noticed was that the morass had vanished. My legs were free. Then my eyes were focused. I had something to do, somewhere to go. Then, my heart was warm – someone needed me. Then, I felt a thrill of satisfied revenge. The bloody Indians had harried me from pillar to post, thinking I was helpless and harmless. They would regret it.

I stood up, and exhilaration flowed in, replacing all other emotions. I thought of what was to be achieved. Was this not precisely the sum of my thoughts that dreadful day at the Pattan Rest House when I asked myself what we had done, to destroy the old India which my ancestors had found, and hand it over to the worst sort of mediocrity? I was being given a chance to start again, to create and preserve instead of destroy.

After a few minutes I came back to the actual question, almost

128

as an afterthought. There was no doubt in my mind at all. I would
take the task and do all that I could to make Chambal free,
independent, and, above all, Indian. And I would meet Sumitra.

I was fast asleep when Ratanbir returned at midnight, drunk.
He stood wavering and teetering and saluting, telling me that he
had got to know the bank guards. The man on duty during the
evening was a Burathoki, the same subtribe as himself; they were
even distantly related; and he had been a *naik* in the 8th Gurkhas.
'He's an honest man,' he said, belching, 'but he drinks . . . weak
head. It won't be difficult.'

I told him to go to bed. Perhaps I should have told him I'd never
meant to rob the bank, that such an idea was degrading for both of
us – but I was too tired and too involved in other thoughts, and I
didn't.

The next day at one I went to Chambal House. After a short
wait I was ushered up a flight of carpeted stairs, along a tiled
passage, and into Hussein Ali's expensively simple suite. I told
him I would accept his offer. He said, 'Good,' and, opening a
drawer, handed me a long envelope, marked 'Brigadier Savage,
expenses (not accountable).' He said, 'Please report to me in
Chambalpur within the week.'

I said, 'O.K.,' and that was that. One thousand rupees.

I took a tonga to the Imperial and sat down to lunch. Before I
was through the first course the *khidmatgar* handed me a note. I
looked up quickly. 'Who gave you this?'

'A man,' he said, 'a *desi admi* – a native. He went away.'

I opened the envelope, which was properly addressed to me,
including my decorations. The note inside read, 'Be so good as to
call on me in my office, Secretariat Buildings, any time after three
o'clock this afternoon. L. P. Roy.'

I finished my lunch, chewing carefully and trying to avoid excessive thought. I might be able to work out what L. P. Roy wanted
of me, then again I might not. I might reach a conclusion, but
find later that it was quite wrong. It is better to have a blank mind
than a mind full of misconceptions.

After lunch I read the *Statesman* and then set out for the
Secretariat. A *chuprassy* told me that Roy Sahib's office was close
to Sardar Patel's. A few minutes later I was announced.

Roy's office was not large and what with piles of books and

papers, another visitor sitting in a cane chair across the table from him, and a secretary bending over Roy's shoulder, it seemed crowded. Roy said politely, 'Be so good as to wait one moment, please, Colonel.' I sat down on another chair, in the only corner free from furniture, reflecting how universally and truly Eastern is the custom of doing business in public.

They talked in the wonderful and fantastic mixture of Hindi, Urdu, and English which had already become the lingua franca of bureaucratic India. The subject was some mines that had been willed by one petty (and deposed) rajah to another. I listened with joy to such remarks as '*Lekin yeh* joint royalties *aur* overriding commission *ke* arrangement *hai*' and '*Agar Ram Singh apne* collateral descendants *ke lie* life interest *dena chahta*' and 'Legal aspect *bilkul* clear *hai, magar* . . .'

Roy finished his business with dispatch, and when he gave the decision there was no argument. A moment later we were alone, and Roy got up and closed the door. He was wearing the same clothes he had worn in the Red Fort, the clothes he wore, as far as I knew, all day and every day – a spotlessly white dhoti and shirt, bare feet tucked into sandals. His square face somehow managed, without the Gandhi cap, to look lean and ascetic, and his mop of grey hair stood out like a halo from his head.

He said, 'I have a short temper, which I cannot control. It is a grievous fault. I apologise for my words when we last met, near the Moti Masjid.'

'I was equally at fault,' I said, 'my mind was elsewhere.'

He nodded. 'Good . . . I have, naturally, held a prejudice against you because you killed my brother. But I am told by many whose judgment I trust that you are, in your way, a friend of India.'

I said, 'Of India? Yes, I think so.'

He said, 'You must not take the appointment you have been offered in Chambal, whatever it is.'

'Why?'

'It would be wrong. How could you then be a friend of India?'

'Perhaps not a friend of your government, or of Mr Patel's plans.'

'An enemy of ours is an enemy of India,' Roy said.

I began to feel that peculiar throbbing behind the temples, with a tightening of the chest, which my ancestors must have experienced when they first came to grips with the Brahmin mentality: the calm arrogance; the cold contempt for anyone else's opinions; the belief that the Brahmin is in direct communion with God, is in fact a part of God, and can do no wrong. It is fortunate that in those early meetings the Brahmins came across perhaps the only other people in the world with the same colossal self-conceit and set in much the same terms. Of course Roy was not technically a Brahmin – but that did not matter. The attitude had been inherited by the new rulers of India.

I controlled myself, and said, 'That is a matter of opinion.'

'Not a bit of it,' he said. 'There can be no matter of opinion about it. The so-called princely states are a part of India – like Goa and the Portuguese colonies – and we are going to have them.'

'Regardless of what the people concerned say or feel?'

'They are ignorant,' he said. 'Some have been oppressed, some misled, all exploited . . . I believe Dip Rao, Rajah of Kishanpur, is a friend of yours?'

I nodded.

'I imagine that your new employers, if you are misguided enough to go to them, will use you to try to influence the Rajah's future course of action. I should advise you, if you really are a friend of his, that we will treat any collusion between him and Chambal as treason on his part and will punish him accordingly.'

'Treason!' I burst out. 'How can a sovereign ruler commit treason? Until 1947 Dip and all the other rajahs acknowledged England as the Paramount Power and surrendered to it all rights in foreign affairs and defence. But we – England – abrogated paramountcy when we left, and told the states they were free to work out their own relationships with the new Government of India – as sovereign entities.'

'We shall regard it as treason if any ruler acts against the best interests of his people – and that means any action which does not guide the people back to the arms of free, independent Mother India.'

'Oh yeah?' I snapped. 'You think that Hari Singh did the right thing then, in handing over to India a people 90 per cent Muslim, who would certainly have wanted to join Pakistan – and still would – if you allowed a free vote?'

'Certainly. Besides, he was a sovereign ruler and had the

131

constitutional right to do as he wished. We merely accepted his decision.'

'But the Maharajah of Junagadh wasn't a sovereign ruler when he tried to join Pakistan and you sent the army in? And the Nizam of Hyderabad wasn't when he wanted to be independent?'

'They were wrong, and wicked,' Roy said. 'They were enemies of India.'

'How's your non-violence going these days?' I asked.

'We shall never resort to violence to resolve our problems,' he said. 'It is the sacred teaching of the Mahatma, often repeated by Panditji.'

'Kashmir and Hyderabad were fought with feather dusters, then?'

'They were in the wrong. They were the aggressors.'

'You mean, your bottomless patience was exhausted?'

'Yes – precisely.'

'I wonder where I've heard that phrase before? . . . You don't agree, perhaps, that aggression might be a matter of opinion, subject even to evidence, factual evidence?'

He waved his hand. 'That's a waste of time. We are a peaceful state, therefore how *can* we commit aggression?'

I longed to possess, for just half an hour, the power my ancestors had used to solve just such impasses as this . . . There was the Brahmin found with the dead body in his courtyard and a knife in his hand. *Yes, I killed him.* That's murder, then. *Oh, no, because, you see, I am a Brahmin; murder is wrong, but Brahmins can do no wrong, therefore I cannot commit murder, and if I cannot, obviously I have not.* Then how did this man here die? *It was the course of events.* I see; well, I'll tell you, the course of events now is that you're going to die, too . . . And in marches a squad of soldiers, the gallows are set up, and amid anguished wails and howls and the thunderstruck disbelief of the populace, the Brahmin is hanged.

But I did not possess the power. The attitude with which I was now faced, the strong belief in its own total virtue, was the attitude of the new India, and it – not I – had that power.

Roy said, 'You interest me. Tell me, why do you wish to serve the Nawab of Chambal, who, as you must know, is a bigoted and suspicious despot?'

132

Just so must old William, my great-great-grandfather, have sent for the other Brahmins, after he'd shown he could hang one of them just as easily as the next man, and said, 'Tell me now, what makes you tick?' And just so, after days and years and centuries, would there stand an opaque wall between true understandings, however clear the paintings each of us put on the surface of the wall, in an attempt to communicate.

I said, 'These states are in many ways anachronisms. I do not think that any one man ought to have the powers and privileges of the rajahs, unless they have been freely voted to him. It is wrong that the people should have no say in their own government—'

'You were not saying that very loudly a few years ago, here,' Roy interrupted.

'Who's sitting behind that desk – you or I? . . . It is also wrong that in a huge country like this, with so many different ways of thought, so many religions, so many backgrounds, so many manners of living, that one party, one group, one viewpoint, should impose itself on the rest by force. The Nawab of Chambal, for all his faults, wants to make a country which is anti-socialist, more individual, more closely linked with the past, with tradition, than you believe in. I believe he has the right to do so, and I'm going to help all I can . . . because I believe in that sort of India, too.'

Roy's face grew suddenly red with anger. 'You wish to preserve your economic stranglehold!' he shouted. 'Economic imperialism! You wish to preserve an India subject to your exploitation. You will sell Chambal anything – guns, aeroplanes, whisky, big American cars, stupid luxuries . . .'

'And are those, any of them, un-Indian?' I asked.

'Yes,' he shouted. 'They are wrong, wicked. Gross materialism . . . exploitation of baser nature . . .'

I let him rave on. Like several other prominent Indian politicians, he was a fanatic. When any of them climbed on to his pet hobby horse, whatever it happened to be – whisky, spinning wheels, the wonder of the Hindi language, economic exploitation – it was impossible to talk to them – as impossible as to talk to the sort of Englishman who claimed that the course of history showed God's guiding hand over England's destiny; or, more accurately,

133

the sort of German who yelled that all his country's troubles were due to the Treaty of Versailles.

When he ran out of breath I stood up and said, 'If that will be all, sahib, perhaps you will permit me to take my leave.'

'Sit down, sit down,' he said. He did not make any apology for his outburst. How could he? He was in the right. He sat very still at his desk, looking at me out of his hot, black eyes. He had a great capacity for stillness. He began to speak, slowly. 'I am sorry for you, Savage . . . You are ready to fight for your ideals. But it is not human beings that you will be fighting against. It is a great river called History. This river sweeps away all who struggle against it. Nor can anyone stand aside, in neutrality, and hope to let it pass undisturbed, because it undermines the foundations and causes the silent collapse of the place on which he stands. By its existence it changes the climate of the time, causing orchards to grow where there was desert, putting a blight on groves where there used to be palaces.'

'True,' I said softly, for I felt close to Roy at that moment, 'but it is not necessary for those riding the crest of the river, downstream, to don garments of unctuous virtue, still less necessary for them to crow over the flood's senseless destruction of much that is beautiful and valuable.'

'It is!' Roy said. 'Cast your mind back a couple of centuries. Did your ancestors, when they overthrew the old India, wail and beat their breasts? Did they not proclaim, rather, the merit and rightness, even invoking God's will, of what they were doing?'

I nodded. It was a good point. I said, 'You are probably right . . . But you agree, then, that at that time you were the ones trying to fight against the river?'

'Yes.'

'And did that knowledge stop you from fighting?'

'No.'

'So?'

'Ah. Perhaps those people did not recognise the course of history. They were, after all, ignorant of the world outside India. You are in a different position . . . Do you know how *I* would look for the course of history, these days? I would think of you, someone like you. You have been floating down on the current, now I notice that you are swimming upstream. Your ideals have not

134

changed, nor has the course of events changed, yet their relation to each other has changed. This is very strange, and only your Einstein or our mystical sages can explain it. Yet one thing is sure, and I feel it in my bones – that you are doomed, like the Flying Dutchman, to swim and sail against overpowering headwinds and currents. So – I can be sure my course is correct if I merely go in the opposite direction from you, eh?'

I said, 'I see. You remind me of a story – by Somerset Maugham, I think – about a naval officer who gets into desperate financial trouble and goes to Monte Carlo, to an old man whose life he had once saved. This old man was always amazingly successful at the gaming tables and the officer begged him to tell him his system. The old man offered to give him whatever he needed, but the officer's pride wouldn't accept that, he only asked for the system so that he would win for himself. The old man said the system would do *him* no good, but the officer kept pressing and pleading, until finally the old man said. "My system is simple. I bet against those who *must* win. They never do." '

Roy stood up. 'I am the old man, Savage. I am offering you the equivalent of the money. Do not let your pride refuse it.'

I was standing, too. 'I'm sorry. I don't agree that history has a course of its own. I think it is influenced by men who are not afraid of it. I don't believe in systems, either. Sometimes you win, sometimes you lose – but you've got to play.'

Roy's voice became hard. 'Very well. Do not expect any preferential treatment when the time comes to settle the Chambal affair. You will pay the full price for whatever you have staked.'

I said, 'That will be the lot, sahib. The whole lot.'

Chapter 9

Three months to the day after I reached Chambalpur I was sitting in my office one morning, wondering what to do next. Wondering is too serene a word, since it gives a picture of a man sitting back in calm debate with himself. It was never like that in Chambal. I had no one job but was involved in everything. I had been imported to bring to Chambal the sahib's direct approach, executive efficiency, the sense of what is to be done and then the going out and doing it. But the affairs of Chambal were run on the system of the *Arabian Nights*, with one grand wazir receiving one set of orders, and another another, and both knowing that they were *really* supposed to do something else entirely. Above all, the ruling principle of government in Chambal was not justice, or right, or even autocracy – it was suspicion. Everyone was suspicious of everyone else, and, usually, with good reason.

There was excessive secrecy. The atmosphere was heavy with mistrust and intrigue. Whispered rumours flew around: 'X is in secret touch with India.' 'Y is ready to turn his private troops against the Nawab.' 'Z is sending money out to Swiss banks under an assumed name.' Everyone was an amateur spy – except when they were professional. I was trusted, but not therefore liked or followed. There were intrigues against me by officers who suspected that I was responsible for having them removed from important posts. There were financiers who wanted to nullify my influence in the awarding of military contracts, so that they could deal more amicably with someone else. I was permanently in a bad temper, curt and ruder than I needed to be, because I felt that the air was tainted by noxious gases.

So when I said that I sat wondering, what I mean is that I sat and glared at the wall map, while angry thoughts crowded for preference in my mind. If A didn't report soon that he had paid

136

the guerrillas now being trained in the north, I would go and shoot him. But it was more urgent to see that the mechanical engineers were actually installing the new machine tools in the tank repair shops and not selling them to factories in the city. But it was more urgent still to see that B was fired at once from command of his brigade as he was a hopeless alcoholic; but to achieve that I would have to put him into a position where he would insult either the corps commander or the commander-in-chief – or, of course, the Nawab. They already knew he was inefficient, but that was not enough, not in Chambal. It had to be an insult, and B was too easygoing to become rude, even when boiled as an owl.

I had expected to be employed in negotiations with Kishanpur, but so far that had not been mentioned and after the first week or two I understood why. They did not trust me yet. My office was in Army Headquarters and a wooden plate on the door announced in gold-leaf letters, in English and Urdu, that I was Brigadier R. Savage, Assistant Military Secretary to His Highness the Nawab. I had a *babu* clerk, a telephone, a typewriter, and a water *chatty* in the corner. A few doors down the passage was the office of the commander-in-chief, General Prince Afif Khan Bokhari, a cousin of the Nawab. He was a dear old boy, seventy-eight years old.

Just as I had decided to take a trip to Digra and have a look at the port defences, an agitated *chuprassy* in full dress gold and green dashed in. 'Sahib,' he said breathlessly, 'His Highness is waiting.'

'Where?'

'Outside, in the car.'

I hurried down the stairs, in and out of courtyards full of dozing servants and sweeper women. I had a telephone, and His Highness could have indicated his intentions well in advance; but that wasn't the way things were done in Chambal.

Sir Mohammed Akbar Bokhari, G.C.B., G.C.S.I., G.C.I.E., etc., Nawab of Chambal, was sitting bolt upright in the back seat of one of the twelve State Rolls-Royces, a vast Phantom III drophead coupé with gold fittings, the top down, and a liveried chauffeur at the wheel. I got in. His Highness was sixty-five, clean shaven, gaunt, pale brown. Still, after four hundred years you could detect a faint trace of the Mongolian fold in the corners of his eyes. His family had come from Bokhara in Central Asia with Baber, the first Mogul emperor, hence the family name, Bokhari.

He wore pince-nez and was a simple man, in that he knew what he wanted: he wanted to keep all real power in his own hands. He was wearing, as usual, tight trousers, slippers with turned-up toes, a plain black achkhan reaching down to his knees and buttoned up to a high collar, with two jewelled stars on the left breast, the Order of the Bath and the Order of Chambal.

We drove off without a word. Chambalpur was a complete epitome of India, in romance, in fable, and in actuality. The old city stood around a mile-square lake. The Nawab's rose-red palace soared sheer from the water on one side, hanging like a vivid dream against the blue sky and the sharply etched backdrop of sand-coloured hills. Other palaces and mansions surrounded the lake – among them Army Headquarters, which was mid-Victorian icing cake. On the other side of the lake an inordinately ugly factory belched foul-smelling smoke from three tall tin chimneys. In the city there were narrow alleys where time seemed to have stood still for ten centuries, and others, nearby, where the squalor was not patriarchal but modern. And there were real slums, and tin cans piled in the offal dumps, and chemicals running down the open sewers from hidden shops and factories.

We passed under one of the immense city gates, with hardly room to squeeze through; and on among the jumble of shacks that had long since spread outside the walls. Near the point where the shacks finally died away and the empty semi-desert spread out in front of us, the Nawab spoke a single word to the driver. The Rolls stopped. The Nawab pointed. 'What is your opinion of that?'

About fifty yards in front of us a deep ditch crossed the road. Concrete anti-tank pillars made a line a hundred yards broad in front of the ditch. An immense amount of work had gone into it.

I said, 'The concrete is up to specification, I know. I have checked it myself.'

He said, 'So have I.'

I had a brief vision of the second richest man in India, perhaps in the world, banging away with a hammer in the dead of night, taking the chip back, bending over a test tube . . .

The anti-tank defences, taken by themselves, were fine, but they were in the wrong place by about eighty miles. They should have been put in the Lapri Gorge or just where it debouched on to the plain; and Lapri was eighty-five miles east.

On the other hand, I had to work with General Gokal Singh, who had chosen the site.

I said, 'The defences look very good, Your Highness. But I know that General Gokal Singh is planning to supplement them by another system nearer the border – at Lapri or Sakti.'

The Nawab grunted. 'Drive on.'

We drove to the main airfield. It was one of the only three all-weather fields in Chambal capable of taking the heaviest planes – and it lay forward of the anti-tank defences. Someone must have seen the Nawab coming, for we were greeted by an Air Force guard, and by the air marshal himself. I followed the Nawab, and said little. This felt much better. There were about fifty P-47 Thunderbolts dispersed around the field, and the Air Marshal – a Chambali prince and ex-playboy – knew his stuff and seemed to have an excellent relationship with the motley crowd of Australians, Austrians, Americans, and Italians who were flying the planes. Also, he had accumulated large stocks of high-octane petrol, and spare parts for the planes. India had already cut off all supply through her ports.

My heart missed a beat when the Nawab said, 'You have been spending a great deal of money on petrol, Air Marshal. Are you sure you need that much?'

The air marshal made the point I had just been thinking about – building up a reserve. The Nawab said, 'You do not need a large reserve. It is just a waste of money.'

I kept my face wooden, though the air marshal caught my eye as he began to defend his expenses. The Nawab grunted and moved on. I wanted to talk to the air marshal about the progress he had made in training supply-dropping teams, but I had to trail along behind the Nawab and only had time to make an appointment with the air marshal. Supply dropping was a vital part of my plans for guerrilla war against the flanks of any Indian advance.

We drove on, round the outside of the city, towards the main barracks. Here, 'by chance', we met Lieutenant-General Gokal Singh, the deputy commander-in-chief, and also commander of the striking force. He turned his car and followed. He wasn't going to let the Nawab wander about unobserved, especially in company with me. Gokal was a Rajput, thirty-three years of age, a very bright and clever young man, sharp as a knife. With experience

139

he might have been a great soldier. As it was, he thought he was much better than the facts indicated.

At the barracks Gokal shot out of his car and reached ours in time to open the Nawab's door with one hand and salute with the other. The Nawab stared at the dozen Sherman tanks rumbling back and forth across the sandy parade ground. After five minutes he said, 'Why is it flying a yellow flag?'

Gokal said, 'That is the troop leader's pennant, Your Highness. Each troop has a different colour, and—'

'They should all be green,' the Nawab said, and climbed back into the Rolls. I saluted Gokal punctiliously, and followed. The old bigot wanted all his tanks flying the Muslim green. The majority of his soldiers were Hindus. I wasn't thinking about that, but about the waste of track mileage. Tanks can go only so far before their tracks and engines need major overhaul or replacement. The tank commanders were wasting mileage because the exercise they were carrying out here should have been done in a classroom. I pulled out my notebook and made a note. Somehow I'd got to persuade Gokal that his tactical brilliance would do him no good if his tanks wouldn't run.

The Nawab said, 'Is he loyal?'

'General Gokal Singh, sir?' I said, startled.

The Nawab said, 'He is a Rajput. No family. I made him what he is, raised him up from nothing, so that I would have a man who owed everything to me. He ought to be loyal. But I can trust no one.'

I didn't answer, because doubts about Gokal had entered my own mind. I had rejected them, feeling that I must not allow myself to be tainted by the universal suspiciousness. If we could not trust our chief battlefield commander, then we did not deserve to stand.

The Nawab dropped me off at Army Headquarters and drove on. I looked at my watch. Another morning wasted. Now I couldn't set out for Digra until the next day.

But I could not afford to waste the day. I went up into Headquarters and looked for the chief of intelligence. I wanted to find out how the corps of observers and spies I had organised along the borders was working. The chief of intelligence had gone to lunch. Tried to find the commander-in-chief, to discuss a training

140

programme for senior officers. He had not left his mansion today, and could not be disturbed. Looked for the commander of the city garrison, to check progress on plans for the protection of radio and power stations against sabotage. He had gone north to his son's wedding. Went disgustedly to my own office, stared at the wall, and wondered how I could make Lieutenant-General Gokal Singh understand that he was not Rommel. Worried about the guerrilla plans for Lapri and Bhilghat ... Sent for the armoured brigade tank history sheets and studied them; situation bad, as I thought; engine replacements due for about 20 per cent already, and the political affairs with India like a keg of dynamite. Wrote all afternoon, went to my house weary and ill at ease.

And so on ... I only give a typical day during the period when my duties were solely military. Then, about another two months later, when I had been in Chambal five months, Hussein Ali sent for me and told me the time had come to use me in the political manoeuvrings designed to bring Kishanpur and smaller uncommitted states into some sort of alliance with Chambal.

My waning enthusiasm rekindled. I needed Dip and his sensible, modern outlook here. Whatever the terms Chambal offered to him, they would have to include a measure of power in the affairs of the new country, and Dip had good ideas.

I do not want to give the impression that life in Chambal was all bad. I was tired, and if there had been nothing but the medieval intrigues of the court and government, I would have given up within a month and crept back to England with my tail between my legs – or perhaps even gone back to Roy. But the thing that I believed in did exist, and you only had to leave the capital to feel it, as real and as wonderful as a dove in the hand. The peasants greeted you outside their hovels, standing upright against a poverty that would have caused many to bow and wail. There were country gentlemen living on their estates, where every man for five miles around behaved and was treated like a member of the aristocrat's family; and on the squire's whitewashed wall hung a sword that had been carried at First Panipat against Baber the Mogul in 1526, and at Laswari against Lord Lake, and finally been broken on a Sikh skull at Chilianwala. There were old men with long white beards, who sat under the village tree and talked not of economic exploitation or democracy or colonialism but of honour and right

141

and obligation. There were women with bright shards of mirror glass let into their swinging red skirts, who primly hung the sari over their heads when I passed; but if I went to the well and stood nearby, and talked to Ratanbir about the kind of woman we would like to marry, looking at them as we talked, then they would begin to laugh and giggle and, not looking at us, would throw out tangential comments of wonderful earthiness.

Every time I escaped from Chambalpur my conviction that all this was worth preserving – not the poverty but the simple dignity – became recharged. At the same time I became more sure that Chambal's hope lay in diplomacy rather than fighting, so I was delighted when Hussein gave me the orders that would, for a time at least, take me away from the charming old historical monument called the commander-in-chief, the Renaissance *condottieri* disguised as twentieth-century generals, and all the other animated museum pieces of the Chambal military establishment.

Dip had long since, in August, invited me to Kishanpur for the Dussehra celebrations, so there was no need to invent a reason for my visit. Then, a few days before I was due to go he wired that the Indian Government had summoned him to Delhi and he had thought it expedient to obey. I arranged to pick him up at Bhowani Junction on his way back, and so, in a beautiful dawn early in October, I set out in the Bentley, Ratanbir beside me and the suitcases and bedding rolls thrown into the back seat.

Chapter 10

I was in excellent humour by the time Dip's train whistled for the station. First, I had escaped from Chambalpur. Second, I would see Sumitra again, and as a new man. I had a feeling that she had slept with me, and later visited me, out of compassion, which galled my pride. Now we could start afresh. Third, I had had time to reflect that Dip, after his visit to Delhi, would probably be in a receptive mood for my proposals. Roy might have frightened him with his threats: the method of getting the states into the Indian Union was quite simple – the iron hand in the iron glove – but it was more likely that Dip would be annoyed at the bullying. Fourth, while buying some matches in the Bhowani bazaar I had run into Tilakbahadur, the *subadar* major of the 1/13th Gurkhas, my own old battalion. He insisted that I bring Dip to the head cutting, always a very moving ceremony to me. Fifth, and last, the news that I was in Bhowani had then filtered rapidly from Tilakbahadur up to Max, who had invited us to have tea at Flagstaff House before setting out for Kishanpur.

So I was feeling happy and almost young again as I scanned the windows of the incoming train, looking for Dip. Blue smoke and the smell of hot steel from the brakes filtered up from the grinding wheels. They stopped, and Dip opened a door, opposite where I waited.

He looked cross, and I understood why when another man stepped down after him, and Dip curtly introduced him: 'Mr Mehta, of the C.I.D. Mr Mehta, this is one of my oldest friends – Colonel Rodney Savage.' The C.I.D. man's jaw dropped, and he licked his lips. It was obvious that he had been lecturing Dip all the way down from Delhi; equally obvious that he had specifically warned Dip to be on his guard against the dangerous Chambal agent, Savage.

143

He had a large padlocked brief-case in one hand. I leaped forward obligingly. 'Can I help, Mr Mehta? Allow me to carry that brief-case for you.'

Mehta clutched the brief-case tightly to his breast, and snapped, 'No!... Thank you.'

'Just as you wish,' I said affably. 'Come on, Dip. I've got the car outside and we're going straight to the lines. Good-bye, Mr Mehta.'

We left the station, shuffling slowly out among the mob of travellers, Dip's servant and two coolies following behind with his suitcases. Dip muttered, 'Bloody man. What right does he have to tell me what *my* duty is?... The lines, did you say? What lines?'

I told him about the head cutting, and he said, 'Really, I ought to get home, Rodney,' but I saw that he did not mean it, and, being also certain that the change of atmosphere would do him good, I had no difficulty in persuading him.

We sent the servant straight to Max's with Dip's kit and, ourselves, headed for cantonments. Ten minutes later we passed a Gurkha sentry at the roadside, and turned up a gravelled road leading towards a row of long barrack buildings. As the car stopped, a dozen officers in jungle green came forward, followed by Gurkhas loaded with garlands. Dip joined his palms and bent his head. 'Marigolds,' he muttered. 'Marigolds and zinnias. Don't you wish people would sometimes use flowers with a less cloying-sweet smell?'

I introduced him round. 'His Highness of Kishanpur, Colonel Mahadev, in command. Major Harbans Singh, Captain Lal... I don't know you. What's your name?' I stopped in front of a burly young man with second lieutenant's badges and a fierce moustache. 'Govind Singh Badhwar, sir. I have your old company, A.'

'Any relation to Hari, of Hodson's Horse?'

'He is my uncle, sir.'

'Good... He's a great man, and a good man. Don't let him sell you any ponies, though. He may be your uncle, but he's a damned horsecoper at heart. Have you still got that *gad* head, the one Rifleman Khagu shot in the middle of a battle in '37?'

'Yes, sir. We always keep it in the champion platoon barrack room now. One of the eyes is missing.'

144

I smiled and turned to the colonel. 'Is General Max coming, Jai?'

'No, sir. He's with the 1/4th this afternoon.'

'Oh, are they in the division too? Well, Dip, the colonel now proposes to hand us over to the *subadar* major . . . Tilakbahadur Gurung, *Sardar Bahadur*, O.B.I., I.O.M., M.C.'

Tilakbahadur was about forty-five, grizzled and powerful. His grip crushed Dip's fingers. I spoke aside to Tilakbahadur in Gurkhali, and Dip said, 'What have you been telling him? To spike my drinks?'

'Just the opposite. I was reminding him that we had a date with the general after this, and then we have to drive forty-seven miles – so would he please see that the drinks are kept at a reasonable size.'

Dip grinned, the *subadar* major saluted. We all drifted to the edge of the parade ground, and sat down at tables set out there under awnings. Huge glasses full of orange-tinted sweet rum appeared at our elbows. The *subadar* major sat on Dip's right, and an alert young *subadar* on my left.

I sighed and settled back. So did Dip. This was the Indian Army. This was a Gurkha battalion celebrating the great Hindu festival of Dussehra. Tomorrow and the next day, in Kishanpur, Dip would preside over more formal celebrations of this same festival. It would be quite different, but it would have something of the same atmosphere as here – a very different atmosphere from the miasma prevailing in New Delhi.

All the battalion's arms were massed in hollow square to our right. Flowers stuck out of the rifle muzzles and garlands hung from the machine-gun barrels. This was the festival of the god of war, and good luck with the sacrifices would mean good luck in all the battalion's endeavours during the coming year. Though there was no shrine or image on the parade ground, the spectre of Kali the Destroyer, the necklace of skulls round her neck and her protruding tongue red with blood, towered over our imaginations. If we did not pay her homage correctly, it was we whom she would destroy.

Tension mounted as a group of soldiers sang Gurkhali hymns. Others dragged a big male buffalo on to the parade ground and tied its head to a post set in the earth. A squad stood ready to fire a

145

salute, rifles raised. A single man stepped forward, in white shorts and undershirt. He raised the heavy sacrificial *kukri*. The blade flashed in the sun and the buffalo's head flew off into the dust. Quickly the Brahmin bent and placed a live coal on the dead forehead. A smell of burning hair, and blood, drifted into our nostrils. Dip looked shocked. I shouted, 'Well done!' Everyone cheered and clapped and stomped. The squad fired three volleys.

The soldier who had done the sacrifice came forward and bowed his head. Colonel Mahadev stood ready, a white cloth in his hand. I whispered to Dip that the colonel would wind the cloth round the man's head, like a puggaree, as a reward and a mark.

But Mahadev turned to me, and said, 'This was your battalion, sir. You made it what it is. We would be honoured if you would tie the puggaree.'

For a moment I thought I would cry. My eyes hurt, but I managed to look up and take the cloth. 'For the last time, then,' I said. '*Ai-ja, choro.*' The man stepped forward, straightened in salute, then bowed his powerful shoulders. I tied the cloth round his head. As I wound the cloth I said aloud, 'You have done your duty cleanly and well. Do it so always.'

More men dragged on more buffaloes. There was more singing, and more blood; more horned heads joined the row in the dust. Small boys strutted out on to the ground, and with their fathers' heavy swords cut cucumbers in two. The rum was strong, Dip had settled into drowsy relaxation. 'A barbaric spectacle,' he said, 'but in keeping with certain aspects of the religion. Very Indian, somehow. You won't see any sacrifices in Kishanpur, only processions, with the State elephants parading the streets and me in the Rawan jewels and the big hat – and my soldiers – all fifty of them – in yellow coats and pikes. A waste of money, but great fun, and a great annual event. I wonder how much longer it will go on . . .'

Soon it was time to leave. All the officers and Gurkha officers saw us off, and we were hung with more garlands until I wondered how Dip was able to see over the top of them, and I could hardly drive. Just before we started Ratanbir ran up and bundled himself into the back seat. I told him it looked as though the *havildars* had been generous with their rum. He grinned amiably but said nothing. We drove away through the dusk, among cheering

146

soldiers, and I had a big lump in my throat and a pain in my chest.

At Flagstaff House the sentry at the gate saluted, examined us, and let us pass. A large table, spread with a white cloth, was set up on the far side of the lawn. Pressure lamps hung from trees nearby and turned the grass into a brilliant, translucent green carpet. Janaki Dadhwal came out on to the veranda, petite and beautiful in a white sari faintly patterned with green. I went slowly up the steps, took her hand and kissed it. Max came out, rubbing his cheek with his hand. 'Phew!' he said. 'Those damned bun-faces of yours are going to wear me out, Rodney. And there's a nautch later tonight. Two more parties, a parade, and another nautch tomorrow . . . Whisky, Dip?'

Dip held up his hand. 'Orange juice, please,' he said, 'and blotting paper.' He helped himself to a curried titbit.

Max said, 'Rodney, have you got any time to spare for a look at the Caves of Konpara? Janaki and I thought of going over next weekend – to recover from Dussehra. Or have you seen them?'

I said, 'They're worth seeing a hundred times, but sorry, I'm booked up.'

Conversation flowed gently round the table. I told them about a ruined Rajput fort I'd found in the southern part of Chambal, and the wonders which I thought a proper excavation would reveal. Janaki brought out some paintings she'd bought, done by a Punjabi artist just coming to prominence.

Someone mentioned Gonds, and Dip said he had a problem with a small tribe of them living in the southern part of his State. They would have to be moved because a new dam and reservoir would flood their land. He didn't know what to do about them.

I said, 'Talk to the D.C. of Bijoli – Ranjit Singh. Sumitra knows him, so does Janaki here. Get him to fetch the Gond chief up from Bhilghat, old Gulu, and send him down to your Gonds. Gulu has enormous influence, and he's learned to adjust his thinking to the new times better than most. But, whatever he says to do, do it, or you'll be in worse trouble than ever – and so will the D.C. Gulu doesn't like to have his advice ignored.'

Janaki said, 'Is there anything you don't know about this country, Rodney? It seems such a . . .'

147

She did not finish, but sat, looking helplessly at me. Such a waste – I finished the sentence for her in my own mind. I felt like that, too. India's time for freedom had come, and I didn't want it otherwise, but why did I have to be thrown on the rubbish heap? Was it inherent in the situation, or only in my character?

A visitor wearing sandals, dhoti, and Gandhi cap came across the lawn, his hands joined in a perfunctory *namasti*, the sentry trailing anxiously behind him. It was L. P. Roy. Max stood up, a look of alarm on his face.

'Oh, please sit down,' Roy said. 'General, I am sorry to upset you at such a time, but there is an important matter . . .'

He glanced round the group at the table. Janaki, as the hostess, had risen and was making *namasti*. Dip and I made the same gesture where we sat.

Roy stared at me. 'You!' he said. 'Colonel Rodney Savage!'

I said, 'No, sahib. Brigadier Rodney Savage, O.B.E., M.C.'

For a moment I thought Roy was going to lose his volatile temper, but he controlled himself and turned instead to Max. 'I did not expect to see this enemy of India at *your* house, General.'

Max said heavily, 'He is an old friend, and a guest.'

'Where did those come from?' Roy indicated the garlands lying piled on the grass beside my chair.

I began to say, 'That is none of your business,' but Max interrupted: 'They were given to him by the officers and men of his old regiment, the 13th Gurkha Rifles.'

'Ah,' Roy said. 'He has been visiting military installations? A Chambal officer, visiting Indian military installations. At your invitation?'

Max lowered his heavy head. He looked like a bull being goaded by a bull terrier. He said, 'Not at my invitation. At the invitation of the colonel commanding the battalion, but with my full permission and approval . . . It's an act of common courtesy.'

'You put courtesy before proper military caution?' Roy snapped.

Max said, 'I put it before anything, sahib . . . Not courtesy, I mean – doing what an Indian gentleman ought to do, or any other kind of gentleman . . . what he *has* to do.'

'I see,' Roy said, pressing the tips of his fingers together and raising himself lightly up and down on the balls of his feet. 'I see.'

148

Max was beginning to lose his heavy Jat temper. He growled, 'Colonel Savage and others like him taught our army to do its duty, at all times. It was not he who tried to subvert the loyalty of Indian troops for political purposes.'

'For political purposes, General? Can you refer to our efforts to attain the independence of our nation?'

Max did not answer, and I thought sadly, Roy's too clever, too intense for him. Still, they were such *bloody* fools. Casting aspersions on Max's loyalty to India was like accusing Nehru of selling out to the British . . . and I'd heard that said, too.

Roy said, 'Well, I did not come here to meet Colonel Savage . . . or even His Highness of Kishanpur.' He bowed perfunctorily to Dip. 'I have some important matters to discuss with you, in private.'

'Excuse me,' Max said and, at Roy's side, crossed the lawn towards the bungalow.

No one spoke. Roy's job was to take all necessary political action, create all necessary political pressure, which would force Chambal and the smaller Indian states into the Indian Union. He had paid one official visit to Dip in Kishanpur, but was in constant secret correspondence with the leaders of the Kishanpur Progressive party. The party contained about a thousand members and everyone knew that their role was to riot for union with India on the signal from Roy – thus giving India an excuse to send in her troops to restore order. To send in Max, in fact.

I caught Dip's eye and stood up. 'I think we'd better be on our way, Janaki.' As though at a secret signal, Dip's servant slipped out of the darkness behind his chair and murmured, 'The Presence's bags are loaded into the car.' Ratanbir was there, saluting.

I did not speak until we were ten miles out on the road to Kishanpur. Dust hung under the double avenue of trees, for bullock carts swung slowly along the wide unpaved verges or in the middle of the road, sometimes with the drivers dozing on the cart. The Bentley's headlights bored a short wide tunnel, which shaded away from white to a dense green-shadowed brown as the dust reflected back the rays. Bullocks, and carts, and occasionally a man on foot loomed suddenly out of it, and once the leaping orange flames of a fire at the edge of a mango grove, where a family prepared to sleep.

The familiar, appalling sense of home, of love that could not be returned, settled in me. There was no sense of time when that mood came, only place – India. I knew that a Roman legion would not come out of that dust ahead – that would be ridiculous, though I'd often expected to see one march out of a fog on the Wiltshire downs . . . but Aurangzeb might come, sick and old, carried in a litter, reading the Holy Koran, remembering all the people, all the beauty, he had destroyed in order to preserve the Faith, and knowing at the last that he had preserved nothing – only destroyed. British infantry might come, with fife and drum, Kipling's infantry, the green flag with the bull, and Kim, and Mulvaney, Learoyd and Ortheris, and Danny Deever in the middle, a rope round his neck and the Pioneer Sergeant on his right with apron and axe . . . Or the Mahrattas, Dip's ancestors. *Can you hear the light horses neighing and the muffled pad of the hoofs in the dust, round shields and steel helmets shining in the light there, and the spears slanting back on their shoulders, and the smell of blood as they canter endlessly past? . . .*

I shook my head violently, shaking away the dream. I said, 'Do you realise that that is the man – L. P. Roy – who will take over rule of your State, Dip?'

Dip made a half-motion, touching my arm and at the same time indicating that Ratanbir and his own servant were in the back. The atmosphere in New Delhi had made him nervous and suspicious. I said, 'A Gurkha *havildar* and the body servant of a Rajah of Kishanpur are to be trusted, totally. When the time comes that such men cannot be trusted, then there will be no need or place for a Rajah of Kishanpur, or for Rodney Savage – or for Max.'

Dip said, 'I don't know what to do.'

We remained silent for some miles. At length I said, 'Feel that you're in a swamp? I've been there . . . There's not much more I can say about the political side which other's haven't told you before, a dozen times, a hundred times, I expect – from both sides.'

'Two hundred,' Dip said bitterly.

'Yes. Well, I'd like to stress another aspect. You know the Indian Government, besides taking away your powers, will also

150

take over the State revenues and give you an allowance instead, decreasing it for your children—'

'I don't have any.'

'Perhaps you will, later ... There's a lot of money in these states, much of it in gold bullion and jewels ...'

'I have a couple of million pounds' worth in the castle vaults,' Dip said.

'I know. And there's plenty more under your moneylenders' beds. That money is doing nothing. It ought to be hiring international lawyers for us, to put our case to The Hague, and the UN. It ought to be employing public relations experts for us. It ought to be buying more fighters and bombers, so that we'll be too strong for Nehru to take the high hand he took with Hyderabad. I say "us", and I mean "us". If we don't hang together we'll hang separately. Even if you don't want to come in with Chambal afterwards, you're mad not to join us in a mutual defence pact. India suspects that we've got such a pact already – and another between all of us and Pakistan. That's the only thing that's prevented them sending Max in months ago. And what do you think they're waiting for now?'

'Kashmir,' Dip said.

'Of course. As soon as that's settled, or at least put on the shelf – you've had it.'

Dip groaned aloud. 'I know, Rodney, I know! But ... however much I hate them individually, however much I dislike some of their ideas, however hard I try, I can't finally see any practical alternative.'

'The new Chambal Federation is the only answer ... Tomorrow I'll give you a long secret letter from the Nawab, written in his own hand, in Urdu so high-flown that no one can understand it – but there is a typewritten English version. It is in three parts: the terms of incorporation into Chambal, the details of a mutual defence pact, and the details of a loan programme, at enormous rates of interest to you. We need money.'

'But I thought the Nawab had all the money in the world, now that the Nizam's out,' Dip said.

'He did,' I said, 'but we really mean to be independent. I'll tell you something that Mr Roy does not know yet. He will tomorrow morning. We have bought a six-inch-gun cruiser and two

151

destroyers from a certain South American country. They will be delivered tonight, at Digra, complete with Italian crews.'

'My God,' Dip said, appalled. 'There'll be war.'

'Not just yet,' I said. 'But I want you to stop thinking we're all helpless, that we're in the grip of something bigger than we can cope with. India is not all-powerful.'

Then Dip said almost exactly what Roy had once said, 'No, but history is.' And I sat silent, half in fear, half in anger.

The Bentley rolled out on to a long bridge. As we always did at this point, we looked upstream. The black bulk of Kishanpur Fort towered above the right bank of the placid river, silhouetted against the lighter southern sky. The smooth water reflected lights from the fort windows, and a thousand lights pricked the darkness from the city huddled to the left of the fort.

'Home,' Dip said.

'For how long?' I said.

I turned the Bentley carefully through the narrow, double-angled entrance to the Fort. An old man in yellow livery made a deep obeisance. The servants appeared under distant arches, running.

Dip climbed out. 'Sumitra's come down to greet us,' he said. 'She doesn't often do that.'

I watched Sumitra sweep forward with the smooth, swinging motion that sent a tremor through my loins the first time I saw her.

She had heard what Dip said. She was smiling, her hand extended. 'Of course I came down when the watchman telephoned. I'm the chatelaine, aren't I? How are you, Rodney?'

She looked stunning – a slim white silk cocktail dress, high heels, a single rope of rubies. As I greeted her I wondered again whether Dip knew of our affair. She had come alone to Pattan once, and Dip knew it was hard for any man to resist her if she set out to seduce him. But that was the time she returned two days earlier than he expected – so perhaps he would believe that I *had* resisted her. I'm afraid it didn't matter very much to me. Whatever the basis of their marriage, sexual jealousy certainly didn't form part of it or Dip would have committed suicide or murder ten years ago. I thought he loved her, and her waywardness hurt him only because he could not himself provide, could not himself become, whatever it was that she needed – and that was much more than a stallion. I was surprised that he hadn't long since decided it would be a kindness to everyone to divorce her and take a new wife. Probably he had thought so, but couldn't do it. He was like me. He just had to go on the way he was going, and take what came.

We went up into the Fort.

Chapter 11

'You are not very exciting company tonight, Rodney.'

Sumitra touched my arm as she spoke. We were leaning over the upper battlements of the Fort, watching the procession forming in the courtyard below.

I said, 'Sorry.'

I was dead-beat. Five days had passed since Dip and I drove in that night. Every day had added up to exhaustion – long, wrestling conferences with Dip; colourful, noisy public processions; fireworks; nautches; State dinners. Dip was as tired as I. I saw his head nodding forward under the big sail hat down there in the caparisoned howdah far below me, and I saw the chamberlain nudge him respectfully. Dip started awake, and sat up. The elephants rolled out towards the lights and the yelling crowds and the rockets already soaring up into the night.

I would not have been tired if I had won. I had lost. Before dinner this night Dip finally told me he would not join Chambal, would not sign a mutual defence pact, would not lend us any of his gold. He was in terrible distress to have to say it to me, and he still did not know what he *was* going to do – only what he was not. I had been plodding round and round in his personal morass with him for so long that I was almost glad to get out of it, even though in the wrong direction.

I had lost. If only L. P. Roy had come, fanatical and threatening, it might have swung the trick. If only Max had moved his troops menacingly closer to the frontier. He hadn't (but his division had been reinforced by an armoured brigade of Sherman tanks, I learned). I had lost. And if Kishanpur kept out, Konpara and the smaller states would certainly follow suit. They had no choice. Without Kishanpur they would be politically and geographically isolated.

154

I looked at Sumitra. She twitched the blue chinchilla cape a little more closely round her shoulders and stared back at me. The starlight showed the clear outline of her face against the distant violet blur of the night horizon. I was wearing a dinner jacket, the coat buttoned against the chill from the river, and a white silk scarf thrown round my neck. I was smoking one of my cheap strong cheroots. She was wearing black diamanté sandals and a slim three-quarter-length black evening dress. Her manner towards me these five days had been warm, but until now no natural opportunity had come to be alone with her, and I had created none. My whole being was concentrated on Dip and my task. Nor had Sumitra made any advance; only watched me with increasing concentration and, it seemed, puzzlement. I had been very much aware of her. There were moments when a purely animal lust stalked upon me like a lion out of its cage. Desperately I wanted to feel those satiny thighs wrap round me; but before the desire could become frenzy, a thought would come about the business in hand – some point I had not fully explained to Dip, some new angle from which I could exert pressure on him ... and lust would slink back to its lair.

As the tail of Dip's procession left the courtyard I said, 'That's that.' I turned to her, dropped my cheroot, and took her in my arms. After a moment's resistance she responded eagerly, and at once my exhaustion left me. In a trice we were locked in one of those bellypressing, leg-twining, rocking, helpless clinches which can only have one proper end. I could feel her sliding down, going limp in my arms, and at the same time becoming muscularly and rhythmically alive. It would finish on the stone roof there, and that would be right. That's that, I had said, and now the lovely beast was out of its cage for good. I moved my hand and slid it up under her dress.

With a tremendous and unexpected effort she fell away from me and stumbled across the roof towards the far parapet, overlooking the river. I ran after her, and caught her shoulders as she leaned over. She resisted the pressure of my hands, as I tried to turn her round to face me. 'Sumitra,' I whispered in her ear. 'For God's sake! We have so little time. In a couple of days I've got to be back to Chambal, and then ...'

And then we'd be cut apart for as long as my mind could

imagine. Win or lose, there was soon going to be no chance for me to revisit India or for her to come to Chambal. I pulled more urgently at her shoulder.

She half turned. 'Wait . . .' she began.

I caught her and kissed her again. Again, for a moment, she gave herself up, and was swept to me by the same violent physical need that made me tug and pull at her dress until it was up over her waist.

'*Rodney!*' she gasped, turning her lips away from mine. '*Wait!*'

I stood back a pace, breathing deep, trembling, utterly aroused, my eyes fixed on her loins, where the high-riding dress hung like a theatre curtain over the remembered dark triangle of hair and the strong curve and countercurve of thigh and groin and mount of Venus.

She recovered some of her breath. 'There can . . . be more . . . time . . . for us . . .' She got the words out slowly, in bursts.

One side of the dress slipped down of its own, covering half her loins. I made a move to her but she held up her hand. 'I can come to Chambal . . .'

The other side of the dress slipped down over her hips and, gracefully, the whole fell in a slow draping until it hung as before, feminine and civilised, covering the female animal.

She said, 'Give me a puff of one of those awful things.'

I lit another cheroot and when it was going well handed it to her. She drew on it two or three times, coughed once and gave it back to me. 'That's better . . . Dip has made up his mind against you.'

She was leaning back against the battlements, the stone pressing into the small of her back. I said nothing. We had never mentioned politics in front of her, and she had never showed any sign, now or before, of taking the slightest interest in it.

She said, 'Dip hasn't said a word. But it's obvious. I am not a fool, and I do have interests outside *Kinder, Küche, Kirche* – perhaps because I am a childless atheist with a good cook . . . What would you do if I told you that I did not agree with Dip? That I thought Kishanpur should join Chambal?'

'I don't know what I would do,' I said slowly, 'but I know you couldn't do anything . . . short of poisoning Dip, announcing yourself as rani-regent, and issuing a proclamation. But the days for that kind of thing are past.'

'What about money?' she said. 'Don't you need money?'

I found myself saying 'Yes,' though our financial manoeuvrings were covered in as much secrecy as our military preparations. (When the news of our cruiser broke, the Indians ordered their biggest ships up to Bombay, which is less than two hundred miles steaming from the Chambal port of Digra. Pakistan promptly sent *its* tiny fleet to sea, on manoeuvres. What annoyed the Indian Government most was that our cruiser hit headlines all over the world. Their interest was always to sweep the whole business under the rug and keep the world ignorant not only of the issues but of the fact that there was a problem at all.)

'I could give you half a million pounds,' she said.

I stared at her in astonishment. Six million rupees was a lot of money. She might have saved a lakh or so, but Kishanpur was not a very rich state. The gold in the vaults had been collected over centuries. Dip had never been in a position to give her a really big allowance, nor had she picked up exclusively with multimillionaires on the Riviera.

'You're serious, aren't you, in this Chambal business?' she asked.

There was something about the tone of her voice, something about the steady, penetrating look in her huge eyes, that made me pause before answering. I began to speak slowly. Yes, I was serious. I had never been so serious in my life. I tried to tell her. I tried to tell her about an Indian land where there could be dignity as well as progress, splendour as well as justice.

'And you think you can attain it?' she asked. 'I mean you, yourself. Or are you fighting for the sake of fighting?'

'I think we can attain it,' I said. 'Myself . . . I feel that I have been given a second chance. For all the time we English have been here, certainly for the past fifty years, we seem to have been heading the wrong way. Now I've been given an opportunity to put that right. At the moment it's a matter of fighting, or being prepared to fight, like Israel. But I suppose Israel has an idea beyond self-defence, something it means to become – and so do we . . . Why aren't people like Max and P. R. Sethi in public life? They and hundreds of thousands like them, some who speak English, plenty who don't. I mean *decent* people, people everyone respects and trusts. Why? . . . Because they won't lie and stoop

157

and fawn. What is right is not always popular – it's practically *never* popular . . . We left the democratic process here, but we did not leave England's real secret – mutual respect among people, tolerance, independence of thought . . .'

My cheroot tasted foul and I threw it far out over the battlements, so that the red spark fell in a long curve down to the river.

'I, too,' she said slowly, 'I, too, have been given a second chance. India was mine. What could I not have achieved with this name, this position – Sumitra, Rani of Kishanpur? I rejected everything. I don't know why. Perhaps because everything seemed so settled. I do not like to have my fate cut out for me. This is a custom-bound country, and Dip is more deeply held by it than you would think. I would obviously have no say in the running of the State, so I never tried. I should have looked further, but I didn't. I went to Europe, and found men I could influence, men who were making something of themselves, against odds. Men like you.' I put out my hand, but she only touched it delicately, then went on speaking. 'I never thought of the British leaving India. I never expected to feel involved in the fate of peoples, only in the fate of people, singly . . . Now I do, I am involved, deeply. I will come to Chambal.'

I felt a little dizzy. If the Rani of Kishanpur came to Chambal, openly announcing her support for our position, it would be a tremendous coup; and it would give us more publicity. No other rani would have served that purpose so well, because the European and American press knew her, and her name and picture meant something outside India. On the other hand, the old Nawab would look on her with deep distrust, suspecting more Hindu trickery. Perhaps not. Who was it said there is nothing so persuasive as a million dollars? She was offering more than that.

'Where is the money coming from?' I asked her. I still could not quite convince myself that all this was not a crazy joke.

She said, 'The Rawan jewels. Tomorrow evening Dip and I will be wearing all that we can carry of them, and the rest will be in the vaults. I can hand the whole lot to you any time in the night. They fill two suitcases.'

The Rawan jewels were very well known. They were a fabulous collection of gems, brooches, tiaras, rings, necklaces, and other Hindu ornaments, such as anklets, and nose jewels, made up at

158

various times over the past thousand years. One or two pieces were valuable simply because they were old, others because of the size of the gems, others again because of the artistic genius that had gone into the shaping of them. The whole collection was priceless in the sense that Ajanta or the Konpara sculptures or Nanda Devi or the Ganges is priceless. They were part of India's heritage. They were part of the whole complex that *is* India.

Earlier this evening Dip had rejected that heritage. Though I understood his reasons, I despised him. If a man will not fight for what is his when the chance is given to him, he does not deserve to keep it. He himself might wish to knuckle under to India, but he could not complain if Sumitra had the courage to fight. It was also peculiarly fitting that she should bring with her not bearer bonds or Swiss francs but jewels. It was very right, and very Indian, that ancient jewels should be used to preserve an ancient dignity.

I would have to devise a plan to smuggle the jewels out of Kishanpur. I had the Bentley. I had Ratanbir. I could ... But tomorrow was another day. Tomorrow would be time enough for that.

Full realisation of Sumitra's meaning flooded into me. 'You will really come to Chambal – with me?'

I could say no more. It would not be quite truthful to say that I loved her. Yearning for her body, longing to learn what made her tick, fascination with her personality, these did not yet amount to love. Perhaps it was an element of self-protection that had prevented me going quite over the edge while she had seemed so inaccessible. I could hardly stand another hopeless love, such as I had given in the past to Janaki and Victoria Jones. But the sudden revelation of her ideals and sense of purpose; recognition of the depths below the narcissistic surface; appreciation of her courage in taking this tremendous step – these set off a trigger, which ignited a charge, which would, I knew, lead now inevitably to love.

I took her hands.

'Wait!' she said again, with a terrible sharpness. 'Rodney, it's no use pretending I don't find you exciting. But I didn't say I would come to Chambal with you. I said, I will come to Chambal ... Think, Rodney. Remember what I said to you at Pattan. I cannot promise to fall in love, as you will. I cannot promise not to betray you, as I am betraying Dip. There is a woman in me who is not subject to any rules of behaviour, or decency, or obligation. When this woman starts to move me, I go.'

I took her hands and lifted them and put them round my neck. I leaned forward and kissed her on the lips, my arms round her. Her hands tightened, her head turned away. She whispered, 'I warn you, Rodney, I warn you!'

I found her lips again and slowly, resisting, they opened to me, and she gave a long sigh against my mouth, and I led her across the rooftop, she leaning against me and walking with dragging drowsy steps, and I took her down to her room, and locked the door, and undressed her, and as she lay naked on the bed I looked long into her eyes, which had grown dull and wide and feverish, and, having lost all frenzy in the knowledge that this was a beginning, not an end, I kissed and stroked and made love to every part of her body, and finally locked myself into and upon her in a passion of love that seemed to have no end, but went on outside time, in the motion and countermotion of a liquid eternity, until a long bar of duck-egg green light shining on the ceiling told us it was dawn.

Chapter 12

Sumitra came to Chambalpur five days after my own return there. My first day Hussein and the Nawab and the council of state kept me so busy I hardly had time to think. I told them first about my failure with Dip. The Nawab questioned me sharply. My enemies hinted that the failure was my fault. I would have found it easy to lose my temper if I had not been thinking of Sumitra. Hussein protected me from the more foolish insinuations by letting out that the mission had been regarded as hopeless from the first. Of course, I thought. How could I have believed that they would let *me* get the credit, if they had expected any credit to be going?

Then I told them about Sumitra. After a few moments of thunderstruck silence, enthusiasm became general. The public relations expert embraced me. The Nawab looked suspicious – but he always did; and even he smiled when I told them about the six million rupees.

The second day I waited with increasing anxiety for Ratanbir. We had left Kishanpur together at dawn the day before in the Bentley, with the suitcases containing the jewels just thrown into the back seat under our own. Five miles outside the city the car I had hired was waiting for us. Ratanbir transferred to it, and they set off southward on a by-road, while I continued west. I drove slowly, and a little later spent an hour sitting in a jungle clearing, the Bentley concealed. Near Bhowani, when over the border, the Indian police stopped me. That was interesting because it showed that Dip had decided to bring them into the matter; which in turn meant his total surrender, because the Indian Government had already announced that they regarded State and crown jewels as the property of the people, hence *their* property.

It also showed that the theft had been discovered early. Sumitra had warned me she could not give me more than an hour's grace, and I was prepared.

While I was at the police *thana*, after they had searched the car and found nothing, the inspector telephoned Kishanpur. Since the Indian telephone system was primitive, and since I was in the next room, I heard every shouted word. The inspector was speaking to Dip himself. He said that he had found nothing. Nevertheless, he could arrest and hold me under Emergency Regulations if His Highness wished. A long silence. No, His Highness did not wish. Then Dip must have asked to speak to me. The inspector called to me, but I shouted, 'I have nothing to say to His Highness.'

I felt no qualm of conscience about the jewels. If he was willing to allow India's claim to them he could hardly treat it as a personal theft for personal gain, which of course it wasn't. I would have liked to tell him, before it happened, that Sumitra was leaving him, but she wanted to tell him that herself. I would have liked to say I was sorry it turned out that she was leaving him for me, because in spite of everything I liked him; but Sumitra was going to leave him sooner or later, everyone had known that for years, and in truth I was not sorry. I was delirious with happiness and expectation.

A little later the inspector let me go. By then I reckoned Ratanbir should be thoroughly lost to view on dirt roads and jungle cart tracks in the south. He should have entered Chambal territory the same night, and reached the capital this second day.

He did not. The third day he did not come. The fourth day I left Chambalpur at dawn, drove to the southeast corner of the State, and spent the day inquiring of police officials, guerrillas, and military outposts whether they had seen such and such a car, or such and such a man, whether they had heard of an accident. Nothing. I reached Chambalpur again at three in the morning, and slept fitfully and unhappily.

At noon Sumitra arrived. The propaganda people had arranged a huge press campaign to tell the world about the accession of the Rani of Kishanpur to our side. I was waiting at the Nawab's palace when she drove up in a big Chambali Cadillac with her maid and the Grand Wazir. A hundred photographers and journalists milled about the reception-room like a racecourse crowd. Flash bulbs exploded, cameras clicked, women scribbled, men shouted questions.

Standing with her on a dais the Nawab looked old and disgusted. He hated publicity of all kinds and could never unbend. Sumitra made a little speech about freedom and self-determination. She was very beautiful. Someone asked her whether the rumour was true that she had brought the Rawan jewels with her. Dip and the Indians had tried to keep that quiet, but something had leaked. Sumitra said she knew nothing about them.

Two hours later they drove her to one of the Nawab's large houses by the edge of the lake, and the press finally left her alone. I was already living in another wing of that house. The fact would doubtless be mentioned by some of the journalists when they wrote up their stories. I did not care.

She came to me as soon as she had bathed and changed. We fell greedily into each other's arms and assuaged our physical hunger. Afterwards, her face again made up, we talked business. I told her that Hussein Ali was coming round after dinner for a formal discussion of her role here. Then she ran through the names of the principal men of the State, their positions, characters, and influence. She knew an amazing amount about them and I had little occasion to correct her.

'And now you'd better give me the jewels, darling, so that I can give them to Hussein,' she said. 'That's the price of admission, after all.'

I said miserably, 'They're not here yet.'

Watching her arrival, making love to her, talking to her, had enabled me to forget my worry, but now it was back. She looked at me with her big eyes, which were momentarily cold.

'Ratanbir hasn't arrived,' I said. I walked up and down the room, beating my fist in my hand. 'I don't know what the hell can have happened to him, but something has. Suppose he was caught and arrested while passing through India . . . I don't think so. There must have been an accident. The poor little devil's lying injured in some hut miles from anywhere . . .'

She got up and put her arm round me. 'My poor Rodney . . . He's all right. The car may have broken down. He would have had to use some pretty bad roads, wouldn't he?'

'Yes,' I said. 'He was crossing India through Bhilghat. The road's awful.'

'Don't worry,' she said, 'he'll turn up soon . . . I can find some other way of convincing the Nawab of my value to the cause . . . though he'd much prefer to have the jewels. What was he going to do with them, by the way?'

'Sell them in Europe,' I said. 'There are ways. We would have raised about half their real value . . . The Indians are watching every road now. Ratanbir may have had to leave the car miles back and come on by bullock cart. I sent a message to the Gonds to look out for him . . .'

'The Bhilghat Gonds?' she said. 'But they're in India.'

'Yes,' I said, 'but they're working secretly for me. They will be ready to rise when the time comes.'

Later, the meeting with Hussein went off well. He advised her to introduce herself to the ladies of the Nawab's household, and the households of all the leading council members and generals. She was to keep her ears open, particularly about the strength of the ladies' attachment to the Chambal cause. She was to visit hospitals and run fund-raising bazaars, and do anything else that would get her picture in the papers.

'Can I not organise women's battalions, for labour and clerical work, nursing, even fighting?' she asked.

Hussein looked a little unhappy. 'That is against the Nawab's policy,' he said. 'We are, after all, fighting for the old ideals. Woman's place is in the home.'

I had a twinge there. This was feudalism, but I could not complain. You have to take people's bad ideas as well as their good ones, and do the best you can to teach them.

Hussein took an opportunity to speak to me alone the next day. He warned me to tell Sumitra nothing that was not necessary for her to know. I was indignant. 'What is the point of having her if we don't trust her?' I asked.

'We do,' he said, 'but in another sense, we trust nobody. You, after all, do not know exactly what I am always doing, do you? Because I tell you only what you need to know.'

'How can you mistrust someone who's giving half a crore's worth of jewels to the cause?' I said heatedly.

'She hasn't, yet,' he said, smiling.

'But damn it, I've told you, that's nothing to do with her. If it's anyone's fault, it's mine.'

I began to tell him that this universal suspicion was the curse of Chambal, but soon gave up. Hussein could not abolish it any more than I could. I turned to my work.

It felt better, more worthwhile now.

Sumitra made the difference, sweeping through my existence like a current of fresh air. It helped her that she shared a house with me, because none of the high Chambal ladies – and they were as suspicious and secretive as a nibble of weasels – could think that she was after their husbands. In two days she had got to know a dozen of the most important women in the State, and became so busy I hardly saw her until late at night.

So I was surprised when she came to my study about teatime on her fifth day in Chambal. I was working on a master plan for the defence of the Lapri Gorge. I pushed the maps away and stood up. She was smiling, her arms out. She hugged me tight, and kissed my face and neck and arms. 'Oh, Rodney, I'm so glad!'

'What's happened?' I asked.

She gave me a letter. It was from Dip to her. He thanked her for seeing that the jewels were returned to Kishanpur. He told her that he had paid Ratanbir the reward. He hoped that she was well. Signed. 'P.S. I shall always love you. Do remember that, wherever you go.'

'Of course, I had nothing to do with getting the jewels back,' I heard her say.

I read the letter three times. I threw it down on the floor. 'It's not true!' I shouted.

She looked at me. Her smile had become sad.

'It's a bloody lie,' I shouted. 'The Indians caught him and handed back the jewels. Ratanbir had nothing to do with it.'

She held my arm. 'Rodney, is it so impossible? He knew that you and I stole them. Didn't you tell me, the other night, that you once had him making preparations to rob a bank in Delhi? You're not Colonel Savage of the 13th Gurkha Rifles any more. You haven't been for a long time. Is it so dreadful that he should not be Havildar Ratanbir any more? That he should have learned these other attitudes from you, in the same way that he learned to shoot and march?'

I could not speak. I could not accept what she said. If it were true, I could trust no one. I could not trust her.

She said, 'It doesn't matter. I'm so glad! I thought you had taken them for yourself.' She caught my look. 'What else was I to think? It didn't seem so very terrible, to me. And you must admit that you are a mass of contradictions. How am I to know when you are going to think like a sahib and when you're going to think like – like one of your merchant-pirate ancestors?'

She hugged me and kissed me again, but I felt miserable. The more miserable I felt the more she warmed towards me. 'What about that P.S.?' I asked. 'Do you still love Dip?'

She said, 'I never did. This Chambal cause has given me the incentive to end a farce. He ought to marry again. I like him, that's all. It's finished.' And she hugged and crooned over me.

Two days later she came in, again at teatime, and began to hug me with a warmth and affection quite distinct from sensual passion. 'What now?' I asked.

'Dwarkanath and the bribe,' she said, looking fondly at me.

'Oh,' I said. Dwarkanath was a man who'd landed a contract for building barracks down at Digra, the port. I had flown down, found the work far below specifications and was even then writing a report to Hussein Ali. Dwarkanath had offered me twenty thousand rupees to keep quiet. I had refused with vehemence and abuse.

'You realise this will put So-and-so against you,' she said, naming three generals and a minister who owed a great deal to Dwarkanath, and vice versa.

'I don't care,' I said. 'I'm fighting for tradition – but not this one.'

'Yes,' she said slowly. 'You are an idealist, after all.' That night, after the love-making, which was as long and as detailed as the night at Kishanpur, she whispered in my ear, 'I love you, Rodney.'

Then she burst into tears, and for an hour I held her against me, while she sobbed quietly and whispered over and over again, 'But I love you, I love you.'

I felt that I had mounted the steed Pegasus. She lifted me out and above the poison gas of Chambal politics. I went at my work with a new vigour and came back at night refreshed and alert, to be transported by the magic of her love and affection to new, more vivid clouds.

I needed all the energy and élan I could muster. India began an economic blockade against us, and it became harder and harder to keep the army and the civilian populace content. Our three Constellations flew in from Europe, via Karachi, as fast as they could make the round trip, bringing in arms and supplies, but it was a drop in the bucket against our needs. Chartered ships plied in and out of Digra at enormous cost. There the cruiser H.M.S. *Chambal* lay to her moorings, conserving oil, while the Italian crew played cards and suffered from *le cafard*. Our puny railroad system began to fall to pieces. We were fast reaching the point where we must force India to act. If we did not, we would collapse of our own weight.

I poured out my thoughts to Sumitra. She soothed me, her hand on my brow. I said, 'There are times when I feel there can be no building until we pull everything up by the roots, His Obstinate Highness included, and start again from scratch . . .'

'That's what the Indians are trying to do,' she said. She took my hand and held it tight. 'And, Rodney darling . . .' she began.

I interrupted. 'But I've eaten the old bugger's salt and, by God, I'm going to earn it.' I jumped up and poured myself a stiff drink. Sumitra sighed, and I mentioned that the Nawab mistrusted her, as he mistrusted everybody. 'I expected it,' she said. 'Perhaps he'll feel different tomorrow. I've unearthed an Indian agent – quite an important one. Ram Lubhaya.'

'My God,' I said. 'Are you sure?'

Lubhaya was No. 2 in the Communications Department.

'Yes,' she said, 'I heard something, and told the secret police yesterday. Today they searched his house and found incriminating letters from L. P. Roy. He's in jail now.'

'That ought to show them about you,' I said.

She said, 'Yes. I think it will.'

Two weeks later I went down to Lapri to run a training exercise for the local guerrillas. I had been to Lapri many times during my time in Chambal, for the gorge and the Sakti plain behind were the keys to any military defence of Chambal. Twice I had seen Margaret Wood. She was looking more composed, though wan and tired. The loneliness must have been getting her down because she gave me tea and obviously tried to keep me, talking about nothing, until I had to break away.

167

Now here I was again, this time standing in thin trees near the edge of the slope, about halfway between Dhain and Lapri, looking down on the gorge road from India. The little village of Gidha nestled halfway up the farther slope. A motley gang of local men surrounded me and I examined them carefully. This was the kind of thing the American magazines would love, if only I could afford to let them take photographs here. I could see the captions now ... *Jungle Natives Fight for Freedom! Intrepid Guerrillas Prepare to Defend Homeland against Armed Might of India! ... Tall hawk-faced ratmouthed Savage (see cut) English mystery man prepares secret hideout.* In my mind's eye I picked out the men who would make the most fierce photographs.

I sighed regretfully. To work ... I had twenty men from Lapri, Dhain, Gidha, and other villages farther west. Five had modern rifles, and all knew how to use them. I had personally given them a course, back in the jungles, earlier in the day. That was a waste of my time – any *lance naik* could have done it – but Gokal Singh had protested his inability to spare me even a *lance naik*, so I did it myself.

The men were mostly ignorant and raw, but most had a spark of patriotic feeling, and one or two some basic knowledge of the problem. I had just appointed a wizened old bird from Dhain as the over-all commander. Age is always important in India, and he was a skilled *shikari* and poacher, though getting a little creaky in the joints. I called him the Marquess, as he looked like Reading, the ex-Viceroy.

Now I gathered them all closer, made them squat down, and began to talk. 'This is where you have to work, when the time comes,' I said, pointing down at the gorge. 'The Indian soldiers will have to use that road for their tanks and trucks, and for the men who march. They cannot defend every inch of it – it is too long, the jungle is too thick. On the other hand, you can't stop them. They are too strong and you are too weak ...'

A few faces showed a glimmer of understanding. The rest stared down in wooden puzzlement, mixed with alarm. I told them they must organise into groups of three or four. They must hit and run away – snipe a single man here, blow up a culvert there. They must prepare several caches in the jungle, where they could hide ammuniton, rifles, and also wounded men. I told the Marquess that each

168

group was to know only the site of its own cache, so that they could not even by accident betray the others. (Or under pressure, I added to myself.) The Marquess raised one wrinkled and hooded eyelid, like a sardonic cobra. The object was to delay the Indians, and to force them to use more and more soldiers on guarding their communications, so that there would be fewer when they debouched on the plain, where our own army would meet them.

More . . . we wanted information about little-known tracks through the hills south of Dhain, and north of the northern escarpment. We must know which paths the Indians used, how many men, how fast, any tanks or vehicles. I would set up an army post at Sakti, ten miles west. All information must be sent there by the quickest means.

We began a series of small exercises. I pointed out a tree or a rock as a pair of Indian sentries. The Marquess divided the men into groups, and I watched while group after group did a quick stalk and pretended to kill and escape. I showed them how to cover each other, so that men in hiding protected the man in motion. We examined various sites for caches and discussed their advantages and disadvantages.

Finally, I arranged a practical ambush. A broken stream bed ran steeply down the hill in a north-easterly direction, from somewhat below Dhain towards the Pattan Rest House and the Shakkar. It was a steepish run of rock, in step and fall, not very wide. I would wait at the top, and after half an hour begin to walk down it, alert. I was supposed to represent a patrol of six men. The guerrillas, acting in concert under the Marquess, were to ambush me before I reached the jeep road at the foot of the hill. They went off down the nullah and I lit a cheroot.

It was time Sumitra and I got married. There were still mysteries and depths in her which I could not get at, and, I felt, never would until marriage gave her full confidence. I suppose there has never been a mistress who is not always aware of the relationship's impermanence, and therefore holds back something vital, which she can salvage from the wreck. I had also come to appreciate the depth of her involvement with her native soil (and mine, incidentally). Her years in Europe and America had passed like a shallow stream, and, except for the occasions when she still wore

Western clothes, might never have existed. I ground my teeth on the cigar. We'd *got* to win our fight for Chambal's independence. Otherwise we would both be in exile, for ever ... if I did not end in front of a firing squad.

I glanced at my watch, stubbed out the cheroot, and started down the nullah. I kept my eyes open, but not unnaturally so. Let's see, I thought, a section would come down here with two men in front, one on each side of the nullah and as high up as they could get; then would come the section commander and the Bren gun team; and two more men would follow thirty yards or so behind. The ambush must take account of all those. They'd probably forget to allow for the dispersion, rush in on the front men, and get caught by the two at the back ...

A slight change of light, from a reddish matt of rock to a darker sheen, caught my eye a little right and ahead of me. Now, would I have seen that? Before I had made up my mind whether to start pretending firing, a man materialised from the shadows, a rifle in his hand. It was Chadi, my old *shikari* from Pattan. A sound behind me made me turn my head and I saw Mitoo and young Ganesha. Both were armed.

'Chadi!' I said. 'My friends! Is the village hungry again? And I see you have rifles. A little old, but good.' They were of an obsolete mark, obviously from Indian arsenal stocks. I smiled.

Chadi did not smile. He said, 'Sahib, you are on Indian soil.'

'Well,' I said, 'we'd probably have to get a map and a surveyor's instrument to make sure of that, wouldn't we?'

The border between Chambal and India ran due north and south here, across this very hill. I realised about now that the three had not seen or heard the Marquess. How could that be? Ah, the cunning old Marquess, really in the spirit of our game, had moved his party downhill off to the side, so that there would be no footmarks or crushed leaves in the nullah to attract the attention of the 'Indian patrol'. Was he within earshot? Probably not, because if he could hear us, these three could certainly have heard him getting into position.

Chadi said, 'We shall have to take you down to Pattan to the head constable.'

I was wearing Chambal uniform, and carrying a long thumb stick. Otherwise I had no weapon. It would be awkward to be dragged off prisoner into India, whatever the legality of the matter, which would be impossible to prove one way or the other. Here, possession would be all ten points of the law.

I had not expected this. I had an organisation among the Bhilghat Gonds, under Gulu, but nothing in Pattan. It seemed to me that the Indians, knowing my close connection with the place, would be too much on the lookout there. But this . . . that *they* should have organised guerrillas, and from my own people! I felt cold, and murderous, but held my face under control.

I said reproachfully, 'Is this how you repay what I did for you?' I looked at Mitoo and Ganesha.

Ganesha was young, and I had been a great hero to him. He muttered, 'Surely we can let the Gora-Raja go?'

Chadi felt the strain, but life in these hills is hard, as I had learned for myself. For a time I had led them towards a dream. The dream had collapsed. Chadi had to live. He'd taken a new allegiance.

'I am sorry, sahib,' he said quietly. 'We have promised.'

I shrugged. 'Let us go down then. Or would you prefer to shoot me here and save yourselves trouble?'

'Don't speak like that, sahib,' Mitoo wailed, 'we have promised . . .'

I started down the nullah, hoping we would get far enough down for the Marquess to hear us before Chadi headed out and east, directly towards Pattan, which now lay almost behind our right shoulders. I hadn't gone ten paces when he said, 'This way, sahib.'

He was as sharp as a razor, Chadi. He had realised that I knew perfectly well where Pattan was. Therefore, if I was heading on down the nullah, I must have a reason for it.

We climbed up out of the nullah, and at the top the Marquess was waiting with his rifle aimed at Chadi's heart. 'Don't raise your guns,' he said in a hungry voice. 'I am not alone.' We heard the rest pounding up the hill then.

The Marquess said, 'You were late, sahib. I came up to see . . . and saw . . . and went back and told them to come . . . and hurried up myself. I know you, Chadi of Pattan. What are you doing on the earth of Chambal?'

Chadi did not answer. The three were surrounded now. 'Take their rifles,' I ordered. Grinning, my guerrillas did so. They were

wildly excited, their eyes shining. The boring game had turned
into reality. I looked at the three prisoners. It would be best if they
did not return home. Nothing would more discourage the people
of Pattan and other villages from doing police and scouting work
for the Indians than to have it leak out that three of the best
shikaris in the district had mysteriously disappeared.

The Marquess was carrying the universal long-handled small-
bladed axe, tucked now through his loincloth. He handed his
rifle to another man and drew the axe. I stared at the three men.
Young Ganesha was quaking with terror, though silent. These
bloody people had betrayed me. They'd all better learn that the
day of the pukka sahib was over. The day of Hodson and Edwardes and Nicholson was coming back, the day of the hard men
of total power, instant decision, and no remorse.

I remembered the warmth of Mitoo's wife's arms round my
neck. These people had given me something, too. We'd shared
everything, during time that could not be measured, and it wasn't
their fault that that time had ended. It was the shape of the
continuum at that point in history.

The Marquess looked expectantly at me. I said, 'Take them to
the jail at Sakti. They are to reach there alive and well. Understand? From there I will have them moved to Chambalpur as soon
as possible.'

I would have them thrown into the dungeons, to join others.
The effect, of total disappearance, would be the same; but sooner
or later they'd get back to their families. If the Indians won, they'd
be released. If we won, I'd see that they were let out. The bastards
ought to be thankful for their lives.

The Marquess looked disgruntled and still hungry, and I said
sharply, 'Remember what I said! Without discipline we are lost
before we begin.'

Ganesha fell to his knees. 'Thank you, Gora-Raja ... Raja,
Gulu has been arrested.'

'Silence!' Chadi snapped. The Marquess hit him hard on the
side of the head with the axe handle and he stumbled, and groaned,
but recovered himself.

Ganesha gabbled on, 'Yesterday, sahib. He and a dozen others
in Bhilghat. The police went. Another man is to answer messages
in his name, pretending ...'

172

'Thank you,' I said. I motioned to the Marquess. 'Take them away, by the hill roads.'

We split up, the others going back up the nullah towards Dhain and I going on down alone. My mind raced and caught.

Gulu arrested. The whole of my guerrilla organisation among the Gonds wrecked. They must have had an eye on Gulu, after I'd given the D.C. a practical demonstration of my special position with the Gonds; but this was more definite. They had something on him. As he kept no papers, couldn't read, in fact, it was something else. I had met Gulu twice since coming to Chambal, once on the border near Bhilghat, once outside Lapri . . . and that time, by pure chance, Margaret Wood had passed, walking alone along a deserted path miles from anywhere. She'd seen us. Jesus Christ, the bloody bitch had told the Indians . . .

I reached the road and strode fast along it towards Lapri and the mission. I'd fix her for good and all this time. His Suspicious Highness was right after all – trust nobody, nobody at all.

At the mission bungalow I ran up the steps and knocked on the door. She came out smiling, an envelope in her hand. 'I saw you coming,' she said. She gave me the envelope and I took it automatically. 'Do come in and . . .'

I snapped, 'You are to evacuate this mission in forty-eight hours. If you are not out of Chambal territory within that time you will be arrested and taken to the concentration camp. You will receive confirmation of these orders, in writing, before—' I looked at my watch, it was five o'clock '—before six.'

I turned and went down the steps. I heard her crying behind me, 'What is the matter?' I heard her footsteps running down the veranda, felt her hand on my arm. 'Rodney! Colonel . . . Brigadier . . . what's happened? What have I done?'

I soon outdistanced her and in Lapri stood over Faiz Mohammed while he wrote out the order. The Nawab had long since given senior civil and military officials authority to put any suspicious or traitorous people into a concentration camp, without inquiry or trial. I watched him walk down the road to the mission bungalow to deliver it. Then I got into the Bentley and drove back to Chambalpur.

There I had a dozen people to tell, a dozen moves to make to counteract the effects of the action against Gulu. It was very serious indeed, because I had counted on the Gonds, with their jungle craft, posing a real threat to the Indians' southern flank. Gond quiescence would release at least two more Indian battalions to come against us. And there was an air of urgency liberated by the act, because the Indians would not have moved until they were on the point of major action. Otherwise they'd merely be giving us time to start all over again.

I did not reach the house until midnight, and only then remembered the letter Margaret Wood had given me. It was dated from Bhowani the day before. It was from Max. It began: *My dear Rodney, Some friends and I got together a week ago, and agreed that your tremendous talents are being wasted in your present job . . .*

The letter went on to offer me any one of five jobs: secretary of a club in Calcutta, another in Bombay; secretary of a racecourse somewhere else; top executive positions with two big industrial firms. It continued:

We have a good deal of influence, and can assure you not only that the jobs mentioned are all available and held for you, but that we can ensure that any previous misunderstandings between you and the Government of India will be forgotten.

In view of that last paragraph, Max must have got on to some of my I.C.S. friends. Senior Indians of the I.C.S. were quite indispensable, and the government knew it. Swallowing my peccadilloes, if the I.C.S. demanded it, would be no trouble at all.

The letter ended. *We – all your friends – do most sincerely urge you to accept one of these offers, and as soon as possible.*

Sumitra came in while I was reading, and leaned over my shoulder. When I had finished I put the letter back in its envelope, and burned it carefully in the grate, where a small fire sputtered – it was winter now, and cold at night. Sumitra said, 'Why do you burn the letter? Don't you want to keep it, for later . . . in case?'

I said, 'Max has to be protected against his own better nature. He could get into a lot of trouble, writing letters like that to English adventurers in the pay of the Muslim despot . . .'

I thought what a damned *good* man Max was. Max, my enemy. Max, the cuckold. Max, too big to think of that, only that I had shared a love for all that he loved, and I had lost. Max, oh, Max, I thought, what a God-damned bloody tragedy.

'What sort of a day did you have?' Sumitra asked. I leaned back and she gently rubbed her fingers through my hair, massaging my scalp, leaning over the back of the chair, her breasts warm and firm against my head. I thought, she talks as if I'd just come back from the City on the 5.06. And what have I done? Crawled about the jungles, nearly had three men executed, thrown a woman out of her house. I began to tell her, and when it was over, drowsily, lovingly, we went to bed. Got to ask her to marry me, I told myself sleepily. This must go on for ever.

Chapter 13

The daily bus left Lapri at seven in the morning, reaching the capital four hours later. Margaret Wood, huddled among the zenana passengers in the back, was grateful that she was a woman, for the lightly drawn curtains, shielding the ladies from the public gaze, also gave some protection against the bitter chill of the upland morning. Later, exhaust fumes filtering up through the floorboards, and the swaying of the bus on the many corners beyond Sakti, made two of the women sick, and she had a hard time holding down her own queasiness. Usually, on these buses, the women chattered like magpies all the way, and she would be asked innumerable questions about her family and children; but the tension of the past months had seeped into the people's hearts. Few talked, and they in low tones.

When the bus reached the alley which was its terminal in Chambalpur, she climbed down and walked stiffly out into the bustling street. There she stopped. Men passed her, gaping inquisitively. The dark eyes of women examined her through the mesh of *burqas*. She stood like a rock, awash in a half-tide.

She realised that during her sleepless night she had decided to come to Chambalpur to protest her banishment from Lapri, but she had not thought whom she was going to protest to. The government? Yes, but who in the government? The only man Henry had known was the Home Minister, and she could not remember his name. Two or three home ministers might have come and gone since Henry died. The army then. It was an army order that Faiz Mohammed had handed her. No, it was the Nawab's own order, but given 'on account of the military emergency'.

Rodney himself had done it, and she bowed her head in the street, remembering the sickening blow, like a kick in the stomach.

176

She had hurried out warm and expectant, and seen his face, cold and harsh ... He was a brigadier, and worked in Army Headquarters. It was him she must face, whatever the pain.

She beckoned to a passing tonga and told the man to take her to Army Headquarters. Sentries stopped the tonga at the gate and she filled out a form, and a *chuprassy* shuffled off with it. She waited. Half an hour passed and the *chuprassy* returned.

'*Nahin hai*,' he said, twisting his hand, palm upwards. Where had he gone, where could she find him? The man said something in Urdu which she could not understand. She asked him to repeat it and he said, in English, '*Millitairy see-crut*,' and grinned tremendously.

The tonga driver, who had been dozing in his seat, the tonga parked under a tree, called out, 'Who does she want to see?'

'The English brigadier sahib.'

'I know where he lives. I can take you to his house. He may be there.'

She climbed back into the tonga and the driver lashed the gaunt pony into movement. Rodney was living with that woman, the Rani of Kishanpur. The Indian papers had said so openly at the time she first went to Chambalpur. Margaret had no wish to meet her again. They had met once, exchanging a few polite words when she and her husband passed through Lapri on the way to Pattan. When she went through later, alone, Margaret had only seen her pass. Well, it was Rodney she had to talk to. The Rani would hardly force herself into such an interview.

The tonga stopped in front of a big house facing the lake. She paid off the driver and walked up the steps. A servant came, took her name, and left her on the wide veranda. The front doors were open, the tatty screen pulled up, and she looked into a marble hall hung with Bokhara rugs and aglitter with brass ornaments. The *chuprassy* returned at once, but stopped inside the hall, holding back a curtain. The Rani of Kishanpur glided through the doorway and towards her. Her violet sari made Margaret's own khaki skirt and white blouse seem sordid.

'Mrs Wood ... Rodney is not in Chambalpur and won't be back until evening, I'm afraid. Can I help you?' She smiled pleasantly.

Margaret said stiffly, 'It is Brigadier Savage I wish to speak to, Your Highness.'

The Rani said, 'It's about the order to leave Lapri, I suppose? I know something about that. I can't promise to be able to help, I'm afraid ... but won't you please come in? You look pale. You must have come up by bus. That's an experience to upset anyone.'

'I didn't think *you* would have travelled much by bus,' Margaret heard herself saying and knew that her face was still set in frozen dislike.

The Rani smiled again. 'Not much – but enough. I have taken many bus rides since coming here. You hear a lot, in buses, if you are hidden under an old *burqa* and let the other women talk, as they're only too pleased to do. . . Please, Mrs Wood, let us be sensible. You have nowhere to go, you look hungry, Rodney won't be back till six at the earliest. Please come in.'

Margaret finally managed to say it: 'Thank you.' She followed the other woman into the hall, through the curtain again held back by the bowing servant, and into a big drawing-room. A voice was speaking in Urdu from a radio in the corner and the Rani listened to it a moment before switching it off. 'Mr Roy again,' she said, 'giving me another personal mention, too. I sometimes wonder whether the propaganda value of my coming here has not been outweighed by India's ability to focus people's dislike on me as a personal symbol of treachery to the cause – their cause. Me and Rodney – the Traitress and the Foreigner. . . The rather ornate furnishings are not *my* taste,' she added with a gesture. 'This is one of the Nawab's guest houses. Make yourself comfortable. I'll get us something to drink.'

She walked out of the room, her hips swaying, and Margaret heard her voice, faint, from farther along the airy house.

The pictures on the walls were dreadful Italian oleos, and a huge imitation-Rubens nude hung over the fireplace. There was a low coffee table, and a Buhl cabinet that clashed with everything else in the room, some chairs and sofas, the radio, and a locked roll-top desk. And on the desk a big picture of Rodney in a silver frame. She stood in front of it. It was recently taken, an enlargement of a candid camera shot of him in his Chambal brigadier's uniform, smiling at someone off the picture to the left, his hair wind-blown and the clear mark of sun tan in the light values of his face. He looked wonderful, there, and so happy, but too thin round the jaw and cheeks, as though he were not eating enough and working too hard. This woman did not feed him properly.

She did not hear the soft glide of the Rani's returning footsteps and did not know how long she had been standing there, in the door. The first that Margaret knew was her voice: 'He is a man.' The voice was sad.

Are you going to get married? Do you love him? Aren't you ashamed of leaving your husband? Why don't you go back to him? A hundred accusing questions flew to the tip of Margaret's tongue; but she said only, 'Yes.'

The Rani changed her tone. 'Do you know why Rodney gave you that order so suddenly?' she asked matter-of-factly.

Margaret sank on to a sofa. 'I have no idea,' she began formally. Then the memory returned, the cold dislike on his face, the ice in her heart, spreading so that she thought she would never be able to move again. The words poured out: 'I don't, I don't! Once, months ago, I said I'd fix him, but that was when he was in Pattan and I . . . I didn't understand him, I didn't *know* him. He was so different from anyone I'd met, and Henry only just dead. But I *didn't* try to fix him, I didn't do anything. I explained all that when I was ill and he saved my life, and . . .'

'He saved your life?' the Rani said.

'Didn't he tell you about it?'

She could not believe that those days of her illness had meant so little to him.

'He saved my life,' she repeated. Her hands weaved and knotted on her handkerchief. 'I suppose he doesn't remember, but he did, and I did explain it to him and I thought he believed me, and then . . . and then . . .'

'Here, my dear, have a drink.' The Rani poured out a small glass of whisky from a decanter that had appeared on the table. Had the servant come and gone while she was talking, and she seen nothing? She could see nothing now, except the Rani's face, and feel nothing except the whisky burning her throat.

The Rani said, 'He gave the order because he believed you had betrayed Gulu.'

'Gulu?' she said. 'Who's Gulu? I've never heard of him.'

'I didn't think you would have. He's a Gond chief, from the

179

Indian side of the border. He was working with Rodney to prepare the Gonds to rise against the Indians when the time came. Rodney had just heard that the Indians have arrested him.'

'Is he a small very black old man, wrinkled skin and ...? He must be the man I saw once with Rodney, near a jungle footpath up the hill behind Lapri. But I never said a word to anyone!'

'I know you didn't,' the Rani said sadly, 'but Rodney believes you did ... I wouldn't worry too much if I were you. I think the clash between Chambal and India is going to come very soon, and then everything will be different. If India wins, it won't do you any harm to have it believed that you did give the information ...'

'But I didn't,' she cried. 'And I don't care what the Indians believe if *he* believes that I was spying on him.' She collected herself. 'Another missionary is coming from England, at last. He is due in Bombay the beginning of next month. I only have to last out that long, and then ...'

'And then what?' the Rani asked.

'The mission will ...'

'No – what about you?'

Margaret wound and unwound her handkerchief. 'I ... I don't know. I was just waiting, staying.'

'And you were as near him as you could get?'

'Yes!' She looked up quickly, but the other woman's face held no gleam of triumph or discovery. It was as unhappy as her own.

The Rani said, 'You are a trained nurse. How would you like to run a nurses' school?'

Her professional interest was touched. She said, 'You can't start a school, just like that. It has to be part of a hospital.'

'There would be no difficulty in getting you a post as senior matron of a hospital, and all the facilities you wanted to turn it into a first-class teaching hospital for nurses as well.'

'Where? Here?'

The Rani hesitated. 'In Chambal – yes. If India succeeds ... my direct influence will be nothing, but I can still manage that for you, anywhere.'

Margaret burst out, 'But what will happen to him, if Chambal loses? India is so strong. Mr Roy has openly threatened him, he

180

has so many enemies, he has done so many things against India –
oh, they're all in the papers, even more than he *has* done, probably.
Where can he go?'

The Rani said, 'I'm afraid he will not live to be worried by that
question. He is going to fight, to the end. If he does not die under
Indian guns – *Indian* guns, O God! – he will die by a knife wound
– someone here stabbing him in the back . . . And there are many
kinds of knife wounds.'

'It's your fault,' Margaret whispered. 'If it weren't for you, he
wouldn't be here, fighting this hopeless battle.'

The Rani's huge eyes burned with a dry flame. 'Some think that
it was the other way round – that he brought me here, Mrs Wood.
That if it were not for him, I would still be with my husband, and,
through him, attached to the Indian cause . . . You love him.
Don't attempt to deny it, please. I saw your face looking at the
picture there.'

Margaret said, 'Yes. For a long time now I've known that
Rodney is all I have to live for. All I have to live *in*.'

'What are you waiting for? Me to die? My God, you are like a
vulture sitting on a tree.'

'I do not think you will stay with him. As you did not with the
others, in Europe. I think, soon, that he will be alone again, and
lonely.'

Sumitra gasped, then said slowly, 'I suppose that is deserved. I
can see you will have him, if he lives. You have the tenacity . . .'

Margaret said, 'I told you. I have nothing else to live for. But he
does not love me. He is not aware of me, except that I betrayed his
friend. I know him well enough to know that he will never forgive
a betrayal.'

Sumitra's hand trembled so that the jewelled wristlet shivered
and clinked on her wrist. Her breathing came in gasps.

Margaret said, 'I will stay here until I see him. He must know
that I did not betray him.'

'You must go,' Sumitra cried, jumping to her feet. 'About Gulu
– I shall tell him myself. Yes, yes, I promise. What is it to me?
Within a week it will be settled, one way or the other. He will be
dead . . . he will be mine for ever . . . or he will never be mine,
and this petty nothing about you and Gulu will be buried, forgotten. . . I shall order your lunch now, and afterwards the

chauffeur will drive you back to Lapri in my car. You will receive an order to Faiz Mohammed delaying your eviction for a week ... Good-bye.'

She stood well away, and briefly joined her palms, then turned and ran out of the room, her sari rustling like a dying wind in the trees.

Chapter 14

'First, we will hear syndicate solutions to the problem. Then Brigadier Savage will bring out the main lessons, and I will sum up.'

General Gokal Singh sat down and I stood up, leaning on my pointer staff. We were running a cloth-model study based on an Indian attack up the Lapri Gorge. I had thirty senior officers of the Chambal Army there, divided into six syndicates. The cloth model, set out on the floor of a huge room that had been a reception hall, was about 30 by 60 feet and gave a very fair representation of the ground between Lapri and Sakti. After explaining the locations of our own troops, and two different versions of what the enemy might be doing, and putting out various flags and toys on the model to represent the troops, I posed the problem: How and where to engage the enemy? An hour later General Gokal made his little speech and I called on Colonel Nazr Ahmed to begin.

After the first two sentences I knew I didn't have to listen to *him*. My mind could run about among its numberless worries. Mid-January and our affairs fast coming to a head. The Indians were ostentatiously strengthening their garrisons along our northern borders. Prince Afif and I were convinced it was a feint. There was too much desert up there, too many miles of nothing, all open to our excellent air force. Gokal Singh, in command of the corps which was our only striking force, wasn't so sure, and we were having a hard time preventing him moving the armour and part of the infantry northward. I said flatly that the Indians would not come from the north. Gokal said with pointed politeness that the responsibility was not mine. I ground my teeth.

Our defence forces were standing by, some at thirty minutes' notice, the rest at four hours'. The morning cold was like a razor

183

these days, until the sun rose. Then the shadows retreated fast, withdrawing like an army across the empty courtyards, leaving the bare stones bathed in dry golden light.

Two more syndicates spoke – unimaginative nothings. I called on the next. A young Rajput major stood up. 'Our object,' he said, 'is to draw the enemy's armour into battle piecemeal against our own armour, concentrated, and supported by all our anti-tank guns.'

I glanced up. This fellow had the idea. I made a brief note on my pad. The young major went on. He was good, at least on the theory of it.

The other syndicates followed. My opinion had been better expressed by Churchill: 'The answer is in the plural, and they bounce.'

... One of the fealty rajahs in the northern part of the State had refused to move his private army unless the Nawab agreed to transfer a few thousand acres of desert from a neighbouring barony to his. That quarrel had been going on for three centuries and now he saw his chance. The Nawab had flown up to beg his rajahs to be reasonable; or, possibly, to throw them both into the dungeons.

L. P. Roy had been on the radio, swearing that India would never use force in the solution of its problems. Nevertheless, India's patience was exhausted. Chambal's provocation, Chambal's suppression of its people, Chambal's aggression ...

Margaret Wood was still at Lapri, saved by Sumitra's soft heart. Gulu was still in an Indian jail.

The last syndicate gave its solution. I made a few more notes and began to dissect what had been said.

The vital point was obviously that Max had to get his armour out of the Lapri Gorge and up on to the Sakti Plain, by one steep, twisting road, in rocky jungle-covered hills. Numerically, our armour about equalled his. If we could attack him, with all our armour, at the moment when the leading half of his tanks had come out into the plain and the rest were still in the gorge, we would stand an excellent chance of destroying him completely – because he would either have to retreat or push forward the rest of his armour and let us destroy that in its turn. Max was no bloody fool, and there were many manoeuvres he could pull to circumvent us ...

I won't go into any more detail. Of the six syndicates only one, the young major's, had produced a sound plan, because only he really understood what we were trying to do. Few syndicates had thought to use our air forces at all, and only two had used them properly.

My suppressed anger carried me into some harsh words. Why hadn't all these matters been studied for the past weeks and months? Because Gokal Singh insisted that secrets would leak out, plans become known. Yes, but there were ways round that, and anything would have been better than to leave these semi-trained officers in any doubt of their exact objective.

When I had finished a brigadier stood up, his face taut with spleen. 'My opinions are entitled to more respect than you have given them,' he said. 'I have twenty-eight years' service . . .'

'So had Frederick the Great's mule,' I snapped. The brigadier turned pale, and I expected Gokal to rebuke me. He certainly should have; and I would have accepted it and apologised. He did not and I thought, even in my fury, he *wants* dissension.

A second cousin of the Nawab got up. Oh, God, here it comes! 'Since I am of the Blood Royal, I *must* be right . . .' It wasn't as bad as that. He wanted to know why I had not given the place of honour to the horsed cavalry squadron of the Nawab's Body-guard.

Gokal summed up. He played both sides against the middle in a masterly appraisal in which he supported my solution in every particular, but ended by pointing out that the battle might not be fought anywhere near the Sakti Plain. Once again I suffered a sharp spasm of doubt, of suspicion. If we didn't fight on the Sakti Plain we would not fight at all. The Chambal Army had its virtues, but it definitely did not have the training or the confidence to fight after a long withdrawal.

I thanked General Gokal profusely and hurried out. I was meeting him again in fifteen minutes at the C-in-C's office. I had to rush upstairs and collect a secret file from my safe. The lock had been tampered with, and I swore, and congratulated myself on keeping all really important papers in the safe at home. Besides, this was very unlikely to be the work of an enemy agent. It was a henchman of the Nawab's, or of Gokal's, sent to learn what I had said to one about the other, and vice versa.

185

In his office the old C-in-C, General Prince Afif, was squatting on cushions on the carpet, being fanned by a pretty girl and smoking an ornate hookah. The girl was some sort of slave. Oh, yes, slavery had been officially outlawed in Chambal a century earlier, to please Queen Victoria, but it still flourished.

Afif was a delightful old man and the soul of courtesy. He had made his battle plan: he was going to drive out to the fight in his Rolls-Royce, the Rolls drawing a horsebox containing his favourite charger. He would wear the full war costume of the Bokharis, and would charge waving his scimitar. At the funeral a *mullah* would recite the appropriate chapter from the Holy Koran.

The business at hand was unfortunately more complicated. Gokal and I squatted on the carpet, facing the Prince. The old boy passed round the mouthpiece of the hookah.

I began the negotiating. I've forgotten now what the problem was, except that it ought to have been solved three months ago by a junior captain. Now a general, a lieutenant-general, and a brigadier thrashed it like a dog, for an hour.

We wrangled and fiddled on, the cloud of hookah smoke thickening and fine perspiration beading the girl's bare torso. Next we had to appoint a new paymaster for the guerrillas. X wouldn't do because he was already responsible for meat procurements – a lucrative post. Y had trodden on the Nawab's great-uncle's cousin's mother's nephew's toe at a reception in 1898. Not *him*, Allah forfend! . . . The centuries surrounded me, not in succession but all at the same time, in a frightening jumble. I was De Boigne, teeth set, trying to convince Scindia that if he didn't patch up his feud with Holkar, both of them would be swallowed by the Peshwa. I was Dupleix, listening while two maharajahs squabbled over precedence and Clive marched. I was a lone Amir of Sind, shouting, 'The English, they come!' to a tentful of torpid despots while Napier brought his troops into the battle line. The disciplined combination of intrigue, diplomacy, and brute force was on the other side, down there with Max and Roy and Nehru. *They* were Warren Hastings, Stringer Lawrence, and Eyre Coote; I, squatting on this carpet, was the old, free, chaotic India . . .

We agreed on a name. Next problem.

Poor old Afif closed his eyes in pain. We were giving him a headache.

Gokal stated his case. I stated mine ... Wrangle, wrangle, wrangle. I had, in effect, won on the first problem, and I knew the C-in-C would rule for Gokal this time, and he did.

Military police to control traffic. There weren't enough. There ought to be. Something must be done ... What?

Two hours later Gokal and I stood up. Afif remained squatting, looking very much his age. A *chuprassy* sidled in with a signal form, and handed it to him. He fumbled around for his spectacles. The girl found them and gave them to him. He put them on. He read the signal. He read it again, aloud. ' "Tanks, trucks and infantry moving from Bhowani towards Bijoli ... Deciphered at 11.30 a.m." ... Why wasn't this given to me sooner?' he said querulously.

'Prince,' the *chuprassy* whined, 'you were in conference. Your orders ...'

It was a strict rule, true enough. No one could disturb the Prince when he had the girl and the hookah in there. It was now two o'clock and I was ready to die of hunger.

'You will move your troops, then?' the Prince said.

Gokal scratched his chin. 'Perhaps we should first inform His Highness ...?'

'We can't reach him till evening,' I broke in. 'He's spending the day out hunting with the Rajah at Maragan. We have his signature, approving this movement as soon as we get this information.'

Gokal said, 'It is a big decision to make without His Highness's knowledge. Action might precipitate war.'

I said, 'Sir, inaction might precipitate some executions.' I saluted, and went out.

In my office I told the *chuprassy* to get me food, quickly. The C-in-C sent me a note, telling me that he had ordered the troop movements, in writing, and I felt a little better. After eating I drove out to the barracks and found remarkably little turmoil. I was congratulating the Chambal Army, in my mind, on a higher state of training than I had thought it possessed, when I stopped behind a group of officers, under the brigadier who had been so angry at the cloth model. I found that they were conducting an exercise. It had only just begun, and they were doing it with live tanks. I counted forty of them out in the plain a couple of miles away.

187

I took the brigadier aside, saluting punctiliously and using 'sir' every other word, and asked him whether he had yet received the order to move. 'Yes,' he said, his eyes glinting nastily, 'but we are to finish this exercise first. After all, remember Drake finishing his game of bowls . . .'

'Yes, sir,' I said, 'but I understand that the C-in-C gave definite orders for the move to begin at once.' By God, over an hour had passed since the order went out. The leading troops should have been ten miles out.

The brigadier became ugly. 'This is my business, Savage.'

I said, 'Sir, I assure you that Prince Afif has given his personal and most stringent orders to move at once, according to Plan Panipat. Any disobedience is likely to be punished by death.'

'That's very funny,' the brigadier said, with a wolfish grin. 'General Gokal told me personally, ten minutes ago, to continue my exercise.'

That's when I became positive that Gokal was on the other side. The commander of our striking force!

It was a moment of doubt and indecision. All at once the full weight of the situation came upon my shoulders. What was I doing, involved with these bunglers and traitors and idiots? How was it possible that I stood here, prepared to fight and kill Max, my friend, to whom I had handed my Colours, my country, my love? What possible hope of success was there, and even if we won, what possible hope of improvement, of progress? From all that I had seen, an independent Chambal, loosened from the stringent supervision of England, would go back to those jolly days when a Nawab could burn a couple of dancing girls alive for some minor peccadillo. (It was undoubtedly his right, since he was sovereign – but that had not prevented the viceroy of the time from summarily removing him from the *gaddi* and appointing his son instead.)

I should leave this bloody mess at once, go to Sumitra and ask her what was to be done. Hold a council of war with her, and Hayden, and the few other Englishmen in Chambal . . .

I remembered that all this had happened before: to Clive in the mango grove before Plassey. If Clive, the boldest man India ever knew, had had his moment of doubt, surely I could be allowed mine?

The thought of Gokal and his friends winning their victory exactly as they planned, from inertia, was too much for me. What a laugh they'd have, in the years to come, over how they'd hood-winked the stupid Englishman!

I drove furiously into the barrack area. Gokal had vanished – east towards Sakti, it was said. I found two dozen tank transporters drawn up on the polo field, waiting. I told the major in command to take his transporters out to Brigadier Narain Singh and say, as from the C-in-C, 'Load! Move!' Then I went to the C-in-C's house and got him to send a personal order to the brigadier – to all officers of the corps – to get going. Then I drove back out to the barracks and watched for two hours while the order was obeyed. At five o'clock the movement was in full swing. Where now? Where was the focal point?

As far as I knew there'd been no diplomatic démarche, no ulti-matum from India. We must get hold of the Nawab and bring him back to the capital. We must expect news that Indian troops were also advancing closer to our northern border. I must prevent the Nawab or the C-in-C detaching any part of our armour to face that threat. I decided that my place, for the moment, was here in Chambalpur.

I went to the palace and found Hayden, the ex-I.C.S. English-man the Nawab had hired as constitutional adviser. There was some commotion in the streets and an unusual number of police about. I was not surprised to hear that half an hour earlier the Indian National Congress had issued a proclamation, calling on the people of Chambal to resist the Nawab's tyranny. Hayden had somehow contacted the Nawab, who was already on his way back.

Hayden said, '*Five* minutes ago the Home Minister ordered the arrest of Dunawal and all his crowd.'

Dunawal was head of the pro-Indian Congress group in Chambal. We had refrained from arresting him, thus far, in order to avoid provoking India.

Hayden said, 'All India Radio announced the arrest *twenty* minutes ago . . . It was all fixed in December. He was to take out an illegal procession, and force us to arrest him, on such-and-such a signal. He got it, he did it, we arrested him.'

'What now?' I asked.

He indicated a mass of paper on his table. 'Preparing this

cable to the United Nations. It'll go off as soon as the Nawab arrives.'

'And what will the UN do?'

He shrugged. 'Just what they did in Kashmir.'

'Pakistan?' I asked.

He lit a cigarette. 'On the edge of bankruptcy. Their only real use was as a threat. Bluff, if you like. Nehru is calling it. Look, you go and get a good night's rest. I'll see that you are told if anything happens or they try to do something silly with the army.'

I drove home.

When I walked up the steps into the house the doors were open, and I left them like that, as I usually did. Sumitra was waiting for me in the hall, and the first thing she did even before kissing me was to go and close them. At once it became quieter in the house, and the load on my back began to lighten. I leaned on her, my hand on her shoulder, and she guided me like a sick man to the drawing-room. As we entered the room she left me and walked over to the radio. Someone was making an angry speech, and probably the speech piled more fuel around us, ready for the spark that invisible demons were even then carrying down from Indra's Abode of the Thunderbolt. At that moment I could not care. As the voice hiccuped into silence in the middle of a sentence I sank back into a chair and closed my eyes.

It took me all the early part of the evening merely to return to a full awareness of myself as a human being with ten fingers, ten toes, one nose, two ears, and the rest. I bathed and changed, I know. I ate, I know, but did not record it until afterwards when the sense of well-being that surrounded me included, I noted, a well-filled belly and a glass of liqueur brandy on the coffee table. I noted, properly then, the closed doors and the turned-off radio. For this night she and I would be alone. Let it be so.

Later we walked together to my bedroom, she now leaning against me, my arm round her waist and under her breast, her legs languid and her pace voluptuous. In the bedroom, having undressed myself, I unfastened the knot of her sari and she stood like Niobe, her eyes slightly averted and downcast, while the heavy silk slid slowly down the coppery satin of her thighs. I loosened her *choli*, and she extended her arms slightly so that I might the more easily draw it off them.

190

There are many degrees of love and sometimes it is easy to know what degree you are experiencing at a particular moment – as when the slim column of a woman's neck is all tenderness, all beauty, nothing else; as when the rough texture of her bush and the slippery passage between, contrasted with the daintiness of the underclothes she may still be wearing, jolts you with the electricity of desire; as when tired hands work for you, tired eyes search for the aches that they can soothe in body or soul, and you know only the dependence of love; as when, standing together against sorrow, there is only the dignity of love.

This was not such a moment, classifiable into its category, but one of the others, rare and so total that there is no experience like it except probably death, when all the degrees and kinds are fused into one, when you are overwhelmed by the simultaneous flooding over of every channel of your being. I saw her eye, large, the lashes curled upwards, brimming with the Madonna's bliss. I felt, pouring into me from her brain, her deep respect for me. Her generous spirit overflowed with no more and no less of grandeur than overflowed the secretions of her loins, soaking the rose petals between. The twin awareness of shared danger and affection thrust into my heart no less and no more than did the rigid, extended nipples crowning her full breasts. I could not tell, when I poured the liquid essence of my love into her, whether it was the commonplace of animal husbandry, the thing every bull has done to every cow since the world began, or whether it really was my life that I was giving her, all that I am, spiritual as well as physical. I know only that I was immeasurably increased – just as Christ said – by giving away all that I had. We did not make love, we were love.

When finally, this state of unearthly union having continued several hours, we could bear to separate the bodies that had served so well as the vehicles of emotions far larger than they could in themselves contain, I laid my hand upon hers and said, 'Will you marry me?'

I thought it sacrilegious to mention marriage after what we had shared, but in a material sense I wanted to weld the link, to let her know that I never would wish to escape from this mutual bondage.

She must have felt the same, for she said, after a time, 'My darling, is it necessary to decide that now? What more can life possibly give us, whether you put a ring on my finger or take me by the hand and lead me round the sacred fire? We have just been living *in* it.'

But now I was obstinately decided that the inward miracle should wear the conventional label for all to see and wonder at. 'Please,' I said, 'I love you.'

'I love you,' she said, and relapsed into silence.

After a time she said, 'Would you want to take me to England?'

'No!' I said violently. 'Here, here . . . Do you *want* to go to England?'

'No,' she said, 'but if you did, terribly badly . . . or if you had to . . . I could not go with you. At least, I didn't think I could before tonight. Now, I don't know. Could you ask me . . . in the middle?'

Neither of us could tell when such a miracle would happen again. And, no, I could not ask her anything 'in the middle'. Nothing existed, during the miracle, outside of it – so how could I refer to some exterior thought or event?

'Why England?' I said. 'We are here. We have work to do here. There is a sink of corruption to be cleaned up before the genuine ideals of the Chambal people can be realised. Who knows, perhaps our son will be prime minister, and finish what we begin.'

She took my hand and placed the fingers to her lips, and kissed them sweetly. 'I can't answer you now,' she said. 'I can say neither yes nor no. There is nothing left of my will or thought except you, and the knowledge that I touch you and lie beside you. Good night, sweet prince.'

I lay on my side, propped on one elbow, for a long time, examining the beauty that seemed to grow more troubled as the body that fed it sank into sleep, so that gradually the exhausted calm of the face began to ebb, the warm, wet lips to move without sound, the rounded thighs to twitch against me, and hair-fine creases to mar the broad forehead. Deeply stirred, and fearful, I thought I would never sleep, but sleep came upon me with so sudden and powerful an assault that I knew nothing until I awoke, tense and alert, in the hour before dawn.

Where was the Nawab? What was Gokal doing down at Sakti and Lapri? Why did I dream our cruiser had opened fire on an Indian submarine? Had Max's boys crossed the frontier? What

192

was Prince Afif doing? Birds chattered, and it was dark, one window wide open. A thin cold mist from the lake filled the world and our room, so that neither eyes nor any other sense could find the line of demarcation between the mist and the night, or between them and humanity – we were all one, beings with no defined limit, Sumitra, and the mist, and I, and the lake.

I thought of Ratanbir. Where was the poor devil now, what thinking? How was he finding it, to live with wealth stolen from my trust? That hurt too much and I turned to curl up against Sumitra's back. In that instant I heard the heavy, dull crash of distant bombs, and the tearing roar of aircraft's multiple machine guns.

Sumitra sprang out of bed in one motion and crouched naked, staring out the window. The first light of dawn was coming, and the mist clearing. The crash and crash of bombs came from the northeast, about five miles away. Two Spitfires flew low over the city and I saw the Indian Air Force roundels on their sides.

I switched on the bedside radio and began to pull on the first clothes that came to hand – the shirt and dinner jacket I had worn last night. The radio was in the middle of an announcement, but it had nothing to do with the air raid. It was the Nawab's own voice, speaking in his classical Urdu. He repeated his announcement: 'We, Mohammed Akbar Bokhari, Nawab of Chambal, being independent of all earthly powers, by the Grace of God, being encumbered by no treaty or other hindrance, do hereby declare ourselves King of Chambal, to be known from this moment on as His Majesty King Mohammed I. In the name of Allah the compassionate, the merciful! There is no God but God, and Mohammed is the prophet of God.'

Then an announcer said it again, in Hindi, Gurjrati, and English, with a note that the announcement would be repeated throughout the day.

'Good!' I said. 'The old boy's showing his mettle.' That definitely committed us to a break with India, even more perhaps than the air raid, still in progress. For the Nawab there was no turning back now, no chance of accepting a compromise. The proclamation definitely divided us into the sheep and the goats.

The announcer said, 'Attention!' This time it was about the air raid. Indian aircraft, without warning or shadow of justification, were attacking the peaceful inhabitants of Chambal. Naked aggression – resistance to the utmost – keep off the streets – take cover – persons spreading rumours will be shot – victory.

Sumitra had dressed while I did, she also in the unsuitable finery of the evening before. She looked pale and frightened. 'Don't worry,' I said, hugging her. 'They're not attacking the city, and they won't, except perhaps with leaflets. They're making a surprise raid on the airfield – but most of our fighters aren't there ... This is it, at last.'

'I'm not frightened,' she said, 'I'm afraid ...'

'What's the difference?' I began.

Knock knock knock on the door. Who's there? Servant. A man to see you, sahib. He says it is very urgent. What kind of man? A village man. The voice of the fat servant trembled with terror. Well, at least he hadn't run away, yet.

'He says his name is the Marquess.'

The Marquess came in, very tired, but his old eyes gleaming. He said, 'At ten o'clock last night, sahib, while I and another were hiding on the escarpment a little east of Dhain, a man came past, moving hurriedly and secretly. We hit him with our axes and he died. He was carrying this.'

He held out his hand and I took the envelope. It was addressed to Lieutenant General Gokal Singh in English.

'I cannot read English,' the Marquess said, 'but the other with me has worked with the cement factory, and he could. He read it. So I brought it to you.'

He was wearing only a loincloth and the high-backed slippers, his legs grey with the patina of age and the dust of travel.

The letter was from L. P. Roy. The text was short and clear: *My dear General, We agree with your proposal to keep your tanks on the south side of the Sakti Plain. Circumstances where a surrender would be proper will probably occur about 12 noon. If you will place yourself somewhere near the Sakti dak bungalow at that hour, bloodshed can be more rapidly brought to an end. We hope that shooting can be kept to an absolute minimum even before then. Sincerely.*

I folded the letter carefully and put it away in my trouser pocket. The old man had brought it eighty miles, through the night. God knows what feats of persuasion and bribery he had performed to

194

get here, probably on returning supply trucks from Gokal's corps.

'All right,' I said slowly. 'Wait down in the servants' quarters. Tell them from me to give you food and drink. Be quick.'

He said, 'I must get back, sahib. There is fighting.'

I wheeled round, 'Fighting? Where? When?'

He said, 'The news has not reached you?... At midnight Indian soldiers left the gorge below Lapri on the north side and began to move west. They crossed the border there, and our men from Gidha ambushed some, killing two. I heard a machine gun just after we killed the messenger. The news of the Indian advance reached the post at Sakti, I know.'

I said, 'Eat fast, then, I shall take you back with me.'

He made a perfunctory salaam and left the room. Sumitra and I were alone, the sound of aircraft faint and far now. The click of the closing latch was like a trigger to my mind.

I said to Sumitra, 'What are you afraid of?'

She stood taller, her back straightening and her head coming up.

'Tell me,' I repeated, 'what are you afraid of?'

A hundred incidents dropped into their proper slots, like the latch, click click click, so fast that there was no sense of progression, rather of a whole pattern falling into place at once. There had been hints, careless words, inexplicable actions. She had not been careful, rather the opposite. Love is blind. Whom the gods wish to destroy they first make mad. There are a dozen proverbs to meet the case.

'You know,' she said.

Yes, I knew.

Once, wounded by bullets, I saw my blood flowing out of me on to the ground, staining it a dark red, and knew that at an uncertain moment the continuing outpour of blood would relieve me of consciousness, which I would welcome because my wounds then hurt severely. While I lay temporarily bereft of awareness and pain the blood would still flow out on to the ground, and after another time I would be relieved of life, and neither awareness nor pain would ever come back.

So it was now with the spirit, the soul, the whatever one calls it, however one defines it, which makes us human. That spirit, which had overflowed in love a few hours earlier, now flowed out of me on to the carpet, staining the whole world a pale grey. This time there could be no doctor, no comrade, no shell dressing to stanch the flow. The sharer and giver of love stood opposite me, the knife still in her hand. She did right to be afraid, but perhaps she did not then realise just why. It was not love for her that was draining out of me, it was my capacity for any love.

She broke down first, and flung herself to the carpet, clasping me round the knees. 'Rodney, my darling, I tried to show you, to let you know, so that you could send me away, at least protect yourself. I do believe in the new India. I know Chambal cannot survive alone, I know it cannot achieve what you believe in, because the Nawab, these men here, don't want it to! Your ideals are not theirs – but that doesn't matter. It's all over, and we can go now. I'll go anywhere with you, do anything for you. I can protect you against Roy, anyone. I have the Prime Minister's own word.'

It was she who had betrayed Gulu and the Gonds of Bhilghat, and allowed the blame to fall on Margaret Wood. She who had kept Gokal in touch with Roy. She who had caused Indian agents, their names given to her by Roy, to be thrown into jail, so that her own loyalty should be above suspicion. She . . . the list was too long. I felt strong, strong enough to strangle her with one hand. The flowing wound still hurt, but already I could feel the waning capacity for feeling. Unconsciousness, sleep of the spirit, would come soon, and then, while it slept, its death. Cauterisation might help. I must get to the fight, at once.

I said 'I am going to keep my promises. Remember, sometimes, what might have come to us if you had kept yours. When they bow down and worship you, the heroine, the lady minister, the ambassador – remember. When you are lonely and alone – remember.'

'Rodney!' she cried. 'I have a car ready. We can go, we can hide in any one of a dozen places and they'll never find us. The Indian Army will be here tomorrow. Then you'll know how hopeless it all was from the beginning, how everybody here tricked you and used you and betrayed you, far worse than I have.'

I said, 'I don't want to know and, with luck, I shall not.'

She clung harder to me. Without deliberate effort, I threw her across the room. She crashed against the wall, fell to the floor by the window, and lay there, pulling herself up on her arms, weeping, her hair in the disarray of the night, after love.

I strapped on my automatic and its belt, went out, locked the door behind me, and called the servant. I told him the Rani was under arrest, on the King's order, and was on no account to be let out, or allowed to pass any messages to anyone. I telephoned Hayden, and after a delay got through, and told him. I tried to ring the commander-in-chief, but was told he had left the house in his car, with an aide-de-camp, a groom, and his charger in the horsebox.

I found the Marquess eating cold chicken, left over from our dinner last night, watched by no one. Most of the servants were out on the lawn, staring at the sky. Some held leaflets in their hands. I took one and saw that it was an official notification from the Government of India, in three languages. In response to public demand, in answer to intolerable provocation, and to end the misrule of the Nawab the Government of India was temporarily taking over the administration of the State. Everyone was to keep calm, stay at home, and take no part in any fighting which the foolish Nawab and his wicked advisers might cause.

The Bentley's tank was full. I backed her out of the garage at high speed, pulled her round, and waiting only for the Marquess to clamber in beside me, rammed her out into the road. It was about eight o'clock. I gunned her along the boulevard round the lake as fast as the cold engine would take. Beside me the grim, fearless old man shook with terror. I patted him on the bare knee and shouted, 'Relax, father! If death comes to us today, it won't be in this machine.' He closed his eyes and held on tight.

There were no police about, and very few people, just one or two huddled inside doorways, staring upwards or reading the leaflets. I went through the winding streets of the city more carefully, and at the far end passed through the Bhowani Gate and out into the open country.

I pressed the accelerator against the floor boards and snugged down in the bucket seat, ready to drive as I'd never done. I saw a khaki staff car racing towards me under a cloud of dust. I recognised it as the air marshal's, just in time, skidded to a stop across the road and jumped out. I ran to his car, saluted (though hatless—a serious military crime) and said, 'What's happened, sir?'

'Lost three on the ground,' he said. 'Shot down one, chased the rest back. What's happening at Sakti?'

'I don't know,' I said, 'but Gokal's in Indian pay.'

He swore. 'That explains ... He's just sent me a message – nothing to report. We have another raid reported coming in from the north and I've sent one squadron off to intercept it.'

I had been calculating and interpreting ever since the old guerrilla gave me the time and place of the earliest clashes. 'I'm going to Sakti, sir,' I said. 'I don't think anything serious can happen until near noon, perhaps eleven. Then we'll need every plane you can put over.'

'All right,' he said, 'I'll do my best ... but the Nawab – the King – just called, ordering me to send *all* my planes north. I'm going in to protest.'

I saluted, got the Bentley out of the way, and we passed. I rammed my foot down, jammed the gears through the box without using the clutch. We had foreseen all this – the Indian feint attacks by land and air to draw our air force away from Sakti. Was the King trying to cut his own throat now? No, probably some bloody tinpot rajahling up north had telephoned that he'd go over to the Indians unless he was protected. Nothing more I could do about it.

The yellow sun climbed straight ahead over the hills. The air rushed past cool and solid, the tyres whined and even that old slow-breathing monster of an engine began to roar. After a minute the blower cut in and we went east behind a banshee shriek that sent chickens and children diving into the ditch and bullocks lumbering away across the fields. We left the Chambalpur plain, and the white stones marking the edges of the road flashed by. Bridges passed, the exhaust wavering against the pillars like running a stick along a railing ... A dak bungalow, white under a red roof, set back in a clearing, whitewashed stones leading to the round arches of the veranda, two men staring at us. I could observe, but not feel. Past, present, and future blended, the material and the immaterial, as in the dawn.

That was the bungalow in the Dun where at dusk I brought back a thirty-pound mahseer after a four-hour fight, knee-deep in the river. Twelve years ago? Ten? I remembered utter exhaustion, and exhilaration, but could feel neither.

198

One, two, five, six, fifteen bullock carts in file, steep hill, swinging down in the whining shriek of the tyres, past, behind. Army trucks, soldiers standing up in the back, staring up at the sky, blare of the old klaxon, past, behind. Tank transporter broken down, overturned, the tank upside down lower on the hill, men squatting round it, smoking, past. Another plain, open her full out again, and again the rising whine of the supercharger. Maize in the fields, women at the well, men with sickles, infantry marching in the slow dust column that infantry carry with them always, like the packs on their backs.

These are the fields, five hundred miles away, I marched through with the two stars of a lieutenant on my shoulders and not a care in the world, a field company of purple-black Madrasi sappers and miners in front of me. They couldn't speak a word of Hindustani, only Tamil and English, and I had to translate their occasional shouted comments to the pert girl children running and leaping beside them, pointing at their black faces. Tall stovepipe khaki hats and names like Coomaramangaladamaswami that made them all address each other by their numbers, very polite, 'Please,'498, adjust my left packstrap, for it is aching into my back.'

Rise of trees and jungle and the sun hot as fire against my eyeballs. Hills and rocks and the whitewashed stones again, dulled under dust, more soldiers, a long reach of scrub and a deer transfixed beside the road, monkeys crashing away in yellow green of the bushes. Down and around, this was the last hill line, the last gap, the plain of Sakti beginning to spread out, seen small, gradually larger through the trees as the road swung, tilting, fading, foreshortening as we reached the foot of the slope. Open land, rocks, almost desert, soldiers waiting in a dry nullah.

Dogras they'd been, a platoon of them under a jemadar, as soft spoken as the Madrasis, but high-caste pale-skinned Hindus, always decorous and well-mannered, escorting fifteen Mahsud prisoners back to the Political Officer after a North-West Frontier fight. Hardly prisoners, just men found wandering about the hills in their baggy cotton, with or without rifles, unable to account for themselves. I rode past with the Dogra colonel, him nearest the prisoners in the narrow nullah. One of them sprang out of the ruck and up at him, dragged him off his horse, a knife flashed, Colonel Dougherty struggling and kicking, both of them practically under the horse.

The nearest Dogra ran his bayonet through the Mahsud. Then no one gave an order, and I was bending over the colonel, pulling him to his feet and holding both horses' bridles with the other hand, and hardly realised what was happening until I looked up. By then only two of the prisoners were still alive, and the shy, quiet Dogras were cleaning their bayonets. A sepoy methodically ran the last two through the stomach. Then they set the colonel on his horse, asked politely whether I was sure I had suffered no hurt, and marched on.

Tanks moving, far to the right, the south. If there was firing, I could not have heard it. Many trucks jammed together at the foot of the hill and the empty road running straight as an arrow across the plain, to the clustered houses of Sakti, and, on the near side, by itself, the white dot of the dak bungalow. In the distance the line of hills, and the cleft marking the top of the Lapri Gorge.

Many transporters were parked off the road. I stopped the Bentley and called to a worried-looking major. 'Where's General Gokal Singh?'

He pointed up the road. 'At the Sakti dak bungalow, sir. He's holding an orders conference, I think.'

'Thank you. Have you got a car to spare?'

'For a few minutes, I think,' he said doubtfully.

'This man is the leader of the local guerrillas, and must get as far forward as possible, quickly. Send him up, will you?'

I explained quickly to the Marquess. He clambered out of the Bentley, his legs trembled so much that he nearly fell down. We shook hands.

Then I went on. I stopped the Bentley off the main road, and walked down the driveway, between the inevitable whitewashed stones, towards the dak bungalow. Staff cars and jeeps lined the drive, nearly all flying pennants showing the commands of their owners. A company of infantry was waiting about in the compound, more or less at the alert.

Two sepoys with tommy guns and a *naik* with a pistol stood on sentry at the foot of the veranda steps. The *naik* held up his hand. I said, 'I carry a message from His Majesty to General Gokal Singh. It is most urgent and important. I showed him the intercepted letter, trusting that he could not read English. He saluted and stood aside.

As I walked up the steps I had no idea what I was going to do.

200

But on the top step I distinctly saw the Dogra who had saved Colonel Dougherty's life in 1937, his face unemotional, thrusting his bayonet forward in the long point just as though he were practising it on the drill ground. I quietly pushed open the double doors which, in bungalows like this all over India, lead into a central hall.

I knew exactly where everything would be. Sure enough, the hall was full of officers. Maps, map cases, and map boards covered the table and hung over the backs of chairs. A larger map was tacked to the far wall. General Gokal Singh, his back to me, was saying in Urdu: 'There is no need — ' It was a quarter past nine.

I drew my automatic as I went in, and shot him three times in the back of the head. He jerked, spewed a stream of bright blood across the maps, then lay still, sprawled on the table.

I said, 'He was a traitor. There's the proof.' I flung the letter on the table and swung round. The sentries burst in. They were Muslims. Holding the automatic on the *naik* I said, 'Wait. The Hindu general was betraying us. I act on His Majesty's own orders.'

They hung back, perplexed and doubtful. A brigadier began to read the letter out loud. 'It's true,' he said at the end. He motioned to the sentries and they backed out.

A colonel retched noisily in a corner. The rest, though they may have been listening with some part of their attention while the brigadier read the letter, stared at the mess on the table. Their faces were an unpleasant grey colour under the varying shades of brown, and, if I'd had to do this earlier, say the day before, mine would have been, too. Gokal's head was twisted sideways, revealing that the bullets had come out mushroomed, blowing half his face, one eye and a mess of blood, brains, and mucus on to the table. Sumitra would not have looked different.

I took back the letter and put it into my pocket. I hesitated a moment, and that moment of standing there, staring at them, may have had important effects later. They must have thought I had come out hotfoot, direct from the King, with orders to execute a traitor; and, obviously, to appoint someone in his place. But for a few moments I did not know what to do.

I could take over the corps myself. Then my credentials might be queried, my authority demanded. Being superseded in command was far more serious to most of these clots than losing a war. Certainly there would be frantic jealousy, and the consequences of that might be worse than the normal and to-be-expected incompetence. Some of the men in that room must also be in the plot to sell out to the Indians – but which? At that instant, not knowing who might have talked, or how much, someone was quaking in his boots, someone was wondering how to put me out of the way.

I made up my mind. I must work through the senior officer. I turned to the major-general commanding the infantry division, and — 'Sir, His Majesty charges you with the command, and appoints you to the rank of lieutenant-general . . . May I have a word with you in private?'

The major-general, Sher Khan, called for the sentries to come in. No one spoke while they lifted the corpse and half carried, half dragged it outside. Sher Khan said, 'The rest of you – get the mess cleaned up. Wait here.'

Then he and I went into one of the bedrooms. He bolted the door. 'There must be other traitors. Who are they?' he asked. 'I need to know. Otherwise I may entrust one of them with some vital job.'

He looked haggard and very old, though he was hardly fifty. You're probably on the edge of the plot yourself, I thought. I said, 'His Majesty did not reveal that to me, sir . . . Can you tell me briefly what is happening?'

Sher Khan stared down at the bed, his hands shaking. He pulled himself together with a visible effort and began to talk.

The Indians were advancing on a broad front – up the gorge itself astride the main road, and wide round both north and south flanks. None of the dispositions we had planned had been made. 'Gokal's orders,' he said miserably. 'He said—'

I interrupted him. What Gokal had said or done no longer mattered. He was dead. 'Have you had any identifications of units yet?' I asked.

'Yes,' he said. 'The 1/13th Gurkha Rifles on the north, and the 3/5th Mahratta Light Infantry on the south.'

'In the centre?'

He said, 'Tanks of the Central India Horse, and infantry – 2/18th Royal Garhwal Rifles . . . They're going to have us surrounded if we don't pull back.'

I said, 'All those are in different brigades. My God, it can't be possible!'

Max and I, both commanding battalions, served in Burma together under a flatulent genius who had read too much American Civil War history and had a cold contempt for men whose skins weren't white. Inspired by this combination, he had launched us not once, nor twice, but three times, on grandiose double encirclements, like a boxer trying to hit his enemy on both ears at the same time. Needless to say, the despised yellowbellies had counterpunched straight back down the middle, smashed the pivot, overrun guns and headquarters, and left Max and me to get our battalions back as best we could, without ammunition, food, or medical help. It seemed incredible that Max was doing the same now. If all three of his brigades, and the armour, were in the line he had no reserve to speak of.

We sent for the intelligence officer and he gave us more identifications, more reports from spies and guerrillas. There could be no doubt about it. Max was committing a cardinal sin.

I talked rapidly to Sher Khan. A great victory lay to hand. His eyes began to gleam. Every soldier dreams of the laurels, of the people in the street saying, 'That's him, the man who won the Famous Victoree.' Sher Khan may have been on the edge of treason and he was not the most intelligent man in the world, but he could see this clearly enough. There were some technical points to be agreed, where to put the anti-tank guns, and when and where to commit the tanks – but the outline was plain enough. 'It only needs energy and decision, sir,' I said, 'and the will to fight.'

He was eager to go, then. 'One moment, sir,' I said, 'I have another message for the officers, from His Majesty.'

The grey look returned to his face, but he nodded and we went through to the hall. The murmur of nervous conversation ceased. I stood there, suddenly aware of my dinner jacket. I took it off, for the day had become warm now. The white shirt and black bow tie did not seem so odd. I gathered their eyes to me. I began.

'Gentlemen, officers of His Majesty ... General Sher Khan sees the prospect of a great victory before us. In a moment he will give us his orders to bring it about ... We have only to do our duty. His Majesty reminds you that you are fighting for the honour of your names as well as his. He repeats that we are fighting for our future as free men, for the right to rule ourselves in our own way, and not by the dictate of *babus* in Delhi. If we fail in our duty none of us will ever be able to stand straight and look another man in the eye. *We have eaten His Majesty's salt.*'

I watched them as I spoke. Some kept their eyes downcast and did not look at me. In others, a spark of spirit began to glow. I am no Churchill and there was little emotion in my words, for I could find none. But there was agate hardness, and ruthless determination.

I ended: 'I have one final message from His Majesty ...' I looked slowly round the room, trying not to load my glance too heavily with menace; I didn't want to *drive* anyone to desperation. 'It is this. His Majesty knows that this treason was not confined to General Gokal Singh alone. The action he will later take depends not on words or thoughts but on deeds – on what is done today.'

I saluted Sher Khan, left the room, and sat down exhausted on the veranda steps. Gokal Singh's body lay on the grass, covered by a blanket. No one went near it.

And the will to fight. Those were the key words. I knew why Max was coming on like an amateur. I had seen that formation many times before – in the military history books, in the diagrams showing the methods used in our old battles against petty rajahs, nizams, amirs, shahs, and mandarins, from Suez to Peking. I could quote the text, written about 1870: 'Against an Oriental opponent, too much manoeuvring is a waste of time and can lead to disorganisation. It is usually best to go straight for him, confident that a determined assault, pressed home, will cause his febrile enthusiasm, unbacked by discipline, to evaporate. A few scattered groups, led by individual brave men, may fight with desperation, and cause considerable damage, while the rest flee, but even this serves in the end only to destroy the enemy's leadership and break his cohesion ...'

Max was treating us just as the old Indian Army had treated his ancestors. For 'Oriental' substitute 'old-fashioned', 'non-progressive', 'reactionary', or any of the other labels the Indian radio had been tying on to us for the past six months, and you had Max's tactical doctrine.

I got up, went back into the hall, and listened to the last part of Sher Khan's orders. The colonels and brigadiers hurried off. I checked with Sher Khan to make sure I knew what was planned. Then I got into the Bentley. Now my real job began – to force the commanders to fight.

I drove south across the plain, on rutted cart tracks, found a brigadier, and listened while he gave his orders. I went up to the battalion in contact and heard the sharpening of the fire, so much so that the Indian artillery, which had been very quiet, opened fire. But our men held them. Returning to brigade headquarters I saw another battalion marching off post-haste to enter the general reserve for the great blow.

At twelve I ran back to the Bentley and drove to the main road. Max was getting annoyed, and now his medium artillery began to fire. The heavy shells whined overhead with an angry roar, and burst far back where the road came out on to the plain, where the transporters were parked. Other guns began to fire on the Sakti dak bungalow, since the heavier fighting had now made it obvious that there would be no rendezvous with Gokal Singh, no agreed surrender there. I found our tanks, concealed in scrub jungle, the men resting, the junior commanders studying their maps.

At two I went forward to the leading battalion on the main road, near the entrance to the Lapri Gorge. Here the shelling was heavy and the raw troops looked nervous as men were hit and trenches destroyed. The brigadier came round with me and I thought his men would hold long enough. They were due to pull back in half an hour. Behind them engineers worked with frantic haste to lay a minefield, on to which we would draw Max's armour when this lot retreated. I visited the anti-tank guns, which were concealed as carefully as possible – not very well, but one or two of our own fighters were always in the air, and the Indians had not attempted to come over.

Going back, on my circuitous way to the northern flank, I found the commander-in-chief's Rolls parked in a grove beside a small stream that crossed the road there. The old Prince, dressed in a magnificent Mogul costume of green and gold silk, was eating lunch off silver plates laid round him on the grass. His chauffeur was preparing a hookah, and the groom was currycombing the grey charger tethered to a tree.

He invited me cordially to share his lunch with him, but I refused. He had no idea what the battle plan was and begged me not to tell him. He was sure it was good, but much too complicated for him to understand. One of the young colonels would come to him when the climactic moment was at hand. He looked very calm and sure, and before I left I knelt quickly before him, and placed my hands between his. He squeezed them and said, 'God be with you, Savage. You are a good man, a real sahib.'

Over to the north flank: the same situation as on the south – one of our battalions holding two or three of theirs, the rest gone into the central reserve. I drove back to the main road, begged food off the headquarters of a regiment of field artillery, and ate it quickly.

Crash! On the stroke of four o'clock Max's artillery opened up all along the front. He had stopped fooling, and begun his attack. Calls for defensive fire began to increase until they came in like a flood. From them, and the occasional situation reports, I could tell what was happening. On the south our men were pulling back, drawing the enemy farther along the slope. Over there I saw shells bursting in the distance, and clouds of dust rising on the ridge. To the north the same, but our men were retreating faster than they should. In the middle, reports of enemy tanks advancing under heavy covering fire. Our anti-tank guns in action. Two Indian tanks on fire, three . . .

Now was the moment. We had them trapped, just as we had planned – half his tanks on the plain, half in the gorge, and no reserve to counter ours. A heavy attack by our fighter bombers had been called for. The anti-tank guns and forward infantry only had to stand firm for half an hour behind the minefield while our own tanks moved up, with the reserve . . . They were on the way now.

The artillery colonel turned to me, his face anxious. 'The planes aren't coming.'

'Why?' I said.

'No reason given.'

Who'd ordered that, I raged. But perhaps it wasn't an order. Perhaps the Indians had raided the fields. Perhaps . . .

'Call for SOS fire on A.36,' the gunner colonel said. I looked at his map. SOS A.36 was right in the middle of one of our forward positions. 'They've vacated it,' the gunner said.

SOS on B.7, also in the centre, also where the men were supposed to be standing fast. The line was crumbling at the one point where it *had* to stand firm. Who was giving these orders?

206

Where was the treachery now? The automatic itched against my side.

'Our tanks ceased their advance. Halted at 403621. That's a mile over there, on the north.'

Prince Afif rode by alone, on his charger, his scimitar on his shoulder. I jumped into the Bentley and tore up the road. Smoke and dust and bitter explosive fumes from bursting shells lashed at me. If I could reach the armour – if I could get to them, shoot the man who had ordered the halt, take command myself, find the young major, someone, anyone who had a fire in his belly . . . I rammed the Bentley along a cart track, turned right, raced it across country.

I knew what had happened: Max was right, the old textbooks were right – that was all. But there was still a chance. If I could just get to the armoured brigade . . . surely someone would stand fast over there, in the centre, when they saw their old Prince riding forward alone? Surely, just for a few minutes . . . ?

The rock outcrops concealed a sunken road. I bounced into it and turned left. The sound of aircraft distracted my attention and, looking up, I saw Indian Spitfires overhead. When I lowered my eyes I found myself motoring at fifty miles an hour straight at the dark-green hulk of a tank – a Sherman tank of the Indian Army. I stood on the brakes, and dived out while the Bentley was still moving. I heard the roar of the tank's '75, and felt the blast of the explosion as the shell ripped into the Bentley's engine. She exploded in flames but by then I was out of the sunken road and running across bare ground. There were other tanks behind the first and their co-axial Brownings tore the air into noisy strips about my ears. I saw a sort of depression near a low bush, and as I dived for it a mad mule kicked me in the back and hurled me into it.

I felt no pain then, only suffocation, and my breath trying to come in heavy groans. My shirt was getting wet.

Three or four co-axes were tearing up the earth by my head, like pneumatic drills, deafening me. They stopped, and a colossal explosion showered me with dirt. That was a turret gun again. One more of those would blast me to pieces. I staggered to my feet, wondering whether they'd bother to stop firing, whether they could. Someone might have his finger on the trigger as I rose.

I stood there a long time, one hand on my belly, blood pouring out over my fingers, hurting badly now, seeing nothing in the low glare of the sun. I thought I was in water, and swimming. Everything was silent. The tank engines must have been running but I didn't hear them. One of the tanks glided close to me and I tried to focus. Someone was leaning out of the turret.

'*Salaam*, sahib,' a familiar voice said. '*Ap kaise hain?*'

My head cleared with miraculous suddenness. The pain grew steadily worse, but I could see and understand very clearly. It was Rissaldar Rikirao Purohit, of the Bombay Lancers. I knew him well, because we had fought in Burma together. Also because he had shown me his family's most treasured possession, a faded letter commending Daffadar Rikirao Purohit of the Bombay Lancers for good work against a Thug gang. The letter was dated March 27, 1826, and signed by William Savage. His great-great-grandfather, and mine.

'*Salaam, rissaldar* sahib,' I said. '*Ap kaise hain?*'

One must observe the decencies. The rissaldar-sahib had asked me how I was, I had asked him how he was. Next must come a formal invitation to be seated, to have a cigarette.

'*Tashrif rakhiye*,' I said. '*Sigrit pijiye.*'

He said, 'Thank you, sahib. I regret I have to be going.' He ducked down inside the turret. On the sunken road the Bentley burned with an orange flame and dense black smoke. The man leaning out of the next tank I had also known in Burma and I saw that he was now a *daffadar*. I congratulated him on his promotion. 'Thank you, sahib,' he said, smiling from ear to ear.

Rikirao's head popped back up out of the turret. 'We have been ordered to stay where we are,' he said. 'There is perhaps a cease-fire. I think the enemy have surrendered.'

Agile as a cat he climbed out of the turret and ran to me. 'Your wound, sahib,' he said, 'it is serious. Does it hurt badly?'

'Only when I laugh, *rissaldar* sahib,' I said, and fainted.

When I came round I was sitting up beside the main road. I don't know how I got there. Rikirao was supporting me in his arms, my shirt was raised, and there were a couple of shell dressings over my wound. My nostrils reeked of iodine and it hurt worse than ever. My *daffadar* friend jabbed a needle into my arm. A group of soldiers were brewing up tea in a desert cooker – an old kerosene oil can filled with earth and soused with gasoline. A few minutes later a young *sowar* brought me tea in a mess-tin, but Rikirao said sharply, 'Not with a belly wound, O outwitted yokel. Are you trying to kill the sahib?'

Dimly I heard other voices. A staff car had stopped on the road. Max and L. P. Roy were walking towards me. Everyone saluted, and I managed to raise my hand to my forehead.

Max dropped to one knee. 'Rodney, are you all right?'

'My pistol went off by accident,' I said, 'while I was cleaning it.'

A high proportion of belly wounds are fatal. Internal bleeding would show its effect soon enough and then I'd go out. I didn't care.

Roy's voice said, 'Colonel Savage!'

'O-B-E-M-C,' I mumbled.

It was getting hard to talk straight, the morphia taking effect but the wound still raging, but one has to keep the natives in their place.

'Armed, in action, wearing civilian clothes,' Roy said. 'I warned you.'

'General Gokal ... invitation to breakfast,' I got out. 'Said, come as you are.'

'And we have half a dozen witnesses to prove that you murdered General Gokal Singh!' Roy shouted. He was furious again.

Max interrupted roughly. 'That can be settled later, sahib.' He rattled off orders: 'Get up the jeep ambulance. Take him direct to the C.C.S. You, go with him.'

Roy said, 'I shall hold you personally responsible for his safe custody, General.'

Rikirao said, 'I'll take him back myself, sahib.'

'Only when I laugh,' I mumbled, seeing no one any more, trying to shout it against the encroaching darkness. 'Only when I laugh ... only when ...' I lost consciousness, my last thought being a certain knowledge that whether this dark slope led immediately to death or not I would never laugh again.

Chapter 15

Major-general Ran Singh Dadhwal, comfortably settled in the canvas chair in his office tent, slowly filled his pipe. Through the open end of the tent he looked out over the plain of Sakti, dull in the twilight. The single bulb, hanging from the ridgepole by its cord, came on, gave out a wavering light, and faded. The general frowned, listening with half an ear for the kick and throb of the generator to start again. When it did, he noted that the current was still unsteady. He took a notebook from his pocket and wrote briefly.

A chill wind blew round the group of headquarters tents and trucks scattered among the trees at the eastern edge of the plain. The sun had just set and an even violet light spread across the sky. A burned-out tank stood like a ruined monument in the plain, about a mile away. Farther off, the village of Sakti lay under the blue haze of its cooking fires. It was the third day after the battle.

The general finished filling his pipe and methodically found his matches. He kept them always in his right-hand tunic pocket. He lit one and held it over the bowl. With the second match the pipe began to draw well. The general blew out each match in turn, held it until he could break it, then dropped the halves into the ash tray on the table beside him. The second time, he noticed a small hole in the green baize laid over the table. He pulled out his notebook and wrote: *Camp Comdt, hole in my baize*.

Behind him, on another table in the far corner of the tent, flowers and offerings of *gur* lay at the feet of a small statue of the monkey-god Hanuman, his own personal avatar. Beside the statue, on one side, stood portraits of Mahatma Gandhi and Jawaharlal Nehru; on the other a portable bookcase, containing the *Mahabharta*, *King's Regulations*, the *Ramayana*, the *Indian*

210

Army List, the *Bhagavad Gita*, the *Life of Robert Clive*, *Memoirs of the Emperor Baber*, and Wavell on *Leadership*.

The general heard a discreet cough outside the tent and saw the tips of a pair of brown shoes. A voice said, 'Sir ... it is Major Gupta. You sent for me?'

'Yes. Come in.'

A small dark fat man sidled apologetically in, saluted, and stood at attention just inside the tent flap. The general said, 'I wanted to ask how your patient is ... Colonel Savage.'

The fat major said, 'The A.D.M.S. saw him again this afternoon, sir. Of course we cannot be sure, but bullet seems to have made clean passage without puncturing intestine or wital organs. He has been suffering from obvious shock, but owing to good general condition he is making rapid recovery from that. He is somewhat weak, naturally. Temperature 101.1, pulse 95, poor wolume, and increased rate of breathing. Unless A.D.M.S. diagnosis is wrong though, and it is confirmed by X-rays, he should recower after suitable period in base hospital.'

'Is he ready to be moved?'

The major said, 'If moved carefully, yes. He has excellent powers of resistance ... I found him out of bed just now, sir, standing by exit. When I insisted he must get back he said he was looking for nurses' quarters. He needed a woman and told me to send him a nurse at once.'

'And doubtless you told him sexual intercourse was contra-indicated until his wound had healed properly?'

'Yes, sir. Of course! I explained the effect on the walls of the stomach tissue and the drawing away of blood, the general strain on muscle. Besides, I said his request was impossible, as there are no nurses with a field ambulance. Besides ...'

'It's against Army Instructions, India, to have sexual intercourse with nurses.'

'Precisely, sir. Also ...'

'Also, it is not a nice thing to suggest, being insulting to Indian womanhood. No, for God's sake, don't agree with me ... I want to talk to him. He has important information I need. Could you bring him here?'

The major said doubtfully, 'I think so, sir. Of course, in absence of military necessity, on medical grounds alone, it is not to be recommended, but . . .'

'Bring him now. Wait – I suppose he has no clothes?'

'No, sir. What he was wearing was evening dress, mufti, without coat, and in wery poor condition, quite u/s. I have made out destruction certificate . . .'

'I'm sure. Give him these. I think they're about the right size.' He got up and handed the doctor a small roll done up in a faded blue *durrie*.

'Yes, sir. Thank you, sir.' The major saluted and backed away.

The general sat down again. Bloody silly little man. With a fellow like that in charge, perhaps it wasn't really necessary to make any special arrangements. Rodney was more than capable of dealing with him. But at any moment they'd send him back to the main military hospital in Bhowani, and that would be different.

Why did so many of the new generation take themselves so seriously? It wasn't like that in the old days. Look at Brigadier Moti Yasurvedan, Moti the Menace, with his monocle and his hackin' jacket down to his knees, motoring off to take over the pacification of Chambalpur. Moti's command car was always followed, at a respectful distance, by a three-ton truck with armchairs, sofas, silver, linen, a small four-poster bed, and a portable bar. Moti, when on outpost duty on the Frontier just before the war, had left his squadron to his *rissaldar*, with a thousand copies of his signature, and flown to Paris. And would have got away with it if he hadn't run into his colonel in Maxim's . . .

The general chuckled and wondered how much longer the teams playing cricket on the plain could continue in the rapidly failing light. With the pitch as rough as an obstacle course, they must have been playing by radar even half an hour ago.

A steady crunching of boots on the dry leaves made him turn his head to the left. He saw his A.D.C. striding through the trees, shotgun on shoulder and English pointer quietly at heel. He called out, 'Any luck, Chop?'

'Not a bloody thing, sir. The birds must have been frightened by the noise the other day. They've probably reached Cape Comorin by now.'

The young captain disappeared. The general relit his pipe. There

212

were good ones in the younger crowd. And certainly the British had plenty of bad ones. All the same, there was a loneliness . . . it took a lot of effort to combat it. He missed them – even Talbot, even Byrne, whom he'd fought to earn his nickname. What a narrow-minded blighter Byrne was – wonder what he's doing now? Never got very far, retired as a lieutenant-colonel right after the war, probably pig farming in Essex. He was a blighter, all right. But no one ever had to tell him when to blow his nose, what attitude to adopt. He made up his own mind, and never asked anyone's permission. No one had to give him lectures about *esprit de corps* or work to convince him that he was the best in the world. He knew it.

That was it – confidence. Very unpleasant when it led to kicking Indians out of first-class compartments and yelling about Wog music, but, oddly enough, it hadn't cut them off as much as you'd expect. They never shouted at *sowar* or sepoy. Their manners to the V.C.O.s were wonderful. Say a word against Dogra or Mahratta or Garhwali – whichever *they* happened to be serving with – and it was worse than imputing sodomy to the King. Their viceroys lived and moved like monarchs – wasn't it Edward P. who said he never really knew how royalty lived until he stayed at Viceregal Lodge? – but the rest didn't give a damn for the Viceroy, and not much more for the commander-in-chief. Ride hard, play hard, don't ask questions, never doubt yourself or your regiment . . . The gap they created was between themselves and the Indian upper-middle class – his own. He'd never seen an Englishman until he left the little village where his father owned land to go to school. Now they'd gone – and everything about him breathed of them, and again the laurels of victory crowned the Colours they had devised and set up as symbols, and now given into his hands.

He went out and beckoned to the Sikh military policeman sitting on a bench ten yards away. The Sikh leaped to attention, saluted, and ran up. The general said, 'Have the *jawans* eaten?'

'Not yet, sahib. We are eating by turns.'

'The war is over. You can all eat together tonight. Go now, and get your tot of rum. You needn't come back until ten. Enjoy yourselves. *Sat sri akkal!*'

'*Sat sri akkal!*' the soldier replied, saluting with a broad smile.

The general looked at his jeep, parked behind his tent, and called, 'Harnam Singh!'

Another Sikh popped out from inside the guard tent. 'You, too. Off you go.'

When the driver had followed the military policeman, the general took his red divisional flag off the jeep's fender, rolled it into its khaki cloth cover, and carried it back into the tent.

Another jeep puttered up. Major Gupta and a medical orderly helped Rodney down from the seat beside the driver. Rodney came forward, leaning heavily against the doctor. Max noticed that the khaki sweater, green trousers, and woollen shirt he had sent fitted him perfectly. About the boots he couldn't be sure, but they looked all right. He saw by a bulge at Rodney's pocket that he had the beret tucked away there. That was important. The M.P.s were demons on correct dress – as he'd insisted they should be.

The general pulled forward another canvas-seated chair and Rodney lowered himself into it. The general said, 'All right, Gupta. You can go now. I'll call you when I'm finished . . . Are you comfortable, Rodney?'

'Yes, thanks.'

'Excuse me a moment.' He picked up the field telephone on the table and said, 'C.I.E.M.E., please . . . Divisional commander. Are you ready to talk about the tank recovery state yet? . . . Good. No, give me a ring here in . . . twenty minutes.'

He put down the handset and smiled at his friend. 'Sorry, I don't have any of your awful cheroots. How are you, really?'

'Not bad. A little weak, but not as weak as Gupta thinks . . . That field ambulance is a bit of a mess, Max. Anwar's a good doctor and so's Gupta, but they've got no idea of administration. The orderlies play cards all day, the jerries aren't emptied, they keep running out of rations . . .'

Max said, 'I've had my eye on it for some time. Thanks . . . Rodney, I don't want to be melodramatic, but you're in danger. Roy got a dispatch out – I had to end military censorship as soon as they surrendered – and now the press and the government know all about you. Did you have to shoot Gokal?'

Rodney said, 'Either that or lie down. I told you I'd fight, one day.'

214

'I didn't like him myself . . . You can go home without feeling you've failed, Rodney. I was thinking, before you came – so much that I see and touch and feel is yours. You're leaving something pretty good, at least I think so, and a few hundred thousand others like me. And you're taking a lot with you, too. You can't leave your memories behind.'

Rodney held out his hands slowly. 'Empty-handed,' he said quietly. 'Beaten . . . How did the 1/13th do?'

'Very well. Forty casualties. I don't suppose they'd have had any, except for you.'

'One does what one has to.'

The general sighed. 'I know . . . Look, there's no time to waste. In a day or two, even by tomorrow perhaps, you will be on your way, put into the machine. To the C.I.M.H. in Bhowani. Then – to Delhi jail, I suppose. Is there anyone you want me to tell? Your father . . .' As soon as he had said the words he remembered, but it was too late.

Rodney said, 'My father is dead. He was killed during Partition, on a very appropriate date as a matter of fact – August 14, 1947, the day before Independence.'

Max said, 'I'm sorry.'

Rodney was looking down at the table. 'I should have been up there with him, with Pete Rees on the Boundary Force. I wasn't. I was in Bombay, seeing about getting a job with McFadden Pulley. Perhaps I would have been killed up there, too. And then we would have all come to an end tidily, no loose ends, exactly on Glamorous Dickie's schedule . . . It's rather wonderful to think of Attlee and the Admiral, with about three months' knowledge of India between them, breaking up in half a year what it took us two centuries to build. Not only that, but getting the whole damned lot loaded on to ships, pushed under the carpet, or at least disposed of somehow. Only they moved too fast for me. I got left over, me and five hundred rajahs. They, poor simple-minded saps, went round waving the treaties in which the Noble British Government guaranteed them their independence. They actually thought the Honest British Sailor would concern himself to see that those silly scraps of paper were honoured. I didn't *have* a piece of paper . . . You had no business to accept the partition of India, Max. No business to ride over the princes like

215

a gang of Nazis. You only had to wait a few years, and do it honourably, even if it meant having us around that much longer. Twenty years from now this won't be the army you knew – you're brutalising yourselves, and India.'

Max said, 'I don't know . . . I feel a bit dirty, in a way . . . But we'd waited a long time already. Time seems different from inside a jail, even though you think the jailer has tremendous qualities. And I suppose there comes a time when you have to tear down something, so that you can start to rebuild. The princes really were out of date, a sort of political slum, somebody called them . . . Janaki's in Bhowani, at Flagstaff House. There's no sentry at the back where that lane runs along the garden hedge.'

The telephone rang. 'Divisional commander . . . Yes, it is urgent, as a matter of fact, and I want to see that damaged gun for myself. I'll be right over.'

He stood up, and picked up his red-banded hat. 'I have to go to the C.I.E.M.E. I'll be back in half an hour.'

Rodney said, 'All right. By the way, you'll find three men of Pattan in the Chambalpur dungeons. Their names are Chadi, Mitoo, and Ganesha. They probably ought to get a medal. Better still, give them some cash from the imprest before you have to go back to peace accounting.'

The general made a note in his little pad. 'Thanks,' he said. 'I'm glad about them. Roy had an idea that we might be able to add them to the charges against you, if we searched hard enough in the jungles.' He went out, glancing back once. His friend was sitting with his head in his hands, staring down at the table. He looked ill and tired and bitter. The general turned back, and said in a low voice, 'For God's sake, Rodney, no more violence.'

The man at the table nodded without looking up. The general went out and walked quickly and quietly through the trees towards a cluster of lights a hundred yards away to the east.

He had hardly reached it, greeted the waiting colonel, sat down inside a tent similar to his own, and begun to examine the chart spread out before him, when the telephone rang. The colonel picked it up.

'C.I.E.M.E. . . . Yes, he's here, sir.' He turned to the general. 'It's L. P. Roy, sir. He's on his way through from Chambalpur and wants to speak to you. He's in your tent.'

The general swore silently. 'Tell him I'll be right over,' he said. 'This will have to wait.'

He walked slowly back to his headquarters. His jeep was still standing behind his tent. A government car with a civilian driver sitting behind the wheel was parked close by. Sheer, rotten luck! Rodney had looked fit enough to drive eighty miles, and, dressed as a sepoy, with his command of Hindi and no M.P. likely to stop him, he ought to have got through to Bhowani without trouble in a couple of hours. Trying to escape on foot, though, in his state . . .

L. P. Roy was seated in his chair and the general felt a small stir of resentment. Why did the damned man have to keep emphasising his superiority over the military? They'd done what they were told, hadn't they?

Roy spoke in English. 'Good evening, General. All is quite well in Chambalpur. We have installed Dunawal as temporary chief minister, and he hopes to form a provisional government by to-morrow. I am on the way back to Delhi to report to the Prime Minister. I am going to catch the night train at Bhowani. I would be glad if you could give me something to eat.'

'Delighted.'

'Thank you. While we are waiting, I would like to see the prisoner, Savage.'

'All right,' the general said. 'Would you care for a drink?'

Roy waved his arm. 'I do not drink, as I think you know, General. In fact, I recall advising you that the alcohol habit was un-Indian and a relic of British imperialism.' He stood up. 'Let us go and see the prisoner now.' He looked fanatical and bitter – as bitter as Rodney, Max thought. What did *he* have to be bitter about? He wished he had the Prime Minister to talk to, to explain to, instead of this hot-tempered, bigoted politician. Nehru had his faults, but ungenerosity was not one of them – and he was a gentleman.

He thought slowly, now what's the best way of holding Roy off for a little? He had promised Rodney half an hour. So far only twenty minutes had passed. Of course, Rodney wouldn't need the time so much, going on foot. He could be anywhere, whereas in the jeep he could only be up or down the road.

'Let us go,' Mr Roy repeated impatiently. His white Gandhi cap sat straight on top of his thick hair, and his dhoti was spotlessly white.

'Sir ... General Dadhwal ...' The fat doctor peered into the tent, saluting. 'Sir, it is my medical duty to adwise you that the patient should return to the hospital now. He has been here nearly forty-five minutes, and that ...' He peered round the tent. His face took on a comical expression of surprise, then fear.

Max thought of saying he'd sent Rodney back to the hospital. Then they'd all go and look for him there – but Gupta had just come from the hospital and could say he hadn't arrived. Besides, Roy was sharp as a knife, and it was too late.

'You left the prisoner here,' Roy snapped, 'with General Dadhwal?'

'Yes, sir,' the doctor stammered, 'forty-five minutes ago. I ...'

Roy waved a hand. 'Go, go!'

He turned coldly on Max. 'We will hold you responsible for this, General! I promised Savage that he would pay dearly if he opposed us. You will face a court-martial, and it will not be packed by your friends. There are some generals who understand there has been a change in India!'

Max said nothing. The longer Roy spoke the longer it would be before he would have to give any effective orders to recapture Rodney. 'I was going to recommend you for a high order, and promotion, for your good work in this affair,' Roy snapped. 'Now I will withdraw those recommendations. Unless Savage is found, at once!'

Max said, 'You must do whatever you think fit. We all must. Personally, I think you are being petty.'

Roy was not really a bad or petty man, just a product of his nature and the political history of the past thirty years. But he was famous for two things: his fanatical hatred of the British and his short temper. Max hoped to stir the latter into further time-wasting fulminations. He succeeded.

Roy raised one shaking hand and waved it in the air, stabbing and slicing. 'Watch out, General! Watch out, you and your Sandhurst friends! We have had enough of this Sandhurst spirit. You are servants of the people now. We don't want your polo ponies and English tweed coats while the people starve! What did you do in our fight for freedom, but toady to the English!'

218

Max said, 'I was taught to stand by my obligations, Mr Roy, at first in my home, by my father, and also, later, at Sandhurst. I was taught to obey constitutionally given orders whether I agreed with them or not. I took the English government's arms, and their training, and if I had betrayed them, how do you know I wouldn't betray you? I have an armoured brigade and an infantry division here. General Usman has a corps in Kashmir. General Rajbir has a corps in the south. Would you like any of us to forget what we were taught?'

'That would be treason,' Roy said. 'You are under oath to defend the constitution.'

'You are wrong, sahib. I am not under oath. The British never made me swear an oath, nor has our own government since Independence. What really matters cannot be put in writing, or sworn to by oaths. That's why you are safe, and that is why my friend Rodney Savage, an officer of the Indian Army, will have at least one more half hour before any attempt is made to find him. Some Indian traditions have to be sacrificed for the future of India, but not personal loyalty. At least, not by me. *I have eaten his salt* ... If you wish to report the matter to the Prime Minister, I shall be pleased to accompany you to Delhi. Now I am going to have a drink.'

He turned his back, opened a drawer in the table, and pulled out a bottle of whisky and one glass.

'Have you got another glass?'

The woman's voice was low and tired. Roy and the general turned. Sumitra, Rani of Kishanpur, stood in the entrance to the tent, leaning against the pole, her palms joined in *namasti*.

Roy hurried forward. 'Your Highness!' He seized a chair and pushed it forward. Sumitra sat. 'I searched everywhere for you in Chambalpur, but could not find you.'

'I was ... in retreat,' she said.

'India owes you a great debt. I have messages for you from New Delhi ... You did not know, General, that Her Highness was our chief agent inside Chambalpur?'

'I did not,' Max said curtly. 'Until the All India Radio announced it after the surrender.'

Sumitra looked up, her hands spread pleadingly. 'I believed in the policy, Max. I made up my mind to do all that I could, months

219

before Rodney came to Kishanpur that time . . . as soon as I really understood that India was free and there was work for me in shaping and building it.' Max continued to look at her, his face stern and sad. She threw out a hand towards him. 'My God, Max, I tried to warn him, but in the end I was caught, just as much as he . . . Where is he? In hospital here, still? I've got to see him. Perhaps he feels better now. He did his best. No one could have done more, and he must see now that what he wanted to achieve was hopeless from the beginning. If only I could have persuaded him of that, before we went to Chambal.'

'Then he would not have gone, or taken the Nawab's pay,' Max said coldly.

She drank the whisky. Roy stood behind her chair, listening, surprise growing in his face. 'But you did not really care for him, Your Highness!' he cried.' He is an enemy of India!'

Sumitra ignored him, and spoke to Max. 'I wouldn't do it again, if I could start at the beginning . . . It wasn't worth it, but how could I know? Anything seemed worth it, for the new India.'

'It is,' Roy said emphatically.

Max said, 'Murder? Deceiving people who love and trust you? Turning in your mother to the police? If you think those are worthwhile, for India, it isn't a new India you'll create but a new Soviet, a new Nazi Germany . . . Rodney has escaped. Sri Roy and I were just discussing the best method of recapturing him.'

The Rani's head sank into her hands. Max saw that she was weeping. 'Alone,' she whispered, 'alone again, in the jungle, wounded. If only I'd come earlier!'

'He wouldn't have listened to you,' Max said. 'Here, have another drink.' He patted her shoulders awkwardly. 'I'm sorry I spoke like that just now. I didn't know you had . . . I didn't know.'

Roy's face was unexpectedly gentle. He had got over his temper. 'I am sorry for both of you, but I, too, have my duty to do – a larger duty than either of yours, if you will excuse me. I shall give the necessary orders myself.'

Max called after him, 'No one will obey you. Just wait a bit, please.'

Sumitra raised her tear-stained face. 'Has he gone?'

'Yes.'

'I couldn't bear the look in your eyes, Max. My father and

220

mother are dead. There's got to be someone in the world who knows. I'm going to have his child. He doesn't know. Only you. Not Janaki, nor Dip, nor anyone else at all yet. Only you. So that there'll be one human being's eyes that will look at me with sympathy.'

She rose unsteadily, and Max, silent and appalled, helped her into the open air.

Chapter 16

Margaret Wood pushed the falling hair back out of her eyes and began on the second shelf of the *almirah* in the corner. *Almirah* was the Hindustani word for 'wardrobe', but to be a true *almirah* it had to be this kind of wardrobe – rickety, creaky, liable to fall over on you if you tugged too hard at the door, the wood warped by forty hot weathers and forty monsoons.

One, two, three . . . four pairs of sheets for the double bed, all of them patched and frayed at the hem from the vigorous beating the *dhobi* gave them on the flat stones by the river below Lapri. She didn't need double-bed sheets. She could cut them in half. But that would make eight pairs – more than she'd need. She glanced down at the wooden, iron-banded trunk on the floor. Everything had to get into that, and one suitcase.

She took two pairs of sheets from the *almirah*, folded them and packed them in the trunk. The others she laid on a pile of linen and clothes in the corner.

Pillow cases . . . face towels . . . bath towels . . . The same insoluble problem every time – no space to pack all that she would need, no money to buy more when she reached wherever she was going.

She was folding the towels too small now, so that they made a needless bulk. They'd go better with only one fold. She knew that quite well. Henry used to say she was a wonderful packer, a wonderful, efficient woman. Where had all that gone? Vanished, with the sense of purpose. Could an aimless, unhappy woman pack well? Thin khaki shirts, four. She'd better take two and wash them herself, like her underclothes. She held up a petticoat in disgust, and threw it on the pile in the corner.

She heard the fast-approaching roar, easily recognisable, of a jeep, and glanced at her watch. Eleven o'clock. She'd have to stop soon or she'd fall asleep over the trunk. The jeep engine stopped outside and she raised her head. Nailed boots ran up the front veranda steps, knuckles beat on the door. She climbed to her feet and opened the door. The light from the narrow hall where she was packing shone on the face of a young Indian lieutenant.

He saluted energetically. 'Mrs Wood?'

She nodded. The jeep headlights shone across the weeds of the lawn towards the chapel and the gravestones. She saw the dim shapes of two soldiers with cradled rifles in the jeep, behind the glare of the lights.

He said, 'A prisoner of war has escaped from hospital up the road. He is on foot, and armed, and we are warning all villages to be on the lookout for him. There is a reward of five thousand rupees for any information leading to his capture.' He looked embarrassed, and his glance turned away from her. 'He's an Englishman, about five feet ten, very sunburned, blue eyes – Colonel Rodney Savage.'

'From the hospital!' she cried. 'He's hurt? But All India Radio said yesterday that he was in jail! If I'd known . . .'

The lieutenant said, 'I suppose they wanted to keep it secret, until they really had got him to jail . . . You know him? He was wounded in the stomach, quite badly, but he was recovering well until he escaped.' He looked full at her. 'It's Mr Roy who has ordered the reward . . . My orders are to advise anyone living alone, like this, to keep the house locked, and to take every means to inform us as soon as possible if they see or hear of him . . .' He glanced past her. 'You're not going anywhere tonight, are you? I don't think Colonel Savage would harm you, or anyone else – but he might give you an awful fright if you ran across him, and . . .'

'Not tonight,' she said. 'The new missionary is due tomorrow.'

The lieutenant saluted again, ran down the steps, and jumped into the jeep. The engine kicked into life, the headlights swung round and away, along the narrow cart road towards the old Rest House and Pattan.

Rodney, wounded! When she heard that he was in jail, charged with murder and treason, a wave of absolute lassitude, and exhausted failure, overcame her. She had hardly stirred herself, even to eat or drink, until she began to pack early this afternoon. He was in jail – but where? He needed a lawyer. She knew nothing

223

of lawyers, and had no money to hire one. He was behind brick walls and iron bars, and she had no strength to climb, no weapons to blast open. She did not know where he was, and she did not have the money to go to him.

She stood at the open door, her mind lifting like a boat on a rising wave. He was wounded, and free, and she was a nurse. Now, if she could find him, she could at last do something to give him an inkling of her love. Later she would give him her body, which he had once asked for and she had refused; and once she had offered, wrapped in her soul, and he had rejected, through indifference more than hate.

She turned to go into the bungalow. The shadow came up the steps almost beside her. She had her hand on the door when she realised, and his voice said, 'Inside, and close the door behind me.' He followed her in, she closed the door, and with one hand he locked it and pushed the bolt across. In his other hand a blue-black automatic pistol pointed at the pit of her stomach.

'Into the bedroom,' he said. She walked down the passage and he stopped at the door, in the shadows. 'Draw the curtains, tight. Lock and bolt the back door. Now the door out of the *ghuslkhana*.'

'It's all right,' she said. 'They won't come in again.'

He stood in the middle of the bedroom, swaying like a poplar tree in a gusty wind. His face was a greenish grey under the fierce tan, and the blue eyes swam in and out of focus in time with his swaying, so that now they were sharp and cold, now dim and blurred.

'Lie down on the bed,' she said, trying to keep her voice calm. 'You're ill.'

His mouth twisted. 'Lie, sit – *prang*, I've had it. Then five thousand chips for you. Didn't they – pay enough for Gulu? Sorry, that wasn't you, was it? What's the difference?'

She drew a deep breath. 'Rodney, the difference is that I love you. I've had no way of showing you, when you so obviously didn't care. You don't care now, and I can't make you in a minute. I only want to tell you, so that you'll know. I never want anything or anybody else but you.'

'That's what – she said – in the end.' His eyes flickered on and off her face. 'They want me,' he mumbled. 'Murder. Listen radio.

224

Killed three Indian babies. Ate them, apple sauce.' He twisted slowly and began to fall.

She had been waiting for it and from long experience was able to judge to the moment when and how it would come. She caught him, feeling her arms strong enough to hold him for ever, and eased him on to the bed. She lifted up his legs and unfastened his boots. In the stomach, the lieutenant had said. She undid the buttons of his shirt and unfastened the buckle of his web belt – Indian Army uniform, she noticed, and practically new, though stained and scratched where he had fallen and stumbled. Six miles, in the hills, at night, from the edge of the Sakti Plain. He lay on his back, his right arm dangling over the edge of the bed, the pistol in his hand. She knelt and gently tried to disengage it, but his grip was like steel and she could not move it.

She eased down his trousers. The exit wound was in the left anterior section of the abdominal wall, two inches from the navel. No granulation yet. Wound lacerated and about two inches square. Some recent bleeding and exudation of serum. The bandage had worked loose and hung round his loins. They seemed to be teaching the Indian Army the Evans Over-Cross Tie for abdominal wounds. The bullet couldn't have damaged any viscera or organ in its passage, or there would have been tubing in him, or signs of an operation. She turned him over gently. Entry wound small, one inch left of the spine at the sixth thoracic vertebra, barely missing the left kidney. Granulation tissue forming. Some recent bleeding beginning to clot. Temperature 101, pulse 108.

Systematically she began her preparations, her hands working with detached, unfumbling efficiency at their tasks, her heart soaring in dizzy ascent, singing like a lark towards the sun. He had come to her. This time she must not let go.

He groaned, stirred, and tried to sit up. She reached his side before he could move, and laid her hand on his forehead. The eyes looked long at her, but dim and blank, and the pistol did not fall from his hand. The kettle boiled. Quickly she made tea, stirred in plenty of sugar and milk, and two aspirins, and held the bowl to his lips. He drank deeply, and when he had finished the first bowl, whispered, 'More.' She made him another, and crooned over him as he drank, his head so close to her breast that there was a contraction in her womb and a swelling of her breasts. Later, in his sleep, he will wet the bed, she thought. She hoped he would, that she could wash and clean him and do, out of the fullness of love, all and more than he had done for her out of indifferent duty.

She cleaned his wounds with antiseptic and retied the bandage. His head fell back on the pillow, and he slept on the instant, but his grip never loosened on the pistol. The sound of the jeep engine, returning from Pattan, grew in the west. She crouched over him, glaring at the door; but the jeep did not pause this time, and in a minute the sound died.

She pulled up a chair and sat beside the bed, staring down at the drawn face. The thin lips fluttered with each rapid, noisy breath, the chest rose and fell in an uneven rhythm and both hands sometimes trembled, the left shaking the top of the sheet, the right causing the pistol to make a rapid drumming rattle on the wood floor.

After half an hour the movements began to quieten and slow, and finally to cease altogether. She took his wrist. Pulse 80, temperature about 99.5.

He said in a low distinct voice, 'O.K., Harry, let's go down to the ford.' Then he spoke longer, in a language she did not understand. Then he laughed, a low happy chuckle, and said, '*Hut teri ma!*' That she knew. It was soldiers' language, meaning 'Up thy mother's!' He was smiling, and she smiled with him.

He said, 'There's cloud on the pass but we ought to ... *Barf, choro, barf*. Snow, my son, snow ...'

The voice changed again. Now it was sharp, yet deep with a tremendous yearning. 'We've got to try. How many of you are going to die in the next ten minutes?' Then edged and confident, '*Achchi bat, choro-haru, advance garnu parchha. Tayyar chhan? Jaun!*' He winced, his jaw set.

It took a long time for him to recover the original calm. Then he whispered, 'Janaki, Janaki, how can your legs be so slim and so strong?'

She looked anxiously over her shoulder, and about the room. The lamp burned steadily on the table. The curtains were drawn. She should not be hearing this, eavesdropping on his soul, until he trusted her. Smiling, he mumbled in a strong Anglo-Indian accent, 'Oah, Vickee, come in out of thee sun, you will get all brown!'

226

The minutes floated by, into half hours, into hours. Like a slowly revolving wheel his life passed. After a time she waited to hear him speak of his mother, of his father; of school in England, of green fields and cricket. He never did. Sometimes he spoke in Hindi, which she could understand a little, sometimes in the other language where only a word that was the same as Hindi came through. The sentences fell separate and disconnected from the fluttering lips, but formed a single world, a single life. Snow glittered on mountain peaks, and men climbed a long slope towards them. Indian girls danced in a closed room, very hot, and she heard the chinking of their bangles and saw his amused eyes fixed on their lascivious bellies. Rain fell, and he lit a cheroot and swore at the cook. There was a battle, and she heard orders given and taken, and the rumble of tanks under his suddenly raised voice. He danced, holding the women desirously in sardonic flirtations, and then suddenly, so that she imagined him still in his dinner jacket, he was striding fast through light jungle, and the sambhur stag was feeding beside the river.

She waited for the anger she knew so well, for the bitterness. Surely he must have hated? All his life seemed to be lust and violence and war. But there was none. A hundred names he spoke, and every one of them, English and Indian, brought a faint smile and a subtle change to the voice, an ache of love which was the same whether he spoke of mountains or of the satin heaviness of a woman's breast.

Yet there is bitterness, she thought, a bitterness too deep for words. Sumitra's name he never spoke, and for the rest, all was of the past. *This* had been. For the future – nothing; except the pistol held tight in his thin fingers.

Her head began to bow of its own weight, as though someone were pressing it gently down against her breast, and she felt a tear fall on her blouse, then another.

He awoke at four, an hour before dawn. The first sign was the clatter of the pistol falling from his hand as his muscles relaxed. She stooped quickly to pick it up, but he was quicker. He grabbed it, transferred it to his left hand and unflexed the muscles of his right. 'Mustn't lose Max's pistol,' he said. His voice was strong, his eyes unnaturally bright.

She sat down again and tried to smile, but the tears rushed up to

227

the very brink, and she looked away until she had recovered her composure.

'I want something to eat. Quickly, please. And I'll take whatever other food you have away with me.' He swung his legs out of the bed, turned pale, and hung on to the bed with both hands.

'Let me!' she cried.

'Cook, woman,' he said, summoning the wide sardonic grin. He bent and began to put on his boots. She saw beads of sweat bursting out on his forehead. She went to the kitchen and quickly lit the fire. She heard him moving about the house. Fifteen minutes later he came through to her, and she saw that he was wearing khaki trousers and a shirt that had belonged to her husband. 'I found these,' he said, 'also a small haversack, full of bottles and bandages. I've thrown them out.'

She made tea, poached eggs, and buttered bread, and put out a pot of jam. He set it all on the mantelpiece in the living-room and ate hungrily, standing. 'Sitting hurts,' he said.

She said, 'Don't go now, Rodney. Hide in the attic. The new missionary is coming in the taxi from Bhowani, and I'm sure we'll be able to smuggle you out in it somehow, if we pay the man enough. There'll be room in the boot.'

He smiled, his mouth full. 'Me, locked in the boot of a car, with five thousand rupees on my head?'

'You must trust me,' she cried. 'You were helpless all night. Besides . . .'

'I know you,' he said suddenly. 'You were wearing a light-blue linen frock, very plain. There were some dark rain spots on it, and you were worried and frightened. I asked you to take your clothes off and you ran away.'

She said, 'I knew you'd remember, one day! It was Independence Day. You were drunk.'

'Yes,' he said. 'And they'd just given me an O.B.E. That's enough to drive any man to drink.'

'And your father had been killed.'

He gulped down the rest of the tea and said abruptly, 'I'm going. Where's the rest of the food?'

She showed him, and he stuffed it all into the first-aid haversack, a loaf of bread, some butter, a piece of cold mutton, half an uncooked chicken, a pound of sugar, a can of bully beef, the pot of jam.

228

'Money?' he said.

She emptied her purse into his hand – 108 rupees. He gave her back five, and turned towards the door. She stepped in front of him.

'Where are you going?'

He examined her. 'I don't know.'

'Are you going to try to reach Bombay? I can speak to Sir Andrew Graham. They'll arrange to get you out of India secretly. Where can I wait for you in Bombay? I'll have everything fixed.'

'No,' he snarled. 'I'm not leaving India. Now, get out of the way.'

She stood aside. 'I love you, Rodney.'

He stared at her in passing. 'That's too bloody bad,' he said.

She fell on the bed, too exhausted to feel pain, and slept.

The sound of knocking on the outer door awakened her. Ten o'clock. He'd had four hours. Drawing back the curtains she saw three sepoys, and a pair of thin, loinclothed peasants wandering round the back of the house. One of the peasants was pointing at the ground as he walked. She called, 'Wait,' washed her face, combed her hair, and opened the front door. The same lieutenant who had come in the jeep was there. He too looked tired. He saluted carefully. 'Did Colonel Savage come here, Mrs Wood?'

'No,' she said.

He said, 'Mr Roy put a couple of *shikaris* on to tracking him. They have followed him as far as this. They say he spent some hours inside, and then went on east.'

'Can they follow his trail farther, from here?' she asked quickly.

The young man said, 'He wasn't so tired when he moved again. He got into the stream over there, and they don't think they'll be able to pick it up again . . . He took me into my first battle. I was terrified, a brand-new second-lieutenant commanding a company attached to the 1/13th Gurkhas for the operation. He was . . .'

'I know,' she said. 'If he came here, I didn't see him. I know nothing about it.'

The lieutenant smiled at her. 'I'll report to headquarters.' He ran down the steps and leaned over the back of a truck parked on the road, radio antennae sticking up from it. The sepoys and the *shikaris* squatted among the weeds at the foot of the veranda.

The lieutenant returned. 'General Dadhwal would like to speak to you, ma'am. He would come down if he could, but he can't leave his headquarters. Would you mind . . . ?'

She climbed into the truck. She sat silent for the short ride, while the driver slammed the truck confidently round the hairpin bends, under the red-rock cliffs and the tall trees. At the summit, where the walls of the gorge fell back and the plain opened out, he turned right down a narrow track recently cut through the trees. General Dadhwal stepped out of his tent before the truck stopped, saluted, and helped her down.

Inside the tent, when they were seated across from each other at the green-baize table, he said, 'You know, Mr Roy can make it very unpleasant for you when he hears the evidence of the *shikaris*. Accessory after the fact, and so on. You'd better leave at once. I don't think he'll bother to have you arrested after that. Especially as I can persuade him that you won't change your story. You won't, I presume?'

'No,' she said, 'I won't.'

'Mind if I smoke?' He shifted his body and found his pipe and matches. His tunic was faded but spotlessly clean, the brass buttons glittering, the double row of medal ribbons bright on the dull khaki. There was a good deal of grey at his temples and along the sides of his heavy head. Like everyone else today, he looked tired.

He said, 'I thought . . . I understood, that you were no friend of his.'

'In the beginning,' she said. She laid her hands flat on the table. 'General, I love him. I must find where he's trying to go, what he's trying to do.'

The general muttered, 'Christ! . . . I am sorry, ma'am. Forgive me . . .' She gestured impatiently. The general got up and paced the little tent. After a few minutes he seemed to make up his mind. He stopped opposite her. 'He's got to leave India, and everything that India has meant, everything he's done. He's got to leave it all behind . . . *all*. He's got to start again somewhere – England, Canada, Kenya, it doesn't matter.'

'That's the only thing he said. What he was not going to do. He's going to stay in India.'

The general again muttered under his breath and sucked noisily at his pipe. He sat down. 'Mrs Wood,' he said, his brown eyes steady on hers, 'Rodney Savage and I have had a special sort

230

of relationship for a long time. He is not just England, he is England-in-India. And I am not just Indian, but a special sort of Indian. I wish that much of what has happened between us had not happened – not just the imperialism and the rest, other things as well. They're all too tied together to explain, even if I wanted to and had the gift of the gab. What matters now is that I will not help you, even if I could, unless I am sure that you can give Rodney what he needs. Something different from what other women are ready to give him. *How* do you love him? Why? Tell me.'

She remembered that Janaki, whose thighs had held Rodney in the night, was the general's wife. She was sure that the general knew. There was a love almost as great as her own here. She had no cause to be embarrassed. She said, 'I came out here thinking I loved my husband, thinking I had religious faith to be a missionary. After he died I found that I had been lying to myself. I did not love him – I respected and admired him. I did not have faith – I only wanted to be a good and loyal wife. The first time I saw Rodney he wanted me to take my clothes off. I hated him and I couldn't forget him . . . But what is the difference between wanting me as a woman and wanting me as a nurse? Which is more insulting? . . . In the middle of that desert where I was, frightened and alone, there was no one in sight but him. He was there for me to hate, to despise, to fear. Then I fell ill, and if he had not come by I would have died. In the weakness and the delirium and the fear – I was very much afraid that I was going to die – my intense feelings about him simply changed round. Or I gave up the struggle of trying to pretend the opposite of the truth. I gave up trying to be loyal to Henry's ghost. I don't know much about psychology, but whatever the reason is, the thing's happened often enough before. Don't they say you only have to worry when the person you love doesn't care, one way or the other? . . . Hate became love, despisal became respect, fear became worship. He felt nothing. He was thinking of Sumitra, if of any woman. Now she's destroyed him, and he feels nothing for anyone, or anything.'

'How can you change that?' the general asked in a low voice.

'I don't know,' she said. 'I only know that there's nothing else but him, for me, in life. Surely, somehow, if I can only show him that, he can begin again.'

231

The general relit his pipe, drew a sheet of paper towards him and wrote carefully. After five minutes he folded the note into an envelope and gave it to her, unaddressed. 'That is for my wife in Bhowani,' he said. 'She's at Flagstaff House. I don't know what Rodney will do, where he will go . . . but I think it quite likely that he will turn up there for help of some kind. You can stay as long as Janaki is there . . . It is also possible that the Rani of Kishanpur may arrive, for the same purpose as yourself. I know how you feel about her – but, if you can, try not to hate her. She has been as badly hurt as you. Perhaps more, because she did have in her grasp everything she wanted – and threw it away.'

'He will go back to her,' she said miserably. 'She is so beautiful. They have shared so much.'

'It is possible,' the general said. 'I hope not . . . Now, I'm going to send you straight to Bhowani in my staff car with my A.D.C. Just stop off to collect your things. You're packed? Good.' He held out his big hand. 'Good-bye, Mrs Wood.'

'Good-bye . . . Did you say something about Mrs Dadhwal's leaving Bhowani?'

He smiled grimly. 'I have been posted to an obscure command in the farther wilds of Assam – a non-family station. Mr Roy is very angry with me. But I have a week or two yet. Janaki will come up to see me off from Chambalpur airfield. Soon after, she'll go to her mother's house in Bombay. I don't suppose you and I will meet again. I won't say "good luck". It sounds cheap. I will pray for you.'

He ushered her out of the tent.

Chapter 17

After leaving the distraught Margaret Wood and the mission bungalow I crossed the road and a ragged field, rolled up my trousers, and entered the shallow Shakkar stream. While night lasted I had to go carefully and very slowly. I could not afford a sprained ankle, and I couldn't afford to scatter water on stones which would normally be dry. They would be after me soon.

When light came I had covered a quarter of a mile. After that I went comparatively fast for half an hour, then turned up a side stream, which came in from the east, and for a time followed the bed of that. It was a torrent that fell down the high escarpment between the old Rest House and Sabora, and I knew that the linked pools of still water only reached the foot of the slope. Before they ended I sat on a rock in the water and took off my boots and socks. I wrung out my socks, spread one over each shoulder and waited for them to dry. The old Rest House, from which the hidden manoeuvrings of politics had ejected me, lay due south of me and less than a mile away. The morning was cold, not bitter-sharp like mornings on the high desert plateau of Chambal, but raw. My wound ached and a mist as pervasive and chilly as the caresses of a drowned army surrounded me. I shivered the whole time I sat there. I could not see more than a hundred yards at ground level, then the trees became blurs and at last vanished in the mist. Above, their tops made cold patterns against the lightening pale-blue sky.

An airplane droned over, east bound, and I froze where I sat, turning my head down, before I realised from that first glance that it was a DC-3, the Indian Air Force's regular mail and V.I.P. passenger run from Chambalpur to Bhowani and Delhi, which had passed over every morning at this time while I was in the C.C.S., after the surrender.

233

When it had gone below the trees, and I could hardly hear the soft throb of the engines, I picked my way to the bank, barefoot on the stones, carefully put on socks and boots, and began to climb fast up the face of the escarpment. Most of the trees were bare of leaves in that season, and I felt all the time, as I climbed up that westward-facing slope, that someone was watching me from the opposite slope, below Dhain. If they saw me, at that distance of about two miles more or less, they could not hit me. But they had cars, and could get round to Sabora in half an hour, to Pattan in less, and from there converge across my path – any path. My only chance was speed.

I climbed up, a little to the right of the line where smooth red stone and long black streaks showed how the stream, in the monsoon, rushed down this face in a heavy waterfall. A long nerve in my stomach pulled all the way from my thigh to my chest at every step. There was no strength in my legs, and my breath came in short wheezing gasps – I, who had once run up and down this slope three times in an hour with young Ganesha.

I reached the top, threw myself down and vomited. A painful spasm in my stomach made me think that my wound had re-opened, perhaps forcing out part of my guts. I dared not stop to look. The vomit spattered the giant teak leaves under my face, and after a few minutes I struggled to my feet and went on eastward. Just here I had killed the sambhur stag and fed the people of Pattan when they were starving. By that pterocarpus I had waited, and there by that patch of heavier jungle I had shot him . . . On, east, the leaves roaring under my feet, earth and rock as dry as splintered bone and the low sun clear and yellow in my eyes.

After two hours I knew that I had passed the first danger line. Sabora was behind my left shoulder by two miles, and Pattan six miles behind my right. I had crossed the main footpath from one to the other, which was the obvious and best place for them to cut me off. The forest ocean rolled away in all directions now, and I stopped under a tree, leaning back against the rough bark and staring all round. Where to go? Bhilghat lay south-east about twenty-five miles. I could not reach it today, but tomorrow I could. There I could find shelter, and old Gond women with prehistoric remedies for wounds, and I could lie in the hut while

234

Gulu's grand-daughters fed me and cared for me until I was fit again.

Gulu was in jail, the settlement full of police, schoolmasters, and probably soldiers. I could not go there. I could not go back to Pattan. I could not use roads or well-travelled paths. Where, then?

I began to walk again. There was no answer to the question, but nor could I stand still. Sometimes problems resolve best by staying in one place and thinking. Sometimes, as when I was in the morass in Delhi, holding the body still produces the same result on the mind – nothing.

Sabora, the McFadden Pulley quarries, and the metalled road to Bijoli and Bhowani were on my left, Bhilghat on my right. I walked between, allowing the sun to climb past my right shoulder ... On through the long morning. Sleep in a dense thicket in the early afternoon. Awaken groaning with thirst, my throat gummed, and on again in the growing cool of the evening. An hour before sunset I came to the dirt road from Sabora to Bhilghat, the same I had driven along with Ranjit Singh and Max, in the beginning. Heavy military tyre treads marked the dust, with the traces of bare feet and goat hoofs. I took off my boots and crossed in my socks, carefully brushing the ground behind me with a bunch of leaves. On the far side I put on my boots and went on east.

A footpath joined my course at a diagonal. Stooping to examine it, I saw that it had once been used, but not for some months. It led east, so I followed it for twenty minutes, drawing quickly behind a tree when I caught a glimpse of stone, glowing red in the filtered rays of the setting sun. I went forward cautiously. It was a shrine, ruined and deserted, giant creepers climbing up the lone standing wall, stones fallen on one another, and a chipped and weather-worn statue of Shiva Nataraja against the inner face of the standing wall. Faded flowers lay on a stone slab below the dancing god, but when I went forward I saw that they had been lying there a long time and were now all but crumbled to dust. That explained the state of the path. This was a shrine to which the people of some neighbouring village – five or fifteen miles away – came to worship once a year. Water lay in a kind of stone urn. I stooped over it and drank. It was black and bitter and tasted of leaves, but it slaked my thirst.

It would have been safer in the jungle, but the shrine attracted me and I sat down on the stone slab, sweeping the dried flowers to the ground, and leaned back against the wall, my head against Shiva's balancing right foot. There I opened my haversack and ate.

As I ate the banked red fires died down in the stone, the sun set, and the surrounding forest began to creak and move, awakening slowly to its life of the darkness. The stone turned cold under me, the daytime world of colour and texture dissolved into the night world of pattern and mass. The bats began to swoop down the dark alleys of the jungle, and I carefully refastened the straps of the haversack.

The direction of the wind changed and in the huge silence I heard the barking of dogs. There was a village nearby then, hardly a mile from me. It was to the south, but I would have to go carefully when I started out in the morning.

Who could I turn to now? I thought of Victoria Jones, the Anglo-Indian girl who had married Taylor the railwayman. She had loved me once. Taylor had got a job on the mineral railway after being dismissed from the Delhi Deccan, and they were living in Bijoli, only forty miles north-east. Suppose I went there. Victoria owed me at least shelter, money, help.

I turned angrily. She owed me nothing, nor I her. Taylor would hand me over to the police, to ingratiate himself with the Indians he despised.

I lay down, put the haversack with its sharp-edged contents under my head, and tried to go to sleep. Jackals began to howl their insane chorus, rushing aimlessly through the trees in the dark. Far in the north I heard the cough of a leopard. The dogs of the village were silent. Such shrines as this are usually the home of cobras, and I thought I heard the slithering of a big snake over the stones as I lay on my back, staring through closed eyes at the darkness, but I was not afraid and did nothing to investigate . . .

Our campfires blossomed like potted geraniums under the trees and Charlie, Beetle, and I were sharing a big bowl of rice against the temple wall. The desolation of the ruins, twenty miles from anywhere, long forgotten even by the villagers, only emphasised the comradeship of our own company. The beat of madals *throbbed up from the far end of the camp, where a sluggish stream ran under a low rock bank. Nearby the colonel was writing a letter to his wife.*

236

We ate rice and dal, and sat back, at peace, in our sweaty clothes. Tomorrow we would march to Telaghat, the day after to Charria, the day after . . . on always to the day after, the same, and the petals of the gold mohur falling in an orange shower over the stone phallus in the courtyard . . .

I smelled hot steel and oil, heard a locomotive breathing in the dusty twilight of an April evening, the metal scorched from its hours in the sun, from its rushing passage through the still, hot jungles, and rock ovens of the Vindhya hills, over the rumbling iron bridges, along the metalled track cut like a sword through the trees, the dust whirling in plumes alongside the wheels. Victoria stood beside me. I smelled the cheap perfume she used to wear, a touchingly innocent perfume trying in vain to counteract the unambiguous femaleness of a ripened woman at the end of a hot day. I smelled my own sweat, strong and male, and, in all, the drifting invisible presence of coal smoke. Then she went and I was alone.

Early in the morning, the light vague and tentative, I awoke suddenly, in my ears the dying tones of what had awakened me – an exclamation in a human voice. I sat up quickly and made out a dark figure below me, crouching on the earth at the foot of the slab where I was. I heard a low mumbling.

He raised his head and I saw that he was an old man, wearing only loincloth and puggaree. I put my pistol back in its holster. He quavered, '*Guru-ji*, you have come back?' With a convulsive gesture he spread his hand. A bunch of fresh flowers fell in my lap, then again he bowed his head to the ground.

I did not remember ever being in this place before, though in plenty like it, as in my dream. *Guru-ji*, the title he gave me, means 'teacher'.

He said, '*Guru-ji*, this time you will stay? After sixty years, the village needs you.'

Sixty years? The old man was in a state of shock, or trance. He was not much more than seventy himself. The dawnlight was growing and spreading fast over the world and I saw him clearly, saw his thin eager face and hungry eyes. I remembered that I had not shaved for three days, that my clothes were torn and filthy, and I myself sunburned and weathered like any Indian. But boots and trousers were surely out of place, whatever 'teacher' he thought I was. He was just not seeing them, any more than he was seeing my

237

age. Time did not exist for the teacher of the shrine, whoever he had been.

The old man said, 'Good morning, Briju. Good-bye, Briju. Be good to your mother. Thank you.'

'Who taught you English?' I asked amazed.

He said, 'You spoke such words to me so many times that I learned them by heart, to please you. Don't you remember? ... We never told anyone you were here. Not once, all those three years, no one outside the village ever knew. You asked for peace and we gave it to you, didn't we? We have told no one since ... You are hungry, *guru-ji*? I will bring food for you! Everything will again be as it was when I was a boy, and we came to you and you talked with us, and sometimes being children we played jokes on you. We were afraid – at first because you were an English sahib, later because we knew we were committing sacrilege against an elect of God, but you only laughed with us. And do you remember my sister – aihh, long since gone! – coming with gifts because you gave her a blessing that got her with child? But you laughed again and said it was her husband's love that had done it. And the days the elders came to sit at your feet when the crops failed, or the deer ate the young corn, or there was bad blood between families, and we boys and girls hid in the jungle close there, lying on our stomachs, listening. It will all be the same!'

A picture of the past came clear. A man, an Englishman, had come here sixty years or so ago, about 1890. He had taken up residence in this shrine – perhaps it had a roof then. He had asked the villagers not to tell anyone. Whether he was a fugitive from the police, or from the world in general, from his own people, or from some particular person, I would never find out. But he had stayed three years as the village's *guru*, the resident spirit of the shrine. The old man's eyes beseeched me – you have returned, stay!

My head swam with hunger, and a lifting of material problems which had seemed reality. Why not? In Pattan I had destroyed my vision by mixing into it a desire for power. I no longer wanted power, or responsibility. I no longer wanted women. I no longer *wanted* anything. I could not be an Indian, they would not let me live as an Englishman – but a tree, a stone I could be, in this soil which had made me.

238

I sat cross-legged and raised my hand to bless the old man . . .
'Grandfather? Grandfather?'

The old man stood up. 'It is my grandson. Wait till he sees!'

A young man of about twenty-five came through the trees on a
path from the south, which I had not noticed the evening before.
He wore trousers, a shirt, a grey homespun cap and spectacles and
I could tell at once that he had some education.

He was saying, 'You did not come back and my mother sent . . .'
He stopped, astonished. 'Who is this?'

'It is he,' the old man crowed. 'Our *guru*, came back to us. Ah,
I knew you thought we old men were dreaming when we talked of
him!'

The young man's eyes were round and his mouth agape. 'I did
not know,' he whispered. 'Is it really you? . . . It is such a long
time.'

'Is there death, or age, for such as these?' the old man cried.

The young man dropped to his knees. Education had eroded the
edges of his simple faith, such as the old man possessed, but the
core was still there. He was not a town man, just a young village
man with a little education. 'You will stay, *guru-ji?*' he asked.

I made up my mind. 'I will stay,' I said.

The old man wrung his hands in an agony of happiness and
tears streamed down his cheeks.

The young man's eyes shone like beacons behind the cheap
lenses. He cried, 'Now we will have a *guru* of our own! We will be
famous all over Bandelkhand and Chambal! All over India! No
other village has an English *guru*.'

I said, 'No one must know. I want peace, total peace.'

The young man's face fell. 'No one?' He brightened. 'But someone will have to know, *guru-ji* . . . for the government census. The
officials are in the next village now, but they will reach us today.
The question is, are you in our village of Chahar or in the village
of Lihur? The *subtehsil* boundary runs close, but it has never been
settled whether the shrine is . . .'

'Leave me out of the census,' I cried, 'I do not exist!'

Now it was the old man who looked worried. 'But there is the
smallpox vaccination, *guru-ji*,' he said. 'Everyone must have it.'

The young man chimed in: 'And in *our* district the officials are
making a *pilot surwey*—' he spoke the words in English – 'showing

239

exact details of land use, number of dwellings, number of inhabitants per dwelling, agricultural and home-industry production per head. It will be *pilot surwey* for all India, so you see—'

'We will discuss that later,' I interrupted, controlling my voice. 'I am hungry. Bring me food. Be sure to enter it in the proper column in the printed paper.'

'Oh, there is no record of that,' the young man began, but I waved, 'Go, go!'

As soon as they had disappeared down the path I grabbed up my haversack and hurried east through the jungle. After two hours, when I thought I would die of melancholy, I lay down and tried to relieve my misery by tears. No tears came and after a time I went on again.

It was a day without purpose, except movement. I walked, saw no one, nothing, only two vultures very high in the blue sky, who watched me until dark. I walked east all day except for an hour, when I got up after a rest and walked west, and did not know it until I fell down a low rock cliff. In the pain and shock of the moment I realised that it was the same cliff I had scrambled up, in the opposite direction, an hour before my rest.

I do not know where I lay down for the night. It was, like the day, a nothing place, non-existent, and the night the same except that it contained aimless stillness instead of aimless motion.

The third morning, after vomiting, I felt better and ate most of the rest of my food, and it stayed down. I would have to use Max's pistol – I had stolen it from the *yakdan* in his office just before I heard Roy's car arriving – to kill some food. That would be easy, but dangerous.

I went on east. Near ten o'clock in the morning, the sun bright and a fresh breeze blowing through the jungle, myself feeling weak but not in pain, I heard the sharp crack of breaking wood somewhere close ahead, followed by a scream and a crash. I was going downhill towards a river, seen once through the trees from the ridge crest. I knew the river must be the upper Harpal. I stopped. I heard a woman crying urgently, but could not make out her meaning. I hurried down among the trees and came in a few seconds to the edge of the river. It ran about fifty feet wide there, between red-laterite cliffs twenty feet high. A wooden cart bridge had spanned the river from this bank to the village crowding the far cliff. Now the rickety structure, a hundred times half-repaired, had broken. Part hung down from the farther side, where a woman shrieked and shrieked, calling up to the village. Part swirled round and round in the pool below the bridge, where I saw too the floating red skirt and hair of another woman.

I hesitated. Some men were running down from the village, others along the cliff to the right, but there was no way down the cliff there for at least a hundred yards. The pool where the woman floated was a whirlpool, but the current very slow. Even a little effort would have taken her to the bank, or to the shallows. Perhaps she had been stunned by the fall of the rest of the bridge on top of her. Perhaps she was already dead.

Cursing my luck, I jumped over the cliff. When I came up the woman was close to me. I caught her and turned her face up. Blood stained the water from a gash in her forehead. I took her under the armpits and dragged her to the strip of sand.

My tiredness had gone in the shock and excitement of action. I stretched her at once on to her stomach, tore off her *choli* and began artificial respiration. Villagers called down to me from the clifftop, others ran up the narrow bank of sand and stones from the washing place downstream. When these arrived I was very tired again, and the particular motions of artificial respiration could not have been worse for my wound. I called to the first arrival, an agitated young man who might have been the husband, 'Watch me, watch!'

'Yes, sahib,' he gabbled, 'I see.'

'Come here.' He knelt beside me. 'Do it with me . . . there . . . there . . . there . . . Now go on doing that . . .'

I stood up and spoke to another man. 'You, watch him. When he is tired, do the same. Let there be no stopping of the work, even for a breath.'

From the cliff above an old grandmother wailed, 'She is dead! *Aiiih*, my daughter is dead!'

I said nothing. Three minutes later, to my surprise, the woman groaned and retched. 'My head,' she moaned. I turned away. It was clear that the blow on the head had been her main trouble. She had not swallowed much water, and would soon be all right.

An old gentleman in clean white dhoti, shirt, and puggarree

241

made a deep salaam. 'I am the headman, sahib . . . She whom you saved has five children. How can we ever thank you?'

I found myself swaying. 'I am hungry,' I heard myself say. 'Is there anything to eat?'

'Of course, sahib. Only our poor *desi* food, I fear, but . . .'

'Let me eat,' I said.

The old man led down the bank to the place where the path went up to the village. Twenty huddled women, who had been washing clothes, smiled at me. We went up the path in a great crowd, all the people chattering like magpies.

A policeman came running out of the village adjusting his puggaree as he ran. 'What happened? Is she dead?' he cried.

'She is alive,' the headman said. 'No thanks to you. What were *you* doing? Sleeping under the peepul as usual? The sahib *bahadur* here leaped into the river and saved her. I saw it.'

The policeman saluted me. Then his eyes widened. He cried, 'This is . . . this the sahib who did the murder! We have captured him!'

'What do you mean?' the headman said irritably. 'He has saved the life of Nathu's woman.'

I edged sideways through the mob, my hand on my pistol. The women crowded towards the policeman, shouting and waving their fists. 'Murder, fool? He saved her life! He is a hero! A sahib *bahadur!*'

Then the policeman spoke the fateful words. 'Five thousand rupees reward!' he said. 'Five thousand rupees.'

I pushed the nearest woman into him and ran. As soon as I was clear of them I drew my pistol and shouted, 'Keep back!' The policeman was unarmed, and they all fell back.

I heard the grumble and murmur of their voices. They weren't saying save him. They weren't saying, he saved her life. They weren't saying, Murder. They were saying, five thousand rupees.

I backed into the woods and when I could only just see them, gathered there staring after me, I fired a shot over their heads. Then I turned and ran. I heard the collective rising yell: 'After him! Five thousand rupees!'

I ran down the valley for a time, then turned up through the trees, and stopped. A young man was coming fast up the slope after me, with two companions. They were young and fit and I

242

hated them. I aimed carefully at the centre of the young man's chest and fired. My hand shook so from fatigue and hate I did not kill him as I had intended. The bullet hit him high in the shoulder. He screamed, fell, picked himself up, and stumbled and fell back down the hill, screaming in pain. His two companions were by then well ahead of him. They vanished and I turned again.

On, over the brow of the slope. On, down the other side. On, miles across a shadeless flat volcanic plateau covered by stunted thorn bushes and spear grass, the sun high and every part of my body aching. On, through the afternoon. On, to the side of a main road, just in time to edge back as a truck passed full of police armed with rifles. On, across the road in the dust cloud behind the truck. On, east, over hill and valley, stream and marsh and plateau and ridge and scrub and field. On, until my legs gave way and I fell in the middle of the game trail I had been following. I crawled under a thornbush to the side, pulled up my legs tight under me and passed away, whether in faint, sleep, or death, I did not know.

It was a long straight road on the outskirts of the old Hira Mandi bazaar in Lahore. Inside there is a narrow lane, stone paved, between wooden houses whose upper balconies almost meet overhead. At street level the whores sit in open-fronted booths, and a dense crowd of men walk up and down the alley jostling and staring at the women, who stare back over their heads, impersonal and impervious. Christ came out of the old city gate below that alley, but it was in daylight, and we were standing to arms at the crossroads, a platoon of Gurkhas and my company headquarters. There had been a week of rioting between Sikhs and Muslims already, over the destruction of a Muslim mosque; and that over the encroachment of a Sikh gurdwara; and that over the building of a Muslim slaughterhouse, where cows were killed; and that ... We had nothing to do with the quarrels but as soon as we came to stop it, of course, we had. The Sikhs took out a procession against the Commissioner's order. They advanced on us out of the old bazaar and down the wide road, waving banners in Gurmukhi. The banners called for Muslim blood, but it was not the Muslims barring their path, it was us. He was their leader, Christ. He had a long, saintly face, very fair of skin, and he had not tied his puggaree, so that his black hair fell over his shoulders in a wave almost to his waist, like the pictures of Christ in old Bibles, only they made Him a blond. The Assistant Magistrate with us gabbled through the formalities of the Riot Act. After that the responsibility was mine. Christ walked slowly on, calling out to the Gurkhas kneeling in the road that they had no business here. Were they not Hindus? He was on his way to throw the moneychangers out of the temple.

I pointed him out to Rifleman Manraj. Manraj jerked his bolt, putting one round in the magazine. I called to the crowd, but spoke to Christ: 'If you pass that chalk line in the road, we fire.'

He did not bother to look down, but came on. When his front foot passed the chalk line I tapped Manraj on the shoulder. Manraj fired, hitting Christ in the left eye. He fell backward and the rest of the crowd dropped their banners, turned and ran. He did not die for a few seconds, but died in my arms as I ran forward. He could not speak but his other eye was open, staring up at me, wonderingly.

The Governor commended the battalion for quelling the riots with so little loss of life – one man killed; after they had already killed nearly two hundred of each other. One man, I thought, that's the trouble with figures, and in the last resort, with democracy. I'd rather have killed two hundred more, but not that man . . .

In the morning, that nowhere under the bush in nowhere became a hillside of stones and brown grass, thinly sown with bushes, and the lowing of cattle not far off. My mind was sharp with hunger and my wounds hurt with a dry pain, like a scab almost healed that is torn open. I was making it too easy for them, plodding on east as though one dawn I hoped to catch the sun rising from its forge and hurl myself into that burning abyss. I must have been seen half a dozen times yesterday after the episode of the drowning woman.

I started off south-westward. When I saw a village I watched it from cover, resting to re-gather my nervous strength – there was not much of any other kind left – wondering whether to invite a little attention to myself, and whether it could be done without causing my immediate capture. Three times I decided against it – because there was no nearby jungle – because I saw an old bus parked – because natural obstacles would channel my flight in a certain, obvious direction.

The fourth time, I saw that it could be done with only a reasonable risk, and, after preparing myself, I walked past the village on the south, skirting small fields and thorn fences well within sight of the backs of the houses. An old woman emptying pots outside her hut saw me, and later two men. They stared, but did not come closer, nor did they run for cover as they would have if they had suspected I was an armed and dangerous criminal. Yet it was enough; they would talk; the gossip would reach the ears of some busybody; the message would go out.

Three hours later I came to another jungle village, this one reached by a telephone line. A telephone line in those hills usually meant a police *thana*, and so I presumed there was one, and again skirted the village in such a manner that I would be seen – but first I cut the telephone line. This was a long and hard business for me, since I had to find a big stick, and climb a tree, then batter at the line passing six feet off. I did it, and then skirted the village much as before, fairly close and keeping my eyes sharply open. This time two small boys saw me. After a long moment of staring under shaded eyes at me across the field, they darted back into the houses. I broke into a run, hurrying over the ploughed earth by the thorn fences until I reached the jungle. Then I ran along a westward path and, after half an hour, eased off on to the leaves and lay down behind a rock, waiting. I was only just in time. Two policemen, wildly excited and calling to each other as though it were only a jackal they were pursuing, came panting up the path, their noses down. Three boys and an older man followed. One of the policemen carried a slung rifle. I watched them, my pistol ready, until they disappeared westward. Then I started south and, going with extreme caution so as not to be seen at all, by anyone, at dusk found a place to lie, and lay down and tried to sleep.

I did not sleep more than an hour or two all night, from hunger, but my body got a rest, at least.

Before dawn, listening to the sounds of the jungle, I knew that I must get some food today or I would not be able to go any farther. I ought to do it at once, rather than look for it while on the move. The human mind has difficulty in real concentration on two things at once, and if I was looking for food I might forget other dangers.

After two hours of daylight searching I had found nothing, and set off eastward once more. The denser jungles and lakes of the Bhilghat area, and the tangled hills along the southern part of the India-Chambal border, now lay behind me. It was reasonable to assume that the hunters, having twice seen me heading towards them, would suppose that they were my destination – especially as the area formed a near-perfect refuge, and had been used as such often enough in the old days – by hunted Thugs fleeing from my great-grandfather; by Pindaris broken in Lake's campaigns of extermination against them; by Mahratta horsemen shattered at the Third Battle of Panipat; by all the defeated and the hopeless, starting with the Gonds four or six thousand years earlier.

In the afternoon I came to a stream, where I drank, and then a road. I lay down and observed it carefully from the edge. I saw bicycle tracks in the dust, but not fresh. Seeing no one, I crossed it with all precautions, and soon after fainted on an open hillside where my body as it lay must have been visible for half a mile in all directions. The relentless sun brought me round with a trip-hammer headache and a return of nausea, but I had nothing to vomit now, and after a time I crawled into the nearest shade, and lay down. A lizard appeared and my jaws ached painfully. Two hours later, when it was crawling about on the rock under my hand and I had not moved a muscle, a sudden spasm of effort brought it into my fingers. I broke its neck and ate it raw. At dusk a crow settled in the top of the tree ten yards from me, and cocked its eye, examining me. I shot it, it fell down through the boughs with a thump to the ground. I grabbed it and went on east as fast as I could, for the road I had crossed was close behind me, certainly within sound of that shot, and it was a time of day when many people besides police might be travelling along it.

In a thicket, two miles farther on, I lit a tiny fire, scraped open the crow's belly with a sharp stone, gutted it, and grilled it whole, burning off the feathers, and ate it, and then stumbled on another mile through pitch darkness before lying down to sleep.

At the edge of the wood, by a dusty road, two peacocks displayed before a hen. I had gone out to shoot peafowl and beside me Man-parsad chattered with excitement, but I could not shoot. The cocks were grave and voluptuous in their appalling male beauty, and the hen crouched and waited so tenderly that I put my finger to my lips, and we crept away, back through the forest. We reached the road near a small village where women bent over the well and brass pots shone in the dusty sunlight. A cow had died there and forty vultures crowded the boughs of the gnarled tree overhanging

*her body, and ten more hissed and trampled, with wings arched
into black and white canopies, to plunge their heads into her anus
and vulva, dragging out long strips of bright meat. The vultures on
the tree flew away when Manparsad and I appeared, and those on
the ground tried to, but it took them a long time, like a modern jet,
slow hop-hop and gradual run across the field, their wings dragging
along the ground and raising dust as they tried to flap, at last they
just got off the ground, but for another thirty yards made so little
altitude that the wing tips still touched the ground and stirred the
dust. I raised my gun to shoot one of the gorged despoilers – then
lowered it. The peacock is sacred to some in India: the vulture to
all. Without them, death would overwhelm life. Manparsad and I
went back to camp empty-handed, but we had walked twelve miles
in the forest, and seen the peacocks and the vultures and the dead
cow and the women at the well . . .*

The next day I stole a chicken from a village and got away
without being seen except by the pariah dogs, which bark at
everything and so are not much heeded. Again I cooked it, this
time by a small lake, and drank well, and was strong enough
afterwards to go ten hours, resting only twice. I did not go fast but
estimated that I had covered about twenty miles. There was no
more food that day, or the next, and in the late afternoon I came
suddenly and unexpectedly upon the railway line. It was single
track, broad gauge, the rails shimmering in the sun, and no one in
sight north or south. This must be the main line from Bhowani to
Itarsi and Bombay. I had travelled this line often during the
troubles of 1946 but could not recognise this exact spot.

I did not cross it, but lay in the shade staring at it. The heat of
the pursuit was for the moment far behind me, somewhere in those
hills which had disappeared into the haze. When I had rested,
should I cross the line and head on towards the rising run – like
yellow-dog dingo, running and running across the endless plain
of Australia – like the kudu of Africa, or the sambhur of this very
land, pursued relentlessly by packs of dogs, relay replacing relay,
always yapping and snapping at their heels until, bleeding from
fifty bites in the tendons, they turn to fight, and die?

No, I would not cross it. I would jump a freight train during the
night, and at last get away from this arena where they pursued me.

The first train was a passenger, going south. It came fast in the twilight, the red carriages hurtling past with a long rhythmic clatter, lights shining out from some windows, others dark and shuttered. If I tried I knew I could remember something wonderful about that train, and someone who had loved me and whom I had been able to give something to. But I could not remember, because my mind, like a baulking horse, came to a point and shied off violently, hurling me, its rider, to the painful stones.

The next train, two hours later, also was a passenger, going the other way, still fast but not nearly so fast. My time in Bhowani in '46 had taught me something about locomotives and I knew from the beat of the exhaust that this last train was going uphill. There were only a few carriages and the powerful engine could still maintain 30 or 35 miles an hour up the slope – too fast for me.

Between one and three in the morning two freight trains passed, southbound, both going fast. At ten past three I heard in the south the laboured roar of an engine coming up the hill with a heavy load. At last the searchlight swung round the distant curve, two miles away, and laid a band of light along the rails. The thunder grew and I crept close to the track, lying among trees ten yards from the edge of the ballast. She came on up, groaning through the night in heavy labour, towering sparks just visible high above, where the searchlight had lost its intensity. The engine and tender passed, and at once I scrambed forward and stood close to the clanking, creaking wagons. First came ten or more boxcars, tight-closed and locked; then open wagons. After letting two pass to gauge the speed and see exactly where the steps and platforms were, I ran alongside, caught a step and swung myself up. My wound shot a bolt of pain through my stomach, but I hung on and by slow, careful effort climbed over the edge of the wagon and fell in a heap down inside. It was empty, and smelled of crushed stone.

I lay there for two hours, while the locomotive up ahead worked north under blazing stars. Near five in the morning the wagon began to clatter over points and switches. I climbed up and, looking past the red glare of the engine's firebox I saw the lights of houses and the square silhouette of others, very black in that moment before dawn. Signal lights shone green and red among the fading lower stars, another track branched out beside us, more jerk and rattle of switches. I climbed down to the outer step and waited. We came up under the first approach gantry, past the bungalows of the railway colony, and from the engine I heard the hiss of escaping steam and felt the first grind of the brakes. I stepped off into the black grit of Bhowani Junction yards. So, I had come here, where Janaki was, whom I had loved, who had rejected me. I would give myself up to her – give her the final satisfaction of handing me over to the new lords of my country.

Twenty minutes later I walked along the side of Flagstaff House and passed through the back hedge. The house was dark, but the french windows on the right, facing this garden, were open. I went in there, and at once a low voice whispered 'Rodney?' It was Margaret Wood. My eyes, accustomed to the night, could see that she was sitting up on a camp bed in that room, which was ordinarily Max's study.

I sat down slowly, very slowly, in the chair by the desk. 'Food,' I said, and could say no more.

She was out of bed, hurrying into a dressing-gown, kicking her feet into bedroom slippers, closing the windows behind me. 'Don't put on the light,' she whispered, 'Janaki thinks the house is being watched. I have something ready for you.'

'Wha'?'

'I have, every night,' she said. 'Wait. I'll tell Janaki, and Sumitra.'

The sound of that name sent a worse pain than any physical one through me and I gasped with it. It was the first time for ten days, which seemed like a thousand years, that any thought of her, even to her name or perfume or the sound of her voice, had come into my consciousness.

Chapter 18

A log on the fire starts to burn with a light, leaping flame as the bark catches. During its maturity it burns more steadily but with a greater warmth. At the very end, often, it flares up again, and again light flames dance along it, and jets of fire, fed by the last reserves of its stored fuel, hiss out against the grate.

Four days and nights they hid me in an attic of Flagstaff House. I lay on a thin mattress on the plank floor, asleep most of the nights and all the days. I saw, the first night, a high valley of Lahoul, the main snow peaks of the Himalaya beyond, and a grey monastery set in a stony wilderness. The monks wore orange robes and tall red hats. The night I reached that place they danced the devil dance in the monastery courtyard. Ten-foot horns of copper and silver rested on the shoulders of acolyte boys, they and the trumpeters standing on a flat roof high above the courtyard. Long flags whipped in the never-ending violence of the dry Central Asian wind, gold and brass gleamed in the shadows of the pillars, and behind smoking oil lamps grotesque statues, carved in butter, loomed out of the echoing corners. Inside – the dark red and swirling yellow of the dancers in the courtyard; outside – one step – the beginning of eternity, of cold and wind, stone and snow . . .

The second night I saw the Bengal famine of 1943. I passed through in a train on my way to the Burma front. Women and children lay dead beside the track as the train clanked through the hot-weather afternoon. Men lay in the fields, fallen where they had been trying to grub a leaf from a dead plant. In Calcutta corpses littered the gutter. I saw soldiers giving bread to children with matchstick legs and arms and huge staring-eyed heads. The children crumbled it listlessly in their hands – only cooked rice was food to them, bread wasn't. Later their heads sank and they too lay down in the gutter. Etched on the copper sky over the train, over the city, kites circled, vultures waited ...

The third night I revisited an orange grove near Nagpur. The time was early February – the same as now. (Often during my flight from Lapri it had come to my mind that in Nagpur and Chhindwara the oranges were ripe and sweet on the trees; and I had to swallow the aching saliva and think only of the stones under my feet.) A caravan of gipsies were camped in the orange groves. They were a criminal tribe on the move, and a couple of policemen travelled with them, to see that they did not steal the oranges from the landlord's trees; but otherwise the policemen turned a blind eye, and all night long men slipped out of the town a mile down the road, and came to the camp, to sit by the leaping fires under the golden Hesperidean apples. Here bears danced on the end of short chains. A blind man played a *sitar* with haunting beauty. Women lay on their backs under the hedge with customers. Their husbands, sons, and fathers picked pockets, danced, beat drums, sold arrack, and escorted more men in from the town ...

On the fourth and last night it was a beach of sand, pale pink in colour under an early sun. Palm trees leaned over the sand from the landward rim, and the sea broke in long waves, alternately blue and white. I did not know where that scene came from in my past, but there it was – just that, the empty sand, the sea, and the trade wind. That was the last vision.

Janaki's servants were old and loyal, and knew me. No one came up to me during daylight, for it involved placing a ladder in the middle of Janaki's bedroom floor. The ladder would have been too difficult to hide or explain away in case of a sudden visit. Janaki came up that first night, with Margaret Wood. Margaret Wood spent a long time on my bandages, almost weeping over what I had done to myself since she last tied them. The second night she came alone, telling me that Janaki had gone to Chambalpur to say good-bye to Max before he finally left for his new posting in the wilds. She was going to have a last couple of days up there with him. I wished I could have at least felt sorry for him. The third and fourth nights it was Margaret Wood alone, twice each night, after dusk and before dawn, working on my wound and bandages, emptying the pot, feeding me, filling the water jug, leaving food for the daytime. I wished I could have at least felt sorry for her.

The fifth night, when the hurricane lantern rising like a will-o'-the-wisp through the trap door awakened me, I saw that it was Sumitra. A physical shock, like a bullet wound, set my head spinning. She saw that I was awake and came on up, but did not look at me again. For a time she set about her business, handing down the pot to an unseen sweeper waiting below, handing down the water jug, waiting for it to be returned full, taking up the tray of food, setting it on the floor beside me. I watched her, and waited. At last she squatted on her heels at the foot of my bed, and said gently, 'Eat, Rodney . . . Margaret had to go to the chemist's.'

I ate. She sat silent, her face averted. When I had finished she handed the tray down the trap door, and returned to her place. 'Have you nothing to say to me, Rodney?' she muttered.

All the time my head had ached, the plates had wavered in front of my sight.

'Come here,' I said. She began to get up, and my hands flexed. The throbbing in my head turned to sharp stabs of agony.

We both heard the creaking of the ladder, then Margaret Wood's head appeared, followed by Janaki's. The pain left my head and my eyes focused. They glanced quickly from Sumitra to me. Sumitra stared at her feet. Janaki said, 'I'm just back . . . I have to leave this house tomorrow, Rodney. The new general is moving in the day after. Sumitra's going to friends in Bombay, and I to my mother. We will take you with us. You must leave India as soon as possible. Margaret is sure she can arrange with Sir Andrew Graham to smuggle you out on a McFadden Pulley ship. If that fails, P. R. Sethi has promised to fly you to Pakistan, from there it will be easy to go on wherever you want to. Max saw Hussein Ali in jail in Chambalpur yesterday – he's being let out any day now – and he has promised to put ten thousand rupees into a Swiss bank for you. You must see that there is no other way, nothing else to be done now.'

I said, 'How do we get to Bombay?'

She stared at me, surprised. 'Well . . . that's wonderful . . . I didn't expect, somehow . . . we will leave early in the morning in the Ford station wagon, Margaret, Sumitra, and I. You will be hidden under the bedding rolls in the back. "Chop" Wazeer, Max's A.D.C., will drive for the first ten miles, and that far we'll be travelling with an artillery regiment going down to the Babina ranges. There is a police post on the road but I don't think they'll search us very carefully, if at all, in the circumstances. After that, you will be our chauffeur, an Anglo-Indian perhaps . . .'

'George D'Souza,' I said. 'All right. Get me some clothes and thin, cheap shoes.'

'I've done that,' Margaret Wood cut in; 'everything's ready. You get to sleep now.'

'The head of the regiment is passing the house at seven in the morning,' Janaki said. 'We must be ready to go by then.'

'All right,' I said.

The three women left the attic, and again I was alone, in the dark.

'Slower, Rodney, please!'

Janaki's voice was sharp. I realised I was doing over seventy, and eased my foot on the accelerator pedal. The old Ford slowed. It was a pre-war V-8 station wagon, much the worse for wear, the springs gone, the body rattling, and a hurricane of dust swirling around inside so that the two Indian women had the ends of their saris drawn tight across mouth and nostrils. Margaret Wood was in front with me.

'You really must drive slower,' Janaki said, not quite so sharply, realising that I wasn't altogether with them. 'The police will stop us.'

There were no police on that southward road from Bhowani, after the post we had passed, without incident, at the edge of town; but I tried to keep it down. Obviously I could not get away from Sumitra by driving like a maniac, when she was in the back seat of the same car.

I drove all morning. Near Itarsi Janaki bought food and brought it to the car while I had the tank filled. We ate later, by the roadside in thin jungle. I drove all afternoon, and at dusk we reached the place Janaki had chosen for the day's destination. I didn't know it, but she had driven this road many times. It was a dak bungalow on a side road which had been by-passed by more modern construction. A faded signpost pointed to *Gonaghar Dak*

Bungalow, 3 miles, and soon there it was, standing back in calm decay in a clearing off the deserted road. Even the bullock carts used the new tarmac now. The ancient *chowkidar* staggered out from one of the servants' quarters, and made a low salaam. 'Will you be staying the night, presences?'

Janaki said, 'Yes', and the old man's eyes lit up. It must have been a year since anyone had stopped there, except a district commissioner or a forest officer, on tour. Perhaps not even one of them. These bungalows were built for men who travelled on horseback. For years they'd been declining as everyone dashed past in cars.

I got out and opened the doors for the women. Then in three trips I carried their suitcases and bedding rolls into the bungalow. Every time I went near Sumitra I felt dizzy. When I returned for the cheap cardboard case they had given me, I started automatically for the bungalow again. Janaki nudged me, glancing towards the servants' quarters, and I headed back there.

The *chowkidar* lived in the quarter nearest the bungalow. He had no woman. I took the quarter farthest from him. It was the usual cell, about nine feet by five, containing a string charpoy and a string chair, both in advanced disrepair. Outside, on a small brick platform, there was a standpipe and a brass tap. I washed my hands and face and went back into the cell. The walls might have been whitewashed ten years ago, but now were cracked and peeling and kicked away at the bottom, showing the dusty brick underneath. The floor was of broken and pitted cement. A door hung on one hinge. There was no window.

Now, in my role, I should drag my bed out into the dusk, and squat on it, smoking a *bidi.* Soon the old man would come down from fussing about the bungalow, installing the ladies, and pull his bed close to mine, and sit on it. We would pass the *bidis* back and forth, holding them in our cupped hands between the outer fingers, sucking in the smoke so that our lips never touched the end. We would discuss our employers, the government, the crops, and the weather. I could not face it, and walked away.

The servants' quarters backed on a mango grove. In the dusk the formal dark-green leaves shone with an oily smoothness, and the boles marched away into outer darkness like a parade of soldiers waiting for some ceremony to begin. Yellow lights shone out of the dak bungalow's windows as the *chowkidar* lit the lamps, giving the impression of lights in a temple. It struck my fancy that the parade and the lights were for a funeral ceremony, the funeral of the Last Sahib. The *chowkidar* would be pleased if he knew he had spoken to a real sahib, a *vilayeti* sahib. It wouldn't disturb him much to realise that it was a funeral he was officiating at. After all, the play's the thing, and if it happens to be a tragedy, it's a tragedy.

The Last Sahib at the Last Dak Bungalow. I looked with a bitter longing at the ramshackle bungalow, the faded whitewash, the warm yellow of the lamps in the windows. These were mine, these and the mango grove, the jungle behind, the invisible hills beyond, and the abandoned road.

The *chowkidar's* voice called me: '*Ohé*, driver, food is ready!' I went back to the servants' quarters and we ate rice and dal off neem leaves. The old man said I reminded him of Golightly Sahib, the Forest Officer. Golightly Sahib stayed here often. In 1906 and '07. Perhaps he was hinting that I might be this Golightly's son, but I repeated that I came from Goa and after we had finished eating he shuffled off to carry their dinner up to the ladies.

After an hour's silent smoking I dragged the charpoy back into the cell, leaving the door open, lay down, and tried to get to sleep. The long dusty day's drive had worn me out, and I did sleep, a sleep absolutely blank of thought, dream, memory, or expectation.

I awoke with a hand gently shaking my shoulder, and a voice saying softly, 'Rodney.' I recognised her voice, but even if I hadn't, the dizziness and the stabbing pain in my skull would have told me. I opened my eyes and vaguely sensed her shape beside me. 'It is I, Sumitra,' she said.

She squatted down on her heels against the wall, her face on a level with mine. She said, 'I must speak. I cannot make you listen. I only beg you to, for your own sake as well as mine . . . Margaret and Janaki have made me promise never to go near you alone, but I must . . . I have had three weeks now to think of what I did, and what I must do. I love you, Rodney. I did wrong in deceiving you, and I ask you to forgive me. I have learned that there is nothing more valuable than love . . . For the future, I must go into politics. India needs women leaders more than men. Our future depends on the women. I ask you to come with me. At first you are bound to be under my shelter. There is no way of avoiding it. [*The probing needles in my head were without pity.*] Soon, though, it will be the other way round. Your mind is stronger than mine, and you know the real India better than I do, in spite of my blood. You will be the brain and the will, and I the hand. There isn't a decent politician in the country who wouldn't like to find, somehow, a way to use you and all that you represent. I ask you to be my lord, my husband.'

My wound gave me a slow long stab of pain, her blurred shape twisted and writhed, though I knew she did not move. Inside my head, I could stand no more.

'Come here,' I whispered.

She knelt forward and leaned over me. The trembling lake was the wet sheen in her huge eyes. 'Oh, Rodney . . .'

I put up my hands and grasped her round the throat. For ten long seconds, while my fingers tightened and cut off her breathing, she knelt absolutely still. Then her hands began to jerk, and she beat frantically at my wrists. I released my grip a little, just enough, and heard her croak, 'Must live . . . not for my sake . . . let me . . .'

I squeezed tight again, and said, 'Beside you. On the chair.' My head was clear, without pain.

Her right hand, reaching urgently, found the chair, and the pistol lying loaded on it. When she had it in her hand, I locked my grip and waited. There was no fear in me, no pain, no emotion of any kind. As soon as I saw this faded dak bungalow by its empty clearing in a forgotten jungle I recognised it as the end of the road. The pistol jabbed and wavered against my forehead now, but she was losing her strength. Another few seconds and she would not be able to pull the trigger. I released my grip, let her draw four wheezing breaths, and squeezed again.

Her head bowed forward, her arms lowered, and the pistol dropped with a heavy clatter to the cement. Her struggles ceased. But it was not the failure of her strength, it was the victory of her will. She had made up her mind that I should not die by her hand.

For a moment longer the power flowed into my wrists, then, as suddenly as the turning off of a tap, it failed – just vanished, leaving my arms and fingers and body full of a chill, trembling water. Even the final gesture, even the forlorn hope, had failed.

I heard her slump to the floor. Her breathing was strangulated, loud, and groaning. Gradually it settled into a painful but steady inhalation. Then I heard the rustle of her clothes as she rose to her feet, heard her stand up, move to the door, one hand slithering along the wall for support, heard her go out. All sound died, and that was the end, the absolute end.

Chapter 19

Margaret Wood watched stiffly as Sumitra stumbled out of the quarters. Sumitra did not raise her head when Margaret put one arm around her waist and under her shoulders and, thus supporting her, helped her up to the bungalow. Still she did not speak while Margaret guided her into her room, eased her on to the bed, and lit the lamp. She lay on the bed, looking up at the ceiling cloth, her eyes wide, while Margaret sponged her blotched face, and her neck with its livid finger marks.

When she had done all that she could, Margaret said, 'Do you have any sleeping pills, or shall I give you some of mine? I got them for him.'

Sumitra said, 'I have some. That bottle on the table.' She drank the water, swallowed two pills, and lay back. 'You followed me? You were there the whole time? Outside?'

Margaret said, 'Yes. Yes. Yes.'

'You didn't want to save me? Or him?'

Margaret said, 'You – no, except for the trouble it would have caused him. Him – I couldn't interfere. It was between him and you.'

'I see,' Sumitra said slowly. 'You hate me?'

Margaret said, 'I try not to. Now will you go away and leave him alone?'

The woman on the bed said, 'Yes . . . You can't really mend a broken jar, can you? What would you have done if it had ended differently tonight? Would *you* have gone away?'

Margaret said, 'No. I have no politics to turn to, no power, no position, no money. You would have betrayed him again, sooner or later . . . What did you mean, when you said it wasn't for your sake, that he should let you live?'

Sumitra's congested, bloodshot eyes turned slowly up to her. 'Nothing. Leave me now, please.'

Margaret turned and left the room. Outside Janaki's door she hesitated. But Janaki must be told, and she was a woman to be trusted. She entered quietly, whispering, 'Janaki?' The other awoke and Margaret sat on the edge of the bed and told her quickly what she had seen. Janaki muttered, 'Is he all right? Will he try to do it again tomorrow? Or kill us all in the car?'

Margaret said, 'No. It's finished.'

Then she went to her own room, and, knowing that she would have no need of tablets, being utterly spent, fell into bed and asleep.

In the morning after breakfast Rodney came, pale and contained, to load their baggage into the car. By eight o'clock they were on their way again through the awakening spring of a warm February day. The hours passed in almost total silence. Sometimes Sumitra talked in a low voice with Janaki in the back seat – Margaret noticed she made no attempt to hide the marks at her neck – but her talk was of nothing, things seen by the roadside, comments on people known, small bursts of human sound that broke up the inhuman silence in the car. She herself spoke occasionally to Rodney, searching for half an hour to find something to say, then saying it. Rodney answered monosyllabically, his voice dry. The Ford raced on, driven fast but safely.

Late in the evening they entered the outskirts of Bombay. At half past eleven, when passing slowly down a raucous street near Victoria Station, Rodney pulled in to the kerb.

Janaki sat up, yawning. 'Where are we? Why are we stopping here?'

Rodney did not answer but went round to the back, opened the door and pulled out his suitcase. 'I am leaving you here,' he said. 'I do not need help any more. It will also be dangerous for you. Thank you for everything you've done.'

Margaret tried to pull open her door, but he was leaning against it. His cold, dead glance turned momentarily on her, and he said, 'Stay there, please. I do not want your help, either.' He walked up to a taxi parked a little in front, and got in. The taxi drove away.

The three women sat without motion for a minute. Then Sumitra said, 'I'll drive. Your grandmother's house is on Douglas Road, isn't it?'

She slipped behind the wheel, and they went on without another

259

word. At the big house they all got out and a horde of women, children, and servants ran down the steps. Sumitra said, 'Would you mind calling a taxi for me?'

Once again, there was no argument, no talk. They waited in the drive, and in a few moments a taxi came. The servants transferred Sumitra's baggage into it, she climbed in with a final 'thank you', the taxi drove away.

Then Janaki introduced Margaret to the people crowding round: her sister; the sister's husband, a banker in the city; two female cousins; a fat aunt; a dozen assorted children, shy, wide-eyed, but yawning, for it was long past their usual bedtime; her mother, a widow for twenty years; and her mother's mother, a widow for forty years and the head of the household – a frail, thin-skinned old lady with piercing black eyes and a plain white sari, who said, as she held out her thin arms, 'Welcome, child . . . you are the first English person to enter any house of mine.'

The mother led Margaret to an upstairs room with the smell of the sea blowing in through open windows, escorted by the whole family so that she felt she was in a football crowd at home. For five minutes they all wandered round, each little boy and girl proudly pointing out a light switch, a cupboard, the table where she could have *chota hazri*, until at last Janaki cried, smiling, 'Leave the lady in peace. We have had a long day.'

Then they crowded out with profuse expressions of apology, and Margaret sat down on the bed. Janaki remained standing. 'What are we going to do now?'

'We?' Margaret said listlessly. 'He isn't your problem any more.'

Janaki said gently, 'I loved him myself, once . . . We are tired, and there's nothing we can do now, unless we call the police.'

Margaret sprang up, crying, 'No!'

Janaki smiled faintly. 'You are like a tigress . . . Of course we cannot. In the morning we will talk, eh? Now, go to sleep.'

In the morning, after the servant brought the *chota hazri*, Margaret got up and looked out the window. Between palms standing stiff in the airless morning, through the heavy sea-laden atmosphere, she could see a corner of the Indian Ocean, and a ship on it, gliding out of Bombay harbour four miles to the south round the curve of the reclaimed land, drawing a trail of strong black smoke across the blue-sheened water. The ship was going west, towards Aden, the Red Sea, and England. She watched it a long time, until only the smudge of its smoke hung above the sea line, then turned back into the room and began to dress.

As she had asked, they brought her breakfast to the room, and at ten o'clock Janaki came.

They sat in high hard chairs by the window, looking out across the Indian Ocean. Janaki came to the point at once. 'Margaret, is it any use suggesting that you should go back to England, now? He doesn't seem to care for you. Excuse me being frank, but it would be foolish to ruin your life out of an illusion. The worry, the strain, are making you ill.'

'Do I look ill?' Margaret interposed.

Janaki said, 'Thinner ... feverish. You look now the way I always expected missionaries to look, but you never did, the few times we met when you *were* a missionary – twice, wasn't it?' Janaki threw out her palm. 'I am not speaking the truth. You do look feverish, but it suits you. You are more beautiful than you have ever been.

Margaret said, 'Now I really am a missionary, with faith, and a cause I believe in, and love – the love Henry wanted me to have for Jesus. I suppose it's blasphemous, but I can't help it.'

'So many women go the other way,' Janaki said, 'turn from men to God. No, it's not blasphemous, not to a Hindu, at least ... I knew it was no use arguing with you. I only wanted to be sure that you understood what a long, hard road you have chosen. What do you want to do?'

'Find Rodney,' Margaret said promptly. That was all. That filled the whole of her thought.

'And then?' Janaki's voice was gentle but insistent.

Margaret gestured impatiently. 'Work for him, look after him, feed him, love him. Sumitra killed him. I must bring him back to life. I don't care what he does. He can beat me, steal from me, make me go on the streets, have other women in my bed, I don't care.'

Janaki sighed. 'Very well. Now, how are we going to find him?'

Margaret could not answer. They sat in silence, staring out at the flat blue sea.

261

'Private detectives?' Janaki said. 'They are terribly expensive, but . . .'

'I'll get the money somehow,' Margaret said. 'I have eight hundred rupees in the bank, and passage back to England that the mission gave me. I can get a refund on that. I can work, too.'

'Yes,' Janaki said, 'you can make a lot of money, with your training, particularly in private nursing.'

'That wouldn't give me enough time, and they usually want you to live in.'

'What about the Wadalia Hospital, then? It's run by the Parsees. It's very good – and they pay decent wages.'

'If only we could reach him with a message,' Margaret muttered.

Janaki's voice had a thin edge. 'What message? That you want him? He knows that. What can you say in a newspaper advertisement that would make him come out?'

'A newspaper advertisement,' Margaret said, 'I hadn't thought of that. Will he read the papers?'

'Not for a bit, probably. Even if he does, what are you going to say?'

Margaret got up. 'I'll think of something. Now, how do I find a private detective agency?'

It was Janaki's turn to be without an answer. At last she said, 'I don't even know if there are any.'

'There must be!' Margaret cried. 'They have divorces here, too, don't they? And cashiers they don't trust? I'll go to Sir Andrew Graham and ask him. And then, if you'll give me his name, to the chairman of that hospital.'

Ten minutes later Margaret left the house in a taxi, sitting impatiently on the edge of the seat all the way to McFadden Pulley's head office in the business district. That was the last taxi she took for a week. That was the beginning of an endless time when every day contained too few hours for the fulfilment of her restless desire for action, and every night too many . . .

Sir Andrew Graham ushered her personally into his office. Although she never said it out plain, he understood the situation clearly, and tried to warn her against banking too much on a man of Rodney Savage's proven instability and violence. She shook off his warnings, and then he answered her question. Yes, he knew of a reliable private investigation agency. Yes, he would be happy to lend her money, over and above what he would give as a small contribution.

'And when I do find him,' Margaret said, 'if he agrees to leave India, will you smuggle him out of the country in one of your ships?'

Sir Andrew fingered his heavy jowls and his Scots accent became more noticeable. 'They are not my ships any more, Mrs Wood. They belong to the new McFadden Pulley, of which I am not a partner, merely the managing director, and that for only a few months more.'

'The ships' officers are still English, aren't they,' she said emphatically, 'even in the coasting steamers?'

'It's a dangerous business for us to get involved in,' he said.

'You owe it to him!' she cried. 'What were you doing when he was being wounded in Burma?'

Sir Andrew held up his hand. 'I will see what might be possible, if the situation arises. I doubt that it will arise.' He walked with her to the door. Just before opening it he said with a half-smile, 'I was sitting at that desk during *this* war, Mrs Wood. But in 1917 I was lying wounded and frozen in a trench with a hundred corpses, at a place called Passchendaele.'

'I'm sorry,' she said.

'Good luck, ma'am. I only hope he turns out worthy of you.'

On to the address he had given her, hurrying on foot through the crowds in the lazily growing heat. A guarded talk with two small dark men in European clothes. Ah, Colonel Rodney Savage. Did Madam realise that if they learned anything about that gentleman they were in duty bound under the terms of their licence to report it to the police? The gentleman had a criminal as opposed to a civil suit pending against him. This was a special case! Yes, indeed, precisely. In the circumstances, provided it was only information, not leading to a situation where their agents could be said to have made actual contact, as in serving papers or the like ... Aah, nothing of the sort, Precisely. In that case ...

On, to the office of Milkwalla and Company Ltd. Wait in the outer office, cautiously scrutinised by fat gentlemen in tall hats through glass partitions. Guided into the presence of Sir Ramatoola Milkwalla, a stern old man in traditional Parsee robes; in the

263

corner, at another big desk, a young man with a huge R.A.F. moustache and hacking jacket. The old man reads Janaki's note, mumbling politely to himself. At the end: 'Mrs Wood, if your qualifications are as stated, I am sure the hospital will be only too glad to employ you . . . but for how long? It upsets the routine of the hospital to employ nurses, especially senior ones, who come for a few weeks and when their, ah, purpose is served, leave. How long a contract of service will you sign?'

No more lies, anywhere. She lifted her chin. 'I am here looking for a man – Colonel Savage. When I find him I will leave the hospital, if he wants me to.'

The young man in the corner turned. 'Rodney Savage? The chap who rubbed out that clot Gokal Singh in Chambal?'

'Yes,' she said.

'I knew him in Burma. Came to our squadron mess once, and broke all our plates. Great binge! Next day I flew him over Homalin in a Harvard. Flack everywhere, no joy. Pranged on landing. Kersplat! No gore.'

'Murder?' the old man said. 'Do I understand, madam, that you are associated . . .?'

The young man said, 'Come into the other office for a moment, Dad.'

They left her alone. When they returned the young man said, 'A piece of cake. I'll ring old Merchant and he'll give you the job. Savage was one of the best brown jobs I ever came across.'

On to the hospital, a large brick building half a mile back from the docks. Crowds of all races waiting under the trees outside, and in the corridors. Interview with Dr Merchant, a tired, over-worked man. Talk about Dr Pallister at the Royal Mersey. She got the job, as senior night sister, medical wards. The matron did not ask her why she wanted night duty, but was only too glad to agree. Start tomorrow, to give her time to get her uniform cleaned and laundered. She would wear the Royal Mersey cap and cape, of course? Of course.

On, back to Janaki's, to eat. Out, working like a hound through crowded streets, staring at every face, until an Anglo-Indian police officer barred her way. His voice was hard: 'How long have you been on the street? I don't recognise you.'

She shook her head, a tired hound coming out of water. The

street lamps glowed, her feet burned. She stared at the man. 'Where am I?'

His voice changed. 'Are you all right, ma'am?'

'Yes, yes.'

She turned and hurried away. Must get a street map of the city tomorrow, mark it out in sectors, search each sector thoroughly. Must sleep. After she started work, how many hours a day could she walk, search? Must remember to visit the detective agency every day, too . . .

On, through the night, the next day. The first night at the hospital, the routines coming back to her hand so that she did automatically what had to be done, and between watched the dawdling circles of the clock until she could go home. Sleep, hurry to the agency, lean over the two dark men. Any news? No, ma'am, we must exert patience . . . Out on to the streets.

One morning hurrying up the stairs at Janaki's at eight o'clock on her way to bed, a hand on her elbow detained her. She tried to shrug it off but it held more firmly, and a voice said, 'Margaret, *stop!*'

She stopped. Janaki linked her arm in hers and walked her up to the bedroom, forcing her to go at her own slow pace. Inside the room Janaki said, 'Sit down in the chair . . . You've been running for a week now. Now you really do look ill. Do you want to get sacked from the hospital? Do you want to make some terrible mistake there and kill a patient? Do you want Rodney to think an old witch is after him, if you do find him? When's your night off?'

'Tonight, but I volunteered to give it up.'

'Oh, no, you don't. I shall ring Dr Merchant and cancel that. We haven't seen you for days, your food is hardly touched . . .'

'I've got to find him,' Margaret said sullenly. This happily married woman did not understand.

Janaki said, 'See, you're so tired you're getting bad tempered . . . Max suggested an idea, in his last letter.'

'What?'

'He said that the only hope of getting Rodney out of hiding was to find what he cares about, and appeal to that. He thinks Rodney still worries about that Gurkha driver who disappeared. Remember Sumitra telling us about him, one evening in Bhowani, a day or two before Rodney came?'

265

Margaret nodded. She remembered, and remembered the Gurkha's face, too. He used to drive often past the mission bungalow when Rodney was at Pattan, and he drove the wounded man to Bhowani, the man Lady Hillburn shot. She said, 'But he stole the jewels, didn't he? For the reward that Rajah Dip Rao was giving. Rodney must hate him. He was the first to betray him.'

Janaki said, 'Perhaps. But Max suggests you put an advertisement into the paper, pretending you're Ratanbir. If Rodney doesn't respond, you're no worse off. But Max thinks Rodney will want to see him again, to find out the truth. He thinks that Rodney doesn't really believe he did it. He believes, or wants to believe, that it was somehow a machination of Sumitra's and L. P. Roy's. . .'

'What will he say, if it does work, and he finds it isn't Ratanbir, but me?'

Janaki said, 'That is a risk you have to take. You can't do anything for him until you find him.'

Margaret made up her mind. 'Very well. I will.'

Janaki said, 'Max said, don't use Ratanbir's name, as the police will know of the connection and it's a distinctively Gurkha name, which would be noticed in a Bombay paper. His old army number was 2588. So many Gurkhas have the same name that the officers often speak to them by the last two figures of their numbers. You may have heard Rodney call him *atharsi* – that's 88.'

'The meeting place would have to be in code. I mean, some place that Ratanbir and Rodney would know, but would not be clear from the text.'

'Yes. Suppose you say, round the corner outside the place where he used to work. Rodney would know that was McFadden Pulley's. There's a café there, a sort of teahouse among a lot of small shops, bookstalls, and so on . . . We'll have to insert the ad several times, in several papers . . . Would you rather I sent a servant to the rendezvous? We could describe Rodney to him, and he could follow him, and tell us where he lives. Better still, tell the detective agency.'

'No, I'll go myself,' she said. 'Where's a pencil and paper?'

When she went to bed an hour later the advertisement was

already on its way by messenger to the newspaper offices. The message, to run a week in all newspapers, was: *Waiting five p.m. every day one hour in teashop round corner from place you used to work – 88.*

That evening, from five to six, she sat in the dingy teashop, waiting. It was a worrying, anxious time, and full of problems, some of which she had not foreseen. She had foreseen that she must not sit too much in view, or he could recognise her from a distance, realise the deception, and again vanish, this time for ever. On the other hand, she must sit far enough forward so that she could see him when he did enter the teashop. She had foreseen that, sitting alone for an hour in such a place, she would be the object of curiosity and perhaps worse, and so had armed herself with a book, and also ordered a quantity of the teashop's sickly sweetmeats, so that she appeared to be taking a peculiar sort of supper.

She had not foreseen the denseness of the crowds, nor their St Vitus's Dance of purposeless motion. For minutes at a time she could see nothing but jiggling legs, waving shirt-sleeves, dark, animated faces. The teashop jerked with them. On the street outside they hurried in opposing streams, met in tide rips of animation, broke into circling groups, rushed off in different directions. After half an hour her head ached and her left eye, catching the restlessness, developed a tic.

She had not foreseen the bugs. Just when the concentrated effort to pick out his face amid the frenzy was becoming nervously oppressive, she felt a bug crawling up the inside of her thigh. Instinctively she jumped to her feet, meaning to ask the man at the counter where the lavatory was. Then she sat down again. She dared not leave even for a minute. A couple of young men standing jammed together close to her table stared at her in amused astonishment, and she bent her head over her book. But he did not come.

The next evening she doused her underclothes with bug powder. As she sat down at the same table, and opened her book, she could not help a smile, quickly concealed, at the typically Indian mixture of high tragedy and low comedy. The powerful smell of the bug powder crept out from under her skirt to mingle with the subtly expensive perfume she had bought that afternoon. The men jammed round the tea urns kept looking about, and at each other, and sniffing. But he did not come.

The next day, fifteen minutes after the appointed time, he came – a stoop-shouldered figure in dirty white trousers and shirt, a newspaper in one hand, a battered topi on his head, dark stubble on chin and jowl – a middle-aged Anglo-Indian, down on his luck. For a moment she did not recognise him, and obviously he had no eyes for her because after staring round the teashop, he turned and left. She half rose, fighting to hold back her tears. The men stared at her as she put money on the table, grabbed her book, and hurried out. She saw his topi above the puggarees and the bare heads, and walked faster. At the next corner, when the snarling, ill-tempered traffic held him up, she caught him. She touched his arm, 'Rodney,' she said in a low voice.

The traffic cleared and he walked on, turning his head. His eyes were dull on hers. He said, 'Oh. It was you, was it?'

'I must talk to you.'

He stopped. 'Well?'

She looked nervously up and down the crowded street. 'Not here. It's not safe.'

He opened the newspaper in his hand, and gave it to her. On the front page a two-column headline announced *Amnesty in Chambal.* The story explained that with the setting up of a democratic Congress ministry in the province of Chambal, and in order to eradicate all previous bitterness, the government had declared an amnesty in respect of acts done during the troubles. A brief editorial comment noted that this closed the cases of half a dozen men – they were listed – now in hiding or in jail awaiting trial. Rodney's name was on the list.

'It's an evening paper,' she said, 'I left the house at three and didn't see anything ... Oh, Rodney, that's wonderful!'

He took back the paper. 'Well?'

'Please let me come with you.'

'I can't stop you,' he said.

He walked on. She walked beside him, wishing she were not so conspicuously clean, so fastidiously dressed beside him, so that men turned their heads and women stared at her.

'Can you smell the bug powder on me?' she asked, forcing a smile. 'That teashop's crawling with the beasts. My panties are full of powder. Yesterday a bug practically went to earth up there before I could catch him.'

He said, 'I can smell it.'

After fifteen minutes' walk through increasingly squalid streets, he turned into a row of mean houses on a mean street. Garbage, offal, and filth overflowed the gutters, the street lamps shone on broken glass and chipped brick, on women leaning out of windows and washing hung from lines strung across the street.

She followed him up one flight of stairs, along a passage smelling of urine, and into a small back room, its bare walls streaked with damp, the wooden floor bristling with splinters. She saw his suitcase and a chamber pot under the bed, and, thrown into the corner, half a dozen newspapers. A single electric light bulb hung from the ceiling.

'As you've got bug powder on, you can sit on the bed,' he said. 'I have to go to work in an hour.'

'Me, too,' she said. She wanted to ask him what his work was, but she had better wait. She said, 'First, is your wound healed properly?'

'It hasn't bothered me.'

'May I look at it?'

He unfastened his shirt and opened his fly buttons without a word. His trousers dropped and she leaned forward. The exit wound was still slightly inflamed. 'Turn round,' she said. The entry wound in his back was clean and healthy, faintly pink, light scar tissue well formed. 'Turn round again, please. You ought to keep that well covered, and protected with sulpha powder until it heals properly. You haven't seen any signs of blood in your urine or stool?'

'I haven't looked,' he said.

Her professional detachment vanished. She became intensely aware of the ridge of hair running down from his navel into the dense forest of his loins, of the muscled columns of his thighs, the unequivocal statement of his male formation.

A tiny movement in the hairs caught her eye. Her arms went out, holding him tight by the buttocks. This she knew only too well, from her profession.

'Oh, Rodney,' she wailed, her voice breaking, 'you've got crabs. And you're covered with bug bites. You must have lice, too.'

'Probably,' he said. He pulled up his trousers, so that she had to take her hands away.

'For God's sake, leave India,' she cried. 'Sir Andrew Graham will give you a passage. There's nothing for you here now, nothing at all.'

She waited, pleading silently for an answer. What there had been for him, what had been offered so generously, he had refused. What he had tried to keep had been taken from him, and broken before his eyes. There was nothing.

'Go?' he said slowly. 'I can't go. I'd be ashamed.'

'Ashamed of what?' she cried.

He held out his empty hands and stared at them, turning them over slowly. He said, 'Nothing. Having nothing. Being nothing. I can only do that here.'

She drew a deep breath. 'Let me look after you, then. I have a night job, too, nursing at the Wadalia Memorial. I don't ask anything else. I won't get in your way. I don't ask you to speak to me even, but . . . I can't bear it!' Tears welled up in her eyes.

He said, 'I have nothing to give you.'

She cried, 'I don't want anything.'

He didn't speak for a long time. Then she heard his distant voice: 'I suppose nothing else will teach you. All right.'

She leaped to her feet, her arms out. In the face of his silent indifference she let them fall to her sides. 'We'll have to get a better room,' she said, 'where I can cook.'

'I'm staying here,' he said. 'The room next door's empty, and there's a gas ring and a cold water tap in it.'

For a moment she felt chilled; but then at once thought, It's better not to crowd too closely on him until he asks me. She said, 'I'll take it now, and move in tomorrow morning' – she found another smile – 'with a gallon of disinfectant and five pounds of bug powder.'

'All right,' he said.

Chapter 20

February: the fresh light pouring a clean Aegean-colour wash over the filth of the city and shading the smoke to pastel. By the end of the month, twice daily scrubbing walls and floors of the two rooms with soap and water, with carbolic acid, with Jeyes Fluid, with potassium permanganate, she had conquered the bugs. By taking beds and chairs into the street, unwinding the *newar*, dousing the frames in kerosene and setting fire to them, she burned the bugs out of the cracks and joints. By soaking his head and her own in kerosene, by shaving and blue ointment and vigilance she freed him and herself of lice, nits, and crabs. By miserly scraping and clearing of scraps she kept away the mice, rats, and cockroaches. The landlord, a fat Muslim living in terror of his Hindu neighbours ever since the partition massacres, at first treated her as a madwoman, but now with a grudging respect.

Rodney was clean, and free of parasites, because she kept him free. Otherwise he had not altered one jot. Every evening he left the house, walked to the Central Station, and took an electric train three stops up the line to the cotton mill where he was employed as night watchman. He had originally given the name of D'Souza when applying for the job, and saw no reason to change it. Every morning he returned, ate the supper she had prepared, then went to bed. At three in the afternoon he awoke, ate breakfast. She washed up and cleaned. He lay on his bed until the time came to go to work.

March: the heat gradually increasing in a double progression, each morning a little hotter, a little closer, than the day before, each afternoon a little hotter, a little closer, than the morning, a blanket-like drugging sea heat, far different from the sword thrusts of the northern sun.

At the hospital she made the mistake Janaki had warned her she

271

would. In consequence a sick Parsee woman spent a night in the oxygen tent, and Dr Merchant spoke in sad warning to her. The hospital could not afford such mistakes, let alone the patients. She grew distraught, snappish, and distant. For a time her job teetered on the brink. But too much depended on it: decent food for Rodney, decent clothes, good sheets, gay curtains, all that could remind him of another world outside the rat-ridden tenement and the overcrowded train to the factory. After a bitter night, knowing that it needed only a touch of his hand, the graze of his cheek on hers, in love, to cure her, and knowing he had no desire to make the gestures, and no love to charge them with meaning, she mastered herself. After that she wiped Rodney out of her mind at the moment she entered the hospital grounds, by a deliberate act of will, like cleaning a slate with a wet cloth; and took him back the moment she walked into the street again in the morning.

In Rodney – no change. He slept in the steamy heat as well, or as badly, as in the Mediterranean beauty of February. Watching him narrowly, trying to learn more about him, she noticed how un-Indian he was. There was nothing strange about his face or his clothes, but people always looked at him with surprise as he passed, even those living in the same block, who saw him every day. It was his manner, she decided. He was a dead-beat, a down-and-out. But those were Western words carrying the notion that he had once been something else, and, but for his own character, might be again. There was no resignation in him, only despair, for he was not in the grip of an all-powerful fate, like the Indian poor around him, but in the grip of his own nature.

She noticed also his absolute lack of possessions. Where were his medals, his uniforms? Most of his civilian clothes he had lost in Chambal, and the rest when he was wounded. When he arrived that dawn in Bhowani after his flight he carried nothing of the past but a wrist-watch, and somewhere even that had gone. She believed it was a presentation watch, perhaps with his name engraved on the back, and he had thrown it away before leaving Bhowani as their chauffeur. In becoming the chauffeur he had lost the clothes she had given him. Now, apart from the suitcase and the minimum of necessary clothes, he owned nothing at all.

April: heavy clouds beginning to move up in dense formations from the Arabian Sea, so that at noon the city lay dark in the stifling embrace of heat, and the sun's rays, grey and hardly visible, poured out from the stone walls, up from the oiled streets, down from the trees. The fecundity of India, which she had once scorned and feared, now twisted her bowels every time she went out. There were always two or three pregnant women squatting outside the houses, always a dozen naked brown babies playing in the gutter. In the afternoon she heard wailing and cooing from every window and doorway. Wherever she turned, women squatted with choli loosened, sari negligently half covering one breast, a baby ecstatically kneading and sucking at the other.

Rodney had not changed, not a degree.

May: a sudden increase in heat and humidity, though she had thought both were impossible. A short violent dust storm, followed by heavy rain, struck on the first of the month, when the Communists marched through the streets waving the clenched fist, banners flying until the wind shredded them and the rain drove marchers and spectators alike off the streets, and ten palm trees blew down in the park. The Alfonso mangoes came in season now, yellow, juicy, firm-fleshed, and sweet as nuts. She bought four, carefully wrapped in ice, gave him two for breakfast, and waited expectantly for comment. In vain: he said nothing.

She almost lost her temper with him then, but controlled herself, and when he had gone, wondered whether in fact he ever tasted anything. His taste buds could not have been physically destroyed, but perhaps the nerves that transmitted the sense to the brain were out of action, like those others that instigated interest, pity, hate. Later, she decided it must be so, for in the middle of the month they were walking together to the end of the block, where he would turn left and she right, when a careening truck swung round the corner and ran over a two-year-old child in front of its mother. The child was half squashed, like a beetle, no longer a human being but an animal dying in pain, gobbling and writhing in blood and crushed flesh. The mother ran out, shrieking. Rodney glanced at it, and walked on, saying nothing. Later that day, punctually on schedule, May 15, the monsoon broke. She discovered a leak in the wall of Rodney's room, the plaster began to flake off her own ceiling, the rats came into the house for shelter from the flooded sewers, and a few nights later she killed two of them in her room with the frying pan.

June: the rains falling in their cyclic pattern, rain every night, clearing a little by dawn; mid-morning rain, clear in the afternoon; rain starting in the evening when she set out for the hospital. Mould forming in the shoes she ranked against the wall, in a single day. The temperature hovering around 90 every day, 88 every night. No change in Rodney . . . A subtle, growing change in herself. She saw a cockroach, and made no attempt to kill it. Half-way to the hospital she would remember she had left the dishes unwashed on the table. Or she would look in the mirror in the nurses' common room, and see that she had forgotten to put on lipstick.

July: July 1, the monsoon broke out into one of its sudden spells of violence. Lightning sizzled across the roofs of tenement and factory, and outlined the ships in harbour with violet fire. Thunder rattled the bedside tables in the wards and the lights flickered off, once for a few seconds in the middle of an important operation and later for ten minutes. The patients grew more nervous and jittery. Lightning struck a tall, old building opposite. The building cracked with a sound like a dynamite explosion, and then caught fire internally. In two of the wards the patients' collective nerve cracked, and hysteria exploded. In the morning she walked back to the tenement through a battered, shell-torn city in the rain, fell into bed, and asleep.

She awoke early, her nerves on edge . . . As soon as she had dressed she opened the cupboard and took out the bottle of whisky she kept there. She poured herself a stiff dram, drank it in a couple of gulps, and began to prepare the tea, bread, vegetables, and lamb chops for their 'breakfast'.

Rodney came in and she indicated the bottle. 'Have some. Have a lot . . . Look at it!' She waved a free hand at the small window. The rain streamed down the panes, and seeped in over the sill with the driving wind. Thunder growled in the distance, clouds hung low over the rooftops, and there was no sign of the sun.

Rodney poured himself a drink. Nowadays he did not drink anything like as much as he used to. As with pain, and with taste, there was nothing there. If she offered him the bottle, he drank. If she didn't, he didn't. Once, trying to stir him to show *some* kind of

274

emotion, she had given him half a dozen pegs in quick succession. Nothing changed, neither in his manner, nor in his speech, nor in his silence.

When they had eaten she pushed the plates aside – to wash them she had to take them down to the drain in the tiny back yard – and poured herself another whisky. Rodney rose, but she said, 'Sit down. Have another whisky. There's nothing else to do today. Pheew, it's close.'

The whisky burned like a small coal fire in the pit of her stomach. How long, how long? The memory of the night crowded in upon her and she felt a hysterical desire to be held tight against fear, fear of loneliness, fear of the dark, fear of the vast and heedless universe. The muscles of her wrists trembled and the tic returned to her eye. In all these weeks she had held herself back from a physical contact she needed as a flower needs water. She had thought, once, that his sheer maleness must sooner or later break out at the provocative glimpses he had of her: half dressed; bending to put on a shoe; standing with one leg on a chair to fasten garters; brushing her hair in front of the mirror – situations which she had not deliberately created because she had not needed to. Living so close, they happened. She had hoped, at first almost subconsciously, later with acknowledged hunger, that animal rut would bring him upon her. Once in her arms he *must* feel the melting totality of her love. From lust she could lead him to tenderness, to hope of a future, to . . .

He never made a move, and she never caught in his eye any glint of interest, nor heard any tremor of invitation in his voice. These, and the gradually deepening loss of confidence, had held her from a more direct approach, so that, although their hands occasionally brushed, and, in those confined spaces, more often, their bodies, that had been all. Besides, she was a woman and knew without having to remind herself that if her permanent availability and her obvious love did not move him, certainly no assault would.

But there come moments of desperation when one must do the thing that is bound to fail, because it is there in one's nature and cannot be for ever suppressed. As she stood up, her eyelid quivering, she thought of Rodney himself, rushing out in the dawn from Chambalpur to the hopeless battle . . .

She went to him, carefully lifted the whisky out of harm's way, and sat on his lap. She muttered, 'Rodney,' and snuggled close against him, her arms round him and her mouth pressed to his cheek. The long-withheld fact of physical pressure went off like a bomb in her, but not specifically in her sexual desires or in their seat. She clung and whispered, kissed and caressed in an agony of love, willing the cold body to come to life, trying to squeeze out her own life into him, so that she could lie at last dead at his feet, if only he could live, to look down on her with the love she was giving him. 'Oh, my darling, my darling,' she mumbled, 'oh, my darling, my darling, I love you, I love you.'

Thus for a long time, which she could not measure, just a long time, until he took her by the shoulders and pushed her away.

The intensity of her emotion again exploded, this time in quick-burning fuses of anger leading from all parts of her body to her head and pouring in fire from her smarting eyes. She stooped and tugged and kicked out of her underpants, jerked up her skirt until she held it above her waist, and thrust her loins into his face. 'There!' she screamed. '*There!* Don't you even want *that!* Forget about *me.* Think of *that!* You're a man, aren't you?'

He said coldly, 'We had a louse inspection the day before yesterday. Pull your skirt down . . . The purpose of making love is to have children.'

She pushed down her skirt, her heart pounding. She said, 'There's nothing . . .'

'When you *can* have children, you can forget that they're the object. You can take sex as lust, as affection, as anything you like. When you can't – you can't.'

She cried, 'Rodney, I would die with happiness if you would . . .'

He said, 'No one can have my child, or will.'

'I will,' she said.

He said, 'No, you won't.' He met her eyes coldly. She knew that nothing of her passion, her desire, her love had communicated itself to him. He was, at least in regard to her, impotent.

She sat down and poured herself a whisky. 'What would you do if you had a child?' she asked.

He said, 'I'd take her away with me.' His hands came forward, not outspread and empty now, but slightly curled, carefully holding the invisible shape of a small baby. 'I'd raise her and love her and think my life had been worthwhile. I could go then, and begin again, because I'd have something to begin with. But, as you see – I shall not have a child.'

'I could have your baby,' she said carefully. 'There are modern ways. One's called artificial insemination. You wouldn't have to make love to me.'

He said, 'A child that came out of love, of its own accord, not planned for any purpose.'

She sat, with head bowed over the table. After a while she said, 'It's time we both had a holiday. I need one badly, and so do you.'

'I don't want a holiday,' he said.

'We could go up to Mahabaleshwar,' she said, 'we could go to Ajanta . . . a rest house in the jungle somewhere. We've got to get out of this.'

Rodney said, 'There's nothing to stop you going.'

'Without you? I'd be miserable,' she said.

As soon as she said it she knew she was lying. At this moment, her head aching from the thunder, her nerves jangling from the night's hysteria and the screaming patients, the lightning flashing through the darkened wards, her body quivering with frustrated love, she knew that she would give anything to be away from this silent, dead corpse to which she had tied herself.

She said, 'Then, if we aren't going to have a holiday, we must live better. There's no need for you to work as a *chowkidar* any more. Last month young Khussroo Milkwallah came to the hospital, and asked after you. I told him what you were doing and he said, "That's a bit of a bind, isn't it? What's the point?" He's right. Yesterday he was in again, and told me they'd be happy to appoint you assistant administrative officer there. The administrative officer is no more than a glorified *babu*, and they want a different type of man, anyway, someone who can deal with the doctors as an equal, but take the administrative load – the actual buying of supplies, the laundry, the catering – off their hands. The *babu's* going to retire in six months, and by then you'll be ready to take over, at a much better salary, too . . . There was no chance to tell you about it yesterday.'

Rodney had given no appearance of listening, and again, for a moment, the furious outburst against him hovered in her throat and in the aching tips of her fingers. Just as she leaned forward to shout at him, he said, 'There's no place for me in that world.'

'There is, if you'd just take it,' she said; 'whatever purgatory you've sentenced yourself to, you've had enough. And it's not only yourself you're punishing.'

He said, 'I didn't ask you to share my life. I told you that perhaps trying it would be the only thing to convince you. Why don't you go away?'

She jumped to her feet. 'I will! I can't stand any more.' She ran the door, sobbing in pain and anger. He sat at the table, his head bent over the dirty plates.

She ran back and threw herself to her knees beside him. She put her arms round him and laid her head on his lap. 'I'm just going out, darling. I had an awful night and can't sleep . . . I'll be back, always.'

He said nothing. She rose to her feet, kissed the top of his head, and slipped out of the room. For an hour she walked in the thinning rain, picking her way over the wreckage of the storm, water gurgling all the while in her ears. She walked aimlessly, seeking a way of escape from a situation which would soon destroy her. Then she would be no use to him. Or perhaps, she thought, only then will I be of use to him, two derelicts together – but the idea repelled her, and she could not think of it as union – the slow sinking through turbid water of two corpses, tied together, even though one was male and one female.

She found herself outside Janaki's house and walked in. Janaki hurried to her, arms outstretched. 'My dear! Why haven't you come before? Why haven't you brought Rodney? . . . I've heard something from Khussroo Milkwallah . . . You look awful, Margaret, really awful.'

'Give me a whisky,' Margaret said sullenly, 'please.'

'At this time? Three o'clock? . . . Sit down . . . There . . . There's no reason why *you* shouldn't have come to see me, though I understand about Rodney. Surely you need a rest sometimes?'

'Not if he doesn't take one with me,' she said. She gulped the whisky. 'Why didn't you marry him, if you loved him?'

'I was married already,' Janaki said.

'Then why did you lead him on? You're the only person he's ever loved. You were the one he dreamed about. It was only

278

when you threw him over that he went to all those other women. You could have given him everything . . . but you just wanted him for a thrill.'

Janaki got up and closed the door. Agitatedly she kneaded her small, soft hands. She said, 'You must understand, Margaret. He overwhelmed me, the same way his people overwhelmed my country. I was mesmerised by his confidence, by his power. I remember the night . . . we became lovers. I'd been out in his car, and we had to come back through Pabbi. There was rioting all over the province then and Pabbi's the worst town in the country. A big crowd of Pathan roughs stopped us, surrounded the car, waving knives, yelling. I was so terrified I almost fainted – I, a Hindu woman among those raving fanatical Muslims. Rodney raised his hand and said in Pushtu, "Gentlemen, you may not have my balls until I've used them properly. Go away, and send your women to me. All of them." For a moment there was an awful silence, then the whole mob burst into shrieking laughter. We had to stay till midnight, eating an enormous *pilao* with them. When we got back to Peshawar – Max was out on manoeuvres – he looked at me, and . . . I couldn't help it, any more than the Pathans at Pabbi . . . I just keeled over. I tried to tell myself it was a reward for saving my life, but really I was helpless. He could do anything he liked with me . . . I fawned on him. I hated him. I loved him. I despised myself – never him. I had been taught never to speak to an Englishman until India was free. You have met my mother and grandmother. Of course I had to meet them when I married Max, but I never had one into our house. At that time I might have gone away with Rodney – he didn't ask me. We were both very young. He had his career. Later, when I knew that he really loved me, Max had got the same confidence. I saw that all the things which had once annoyed me in Max – his slowness, his acceptance of the British, of insults, his ox-like good temper – were really the signs of a man who had as much strength as Rodney . . . and he was my husband. I fell in love with him . . . What could I do?'

Margaret's head sank. 'What am *I* going to do? I can't get him to live, to think, anything. He won't move . . . Is one of your children his?'

Janaki exclaimed, 'Margaret!'

279

'Well?'

Janaki said, 'No. Both my children are Max's, though you are right, I was foolish to object to the question.'

'What about that Anglo-Indian you mentioned, the one who was in love with him in '46 and married the railwayman? Did she have a baby?'

'Victoria Taylor? She had no children. But—'

Margaret looked up sharply. 'But what?'

Janaki went to the window and stared out. 'Nothing. I think you ought to . . .'

Margaret jumped to her feet, knocking over the whisky glass. 'Sumitra!' she gasped. 'She's going to have his baby! That's what she meant when she said it wasn't for herself alone, the night he tried to strangle her! That's why she looked so pale in the mornings . . . Oh, what a fool I've been, blind, blind idiot! Where is she?' The whisky dripped loudly on to the tiled floor.

Janaki sighed. 'Yes, Sumitra is pregnant. Her baby's due early in September. It must be Rodney's.'

'Unless she was sleeping with other men at the same time,' Margaret said viciously.

'You know that's not true.'

'Where is she?'

'What are you going to do?'

'See her . . . I don't know . . . This has gone on long enough. He talked about a child this morning. Something's got to be done, and done now. I love him too much to see him fall to pieces before my eyes. Where is she?'

Again Janaki hesitated. Margaret got up. 'I shall find out.'

Janaki said, 'You will never find out.'

Margaret flared. 'Perhaps not now – but the child's going to be born. She's not going to keep it locked in a cupboard for ever. If she doesn't bring it up herself she's not going to give it to just anyone. It'll go to someone who knows and loves Rodney. I'll find out, however long I have to work. This is Rodney's baby!'

Janaki sat down. 'You are implacable, Margaret. Don't you understand? Sumitra said that Rodney must never know. She made me swear.'

'In case he felt it his duty to marry her? She can say no, can't she?'

Janaki said, 'What should I do? What would Max do? . . . It is Rodney's baby. She's in a flat, at 78 Reclamation Road, fourth floor. She sent for her old ayah from her home, who lives with her and does all the shopping and cooking. Sumitra never leaves the flat, and sees no one.'

Margaret said, 'Thank you,' and hurried out of the house.

Chapter 21

She paid off the taxi driver and stepped out into the rain. She had meant to stand outside the building for a time, while she had a look at it and rehearsed once more what she would say. But the slanting rain beat on her cheek and she ran across the sidewalk, into the hall, and straight up the stairs. There were only two apartments on each floor. At the fourth, panting heavily, she looked at the two doors and wondered which was Sumitra's. One of those apartments would face the sea and the other the city. Sumitra would have the sea. She rang the right-hand bell.

No one answered. After waiting a full minute, she rang again, long and firmly. This time a cracked old voice from immediately behind the door said, '*Kaun hai?*'

She said, 'Wood Memsahib. Give my salaams to the Rani Sahiba.'

'There's no Rani here.'

It was a new building, cheaply constructed. She could hear the old ayah plainly through the door. Sumitra must be within earshot. Raising her voice she said clearly, 'Sumitra, this is Margaret Wood. I intend to see you if I have to stay here a week, or call the police.'

Ten seconds later the door swung suddenly open. Sumitra stood there. She said curtly, 'Come in.'

She turned and walked ahead of Margaret into the apartment, and sat down on a comfortable sofa by the window. Just over seven months, Margaret had worked out. She was showing it more than most primigravidae at this stage, the bulge of pregnancy heavy under the sari. Her enormous eyes looked even bigger in the thin pallor of her face, and were further accentuated by the deep, dark circles under them. She wore a dark sari and a pearl necklace, and her hair hung to her shoulders, loosely gathered by a silver cord at the back of her head. She said, 'Well, now you have seen for yourself . . . Is he dead? Is that why you've come?'

Margaret said, 'No. I forced Janaki to tell me. Don't blame her.'

'Are you going to tell him?'

'That's what I've come about.'

'I shall have to leave then. This time no one will find me.'

'And after you've had the baby? Are you going to bring her up yourself?'

'I don't know. Sometimes I feel that I shall die of misery, whether . . . What's it got to do with you?'

'Everything. Answer me, please.'

Sumitra shot her a defiant look; but she needed to talk. Somewhere in the background, from the kitchenette, Margaret heard the breathing and shuffling of the old ayah. Sumitra had seen no other human being for five months.

Sumitra said, 'It's the old question, and there's still no answer. I talked to you about it that day you came up to Chambalpur, but you didn't understand then. What *am* I, a mother or a political leader? What kind of mother? It would be no problem for you. It would be none for me if . . . if I hadn't done what I did to Rodney. But even that would be no problem for you. You would have betrayed England for him, wouldn't you?'

'Yes.'

'Without a husband or a home I can't be a mother. I can't raise the child and give him—'

'Her . . . Rodney always says "her".'

'He knows already?'

'No – just talking about babies.'

'Him, her, I daren't think that far . . . I can't give her a home, I can't bring her up, if I am to travel round the country organising the women of India, as the Prime Minister wants me to. Without a husband I love, why should I stay in one place? I couldn't do it for Dip. For Rodney, yes . . . but I finished that.'

Margaret waited till the other woman turned her head slightly to meet her eye. Then she said, 'Come to Rodney. Show him yourself, and his child. I've lived with him for nearly five months and I know that nothing else can save him.'

Sumitra laughed rather unpleasantly. 'Has he thrown you over, too? And you want to see him finish me off properly this time?'

Margaret said, 'You still love him, don't you? Don't you? You owe me the truth . . . *Don't you?*'

Sumitra shouted, 'Yes! . . . But—'

'Come to him then. He doesn't know about the baby. But it means so much to him that he may ask you to marry him. If he does, you've got to say yes. On any terms. Even if you have to give up politics, and power, and independence, and just be a woman like the rest of us.'

Sumitra's eyes darkened. 'Would . . . do you think he'll speak to me?'

'I don't know. All I can do is put you in the same room, alone, with him. I know he won't do you any physical harm. I know that that' – she indicated the other's generous belly – 'will move him as nothing has been able to ever since you betrayed him.'

'What are you doing this for? What's the trick?'

'I've told you once. I love him . . . Come with me, now.'

'Now? No, no. I look dreadful. Tomorrow, perhaps, when . . .'

'No. Now.'

She put out her hand and slowly pulled Sumitra to her feet. 'All right,' Sumitra said, and again, 'all right . . . Will you call a taxi? 11904.' Margaret made the call and then watched as Sumitra slipped into a pair of low-heeled sandals, touched up her lipstick and applied a *tika* in the middle of her forehead. The woman moved with an ungainly heaviness, and her muscles were in poor condition. What else did she expect, shutting herself up here so long? There were exercises she must and could do, even if she refused to go out.

Margaret led the way carefully downstairs, and after a short wait in the hall the taxi came.

At the corner where they lived the driver turned with a look of astonished disgust. 'Here?'

'Yes, here. Number 27, on the right . . . Wait here.'

The rain had paused and half a dozen women peered at them from doors and windows up the street. Three naked children stared up from the gutter. Sumitra whispered, 'I'm trembling . . . What shall I say?'

'That's up to you. You know what you want, don't you?'

They climbed the narrow, creaking stair. Rodney's door was shut and she tapped on it. 'Rodney?'

284

His voice answered, 'Yes.'

She heard Sumitra's sharp intake of breath beside her. Through the door she called, 'There's a visitor for you.' He might be lying naked on his bed. What did it matter? She opened the door and slowly Sumitra stepped forward. She could not see Rodney, and closed the door.

In her own room the dirty plates from breakfast cried out accusingly at her. She swept them up, hurried down to the filthy square of black gravel below, washed them, and ran back upstairs. She tidied up her bed, removed the tablecloth, and scrubbed the tiny table. Then she sat down.

Five minutes. She heard the mumble of voices through the wall. It was hard to tell but most of it sounded like a woman's. Ten minutes. She wondered that her eyes were dry, but they were, dry as dust and beginning to scratch so that she had to rub them with a damp handkerchief, then wash them carefully. Still they hurt.

After fifteen minutes she heard the squeak of Rodney's door hinge and tensed in her chair. A man's footsteps came along the passage, but these were fast steps, unlike Rodney's slack near-shuffle. Through the open door she saw him pass. There was a cold set to his face and jaw, and pinched lines round his nose, and his lips were thin and tight locked. His footsteps receded quickly down the stairs. She hurried to his room.

Sumitra was sitting on the bed, head down. She looked up, her face hardening from its expression of utter misery to a cold stare. 'Well,' she said, 'whatever it was you were trying to do, you did it.'

'What happened?'

'At first I don't think he saw me. Only this.' She put her hand on her belly. 'He touched me. He felt it kicking. For a moment I thought everything was going to be all right. Then he realised it was I carrying it. He looked as if he would rip me open to take it away from me . . . I asked him if he would marry me. He said no. I begged and pleaded and promised. He said no. At the end he said a marriage had to have love and he did not love me, and never could. He told me never to come near him again . . . So you showed him his child, and proved that having me too is too much of a price to pay. That ought to be torture enough, for both of us!'

'What are you going to do now? No, first tell me why you didn't get rid of it.'

Sumitra said, 'I have had two abortions in Europe. This was Rodney's. I couldn't.'

'And now?'

'I haven't made up my ... Why are you tormenting me? Why do you bully me?'

'This is Rodney's. Are you going to bring her up yourself or let someone else adopt her?'

'I *can't* bring it up. Without him, I just can't ... Three people have told me they'll bring it up as their own.'

'Who?'

Sumitra did not answer, sullenly looking out the window with pursed lips. Margaret said, 'I can guess – Max and Janaki – your husband.'

Sumitra turned her head and said bitterly, 'You do know us all well, don't you? Yes, those two, and the other. What choice would you make if it were yours – to be the foster child of a general, a rajah, or a prime minister – a prime minister's sister, to be exact.'

Margaret said, 'Give her to me.'

Sumitra stared at her for a long, long time. She said, at last, 'So that's it.'

'Of course it is!' Margaret cried. 'You must have known all the time. But I gave you every chance. I didn't cheat. I thought Rodney would forgive you, and forget, when he saw that ... Now you know, and I know, that he can't forget, and if he can't, he's right not to marry you.'

'But you think that if you have my child he will marry *you*?'

Margaret said earnestly, 'I don't know, Sumitra. I only know that unless he has the child he will continue to sink into the earth, as you can see he has been sinking, and will soon die. But if you gave the child to him, what could he do? At best he would have to hire a nurse or housekeeper of some kind. At worst he might marry some slut. If you let *me* adopt her, though, I am responsible – and I shall never leave him.'

For five minutes Sumitra said nothing.

Margaret said, 'It was not you alone who brought him to this state. I know that it was mainly himself. But it was you who finally stabbed him in the back. You owe him a new life.'

Sumitra burst out: 'But I hate you! Yes, you! Knowing what you want with such utter finality. Untorn by the slightest doubt

286

about anything. Totally in love with one man, troubled by not a thought, not a worry, never thinking, what shall I do ? – only, how shall I do it ?'

'You want the child to be brought up in India, then ? So that you can see her every time you meet Janaki, or Dip, every time you go to New Delhi ? So that you can watch her growing under someone else's love ?'

'Stop!' Sumitra screamed. 'You can have her, you ... you merciless demon. You cubless vixen. You can have her, but you've got to take her out of India within a month, and never bring her back. And Rodney.'

Margaret sighed. The trembling in her body ceased, the queasy fluttering in her belly calmed. She said, 'Are you having regular prenatal inspections ?'

'No. No one has seen me. No one's going to.'

'Where do you plan to have the baby ? What doctor is going to deliver you ?'

'In the flat. Or out in my beach hut at Pabal. No doctor. There is nothing wrong with me. I am a healthy Indian woman, and ayah will deliver me, as she delivered my mother of me. No one shall know who does not already know.'

'You are not healthy, Sumitra. You've got to start the proper exercises at once ... Who does know ?'

'Max – I told him first. Janaki. Ayah. Dip. The Prime Minister and his sister. Now you and Rodney. That's all.'

'When is the baby due ?'

'I began my last period on December 24.'

Margaret had asked the question so many times that she had an obstetrical calendar in her head. She said, 'About September 24, then. Just under three months from now. You look a little later than that. You must have antenatal examinations.'

'I will not.'

'Will you let me ? I am not a doctor, but I have a lot of experience. There might be some simple defect which can be easily fixed now, by medicine or exercise or dieting, but could be fatal to you or the baby, or both, if we don't do something about it.'

'Oh, all right.'

'I'll bring what I need to your apartment tomorrow morning as soon as I come off work. Please have a urine specimen ready.'

287

'How are you going to get it tested?'

'It shall be mine,' Margaret said. 'When we get nearer the date I shall have to leave the hospital to look after you full time, and that will make a good excuse. I can pad myself out a bit.' She laughed almost gaily. 'But you must have a doctor. You really must. It's not only your life and the baby's, that depend on this, but Rodney's.'

'And yours?'

'In a way.'

'I don't care. I will not have a doctor.'

'Then I shall have to deliver you myself, with your ayah.'

'Ayah can do it without you,' Sumitra said rudely.

Margaret said calmly, 'I am sure she can, if there are no complications. But I shall be there, and I shall warn the best obstetrician in Bombay to be ready, if I have to call on him in a hurry.'

'I will not . . .'

'You may not be conscious,' Margaret said. 'The taxi's waiting.'

Two minutes later Margaret slowly climbed back up the stairs, threw herself on to her bed and burst into tears, her hands clutching and kneading at the wet pillow under her head.

Rodney's voice, sharp and angry, brought her to her feet. 'Where is she?'

'Sumitra?' she dabbed at her eyes. 'She went back to her flat.'

'She told me she's living alone with her old ayah, and no one else is going to know about the baby. She can't do that. Something might be wrong.'

Margaret said, 'I'm going to look after her.'

'You? . . . And a good doctor.'

Margaret said nothing.

Rodney slammed down into a chair. 'Then I suppose she'll find foster parents for her. Probably Max and Janaki. I could become their night watchman. Or chauffeur. They wouldn't have to pay me anything. I have a small pension.'

'No, you couldn't,' Margaret cried. 'They wouldn't take you. They *couldn't*! You must see that.'

Rodney stared at her, his face dark with congested fury. 'You're right. So I'll never see her, touch her. She'll never know I'm her father.'

Margaret said, 'Sumitra is going to give her to me.'

288

Rodney's brows came down. 'You? My baby?'

Margaret said, 'She doesn't want to raise it herself – not without you. She realises that she can't even have it brought up in India. The strain would be too much for her. So I am to have her, but I must take her out of India within a month, and never . . .'

Rodney stood up. His hands were like powerful claws, slowly opening, outstretched in front of him. He took a pace towards her where she sat on the bed. His voice was almost casual. 'She is my child,' he said. He stood directly over her. 'I could kill you now for trying to get her – but I won't. You are needed, until she is born. But if you try to take her away from me then, I will kill you. Do you understand?'

Margaret put up her hand. He caught it, and she heard her bones cracking in his grip. She said, 'The baby is yours, Rodney. She will always be yours. You will need a housekeeper, a nanny, won't you? Are you going to change her nappies ten times a day, yourself?'

'Yes!'

'Are you going to pot her, and mix her bottle, and sit up all night with her while she's teething?'

'Yes!'

'Then, in what place? In a hovel like this, somewhere in the slums of London? That's all you'll be able to afford, if you can't work . . . You're a man, Rodney. A little girl doesn't want a man for her mother. No child does. She needs a father who is a man, and acts like a man, and smells like a man. Let the housekeeper do the things a woman must do.'

The grip of his hand relaxed. He turned away. 'All right,' he said, 'but remember, that's all you will be – a nanny. If I catch you trying to become her mother . . . Sumitra means nothing to me, except through the baby. You – even less. Is that clear?'

'Yes.'

'Remember it . . . When are you starting to examine her?'

'Tomorrow morning. I shall be late back.'

'Good. Are you well enough trained? What do you know about midwifery?'

'Enough,' she said wearily. 'But tomorrow I shall buy a textbook and study it again. And I shall ask to be transferred to the

K
289

Obstetrical Ward under Mr Dutt. I'll do everything I can, Rodney, everything that she'll let me do.'

She watched his hard face soften slightly. 'I shall find a name for her. The name of a flower. A Himalayan flower ...' His lips tightened again and he said, 'I've got to go to work.'

A moment later she was alone.

Chapter 22

Mr Dutt, M.D. (Lon.), F.R.C.S. (Edin.), pulled out a chair for her and she sat down. Then, rummaging around in his desk, he found a bottle of orange juice, and filled two glasses. 'Why do babies always choose three or four a.m. for entry into the world?' He sighed. 'Especially if it's a difficult entry ... You look tired, Mrs Wood.'

She smiled wanly. 'I am.'

'I shall be very sorry to lose you. Too few of our Indian girls can exert that authority in the wards – like a good sergeant-major, if you will excuse me – that you British do ... You are not, of course, pregnant yourself?'

She fiddled with the juice glass. She was too tired to go on pretending. Mr Dutt was a short plump man, bald, with protruding eyes and fat, strong hands. She had learned a lot from him. This morning's case had been a nightmare. She felt queasy, imagining that she might have to deal with such a case alone.

'No,' she said, 'I'm not pregnant.'

'I presume, then, that you are preparing to act as midwife for another lady, who refuses for some reason to have proper medical attention?'

'Yes.'

'And from the intensity with which you have studied obstetrics, and have watched and questioned me, I imagine you are worried about it.'

She hesitated. 'It's not the case, as such. As far as I can tell she's perfectly normal and healthy, except for lack of exercise and a slacker abdominal wall than she ought to have at her age. But it's important. Personally.'

'Ah. Personally. You know it is dangerous for a medical attendant to be too involved personally with a patient?'

'I know, sir. But I have no choice. If I hadn't insisted, she would have had no one but her old ayah. She absolutely refuses anyone else. I was going to tell you, when the time came closer, and ask you to be available in case it developed badly. I wouldn't try to deal with any serious complications. I've been studying so that I can recognise them ... but there's really no reason to imagine that there will be complications. Except perhaps that, at the moment, it's a transverse lie.'

The doctor pulled a pad towards him. A lurid sun hung on the horizon, giving out heat but only a confused light. The electric light still burned, though it was past seven o'clock. A long bar of pale-violet light hung over the sky to seaward, and overhead it was dark and heavily overcast.

'Primigravida? ... I see. Well, with two abortions she's really not a primigravida ... Pregnancy clinically confirmed? Blood pressure ... Date of commencement of last period ...'

Her weariness faded as she plunged into the familiar technicalities. Height of the fundus of the uterus. Pelvic measurements. Ah, a good gynecoid arch! Mr Dutt beamed. His voice became lyrical and his eyes sparkled over a good gynecoid arch the way other men's did over a pair of long, well-shaped legs ... General health and mental attitude. H'm, that's bad. Drugs. Get these at the dispensary. Doesn't seem to be anything to worry about, except – except perhaps the dates, coupled with the transverse lie. And didn't you say you thought, at first, she might be further advanced? Well, an obstinate transverse presentation can be dangerous. If it's still obstinate close to term it ought to be corrected by version ...

The doctor stood up, yawning. 'Excuse me ... And, Mrs Wood – do please have the courage to ignore the patient's protests the moment you have any doubts. Millions of women have been happily delivered by midwives far less competent than you, and thousands have died though treated by doctors far more competent than I ... but there is a middle ground, not large in percentage but far too large in terms of human suffering, when you think what a baby really is – our projected selves, our dreams, our hopes, our future – where a midwife can do nothing, a doctor, perhaps, can ... I am at your service whenever an emergency develops – preferably before that. Good luck, in everything, and thank you for all that you have done for me – all of us – here at Wadalia. Are you going to see the patient now? . . . Good. Give me a ring at eight p.m. Or come round, if you want to.'

Half an hour later, the prescriptions made up and stowed into her capacious handbag, Margaret left the hospital. She ate 'supper' in a nearby café, as was her custom on days when she visited Sumitra. Out in the streets the air felt even more close and oppressive than in the hospital. The violet light had turned to a dull purple and was spreading slowly upward across the sky from the west, though no breeze stirred at street level. The sun had vanished.

She took the bus, as usual, to the corner nearest Sumitra's apartment, and walked along the familiar street, through the door, and up the stairs. The old ayah greeted her with a small softening of her wrinkled face. Margaret thought that in herself the old woman wanted to like her, but Sumitra's attitude made it impossible for her to show it. Perhaps also she resented the English-woman with her Western notions interfering in a responsibility that had been hers alone.

She entered the big room, and almost before she was inside the door Sumitra cried, 'You again? I don't want to be examined today.'

Her voice was ill-tempered and the dark rings very noticeable under her eyes. She lay on a couch under the window, her feet up on cushions, her belly rising in a hump in front of her, her hands stretched over it, not calmly or protectively, but with fingers outspread, in anger.

Margaret said, 'I'm afraid I must. It won't last much longer.'

She went to the closet and got out the brown suitcase which she had stocked with all the necessities of private midwifery. She washed her hands and prepared for examination, while Sumitra pulled up her sari and lay back, staring at the ceiling.

Margaret set to work. Half an hour later she had half convinced herself that Sumitra must be wrong with her dates. She had looked for the signs that Dutt had told her of; she had measured and palpated; and she felt sure – almost.

After helping the other woman rearrange her clothes, she sat down opposite her on a hard chair. 'I forgot to ask you your full menstrual history, in the beginning. Are you normally regular or irregular?'

'What on earth has that got to do with it now? Will you never stop asking me questions, pawing and pushing? You're not a doctor, what do you know about it?... Oh, all right. I have always been irregular.'

'Have you ever had any flow which you have mistaken for a period, but which later turned out not to be?'

'Yes. When I was seventeen my mother took me to a doctor for it. I used to have two-day haemorrhages in the middle of periods. The doctor said there was no physical cause, it was due to nerves. I was very unhappy at the time.'

'Now – the period from which we are basing our calculations, the one of December 24. Was that on time? How long did it last?'

'Yes. No. How can I remember?'

'I'm sure you can remember if you try. A woman who thinks she is pregnant by her lover is going to remember very well.'

Sumitra glared at her. 'It was ten days late. It lasted two days.'

Margaret leaned back. Suppose it had not been a period at all, but a haemorrhage? Then the calculations should be made not from December 24 but from the last true period before – November 17. In that case Sumitra was at or past term now.

'You're dripping sweat on to my feet,' Sumitra said, 'sit farther away, please.'

'I'm sorry. It's awfully hot.' She mopped her forehead.

'What's the matter?' Sumitra said. 'Is there something wrong?'

Margaret rose and found a smile. 'Nothing at all, that I know of. But you may be closer to term than we thought. If you are, then we ought to get a doctor to alter the lie of the baby. It's lying across instead of head down. It's simple to move before labour begins.'

'No,' Sumitra said. 'Ayah will be quite capable of dealing with it, even if you aren't. She looked at me only yesterday and said it was fine. I don't think you know what you're talking about.'

Margaret controlled herself with a huge effort. She said, 'Wouldn't it be much wiser to get another nurse instead of me? I can find a good one for you without any trouble...'

'No.'

Margaret let the sweat run down her cheeks. 'Please, Sumitra, let me get a doctor, now. You need one badly.'

'For the last time, no! You shall deliver the baby, and if you do

294

make a mess of it – how wonderful that will be, won't it? Or suppose it's born a cripple. Or an idiot. It's yours already, you see. I don't care. I just have to lie here and grow it and give it to you.'

Margaret repacked the case, and stowed it in the closet. Sumitra lay silent under the window, staring at the ceiling. Margaret turned to go. Ayah opened the door for her and she went out.

Her clothes were soaked through with sweat when she reached the tenement, and the purple-banded sky was dark violet in the lower segment, black as pitch to the west. The landlord was standing on the front step when she entered. He waved a hand at the sky: 'Storm coming.'

She nodded and forced her weary legs up the stairs. She prayed that Rodney was asleep. These days he had to make his own meals. The dirty plates greeted her – let them lie. This was her last day of treble responsibility, thank God. From tomorrow, there would be only Rodney and Sumitra. She pulled off her clothes and fell into bed. Must call Mr Dutt at eight.

A heavy shaking and roaring awakened her, and a ketchup bottle fell off a shelf, smashing on the floor. She tumbled out of bed, her head aching, and slammed the creaky window down against the violence of the wind. The sky was now totally dark except for a thin red line across the centre of the sky. She switched on the light and found her watch. Half past five. The window rattled, the walls shook. She found pan, bucket, and cloth and began to clean up the mess. The door opened and Rodney stalked in.

'You were late getting back this morning,' he said, 'I fell asleep waiting for you.'

She said, 'Mr Dutt kept me, and then I had to spend longer than usual with Sumitra.'

'Why? How is it?'

She wrapped the mess into newspapers, dropped it into the bucket, sat down, and tried to explain her doubts. He listened intently. Ever since the day of Sumitra's visit he had eaten little and, though now suddenly beginning to take care of his person and clothes, he had thinned and his eyes had developed a starved, luminous intensity. His movements had become sharp and jerky, and when he spoke it was in clipped phrases.

She ended: 'There might be no cause for worry. But I'm going

295

to go and see Mr Dutt, because a transverse lie at term can be dangerous. The uterus . . .'

'Call it the baby, for God's sake.'

She put out her hand. 'Rodney, it *isn't* a baby yet. It's a foetus, inside a uterus. Even if you don't think of it like that, and Sumitra doesn't want to – mothers never do – I have to . . . She's in a bad state. She ought to be living with a friend, someone she can talk to.'

Rodney stared at her. The longing came over her that he might look at her like that about her own baby – distraught, intense, involved. It would not do to think about it. He shook off her hand and began to pace the floor.

He said, 'This damned foolishness has gone on long enough. If there's the slightest doubt, she's got to have a doctor.'

Margaret said, 'I told you, I'm going to see Mr Dutt. But what can he do if she refuses to let him examine her, even let him into the room?'

'Why don't you smuggle him in? Hide him in the cupboard where he can see?'

She smiled wanly. 'That's impossible . . . If we could only carry out an X-ray examination, we would know what we needed to know.'

'She's got to go to hospital for that . . . I've got it! Make her ill. Give her something that will make her feel so awful she'll *want* to go to hospital. Once she's there the rest's easy. Put her out, for Christ's sake. Give her a knockout drop and have the ambulance waiting outside.'

'I can't do any of those things,' she said, marvelling at his persistence. 'There's no illness I could induce, no drug I could give her, which might not harm the foetus at this stage.'

'No, not that. All right, I'll go and see her. There's nothing else for it. I'll take her to hospital by force.'

'That would really harm the – the baby.'

'I'll . . . I'll promise to marry her. I can't stand this.'

Margaret turned away and began to dress. The misery didn't seem any greater than usual. Perhaps Sumitra had been working towards this all the time.

Rodney said, 'I hate her, but . . . the baby. I'm going round there now. You'd better not come with me. I'll have her at the hospital by eight.'

296

The door slammed behind him. She sat, unseeing, at the table until half the window shattered and burst into the room on the wings of a shrieking wind. She went again to her brush and swept up the glass. There was nothing to be done about the window. She pulled her bed farther from it and anchored all light objects under pots and shoes. The wind lifted the bedclothes in long waves and, under its howling, in the blackness outside, she heard isolated shouts of fear and the crash of a falling chimney pot. She tried to cook her evening meal, but the wind blew sparks and burning charcoal sticks round the room, so she doused the fire, found some bread, and ate that with butter and jam. The milk had turned rancid and she could not make tea. Twice the light went out and twice came on again. The third time it did not come on.

After an hour and a half of waiting, ten minutes after the light finally failed, she saw a taxi struggling up the street, almost like a man bent against the wind. It stopped and Rodney jumped out. She caught a glimpse of his set face as he hurried across the sidewalk. The taxi waited.

He burst in. 'She's gone. Come on.'

'Where?'

'Ayah doesn't know. Come on.'

She followed him down the stairs, and into the taxi. The taxi drove off, the driver shouting over his shoulder, 'This is my last trip today, even with double fares. Look at that . . .' A chute of heavy slates whistled diagonally across the street, ripped bodily off one roof and sent like shell fire against the upper front of the house opposite, thence to fall shattered on to the sidewalk. Huge drops of rain began so spatter against the windows.

At the apartment house Rodney said, 'Wait here.'

The driver shook his head. 'I'm not waiting, sahib. I didn't want to wait back there.' Before Rodney could pay him he slammed the car into gear and raced away down the street.

Up in Sumitra's apartment the walls creaked under the wind. Ayah squatted in a corner looking fearfully at the blind windows and the darkness beyond. Here the lights still burned.

'*Rani Sahiba wapas nahin agya?*'

The ayah rose, pressing her bony hands together. Her face was clammed with fear. '*Nahin, sahib.*'

Rodney flung himself into a chair. 'She left here about five o'clock. She told ayah she was going for a walk. That's all. The *chowkidar* didn't see her go out. No one did ... She might be taking shelter from the storm, but I don't think so. The storm had just started by then. She went out into it. Where?'

'Janaki's?'

Rodney grabbed the telephone. 'What's the number?'

'24096.'

He dialled and soon after spoke in Hindi. He put the phone down. 'Janaki's out of Bombay, visiting relatives. But Sumitra is not there, and has not been.' He turned to the ayah and Margaret could understand he was asking her who else had visited the flat.

'No one,' the ayah wailed, 'no one!'

The lights failed. Ayah moaned. A long torrent of lightning poured slowly down the sky and in its glare Margaret saw the sea stretching away in violet and white, running mountain high towards the black outline of harbour and city to the left.

Rodney spoke out of the darkness: 'How long do we wait here? And then, what do we do? ... Nearly eight o'clock. The telephone's going to go any moment. Use it while we can. Get on to Dutt.'

He lit a match and she dialled quickly, asking, 'What am I to say?'

'Tell him first what you learned this morning ...' Margaret held up her hand. 'Mr Dutt? It's Margaret Wood ...' Quickly she gave him the details. The surgeon's voice was strained. 'Get her to the hospital, Mrs Wood. She must be put under the care of an obstetrician.'

Rodney, listening with his head close to hers, took the phone from her. 'This is Rodney Savage, doctor,' he said, 'the woman is Sumitra, Rani of Kishanpur.'

She heard Dutt's gasp, the Bengal accent suddenly strong. 'Oah, my Goad!'

Rodney continued harshly: 'The baby is mine. Sumitra's disappeared. Went out at five. Please get all your things, come round here in your car, and we'll go and find her.'

'It is impossible.' Mr Dutt's voice was faint but decisive as she strained to hear. 'I have every sympathy with you, but I cannot spend my time looking for a lady who *may* not be in urgent need of my help if we do find her, while half a dozen women are even now awaiting my attentions. I am going to the hospital now.'

'You've got to come here,' Rodney snarled.

'I cannot,' the doctor said. 'Put Mrs Wood on the line.' His voice was loud and emphatic in her ear: 'Mrs Wood, the storm has produced a rush of cases, prematures, frightened women who weren't going to have a doctor and now want one, miscarriages . . . They're snowed under at every hospital in Bombay. Find the Rani and take her to the nearest hospital. Then ring me. Good luck.' The phone went silent.

Rodney glowered at her, his eyes shining in the lightning with a luminous glow.

She said, 'What about the police?'

'Not a hope. They'll be even busier than the doctors . . . We'll go to Janaki's. Someone there might know where she'd go. Come on.'

'Wait!' She dragged out the midwife's case, and he snatched it from her. They ran down the stairs and into the street. 'No taxis now,' Rodney yelled. His hand pressed hard on her shoulder, forcing her forward into the lashing rain and wind.

'This is a hurricane,' he shouted. They struggled to run against the wind along the esplanade, but could only make the slow and painful progress of mountain climbers against a blizzard. On the left the sea battered against the stone retaining wall. Every few seconds, with a heavy shudder that shook the stone under their feet, a wave smashed over the top and poured in dirty yellow froth across the roadway. A few street lights still shone, though most had their glasses smashed and one lay twisted like spaghetti in the middle of the road. Once a fire engine passed, its bell clanging, but it was going in the opposite direction.

After half an hour they reached Douglas Road. There the tall concrete apartments sheltered the road from the wind, and it was easier to breathe. They leaned against a wall and rested. The water poured from Rodney's hair and clothes as though he had just climbed out of a swimming pool. His eyes burned dully behind the curtain of drops falling from his eyebrows. He said, 'Is this case waterproof?'

'Not very,' she shouted back, 'I never expected I would have to take it out in anything like this.'

'Come on.' He lifted the case, grabbed her hand, and pulled her on down the road, now at a run. Fronds and boughs of coconut palms littered the street, and a small car stood in the middle of the sidewalk.

At Janaki's house they had to pull four times on the old-fashioned bell and shout and hammer for a minute on the locked and bolted front door. Then the door burst open, held feebly by three struggling women and two children against the force of the wind. They shot in like projectiles, followed by a shout of the wind and a gunshot spray of palm fronds, mud, and water. Rodney put down the suitcase and applied his shoulder to the door. Slowly they forced it shut and slammed the bolts into place.

Janaki's mother stood near, wringing her hands and crying out in Hindi, 'Ah, Margaret! What misery! What is the matter?'

Rodney turned to her. 'It is Sumitra, *mā-ji*, the Rani Sahiba. She has gone. . .'

Margaret interposed. 'She doesn't know.'

Rodney said, 'She is going to have a baby.'

'*Aiih!* In this night?'

'We don't know. She has run away from the flat where she was hiding. Do you know where she could have gone?'

The old woman waved her hands. 'I don't know. I have only met her two or three times, in the old days. If Janaki were here . . . She is not far, in Panvel . . . If only we could telephone . . . Bring towels, children, bring hot tea. Bring your aunt's whisky. My poor friends . . .'

'We cannot stay, *mā-ji*,' Rodney said, 'you have no idea where she can have gone?'

A dozen women and children and two or three servants were crowded in the hall round the two soaked English. They all stood in a widening pool of water, the sound of the hurricane increasing outside.

'Wait!' Margaret cried. 'When she first came to our house, and I asked her where she would have the baby she said, "at the flat or" . . . somewhere, a beach hut . . .'

'Juhu?'

'No, I would have known that. Oh, I can't remember the name.'

A thin old voice cut in. 'Of whom do you speak?'

The dense crowd parted. Janaki's grandmother stood on the stairs, all in white, her thin white hair drawn tightly back from her forehead, her sari looped lightly over it, for she was in the presence

of a man of her own class. She made a short *namasti* to him, then
her head went up. Rodney knelt quickly, and touched his hand to
her emaciated foot. He rose. 'You are Janaki's grandmother,
bari-mā?'

'Yes.'

'I am Rodney Savage.'

The hooded old eyes opened with a sudden flash. 'Ah! Of you,
she spoke, to me, once. To me, alone.'

'*Bari-mā*, we talk of Sumitra, Rani of Kishanpur. Do you know
where she or her family have a beach hut?'

The white head nodded slowly. 'Certainly. At Pabal.'

'Where is that, *bari-mā?*'

'It is near Alkhuti. The road turns off at Khed. It is twenty-five
miles from here.'

'I know it,' a tall girl of about sixteen broke in, blushing
furiously. 'It is a sort of little peninsula, an island at high tide and
in the rains. There are four huts on it. I have been there, but did
not know that one of the huts belonged to the Rani Sahiba.'

Rodney said, '*Bari-mā*, is there a car here we can borrow? We
must get out there at once.'

The mother cried, 'In this? It is madness, children! Wait till
tomorrow. Get . . .'

The old matriarch raised a wrinkled, spotted claw of a hand.
'There is my son-in-law's car. Take that. You, you – see that it is
filled with petrol.'

Rodney knelt again, and again touched the old woman's foot.
She put her hand lightly on the top of his head, and then he stood
up. He picked up the suitcase, and turned to Margaret. 'Come on.'

She said, 'Wait!' She turned to the young girl. 'Do they have
electric light out there?'

'Oh, no!'

'Fresh water?'

The girl went pale. 'I think so . . . Not out of a tap.'

Rodney said, 'We'll have a long way to walk. We can't carry
water. We'll just have to hope. There'll be kerosene oil and lamps,
or Sumitra wouldn't have gone there. We have a torch. . . Come on.'

They fought their way out the door and along the front of the
house to the little garage. Inside, one of the servants poured fuel
from a two-gallon can into the tank of the pre-war Austin, then

301

Rodney slipped into the driver's seat, pushed the case over into the back, and started the engine. Margaret got in.

'Hurry, hurry,' she said, 'I have an awful feeling that we're late already.'

'Got to wait till the engine's warm, tonight,' he said. He switched on the headlamps, while the servants stood ready by the double doors. Minutes later he called out, '*Darwaze kolna!*'

The servants struggled with the bolts. She muttered, 'Rodney, I'm frightened.'

He turned his head and for a moment she thought he was going to curse her for a cowardly slut. Instead, his hand went out and rested on her knee. 'No, you're not,' he said gently, 'you've never been afraid when you're with me.'

The doors flung open and they drove out into the storm. Almost before they had left the shelter of the garage something struck the window beside Margaret's head with a heavy crash. She ducked, crying out. Rodney's smile was cheerful in the thin light from the dash. 'Coconut,' he said, 'it hasn't broken the glass, has it?'

Trembling with relief, she looked at the pane, and saw that it was starred from its centre, but not broken. In the road Rodney turned north, the windshield wipers hurrying across the streaming glass and the lights boring a short, enclosed tunnel into the rain. The road lay inches deep in water and debris, and their wheels threw up angry waves on either side. For a time they drove without hindrance through factory and suburb, but the speed never rose above fifteen miles an hour.

'Get that road map out of the pocket,' he told her. 'And the torch out of your case . . . Note the mileage. We started at 3419. How many, on the map, to Khed?—Then look for the turning from 3438 on. That's about the only way we'll recognise it tonight . . . Have we got everything the baby will need after she's born – blankets, clothes, food?'

'Yes . . . *Why* should she run away suddenly? And how could she get there in this?'

'Why? – God knows. Perhaps she'd decided she couldn't let you have the baby, after all. How?—At five the streets were probably full of taxis still. She'd have just about reached Pabal before it got really bad . . . How long will it be before we can take the baby away? One week? Two weeks?'

'It depends – *look out!*' The car was already stopping under the hard pressure of the brakes, throwing her forward on to the dash. A blue flash lit up the wet road, flailing trees and a line of hovels to the right. Another flash followed, and another, each one lighting up the inside of the car with a livid glow. Dimly seen, giant snakes coiled in the road ahead.

'Power cables,' Rodney said, 'two, three ... Take the wheel. Give me the torch. Follow the light.'

'Rodney, we can't!'

'Yes, we can. Just follow me, put the right wheel where I shine the torch.'

He got out and the door slammed. In the interval when the door was open another flash lit the car and she heard the crackling snap of the short circuit. For a moment blue fire ran along the seething gutter. She slid behind the wheel.

The thin beam of the flashlight shone down. Clear in the headlights she saw a looping coil of high-tension cable lash down and across the road, curled like a whip by the wind. Rodney stepped back without ducking, and shone the flashlight upward. The cable had looped into a tree, its end pouring out smoke. The other cables lay across the road. Rodney turned and signalled her on with the flashlight. She slipped the car into gear and crawled forward. He was standing close beside the cables and she saw that there, where the light shone, they lay flat in the water, hissing and sparkling. To the left they rose in waving coils. He jerked the light and she drove over the cables. The lights flickered and came on again, and her hands tingled on the wheel, then it passed, the door beside her opened, he was pushing her across the seat. The car moved again, faster now.

The car lurched steadily on down the empty road. Three times Rodney and she had to get out and pull tree limbs out of the way. 3431. 3432.

The headlights shone on a heavy truck drawn across the road. A wildly swinging red lantern hung from its side. Rodney got out, the door slamming behind him. She saw him walk past the truck, return, go to a hut beside the road, bang on the door. Eventually the door opened and he disappeared. Five minutes later he returned.

'Bridge gone,' he said; 'it's not much more than a culvert, but

303

it's gone. They say we might be able to cross on the railway bridge.'

He turned the car and they went back the way they had come. After a mile a cart track branched off on the left. He changed down and turned on to the flooded cart track at an even pace. Sideslipping, skidding, but always moving, they came after a mile to the railway. Rodney turned on to the tracks, and began a slow bump bump bump northward along them, the catenary wires of the electrified line arrowing down the upper blackness, the lights glinting along their undersurfaces.

'Here it is,' he said. He took the torch and jumped out. She saw him walk across the bridge, the torch flashing to right and left. When he got back into the driver's seat she said, 'Is it all right? Can we get over?'

He said, 'It's two bridges, one for each track, so we can't go on down the middle, like this. Damn narrow. Guard rails inside the running rails, so there's no room for the car wheels. I'll have to put one wheel on the outside. Get out. Take the torch and the case. Walk over. If I don't make it, get back to the main road and bribe someone to take you on.'

'I'm not going without you!' she cried. 'We can't go on if it's as dangerous as that.'

He pushed her forcibly out into the wind. She started across the bridge. Her head swam, for though it was a short span it had no railings and no side path. An inch below the concrete lip black water ran towards the sea with a sullen roar.

At the far side she turned and waited. By then Rodney had forced the car up on to the rails. The headlights crept towards her, heavily tilted to the right where one pair of wheels rode on the narrow band of ballast outside the rail. If he slipped off that, he must lurch into the flood. The lights came on, bigger and brighter.

They reached her. She pulled the door open and sank into her seat, shuddering and weeping. 'Rodney,' she moaned, 'it's not worth it, nothing's worth it . . . We don't even know whether she's there, whether she needs me, whether I can do anything!'

The car bumped over the ties, and again his hand fell on her knee. He said, 'None of us can do more than his best. That much we must do.'

Soon they reached a grade crossing and, turning sharply on to another waterlogged track, regained the main road.

'What's the mileage now?' he asked.

She peered at the speedometer: '3437 – five to Khed, allowing for that diversion over the bridge.' The car ploughed on.

Houses loomed up in the slashed blackness, all lights extinguished, and the street covered with bricks, slates, tiles, and balks of timber. At a crossroads in the centre of the town the lights shone on a black arrow pointing left, and the message: *Alkuthi – 5*.

'Across the Salsette Marsh,' Rodney said, 'the wind will now blow – for a change.'

The road ran at first among the walls and bending trees of small farms and market gardens. The palms danced like madmen in the headlights. Every few yards one or both of them had to leave the car to drag wreckage out of the way. They were both as wet as swimmers, but they had been since leaving Sumitra's apartment. After two miles the palms and the walls and the spectral huts cowering in their lee vanished. The road became clear.

They were out on to the open marsh. The untrammelled wind struck the car on the left side. Rodney swung the wheel sharply to present the front to the wind, and at the same time stood on the brakes to avoid running off the road. Margaret's knees shook so violently together that the bones hurt. If she tried to speak just now she would scream.

Rodney looked at her in the dim light and said, 'That was a bad one . . . Open the back windows. We've got to reduce wind resistance – it's coming straight from the side, across the marsh. No more trees or other shelter till we reach the coast, probably . . . But take the case out of the back and hold it on your lap. There'll be a lot of water coming in.'

She did as he ordered. As soon as she began to wind down the windows the wind shrieked through like a crazed animal, and she huddled forward beside Rodney, her body spread over the case.

He said, 'Suppose it's a difficult delivery . . . and you have to use forceps or anything like that . . . it won't affect the baby, will it, I mean, her bones or head or anything?'

She said, 'Rodney, you must stop thinking so far ahead, about the baby. We've got to get there. We've got to find out how Sumitra is. She may still have a month to go . . .'

He didn't seem to be listening to her, and she allowed her voice to die away. The little car moved on in a universe of wind and water, the world of human beings drowned or blown away. The lights shone down a straight causeway, shiny-wet with water, the surface mottled by the bursting of the rain drops upon it. To right and left stretched an ocean, also black, also shining, also mottled, but marked too by long wind streaks and, over all, a dense curtain of driving spray. Straining her eyes ahead Margaret could only just tell the difference between the causeway and the flooded marsh, whose waves lapped over the road.

The car crawled on, lurching over to the right under the rhythmic pulse of the wind, crunching back on its springs, grinding on in low gear.

The lights went out. The Austin squealed to a stop. Rodney got out and dragged himself forward along the side of the car. When he returned, he beckoned her to the driver's seat and bawled in her ear: 'Glass blown in, bulbs smashed, all of them. Follow me.'

She looked at him, her eyes almost closed against the rain and wind that poured past his bulk. It was impossible to go on, it was madness. She smiled into his eyes. 'All right.'

The beam of the flashlight crept forward and she engaged gear. Following at five paces behind him, she saw only his legs moving slowly, one after the other, down the left side of the road. He was leaning so far to the left, against the wind, that his upper part, seen dimly in outline, looked like one of those movie trick shots where a comedian leans over, past the borders of reason, on nothing.

After ten minutes the light swung in a pendulum arc and then shone its beam left. The road made a full left turn. She inched round, more than ever conscious that she had no guide but the torchlight ahead. Now she could hardly see that. She could detect no difference between the texture of the road and the flood.

When she finished the turn the torch was almost under the wheels and she jammed on the brakes. Rodney was doing something but she could not make out what – fighting, wrestling . . . one leg rose in the air, kicked forward, then shot back. She heard and felt a crash as the wind threw him back against the hood. The light disappeared and she tugged at the door.

The light came again, low to the ground now, but moving forward. The dim aura above was the shape of a man's back, a man on his hands and knees. Rodney was crawling into the wind.

In that instant she knew they would reach the hut. No one else could have done it. Only this man, her man, Rodney Savage, could drive body and will and machine through such opposition as this. The spine of a book appeared before her straining eyes, the moving flashlight in the middle. She saw the title – *Meru 1911–1921* – above the author's name – *Peter Savage*. Now her father's face – *the light in the middle of his forehead* – talking always of mountains from his armchair. Herself, pigtails, twelve, thirteen years old, rainy day – *the light jerking on behind the swinging wipers* – red binding, heavy book, idly leafing through, rain on the window, liner siren mournful in the Mersey ... pictures, old-fashioned to her eye; reading a few pages until fear came, with dark visions of terror; the fear was not of the blizzards and precipices, it was fear of the man who wrote, his remorseless advance against overwhelming fate. *The light crawled on.* She had put the book away, never opened it again, never till this moment on the Salsette Marsh recalled it, or associated the name with her own man. He must have been Rodney's father, who died the day before Independence.

She gripped the wheel more firmly. Perhaps she had shown Rodney something of determination, too, and could show him more.

The road made another full turn, to the right, resuming its original westward course. Rodney struggled to his feet and walked on. Half an hour later he signalled her to stop. The wandering flashlight shone on an uprooted palm, others struggling in the grip of the wind, a house. The light vanished. She waited alone in the heaving car, keeping the engine running fast. The light reappeared, flickered, now shone in her eyes, now downward on the water through which he splashed back towards her.

He tumbled in and flopped forward over the wheel as she squeezed away to make room for him. His breath came in long shuddering gasps. She put out her hand and stroked his streaming hair. He did not shrug her off – but perhaps he did not notice. After a time he raised his head. 'Alkhuti,' he said, 'she came through just after six, and went on to Pabal. The taxi came back at once, without her ... But we can't take the car farther than this.

307

Tarmac ends – sand track beyond, all flooded now.' He edged the Austin into the lee of a hut and switched off the engine. 'Close the windows . . . Ready?'

She braced herself. 'Yes, I'm ready.'

'Here, carry the torch. Walk on my left, hold it in your left hand, hold me with your right. Straight ahead to the beach, a couple of hundred yards, then right, quarter of a mile on beach road, over bridge.'

He forced open the door and got out. She passed him the case and then struggled out herself. Hands locked, they began to walk. Walking was hard, breathing harder. The wind blew so strongly that sometimes it sucked the air out of her lungs and sometimes rammed an emulsion of air and spray down her throat, at a hundred miles an hour. She could only breathe through clenched teeth, but she needed more oxygen than that to move. Rodney, the heavy case dragging and flapping in his right hand, often at arm's length, dragged her forward. The wind came in an alternating pattern of shriek and roar as they passed among and between the hovels of the village. All the time they walked in wind-whipped water, shifting sand under their feet below. All the time, too, a heavy throbbing, deeper than the boom of a liner's siren, deep as the deepest thunder, grew steadily louder and closer, and above it a rising hiss. The water in the wind now tasted salt, there was froth on the road, and the palm trunks were rimmed with white. The last trees fell back and without warning they came upon the sea.

It offered no hold to any sense except hearing. The beam of the flashlight could not reach even to the nearest outflung fingers of the waves. Smell and touch were numb. Only through sound did she know that it had passed the high marks of the highest tides. In sound she 'saw' the short waves crashing down, hurling forward with the long sibilant hiss, being dragged back, hissing louder. In sound she 'saw' the deep swell from a thousand miles out, slowly rising and falling under the surface waves, twelve waves to every surge of the swell. In the upper registers she heard the wind dragging the surface off the water, as one drags a carpet off a floor, and hurling it inland, to coat with salt the palm trees and the huts.

Rodney dragged her round to the right and immediately she

found herself floating in huge strides, the wind forcing into her back and up under her buttocks in violent thrusts. In the jumping light she saw that they were being carried like sail planes down a beach road that ran along the top of what was normally a high, flat dune, now a ridge hardly above the level of the water. Rodney, offering more surface to the wind in his body and in the case gripped in his right hand, flew in longer strides beside her, and twice pulled her off her feet so that she dived on her face into the flooded sand. Then the wind held her down, and it took their combined strengths to get her up. On again, the sound of the sea lessening . . .

Rodney leaned back, pulled hard at her arm. 'Bridge,' he screamed against her ear.

She swung the light and it picked out a wooden railing in the sea. Waves raced past – not full ones, or nothing could have survived, but short, steep waves, near the end of their force as they rushed up into the long re-entrant leading to the marshes.

'Walk behind me,' Rodney shouted, 'hand in my belt.'

They went forward into the water. Ten feet out the railing began. By then the water was up to her knees. At the railing he leaned forward, grasped it firmly, and extended one foot to the right.

'No, left,' he shouted. He transferred the case to his left shoulder, gripped the railing with his right hand, and again carefully extended his foot. 'O.K.'

They advanced slowly. The waves surged past at waist level, the crests tossing over the top of the railing. On, one foot at a time, feeling for the surface of the bridge under the water, cautiously placing some weight on the leading foot, then more, then all. Shine the light forward, past Rodney's body. Anxiously look at the case, the white tension of his knuckles.

'Hold!'

She braced against a wave that almost knocked her off her feet.

Rodney moved a little faster. He jerked downward and she lost her grip on his belt. The weight of the case dragged him sideways. The railing shuddered. He recovered his balance. 'Surface gone,' he shouted. He edged left, away from the railing, two, three, four sideways paces. Tried again. 'O.K.' On. Railing ended. 'Bridge may have gone, too.' Test . . . 'O.K.' One pace, another, another, the water thrusting like an animal against her, between her legs, wrenching at her skirt. Sudden step down, stumble, scream, regain footing. Shallower, shallower, up on to sand, churned sand strewn with foam and wreckage.

'We've done it! Rodney, we've done it!'

The flashlight showed a hut at the head of the beach. They struggled up the steps, banged on the door, shone the light through the windows. Empty. Fifty yards farther, another hut. Empty. And another. The light picked out a chair, a couch, a pair of feet, Sumitra's face and wide frightened eyes.

Rodney said, 'Door's bolted from inside. Through the window. No glass ...' He hoisted and pushed her head-first through the small window, which had never had any glass, only shutters now torn from their hinges and vanished. She hurried to the door and jerked back the bolt.

Sumitra's voice called feebly, 'Who's there?'

'Margaret,' she shouted, 'and Rodney.'

The only response was a long-drawn fluttering moan. Rodney came in. Together they pushed the door shut and refastened the bolt.

Margaret hurried to the couch. 'Is there a lamp here, Sumitra?'

'I don't know,' the voice muttered, 'doesn't matter.'

The flashlight hurried round the room. A cupboard in one corner, an *almirah* in another, two cane chairs, some deck chairs stacked against the front wall, door at the back. Rodney ran to it, opened it ... the light shone on a small kitchen, shelves stacked with cans – and a hurricane lantern, matchboxes. Rodney brought them out. Margaret found Sumitra's hand and gripped it. A match scratched, the glow of the hurricane lantern spread through the room. The gurgle and slap of oil as Rodney shook the lamp. 'Almost full,' he said. 'More oil in the kitchen.'

Margaret said, 'Now it's my turn.' She said it aloud but no one heard. The light showed bare walls, the open window through which they had made entry, water lying below it. The wind howled into the room, the rain spattering her where she sat beside Sumitra. 'Block that window,' she said.

Rodney dragged and pushed the *almirah* in front of the window. Margaret noticed another door beside the front door. 'What's through there?'

Rodney opened it, and the howling wind entered. He peered into

310

the outer darkness for a moment and closed the door. 'Bedroom, but most of the roof's gone there.'

He came to the couch. 'Why did you run away? Were you trying to have the baby secretly and get out of your promise to us?'

'Don't worry about it now, Sumitra,' Margaret said, throwing a warning glance at Rodney. 'When did the pains begin?'

'A long time ago. I don't know. What time is it?... I thought I'd give you a fright. You were going to get everything. I didn't believe... I'm frightened, Margaret.' Beads of sweat broke out on her forehead and a groan was forced between her writhing lips.

Margaret said, 'Hold me... Rodney, get sheets out of the bedroom. Knot one into a rope. Tear up others for rags and cloths. I've got to have hot water, too. Quickly.'

When the pain was over, Margaret asked again, 'When did they begin?'

'The waters broke just before I got here, in the taxi. Six o'clock.'

Margaret looked at her watch and started with horror and astonishment. Half-past two. They had taken over five hours getting here. Sumitra had been in labour eight and a half hours.

Rodney gave her the knotted sheet. She tied one end quickly to a leg of the couch and gave the other to Sumitra. 'Here, pull on that.'

Rodney said, 'No fresh water. The tank outside's been overturned. I can boil salt water. Make a desert cooker with sand and kerosene. It'll take about an hour to boil any quantity. A basinful. That's all there is to boil it in.'

'I can't wait that long,' Margaret said, 'I must examine her now. Take off her sari. Put a sheet or blanket under her.'

'No blanket. The sheets are all soaked and filthy, like that one.'

'Leave it then. Go and get the water boiling. I'll need it later.' She took Sumitra's wrist and felt for the pulse.

Pulse 109, temperature about 101. She took the surgical gloves out of the case and began to spread them with Dettol.

The couch on which Sumitra lay was a cane-bottom lounger, its end curved up to support the head. Margaret pulled her chair closer and said, 'Raise your legs. Spread them. Tell me when you feel a pain coming.'

'It hurts all the time now.'

Margaret bent forward... Transverse presentation for certain.

That showed from the markedly transverse arch of the swollen belly, quite unlike the usual downward pointing egg. Gently she inserted her right hand into the birth passage. Feeling cautiously upward through the thin rubber of the glove she came upon a small protuberance. She slid her finger over it, and bent her head to stifle a gasp. She had felt a hand and part of a forearm. 'Hurry,' Sumitra cried. Margaret slid her hand farther up and tried to feel inside the pelvic cavities to right and left. She could not, because both appeared to be filled, the foetal head and shoulder being in the cavity to the right. She withdrew her hand just in time before Sumitra's next pain began.

Slowly, with the vast force of the mother's reserves of birth power, created for this final act, the hand and wrist of the foetus came into sight. She saw Rodney, passing with a kerosene oil can full of sand, pause and stare. His dark, drawn face turned pale.

Margaret got up. Whatever might or might not have been done earlier, Sumitra had now arrived at a situation where the amniotic fluid had long since drained away, and could not perform its function as a lubricant of the birth passage. The foetus, pushed downward by her contracting muscles, had jammed sideways into the pelvis, one arm out-thrust. Every succeeding pain would impact it still more firmly.

Black smoke and particles of oily soot swirled round the room. Quickly she pulled Sumitra's sari over her upraised knees, sheltering the vulva. 'What are you doing?' she called. Sumitra began to gasp, tugging at the knotted sheet.

Rodney called, 'It'll be better in a minute. I'm going to wedge the front door open an inch or two, and the kitchen door the same, to make a draught.'

She heard him pushing and pulling behind her, the scrape and creak of furniture, the roar of the wind. The smoke lessened. She shook her head, willing herself to think of nothing but her medical task.

She must try to turn the foetus, though it was almost certainly too late to do so. If she failed, an expert obstetrician, with all facilities ready at hand, would be needed immediately. Suppose she sent Rodney back at once . . . he could reach Khed in about three hours. Supposing he found a doctor at once, he could be back in three more . . . six hours. But suppose the bridge went?

312

And how could he drive across the flooded marsh alone, without lights? She would lose them all then – the baby, the mother, and Rodney. That she must not think about. Her responsibility was the mother and child . . . Six hours was too much. She must act sooner than that, and when she did she would need an assistant.

Rodney stood beside her, staring fixedly at the hand and wrist of his child protruding from Sumitra's body, just visible under the arched sari. Sumitra saw his face concentrated only on her loins, and closed her eyes.

Margaret took his arm. 'Come over here.' In a corner of the room close to the door, where she had to raise her voice to be heard above the bellow of the sea and the roar of the wind, she said, 'I am going to try to turn the foetus. You'll give her chloroform. Move that small table to be ready beside you, at her head. Five drops on to the pad, and when I nod, hold it gently on her face. Hold her pulse in the other hand, and count it aloud, so that I can hear. At "ten" raise the pad, and don't put it on again until I say so, and then only for a count of five. Do you understand?'

'Yes . . . My hand's shaking . . . What's the matter?'

'I can't explain now . . . hold the pad loosely. Don't tense. If I say stop, take the pad off at once. It means her pulse rate is getting dangerous. Pull her sari up – right up. More Dettol on the gloves. That's enough. All right, there's the chloroform, and the pads. Get ready.'

She bent over her patient. 'I've got to put you to sleep for a bit now, Sumitra. Count aloud.'

'One – two – three—'

'Head back. Relax. Just breathe easily, between counts, not too deeply.' She saw that Rodney was ready, and nodded. He lowered the pad on to Sumitra's upturned face.

'Seven – eight – nine – ten.' The counting turned to a mumble and died away.

'Pulse,' Margaret snapped.

Rodney jumped, took Sumitra's wrist and began to count. Margaret inserted her right hand into the birth passage, pressed her left hand firmly into the drumlike belly from outside, forcing down until she felt the head and shoulder of the foetus. She began to try to turn it out of its position . . . The hut trembled continuously, the bottles and instruments rattled on the flimsy table.

313

Rodney's voice intoned on, sharp and nervous, counting beats of the pulse. The patient moved. 'Pad,' she said.

She had never done this before. This was a doctor's job, always. Once, at the Royal Mersey, a sardonic young intern had told her to feel the position, so that she would know what they were up against. The forces of the birth pains, which had been spaced apart, had now become a steady bursting pressure, like an over-inflated balloon. The sweat ran down her face, but her body was clammy and cold. Using all her strength, pushing up from inside and forcing up from outside, she could not move the foetus an inch.

She stood up. Rodney kept his eyes down, counting on. Pulse rate rising. She would be conscious in a moment or two. Temperature still raised.

'What's happening?' Rodney said, breaking the rhythm, – 'five, six, seven – for God's sake, what's happening? – eight, nine . . . Is the baby all right?'

She did not answer. Should she bring Sumitra round, knowing that she would have to put her out again soon? How strong was she? Not very. She'd have to come round. Coming now . . .

A long moan. 'She'll be sick,' she said. 'Hold her head. Wash her face, then clean up.'

She turned away. Behind her she heard the sound of retching mixed with groans and, later, Sumitra's faint voice, 'I'm alive . . . Margaret.'

'Yes?'

The hot hand reached up for hers. She smiled, withdrawing her hand. 'I can't touch you, Sumitra . . . gloves.'

'Margaret, there's something wrong, isn't there?'

Margaret held the smile on her face. 'Not exactly wrong – just a little difficulty.'

'Don't lie, Margaret . . . I'm not afraid now . . . I think I have nothing to live for. You can save the baby, at least? Then I will live on, through her. He'll love that much of me, all the rest forgiven . . .'

Rodney's face, tortured into ugliness, stared at her across Sumitra's body. Margaret turned away and gazed at the *almirah* that blocked the window, willing her vision to see through it to the open air beyond. But beyond there was a storm of wind and rain, night, and the sea, no peace, no distant view.

Only a Caesarean could now save the baby. It was a major operation, only to be performed with safety by a trained surgeon in a well-equipped theatre, with all the proper assistants. She looked at the thin catgut and fine needles in the case, suitable for the repair of a minor post-parturition tear, never for a Caesarean. She looked at the muddy slop on the floor, the streaks of sand and mud on Rodney's face, the filth and stains on her own blouse and skirt.

She remembered a film where some man marooned in a cabin miles from anywhere had done some tremendous operation directed by a doctor over the radio. But that was a film, this was real. She knew more than the man in the cabin had known, she had seen many Caesareans performed under her eyes. She knew too much. There was the sheer skill at the cutting and sewing, the time in which she must complete the resewing before haemorrhage killed the patient. If it were a matter of life and death, with no alternative, then she would have to try. But there was an alternative. She could cut the foetus in pieces and deliver them, one at a time, through the birth passage. Barring infection under these appalling conditions, that would save Sumitra.

But supposing she *could* do the operation? Once she cut into the skin would not a miraculous skill come to her from God, from her experience, lending her for those vital minutes the incisive certainty of Mr Dutt, Mr Mackenzie at the Royal Mersey?

She looked at her patient. She needed another ten minutes to recover from the anaesthetic before she went under again. No more, as the pains were coming close now.

She said to Rodney, 'I want to look at that hot water . . . We'll be in the kitchen, Sumitra, and I can see you from there.'

In the tiny kitchen she stood pressed close to Rodney in one corner, by the open door from the big room. In the opposite corner the wind whipped flames and oily black smoke round the basin set on the kerosene oil can. She said, 'We don't have much time to spare, but you've got to understand. The baby can't be born normally because it is jammed. A surgeon in an operating theatre could perform a Caesarean, but I can't. So . . .'

'Of course you can, Margaret! I can help. My hand will be steady, for that.'

Again the temptation assailed her. She saw the film, the trapper's hand moving surely over the bare skin ... Her own hand shook and her voice, when it came, was high-pitched and tremulous. 'I can't! I'd have to cut through the skin, through the fat, through layers of tissue, and finally into the womb. The womb's bursting under pressure, the covering is as thin as paper! As soon as the knife cuts into it, terrible arterial bleeding will begin, gushing out everywhere. In that I have to extract the foetus – the baby – and the placenta, sew everything up from the inside out, layer by layer – with those needles! I've seen a surgeon with an assistant, three trained nurses, and an anaesthetist only just finish in time, and the woman on blood transfusions afterwards, actually during it. We cannot give her a transfusion. *I . . . I . . . I dare not and will not do it!*'

'What do you want to do?'

'*Want* ... I *must* remove the foetus, in pieces, by the normal passage.'

'But that's murder! ... Can't you wait? It's past three. Someone will be here in the morning ...'

'No. Her womb is stretching thinner with every pain. In an hour or two, if I don't take out the foetus, it will burst, and she'll die in a few minutes from loss of blood ... Help me, Rodney! Give me the courage to do what I must do, the way you did getting us out here from Bombay. How do you think *I* feel?'

Rodney pressed back against the wall away from her. Past his tense, bitter face she saw Sumitra lying still on the couch.

She stretched out her hands to seize his arm, to dig her nails into his flesh. The sheen of the surgical gloves caught her eye and she jerked back her hands, but they hovered in front of her face, between her and Rodney, the fingers crooked and tense. She cried, 'Do you think I don't know what this means? But what kind of future can we have, paid for with her blood, and my respect? She said once, twice, three times, that I was nothing but a woman, in love with you. I believed her. But now, here, I've learned it's not true. I'm also a nurse, Rodney.'

Sumitra began to stir uneasily, her legs moving up and down, down and up. Slowly Rodney's head swung to the right, then to the left. Then he turned completely round, looking away from her. But there was no help, no other solution but the echo of her words, and the wind.

Her voice came out flat and unemotional: 'We must start now.' The water in the basin looked to be hot but not boiling. Since she had no cold to mix it with, that would be good. 'Bring the basin through, put it at the foot of the couch. Then get ready to use the chloroform again, same as last time. It will be very bad to watch. I would give anything to save you that, at least – but I can't. I need you.'

She walked into the big room and began to make ready.

From the case she took the razor and, kneeling expertly, shaved off the lower part of Sumitra's pubic hair. This she had done a thousand times, she thought with weary bitterness . . . if this were all! She spoke to Rodney: 'Put the basin down here beside me. Pour in three capfuls of Dettol.' She dipped her finger in it. She'd never heard of sea water being used for sterilisation and cleaning, but no reason why not – except for the sand lying in the bottom. Must wait for that to settle. And it would sting. Since it wasn't boiling, sterilisation of the instruments would have to be done in pure Dettol. Sumitra was deadly pale now, not far from the final collapse of exhaustion.

Margaret carefully washed her gloved hands, then washed the exposed vulva and extruded hand. She stood up.

'Head back, Sumitra, look at the ceiling . . . think of rest, think of sleep. Ready, Rodney. Start counting . . . When you wake up this time it'll all be over.'

Sumitra said, 'The baby . . . baby . . .' Her mumbling died away under the pad as Rodney's hand came slowly, shaking, down.

Margaret took up the bottle of Dettol in one hand and in the other the long surgical scissors. From Rodney she heard, amid the dead monotone of his counting, a falling sigh that sounded like the stifled scream of an anguished child. She poured the antiseptic liberally over the scissors, put down the bottle, and bent over between Sumitra's raised spread legs.

Half an hour later she stood up. At once she clutched the side of the couch to prevent herself from falling. On a torn sheet at her feet lay the separated head and body of Rodney's child, with the placenta and umbilical cord that had so long nourished it. A pool of blood congealed under Sumitra's body and the cane latticework of the couch was sticky with blood. Rodney stood like a dead tree, brittle and white, at the head of the couch.

Margaret dropped the scissors into the basin, dipped her hands, and began to massage the outside of Sumitra's belly. As she worked steadily away, neither seeing nor feeling anything, Sumitra returned to consciousness. 'It's over,' Margaret said dully. 'Look at the ceiling! Rodney, do this ... dig in with your fingers, not too hard, knead gently ...'

Rodney stepped forward, two wooden paces, and did as she told him. Margaret knelt to gather up the sheet bearing the remains of the baby.

Rodney said, 'I'll do that.'

She stood up. Rodney was right. She should stay with Sumitra – but to expect him to carry his own dead, mangled child was too much. He went into the kitchen and she heard the door being forced open. The wind seemed to have lessened a little, though it was still strong. He came back, lifted the sheet, and went out. She closed the door after him and returned to her place, massaging to help Sumitra's uterus in its contractions.

Sumitra's voice was faint. 'Was it a girl?'

'Yes.'

'Is he burying her?'

'Yes.'

She filled a syringe. 'I'm going to give you an injection in the arm. It's to help contract the womb. There.'

'I ... I think I'm going to sleep. I'm terribly, terribly ... tired.'

'Yes. Sleep. I'll be here.'

She sat down on the hard chair and waited, watching the other woman. After a time she picked up a wrist and felt the pulse. Still weak but rebuilding. Ought to give her some hot tea when she awakes. No water. Temperature still high. Ought to get her to a hospital at once, too. Penicillin. Hardly could have avoided infection, in these conditions. Janaki and Mr Dutt would come. When? Noon, perhaps. Rodney was being a long time. Burying his daughter. Burying his future. And hers. Where had he gone? He should have waited for her. She had to stay by the patient, an hour at least, after the delivery of the placenta. That was the rule. More if no one else was present. Past four o'clock, everything absolutely blank, no smell, no hearing, no touch, no taste, no emotion, sight fading.

318

Five o'clock. Six o'clock. Dawnlight, green and pale, the patient sleeping soundly. She rose stiffly and went to the door, opened it, and looked out. Something moved along the dunes on the mainland, about half a mile away. It was a Weasel, one of the army's small amphibious vehicles. She watched as it came closer, and at a quarter of a mile recognised the bald dome and round figure of Mr Dutt, standing up in the back with Janaki and a sepoy. Two more soldiers were crammed into the front seat.

She turned, walked through the room without another glance at the patient, and went out the back door. The peninsula was covered with palm trees, sparse beach undergrowth, and patches of long grass. The trees waved and swung in the wind but now merely with energy, instead of frenzy. After ten minutes the palms fell back and she came out on the final point of sand.

The wind blew strong, the sea heaved and plunged to the horizon. Driving sand thrust sharp arrows into her skin. The beach was littered with wreckage, wreckage of huts, of trees, of a world. At the farthest point of the peninsula, where the sea raced past, furious and yellow and deep at the edge of the steep slope, a man stood, his back to the land. She went out to him.

When she reached him he spoke at once, as though he had been expecting her. 'I never knew I was a coward until now.' His voice was loud but full of doubt, like a man who shouts and does not know whether he will be heard. 'I've been here since I buried her. I meant to come, walk into the sea, keep on walking. I wouldn't have lasted a minute. Look at the tide, look at the sea! ... I couldn't do it. I was lonely.'

She took his hand. 'I'll go with you,' she said. She had taken his life, she would give him hers in return. She felt so weak she could hardly stand. For her, it would last less than a minute because she could not struggle even if she wanted to, and she did not want to. She had killed any hope of his love far more effectively than Sumitra had done. Without him, there was nothing. She knew now inside herself exactly what he had felt during those long months: nothing, absolutely nothing.

She walked into the sea and he followed. The sea tugged greedily at her ankles. Another step and it fondled her knees. The hand was restraining her, pulling her back.

'Wait,' he said. She stopped, head down, unfeeling. 'You didn't give me time to tell you. A few minutes ago before you came, I found that though I didn't have the guts to die I could find the guts to live. What I saw and did tonight turned from an ending into a beginning . . . from a final, terrible experience into a command for the future. Look, my hands are strong, my eyes steady. I can learn.'

'What?' she asked dully.

'To be a surgeon.'

She turned and stared at him. 'You? A surgeon? It takes a long time . . . Yes. You could be a surgeon. You have the nerve . . . Let me go.'

'No. I need a housekeeper. Someone who will earn a living for me, too, while I learn.'

'Is that all you want?'

There was no answer, and after a time she raised her head again and looked at him. He was smiling. At the sight of her the smile, shining white in his dark, filthy, weary face, turned into a low, long laugh.

She said, 'But . . . but you said you'd never laugh again!'

His face returned to its seriousness, but without any trace of sadness or bitterness. 'My baby's dead, yet I can laugh. It's like a funeral in the army. We march to the grave in slow time, with arms reversed and the pipes playing a lament. We come back in quick time, the bugles blowing and our heads up. You know, all those things that you did for me, all that you have been, and are – I didn't feel them at the time, but I did see them. They have been stored away, like film – waiting to be developed. I've been doing a lot of developing, standing here on the brink . . . Well, will you take me on – for life instead of death?'

The hand pulled her steadily out of the sea and along the sand. The small waves lapped at her feet and the spray tingled in her eyes, but the wind lessened as they turned the corner of the point and reached the lee of the peninsula.

37/14